The following works are written and illustrated by Elizabeth Wang, and also published by Radiant Light:

Teachings-in-Prayer: An Introduction.

Teachings-in-Prayer Volume One: Spiritual Training.

Teachings-in-Prayer Volume Two: Spiritual Nourishment.

Teachings-in-Prayer Volume Three: Spiritual Work.

Teachings-in-Prayer Volume Four: Spiritual Life.

Living and Working for the King of Kings, Christ.

How to Pray.

The Holy Sacrifice of the Mass: Mass Poster.

Prayer Paintings: Sets A and B
(Previously called Sets 1 and 4).

Prayer Paintings: Sets C, D, E, F
(Previously called Sets 2, 3, 7 and 8).

Radiant Light *books, paintings and posters are available to buy in person or by mail-order from:*

St Pauls (By Westminster Cathedral)
Morpeth Terrace, Victoria, London SW1P 1EP, UK.
Tel: 0171-828-5582 - Fax: 0171-828-3329

FALLING IN LOVE

A Spiritual Autobiography

Written and illustrated by
Elizabeth Wang

This book serves as a prologue to several
volumes of *Teachings-in-Prayer*

This book is published by **Radiant Light,**
25 Rothamsted Avenue, Harpenden, Herts., AL5 2DN

Written and illustrated by Elizabeth Wang
Front cover painting (OIL:104) by Elizabeth Wang
(See p.26, T:104, in Volume One of *Teachings-in-Prayer.*)
Text and illustrations copyright © 1999 Stephen Wang
Photographs copyright © 1999 Elizabeth Wang
ISBN 1 902960 04 1

Quotation from *Patrick in his own words* by Joseph Duffy used
with permission, © First published by Veritas Publications

Scripture quotations have been taken from *The Jerusalem Bible*
published and copyright © 1966, 1967 and 1968 by
Darton, Longman and Todd Ltd and Doubleday & Co. Inc,
and used by permission of the publishers.

"I am, then, first and foremost unlearned ...

But this much I know for sure. Before I had to suffer I was like a stone lying in the deep mud. Then he who is mighty came and in his mercy he not only pulled me out but lifted me up and placed me at the very top of the wall. I must, therefore, speak publicly in order to thank the Lord for such wonderful gifts, gifts for the present and for eternity which the human mind cannot measure.

Let you be astonished, you great and small men who revere God! Let you, learned clergymen, heed and consider this! Who was it who called me, fool that I am, from among those who are considered wise, expert in law, powerful in speech and general affairs? He passed over these for me, a mere outcast. He inspired me with fear, ...

My decision to write must be made, then, in the light of our faith in the Trinity. The gift of God and his eternal consolation must be made known ..."

(From: *Patrick, in his own words* by Joseph Duffy pp.16-17.)

FALLING IN LOVE

CONTENTS

CONTENTS, Continued

Page

CONTENTS, Continued

LIST OF ILLUSTRATIONS.

i

LIST OF MAJOR QUOTATIONS.

"I am, then, first and foremost unlearned ..."
(*St. Patrick in his own words*, by Joseph Duffy,
pp. 16-17). .... Just before 'Contents'

"God's foolishness is wiser than human wisdom ..."
(1 Co 1:25-31)... page 3

"Everyone moved by the Spirit is a son of God ..."
(Rm 8: 14-32).. page 177

"Do not let your hearts be troubled ..."
(Jn 14: 1-16) .... page 407

"But still we have a wisdom to offer ..."
(1 Co 2: 6-10) .... page 533

"This, then, is what I pray, kneeling before the Father ..."
(Ep 3:14-21) .... page 697

PREFACE.

Many years ago, as a young adult, I thought that I was looking for God. I didn't realise that He is infinitely kind and had already been 'searching' for me, so to speak, in my darkened heart and mind. He had been drawing me towards Himself, by His grace. I began to practice again what I believed were the essentials of the Christian faith, as it had been taught to me in childhood in my Anglican home.

When I turned in prayer to God, at twenty-one years old, I was a free soul, at last whole-heartedly acknowledging my dependence on Him; and I was able to pray with confidence and hope because of the grace given to me long before, in Baptism. Even though I had forgotten or ignored for a long time that great gift of Divine Life, I discovered, through prayer, that the Giver was still living within my soul, ready to receive me into His life and love, through Christ. Resolving to pray regularly, I began to behave as well as I thought a Christian ought to behave, trying to be more charitable and - through my struggles - becoming aware of my many faults.

I met many difficulties. I was not only ill for a long time but was lonely, and afraid. One night, I called out to Jesus, and I asked for help, with more faith than I knew I possessed; and suddenly He was with me. He had responded, in Love. He came to me instantly. I didn't see Him with my bodily eyes but with the eyes of my soul. I saw Him standing beside me; and I was dazzled by His blazing Glory! How foul and dark I saw my own soul to be. I saw years of selfishness exposed in the brilliance of that burning radiance, and so I turned away, appalled, but wholly repentant of every failing, and determined to do what was necessary to 'put things right' with God. My faith was obscure and inarticulate, but nothing could have kept me from reparation, penance, prayer and thanksgiving.

Soon afterwards, I discovered the existence and the sure teachings of the Catholic Church. I worshipped in familiar ways for three or four years; then, after much study and prayer, I asked if I could be received into the Catholic Church. I entered into full Communion on February 22nd, 1968, on the feast of the Chair of Saint Peter, in Manchester, in the church of the Holy Name. Amidst the pain and loneliness of that time, I was honoured by the extraordinary, invisible presence of Our Blessed Lady, suddenly made known to me on the day of my First Holy Communion, in a church full of strangers. I didn't know what had happened, and soon forgot about it, as I plunged determinedly into regular and silent prayer at home, no matter how busy I was each day. I marked the hours by simple prayers, whether the 'Our Father' or the Rosary; also, I prayed the psalms from a small Breviary, every lunch-time when my first baby was sleeping; and I recited the "Jesus Prayer" whenever possible, devotedly and silently, from morning until night, for the next twenty years.

***

After many years of gruelling work, and struggle and failure, with illness, too, and other trials, and - throughout - utter darkness in prayer, I was near despair, but was unwilling to turn away from God. I was a failure in more than one sense, and was ashamed of setting a bad example; but, thanks to God's grace, I didn't give up prayer; nor did I lose hope. I struggled to be faithful in the darkness, not realising that Christ was waiting at the bottom of the pit.

Then, one terrible day, I was reminded of the extent both of my sinfulness and God's holiness. I was appalled by the chasm. That very day, I decided with all the power of my heart to turn to Christ in faith and trust, in every circumstance. I vowed that I would never compromise; I would love my neighbour as Christ had loved me: that is - at any cost. I would do God's Will at every moment, rather than my own. I would bear sickness patiently, relying on the grace of God; and I'd shoulder all difficulties for His sake, even if interior darkness were to continue for the rest of my life. Also, I resolved, I would never, ever, willingly or deliberately offend against Him or against His love or against His laws again, in the least degree.

After Reconciliation in the local church I went about my work in darkness again, but my heart was at peace as never before. At last, I was willing to let Christ lead me into whatever way of life He had chosen for me. I was content to accept outward and inward changes for His sake, and to walk silently - in the spiritual life - along the bottom of my particular ditch, for as long as He permitted.

***

Soon after I had made that resolution I was utterly astonished to find that the habitual darkness of prayer was occasionally lit by great shafts of light. As I shall explain more fully later on, my usual dry, dark, humiliating prayers during Holy Mass or after Holy Communion were frequently "pierced" by an unsought and wordless "knowledge" which explained or unfolded aspects of our Faith.

In this way, every few weeks and then every few days, I was taught much more about God, and about Heaven, then about Christ and His Church, and about grace, prayer, and souls. I learned nothing new; but many truths already known by faith, study, and worship were marvellously given anew and were clarified.

I didn't choose what I would learn in prayer; but each "teaching" was given suddenly and unexpectedly in the silence of my wordless prayer during or after Mass and Holy Communion. Each was about some aspect of our Catholic faith, usually about the spiritual life, but with frequent stress on God's Love for us and on our duty to love Him, and to love our neighbour for His sake.

Throughout my years of study, I had learned from the great teachers and writers of the Catholic Church that we're foolish if we try to cling to experiences of a Person, rather than to the Person Himself; so, although I longed to know God, I neither looked for consolations in prayer, nor hoped for unusual spiritual experiences. I knew that we please Christ most surely when we continue in our usual fervent daily efforts to love Him and our neighbour. I eventually realised, however - despite all my sins and failings - that God sometimes chooses to teach us things in prayer, for His own purposes. Our initial fear and reluctance about paying attention to His 'showings' is praiseworthy; but if God Wills to teach us in this way, I have found, He will do so. Nothing but our ill-will or lack of love can stop Him; however, when we have tried to keep to the usual paths in prayer, but have been thwarted, and are puzzled by our experiences, we ought to turn to our advisors in Christ's Holy Catholic Church.

***

iv

The whole notion that God can teach people in this way was foreign to me, since the early "teachings" - by their simplicity - bore no resemblance to the visions which I'd seen recounted in various spiritual biographies. Also, I was amazed that He should teach a person like myself. But when it became plain that the "teachings-in-prayer" ought to be written down so that others could share them when the time was right, I tried to record in very simple manner what I had learned through Christ about His love for us, about the Most Holy Trinity, about the Incarnation of Our Lord through the Blessed Virgin Mary, and about other truths of the Catholic Faith.

The reader should take for granted that everything explained here in the "teachings" about the Christian faith and about the Christian spiritual life rests upon the sure foundation of the teachings of the Catholic Church as held and preached by her throughout the whole world and in every age. If I had found I was being given a teaching which contradicted any of the truths of our Faith, I would have rejected it with all my power. I would never have recorded anything contrary to the teaching of the Church, since I know that God doesn't contradict Himself; and so I knew that anyone receiving such 'teachings' would be receiving them from another source.

Many of the "teachings" were personal, and so don't appear in this book. Some which were strictly private haven't been written down at all. But I'm duty-bound to share the others, as Christ explained to me quite plainly, in order to strengthen the faith of my brothers and sisters in Christ and to bring others to know and love Christ, and to delight in the Glory of the Holy Trinity.

Certain of the teachings which have been given to me - whether wordlessly or with words - have been accompanied by an image; and that's why, during the past ten years, I've drawn more than one thousand pictures which represent aspects of the Truths that I've been taught by Christ in this way; also, I've written brief accounts of what He has explained on hundreds of occasions, with the words He has used. The greatest of the "Teachings-in-prayer" were wordless and imageless, as I said, and also infrequent, and puzzling at first. None of them can be fully explained or displayed; but those which I've tried to describe are "displayed" only because God has made His Will plain to me in several ways, more recently by inviting me to translate His wordless teachings into my own language, so that other people can delight in His encouragement.

When I plucked up courage to record the teachings, that "First Version" was hesitantly-written and poorly-arranged. Not until late 1994 did I write a "Second Version" which clarified the content of the "teachings" and also the way in which I was taught. However, the "Third Version" was compiled solely because, on November 3rd 1995, Christ invited me to re-write His 'teachings' in a different manner. My new task, I learned, was to list most of His plain instructions about what I must do if I sincerely wish to please Him and to become holy; and Christ invited me to write 'in the first person', so that other people can receive His teachings in the sort of direct and simply way which it's been my privilege to experience.

***

It seems to me as though these teachings have been "squeezed" by Christ through the substance of my daily life as water is squeezed through a sponge; and the image I'm using is of the sort of blood-soaked sponge which is used to wipe the face of an exhausted man in the corner of a boxing-ring. Without the pressure of Christ's urgings towards greater fervour and self-surrender, and without my at times agonised consent, the 'water' of His instruction about our spiritual journey couldn't have 'poured out' for so many years, through prayer, into my daily life and so into my notebooks. I mention this because Christ has been producing, through my daily life and work, a sort of catechism of the spiritual life. Of course, He has already given us all that we need for Salvation; but it's His wish that we be reminded of various truths about the Holy Mass and about prayer, and about sacrifice and penance, for example; and He longs to remind us of His tremendous love for us. He wants to offer a reminder - from within the life of someone fearful and sinful, whose days have been cluttered with problems and anxieties - that His is a constant and forgiving Love. He admires our weak faith and our pitiful efforts to love Him and to love and serve our neighbour.

Throughout His instructions and occasional reprimands, Christ has scattered numerous compliments. He has been encouraging me just as any good teacher encourages a child; yet I've omitted some of the compliments from my writings; and I was tempted to omit even more, and also to omit my own name from the text; but I'm loathe to remove this evidence of Christ's kindness. The 'falling-in-love' of the title of this book was made possible precisely because of Christ's constant kindness and tenderness towards me. It once seemed to me as though I was 'falling' into misery and near-hopelessness at the knowledge of my real nature; but that falling was followed by the astonishing discovery that we not only live 'in' God, as creatures of a Divine Creator; we can live 'in' His own heart, so to speak, and can share His Life.

I discovered the strength of His love for us, and also the depths to which He has stooped in order to help us. I experienced His tenderness in prayer; and so began my 'falling-in-love' with God, as His radiant Light began to shine within my soul. And that's the reason why I hope so fervently that people will believe in His Love as well as in His scorching purity and His infinite majesty; and we are reminded of this marvellous Love in Holy Scripture, where God says: 'I HAVE CALLED YOU BY YOUR NAME; YOU ARE MINE!' (Is 43:1)

It was a marvellous discovery for me, when at last I realised that Christ's Love for each one of us is personal and tender; and I long for everyone to know it.

***

When Christ first began to offer me His 'teachings', He was addressing them, for His own good reasons, to someone who was already baptised. He Himself taught me the importance of repentance, and so I made great efforts to serve Him. Despite my failures, I kept turning to Him in regular prayer. As the teachings continued, He was building, therefore, on a foundation which He Himself had placed within my soul.

Stage by stage, as this work has progressed, Christ has revealed to me further details of His plan. Many people will be helped by the 'teachings', Christ has shown me; and others will shun them. My only concern, He says, must be to produce them, obedient to Him, and to leave the results in His hands. But those who are glad to read them can be assured that everything within these pages was taught to me - whether implicitly or explicitly - by Christ Himself, usually during prayer.

The publication of this story about my journey of faith, and also about the "teachings", is an act of obedience to the One Who asks that I "STAND UP AND TELL THEM ALL I COMMAND YOU. DO NOT BE DISMAYED BY THEIR PRESENCE" (Jr 1:17). I bear in mind, too, another passage from Holy Scripture: "FOLLOW RIGHT TO THE END THE WAY I MARK OUT FOR YOU" (Jr 7:23). "THEY HAVE NOT ... PAID ATTENTION; THEY HAVE GROWN STUBBORN AND BEHAVED WORSE THAN THEIR ANCESTORS ... YOU MUST SAY ALL THESE WORDS TO THEM" (Jr 7:26-27). ... "COME IN; LET US BOW, PROSTATE OURSELVES, AND KNEEL IN FRONT OF JAHWEH OUR MAKER, FOR THIS IS OUR GOD ..." (Ps 95:6-7.)

Christ has shown me, on several occasions, what He witnesses today; He sees that many people - even in the Church which He founded - not only disobey His Commandments but mock the teachings of the Church and lead others to do the same. He sees, too, how few have given Him their hearts, entirely, and how few make sacrifices for His sake and for the sake of the Gospel given through Himself and His Apostles. This was true in past ages, and it's still true, today; but Christ strengthens the faith of His children in ways which He devises, and He has told me that these writings are to play a part in His work of encouragement. Since April 1992, in accordance with His wishes, and longing to comfort and encourage others and to bring them to a renewed friendship with Christ, I've been speaking more freely about His teachings, to family and friends and acquaintances. I've handed out books of teachings to anyone who has expressed a wish to read them.

***

In all my own failures, I've come to see that Christ understands our human weaknesses. He knows the trials and temptations and agonies of this earthly life. He sees that we, His children, are struggling daily amidst all sorts of things that might lead us away from the practice of our faith; so He assists, by his grace, everyone who turns to Him; and He forgives every repentant sinner. It's when we consent wholeheartedly to His action or grace in our hearts, admitting our faults and resolving to love God and our neighbour, that we find that we don't struggle alone. Christ our Lord guides us; His Holy Spirit strengthens us and leads us towards the Father, in the company of all who belong in the One Body of Christ, which is therefore truly called Christ's Holy Catholic Church.

That is why I've plucked up courage to write the story that Christ wants me to tell, though I couldn't have undertaken such a task if I hadn't been sure, first, that it was my duty, and, secondly, that nothing I'd written would contradict the teaching of the Church. Since the Church is guided by Christ now, as in every century, through the Pope and the Bishops, and also through the Bishops' representatives - our priests, I've gone to our priests for advice; and I've been reassured about this present path.

By the time I began to make notes about the 'teachings-in-prayer', I'd been praying regularly for more than twenty years, attempting to love God and my neighbour no matter what the cost, though failing often. For every 'teaching' or extraordinary occurrence mentioned in this Prologue, I've left out ten or a hundred episodes of simple prayer or acts of faith. It should be taken for granted that my routine prayers consist of the sort of Catholic devotions which I describe in various writings Like many other people, I pray the "Morning Offering", centred on the Holy Mass, with acts of faith, hope and charity, and with devotions to Our Blessed Lady and to all the Angels and Saints, as well as Scripture-meditation. My prayer-life has always been very ordinary, based upon vocal and mental prayer and attendance at Holy Mass, whether or not 'extraordinary' experiences have also been given to me - for God's own purposes. It's true that prayer has become altogether more simplified and joyful in recent times, as I've learned to follow God more swiftly and frequently into the prayer of contemplation; yet I hope that I shall never think of entirely discarding the vocal prayers which, at different times of the day or of the week, are so expressive and fruitful. What a wonderful treasury we have in our Catholic prayers: so many long-cherished, safe, good and useful methods of expressing our love for God and our sorrow for sin.

Although I have written, here and elsewhere, about the degrees and categories of "prayer-in-union", generally known as "contemplative" prayer, I ought to add something here about the manner of my 'seeing' truths in prayer. All that I've seen - whether images or persons - has been seen solely with the 'eyes of the soul'. I have never seen anything before me, with my bodily eyes, except what anyone else would see there, too, in normal life.

I've rarely used mental images in my worship of God. I've used my imagination when meditating on the Gospels, and also in intercession, as I remember, visually, those for whom I'm praying; but in 'pure' praise and adoration I've followed the traditional Catholic teaching which recommends a whole-hearted reaching-out of the heart and mind and will towards the God Whom we cannot see, but Whom we approach with confidence because of our union with Christ.

Long ago, I began my determined efforts to brush aside, in prayer, all images and distractions, ruthlessly trying to seek God as He really Is, just as I tried to seek His real Will, without trying to picture the future, amidst the hum-drum tasks of daily life.

It must be emphasised that my ordinary, daily life and worship centres on normal Catholic prayers and devotions - above all, on attendance at Holy Mass. I've looked for nothing novel or extraordinary in prayer. It's best that we try to turn to God in sincere love and repentance, week by week and year by year, following in the footsteps of our spiritual ancestors, and also 'open' to the continuing guidance of the Holy Father and of the other Catholic Bishops who are in communion with him.

It still astonishes me that Our Lord should have given me this work to do. I'm astonished and delighted, daily, thinking about all the gifts and graces to be found in the Catholic Church, which I entered as an awed and grateful convert thirty years ago. But when I entered, and began to make even greater efforts to meet God in prayer, I had no desire for novelty; nor had I any understanding of how God can teach people in prayer in a swift and lavish infusion of knowledge; nor did I understand what I've heard in the Gospel about Christ leading us to the Father; so that's why I took almost no notice of the earliest 'teachings' - although I never forgot them; rather, I continued with my fervent efforts to find out more about the Catholic Faith through the normal channels, to the degree that this is possible for a busy wife and mother. Through those early years when God was persistently teaching me in the silence of prayer I was content with the authoritative teachings of the Church, on every subject. I sought advice from reputable, wise and saintly authors, and gratefully absorbed the truths which come to us through the Holy Father, the Pope, and through the prayers of the Liturgy, the Scripture readings and the homilies.

I was first aware of 'being taught' when I was fourteen years old. There were two long periods of my life when such teachings ceased, as part of my spiritual training; but this way of learning spiritual truths in prayer eventually become a part of my life of prayer: first, at intervals of several weeks or days, and now, daily. When I was being first taught by God in prayer I had no idea of the mission for which He was preparing me; whereas now I know that His plan is to provide encouragement, through this work, to members of the Catholic Church in an era when the Faith is under attack not only from outside but from within, and in a time when the concepts of duty and obedience are widely derided.

**

In order to please Christ, I've written a great deal within these pages about sadness and spiritual darkness. It's been necessary in order to explain those periods of the spiritual life which are unusually called the 'night of the senses' and the "night of the spirit." I shall say more about those, later; but I can't even mention them without saying that today, the darkness has vanished. Through the astonishing goodness of God my life was changed profoundly on December 11th, 1985: on what I now call the 'Alpha and Omega day'. Christ has rewarded me for my efforts, Love for love. He includes in His gifts a pure joy for me at the mere sound of His Name. I hear 'Jesus', or say it, and can hardly bear the joy which the sound or the thought or the Presence brings to my heart: such a pang as I never expected to feel again, when I was merely enduring everything for Him, sustained in hope and love by dry faith alone. I've learned that there's no music, sound, sight or touch more sweet and beautiful than the silent, invisible and true presence of Christ within the soul; and it's a marvel to me that this should have happened in the life and soul of someone who has been so reluctant to serve Him. And now, I live in hope that many people will be led to love Christ more fervently, undaunted by transient worries and difficulties, and therefore to love His Holy Will, which is our only lasting happiness. I hope that, despite the evident flaws in my writing, someone will become more interested in God and perhaps will dare to believe that it's true that God is alive and active - and good.

Everything that I've written here was put down in obedience to Christ; and everything contained in these pages is the truth as I see it - though it might not have been explained very well and some minor inaccuracies might have occurred: for example, about dates. I've been writing at great speed and haven't had the leisure to check every word several times.

**

It is no use my apologising for the stilted style, or the laboured phrases; I'm not pretending to be a professional writer, and besides, this task was extraordinarily difficult, because I could hardly bear to put pen to paper when I first began writing about Christ's work in my life. I was appalled at my impertinence at attempting such a task, whilst being utterly convinced that it was what God was asking me to do.

I haven't attempted to produce a lively script or witty pages. I'm not capable of it; so I hope that this can be seen as just a simple story, simply told. And since the colloquialisms of one era are frequently the dead phrases of another, I've tried to avoid them. Some of this work, I believe, will be used in times and cultures unlike our own.

ix

A further reason for a very plain recital of my experiences is that - as I'll explain - the "Teachings" which God sometimes gives to the soul in prayer are always light, clear, calm, and simple, yet stately. So it seems appropriate that simplicity should be my watchword not only in my recital of the "Teachings" but also in this "prologue" or spiritual autobiography.

***

It's been necessary for me to say a great deal about the reasons why I felt impelled to ask for Reception into the Catholic Church; and now it occurs to me that perhaps I shall be challenged for saying so much that seems critical of Anglicanism. I must proclaim that I believe that God is at work in the Church of England, as He is at work wherever those who belong to Him or yearn for Him pray to Him in Christ's Name and cherish the Holy Scriptures. Yet since I don't believe that any ecclesial body except the one which I entered in 1968 is the One Holy Catholic Church which Christ founded on the Apostles, I've had to explain in detail exactly what I was taught in childhood about the meaning of 'Church' and why, not unreasonably, I grew dissatisfied with that explanation.

NOTES ON THE 'TEACHINGS' WITHIN THIS BOOK

- There has occasionally been a gap of several days between teachings. That's why the subject matter sometimes changes quite abruptly between one sentence and the next.

- Every 'teaching' is numbered. Each 'T' (for Teaching) is followed by a number, and sometimes by a paragraph (#) number; and these correspond with the numbers of the same 'teachings' in earlier versions, and with the numbers in my notebooks, and also with the numbers on the associated illustrations in either water-colour or oil, which can be seen elsewhere.

- I've recorded most of Christ's instructions chronologically, as clearly and as simply as possible. Where a teaching has been given to me as a pure, precious and clear but soundless instruction, I have made it 'concrete', in my own choice of words, as He has requested.

- This 'making concrete' is more like a work of translation than of composition, since I have 'translated' real but inaudible teachings - given on specific occasions - into English, the language I know best; and you might see, therefore, that any grammatical errors or clumsy phrases - though regrettable - are like flaws in the work of a poor translator; and the 'original text' is Christ Himself, Whom I believe to be my Infinitely-wise Teacher, and indeed to be the source of all Truth ever found in prayer.

- There's a wealth of detail later in these volumes not just about Christ our Saviour but also about the life of all Three Divine Persons within the One Godhead. Whenever you read an instruction which mentions "Us" or "We", Christ is explaining something about the Most Holy Trinity - in Whom we believe because Christ, when on earth, revealed more than had ever before been known about God's Life and God's nature, and Christ the Son of God spoke - as we Christians believe - "with authority". Because of the revelation given through Christ and His Apostles, we believe in the Father Who created us, in Christ the Son Who redeemed us and in the Holy Spirit Who makes us holy: Three Divine Persons Who are a Trinity-in-unity. They are One God, Whose Life we now share in a marvellous way, because of our baptism.

Jesus Christ, we believe, is the second Person of the Most Holy Trinity. He is the Son of God. We say that He 'descended' from the Father in Heaven in order to come to earth to take flesh from Our Lady, so that as God-man He could live on earth amongst us, instruct His disciples, die for our sins on the Cross, rise from the dead and ascend to Heaven in glory. Thus, Jesus the Saviour and Redeemer made a Way in which all who believe in Him can follow; and we can follow with confidence, despite our weak nature and life's difficulties. Even in our own time, Christ is at work. It's through His Spirit that He guides the one Holy Catholic Church which He founded and of which we can seek membership. Within it, we can follow the Way of the Saints and feed on the Sacred Scriptures. Christ Himself is teaching us through the Holy Father, and also through the Bishops who are in Communion with him. Successors to St. Peter and the Apostles, Our Pope and our other Bishops - as one - preach Christ, preach repentance and salvation, teach us truth, lead us in the Sacred Tradition, and give us Christ's Divine Life and graces through the Sacraments.

As Christ's Divine Love pours within our hearts and transforms us, it can lead us to a deeper repentance of sin and a greater determination to love and serve God and neighbour. We can prepare for Eternal life where we hope to enjoy, in the presence of the Holy Angels and in the Company of the Saints who have gone before us, the glorious and blissful sight of the Father, Son, and Holy Spirit - One God, Who is more holy, loving and beautiful than the most fervent heart could ever begin to imagine.

Scattered throughout the teachings are passages which convey what I can only describe as God's 'knowledge-given-in-words.' God the Holy Trinity - Father, Son and Holy Spirit - has sometimes communicated teachings in whole phrases or sentences as if from Mind to mind, in prayer, and wholly beyond the realm of imagination. These words are reproduced in lower-case italic type; and whenever such words are shown with speech-marks it is because these particular words were spoken to my soul in prayer in a real though interior conversation, rather than being simply 'given' in a way which I've tried to explain in the Appendix.

A different typeface is used for the major teachings which I have received from God our Father. Nothing like this appears in the early part of this spiritual autobiography because I hadn't received teachings of this type during the period from 1957 to 1993. I have recorded these real but wordless teachings by 'translating' them into my words; and I distinguish them from Christ's own teachings - by the use of a different typeface - only to emphasise God's generosity. That the typefaces are different doesn't indicate that Father and Son are not equal in dignity; and of course we Christians believe that Father, Son and Spirit are One God. Yet when I'm being taught nowadays, in prayer, I am taught not only a particular spiritual truth; I am also taught which of the Three Divine Persons is at that moment instructing me; and this is why I speak of God's generosity. I believe that this is more for the eventual benefit of other people than of myself; and so I've made special efforts to record these things as accurately as I can.

I must say a few words about the use of a special typeface, from Volume Three onwards, to indicate which are the special teachings of the Holy Spirit. The method of identification used at first, in Volumes One and Two, to make plain the teachings of Christ and of the Father, was sufficient; and I explained - about the Holy Spirit, and His 'part' in these teachings - what I believe to be true: that the whole work is His 'script', in the sense that it's only in the Holy Spirit that we can pray "in Christ" to our Heavenly Father, or be taught in prayer, or receive good inspirations or moments of 'illumination' about the truths of our Faith. I believe that some of those who know Christ's Spirit will recognise His signature on what I've produced at His prompting, recognising it despite all the flaws and weaknesses; but when I had begun work on Volume Three, I was shown, in prayer, that the time was ripe for me to identify the particular teachings of the Holy Spirit much more plainly; hence my use of italic capital letters.

There were three reasons for my efforts to be obedient in this matter. First, it was the Will of God; and that was sufficient reason for me; but, also, I'd been shown that the Holy Spirit will be more glorified, if I show out His work in a clearer fashion; and those who read several volumes of this work can receive a 'picture' not just of a soul being led by Christ to the Father, but a 'picture' or an education - albeit through someone very weak and ignorant - of life lived in a true union with God at the 'Heart' of the Most Holy Trinity where the Three Divine Persons are 'at work' as They share Their joy and Their knowledge of Themselves not only with One Another within the unity of the Godhead but with someone who has been drawn into that Divine Life. Now that I've been taught something about the ways in which They are 'at work', I've been shown that it's both my duty and my privilege to share that knowledge with others, as an encouraging reminder of God's great love for us.

In response to Christ's promptings, I've tried to show, throughout the whole body of teachings which I've recorded so far, that Christ's teachings are received by me - through His Will - in a different manner from that which is used by the Father; and the Father's awesome teachings are different from the sudden 'illuminations' of the Holy Spirit. But the difference lies not in the Persons Who, though distinct, share the same Divine nature. The difference of which I write lies in my perception of the different methods of approach which, I notice, have been adopted by the Divine Persons. I can only try to explain this by declaring that Christ's teachings are received with heart-aching tenderness (or grief, as when, long ago, He occasionally rebuked me), whereas the teachings of the Holy Spirit are received with heart-lifting clarity and brightness; and the Father's teachings are received, it seems to me, (and this is why I have to show the difference, through the use of different typefaces), with an astonishing combination of heart-stopping intimacy with unquestionable power. It's my belief that through His differing approaches in prayer God is giving reminders of various aspects of His loving nature, aspects which, when considered all together, might convey something of the astonishing Majesty of the Holy Trinity, whilst also indicating the tender concern of God for every unique soul which He has created: as I shall explain in Chapter 20.

Although I had no plans to alter the style of the books, as I began Volume Four, I was shown that each of the teachings in the fourth volume should be prefaced by one of my brief prayers to the Most Holy Trinity or to the Saints. Only in order to obey Christ, therefore, did I put my sincere but common-place words near His own; but He had shown me that people will be helped if they see how kindly and generous a response we receive from God to our most common-place or even trivial requests, even though nothing in our lives is really trivial in His sight, since He loves us and therefore makes our concerns His own. He can't be repelled by our foolish preoccupations. But He explained to me, as well, that those who see the beauty of His Wisdom set beside my modest phrases can see something like the counterpoint which is found in paintings or musical compositions. His Wisdom can shine out more brightly when His teachings are set beside some of the phrases which reveal so plainly my human weaknesses. He wants to encourage weak people to put their trust in Him, and to believe in His undying love for each one of them - whatever their problems and however dreadful or merely tedious the circumstances of their lives.

It's the Will of God, also, that - through the visible 'counterpoint' of His generous answers placed beside my little queries - people are reminded of various 'aspects' of His nature. It's evident that when He so marvellously replies to my questions, He answers some of them very simply, yet answers others in an 'oblique' manner, and thus casts light on some aspect of the subject which I've 'held' before Him in prayer, yet also gives me knowledge about associated subjects, where a different 'angle' or a greater knowledge of things would be beneficial to me. At other times, for various reasons, His answers have been 'minimal', though always loving; and it's His intention that the 'demonstration' through this book of every sort of answer will demonstrate - despite my deficiencies both in understanding and writing - His extraordinary goodness.

Some of the teachings appear in a style which might seem, in our day, to be strangely formal. The reason is that although Christ - Who is true man, and very tender, as I said - is never less than loving and courteous in His dealings with me in prayer, He is never 'less' than Risen-and-Glorious: my Incarnate God. So even His briefest and most personal remarks have a majesty about them which I can't convey very well but which I'd entirely fail to suggest, were I to translate His teachings into more 'colloquial' language. Of course, the teachings which I receive from the Father and from the Holy Spirit inspire in me the same degree of awe and astonishment, mixed with gratitude. Some formality is evident, therefore, in all of the teachings, even when - on various occasions - the teachings have also been intimate and gentle. [By the way, I'm known to my family and to my childhood friends as 'Lizzie'; hence Christ's use of that diminutive - as you will see later on - whenever He speaks my name.]

- You can see that the numbering system is peculiar. When the 'Teachings' commenced, I was very puzzled and extremely cautious. I had no idea that the first two hundred teachings would be followed by another two thousand and more. I numbered things as well as I could; but by the time I realised how much more efficient I might have been, it was too late to begin again. Hundreds of paintings bore numbers which corresponded with parts of the lengthy text; so the 'system', I have decided, must remain as it is.

- During the early stages of 'teaching' I numbered a few incidents in prayer which were private, though I learned later on to record only things which were to be shared with other people. But this explains the few dozen gaps in the first half of Volume One of the "Teachings-in-prayer".

- The illustrations which I mentioned earlier are monochrome reproductions of the images which I have received from Christ in prayer: simple images which for a long time I tried to ignore, but which I've realised, at last, have an important place in Christ's lengthy programme of 'Teachings-in-prayer'. That's why a few of them can be found in each of the volumes of the 'teachings'; and that's why, at the end of certain teachings, you will see (WC ....) which means Watercolour, or (WC + OIL ....) whenever I've completed the same image in oils, also.

- The reason why I've placed only monochrome illustrations in most of my books is that my blue watercolour sketches reproduce most truly the various images and sights which Christ has graciously shown me in prayer. Almost everything which I've seen with the eyes of my soul has been 'composed' of mixed Glory and darkness, and almost never of colour, whether in the background or in the details. It's as though colour is something which is admirable, yet earthly and emotional rather than spiritual; and so it's not something which is needed during moments of 'Teachings-in-prayer'. I've used colour, later, when I've reproduced some of those same images as oil paintings; I've done this as an artist who makes legitimate re-workings of a simple original, in order to emphasise aspects of the message implicit within the primary image. A few of these oils are reproduced in the Appendix; and, as some readers will have seen, I have placed colour reproductions in the book entitled "My priests are sacred": and it was Christ's wish that I included so many.

- Volume One of 'Teachings-in-Prayer' is entitled: "SPIRITUAL TRAINING." It covers the time immediately around conversion, and beyond. It has a blue cover which signifies the spiritual cloud in which the soul is hidden during its spiritual infancy.

Volume Two of 'Teachings-in-Prayer' is entitled: "SPIRITUAL NOURISHMENT. It covers the time of painful but sure growth in the spiritual life. It has a green cover which signifies the good Food which the soul receives through prayer "in Christ" and through the Sacraments.

Volume Three of 'Teachings-in-Prayer' is entitled: "SPIRITUAL WORK." It covers the time when the soul experiences a more profound and more fruitful Communion with the Most Holy Trinity. It has a red cover, which signifies the fiery Life and Light of the Holy Spirit, by Whose gifts the soul is drawn into the Work of contemplation.

Volume Four of 'Teachings-in-Prayer' is entitled "SPIRITUAL LIFE." It covers a time of almost unbroken joy and Light within the soul. Its yellow cover signifies the brightness of the Glory into which the soul is drawn as it reaches the 'heights' - or 'depths' - of the soul's friendship with God the Father, in Christ, and through the Holy Spirit. The new format - of excerpts from what can truly be called conversations between myself and the Three Divine Persons - has been used only in order to obey Christ's request; and I call this a true dialogue, even though several "voices" take part, because it consists of one human being speaking with the One God: the Holy Trinity.

Volume Five of 'Teachings-in-Prayer' is not yet completed, but is entitled "SPIRITUAL PEACE". In it, the dialogue continues, as I am reminded of various truths - already known through Christ and His Church - about the life of grace, about Salvation, and about the Holy Trinity: both about God's Work and God's Nature.

xiv

Falling in Love

A NOTE ABOUT THE VARIOUS TYPEFACES USED
FOR THE TEACHINGS TO BE FOUND IN
THE INDENTED PASSAGES
IN THIS BOOK.

Normal type is used for Christ's clear but soundless prayer-time instructions, which I have 'translated' into words.

Lower case italic type is used for words which were 'given' to my soul by God: by Father, Son or Holy Spirit, although the words were not spoken. This typeface is used, also, where the words are enclosed in brackets, to indicate some of my own prayers to God.

Lower case 'italic type with speech marks' is used for words which were spoken to me by God: either by Father, Son or Holy Spirit, yet which were spoken only within my soul, during prayer.

SMALL CAPITAL LETTERS, also, are used after T:1264 #4 for the silent yet powerful teachings which I have received from God our Father. I have 'clothed' these vivid but soundless teachings in my own words - and have placed them at the centre of the page. Italic type has been inserted wherever - in the same teaching - God's own words have been received, either 'given' or spoken. (See above).

ITALIC CAPITAL LETTERS, also, are used after T:1750 to show out the specific teachings which I have received from the Holy Spirit. Such an identification was not requested of me at the time when I was writing Volumes One and Two of "Teachings-in-Prayer"; but it has been the Will of God, from the time of writing Volume Three onwards, that I use this means of providing a clearer 'picture' of the work of all Three Divine Persons within the soul, when the soul is more fully 'immersed' in God's Life in the later stages of the contemplative journey.

Bold type is used throughout for teachings which were given to me with especially-great power or glory.

PART ONE

CHAPTERS ONE TO SEVEN

FAITH

IN GOD THE SON:
JESUS CHRIST
OUR FRIEND AND REDEEMER

" ... God's foolishness is wiser than human wisdom, and God's weakness is stronger than human strength.

Take yourselves for instance, brothers, at the time when you were called: how many of you were wise in the ordinary sense of the word, how many were influential people, or came from noble families? No, it was to shame the wise that God chose what is foolish by human reckoning, and to shame what is strong that God chose what is foolish by human reckoning; those whom the world thinks common and contemptible are the ones that God has chosen - those who are nothing at all to show up those who are everything. The human race has nothing to boast about to God, but you God has made members of Christ Jesus and by God's doing he has become our wisdom, and our virtue, and our holiness, and our freedom. As scripture says: *if anyone wants to boast, let him boast about the Lord.*" (1 Co 1:25).

1 INITIATION
(1942-1953)

IN THE BEGINNING. BAPTISM. WAR. WORSHIP.

Life, like a river.

Today, I was gazing once again at the waters of the River Cam. It's a warm sunny day in Cambridge at the end of September, 1998; and I'm here on a short break, to finish writing this book about my life: such a peculiar subject which I would never have dreamed of beginning, if Our Lord hadn't asked me to write a spiritual autobiography. He's told me that weak people will be helped by the story of someone weak who has found peace and joy through His love.

The whole of my Catholic life has gone by, as if in a flash, in the time since I stood on this very same bridge at nineteen years old, gazing at the river, but then accompanied by my fiancé and a crowd of friends. We were posing for a group photograph before dashing off to drink and to dance for hours; and I was happy and puzzled, worried and excited, all at once: living in a haze of uncertainty which was life-without-Christ; and I wouldn't swap the peace I now enjoy, or my present bliss and fulfilment, for any past worldly health or hope, or strength, agility or youthful radiance.

My adult life has consisted of nearly thirty years of struggle and pain - though with many huge and marvellous joys which I can't describe in this story, which must be primarily about the soul's spiritual journey, from the beginning until almost the end. But my present joy is so great that I'm yearning to assure those who will listen to me to put their trust in Christ, and to step out bravely to do His Will no matter what it costs. There's no better or safer way of living, and no surer way of pleasing Him and deepening one's friendship with Him; and it's in order to obey Christ and to share my story that I've begun, tonight, by speaking about a river.

As I leaned on the balustrade once more to look into the darkening water, I saw that my very ordinary life shares something of the water's mystery. The river below the bridge has a surface coating of pond-weed which is swept aside by each passing swan, or by the oars of the punts, in summer; and yet the river, in its depths, races swiftly and unhesitatingly in one direction. My life, like the river, might be judged, at first glance, as being only shallow and sluggish. It is overlaid on the surface with several preoccupations; it is interrupted by strange events and new responsibilities; and yet, in its depths - I trust - it is flowing swiftly and serenely towards the complete union with God in Heaven for which I long.

Shadows and sunlight.

It's in obedience to Christ, only, that I'm writing about myself; and it will be plain, quite soon, that this examination of spiritual problems and struggles has produced a story which sounds far gloomier, at first glance, than someone else's glowing account of successful pastoral work, or another person's lively piece about conferences and travel. I hope that anyone who perseveres with this book will see, towards the end, something of the Light and Bliss which are God's gifts to all who try to love Him and who are willing to accept His purifications; but the descriptions of darkness seem to be necessary if I'm to do what Christ wants, which is to describe the traditional path of the spiritual life in its entirety: from childhood, through the 'Dark Nights' of the soul, and onwards to the transforming union.

If I say that much of this story is 'dark' and sad, the dark patches can be compared with the shadowy areas which I just mentioned in writing about a river. Caught forever in these depths are wrecks and relics which no-one knows about except those who have shared bits of my life with me - whether family members, friends or priests; and some of the things which are scattered about in the darkness have never been seen by anyone except myself; and I have explored the darkness so thoroughly only because of the Light which God Himself has shone down fiercely in prayer in order to change me and to make me ready to do His work; and this work includes several volumes of 'Teachings-in-prayer', as well as this book, and numerous other parts of Our Lord's whole project.

The task given to me by Christ, therefore, is not to write much about persons and places but rather to examine the 'depths' where prayer begins, just as scientists who study aquatic life-forms begin by exploring the rich mud on the river bottom and not the clear bright water. I suppose the richest-possible story we could read would be one in which several levels of someone's life were examined, but this is not that sort of book: apart from a small number of brief ascents to the 'surface,' to make the chronology plain.

A very simple examination is required of me, by Christ - as is usually required, I believe, whenever people write about the spiritual journey and the life of the soul. There just isn't enough room for an adequate presentation of all the 'layers' of this 'river' - nor is it necessary to write about them all. But the mere fact that so much has had to be left out is bound to make the story appear rather gloomier at first than it might otherwise have been. I suppose that few people would imagine that a river were something to be enjoyed for boating, swimming, washing - or fishing - if they had only seen a film of the areas which lie in near-darkness.

God's 'Canticles'.

Having spoken about 'gloom', I must say that there's a great deal here about love: not about my love for God, although that's included, but primarily about God's Love for me: and for everyone. I can't compare the style or approach, but I can say that the subject is the same as that of Saint John of the Cross, in his "Spiritual Canticles" - though I've only come across little extracts. The Lord, I have to say, has 'sung' me His 'canticles'; and He wants me to record them, and also to reveal my spiritual journey, to make plainer to other people how 'mad' with Love He is - for all of us. He delights in us. If people really knew what He's like, they'd refuse Him nothing; yet so many of us have chosen, at times, to be blind, and to fulfil our own ambitions rather than to make the sacrifices which are necessary so that we can allow all that 'blinds' us to God's Love to be torn away. Only when we are single-minded about God can His Light, beauty and astounding Glory fill our souls and our lives.

It's true that I haven't yet reached 'Home'. But I hope and pray that God will keep me faithful, and will let me see Him face-to-face one day. What would be the point of life, without that hope? Meanwhile, He keeps me close to Him in a way of prayer and conversation which, when I first began to learn about prayer, I had never even dreamed might be achieved on earth; and I'm writing this not to boast about where God has led me, but in order to be obedient to His wishes.

He wants other people to read the story of a weak and reluctant Catholic Christian so that they will see how faithful and patient He is: never put off by anyone's sins, but always tender and encouraging. I know from experience that God truly guides and teaches all who turn to him in sincere prayer; and I'm encouraged by the verses in the Acts of the Apostles which describe the rulers' astonishment at the activities of Saints Peter and John "...CONSIDERING THEY WERE UNEDUCATED LAYMEN; AND THEY RECOGNISED THEM AS ASSOCIATES OF JESUS" (Ac 4:13); and that's all I want to be: not a priest - which is impossible - or a leader, but an "ASSOCIATE OF JESUS" (Ac 4:13): someone who spends a lot of time with Him, and who loves to share with others the joy of that friendship; and it's now, when Christ has invited me to tell this story, that I can share the "GOOD NEWS" of that friendship (Ac 8:25) more widely.

A further request from Christ has been that I place a sequence of little photographs of myself within this book. That's why each chapter title is aligned with a snap-shot, despite my reluctance. By this evidence that this book has been written by a real person, in a particular place and era, Christ wants to demonstrate that He chose me for this unique work, as He chooses each one of us to do a different task.

It's not as though Christ sat in Heaven, ready to offer this particular task to the first person He happened to see. When there's special work to be done, He's not like a farmer who asks every passing stranger to come and help with the harvest and to earn some money at the same time. No, that's not how He works in times when there are special problems; and it's because there's so much loss-of-faith in this era that Christ chose me, taught and trained me, and invited me to put Him first and to undertake this work - a work tailored to my weaknesses - so that people in this place and era can be given a vigorous reminder, through books and paintings, of the eternal truths of the Catholic Faith.

[A personal story.

Except for the very early part of the book, in which I've written about a Christian upbringing and about conversion, there's little information here about my immediate family: about personalities and foibles, and almost nothing about highlights or holidays. Quite deliberately, I've scarcely begun to describe the numerous places where I've lived; nor is there much about my friends.

My husband and children are very much alive, for which I thank God; but none of us is entirely free to write about family life or about friendships without considering the thoughts and feelings of the precious people involved. A particular respect is due between spouses. No married person should forget that he or she is half of a couple, whether in the present way of life, or in shared memories, or in matters of mutual loyalty on certain topics. Furthermore, Christian married couples who have experienced the wonder and sense of responsibility which come from having been allowed to 'create' and to carry to birth and beyond other human beings have become founders and foundresses, we can say, of little Christian communities of the family; and we who have been so privileged are not free, therefore, to lay bare the details of the lives of the members of our families. All that is good is a cause for gratitude to God; anything not-so-good is already forgiven; and I who write this hope and pray that I'm forgiven, too, for every scrap of pain or bad example.

Aspects of life and society.

There's very little within these pages about the society in which we live, or about national or international events; nor is there much about social or cultural events, or politics. But this doesn't mean that I've led a sheltered life, or that I'm not interested in any of these things. I've had to concentrate, in these writings, on the highways and byways within the human heart and soul; and it's not part of God's plan that I include much material about external matters.

Having said that, I must say very briefly that every good aspect of our earthly life has fascinated me. So much of what we see in persons or things is either beautiful or intricate, or puzzling or awesome. I've been stunned by the sights and sounds of earth: by beauty in art and nature and music - and also in human hearts; and there's no denying that we can be led some way towards God through the beauty which He has created. I'm aware, also, that the ways in which we develop spiritually during earthly life are bound up with the ways in which we live, move, suffer, celebrate and ponder, in our bodily lives in a material world; and I know that the tactile and practical ways in which we express love for our neighbour, as we help and console by physical work and gestures as well as by prayer, can have eternal consequences.

Nevertheless, few of those things are relevant to the telling of this story. I must deal, here, with my more immediate and direct discoveries about God through thought, and through the gift of faith; and I must say even more about the subject of prayer. These topics will serve as an introduction to Christ's instructions, which have been given to me first through His Church and then through His own Person, in prayer.]

God's invitation.

It seems timely to repeat, here, that only God's invitation has led me to write about my own life at length, as an introductory volume to several volumes of "Christ's Instructions." Nothing could have made me sit at my desk to write this book except Christ's explanation that it's essential to the whole task; but now that I've started, I'm aware that some people will ask why on earth this work has been entrusted to me - to a married woman. Why hasn't it been given to a priest in our Church, or to a nun, or to a single person in 'the world' in a position of influence?

It is so that someone who is involved in a very ordinary life - the sort of domestic and social life experienced by so many other people - and who has known 'ordinary' yet wonderful human love in various forms - as child and as daughter, as wife, as mother, and as friend - can say to every other 'ordinary' person: "The Love of God has been shown to me; and I assure you that His Love surpasses, astoundingly, everything that is known in the most fulfilling and joyful good human relationships. His Love is worth any sacrifice." This is something which - the Lord has decided - needed saying by a married person at the end of the twentieth century: in an age when, sad to say, celibacy and religious life are derided and when, therefore, the wise words of celibate monks, priests and nuns are discounted. But there's something else to be explained.

It's God's wish that people be shown, through my life, with its mixture of shame and glory, and struggle and fulfilment, that union with God is possible for anyone who will respond to His loving invitation. It's possible for those who love the world's beauty and also for those who are meditative and solitary. He wants to demonstrate, through me and my weakness, that union with Him is possible for housewives as well as for priests or religious. It's possible for those with no advanced education, as well as for the sick, and the lonely, or for those with a thousand pressing tasks to do, and for those whose hours of pain pass by very slowly.

There's no age at which we're disqualified from finding God. No state of health, enemy, place or group can chain us in a Godless darkness, if we are willing to take the steps which will lead to union: if we are brave enough to abandon ourselves to God's care, in love and contrition: utterly determined to please Him; and it's because I want to say more about that sort of abandonment that I'll now dive deep into the 'river', to return to my life's beginning, and to speak about how I was led steadily towards Christ despite early parental problems, confusion, unhappiness, puzzlement, ill-health and hesitation. He cannot be defeated; I mean that He cannot be prevented from giving His gifts and joys to someone who is willing to keep looking in His direction and who pleads for His help.

A special date.

If I look back to the very beginning, I can say that the date of my birth has given me more joy in adult life than ever it did when I was a child.

When I was small, I was told that the twenty-fourth of August was the feast-day of an obscure Apostle called Bartholomew. But I discovered many years later, with increasing glee and thanksgiving, that August 24th was the date on which one of my heroes had died after all his literary and spiritual labours. His name was Father Ronald Knox: an author who had cheered me with his "Spiritual Aenaeid", and with "The Creed in Slow Motion." Also, the great Saint Teresa of Avila had founded the first of her reformed monasteries on that day. Even better, it was the date on which the astonishing St. Rose of Lima had entered Heaven; and I was delighted to realise that the French Bishop, Saint Ouen, whose feast-day is August 24th, was the very Saint whose church I had explored in Rouen when I had wandered around as a lonely adolescent, marvelling at the echoing interior of the church dedicated to his name; and the reason for my delight in these discoveries was that I had entered the Catholic Church, in full

9

Communion, at twenty-five years old. I was thrilled with all the riches she offered me, treasures which included real friendships with the Saints.

But on August 24th, 1942, I was born in a nursing home near Slough, and then was brought back to Broad Oak Court where there was a two-year-old sister to greet me. Our parents were devout and hard-working Christians, temporarily separated by war-time duties. My mother was a Leith from Fifeshire in Scotland; and although she was christened Catherine Isabella she was known first as "Kitty" and then as "Kay". My father was a Morley from Rochdale in Yorkshire. He was baptised Alec - and always regretted not having received what he called a 'proper' name. 'Alec' was seen as a pitiful abbreviation.

At the time of my birth my father was somewhere far away, serving with the Royal Corps of Signals, in the British Army; so my mother took me for christening at St Peter's Anglican Church, Chalvey, within a few weeks of my birth, without him. I was baptised "IN THE NAME OF THE FATHER AND OF THE SON AND OF THE HOLY SPIRIT" (Mt 28:19) on what I would later recognise and celebrate as the feast of Saint Francis of Assisi: on October 4th. But in infancy - at the pouring of water, with the invocation of the Holy Trinity, and the gift of the names of Pauline and Elizabeth - I was brought into the life and grace of God unaware of my Heavenly friend, and temporarily ignorant of the great gifts that I'd received; but I lived a life of wondering innocence, despite my failings, until later, in a time of prolonged misery, when I carelessly turned away. This book is the story of that early 'life of grace', and of the path along which Christ led me when at last I'd decided to give Him first place in my life. It's also about many of the setbacks, failures and torments which I have endured in the course of the journey.

Trust and confusion.

There seem to have been three main dark 'areas' or eras of my life. The first of these was brief. It lasted from my first memories of faces, places and furniture until the sudden arrival of light and consolation when I was three.

My general impression, from about one or two years old, was of confusion about the various people who looked after me. It seemed that I was frequently led away from a familiar room to sit and play somewhere else. I never knew what to expect next, and my mother only appeared in the evenings when I was tired. I didn't understand the reason for all this moving about from place to place.

Since I was puzzled and even lonely I was sometimes cross and impatient. But I never had temper tantrums. For the first few years, I was trusting and docile, and very affectionate. I suppose that some longing for warmth must have remained in my heart when I was eased off my mother's lap by the baby brother who appeared when I was sixteen months old. It was the absence of any steady pattern of family life, in war-time, that also contributed to my general sense of puzzlement. My father appeared occasionally, on leave from active service, and then disappeared once more. When I was a toddler, there was no sense of routine. I blindly followed instructions, learning to accept all that occurred, though doing so with more bewilderment than joy. In different ways we experienced grief and fear and darkness. We never knew whether, in an hour's time, we'd still be playing in the garden, or would be hiding in the chest-of-drawers again because the bombs were falling on the town once more; and every evening was spent huddled in our little kitchen. The rest of the flat looked utterly forbidding, from that oasis of light. All of the windows were covered in 'black-out' material, and we couldn't afford to run up large electricity bills. It must have been gruelling for my mother, coping alone with three lively toddlers in an small flat, with all the sleeplessness and trials brought by childhood diseases, war-time regulations, and sheer loneliness. With very few luxuries, she was struggling to make ends meet on the pay-packet of a private in the British Army.

A Providential meeting.

Hardship was no novelty to my mother. Both of her parents had died by the time she was sixteen. To use her own words, she had been 'devastated' by the loss. Also, her life of devout but leisurely gentility with her music-teacher mother had ended. When she had spent two years living with her sister and their two elderly guardians, and had finished her school studies, she left for St Hild's College, Durham, where she trained as a teacher.

It was in Durham, when she was staying at a youth hostel near Gilesgate, that my mother had a brief encounter with a person who seemed as lively, strong-minded and high-principled as herself: and as ready to share a joke: the man who would be my father. And when, by Providence, they were unexpectedly brought together again in the Lake District, on holiday, after a six-month gap, they were overjoyed. They married in 1936, and moved 'down South' to begin what they both hoped would be a better and more prosperous life. My mother was twenty-one years old, and my father five years older. When they were eventually able to buy a little house of their own, they named it "Gilesgate."

My father, too, had trained as a primary school teacher, and had managed to find work in Aylesbury before their wedding. My mother resigned her teaching post on marrying, to become an adventurous housewife. She learned about cooking and entertaining; and the pair of them enjoyed the company of French friends at a southern seaside resort in the long, hot holidays each summer.

From what I was to hear later on, they were very happy during the first three or four years of married life. She was a fervent Anglican and he a devout "Quaker", each tolerating and visiting the other's place of worship. Or perhaps 'tolerate' is too mild a word. They were very strongly bound together by their trust in God and in Holy Scripture. I learned from my mother that in early married life they had embarked on a six-month residential training course, expecting to be posted as teachers to a Quaker school in Madagascar. My father reminded me on many occasions that I might have been born there, instead of England. For fun, he used to call me not just "skinny Lizzie", but "my Malagassy lassie!"

But there was something sad connected with that episode. What he didn't tell me but what I learned much later on was that before the course had ended, it was gently put to my father that he wouldn't be quite suitable. Whether the reasons were to do with education or social standing, or with my mother's unwillingness to leave the Church of England to join the Society of Friends, I can't be sure; but although my parents were disappointed, they didn't let their sadness diminish their faith. My mother's missionary instincts were not to be frustrated. She became vigorously involved in Anglican church life in the town where she was to spend

11

much of her life. She also demonstrated her commitment by teaching Religious Education for many years at the Secondary Modern School where she was first a form-teacher, then deputy head-teacher, during the nineteen-fifties and sixties; and during the same era, my father was promoted, to become head-master of a little Church primary school; then he trained enthusiastically in his spare time to become a lay-reader in the Church of England. I remember him making a new wooden box for his preaching expeditions.

He used to fill it very carefully with his new surplice and stole, with his bible and prayerbook, and other items. He was thrilled by his additional qualification. Once a week, he set off to preach a sermon in one of the tiny villages which could no longer support a resident vicar.

Defence of the family.

To return to the nineteen-thirties, my parents enjoyed only three years of normal married life before the sudden and horrifying approach of 'World War Two' brought turmoil to the whole nation. In the last days of August, 1939, they were in the South of France, visiting friends; and then they made their way back to England unaware of the narrowness of their escape from a country whose approaching conquerors were trying to extinguish Christian civilisation.

My father didn't remain a teacher for much longer. As a 'Quaker' he had supported the pacifist movement sincerely until the moment when Britain was threatened by a Nazi invasion. Then he became convinced that it was his Christian duty to defend his wife and baby. He decided, too, that he couldn't stand aside and let another man "do his fighting for him," should Nazi tanks roll Northward from English Channel ports. He believed that plain evil shouldn't go unchallenged.

Within a year or two he was a soldier in the 'Royal Signals,' far from home, although allowed back on leave a few times during a five-year campaign: hence my own birth in 1942 and that of my brother in 1944. But those years brought him more than the noise of battle. During a time of quiet endurance in the North of Scotland, long before the Normandy landings in which he would play his part, his musings on duty and Church led him prepare for Confirmation and so for communicant status in the Church of England; and when he returned home on leave and told my mother his news, it was greeted with delight.

From what I've heard, my mother coped very bravely without him. It was during the war, and before any of us was born, that good school positions became available because so many male teachers had left to join the Armed services. Married women were delighted to fill the vacant posts; and my mother seized the opportunity to use her training: determined to keep on teaching even after she became a mother.

A sense of order.

My mother so enjoyed her work, and the company of fellow-teachers, that she left my elder sister and me - and then our new young brother - in the care of various neighbours during the day. We were sometimes unhappy, although my mother wasn't unaware of it at the time; but we were too young to make comparisons. Moulded by circumstance, we became very stoical and adaptable, accepting it as normal that our mother had a full-time job.

Our way of life changed dramatically, however, when our father returned home to stay. Life in our flat was wonderfully transformed by his breezy affection, imaginative ideas and sense of order. I was three years old when he arrived as a strange soldier at the front door. I remember the very moment of his arrival. As he scooped me up for a big hug, I felt his moustache tickling my face and his uniform jacket scratching my arms; and I wondered who on earth was this man who acted as though he knew me, when I thought he was a complete stranger.

In only a few hours, I was thrilled to have someone in our home who was so generous and amusing. He was very strict about good manners and telling the truth, and about doing one's chores before amusing oneself; but I didn't mind a bit.

Things were rather different for my mother, of course. I learned in later years how difficult it had been for her to re-adjust to a normal family life. She had grown used to making all the important decisions during my father's absence; and he had been conditioned by war both to give and to demand instant and absolute obedience: something easy for a child to adapt to, but not for an independent-minded wife.

He was a good, generous-hearted man, trained in a hard school, who expected others to embrace life and its toil with the same fortitude and single-mindedness. During the past year he had jumped off a landing-craft on "D-day plus one" to help in the liberation of France. In addition, he had entered the camp at Belsen only twenty-four hours after the gates were opened to the liberators. His force was part of the 'clean-up' squad. Never in my life did he speak about what he saw there; his tears told me. But it was partly because he had witnessed and endured so many horrors during the war that he found it hard in later years to be patient with people who were hesitant or complaining as they faced lesser trials.

I saw him weep only twice in my life: once when I, the first of his daughters to 'leave' him, was ready for my wedding service, and once - only a year or two earlier - when we had heard a radio programme about the war. My father had sat listening in silence as tears poured down his cheeks. We longed to know what was troubling him, but he didn't utter a word.

A different flat.

Just before my father's re-appearance in 1945, we had moved a few yards along the road to a downstairs flat. A short path led from our new home to a small back garden, where we could sometimes help with the weeding and play with our friends. Until then, we had been forbidden to run outside. Air-raid shelters - vast holes in the ground - had been constructed in the grassy space between our flats and the main road; and so we had rarely played outside unsupervised. Our flat was dark and unattractive, and it grew even more crowded every few months, when our only living grandparent came to stay. She was confined by illness to a bed in a dark back room. My mother took care of her to relieve her sister-in-law who cared for her day after day in Reading. But that's why we were thrilled by our new freedom to go outdoors.

As I shall tell, we had very few relatives; but those we had were valued. For example, we left home each Sunday morning throughout my young childhood to drive to church, but would rarely return before three o'clock, or even later. When the church service was over, we children were taken to Reading, then were left to amuse ourselves by playing outside. My parents spent the time visiting Granny, no matter how tired they were; and what good lessons we learned, by example. Those were outwardly fruitless visits to someone barely able to speak; but they were part of the warp and woof of a faithful family life: simple duties to be undertaken without excuses or complaint.

A Catholic school.

Soon after my father's return from abroad, and when I was still three years old, I was greeting a further new experience not with delight but with howls of fear. I remember the short walk across the grass on the day when my mother took me to St Anthony's school, a mere hundred yards away from our flat, for my first full day in a nursery-class.

The peace and order which I experienced there were so far beyond my experience that they were rather unnerving. But I grew to cherish the atmosphere of calm and safety. None of the staff was ever hurried or angry. The lessons and the afternoon naps delighted me, although some uneasiness persisted in the playground. For a reason unknown to me, we were made to feel that we didn't belong. My later discovery that St. Anthony's was a Catholic school brought no enlightenment; I didn't know the meaning of the different religious labels. My Anglican mother had been welcomed there, on her return to infant-teaching; and of course it made sense for her to have her own children taught in the same establishment. My father would never have chosen a Catholic school; but he was away when the decision was made. My mother had learned to make her own decisions, as I mentioned earlier, as she coped alone during the course of the war.

God and His Creation.

The pattern of life had improved by the time I was four or five years old. My most vivid memory of that time is of the large crucifix on the wall of the school Assembly Room. I used to look at the figure on the Cross - far above my head - as I wondered to myself who He was, and why He was there. I was untroubled by the sight, because He had a peaceful face; but I loved to learn more about Him from our teachers. Everything I heard about Him in class seemed reasonable as well as exciting; and for a little while longer I found some similarity between what I was told about Christianity at school and what I learned about it at home and at church.

Church-going was central to my parent's life, so we three children were shepherded, weekly, to St. Peter's Anglican Church where we had each been baptised. Children were made thoroughly welcome; I remember being fascinated by the coloured Gospel pictures on the stamps which were handed out to us each week. It was thrilling for me to stick them in a book of my very own.

During that time, my great delight in church-going stemmed not only from the stamps, but also from enjoyment of the lavish breakfasts provided for the whole congregation after each Communion Service. This was in the days when food was severely rationed; and the generosity of those who made us welcome led me gradually to relax and observe, and pray. Everything to do with God proved interesting to me, and I was happy to kneel in prayer, to sing hymns or to watch the people around me. It was impossible to be bored, since I had a strong and fascinated belief, even at that age, in God.

The notion of God as our Creator seemed self-evident, because of the wonders of nature. Birds, leaves, cloudy skies - even worms, bees and snails fascinated me; and new marvels could be seen each time we were taken for a walk along the leafy roads near Farnham Royal. I was amazed by all that God had made.

A special name.

It seemed as though I had a special connection to God through my own name, as well as through the natural world, and through my prayers in church. My mother had said, when I was young, not that 'Elizabeth' was a Saint's name, but that it was a Bible name which meant "Beloved of God"; and that delighted me. I wasn't as happy with my second name, Pauline, which I associated for several years with a book called "The perils of Pauline." It was a name more suitable, I thought later, for rich girls in gymslips who played lacrosse, and who always had neat clothes and shiny hair. But when Saint Paul became my favourite Saint, after Our Blessed Lady, I was more than content to have the feminised version of his name.

Looking for truth.

As firmly as I believed in God, at five years old, I refused to believe in some of the other things which people spoke about from time to time. I couldn't persuade myself to believe in fairies, or Father Christmas, whatever other people said. There was no proof - and I had no power of invention. One year, when I was about five, I kept myself awake after hanging up my Christmas stocking, determined to prove to myself that the gift-giver wasn't a mythical "Santa", but was my own father. I succeeded, and felt very gratified by my experiment. Knowing the truth was more important than allowing myself to slide into pleasurable fantasies based on falsehood.

It seemed extraordinary to me in later years that some children cherish 'imaginary' friends. I was taught so firmly in childhood to distinguish between fact and fancy, and all lying was regarded by my parents with such utter horror, that I was quite unable to 'invent' anything at all.

One great blessing which arose from that ruthlessness was that I can't recall ever having been frightened by 'the dark', or by "the Supernatural" as it was commonly portrayed in comic books or advertisements. I knew that God is invisible, but I accepted that fact happily. I also learned that He is all-powerful; and my faith in that truth was so great that I never worried about ghosts or goblins, nor about other creatures who were rumoured to interfere with our lives. My parents and teachers told me boldly that God is Good; and it seemed to me that the "God" whose existence I accepted so easily had distributed plenty of evidence of His Beauty and Intelligence. Furthermore, the concept of God as some sort of judge seemed logical, since I understood even before I was seven the difference between right and wrong. My conscience was at work: very well-formed by my mother and father.

Quarrels about truth.

In that secure and contented time of my life, there was only one cause of real alarm. I encountered jovial scorn whenever I repeated at home certain truths put forward at the Catholic primary school. I was full of questions, as many children are; but the answers were contradictory. Home and school authorities disagreed. Most of our queries at home - whether about God or Creation - were welcomed, and answered; yet if ever I spoke at home of what I had learned at school about the Pope being the successor of Saint Peter, to whom Jesus had given "THE KEYS OF THE KINGDOM OF HEAVEN" (Mt 16:19), or about the Blessed Virgin Mary, I was told that my teachers were wrong and that I'd been misled. This was distressing for me, for a simple reason; and I didn't even consider that my feelings had been hurt. I wanted truth, even at that age. It seemed astonishing to me that I'd been sent to a school where un-truths were taught; and I wondered why my parents had permitted this, if truth - as they insisted, at home - were paramount.

On a few subjects, parents and teachers were in agreement. For example, in further lessons at school, I learned more about the soul, and how it can become "stained by sin". This truth seemed obvious to me, and my parents didn't disagree. I wasn't quite sure where my soul was, but various adults said quite firmly that it lay "within". I pictured it, briefly, as a large, round, white object lying somewhere in the region of my stomach. I supposed that it became 'spotted' here and there whenever I was rude or selfish, but that it was restored to its pristine whiteness by some marvellous invisible action of God, whenever I was 'sorry'. The knowledge didn't upset me; far from it. It made me happy because I believed in the essential truth of this process. It seemed logical, and it harmonised with the way I felt about wrong-doing, whether or not I was found out or criticised. My 'soul' or conscience felt 'spotted' if ever I was unkind or greedy, even if no-one else knew about it; and whenever I said 'sorry', I was forgiven, and felt better; and since my parents didn't harbour grudges, I received wonderful lessons in the beauty of repentance and reconciliation.

In every aspect of life, I wanted to know the truth about things, and to reach to the heart of each mystery. I asked 'Why?, How?, Where?' and 'When?', not just about spiritual teachings but about the working of the gadgets on my father's carpentry bench: indeed, about everything which I couldn't work out for myself. My sometimes careless investigations seemed to bring me nothing but trouble.

A symbol of their love.

When I was four or five, I was given a doll by my parents, at Christmas. It wasn't a rag doll, but a proper doll, with a moulded face and limbs. It even had a beautiful nylon hair-do, and I was pleased and very grateful. It was a total surprise to me. Children like us didn't make lists of things we required.

16

Only much later did I realise that such gifts were not only unusual but expensive, so recently had the war ended. The gift delighted me because it was beautiful and had moving parts. I had no desire to cuddle it, since it wasn't soft and warm like my old knitted Teddy; but what I marvelled at most were the eyelids which opened and closed, and the lashes which stood out in a stiff fringe around each perfect glass eye.

Alas, I forgot my manners. After a brief and delighted "Thankyou!," I looked at the doll closely, but failed to do the expected thing. Kneeling on the floor, I began to take the doll apart, fascinated by how it had been fitted together. Immediately, I was roundly condemned for what was seen as vandalism, but which was truly - although I could hardly have pronounced the words - an act of scientific enquiry. When I protested that I'd only wanted to see how it was made, I was told how much it had cost and how thoughtless I was. Alas, I'd been careless. First, I hadn't behaved as little girls were expected to behave; and - much worse - I'd failed to see the doll as a symbol of my parents' love. I'd treated it merely as an object, just as I treated my brother's construction set: the 'Meccano' which kept us busy for hours, and which I preferred to girlish things like miniature tea sets or embroidery hoops.

Security and joy.

After two years spent in the nursery, and a year or two in the primary school, in Slough, I was very pleased when we were asked by our father if we would like to leave in order to attend a school in Amersham, many miles away, to which he had just been appointed as Head. With great excitement we accepted his offer, even after learning that for many months we'd have to travel a long way each morning and afternoon, the five of us crammed into a little car: five, because my mother would come with us as well, for part of each journey. She was to be dropped off daily at the village school to which she had recently been appointed as Head; and we'd collect her on our way home.

Our father organised the daily departure with military efficiency. But it was wonderful to be with him and none of us complained. When, eventually, we moved to a council house three miles away from the new school, we attended the local Anglican Church and made new friends. My father's new post was in a "Church of England Mixed Infants School", called St. Mary's. We had strict instructions to call him "Sir," not "Daddy", between nine o'clock and three-thirty, in an attempt to spare us being teased as "teacher's kids."

Sad to say, future punishments were more severe than those meted out to other children, who might occasionally experience lenient judgements; but my father dared not act "soft" with us, he later explained, in case what might have been seen as favouritism should cause discipline to be eroded.

For at least one year, he was my class-teacher as well as my Headmaster. I found out first-hand that he was a gifted teacher. Every subject was brought alive by his enthusiastic explanations. He knew his subjects and had a fund of fascinating stories. After giving a vigorous explanation of some science problem or history theory he was able to bring things alive with home-made visual aids. He could draw and make models, effortlessly, with any bits of available material, doubtless helped by his years of 'make do and mend' in war-time army camps; and his crisp and comprehensive diagrams clarified Old Testament history so marvellously that I was sad when each lesson ended.

Childhood impressions.

When I was a child, I heard my parents speak reverently of "THE WORD OF GOD" (Lk 5:1) or of 'The Bible' through which, I was informed, God spoke to us. But despite all that I was taught, I didn't understand how God could 'speak' to us through a large, dusty black book which was too heavy for a child like myself even to lift onto a table from the bookshelves. However, for a few years, I listened to my elders and betters, very puzzled about all sorts of things, but interested in God and in Creation. I was happy to believe that others knew much more than I did, and that every mystery would be fully explained one day; and so I enjoyed the lessons from my father in which the Bible was explained to some degree. We were told, in simple words, how God had revealed himself to the Jewish people, long ago, and how He had prepared them for the coming of Christ.

It made me very happy to listen to Old Testament stories, and to draw pictures in my exercise book, as instructed, and to copy lists of Israelite Kings or Prophets. Most eight-year-olds enjoy drawing and painting. But the New Testament presented me with problems. I remember wondering exactly who Christ was. How could He be the "SON OF MAN" (Mk 10:33) and also the "SON OF GOD" (Mt 14:33); and why should a person be called 'The Word'?

My other cause of mild distress was the archaic phrasing of our King James version of the Bible. I was never happy, trying to read large chunks of text. Middle-aged people said it was beautiful; but it sounded merely obscure to me. Later, in my 'teens', when I began to prefer everything 'modern', and when my heroes were not just Matthew Arnold and Rupert Brooke but Elvis Presley and Buddy Holly, things were even worse; I became thoroughly repelled by what I had decided was merely quaint and old-fashioned. There seemed to be no place for those ancient texts in my anguished adolescent life in a non-religious state school.

Thoroughly happy.

From the ages of seven to eleven, however, in the junior school, life was wonderfully fulfilling. I was never bored, and was rarely frightened. My stutter disappeared. All that had made me feel an outsider at the Catholic School was forgotten, as I went gladly to my class each morning, happy to be amongst friendly people and thrilled to have so much to do and to learn. I didn't realise that - through the weekly religious instruction, with visits to the Parish Church of St Mary's - we were all being led firmly along the Anglican path, away from the 'Roman' influence which my father deplored. Meanwhile, all the activities at the school thrilled me.

I accepted the peculiar lunches, which were kept warm for hours before their delivery at school in huge metal containers. The strict discipline, the outside lavatories, and the teeth-chattering play-times in winter when the wind swept over the fields behind the school: these were already part of our daily life. But the school building was small and cosy. I loved the work and the busy jolly atmosphere. I was never half-hearted or idle, and took for granted the little successes which came with my new security and happiness. Even the punishments were an accepted part of normal life: silently endured, since I was determined that I wouldn't give further satisfaction to the punisher by weeping, but soon over and forgotten.

A deliberate sin.

During that period of my life I can remember only once being truly unhappy; I don't mean that I didn't experience pain or teasing. These, with cold weather and other trials weren't a worry. Once, and once only, during that time, I was weighed down - and for the first time - by an uneasy conscience.

Thirty years later I was to describe to my elderly father an incident in the recreation ground opposite our school where we children had been allowed to play each day, supervised by a teacher. I confessed that one lunchtime I had grown impatient of queuing half-way up the steps on the children's slide. Deciding to bypass the queue, I jumped over the hand-rail; and although I was normally agile, I tripped and fell onto the concrete paving, breaking my arm. I wasn't upset by the injury but by its aftermath. I was so desperate to avoid punishment for my silliness and impatience that when I was questioned by a teacher about the fall I claimed that I'd been pushed. It was my first deliberate sin and I was seven years old.

I knew I'd done wrong, not just because my parents had always praised us for being truthful, but because the whole issue was so obviously 'black and white'. Any lie is, by definition, an un-truth, against Truth: a misuse of mind, heart and tongue. I couldn't have explained it, but it was written in my bones.

What I said was: "Someone pushed me." As soon as the words were out, I was appalled at myself. I didn't know how to put things right, feeling too cowardly to face the consequences of a confession. Broken arm or not, I would have been punished. So I kept silent, and the incident was eventually forgotten by everyone else, though so strong was my sense of alienation from God, Whom I now know to be perfect Goodness and Truth, that I've been scrupulously careful about telling the truth, ever since.

At least the experience of a private tussling with conscience was to lead to renewed efforts to be straightforward and good; but what appalled me at the time was that by that single act - and without exaggeration - it seemed as though a door had opened, inviting me into another world. It was a place where, alas, in future years, I would see that lying can be seen as normal, as is every sort of sin, for those who live in the grim slavery of rebellion against God and against His loving laws, a slavery which always masquerades as "choice".

By the time the plaster was removed from my arm, or within a few months, my parents found a house within reach of all our schools. They informed us that our long journeys from Slough to Amersham would soon be unnecessary.

Village life.

My father's school - St. Mary's - was in Old Amersham; and high on a hill above us, in New Amersham, was the Anglican Church of St. Michael and All Angels, which was favoured by my mother for its "high" churchmanship. We remained faithful to that congregation for the next decade and more. The only place of worship close by our new home was a Congregational Church. My parents explained that it wasn't like the Anglican Church, in which we had a hierarchy of Bishops, Priests and Deacons.

From the edge of Slough we had 'graduated' to a pretty country village called Hyde Heath, only three miles from Amersham; and there we took joyful possession of a spacious 'semi', which was newly-built on a small leafy Council Estate, amongst high-hedged lanes. We thought the whole experience Heavenly: with plenty of space, and our own path to the front door - and a front garden. In and around our new home, soon after the move, I was almost overwhelmed with joy at all my new discoveries.

We children explored the village common, then the nearby farm, and, not much further away, a little wood beside a railway line, where we'd soon be leaping almost daily onto the footbridge, to cling to the guard-rails and to shriek with exhilaration as each steam-engine thundered past beneath us. Never before in my seven years of childhood had I been able to run about freely without worrying about traffic; and I was fascinated by everything to do with country life.

Explorations.

During our first two or three years in the Council house, while we were still small, we were driven to school each day in our 'new' car, a little "Morris 8" which my father had bought so that he and my mother could arrive punctually and dry-shod at their respective schools, each day in term-time. But as we children grew older, we frequently walked the six miles from village to town and back. I was energetic, healthy and adventurous; and for a few years more, I was contented and obedient in class and at home, indeed, I was so happy that I can say about that period of my life that it was idyllic - on both the natural and the supernatural plane. All was peaceful within my soul, because I had a clear conscience, since I was never aware of deliberately doing wrong, although I had innumerable faults, such as impatience, and was very thoughtless about the needs and worries of other people; and in everyday home life, I felt secure.

The framework of our lives meant that there was usually someone to turn to in little crises. Some of our friends had stay-at-home mothers who would always welcome me with a smile and a kind word - or an offer of a sandwich. There were always new and exciting things to do in one's free time - and a whole horde of friends to play with. I used to work hard at school, and also when school was over: tearing through the chores-of-the-day which were listed on a notice board inside the kitchen door. None of us dared to start playing before the work was done. But eventually, I'd be free to play outside whatever the weather and to explore the country-side with friends: and everything I saw outdoors entranced me.

During each passing year, I was thrilled by the seasons, and by all the wonders I could see in the lanes and fields which surrounded our village, whether I was looking at horse-chestnut trees with "sticky-buds", at little birds in spring, or at hedges covered with soft white veils of "old man's beard". We could have told any questioner excitedly of the nuts and berries which appeared on hedges and low branches at different times of the year. We knew when the coots were nesting on the pond, which chick would hatch first amongst the birds in the garden, and what sound a hedgehog made as it plodded round the house at dusk, its quills covered with dead leaves which brushed against the wall

When I watched migrating birds flying in formation I was astounded by their beauty and precision. As for summer sunsets, and intricate ice-patterns on our windows in winter, spiders' webs, and ripples on the village pond: when I wasn't marvelling at these things and at many others, or working, I was racing through woodlands with a gang of friends. We collected items of interest for our 'nature museum'. We climbed all the tall trees on the common, and played 'hares and hounds', rushing across the dry grass in the summer holidays, taking turns at being the hunter or the hunted.

On a more practical level, my store of country-lore was tested and enlarged in the village hall, in the Brownie pack, and, later, in the village Girl Guide troop, when young Guides still cooked soggy pastry on camp-fires and learned how to send semaphore messages with flags.

An August heat-wave.

On three occasions in that time of great joy, when I was still at primary school, I was taken away to a summer camp: twice with a group from our school, and once with the Girl Guides. I remember the pleasure of walking in the dewy grass at five or six o'clock in the morning. We went swimming, just before the 'polio' epidemic, in the river which meandered through the field where our tents were pitched. All of this incredible pleasure was to be renewed in my heart several years later when I discovered Wordsworth and the nature poets. They described so perfectly the pure, glad wonder I felt in the freshness of the early morning air, and described what I had sensed: the Presence of God gracefully infiltrating His creation.

Each day took me tumbling through a succession of joys, each delivered like a blow to eyes or ears or heart; and the sight of a dewy spider's web, or a sudden flight of birds, would distract me from any activity or conversation. As an untrained puppy darts off towards every sudden-appearing delight, I darted, temporarily undisciplined, towards wonder upon wonder. Several times each summer I'd be lying in the dry, pale yellow grass at the height of the August heat-wave, gazing up, first, to the astonishing turquoise of the sky, then looking down to the ever-present little insects which were making their way up and down grass-stalks or crawling across my little hand; and my heart would be aching with wonder at it all: almost bursting with longing to tell someone about my wonder or to thank Someone for the beauty. This was a true, spontaneous instinct for worship; yet it didn't occur to me to pray out-of-doors. Prayers were something that people recited at bed-time, to the invisible Law-giver; or they were offered up in church by a respectful and properly-garbed minister.

It didn't occur to me that God would delight in hearing my expressions of delight in His creation. I was sure I was far too unimportant to be of much interest to Someone so grand. Yes, I'd heard that Jesus died for us because He loves us, but I had no notion of what it really meant.

Discipline.

It seems right to interrupt my reflections with a declaration that in these early years I enjoyed many other gifts and blessings which were quite unrecognised by me. As I've thought about how predictable and therefore how stable was our usual family routine, I've begun to appreciate my good fortune at having parents who remained married, and who set me a great example of obedience to God's laws and of loving concern for one's neighbour, though I didn't appreciate the fact for many years. Despite their very different temperaments they remained loyal to each other until death parted them, forty-four years after their marriage. For much of their lives they differed earnestly on various aspects of religion, yet set a tremendous example both to neighbours and children by the simple goodness of their Christian lives.

During my first eighteen years on earth, truthfulness was like a steel thread woven through the fabric of our family routine. It was a thread so fine that I barely noticed it, yet so strong that it supported all the other 'threads' if ever they were under strain.

Something else I took for granted was that we generally had neighbours who were friendly and kind. In our society, then, people could be relied on to keep their word. Nobody was seen to sulk for hours, or to leave work for others to do. Discipline was strict, in all the homes we knew; and we were expected to be cheerful and punctual; but the various rules and regulations gave much security.

It was taken for granted that everyone who was well would be employed in some way: some in paid work and others working for the church in voluntary organisations. It was an age in which it was easy to find employment, but also an age when the people we knew wouldn't have been content to be idle: job or no job; and so we children were never surprised to be given work to do; and we expected to leave home to earn a living for ourselves, not to stay at home supported for a moment more than was necessary. It was also taken for granted that we could draw encouragement from our Christian beliefs in order to behave dutifully and unselfishly to everyone around us; and so the whole community shared the same outlook, tried to be neighbourly and provided some "RICH SOIL" (Lk 8:8) in which good influences could take root.

An 'Anglo-Catholic' parish.

For a few years I was co-operative at home and prayerful in church, glad to join in the activities which were suitable for a youngster. I believed in God, as I said, and relished the external joys of Christmas time, especially the fun of acting in the Parish Nativity Play. I was tremendously moved by our lovely hymns, and by the sad ceremonies of Holy Week. Each year, we looked forward to gazing at the Easter Garden, with its mysterious cave, which the vicar had created during Lent and had placed on a table set against one of the side walls in church.

There was an impressive santuary lamp in church; but the most exciting feature, for me, was the newly-installed reredos behind the altar. It was deep blue, and was patterned by a stylised 'Tree of Jesse', in gold; and the little tree-trunk at the centre bore an image of the crucified Christ.

Every Christian sign or symbol helped me to learn something more about the Christian Faith - and also about reverence and about communal worship, in that soothing prayerful place. I loved the picture of the "Virgin Mary" embroidered on the Mother's Union banner which was prominently displayed in the sanctuary; but it puzzled me. I wondered why these women should be proud of a picture of Mary if what my father had said was true: that we had been freed, three hundred years ago, from Catholic superstition. I had no idea that ours was an 'Anglo-Catholic' parish.

22

The pictures which were scattered around the church were fascinating. At home, I could find Bible illustrations, as well, and a few reproductions of paintings by Margaret Tarrant or Holman Hunt. Then one day I saw a wonderful image of Christ's Face; I spotted a "Sacred Heart" picture, when I visited a neighbour's house, on our new estate. On seeing my interest, she gave me the badge. It had a label which read "The Apostleship of the Sea", which meant nothing to me then; but the picture became my greatest treasure, even though I wasn't sure exactly Who was on it, or why He was pointing to His Heart.

My mother was greatly encouraged at seeing my interest, and imagined I was very devout. She bought a small luminous crucifix for my bedroom wall. That was precious, too - but mostly because we had few personal possessions; I was thrilled by gifts of any kind.

Prayer to "Our Lady".

One of our friendly neighbours spoke very confidently about the holy pictures in her house and about the truths of her Catholic Faith. She was quite matter-of-fact about it all and seemed dumbfounded by my ignorance about certain feast-days and Saints. She explained something about "prayer to Our Lady" and said that the Blessed Virgin had sometimes appeared on earth, and had even worked miracles through pictures and statues.

Eventually, when I was about ten years old, I put on my bedroom wall a picture of the "Blessed Virgin" - a gaudy thing made of blue and silver tin-foil which I'd probably found in one of our local jumble-sales. I stared hard at it, once, for about two full minutes - but was quite unable to persuade myself that the "Blessed Virgin" had moved, or had spoken to me; so I moved on to the next task quite unconcerned. That was the first and last time in my life that I half-hoped to see a vision. I assumed that if ever she had come down from Heaven, Mary had appeared only to Catholics, which seemed logical. I've learned that many Anglicans revere Our Lady: but amongst my own family, I only heard her described as a long-departed holy woman who, though once important, had fulfilled her task nearly two thousand years before, and had been buried in some unknown grave, and was no longer of much interest.

When I became a Catholic, later on, it didn't occur to me to hope for 'favours' or apparitions. As soon as I'd committed myself to regular prayer, I was content to accept - in prayer - whatever God chose to give me: whether darkness or light: His Presence or His apparent absence. His Will alone counted. By then, I knew so much about my own sinfulness that I was content to rejoice in the appearances of the Mother of God to her dear Bernadette and Catherine - and to Lucy, at Fatima - who, unlike me, had been patient and good.

Christian family life.

Despite my genuine ignorance in childhood about many Catholic teachings which I now know to be enormously important I can see what a great grace it was that I was educated in my early years in a firm Christian tradition, and that I spent a few years experiencing Christian family life. Despite failures, we were shown that we ought to attempt to care for one another, not only in routine work, but in feasts and festivals too. Although some aspects of life were strange or downright sad, an attempt was made to live in harmony. Sunday lunch together was important, despite the squabbles and the food rationing. We sat together round the table, supervised with strict discipline, sharing our news and opinions for half-an-hour, grievances usually suspended. Also, worship as a family was regarded as a normal event. We had no tradition of praying together at home, beyond a brief recital of 'grace' before our Sunday meal. But in our parish church we were welcomed by worshippers of all ages; so I looked forward to the weekly Holy Communion, and to the social events, especially the jumble sales which provided the treasures we could neither make for ourselves nor afford to buy at the shops.

We all spent a lot of time in church, because of choir practices as well as other events. It was through twice-weekly practices and regular singing at the Eucharist in the Church choir that I learned psalms, hymns and beautiful prayers - and was grateful for the few extra pence earned at weddings. We misbehaved a great deal, and played the fool, but it was wonderful to be able to follow the seasons of the church, and to celebrate glorious feasts year by year. I liked Christmas and Easter, each for its own mysterious holiness, and for the traditions and festivities. But the Feast of the Holy Trinity fascinated me above all, as I considered the great Mystery in quiet puzzlement and wonder. Even as a child, I was happy to sit still and think about the Godhead. I was content to believe in Something or Someone too grand and glorious for a mere human mind to comprehend.

Disappointment and distance.

Obediently following my parents in the Anglican way, in both worship and Confirmation, I understood little, but was happy - for a few years - dutifully trying to believe that others knew much more than I did. Yet when rebellion came, it wasn't puberty which fuelled it, primarily; nor was 'religion' pushed aside by time-consuming hobbies. It was thinking that unsettled me, or, rather, not thoughts, but unsatisfactory answers to the questions I framed, after thinking. But before that turmoil arose I was confirmed as an Anglican in the church of St. Mary's, which was intimately linked with the Church-of-England Primary School in which we'd attended Confirmation classes.

After listening to weeks of instruction in preparation for my Confirmation, I was ashamed of myself when I felt no surge of power from the Holy Spirit during the solemn ceremony; after all, we had been told that God would be with us even "more strongly". I assumed that God was displeased with me for being distracted at the very moment that the Bishop laid his hands on my head. My mind had been full of half-a-dozen things at once, as usual: thinking where to go, what to do, and - longing for a familiar face - looking at the choir stalls to see if my friend David was looking in my direction.

At only eleven years old, and puzzled at what seemed like a 'non-event', I accepted disappointment and distance as the essence of my relationship with "Almighty God". So many times, I seemed to fail. I'd been frequently assured that He is an ever-watchful guide and that a stern morality is the "WAY" (Mt 3:3); and so I couldn't see how He could possibly be pleased with someone like myself who was impulsive and impatient. I had no idea how one could grow close to Him, if one were so very imperfect. Heaven seemed a long way off, as if at the end of an incredibly-long earthly life; and I imagined that since it was a place for old people it was bound to be boring.

Regular worship.

As we grew older, the rules and regulations seemed to multiply. I realise, now, that devotion to God-made-man as a personal and loving Companion didn't predominate in what we were taught at the time. There was mention of 'Christ' in discussion or casual conversion, at home and at school. We heard about 'Redemption' and 'sin'; but I couldn't understand quite who Christ is. His Divinity was understated, and His titles confused me; so I continued to be puzzled for several years. Also, I wasn't sure of how to find Him. It didn't make sense to hear from my mother that she received Christ in Holy Communion, through obeying His command that she "EAT MY FLESH AND DRINK MY BLOOD" (Jn 6:54), when my father's belief - about the same Holy Communion Service - was that he only received bread and wine.

Much more straightforward were the routine lessons given in the Church Primary School about Old Testament History, and then about the travels of Saint Paul. These were to prove extremely valuable later on, as was the firm teaching about a Church Militant on earth and a Church Triumphant in Heaven. At about ten years old I couldn't have explained to anyone the real meaning of "Church" or sin, redemption or salvation. But for that short stretch of life I grasped the broad picture given to me, that all the apparatus of church rules and organisations and celebrations served one main purpose, which was to make sure that God Our Creator was properly worshipped and that we poor creatures improved our terrible behaviour.

My faults seemed ineradicable. They were listed out loud so frequently, and I saw so often what a nuisance I was, that I couldn't imagine how God could ever be pleased by my words or actions. I used to jump up and down with impatience; I was always in such a hurry to go and do exciting things that I was clumsy and sometimes forgetful. But I was full of goodwill, and liked to make other people happy. I even enjoyed praying in Church, where I felt that since I was surrounded by so many good people God wouldn't notice me or my faults and I could just enjoy taking part in the lovely hymns and prayers which ascended from our community.

Saint Michael, and other Saints.

Our vicar was an intelligent yet marvellously simple man who loved Christ dearly. The sermons were rather long, and I found it hard not to fall asleep half way through, but some of Father Caunter's reverence and awe filtered through my childish understanding. I liked to hear him speak about Angels and Saints. He gave an inspiring talk at the end of September every year, on our patronal feast of St. Michael and All Angels, but I was puzzled once again by the apparent importance to him of Saints and Angels when they had little importance in the life of a devout Christian such as my father, who was even then training to be an Anglican lay-reader.

As I mentioned earlier, I'd been told that Protestants like us shouldn't pray to the 'Saints', since that sort of practice was unnecessary for modern Christians who had been freed from foolish mediaeval ideas. That's why I came to see the Saints only as dead persons, now reproduced in stained glass, or listed in encyclopaedias. Their very names were old-fashioned, for example: Cuthbert, or Dunstan. They had all lived a thousand years ago, it seemed to me, and their exploits were as remote and irrelevant to me as King Alfred with his burning cakes.

We were encouraged to honour the role of the "Virgin Mary"; but she was only one more legendary figure from Biblical times - nothing more. Our only source of information about her, the Bible, seemed to suggest that Christ had kept her in the background. We were taught to pity all the Catholics who "idolised the Blessed Virgin". It was quietly suggested to me that the Church which they obeyed with great loyalty was a superstitious organisation whose members took part in idolatrous practices and who were as muddled and unenlightened, although in a different way, as an extreme Protestant group which was also spoken of with amazement. It was mystifying, I was told, that apparently good persons could steadfastly believe what they were taught by their Italian Pope. This was said to me with real pity and exasperation.

It can't have occurred to my informant that the 'mysterious' beliefs of Catholics might have been the cause of the manifest goodness of some of our neighbours. Despite this extraordinary information, it seemed to me that everyone I knew was kind and devout, and local families were always helpful and polite to one another.

Busy in the garden.

There was usually a friendly atmosphere on our estate. My brother and I were part of a gang of children who played together at every spare moment. When not attending our separate schools, we all played together on the common, or helped on the nearby farm; and when there were fewer friends around, I'd build little altars in the flowerbed, decorating them with flowers and small pieces of lace. I was very happy, except when busy with housework or gardening; and when I could escape, I'd be off to explore the nearby woods again, and the beautiful village common, longing to climb trees and to build secret 'dens'.

The gardening I mention was sporadic. I'd been given a little patch to cultivate, near a six-foot laurel hedge, but I despaired of being able to keep it under control. Then one day someone showed me how to make a miniature garden in an old sink - or an old roasting tin - and I was entranced by the resulting beauty and order. I planted miniature hedges, and made imitation ponds out of old mirrors which we'd found in battered leather handbags at jumble sales.

Much time was spent in inventing 'clubs' - with a friend or with my brother - with hand-made badges and membership forms, and special passwords and rules. I also found time to complete my Brownie projects, and to bury dead birds and animals in a little cemetery near the compost heap.

A musical event.

In writing about the joys of those years, I must say a few words about music; all five of us were untrained, but fairly musical. We were content with simple instruments: with the human voice itself, and recorders. We couldn't afford extra lessons of any kind: but through the school choir and the church choir, too, we fulfilled our longings to be involved in such beauty. We sang together, lustily, on every family outing in the car, belting out "Tipperary" and "Gentille Alouette" or English folk songs such as "The Ash Grove," or "Greensleeves," as well as our favourite hymns.

A Christmas gift I received during that time from generous and puzzled parents gave me tremendous joy. Quite oblivious to the noise which I was about to inflict on the family, I proudly unwrapped and played the small ukulele for which I'd been yearning. Wind instruments bored me; it was harmonies which thrilled me, rather than a succession of individual notes; and so I'd asked for what was a possibility - a ukulele - instead of foolishly pining for something expensive, such as a violin. If I carry the story a little further, on the subject of music, I can explain that after about five years of my energetic strumming, I persuaded my father to buy a guitar for my birthday, from the local music shop. I yearned to produce music that was haunting and beautiful; I was tired of cowboy songs and George Formby ditties. But I'm only mentioning this because it seems strange to me, even now, that by our comparatively minor choices or enthusiasms, God's Providence can lead us into pathways which, otherwise, we might never have taken. I mean, for example, that it was only through my guitar-playing that that I was invited, many years later, to join in a certain musical event; and through it, I met my future husband; and therefore I bore the particular children who have given us so much joy and who, I am sure, will play a part in God's wonderful plans for His Church.

Jesus' Real Presence.

If I were to choose the most strange and mysterious event of those early years, I would select without hesitation the occasion on which I was taken by a Catholic neighbour to visit the "Blessed Sacrament" at a local Convent school. Our little outing might have seemed entirely insignificant, but I realise now that it was a special gift from God: a gift I didn't brush aside when it was offered.

New facts excited me, although I don't mean gossip. I'm speaking about nuggets of information about our family tree, or about nature-study - or about the towns and villages through which I passed with my father on occasional outings in the car. He was a fount of information. So when I was offered facts about the Catholic Faith by someone who knew about it I was delighted. I'd been very interested to learn one day, in a casual conversation, that Jesus was there in the school, which was dedicated to Our Blessed Lady, and that we could go to the room where He was Present. I was invited to visit the chapel, assured that the Blessed Sacrament could be found there, in the Tabernacle. I was very interested, yet puzzled. The same 'Blessed Sacrament', my mother said, was in the local Anglican church, where some worshippers genuflected before it. However, no-one had spoken to me with quite the same confidence as my Catholic friend. It wasn't implied that Christ could be found in some vague and 'spiritual' way which depended on one's faith. I learned that He was Really Present, and that we could go and meet Him, even though He'd be invisible to us. He'd be hidden within the tabernacle above the altar. What a marvellous piece of news this was. I believed it.

We were led through the school corridor by a nun, the first I ever saw in my life. There was no-one else around; we'd gone in the school holidays. At the last moment, as the Sister opened the chapel door for us, she hesitated, perturbed that I had no covering for my head:- not even a handkerchief? Then she took pity on me, and let me in; and I saw an altar and a tabernacle a few feet away, beyond the chairs. The furnishings in the room were plainer by far than those in the Church where I usually worshipped; but I recognised in the silence a vast, wordless Sanctity, and I was content to sit quite still for a few moments knowing only that next to this Presence it was as though I knew nothing at all.

There was something new in the peace of that strange moment. It was vaguely connected to the great pangs of joy I felt when I ran across the fields in sunlight, and also to my puzzled thoughts about our being alive on earth. But I forgot all about it within a few hours, rushing on in my familiar routine. I'd believed what my friend had told me, but I couldn't connect that information to my own life. It didn't occur to me to ask to be taken back again.

2 HESITATION
(1953-1957)

A simple way of life.

It was thanks to the goodness of God and my parents that I lived in innocence, joy and grace for eleven years. Life wasn't without ordinary hardships which were accepted as routine. We suffered, as youngsters do, terrible childhood fears. The punishments we endured were ruthless, and were accepted without question. Yet now that I've heard from other people how strict was the upbringing of children, generally, in the 'forties' and 'fifties', if compared with trends of the present day, I see how fortunate we were to have parents whose whole longing was to be good and dutiful and to raise up children who would have the same outlook.

As for the discipline and the punishments, what was the appropriate in the armed forces was perhaps not adequately adapted for use with small children; but what a marvel of grace it was that parents who had each suffered greatly should have remained generous and cheerful. Their optimism and charity shone from their faces. They bore no grudges. I never heard a malicious phrase from either, even about their former 'enemies'. It didn't occur to me to analyse my parents, or to wish that they were different; and what a wonderful thing was their loyalty to one another.

Other things puzzled me more. I was full of questions about life itself: about who we are, and why we do what we do, and why is life thus? I was told, flatly, that there were no sure answers to many questions, told that I should stop "worrying your head" about them all.

The Christian life, I was told, was a simple matter; one need only believe in God, say one's prayers, avoid sin and do "what the Bible said." Sunday worship was essential; Communion would help me to be good, and go to Heaven. I tried to accept what I was told, even accepting 'Confirmation' at eleven. Blithely unaware of how impatient and selfish I was, I nevertheless lived in true faith and trust. I was unformed, and was puzzled by many things; but I was eager to please people, and so I dumbly accepted both joy and pain from day to day. All that was impure or unkind saddened me, but I was wholly optimistic and secure.

It was impossible to be unhappy for long, even after disappointments, small betrayals or punishments; nor was I bored at that age in our village. One could always run off to find a friend, or to do more work. Every week, voluntarily, I cleaned out the chicken sheds on a nearby farm. The interior of those wooden huts was indescribable, but I earned a few extra pence. In the school holidays we would call in at the farm beyond the allotments. We drove the cows home from the farm every evening, for milking. It was tremendous fun for a ten or eleven-year-old child. Yet whenever I thought about our way of life, in quiet moments alone, usually kneeling on my bed looking out of the upstairs window, I wished that my thoughts and my physical movements could be entirely 'liberated'. I was happy, but I yearned for a greater and unimaginable liberty, which I instinctively felt was attainable, even if I was too ignorant to know how it could be achieved.

Puzzled thoughts.

Frequently, at twilight, I used to gaze at the birds which were soaring around the house. Their flight paths carved great arcs in the sky, wholly unhindered. Watching them was as pleasurable as listening to beautiful music, but my thoughts kept intruding. I envied the birds their freedom, and tried to imagine what it would be like to be able fly Peter-Pan-style over the neighbours' roof, and to swoop down into their back garden.

When I say that it seemed to me as though my thoughts were restricted, I mean that I felt strongly that I was imprisoned in time. I would think about the events of the day, and about the fact that time had passed, and also about the fact that I didn't know what would happen tomorrow. It all seemed astonishing and mysterious. I know I was awed by the concept of the passage of time. But I saw the present moment as a sort of prison beyond which we are unable to project our minds. I accepted the fact of my mind's confinement, but I was awed and puzzled whenever I considered the idea that someone, somewhere, perhaps God Himself, already knows what, to us, is something that shall happen at a certain point in the future. After all, if He's unhampered by human limitations He must know everything already, even future things. That's what I began to believe, because I'd worked it out.

I kept a diary at that time, merely jotting down all the routine tasks and errands which had kept me busy during the day, and the names of favourite programmes on television. It had never occurred to me to write about personal hopes and fears. I knew and remembered my own thoughts. I had no secret wish to read them or to show them to other people; hence my diary was a very pedestrian collection of lists. But now and then, after puzzling alone again with the mysterious fact that we are alive now, though once we were not, and that one day we shall die a bodily death, though we will live forever, I would write something a bit different.

The entry would usually be something on these lines: "In three weeks or three days I shall know that I have passed my exam, or I shall know that I have failed." I felt that there was a point beyond which I couldn't push my thinking. I was utterly absorbed, puzzling over the fact that I couldn't use will-power alone to make complete my present incomplete knowledge, even though I was sure that, somewhere, certain things had already been decided.

Frustrated by my ignorance, I was frustrated, too by my ignorance of what it was that was eluding me. Despite my instinctive and painful longing for a greater understanding of our existence, and of our abilities and of the cause of things, generally, it seemed that something held me back. I was earth-bound, though my thoughts seemed to press against a ceiling which was 'soft to the touch'. It made no sense. I knew nothing of philosophy. But what seems more cruel to me now is that I had no real understanding of the meaning of faith. Nor had I any idea that it's by faith, which is given by God, freely, that we can pierce the 'barrier' which I had sensed, and that it's in prayer that we can encounter true Wisdom: in God.

For anyone who can't see the point of this long explanation, I must say that even when I was very young I longed to be able to understand life. All my future questions about Church and Faith stemmed not from bored curiosity but from a passion for truth. Never having heard of "philosophy" or "theology", and quite unaware that church attendance had any connection with time, space, pre-destination or the fact of our existence, I tried to work things out alone, whilst becoming ever more amazed at the fact that we exist and that our bodies 'work' and our minds think. Yet I grew ever more uncertain of what we human beings are 'for'. I was sure that earthly life had a purpose but I didn't know whom to ask about it.

Feelings of gratitude and wonder.

One summer afternoon, I remember, I stood outside in the street with my brother. We were chatting to a crowd of local children; and for a moment I was distracted from the conversation by thoughts about the heights of various children and about the fact that we were growing all the time. In looking at my little hands and sandalled feet I marvelled about the fact that, in a year's time, my body would inevitably be larger. I mean that I was so amazed at the marvel of the orderly growth of the different parts, growth which is entirely independent of our wishes or moods, that I felt strangely frustrated at not being able to exclaim out loud about that marvel. To have been able to cry out: "Oh God, you're marvellous!" to the Author-designer-creator of that little body would have satisfied all my longing; yet I didn't know that passionate gratitude and wonder - expressed in that way or in any appropriate way - is a tremendous prayer of praise.

Praise, for me, meant singing long hymns to an invisible 'Headmaster', not shouting for joy to the Invisible Lover of birds, flowers and bodies.

Sad Sundays.

Whenever I thought about religion - as we practised it - I used to notice, once more, with gloom, that everything I thought interesting was forbidden on Sundays. Our father's word was Law. I was happy to obey rules out of love for him, and also because his basic rules had seemed reasonable. But I grew more puzzled each year by our restrictions, and wondered why Sundays need be so unpleasant and grim, if they were 'holy days' of celebration.

No games were permitted, or trips to the cinema, or social events except the "Eucharist". I couldn't understand why adults thought that our boredom would be pleasing to God. If He were good, why should He want us to be bored beyond endurance - as it seemed - on His Holy Day each week? I asked my father, but he said something I didn't understand about our duty to "KEEP THE SABBATH" (Ex 31:14).

The reason for his regulations lay far back in our family history. My father had moved from childhood Methodism, through the Society of Friends, to his Anglican allegiance; this was because he developed, first, a vigorous faith in God and in Christian Community and, later,

31

added to his faith the notion of an hierarchical church founded by Christ, and of a sacramental life. However, since one's youthful training exerts a powerful influence, any questions about Sunday amusement disturbed him. He hadn't 'thought out' all his views. He became more lenient in later years, but, for a long time it seemed as though any pleasurable activity on Sunday was regarded as sinful. How peculiar it was, I decided, that everything bright or colourful or lively was frowned upon. How strange to think that God was delighted by long faces, and drab clothes, or was irritated by what was called loud or spontaneous, eye-catching, or decorative.

There was much that was admirable in our way of life, yet some of the rules we followed were rather puritanical. The only Sunday activities which I can recall as wholeheartedly encouraged even though they weren't strictly useful were the outings we made as a family in the school holidays, to have a picnic on Coombe Hill, or at Ashridge or Burnham Beeches. They were tremendous fun, but were one of the few leisure-time pursuits which were permitted. Swimming was regarded as strengthening, therefore useful, as was gardening, and walking. But no one I knew had ever been to an art-gallery - or to a circus or to a dance. The problem wasn't money - or the lack of it - but a suspicion that anything enjoyable was dangerous, and that God wouldn't be pleased unless one kept one's "nose to the grindstone".

A glimpse of colour.

We've been told in Holy Scripture that "THEY CANNOT CHAIN UP GOD'S NEWS" (2 Tm 2:9); I've found that colour and beauty cannot be 'chained', in any community or country. One of the most magical sights of my childhood was the view along Old Amersham High Street on a dark late-September evening, only once each year, when thousands of multi-coloured and brilliant bulbs shone out from the Michaelmas funfair. To a little child of eight or nine, looking upwards, it seemed that half the Universe was filled with light and colour; and in those early years, before I had experienced the joy of singing in a large choir, and before I had heard an orchestra playing, the hurdy-gurdy music which was surging loudly around us nearly lifted me into ecstasy.

Half an hour only, I think we were allowed, before being taken away from all that brilliant light and colour, through the winding lines, to the grey and black of the countryside in winter, and to the beige and brown and navy blue of our everyday furniture and clothing.

Grammar School

When I was ten years old, big changes were imminent. I sat what was called the "eleven-plus" examination and was astonished to hear that I'd passed, and that I'd follow my sister to the Grammar School. On my first day at "Dr Challoner's", I was swamped by the uniform: a small skinny child, the youngest in my class. I felt exhilarated, as though ready for a great adventure. But I wasn't very successful in my efforts to make friends amongst my new class-mates. I found within a few weeks that most of the newcomers had drifted towards membership of one of several recognisable groups, and I seemed to belong to none of them. The fault was partly mine; having been very happy and active in the playground of a primary school, I expected to find the same co-operation in games and explorations from new class-

32

mates. Alas, most seemed content to sit on the steps of the classroom, peering at passers-by, exchanging views in a confident way that both awed and alarmed me.

The games I suggested were looked on as childish and undignified. Attempting to be friendly, I matter-of-factly asked questions about their churches and Sunday-schools, only to be told, equally matter-of-factly, that few of my new class-mates had ever prayed or attended church. I was astonished to discover that few had parents who were practising Christians, so my 'church-going' contributed to my feeling of apartness.

Although this was something I couldn't have articulated at the time, I knew that the children at my Church Primary School had shared the same values and had talked freely about Sunday School and about God. I might have seemed hopelessly naive, or merely priggish, but I was quite bewildered by conversations with new acquaintances who unashamedly told lies, deliberately caused trouble for other people, and who laughed at notions of right and wrong.

In my first few weeks at the grammar school, I learned that few classmates spoke the same 'language': the prevailing 'gospel' was a vague ethical code. Hard work and 'responsibility' were encouraged by the staff, but there was only a stern God to guide us or to point out the way. With no loving Saviour for whom we would undertake the hardest tasks, the code had no solid foundation.

Some of the children were kind. But some were thoroughly ignorant, probably through no fault of their own. God and the Ten Commandments were treated as a huge joke. They saw Christianity as a subject and a way of life which pre-occupied 'boring' old people who led unhappy lives and who fantasised about future rewards. Many of the children had adopted, as their guiding motto - "As much fun as possible, as little work as possible, every day". It was a motto not unknown, I gathered, in Christian schools, but it contradicted everything that I'd ever been taught at home. Quite soon, therefore, prayer and church-going became private matters to be spoken of only with sympathisers: at the Church youth-club, or at home.

Unspoken rules.

Quite apart from the question of religion, I had no real idea at eleven years old of how to 'make conversation'; nor had I many of the social graces. And, quite guileless at first, I was unaware of differences of culture. Persons like myself were 'council-house kids': easily distinguishable in those days. Later, I saw how our speech, clothes and accents, and our pastimes, set us apart almost as foreigners from the girls who led a different way of life, and who were engrossed in talk about tennis matches, piano lessons and holidays away. Naive and uncomprehending at first, I failed to observe the unspoken rules of a different society. I was so ignorant that I'd gone along by myself to a "music competition" at school, taking my Ukulele with me, only to meet with the embarrassed smiles of parents and staff who had hoped to hear a violin piece, and not 'Home on the range.'

At play-times I used to hang around the fringe of any friendly gang. Then as I became bored by the topic under discussion, I'd drift away, and so find myself on the margins again: energetic but impatient, longing for something interesting to do.

Boredom and misery.

I tore about in those first few months, dreadfully unorganised, hoping against hope that I'd have all the right books in my bag as I rushed from room to room when each lesson ended instead of waiting snugly, as at primary school, for a new teacher to appear. When my timetable was under control, and I was able to think clearly, I became calmer and happier for a while - but only until I realised that in leaving behind a familiar routine and encouraging faces I'd left behind the framework which had once made it easy for me to be obedient and hard-working. As I was confronted with a multitude of choices - with no father at hand to prompt or punish me, and surrounded by what seemed like an army of loud and demanding teenagers who had no personal interest in me, I began to find how powerful a force is our free-will. Just as I found myself free to mix with one group and then another, I learned that by my free choice I could decide whether to pass exams or fail, and whether to be kind and obedient, or rebellious.

Until that time, it had never occurred to me to be unhelpful; nor had I ever worked less than whole-heartedly. I grimly observed - at eleven years old - that whenever I worked hard, I did well, and whenever I let boredom distract me, I did badly. Having taken it for granted at primary school that I would be top or second in everything, I was annoyed at the effort needed to tackle strange subjects like Chemistry.

Most of my earlier efforts to be successful in daily activities had surely been fuelled by joy in pleasing my father; but with no such incentive at the Grammar School, I grew lazy. And I was appalled by new experiences in the classroom, where threats and shouting were commonplace, and physical abuse not unknown. I quite soon became generally indifferent about pleasing members of staff, beginning to look upon some of them as being like rather eccentric and dangerous prison warders.

Furthermore, there was no art-room, and therefore no art lessons. Henceforward, I regret to say, I worked at what I enjoyed, and in everything else did the bare minimum, thus stepping for the first time onto the "broad road" which leads downwards. The direction was fixed by a growing discontent in almost every area of life. It was just when daily life at school seemed to be entirely grim that I began to ask myself further questions about family life and attitudes. Every apparent cause for dissatisfaction made me more moody; and ever hour of gloomy reflection led to greater discomfort. I had a home, two parents, food to eat, and much security; but this way of life was so common amongst fellow church-goers and amongst many neighbours on our estate that I took it entirely for granted. For comparatively minor reasons, I began to think our way of life unjust. Certain annoyances, combined with worries about homework and loneliness at school, made me more volatile and critical; and I was lonely at home for a new reason.

Growing apart.

My brother and I had been as close as twins, almost, until I began to mature. Our clubs, explorations and adventures had been pursued in puppy-like joy and good-natured agreement, unspoilt by competition or by much difference in age or height.

Suddenly, I found that we were being treated differently. He escaped to the common with friends, as usual, yet I was expected to do many more chores in the house, and was advised to be 'lady-like' and quiet. I began to wonder why young woman-hood should be so awful in several ways, and envied my brother his greater freedom. I complained mildly about my miserable fate, unaware that boys have problems of their own, and forgetting how much more was expected of him, in many ways, and how much more severely he was punished for each misdemeanour.

Self-conscious and shy, it seemed as though I was dragging myself reluctantly into woman-hood. I still longed to tear about the countryside freely like an inquisitive child, yet longed fiercely as well for something else to satisfy my heart: something indefinable, something resembling beauty, colour or contentment. But I didn't know where to find it.

Drabness and austerity.

In my fifties, now, I marvel more and more at the goodness of my parents, and at the goodness of God who gave me so many blessings in childhood, with opportunities for learning and thinking; however, I must confess that one of the things which irritated me in adolescence was the sense of grey-ness in large areas of life in that era, and in our section of society.

It seems to me as though our already-plain and austere home was further 'veiled' to some degree by the general drabness of post-war austerity; and that gloomy veil was held firmly in place by the nails of puritanism, but which I mean a general sense that anything or anyone who was colourful, lively or exciting was to be regarded with pity, disdain or incomprehension. Such a veil hung heavily on persons already burdened by the responsibility of being British and therefore being obliged - I was informed - to be undemonstrative and uncomplaining. It was emphasised that to 'wear one's heart on one's sleeve' - which meant, to be emotional or to be visibly excited: whether in anger or gratitude - was to be undisciplined, or frivolous. Within our little community, it was not only sinful or frivolous persons and activities that were shunned. I couldn't have explained this at the time, yet I could feel, as a child, that even possessions were rarely tolerated unless they were worthy or useful. Nothing was ever bought simply because of its beauty.

An absence of frivolity.

Looking back, I remember that bright colours - in homes or on public display - were unfashionable and were described as 'vulgar'. There was little music to be heard at home except of our own making. Record players were still luxury items, and the radio was strictly-controlled, and was used mainly for the six o'clock news. A luxury item such as the little T.V. set was bought only so that our neighbours could share the joy of watching Queen Elizabeth the second's Coronation, when half the street crammed into our living room whilst the children were entertained elsewhere.

My bright, vivacious parents were squeezed, so to speak, between the grim pull-your-socks-up mentality which was necessarily adopted by many people in order to keep going during the war, and the Calvinistic gloom which still filtered through some of their theology. All the furniture my father so skilfully made or mended was plain and functional. Alcoholic drinks were served to adults once a year, at Christmas, with some timidity and only if a bold friend had generously provided a bottle of sherry. The same bottle would be standing on the sideboard, three quarters full, the next September. It was only through the kindness of one of my mother's friends that we possessed a few clothes which were unusually bright and cheerful, given by a woman with older children. But any item which was bought new, in a shop, was chosen only if tough, dark and long-lasting.

In the same spirit, the inside walls of our house were quite plain. They were distempered pale pink or green every four or five years, since cleanliness was next to Godliness. But I remember being astounded, later on, to discover that more adventurous and richer families chose to put patterned paper on their walls. Anything to do with decoration and colour, in our circle, was vaguely suspect.

My delight in line and colour was so strong, that at the least excuse I'd create birthday cards from old cereal packets, using coloured pencils on special occasions, or poster paints. Both my mother and father praised my little efforts. Each of them was able to produce a competent landscape; but 'Serious Art' meant very little to us. It had something to do with the gloomy portraits to be found in ancient country mansions, or large sculptures left lying around "the Continent" by ancient Greeks and Romans - as illustrated in the Encyclopaedia Britannia. 'Art' was a hobby which preoccupied only rich and powerful people.

I can't remember seeing any modern paintings when I was young. In later years, my mother put two examples of her own work on the walls. But our prime decorations were old college shields and a photograph of my father's Rugby team, with a palm cross from our church, and one or two small religious prints framed in "passe-partout".

Christian virtues.

As I edit all these my memories and reflections I'm becoming even more amazed at my parents' virtues. I find it a marvel that my parents so steadfastly and bravely ran a home on "Christian" principles and provided a welcome for all sorts of people. It's quite plain to me that our whole way of life was geared to encouraging thrift and discipline and cleanliness, and to stimulating a real interest in God, for Whose sake one struggled to be virtuous; and I believed that God ruled the world like a loving army officer, ever-ready to call back into line any rebel who dared disobey the smallest regulation; yet I know that the boundaries set around my life gave me, for a few years, the firm discipline which kept me from disaster.

It's a cause for gratitude, too, that ours was a home where people talked to one another. There were frequent discussions and even arguments; but a halt was called if anyone became rude or uncharitable. I remember few lengthy disagreements taking place, when I was little. It was recommended that we follow the teaching of Saint Paul, who wrote: "NEVER LET THE SUN SET ON YOUR ANGER" (Ep 4:26); and my parents set a good example in this matter.

Although these two strong-minded and articulate spouses disagreed on all sorts of subjects, they shared - and relished in discussion - an interest in history, the English language, and of course children's education: with additional exchanges of information about her gardening and his woodwork. They were never idle except when physically exhausted, but were generally

36

happy with their various tasks. "The devil makes work for idle hands" was an oft-stated phrase, as well as comments about thrift - "Waste not, want not" - and about good manners and respect for "elders and betters".

They weren't at all over-earnest except for certain subjects and occasions. Much time was spent in good-humoured banter: my father, gently mocking my mother's ideas about good manners and "refinement", and she - chuckling - scolding him about his frank and earthy sense of humour. He was proud of being one of six children from a tough Lancashire weaving family. He thwarted all her subtle or plaintive efforts to improve him, and said: "You can't make a silk purse out of a sow's ear!"

My father's most oft-used quotation was a phrase from one of Cardinal Newman's hymns: from a hymn equally popular with Protestants and Catholics. Whenever my father was exasperated, and when other men might have grumbled or sworn - or even when he was sometimes pleasantly surprised - he would shake his head in amazement at whatever stupidity, unkindness, or astonishing act of charity he had just witnessed; and he'd exclaim: "Lead, kindly Light!" We children had no idea what he meant. But since he was obviously self-controlled, if astonished, and since he wasn't swearing, it seemed to us that he must have been saying something good.

Cheering up sad hearts.

The true love of God shone out from my parents' school of Anglicanism. It was precisely because they both wanted to please God, and because Christ - in the Bible - asked His followers to love their neighbour that we were advised always to be gentle and patient with "difficult" persons, and to be helpful to anyone in need.

There were strict rules - for the sake of charity - about privacy, about not opening anyone else's post, and about the menace of tale-telling or of listening to malicious gossip.

Everyday falsehoods and hatreds and slanders were recognised for the evils which they are. If someone outside the family were criticised, we could be sure that some of their apparent virtues would be mentioned in the same breath.

Although I never met anyone in those childhood days who wasn't English or Scottish or Irish, I learned in one way or another that people of every country and race were to be valued and never scorned. Other customs and life-styles might have seemed strange, from what we read in the newspapers or would find out, later on, on T.V; but every single person on earth, we were assured - even someone from whom we were told to stay away because he was 'a bad influence' - was precious in the sight of God, who had given life to everyone who had ever existed.

That's why our parents welcomed, or "inflicted upon us", as we saw it, an assortment of distressed or eccentric persons, at odd times throughout the year, or over the Christmas holidays. As they put up with our sullen agreement and the embarrassing, stilted conversations at meal times, they routinely cheered up sad hearts for a while, glad to have done their simple duty as Christians who were anxious to please God.

Cleanliness and Godliness.

There lurked within our culture, however, a feeling that tired or emotional "inadequates" must have brought their troubles upon themselves, perhaps through being spendthrift or undisciplined. It seemed as though some of the poor 'weak' ones whom we met during parish activities were spoken of with a mixture of pity and exasperation, as though if they had only kept the Commandments and worked hard, and had been thrifty and not emotional, they would have been rewarded by God with strength and a reasonable prosperity, and would have been able to thank Him for enabling them to be happy and successful.

History has taught us that a great love of the Gospel teachings can be tainted, sometimes, by an exaggerated love of respectability, and a concern about outward appearances. So there was much talk about 'standards' in our circle, and much exasperation. Certain neighbours who didn't appear to be 'respectable' were shunned. We were forbidden to play with children from such homes. People who seemed unable to conform in externals were seen as failures. It seemed as if it was our duty to preserve in daily life a veneer of success and of brisk efficiency. Cleanliness was next to Godliness. No-one had heard of St. Benedict Joseph Labré.

It was inevitable that I would come to see the Christian life as being, above all, a matter of right behaviour, rather than of right belief and therefore of a right relationship with a loving Heavenly Father to Whom I had been led by a loving Saviour. There was so much sheer goodness shining in the hearts of faithful church-goers in our area, in the 1950's, as well as today; but I believe it's tragic that many Christians grow up learning little about the details of the life of grace known to Catholics, little about union-of-heart with Christ, nothing about penance or reparation, or the "offering up" of our earthly pains and troubles by which we can help other souls - and which can make our sufferings easier to bear.

It seems so strange to me now that throughout the whole of my life, until I was twenty-one, I had never prayed for the souls of people who had died, nor asked for the help of the Saints: the heavenly friends who provide wonderful help both in everyday matters and in especially-difficult times. And I'd never even heard of the greatest marvel: of the Holy Sacrifice of the Mass.

As I began to explain in Chapter One, we were given a good grounding in many Christian truths: told that our purpose on earth was to love God and our neighbour and to avoid sin. We'd been told in a dozen ways that lying, murder, stealing and bad language were forbidden. But I had no sense of purpose from year to year: no sense of God's Will being a sure and reliable guide amidst day-to-day problems.

No one seemed to know His Will in any great detail. There was no notion put to me of a 'teaching church' but only of Ten Commandments which spoke of idols and oxen, but which said nothing about the many moral and ethical 'dilemmas' of modern life. It was very puzzling. My father said that in any quandary about a subject which wasn't mentioned in the Bible, we had to make up our own minds about whether it were right or wrong; and I couldn't understand this. I'd imagined that an All-knowing Creator would have an opinion to share on just about everything.

Loneliness.

One day in summer, when I was still a skinny little child of about twelve, my trust in adults was rudely shattered; and so ended my childhood 'honeymoon' of faith. Triggered by such a small event there began the great loneliness which lasted until adult life.

During those warm, glorious, busy days, an entirely innocent and lengthy conversation with a local boy was treated with suspicion and disapproval. There was uproar one evening when I was late home from play. I'd been busy and happy outdoors as usual, and, alas, was oblivious to the time. I had no watch, and no idea why such a fuss should have been made about my coming home a bit late. I quite ignorant of every adult cause for concern, and listened with disbelief as I was told never to go and play with him again. It made no sense to me.

When all the fuss and the questions had ended, I was astonished and hurt to have been treated with suspicion, when - apart from that single lie, earlier - I wasn't aware of ever having done a deliberate wrong. It was true that I was sometimes argumentative, or reluctant to wash the dishes. But, generally I loved to make my parents happy. So I assumed that for some reason which I was too stupid to recognise I was unlovable, and unworthy of love. I rushed ahead from day to day, from then on, wondering why it was so hard to please people. I felt irretrievably flawed, yet I couldn't work out what was wrong. I knew I was sometimes careless, but I was never disobedient.

My mood veered between puzzlement and sadness. In the same year, I was still hovering uncomfortably on the fringes of several groups which had coalesced at school. So at school and home my growing loneliness - combined with the beginnings of adolescent irritability - drew me slowly away from the dutiful obedience which had fuelled all my activities so far.

A house of our own.

The fact that we moved house at that time meant that I lost the gang of friends whom I'd seen daily for six years. Much joy sprang from the novelty of packing, but the move increased my isolation. Within a few weeks of the change being announced, we left our village in the countryside to move to a little semi-detached house only a mile from the Grammar School. My parents were glad to have somewhere of their own which they could alter or decorate without asking permission of "the Council". We children were thrilled with it, initially, because we spent hours in the echoing rooms of our new home, the five of us working hard to make it fit for habitation. We cleared up much of the builders' rubble, then sat together on the floor in a circle, eating fish and chips with our fingers, exhilarated by our labours. The whole project seemed wildly exciting. There were neighbours to meet, and a new garden to create from a sea of roughly-turned clay. But the excitement was short-lived. When our few items of furniture had been delivered on the back of the local coal-lorry, and we had settled in, I discovered the drawbacks.

Our new home was at the centre of a frenzy of new building. We were on the edge of a rapidly-expanding town; and while it was certainly easier for us to go to church and to school we had far less privacy inside the house, and nowhere to play outside with our former freedom and gusto. We had moved away from the pond, the Common and the river, and from my beloved beech-woods and cornfields. There were few children in our neighbourhood and so I had no-one with whom I could share my former interests. I missed my friends, and I had to share a room with my sister, who, understandably, wasn't very pleased to be encumbered with someone as busy and talkative as myself. I've already said something about how shy I always was with strangers or with adults; but I had a torrent of enthusiastic words with which to swamp any equally-enthusiastic child who shared some of my interests.

It was true that friends on the estate were only three miles away; but the long ride on an unreliable bicycle was the smallest obstacle, compared with other problems. We were at different schools now, all maturing at different speeds. I went to see a friend once or twice, when the weather was fine, but our conversation was stilted. We hardly recognised in each other the children we had been the summer before. Our interests were unalike, and besides, I was laden with homework. Little by little, but steadily, my loneliness grew; and, for the first time, self-pity crept in.

Within the family, we three children began to pursue our different interests, spending days and weeks apart except for brief conversations with our parents at Sunday lunch. Each weekday morning, five busy persons dashed passed one another, fighting for bathroom space: each dreading being late for school. Each evening, exhausted parents marked text-books, watched the television news and encouraged us to go and do our homework. Conversations were few, and during the next few years, our parents grew busier than ever, bearing heavy responsibilities. They were usually late in returning home from work.

Numerous time-consuming projects.

When we had settled in thoroughly after our move, and when I had grown used to the new routine at school and was more competent at my regular household chores, I wondered what to do in my leisure-time. There were no close friends nearby. I could hardly run around the fields by myself at thirteen; and I was bored. Then I realised that although I was too shy to talk much with the woman next door, this new neighbour was frequently ill; so for three or four years - now that I'd left behind our Guide pack and its good deeds - I devotedly took her babies for long walks, and gave them some of their meals, so that she could lie down and rest. I was delighted to be able to feed them and to encourage them to talk, treating them with affection, much as I treated our pets at home. We had tortoises, mice, rabbits and a cat. I longed to have babies of my own.

By the time our neighbour was well again, with her children out at school, I'd become more confident, and more observant. My interests broadened. During my time alone - and when I'd finished my designated household work - I undertook great projects, partly to stave off boredom, but, also because I was fascinated by many new ideas. A whole holiday was taken up making a model theatre from scraps of wood and cardboard, painting paper figures from "The Mikado" to push and pull onto the stage. I made a set of tiny curtains which drew together on minute wires and rings. My neighbour let me listen to the Gilbert and Sullivan music on her record-player. I came to know all the songs by heart.

Another holiday was filled by Heraldry, as I passed long hours memorising the symbols, studying the meaning: intrigued that so much of the pageant of history could be compressed into such a colourful code. Thrilled by the work, I made copies of all the shields illustrated in my text-book, having been fortunate enough to find a half-used tin box of paints in a church jumble sale. I put the vast array of colours to good use.

Scottish ancestors.

Throughout another holiday, I spent six weeks of my free time skimming through the entire Bible, drawing up a family tree of everyone named there between Adam and Jesus, gradually extending the sheet of paper until it was nearly three feet long. But an even larger book which enthralled me was a volume I'd unearthed at a jumble sale. It was full of huge photographs of Scotland, with only minimal captions. I was entranced by the thought of learning more about my mother's home country from which had sprung the reels I'd practised once a week at primary school, where a jovial instructor had introduced us to country dancing. Here before me were dozens of extraordinary views of the Highlands; and I decided that these were scenes which must have been familiar to my ancestors; and so I fell in love with all things Scottish, devouring history books for stories of Stuart bravery, and learning Scottish songs.

Having pestered my mother for stories of her family, I was disappointed to hear that the Leiths hadn't even a tartan of their own. My long-dead grandfather hadn't been a Highlander but a marine engineer. But I still amused myself by making what I imagined was a Scottish 'outfit', after spying a little kilt in the bundle of second-hand clothes which descended upon us like manna from heaven each year.

For months, until I out-grew it, I wore the kilt proudly instead of my usual jeans. I made myself a sporran to wear, and found some imitation ballet shoes and a white shirt to complete my outfit.

Old books, and poetry.

Throughout my grammar school years, each summer holiday, my mother was painstakingly composing her own school's new timetable, or leading a party of her pupils on a trip abroad. So, encouraged to amuse myself whenever chores were done, and whenever I was really bored, I gave in and found a book to read. There were no colourful paperbacks available, or modern novels. I read whatever was available from the dining-room shelves. There was nothing un-Christian in the house, unless I count Grimm's fairy-tales, which I disliked for their cruelty.

From poetry and plays, I turned to non-fiction: travel books and biography; and I found a variety of religious works at the second-hand bookshop. Bunyan's "Pilgrim's Progress" enchanted me. The ideas were simple yet profound. I saw, revealed there, the truth of the struggle in our souls between selfishness and sacrifice, but no-one was interested in discussing it, at home, and I was too shy to talk about such things in Church or at school. I painted half of a huge picture which I'd drawn of Christian's many adventures; then I gave up as another idea occurred.

Discovering Bernard Shaw, I was excited by his 'Prefaces'; though I wondered which ideas were right and which were wrong. He was so persuasive: so clever and amusing. I read one of his plays - 'St. Joan' - several times, astounded by Joan's courage. But she wasn't a 'Catholic Saint' to me, but just another misty legendary figure like King Arthur or Beowulf.

At a later date, and after idly browsing through my father's old books, deeply stirred by the words of Longfellow and of Matthew Arnold, Rupert Brooke, and Verlaine, I composed poetry, secretly, loving the sound of syllables moving in a rhythm of one's own choosing: amazed at the scenes one could evoke by a few words on a blank page.

I made an anthology of my favourite poems, many of which were about love, and 'nature' - and death. It included a few pieces of prose which had impressed me, even an excerpt from the writings of Pope Pius XII, which I'd clipped from the daily newspaper in the week when he died. I was quite amazed to find that such a terrible despot - as he had been described to me - had written something so profoundly Christian as the thoughts which were expressed in his last will and testament.

Almighty God.

Much of my free time was spent in church. I felt just as much at home there as in our own living-room. I loved to think about God, but found people more difficult to comprehend. Being too shy to hold a conversation with any of the adults at church, I saw them as so wise and articulate that I was hardly worthy to be amongst them. But I felt comfortable in silent prayer-times. I know that I was seen by my mother's friends as lively and undisciplined but rather devout.

In those early teenage years, and in a quiet and uncomprehending way, as I've indicated elsewhere, I worshipped God very solemnly as Almighty and Omnipotent. I understood and was thrilled by that aspect of God's Nature revealed to us in Church whenever we heard the words of Isaiah in Holy Scripture. I listened in awe to the story of how the Angel had touched Isaiah's lips with a hot coal, when the prophet had said: "WHAT A WRETCHED STATE I AM IN! I AM LOST, FOR I AM A MAN OF UNCLEAN LIPS" (Is 6:5). The prophet knew himself to be unworthy to stand within the temple looking towards the Glory of Almighty God; and that's just how I felt, kneeling in church after Holy Communion; and I assumed that everyone else felt the same way.

It was easy for me to adore the God of Creation, the God of Isaiah, and the God Whom we heard about in stories to do with Abraham or Joshua. But a God of silence or intimacy - God in "THE SOUND OF A GENTLE BREEZE" (1 K 19:12) - was unknown to me, at that time. It couldn't have been otherwise, since all that I'd learned about God had led me to see Him only as authoritative and powerful; and most of the people I met who were in positions of authority were loud, confident and overpowering. I knew something of the meaning of vigorous, determined, loyal and practical love; but since I knew very little about tenderness or mercy, I couldn't imagine how God could be interested in anyone weak or faint-hearted.

Missionary instincts.

The Christian faith was something I admired, and thought worth sharing, nevertheless: and for some of the time in my childhood I was possessed with a longing to be a missionary. It had

42

been explained to me by forthright parents that we should always be prepared to stand up for our beliefs - and even to work hard to spread them. I became gripped with excitement on reading about the past exploits of missionaries in Africa. The stories of Protestant heroism enthralled me. I toiled over maps for long weeks, using the Encyclopaedia Britannica as a source of information, plotting all the journeys of David Livingstone and Mary Slessor, and writing brief biographies, and lists of dates. Inspired, too, by memories of a family friend who had once worked in India, and who had learned 'Hindustani', as it was called then, I spent my precious pocket money on a "Teach-yourself" language book, during a quick family foray in London. I taught myself to count, and learned a few new words, greatly stirred by sentimental pictures on the Mission-fund boxes in our church and on the front of 'Mission' magazines.

The concept of 'evangelism' seemed very simple to me. Surely if one risked one's health to go to faraway places, the people there would be thrilled to receive the Good News of God's love for them; they would turn away from polytheism and embrace Christianity with ease! Alas, my longing to feed the souls of other people went hand-in-hand with an implicit belief in British cultural superiority. In my support for 'The Missions' I hoped to be charitable and clear-sighted; but I was ignorant of different ways of life, especially of honourable traditions which are indeed compatible with Christian faith and practice; and this ignorance was unsurprising. In those days, we led a quiet "God-fearing" life, in a little market-town with few sources of information other than parents, a small circle of friends, and one second-hand bookshop. 'T.V.' and radio were strictly controlled. We travelled very little and met few persons not involved in teaching or in local Anglican Church life. In the adult conversation which we heard at that time, a respect for individual human-beings didn't always include a respect for their cultures.

But my solitary passion for evangelism didn't last for more than a few months.

Self-pity.

At the age of about fourteen, I was still unhappy at school, bored by several subjects which, although not 'difficult', seemed irrelevant to my life, then or in the future. Daily, I felt more and more lonely and isolated at school as well as at home; and I came to see the imposition of a brace on my teeth - with pink National Health spectacles perched above - as the final nudge which pinned me in a corner, as it were, too embarrassed to speak and to draw attention to myself, yet longing for companionship - and for something really interesting to do. I was immensely bored by most of the lessons at school, regarding them as hurdles to be crossed as efficiently as possible so that I could rush home and do exactly what I pleased.

Soon I felt more-or-less permanently irritable and unhappy. There was no-one I could talk to about my miseries, but it wouldn't have occurred to me to grumble. I'd been told many times that life was hard, and that I ought to 'like it or lump it'. Yet sometimes self-pity welled up in my heart, as I said, or the beginning of anger.

Since my mother worked full-time, she knew - during our first few years in that house - only the immediate neighbours. We had few living relations; and since the nearest lived over forty miles away, we had few houses to visit, and were isolated even in sickness, when we were left at home alone. I suffered nothing more serious than chickenpox and appendicitis; and arrangements were always made that we should telephone an acquaintance in another street if we were in distress; yet all our training prevented me from asking for help. Having been taught that 'phone calls were expensive - they had to be listed in a notebook, and paid for - and taught, too, not to "pester" grown-ups, I dared not ask for help - well or unwell. Our very English tradition of 'stiff upper lip' kept all expressions of feelings rigidly under control. This was undoubtedly a great help, outwardly, for any home or community. But although I don't want to encourage anyone to have a life-long pre-occupation with his own "needs", I would suggest that little miseries, even normal miseries, can be made more bearable by occasional sharing, otherwise wounds can fester. The "stiff upper lip" can hide a fatal affliction.

Each illness meant that we had to be alone at home for a week or two. It was unpleasant, but we thought it normal, and learned to occupy ourselves and to be self-sufficient. My brother was out of the house almost every waking minute; and my sister - if not at school - was invariably alone upstairs, her head buried in a book.

'Latch-key' kids.

At fairly regular intervals, my mother would be stricken with pangs of conscience about having three 'latch-key kids' - and she, a teacher. The phrase had only just been coined, and made her feel guilty. She would immediately arrange for an elderly neighbour to come in to prepare a snack and to offer it to us after school: orange squash, and bread and margarine; and each time we were appalled, blithely indifferent to our absent mother's concern, thinking only what a bore to have to wash our hands and make conversation, instead of being free to charge off to our own hobbies, satchels flung onto the hall floor. We would beg to be allowed to continue as usual; then we'd slide back each time into our 'latch-key' existence, which was familiar, and therefore was preferable to any other routine.

Once, visiting a friend's house some distance away, immediately after the school day ended, I felt strangely moved and yet uneasy, as I watched the mother at the door plying her child with questions about her day. She made leisurely conversation as she put out cakes and squash for us both, obviously delighted to be with us, not over-worked and tired like my mother.

That little glimpse of another way of life was enchanting - but was as unfamiliar as the view of a distant country on a television screen. I half-wondered what it would be like to have someone hovering attentively around me all the time, then forgot about the incident and went back to the way of life which I thought of as normal.

Naughtiness.

Sad to say, I remained so lonely, and became so anxious for friendship that I began to conform, and to behave, little by little, like some of the other children I'd met, so that I'd be accepted and not be so lonely any more. It began to seem important to be daring, and amusing. For the first time in my life I became mischievous and unruly.

I don't mean that I had once behaved perfectly and then suddenly lapsed. But my loneliness -

combined with the inclinations arising from natural human frailty - led me to court popularity in silly ways. I grew less sensitive to others' feelings; yet this wasn't perhaps entirely my fault, since it was made plain to us that children were a nuisance.

One or two of the staff at school were routinely sarcastic and scornful. Someone who talked most about good manners shouted rudely at any child after the smallest mistake. Someone else regularly left children weeping, after heaping humiliations upon them for up to half-an-hour, before embarrassed class-mates.

If one asked questions, one was called "cheeky". If one struggled with a problem, one was berated as a "brainless idiot" or a "fool". Such examples of adult behaviour led me to think that all who preached about responsibility and good behaviour were hypocrites. I was quite unable to feel respect or admiration for them, but only fear and puzzlement; and I began to 'lump together' in my mind all teachers, developing a 'them against us' attitude. I began to be influenced by some contemporaries to adopt new standards, or rather, to abandon Christian standards. The new creed was evolving: "Aim for fun and pleasure if you can - provided you don't deliberately hurt anyone, and don't get found out".

This was a Godless creed which led those who followed it away from Christian life. It damaged souls, relationships and family life bit by bit. Secretly but surely, I was influenced by the mainly secular opinions which I heard expressed day after day throughout those formative years; and I found that my cheekiness and pranks were punished three or four times a week when I was kept in detention at school for a further hour after the final lesson.

A kind enquiry.

I owe great thanks to certain members of staff for kindnesses which changed my life; but I'm sad to say that as we grew older and bolder, some of us began to regard members of the teaching staff as 'fair game' for all sorts of pranks and disobedience. I could weep, now, for the small miseries which we inflicted on young inexperienced teachers, now that we had 'lumped together' in our minds all teachers, seeing them - in a jokey way - as the enemy. Egged on by boys who longed to prove their bravery, we scuffled about in class, changed desks, interrupted every instruction, and played various secret tricks: all from a riotous sense of fun, mixed with disrespect and thoughtlessness. Yet never did our jokes progress beyond a certain stage; we were frightened of the Headmaster, and so were obedient in important matters, preferring work to punishment.

A member of staff took me aside one day, in a kindly manner. He led me to an empty class-room, sat me down, and asked very gently why I was always so naughty. Quite sincerely, he continued: Was I unhappy; and could he do anything to help? But I was so overcome by his tender concern that I burst into tears, unable to utter a word about my various miseries. He gave up in the end, helpless to assist someone so genuinely shy and inarticulate.

Nothing short of torture would have made me speak to a stranger like him about my feelings or my family, so strict had been my cultural training. Some of you who read this book will understand how much I've had to unlearn, in order to obey Christ and to write about my life.

45

'God is Love'?

By the time I was fifteen, I felt generally sad, bored and unloved. I was reading far fewer books, snatching only occasional hours with old favourites before rushing off to school lessons or to homework or to household chores. Many of my friends were involved in sport; but I still detested hockey matches and other team games. Obviously, they can be used as a great way for youngsters to 'let off steam', and some people enjoy them. I liked athletics, for the beauty of the movements of the athletes, and for the beauty of the soaring arcs we made in the summer sky with our discs or spears. But I cared not a jot whether team A was more successful than team B in driving a ball into a goal. I had no competitive spirit. It seemed pointless to rejoice in our success and in someone else's downfall.

Very soon, even church-going seemed very dull. 'Prayers' became a chore. All that had to do with God or Creation still held a strange and disturbing attraction - whenever I stopped to think about such things. But I didn't understand the truths which lay at the heart of the Christian faith. It seemed easy to believe that God loved cheerful, hardworking adults who wouldn't dream of behaving badly, and who probably possessed all sorts of virtues about which I knew nothing. How could I understand, I thought - I who was so stupid and untidy, so irritating, and so impatient? My faults were so evident. How could Almighty God wish to have anything to do with a nuisance like myself? I believed that He had made me; but it was difficult to believe that He loved me.

There was something else which puzzled me. I'd been assured that religion was designed to make us happy; but I found it difficult to be patient and uncomplaining; and it was hurtful to have to complicate simple friendships by having to explain our practices to non-churchgoers.

I remember myself at sixteen blushing before some school-friends who were lounging on the steps of the local cinema, chatting, on the way home from school. When I'd explained that I had to leave, to go across the road to make my 'confession' at Church, I felt not brave, but foolish, grudgingly going to fulfil what I saw as an extraordinary practice urged on me by a mother who belonged to a peculiar sort of 'club' which now seemed old-fashioned and irrelevant. I was especially resentful because my father said that 'confession' was quite unnecessary for us Protestants. I didn't know whom to believe.

Refusal to conform.

So muddled were my beliefs that it began to seem pointless for me to go through the usual rituals. And when the questions I asked my parents about church attendance stirred up not encouragement but exasperation, I became even more reluctant to take part. But my eventual refusal to conform, outwardly, by sitting in Church for an hour each week with the family, was due only to a passion for truth, and not from a joy in rebellion.

In different areas of life, I'd been offered a picture of God which was far from attractive. I was told that God was tender and compassionate but I had no idea what the words meant. I was told that the answers to life's mysteries lay there 'in the Bible'; but that large dusty book seemed to have little to say to a 'modern' girl who couldn't penetrate its peculiar prose; and so I came to see God as a Divine Judge who wasn't very fond of me, although He might reward me one day for my good actions if, that is, I managed to avoid all the traps on the way to Heaven. I believed that He would leap up and punish me, as others did, for the least carelessness on my part; and, worse than that, He would do so quite relentlessly throughout the next fifty years.

That prospect was so unendurable that I couldn't understand what was meant by the phrase that "GOD IS LOVE" (1 Jn 4:16).

As I realised in the end, I had false ideas about God which would one day, by His grace, be pushed aside. But, meanwhile, I had wrongly come to understand the Christian life as being a way of fear and drudgery: utterly joyless - as some of our Sundays had been, when everything joyful was banned.

By the time I started questioning the need for Church attendance I had no thoughts of 'Church' as a family place. So many members of the congregation seemed to be old or ailing, and I ungraciously assumed that they went there for the company or perhaps for the music. After all - God wasn't very attractive; surely they knew that, too? For the past two years I had attended church solely because I'd been told to go. I resented being chivvied into attending, and I resented having to fulfil duties which no one could explain to my satisfaction, and which seemed to me to be humiliating and quite unnecessary.

What a nuisance I was, in many ways: either moody or worried, although my bad moods were short-lived, and I tried to be kind. When I chattered at weekends, I was told I was noisy. If I asked questions, I was advised to get on with my work. I was told that: "you think too much" - which disturbed me. Was life entirely 'about' getting one's work done? Were thinking and knowing not important? Were there no answers at all?

It was as though 'God' slipped over my horizon; but I wasn't allowed to forget Him. Things were to happen later which would to widen my understanding, though it would be many years before I would look back in amazement at the glimpses which God had given me of His plans.

Self-consciousness.

Few human beings can have passed through childhood to adulthood entirely undamaged; and certain episodes in my 'teens' gravely wounded and embittered me. It's not nostalgia that prompts me to mention them here, but an aching regret that I was so over-sensitive, coupled with a plea for more watchfulness on the part of all who love and look after children of any age.

At a time when I was already lonely, puzzled and miserably self-conscious about my outward and inner failings, a new torment was added. Adolescence as such was not a problem: just the fact that in a mixed class, in a mixed secondary school, every new, visible and embarrassing lurch into woman-hood was noted with vulgar glee by some of the dozens of ungainly boys who shared our life in the classroom or the sportsfield and who - it seemed - had never heard about modesty or purity.

What might have remained mildly discomforting moments - in a girl's school - were elevated into torture. There was no escape on the tennis court or the hockey pitch; in fact, we were more exposed, since we were routinely mocked or applauded for our faces or figures by the whooping lads who were playing football only a few yards away.

Until that year I had been unselfconsciously thin, lithe and energetic, taking for granted my stamina, no more aware of my body or appearance than a little cat which is sitting poised under a hedge ready to pounce on a bird. I had been that kitten, eyes wide with delight at all the birds: that is, all the little feasts or various delightful occupations that nature or Providence had placed before me. I took for granted my agility, but rarely gave a thought to my appearance.

My new gawky self-consciousness was elevated to near-panic when our sports mistress announced one day that the newly-built showers were to be used by us - compulsorily - after every sports lesson. We would be expected to run naked beneath the shower-heads, from one end of the building to the other, with all the girls in the class.

Whether the practice lasted for very many years, I don't know, but it was a crude and unnecessary abuse of authority. And because it had been vigorously drummed into me that I ought to obey my superiors, I was by then terrified of anyone in authority. From habit, I'd fearfully obeyed instructions given to me by parents or teachers, blithely confident that they knew best. It hadn't occurred to me that any of them might not know right from wrong , or that - unimaginable - they might command me to join in something sinful. So I conformed, defeated by that official promotion of immodesty.

A foolish proposal.

It seemed outrageous to me that others should have so much power over me, when I thought the recent decision appalling.

Who was I, to criticise others? My own behaviour at times was hardly perfect. I must have believed that there was a great difference between moments of thoughtlessness and calculated wrong-doing, although I was so inarticulate that I couldn't have put this into words.

I hope that if I'd been ordered to torture an animal, or to cheat in examinations, I'd instinctively have refused to comply, despite threats or flattery, perhaps pitying whoever asked such things, and supposing that he was merely ignorant. But a crassly-implemented and silly elevation of 'hygiene' above all other ideals was so vague and peculiar an evil, and I was so badly-instructed on anything to do with such matters, and so tongue-tied and uncertain, that I had no idea what to do except to conform. Perhaps that's how people feel today as further foolish proposals are pressed upon children, teachers and parents. Only very brave and clear-minded people can protest with any hope of success in an age when primary-school children have thrust upon them, and supposedly in the name of health-and-hygiene, information about sexual problems. This is now an age, too, when older school-children are told in very great detail much about life-styles and parenting: frequently with no mention of family, morals, and duty.

To some people, it will seem that my distress was caused by such a little thing. But it meant that, as one of a crowd, I took the broad road offered to me. Angry and embarrassed, and yet compliant, by one small step I was made hard-hearted; and another humiliating experience in

48

that difficult time made me miserable and untrusting. It happened when I was a very shy fourteen-year-old, and when I'd gone to France for a month to stay with friends of my parents; the couple whom they'd known since pre-war years.

Experiences in France.

It was a privilege, in the nineteen-fifties, to be able to go on what was called a French 'exchange'. Every second of the journey across the Channel was exciting; and then there were two teenaged children to meet. All the members of the family were kind. After my welcome, there followed a traumatic initiation when I had to speak French, and was greeted by hoots of laughter. But the whole family was delightful. We had a lovely meal, and I grew more confident. It was hoped that my French would improve in leaps and bounds; and that's what happened, just as the spoken English of the French children improved, when their turn came to stay with us, in England.

But after the first day of my stay, and because the family members were all busy, I was free to wander the streets of Rouen. For a month, as long as no special outing was planned, I was free to explore as I'd never been free before. Holidays with my parents had been a rarity, and then had been thoroughly organised every day.

After brief visits to shops and cinemas, I made my way to the swimming pool, having planned to go there every single morning; but I was briefly, though shockingly, assaulted in the changing-room on my first visit, and so I dared not return. It didn't occur to me to mention the incident to anyone. My French was so poor, and my fear of persons in authority so great; and I'd been taught never to complain. So, in order to pass the time, and when I'd finished looking at the shops, and in spite of my feelings about church-going at home, I found myself wandering into every church I passed. I was alone, and curious, with many free hours to spend where I chose, so I looked around me, unhurried and undisturbed. All the churches were open! I was enchanted.

I can't recall seeing any crowds or celebrations when I strolled in, feeling like an intruder; nor was there music or much light. The churches were dark caverns, apparently empty and not much used. Yet I know I sensed a Presence there, and returned to one or two of them every day. St Ouen, the Cathedral, St Maclou - all had vast, cold echoing interiors, full of something or Someone who made me linger and wander and stay. He was familiar; but He remained unrecognised for a while.

It's true that my French 'auntie' took me to Mass with her on Easter Sunday in the Cathedral - quite near the building where Joan of Arc had been questioned before being put to death in that same town. The size of the crowds, however, with my total lack of understanding of the liturgical event in the far distance, caused me to look upon the whole outing as something peculiarly French; it didn't sink in that this was a Catholic celebration, or that the numerous churches I'd visited were Catholic. There was a majesty and beauty about them, as well as a Presence; and these things weren't what I'd have associated with a religion which I'd only heard described as suitable for superstitious and mediaeval people who hadn't had the benefit of Protestant enlightenment. What I'd been given was a glimpse of the glory of the Catholic Faith, and therefore a suggestion of "THE CITY OF THE LIVING GOD, THE HEAVENLY JERUSALEM WHERE THE MILLIONS OF ANGELS HAVE GATHERED FOR THE

FESTIVAL" (Heb 12:22).

My ignorance about France, and about the Faith in France seems astounding now; but we'd met few people who had travelled 'abroad'. I knew little about how others lived: about their cultures and customs.

For the whole month, I continued to explore Rouen with an almost breathless interest as I darted in and out of those echoing sanctuaries. Then I came home to face the next crop of examinations and to cope with teenage 'crushes,' athletics meetings - and continuing loneliness. I soon forgot about that most marvellous aspect of my stay.

[Childhood problems.

How greatly each one of us differs in our reactions to pain and difficulty. How I winced in future years, when I remembered my childhood problems and was appalled that a handful of incidents should have made me so self-pitying and moody. My emotions had lurched, daily, from joy to anger and back again, as my mind darted from one problem to another, unaware of the deeper progression now taking place. Loneliness made me cynical and argumentative. Those two faults helped me to turn away from prayer, and without much prayer I became impatient with those who prayed and who spoke about God. In my heart, I began to despise their blithe satisfaction with their lives. My mind dwelt uncharitably on some of their evident weaknesses; and since our religion was supposed to make us upright and worthy I concluded that all who preached without practising perfectly had thereby proved it to be useless; and I included in my sweeping inner criticism half the staff at school, as well as my own parents.]

---

3 EXPLORATION

(1957-1963)

Questions about the Creed.

An intermittent and ruthless probing into truth was important to me, however, even in the midst of all the turmoil and half-belief of that time. My conscience was active even as I resented my Christian "shackles". Whilst secretly half-ashamed of our faith, I was unable to step outside, as it were, and to disregard conscience. The way of life which had been put before me for admiration and emulation seemed dreary and grim. I half-thought that an active conscience was a sign of childhood 'brainwashing'; yet I hadn't the courage to blot out its voice. From time to time I asked questions: longing for a firm explanation of our traditional beliefs, one that made sense. But none was forthcoming. Adults, it seemed, made bold statements about morality and duty, but couldn't give me answers which satisfied me, for example, about the Church.

No-one I knew had been able to tell me why we recited, in the Creed on Sundays: "I believe in One Holy Catholic Church". I asked: "Where is it?" and was told about the 'branch theory'. I was informed quite firmly that the Church had "broken up" into three parts, long ago, and that it was no longer 'Universal'. No Reformation Church was Catholic, I was told - except for our little bit of the Anglican Church: the Anglo-Catholic part. Christian bodies were 'Protestant', 'Roman', or Orthodox - with the Anglican Church sitting astride the first two groups.

It seemed strange to me that when a Church founded by God could have collapsed in that way, Christians continued to express their unswerving belief in its unity, week by week; and meanwhile I asked questions - sincere questions - about the Bible, wondering: what Authority had insisted that we pay attention to this particular Old Book? I asked why we ignored all other Old Books in the World, for the sake of our 'Bible', when the 'Church' from which it had sprung had disappeared.

My father, when pressed about the meaning and existence of a 'Catholic Church', agreed that the "early Church" had composed the Creed he revered, and that it had selected Scriptures from a vast number of inspired writings to produce the Bible which he now cherished; but he insisted that the Early Church had split asunder; and he insisted, too, that no Church, therefore, taught any longer "with authority". No "authority" existed. All Ecumenical Councils held after the split between Orthodox churchmen and Rome, in the eleventh century, were incomplete and unrepresentative, he announced, and so had no claim on our attention.

So I had no clear notion, in my childhood, of one of the 'foundation-stones' of Catholicism: the conviction that the 'early Church' of Apostles and Martyrs had continued - "One, Holy and Apostolic" - until the present day, and that she clarifies doctrine, still: defines what she herself knows to be the essential to the Christian Faith. It was because she clarified the Faith in the twentieth century as boldly as in the third or fourth that my father was upset by what he saw as "Roman" arrogance. I wasn't sure what to think. My father plainly knew more than I did, but the things I heard didn't seem to 'fit' together.

As for the Scriptures presented to me at ten or twelve years old in King James' impenetrable English, I was ashamed to confess my difficulty in understanding the quaint phraseology. Some parts were certainly beautiful; I grew to love every word we sang in the church choir - especially the Psalms. But although I found excuses for the use of old-fashioned language in musical compositions, I thought it was hopelessly inappropriate for straight forward reading-out-loud in church. After inching my way line by line through a Shakespeare comedy at school, I had no patience left to tackle Saint Paul's letters, also offered to me in medieval phrases.

With my respect for authority dwindling generally, and with my hope of understanding Holy Scripture receding, I inevitably began to wonder, one day: "Christ wrote no book" ... so why should we be constrained by the Commandments, today, as presented in the Old Testament? But even as I asked myself that question, I remembered glimpses from the Scripture-readings at church of a powerful Christ who resembled someone from the stories about Abraham and Moses. The quiet Jesus of the children's story books seemed to be a pale shadow of the One who said that He had come to bring not peace "BUT A SWORD" (Mt 10:34) which would divide families: the One Who rebuked Saint Peter, argued with Satan, and calmed a mighty storm.

"Difficult" issues.

It was doubtless because of my father's vigorous defence of Protestant reformers that, in my 'teens', I examined the very un-Catholic idea that one might join any church which one found congenial. I had been taught, and firmly, that we Anglicans were right to have Bishops and priests and deacons. We were told that our 'branch' of the Church was mediaeval Catholicism now purified of unnecessary additions-to-belief and superstitious practices. Yet there was no criticism of Presbyterians or Baptists who didn't have a hierarchy like ours. It was suggested that the differing styles of worship practised in the numerous denominations provided various sorts of enjoyment for people of different temperaments. I explained, earlier, that my father's reasons for leaving the Quaker fellowship, which had been selected by him as being the most admirable and welcoming of all Christian groups, were based more on reasoned arguments than on fluctuating emotions; but he regarded himself as a special case. He quite happily accepted that other people had far flimsier reasons for changing their allegiance from one church to another. The main thing, in his eyes, was not what denomination one joined, but whether, in the general sense, one acted as "a good Christian."

Strange to say, it was one of the good things in modern life, preached regularly by persons in authority, that re-inforced, for a while, the proposal put before me that the only worthwhile Christian doctrines are those on which the greatest number of persons in any group or nation happens to agree. Of course, I wasn't taught the Catholic idea that if an article of faith, revealed by God, were disbelieved by ninety-nine persons out of a hundred, it would still be true. I could see for myself that the mere numbers of supporters couldn't alter the truth of anything revealed by God. But it was the concept of democracy, as lauded at school, and on television and the radio, particularly in those post-war years - and in my father's daily newspaper - which put at risk, in my mind, the notion of truth or false-hood: absolute good or evil.

It seemed entirely right that 'ordinary' persons like ourselves should be able to eat, work, marry, build homes and sleep in freedom and should take part in choosing who amongst us would govern the country, now that our monarchy's role had become largely ceremonial. It seemed right that newspapers could publish reasonable criticism about public figures, and that wealthy, titled persons shouldn't be counted as more precious or intelligent than those with no money or education. Certain attitudes which had prevailed partly through the ascendance of "democracy" were just and praiseworthy.

But I came to see that I was being steadily encouraged to believe that, in any institution, what is morally right or wrong can be decided according to the will of the majority of its members. When I saw this principle at work in political life, I was in danger of being led to think that it underpinned even Christian thinking.

Some of Christ's "difficult" statements in the Gospels were explained away, I knew, and by Christian writers, as being too harsh for ordinary mortals to obey. Over the next few years I would see 'the will of the majority' held up as the means by which we ought to make Christian decisions on every so-called "difficult" issue in the twentieth century: issues on which the Catholic Church in every century has always offered wise, authoritative and Divinely-inspired answers, no matter whether those answers have been popular or not.

Sin and ambiguity.

One day, as I browsed through a history book, at home, I learned that during my father's childhood - and boldly disregarding ancient wisdom - a conference of Anglican Bishops in Lambeth, in England, early this century had given their approval to sinful acts never before tolerated by a Christian body. And on another famous occasion, I would shortly find, a new 'church' had been created in India, where members formerly regarded as lay-persons were prepared for Eucharistic ministry in the 'Church of South India' through the use of a deliberately ambiguous act of worship. It's true that one question concerned morals, and the other Church order; but what these had in common was that they were permitted because it was the 'will of the majority'.

It seemed extraordinary to me that if sufficient numbers of Christians were agreed, then long-standing and God-given moral prohibitions or disciplines could be pronounced legitimate. I longed to know what was really true, and what was or wasn't acceptable in God's sight. Surely the advice He gave about sin and sanctity and wrong was permanent?

Enormous evils.

[It was to come as an enormous relief to me, a few years later, to discover the teaching of the Catholic Church not only on morals but on systems of government. The Church sees herself as bound to no particular scheme for organising human society, but sees merits in the various systems. So - as I had decided - there might be as much danger in men and women being governed by representatives from their midst, if those representatives were wholly devoted to something un-Christian, as in their being guided and guarded by a benevolent dictator. The will of the majority in any country might as easily enthrone a racist or an atheist as a wise Christian leader. In our own times, by the will of a majority in Parliament, some of our doctors have been given permission to kill unborn babies - something now legal in certain circumstances yet still wholly immoral in the sight of Christ and His Church; meanwhile I could see, long before that Act was passed, that whilst a democratic system might in some circumstances be admirable, it might, in others, be responsible for the introduction into a country of enormous evils.]

At home on Sunday mornings.

I didn't know who could give me answers to all my questions, but I never doubted that I could find answers somewhere, if I persevered. Meanwhile, although I was loathe to disappoint my mother, I decided to be honest. Since I believed that the main reason for attending Church was to profess one's love of God and to adore Him, and since I couldn't do that wholeheartedly, or, rather, since I had no faith in the Church which seemed so muddled, yet which organised our worship of Him, I didn't want to be a hypocrite. So, quite soon, convinced that God Himself probably disliked me, full of troubled questions about the Christian life, and unwilling to sing the praises of the disapproving and Divine tyrant of my imagination, I deliberately disregarded my mother's wishes for the first time in my life, and stayed at home on Sunday mornings. I half-expected my father to lay down the law about worship but he hardly said a word, except to comment that I should do whatever I thought was right.

It surprised me that my father was so uncritical of my decision; but I suppose that, since he had made prayerful choices about his own way of life, as an adult Christian, first, by joining the 'Quakers' and then by leaving, he felt watchful respect for the decisions I made, happy to see me reflecting in this way. On religious topics - with the exception of Catholicism - he preferred to see me argumentative rather than indifferent.

His antagonism to all things 'Roman Catholic' stemmed, quite obviously, from the teaching in his childhood. It triggered all his fervent denunciations of 'Rome'. This made it difficult for him even to speak about the teachings of the Catholic Church without exasperation. One morning in 1950, as we sat at the breakfast table, eating cereal and watching him read the 'Daily Express', we were all astounded by the vigour with which he suddenly looked up from a news item and angrily mentioned the Pope. He criticised him for having "added new bits to the Creed" by a definition of the Assumption into Heaven of the "Virgin Mary".

Since my father believed that "The Church" had broken apart many centuries ago, he believed - as I mentioned earlier - that no-one today could define anything about the Christian faith; it was an impossibility. So he was shocked by what he saw as the effrontery of Catholic leaders in making firm statements and claims of any sort. To him, Catholics were deluded foreigners. It never occurred to him that Christ's Church couldn't die, but remained a visible institution which still challenged the world by its faith in the supernatural and by its demand to be obeyed as if it were Christ.

I can see now that his study of Church history was sincere but rather 'patchy'. He spoke as though the Creed and the Bible which he revered had been given to him without earthly agents. He didn't hold the Catholic belief that, whereas God had indeed delivered His Revelation of Himself "once and for all" through Christ and His Apostles, the infant Church - which was governed by successors to those Apostles - gradually defined and clarified that same Revelation. My father didn't believe that papal influence had counted for much when dogmas were being formulated in solemn Councils throughout the first Christian centuries; and he was adamant that none of the Councils which had been held since the rift with the Orthodox had been valid: had been truly inspired and empowered by God to speak clearly against heresy and to teach sound doctrine; nor would he recognise that Catholics followed early disciples in being "FAITHFUL TO THE TEACHING OF THE APOSTLES, TO THE BROTHERHOOD, TO THE BREAKING OF BREAD AND TO THE PRAYERS" (Ac 2:42).

Ignorance of Catholicism.

Earlier in this story, I mentioned the confident teaching given to me at a Catholic infant school. Not once after nursery school did I hear that the Roman Catholic Church was at work world-wide, and was thriving. I hadn't a single Catholic friend amongst my close contemporaries - nor did I meet a Catholic priest face-to-face until the day I sought one out a few years later on, to ask to be received into the Church. Astonishing as it seems, I've realised that until I began to read more widely in my late 'teens', I remained almost entirely ignorant of the existence and teaching of the Church which has not only gathered together the Scriptures for our guidance, but which - with the same authority, discernment and unity of faith - gathers and guides its members in the twentieth century. When I found the Catholic Church, a few years later, all my questions were answered.

Until then, I had no idea that there were Catholic parishes all over the British Isles, nor that Catholic Missions in far-distant parts of the world had become thriving Catholic Dioceses, with Bishops, priests, deacons and people united in faith, government and worship. Surely David Livingstone had been the sole explorer on the African Continent? Wasn't Gladys Aylward, in China, the first Christian to penetrate that part of Asia? St. Francis Xavier, and others who had toiled across the world for Christ, were to be unknown to me for several years. The only Catholic hero I'd heard anything about was the 'leper-priest', Father Damien, who had died on an Hawaiian Island with his flock around him. He alone, of all Catholics, was mentioned admiringly by adults I knew, because of his heroic work and despite his peculiar beliefs: and also because his virtues had been lauded by a well-known Protestant writer: by Robert Louis Stephenson. I'm astonished, now, to reflect that whole families and communities in England in the nineteen-fifties could have been so ignorant of the true history of this Island Kingdom, where the Catholic Faith flourished for a thousand years.

No-one who is alive now in the nineteen-nineties, when communications are so swift, wide-spread and vibrant, can have failed to have learned about some of the evils perpetrated by Christians - by Catholic Christians too - throughout two millennia. There's been much in Catholic history that has been frankly appalling. Yet I've learned, however, that the price paid supposedly for the eradication of some of the Church's worst abuses has been even more appalling. Those who - from religious zeal, apathy, fear, or personal gain - once worked to overturn Catholicism in this country bequeathed to their descendants, I believe, a weakened faith. By the good which remains within it, it can bring its devout adherents to Baptism and so to the hope of Salvation; but it lacks the richness of the true Catholic Faith which can be glimpsed, reflected, in all the best of England's old art and architecture and literature and law, and medicine, and which could only be found - I was to discover, in my twenties - in its glory and purity, in the Catholic Church which returned from 'exile' after three hundred years, when the penal laws were abolished and the Catholic hierarchy was restored.

Anti-Catholic propaganda.

My ignorance of Catholic teachings and practices was due, in part, to the fact that four centuries of savage anti-Catholic propaganda had been tremendously successful. The "reformers" of mid-sixteenth century England not only offered a new interpretation of the Catholic Faith, through their laws and proclamations; they executed Catholic priests and banished - most horribly - the Sacrifice of the Mass. They abolished, too, prayers for the faithful departed, and petitions for the help of the Saints and of the Mother of God. Whole towns and villages, by the twentieth century, were ignorant of many basic truths of our history and our Christian traditions.

That's why it seems to me that - especially in England - the weight of responsibility on individual Catholics remains awesome, when, in each generation, many ordinary family members must expect to be at least gently mocked for their faith by those who share the same street or the same village. My former neighbours had stood almost alone in my childhood as they proclaimed - at the very least - one or two important aspects of the Catholic faith by their quiet but steadfast witness.

It shocked me later, when I'd discovered the richness of the Catholic Faith, to look back at all that I'd heard, over the years, in matter-of-fact comments about life and religion. Much of the understanding I'd been given at school about 'Civilisation' was flawed. All that was British, Protestant and 'modern' had been held up before us with admiration. Catholics, I gathered, were not generally to be regarded as sensible or well-educated. Their superstitious religion with its "semi-pagan" rites was a religion enjoyed by the ignorant, not by educated Britons like ourselves - so I was informed. Catholics were foolish in having large families, I was told. The Anglican Bishops who spoke at Lambeth in nineteen-thirty were held up before me as spokesmen for all sensible persons who wanted to oppose the unenlightened taboos of a down-trodden people.

A 'mediaeval' Religion.

It seems that even today, good Christians are unaware that many Catholic words we hear are accompanied by abusive adjectives. Every particle of Catholic teaching or practice which was mentioned, in my youth, in books or conversation, was labelled "superstitious" or "foreign", and never simply "Catholic". This ensured that we grew up knowing, vaguely, that England had once been a Catholic country; but we assumed that Catholicism was an early medieval fad which had been largely overcome. Entirely ignorant of the fact that the entire Catholic Church still taught a holy, Apostolic and admirable faith, I was ignorant of the very tender or powerful devotions long-recommended by Catholic Saints.

Almost every word we learned which was connected with Catholicism, such as 'sanctity', 'dogma', 'relics' or 'penance' was used only in phrases about 'mediaeval' ways. We heard about the virtues of Edward the Confessor or Thomas Becket - or learned about ruined monasteries or shrines; but these were all presented as persons or things which might amuse or entertain us, but which hadn't the slightest relevance to any 'modern' mind. All the devotions which we heard about had been swept away at the Reformation - so we were told. Religion nowadays was English, and sensible, and up-to-date - unless one went "abroad".

Few of us in our Grammar School were aware that it had been founded when the country - and the education - was Catholic. Teachers of history and literature doubtless spoke from ignorance and not malice; yet we were thoroughly misled. As I've discovered, there's no such thing as a 'neutral' view of history. The author of every text-book will have brought his own beliefs and prejudices into his writings; so there was little chance of us learning to admire Catholic heroes and heroines, when we were being educated in a vaguely-Protestant, modern English grammar school in the nineteen-fifties.

I remember clearly from those school-days the sight of a slim, dark-haired boy sitting alone in our class-room as all the rest of us dashed out into the corridor to go to morning Assembly. I was told that he was a Catholic, and wasn't permitted to worship with us. Yet not once did we ask about his faith; after all it was 'rude' to ask personal questions. It was 'un-English' to discuss religion or to reveal one's deepest feelings: so we had been taught. He was left alone by himself.

[False Ecumenism.

Despite all that I've said about my ignorance in childhood, I can't think that the relationships between Catholics and others have been solved by Ecumenism as I've sometimes seen it practised in parts of the country today.

True ecumenism, in its purest form, is a modern marvel which has overcome some long-standing prejudices. It has brought Christians together more frequently, in social life, social work, study, prayer and witness. Every Christian ought to be glad, I believe, that nowadays, others who try to love and serve Jesus Christ are revered as Christian brothers and sisters. The fact remains that Christian churches promote very different teachings on a number of serious topics.

I know I haven't been alone in thinking it not only foolish but dangerous to gloss over such issues, nor have I been alone in being saddened at realising that some enthusiasts would like to see Christianity 'rationalised', in the sense of Christians agreeing to proclaim a 'core' Christianity which leaves out every dogma or tradition which causes distress to ecumenical enthusiasts. This is what I call 'false ecumenism', and it cannot bring about true unity "in Christ". How can it do so if it keeps silent about Christ's firm teachings, for example, on morals?

So many good people who work in ecumenism are discouraged by an apparent lack of progress, but some of the 'solutions' which have been put forward are incompatible with Catholic belief. With my own ears I have heard it suggested, time after time, that the Catholic Church is the same as any other denomination, only with more rules and regulations and, sadly, a strict and fervent Pope. It is suggested, by Catholics as well as by other Christians, that if only we at 'the grassroots' could be brave about surmounting our differences of doctrine, and could ignore the ban on intercommunion, stop bothering about 'private' moral problems such as artificial contraception, abortion, re-marriage and other 'disputed questions', then a new united superchurch could emerge, composed of tolerant and loving Christians who can work unhampered by rules and regulations. Of course, this commonly-expressed view is quite contrary to Catholic teaching.

It's true that the rather 'stand-offish' attitudes of thirty years ago may at times have seemed uncharitable; but some of our divisions have the merit of truthfulness. Many persons today seem to wish to brush aside the differences; and such 'minimalism' can lead to Christians treating as unimportant things about which Christ himself spoke with great earnestness.

It saddens me to see that such words such as sacrifice, salvation, martyrdom and Heaven are disappearing from the ecumenical vocabulary, to be replaced entirely by more popular words about 'wholeness', tolerance, peace and fulfilment - all very good words, but not words which summarise the faith which Christ claimed would be "A SWORD" (Mt 10:34); and He warned us that "A MAN'S ENEMIES WILL BE THOSE OF HIS OWN HOUSEHOLD" (Mt 10:36). Quite simply, truth is at stake, whenever Catholics gather and speak with other people who won't share the fullness of the Church's Faith.

There's no question of judging others, nor of denying the good things which are done for the love of God. However, every little failure and evasion by Catholics in ecumenical circles contributes to the false vision which is growing in other Christian minds - of the emergence of a united 'Church' which is free of dogma, discipline and sacrifice: a Church which is heroically committed to the second commandment but which sees no need to remain faithful to our ancient, apostolic ways of honouring the first.

It's a cause for gratitude that Christians have achieved true unity in several areas of life. Nevertheless, the truths taught to us by Christ and shown afresh through the Catholic Church to each generation mustn't be quietly ignored for the sake of ecumenical friendships. Such friendships would be built on shallow foundations. We shouldn't be using tactless language in our discussions, of course, or referring unnecessarily to minor questions on which agreement is impossible at present. Yet important things are rarely discussed, I've found, as being too divisive; and yet these are the very things which need to be discussed if ever we are to pray together, as Our Lord wishes, "IN SPIRIT AND TRUTH"(Jn 4:24); and the Church herself has said, through the wonderful 'Lumen Gentium' of the Second Vatican Council, that it's essential that Catholic doctrine be presented in its entirety. We're urged to avoid a false conciliatory approach which waters down the Catholic Faith and so confuses those who aren't Catholic.]

Opposing advice.

In my mid-teens, when I knew very little about the Catholic Church, and when I'd been made unhappy, whenever I spoke with my parents about religion, by the plain inconsistencies revealed about Anglican teaching and practice, I stopped going to Church on Sundays, as I said: then I also glanced at the subject of Confession, and couldn't see why I should endure it any more. I'd confessed my sins to our minister two or three times a year for several years, in order to please my mother, who'd said that it was what good Anglicans did. But now I'd discovered - through my surge of recent questions - that my father thought it unnecessary. He said, moreover, that it wasn't normal practice for members of the Church of England. He could confess his sins quite well to God, he assured me, in the privacy of his own room.

I'd also discovered that, strictly speaking, we had only two sacraments: Baptism and the Eucharist; and the practice of Confession that was urged on me by Anglo-Catholics was a Roman practice, which was quite unnecessary for English Protestants.

With two members of the same Church giving me opposing advice, and no authoritative leader in Anglicanism to whom I could turn for a reliable opinion about my problem, I followed my natural inclination, which was to avoid unnecessary embarrassment; but when I stopped going to Confession, and so no longer entered the church either to prepare for Confession or to receive the Eucharist, I almost ceased praying altogether. It wasn't a conscious decision. Night-time prayers had ceased long before - indeed, I couldn't remember ever having prayed outside church, except to say grace at Sunday meals. But with each cultural or religious opportunity for prayer now avoided, I became spiritually quite rudderless in all the turmoil and agitation of those difficult years. I've forgotten to say that I'd also abandoned the church choir.

All through those teenage years, beneath the surface enthusiasm and behind the energetic facade, I was blindly looking for a great Love which I felt sure loved me and awaited me. I longed to find the Person whom I knew would be the perfect recipient of all the love that I longed to give. Perfection, in some guise, seemed a possibility, if only one looked hard enough or knew where to look. In yearning for that Extraordinary Person - and although I was very keen to have a boyfriend, and then a husband - I was yearning for someone wholly 'Other' who was perhaps incomprehensible and even unattainable; but I believed, obscurely, that he was waiting somewhere in the wings.

Distractions.

Then almost overnight, it seemed, the boys in our form grew tall and manly. I thought them so witty and attractive that for much of each year I was infatuated with one person or another, admiring their grace and beauty, longing - like a child - for affection: and beginning to forget my yearnings for Someone or something spiritual, transcendent and holy. The whole class became preoccupied with the new 'romances' which were developing or changing. In a single-sex school there might have been some respite for teachers as well as pupils from the turmoil and drama of adolescent crushes; but what happened, sad to say, is that new criteria were suddenly used to measure a person's popularity and 'success': neither academic nor sporting prowess, neither kindness nor wit, but only one's physical attractiveness and whether or not one had a 'date' or a steady boyfriend.

My own hopes for human friendship continued to soar and then to descend according to the degree of boredom or impatience I felt amongst various groups. I remained lonely, in the midst of the grim relentless Dance of adolescent life. What I chased then - like a child amazed by the beauty of soap-bubbles - were caricatures of love. I longed for warmth and affection; yet people were so unreliable, and I was so inadequate. Why were our hopes so tremendous, I wondered? Why did I instinctively believe that I could find a perfect and fulfilling Love when I was neither attractive nor praiseworthy? Why was I convinced that perfect Love awaited me, somewhere, despite my imperfection?

Father Caunter, our vicar, was very patient. Occasionally, at the Youth Club, I would ask his advice and mention my unhappiness. I know I asked him questions about life on earth, and about God, and even about why parents were so demanding. He said that I'd never be completely satisfied with anything in "this world". I didn't know what to answer. Our being alive on this earth seemed an extraordinary thing; what was the real "meaning of life"? Yet I felt like a freak for being disturbed by such matters. None of my contemporaries seemed much bothered about the reason for our existence.

Knowledge about earthly life.

Sometimes, during the sharp joys and pains of my childhood, I was physically stunned from time to time in my heart - or so it seemed - and at the same time I was suddenly aware of a terrible pang of yearning. This usually happened when I was alone, and happened once when I was fourteen and was walking home alone from school, totally unprepared for any new experience. It is hard to describe this, but the 'yearning' in my heart was answered by and accompanied by a sudden clear 'knowledge': an astonishingly rich and deep gift of information - or understanding. It was what I would later call a 'Teaching-in-prayer'. It arrived within my heart and soul without words; and yet since I must describe it here, I shall use words, from now on, to 'encapsulate' something of what I was shown on such occasions in this peculiar manner.

This is what I was told on that summer afternoon, by a Source outside myself, a Source which, as soon as I began praying again, several years later, I recognised as having been our God:

> **Recognise your importance, in My sight.** *You have been made for great things.* **(T:7 #1)**

> **Don't expect to feel entirely "at home" on earth.** *You are like a stranger, on earth.* **You are made for another home. (T:7 #2)**

> **Don't depend for your complete happiness on anyone on earth. Put your hope in Me alone. (T:7 #3)**

Ignorant of the Source of knowledge.

Something good and simple had happened. There was no reason for fear. I was ignorant of the Source of the knowledge, and ignorant, too, of its significance. Therefore I moved on. I had no idea that it's possible for God to teach human beings by infused knowledge, nor had I the faintest idea that a person like myself could be the recipient of such generosity. Absorbing the information, I had my tea and did my homework, beginning to let go of the strange event. I thought no more about it for several years.

If we're made for life with God, then of course in a life without Him, we have no home, and no security; and in this sense I had no true 'home' for the next six years. More and more, my thoughts about God were pushed aside by everyday miseries. By the age of sixteen I'd even begun to have scornful thoughts about those who were 'good'; I began to think that people who were docile and obedient were rather spineless and unadventurous. However, God never let me go entirely away from Him despite my foolish attitudes. The awful yearnings, which nothing on earth could satisfy, came again and again. It didn't occur to me to speak about them. I'd concluded that life was to be full of unsatisfied yearnings. I'd been told that there were no answers to most of our questions; so heartache was a permanent companion, day after day. It was labelled 'teenage moodiness'; and it was quite true that I was usually either grumpy about one thing or wildly enthusiastic about another: regarded by my parents as a bit emotional and over-dramatic; and so I felt not loved but merely tolerated.

Life seemed to consist of a long procession of dreary tasks interspersed with new causes for embarrassment; and there was no comfort from religion. Although I believed in the existence of God, I no longer knew what to believe about the spiritual life as it was presented to me, or about prayer. I longed for happiness, and for peace of mind and comfort, but I felt no hope of finding any of these in church. That was where I expected to meet only the Almighty Judge of my childhood, Whom I'd grown to fear and dislike.

A troublesome yearning.

Week by week, in my mid-teens, I followed the school time-table, and reluctantly did my chores; and when I became Church-free, and almost God-free, as I imagined, I became less happy, not more. But even then, the great mysterious 'yearning' in my soul ebbed and flowed. It distracted me from work, and spoiled my leisure. Yet my head wasn't burdened with romantic prose or cinematic images; this was a fiercer, deeper yearning which I didn't understand. It wasn't some secret, deep desire for glamour or excitement, stirred up by conversations or books or films.

A strict enforcement of work-times and bed-times meant that leisure hours were rationed, but I accepted that our lives were fairly austere. I'd learned to control my speech. I thought my own thoughts, accepting that questions at home were greeted with limited enthusiasm, or regarded as a bit of a chore. So the strange yearning within me was wholly independent of any feelings of resentment about parental decisions. It was independent, too, of any of my fretful thoughts about boy-friends and school. It remained within me, unidentifiable and unsatisfied.

That strange spiritual pang was sharpened by sunny weather and by beautiful sights, and by poetry. Matthew Arnold's "Labyrinthine Mind" made the yearning almost unbearable, so I learned to read poetry in 'short doses;' but I wrote poetry: half-formed verses about half-formed ideas, which of course I kept to myself. Poetry-writing might have been seen as a bit self-indulgent and useless, unlike hobbies such as woodwork or knitting; and I kept on painting. It was as easy as breathing, though there was always more to learn. And since my "A-levels" studies included Art, I continued to paint every week, in term-time. In all that I painted, Christ's face appeared. I couldn't explain it; but there He was, and His Mother, and His Cross; or rather, three crosses appeared somewhere in my pictures, whether they were paintings of dark nights or sunny cricket fields.

Who Christ really was, I didn't know; but beneath all the daily distractions Someone stirred me. Either my memory of Him or His own Self was somewhere in my soul. It seemed I couldn't escape Him. But I would have denied at that time that I was at all 'religious', admitting only to my vague belief in a Creator-God. As for the writings - Christ was there, too, in lines and thoughts, and in little sketches at the sides of the page. I didn't connect the Person Whose presence sometimes touched me with the fiery, terrifying Saviour of some of the Gospel stories, particularly those in which Christ spoke harshly to the Pharisees. What would He make of me, I once thought, if even good earnest people like the Pharisees couldn't satisfy His exacting standards? Such was the sort of reflection - in my ignorance - that kept me from prayer, which could have kept me 'cushioned' by God's grace, and might have protected me to some extent from unwise decisions and attacks of self-pity.

Meanwhile, my unspoken, hopeless longing for a Perfect Being remained a never-healing wound. I loved 'Him' hopelessly; yet I had no idea where to look for Him, and I felt lost.

Saint Teresa of Avila.

It's true that I was no longer reading much besides essential books for schoolwork. Rebellion had made me miserable; self-pity led to boredom; and - sad to say - on those occasions when I wanted to ask for advice or information, pride held me back, lest my mother think that she had won me round by what I saw as her earnest, "do-gooding" outlook. But she never gave up. She was always kind. She patiently accepted my routine refusal of almost every 'worthy' book she offered me. But one evening when I was idly browsing through our living-room bookshelves, and, despite my aversion to organised religion, I picked up an interesting spiritual 'paper-back'. It was a volume entitled: "St Teresa - A Life". I read it that night in one huge gulp, as though I were sitting at the feet of some lovely, lively contemporary who poured out her life-story with vivacity and joy.

The scene which was laid out before me by St. Teresa was a magnificent description of the Catholic Christian spiritual life. It was quite new to me. I'd never before experienced the whole marvellous world of Catholic life, as pictured by her. I'd half expected to read something about Tudor villains, scandalous convent-life or wicked Popes. What astonished and delighted me was a glorious panorama in which I could identify the quest and the journey, the holy Communion, the sacrifices, the adventures, and, all the time, in view, a Castle where a King lived - and such an attractive King - whom Saint Teresa served with such passion and such joy. What astonishment I felt, at seeing Christ as a hero, and also as a chaste but passionate lover.

I didn't analyse my feelings; but it was as though I'd been taught throughout my life that the service of God was a grim and miserable progress which might one day bring us to a place of rest and reward. St Teresa presented a different picture - of sacrifice, certainly, yet of glad toil in the service of Someone Who is so glorious that we should count it a pleasure to be permitted to do anything for Him, now, rewarded or not.

The experience of reading her work after a diet of worthy but "low-church" writers was like seeing my first Cathedral, after thinking that all churches, everywhere, resembled plain Scout-huts. However, I was rather depressed by the information on the back cover. It seemed that this fascinating author had died many centuries ago; also - she was a Spanish mystic. Despite my interest, my suspicious mind began to dismiss her reflections as the gushings of a mediaeval woman who would have been seen as a 'fanatic' in twentieth century life; so I met her, briefly, and then forgot her, despite my attraction. I had no notion that the creed which she professed was still being taught in all its richness and clarity. I didn't know that, for love of Christ, men and women still entered monasteries to devote their lives to God in prayer. My Anglican father had assured me that miracles and visions had only been produced in the early Apostolic Age. That's why I began to wonder whether St Teresa's writings were just fantasies woven in a superstitious mind.

When I was hungering for spiritual guidance, several years later, I bought but didn't read three volumes of her works. One glance at Teresa's rich and splendid prayer-life made me decide that it had no relevance to my own. By then, I believed that I deserved nothing but opportunities for reparation. I turned to other books, which spoke at greater length about my real needs: about earnest prayer for perseverance in utter darkness, and about the avoidance of sin. I felt that St Teresa had never been unhappy for long. She obviously had a gay, loving heart; and mine was overburdened with grief. She seemed happy and optimistic, whereas for many years my only optimism came from pure faith.

It was true that the grace of God kept me outwardly bright and cheerful, once I had given my life to Christ; I would have thought it a sin to appear gloomy in His loving service. But my days were spent in dumb endurance. I thought that St Teresa had never known difficulties as great as mine; I knew she had never been so wicked.

Teenage joys.

It wasn't all doom and gloom, I'm grateful to say, in the nineteen-fifties. Happy experiences came my way for a while. By the time I reached the sixth form, I'd been befriended by a little group of kind-hearted boys and girls whose interests overlapped my own, and who enjoyed the same sort of music. I learned to dance - and loved it. There were jolly evenings spent with a gang of friends and a record-player, with soft drinks, jiving, and much teasing and good-humoured banter. We met on Friday evenings, to listen to 'pop' records in someone's front room.

For a little while, I was happy. Weekdays had always passed fairly quickly, in term-time, with chores and school-work to be done. But what had once been long and lonely weekends were transformed, because of simple things. Now that I had friends I could go for cycle rides, or attend the youth-club; or we could meet together to listen to music. There was no money to spare for travel or amusements; I'd rarely seen a magazine or bought a new book, and I'd only once been taken to a theatre to see a serious play. But my new-found social life was thrilling.

This was the era when 'pop-music' really began, and skiffle-groups were widely admired; so my guitar - and my few dozen folk-songs - were welcomed at parties and other gatherings. My guitar was a great luxury for which I was extremely grateful. Music never failed to stir me, though it filled my heart with as much pain as wonder. I found much delight even amidst the unending stream of misunderstandings and embarrassments. Even at school there was much that was enjoyable. Besides taking part in school plays with gusto, I ached with joy at the music we sang in the school choir. Plays and concerts resurrected interesting ideas or made beauty almost tangible.

Every week seemed to bring a new joy - or a new crisis. If I was happy, I was radiant; but if another brief romance fizzled to an end, it left me devastated: further proof, I believed, that I was simply unlovable; and my lack of confidence blighted my early adult life. Yet I have to state right now, and firmly, that no sad experiences ever made me undemonstrative or 'over-spiritualised', in the sense of being "anti-body", that is, despising all warm, real, marvellous bodily beings created by God. Rather, I was always thoroughly in awe of bodily beauty, regretting that I was plain and uninteresting but admiring every sort of physical grace or beauty wherever I saw it. Moreover, longing to capture beauty, I yearned to draw and paint whatever entranced me.

Another embarrassment.

What embarrassments there were, amongst the joys of that time, and the nice surprises. How deeply I yearned to be beautiful and attractive. Once, I wished I could vanish into thin air sooner than endure another difficult occasion. It was when I was sixteen and had just come back to Amersham on the train, after an interview in London. My own clothes had been unsuitable for an elevated occasion such as a meeting a potential employer, since I possessed only a school uniform, some jeans and an ill-fitting outfit that I'd made for myself. I stood crimson to my roots, after bumping into a bunch of friends in Amersham High Street, while I was still clad in one of my mother's knitted suits. It was four sizes too large, and I'd had to wear it to my interview with the waistband turned over twice.

How I wished I could have looked elegant. I'm ashamed to say that because I was so unspiritual, my attention was focused for many years on exteriors. I'm also ashamed to say that I often failed to appreciate a warm heart or a kind nature, put off by odd mannerisms or superficial characteristics.

Moving out.

Throughout the last few months at school I was in a ferment about exams, beset by numerous fears and miseries; but I masked my feelings with a surface gaiety and endured inner torments in silence. I was moody, becoming exasperated by the social niceties which seemed so important to others, and unutterably bored by what was called "small talk" or by the endless questions asked by adults about school-work. I did my homework solely to avoid being punished, though I found myself enjoying the literature I studied in English and French lessons; the images I found in Milton and Wordsworth thrilled me.

When it was almost time for me to leave school, at nearly eighteen, I was told I should study at university or college, as my examination results were reasonable, although I'd done only the bare minimum of work. But I was so ignorant about form-filling and about grants, and so appalled at having to choose one subject from amongst so many, that it suddenly seemed easier to follow a course I'd initiated two years earlier. At sixteen, I'd gone for an interview at a large teaching hospital and had been accepted for training as a nurse; I was told that I could start there when I was eighteen; and since one of my childhood ambitions was to be a nurse, as well as a missionary, a mother, and an artist, I slid effortlessly into a pre-arranged plan, looking forward to earning my own living, too, when I studied and worked.

I left home at eighteen, taking a suitcase onto the train to start my new life. All the gloom and self-pity of the past two or three years vanished overnight. Once the decision had been made, I'd become exhilarated at the start of what I saw as a tremendous adventure. Yet at the same time I was nervous, incredibly naive, and very shy. My few pathetic attempts, before leaving school, to make independent, adult choices - whether about wearing make-up, or deciding at what time I'd come home after a party - had been foiled by anxious parents, highly responsible and eager to protect me from danger. So I was quite unprepared for life away from home, and had no idea how to sit down calmly to work out a few priorities. Blind enthusiasm was going to precipitate me into a variety of dangerous situations.

With dozens of other young women, I was pitched into a totally strange, hectic and demanding routine, which alternately thrilled and appalled me. After six weeks of classroom studies I was sent to a surgical ward to work full-time. The discipline was tough, but no different from what I'd experienced at home and school. The scenes I saw were shocking, but my childhood training ensured that I didn't bat an eyelid when confronted with what I saw as unbearable. Whatever I felt inside, I briskly pressed on with whatever was required. And besides, my concern for the patients over-ruled my revulsion.

It's with horror that I now look back at my blithe, youthful lack of understanding of the pains and problems of the elderly, whose aching joints needed kind, careful movements, not the swift, ruthless efficiency of someone quick to finish the day's work. Meanwhile, in huge leaps of experience, I grew accustomed to the horrific sights, though not to human heart-ache and grief. With the initial advantage of a disciplined childhood, I coped with the poor bodies and limbs so grievously wounded and damaged, and - later on - learned to love poor aching hearts, too, and admired those who were patient and cheerful.

Exhilarating entertainments.

Life outside the ward was almost overwhelming. I had never been to a restaurant, a 'hairdresser', or an hotel; but now I enjoyed the social life typical of a large institution. There were many rules and regulations, but exhilarating entertainments as well. I enjoyed them all; but, sad to say, I longed to "fit in" and to be popular. My standards declined further, the busier and more sociable I became.

A novelist couldn't have described me as a farm girl or a country bumpkin; but I wasn't far removed from those images; and believing myself to be almost at the centre of the "civilised" world - in London - I wanted to change my image. If I could not be - was not - beautiful, then

65

I would be glamorous and sophisticated.

The glamour could be trowelled on with the make-up, but sophistication eluded me. Excruciatingly tongue-tied with older people, I blushed scarlet at each new social event, appalled at my own blurted schoolgirl opinions, yet still with no training in listening or showing an interest. In short, I had no self-assurance and not much real charity. Allowing myself to be propelled along by events, I grew not happier but more bewildered.

Every few weeks I dashed home on the train for a short time, longing to see familiar faces. I blithely hoped that my home had remained the same; if I compared it with the Nurses' Home where we were regimented and inspected, it seemed very cosy and private. However, when I arrived home, on my first visit since leaving, and hoped for a weekend of relaxation in a familiar room, away from anxious eyes, I was told that all my possessions had been thrown away. Moth-eaten toys, school books, essays, the model theatre, too - all were gone. I owned nothing but what I'd managed to carry away to the station, early in September.

I was surprised but not shocked, and quietly accepted the very logical explanation that there was too little room for everybody's old things. It's true that I felt a bit depressed. Perhaps I felt that if things which I'd either made or treasured were unimportant then so was I, and the fault must be mine. Also I found that - quite reasonably - the bedrooms had been 'changed around'. I was to sleep in the box-room. Although I didn't mind where I slept, I no longer felt "at home" at home. So I returned at regular intervals from then on, longing to see the family, and yearning for affection; but it became a great relief, after each visit, to escape back to my exciting new life in 'town'.

[Painting, and colour.

I still possess the bundle of sugar-paper paintings which escaped the "blitz". I had dashed them off enthusiastically, in powder colour, at primary school. Perhaps they had lain in a folder under my bed, or had been taken to my room in London; it's one of the details I can no longer remember; but I'm glad they survived. They're reminders of a time when, as a child, I could put down clearly and unselfconsciously, in colour, what I either saw before me, or could draw up from my visual memory.

It was to be another forty years before I'd come full-circle, able to do the same again:- with less uncertainty about composition, and with the power of a few new techniques, but, during the moments of time that spanned the picture's creation, with the same joy and self-forgetfulness. Also: it's only been during the simplicity of childhood, and in recent years, that I've painted for the right reasons: not only because it's possible, but because it's the Will of God for me at that moment: by which I mean one more simple task of all the day's good tasks, rather than an impulsive leap or a means of attracting notice or reward.]

Expressionist Colour.

In the midst of my youthful chaos and excitement came an invitation to accompany a friend to an Art Gallery; I think it was my first-ever visit to a major collection of paintings.

What a soaring joy I felt at the sight of the strong, clean colours of the Expressionist paintings which I saw reproduced in the Gallery Shop: colours unseen before in my daily life. Derain, de Vlaminck, Macke, and Monet sent their lavish harmonies and unorthodox contrasts straight to my grey-coated heart. I was irritated with myself for liking Franz Marc's "Blue horses", since I had no especial love of horses - but I didn't realise that my glimpse of those colours and their interactions was a brand new gift which I wouldn't "unpack" properly for another thirty years.

At the same time, I saw, reproduced - not as gaudy and exciting as Expressionist works, but very beautiful and gentle - the Monet paintings of Rouen Cathedral. I was enchanted to recognise the deeply-recessed doorway through which I had stepped with delighted curiosity at the age of fourteen, during a visit to our French friends.

Alas, my resolutions about starting to paint again came to nothing. Still dashing from one activity to the next at top speed, always wildly excited about some new interest or anxious about another problem, I was quite incapable of setting aside enough time in order to concentrate on an activity so contemplative and peaceful.

Work and leisure.

I nursed for two years. I met life and death. I fell in love, laid out dead patients, comforted live ones, and tore between theatres and parties at breakneck speed. I worked with great enthusiasm and took part in hospital shows; but I was no happier than before. There was more pleasure, certainly, than in my childhood, but there was still no answer to the question - who are we, or why are we here? It was all 'surface' fun. I grew accustomed to the frantic pace of life as day-duty was followed by months of night-duty - twelve nights in a row. I became so overwhelmed by work, leisure activities and new friendships that I hardly thought about God from one year's end to the next.

The whole business of being 'grown-up' was overwhelming, although I was still somewhat sheltered by living in the Nurses' Home. It was astonishing to earn money and to be free to spend it. I was just as astonished that I could occasionally buy new clothes, and go to the cinema without asking permission.

Each Christmas, I followed friends to a local Anglican church. However, I felt that I was an outsider, despite my familiarity with the music and the prayers. Now that I was no longer pressurised into church-going, the services seemed to be not boring, but mysterious and beautiful; but God seemed very remote, and His interest in me almost unbelievable; and it didn't occur to me to attend public worship for any reason except to pay homage and adoration. I mean that since I couldn't bring myself to adore Someone I neither knew nor liked - my Headmaster God - I saw no reason for weekly attendance. It would have seemed merely self-indulgent to have gone there just for the music, the beauty and the warm feelings of nostalgia.

A sure symptom of a partial alienation from God and a real lessening of charity at that time was my growing attraction to outwardly-appealing persons and a neglect of those who seemed boring or unattractive. I was too well-trained to be openly rude or unkind; but what a shameful superficiality had overtaken me. Even worse, I who so loved beauty that I wished I were beautiful not only for vanity's sake but to give joy to others, went 'over the top' in my use of cosmetics and hair colourings. I wanted to create a more acceptable face than the plain, pale freckled oval which had faded into every crowd at school and afterwards.

Alas, I fell into a sort of double spiral, downwards, trapped by my own ploys. Knowing that anyone who showed an interest in my new self-creation would be disappointed were I ever to appear in my true colours, like Cinderella after the Ball, I found my efforts to appear stunning were tinged with desperation. I longed to be appreciated, and yet secretly despised anyone who responded to my worldly overtures. How very little I knew about real love.

A brief conversion.

Within a couple of years, God stepped in, to fascinate me, and so to teach and change me; or rather, I reached out, and found God: the loving God behind the monster-mask. But first, there was a false start.

When I was still nursing, and after yet another day of frantic activity, I happened to be walking past a hall in central London where fervent Evangelical Protestant Christians were singing and preaching, hoping to bring sinners to God. I was lonely, and went in. I took part in their prayer-service reluctantly; yet eventually my heart and emotions were touched; it was because I recognised the truth of their message: that we're all full of sinful desires, or perhaps full of good desires, uncontrollable or wrongly directed, and that because of our selfish ways we're in need of forgiveness. I heard, more clearly than ever before, that everyone who asks for mercy is welcomed by Christ, Who came down to earth to save us, and is led into a marvellous new way of life.

Suddenly, I was weeping with shame at my brash, thoughtless behaviour. Since I was still lonely, as I said, and young and impulsive, I overcame my embarrassment in order to approach the stewards, when I didn't even know who they were or where they had come from. I gave them my name, and was told that someone would keep in touch. My thoughts were still muddled, however. I wasn't sure just who Christ is, although I felt a great attraction to Him. But no emotion was strong enough to enable me to examine and change my life. To be led forward on a sure Way, I needed more than a moment's shame at the knowledge of my wrong-doing. It was true that, through contrition, I could help my faint spark of faith to grow into a flame; but I also needed truths about the Divine Person to Whom I was being asked to entrust myself. I needed sure answers to all sorts of questions about sin, duty, worship - and Church. I needed a firmer foundation. The "conversion" lasted for about three days.

Back at work, I became embarrassed that I'd confided in strangers, and regretted that I'd let them 'bludgeon' me with emotional preaching and soft music. I began to despise the kind woman who had been thrilled that I'd 'decided for Jesus' and who pestered me with 'phone calls for days. Exasperated, eventually, by her frequent invitations to spend my precious free time in her room, reading the Bible, I fobbed her off with excuses which she - good woman - happily believed. So cynicism and pride ruled again, as far as my soul was concerned, and religion remained just an annual event: to be observed at Christmas in any church, anywhere, with a party of friends, and then to be forgotten for the rest of the year, except for when I blindly and instinctively called out for God's help in a moment of crisis.

Wanting to meet Love.

If I analyse that incident today, it seems to me that I had a sincere longing to meet the Person Who could forgive my sins. Had I been less impatient and more thoughtful, I might have met Him immediately, in prayer. But at the heart of my disappointment lay the fact that I was yearning to meet Love in Person and yet was offered a book; and it was the very Book that people in my childhood had revered, but which had seemed very dull to me because it was written in such old-fashioned language. Only when I'd given my heart to God in prayer, a few months later, would I turn with reverence to His nourishing Word in the Holy Scriptures.

Marriage.

Very suddenly, at around that time, when I was still lonely and muddled, my whole life changed. Despite all my faults, I began to go out with someone who was kind and had lovely manners, and also a great sense of humour.

He was devoted to his family: to parents and siblings, nephews and nieces; and he was faithful to his religious duties; and on top of all that, he was not only hardworking in his own subject but very musical; and so it was that one month before my twenty-first birthday my fiancé and I were married - in a church - out of reverence for his Christian beliefs and for my vague Creator-God; and I'm full of gratitude that even today, as we approach our thirty-fifth wedding anniversary, I can say that that everything I've just written about him is still true.

We were both members of the Church of England; and so the wedding was in an Anglican church because although I seldom prayed I was quite happy to stand up in front of family and friends, to make public and solemn vows of loyalty to my chosen husband - in a building consecrated for God and for Christians. I had never denied my Baptism. Indeed, I had an agreement with my fiancé that any future children would be baptised Anglicans; and my views on marriage, doubtless imbibed at first from my parents, but truly right and reasonable to me, were crystal-clear. Married couples ought to be loving and faithful until death, I believed, since it was plain that we ought to keep our vows, and never to tear apart a family; and I understood that marriage was primarily about having children and making a happy home: a place of welcome, warmth and safety.

[Different races.

Perhaps it's necessary to mention something else here, though only very briefly, before I move on with my story. I mean that some people who read my surname suppose that I'm Chinese, when I'm not. My husband was born in England of Chinese parents, hence my name; and the reason why I'm writing 'briefly' is that we haven't paid much attention in our own lives to what other people sometimes need to call 'the race question'.

There was no reason why we or our families should pretend that people of different races don't sometimes have different outlooks on a number of issues, or don't approach certain things in different ways. We and our parents knew, however, that there were no disputes amongst us about what was supremely important. We were all Christians, which meant that some things could be taken for granted about customs and traditions as well as belief; and so there was a sound hope of some harmony being maintained. We were all convinced of the importance of a loyal, warm and yet sacrificial family life which makes demands on its members but which provides an emotional haven not only for the members but for a network of friends.

Saint Paul said that we should "BE FRIENDS WITH ONE ANOTHER, AND KIND" (Ep 4:32); and it's obvious that love, goodwill, tact and courteous speech are especially needed wherever people meet who are of different races or cultures. In having the same faith, however, my fiancé and I, and our families, had a sturdy platform on which to build a good relationship. Besides, it would have been regarded by both 'sides' as needlessly offensive to keep pointing out differences in our cultures. This was the era, remember, when it was regarded as impolite to make what were called 'personal comments' about other people; and to have spoken about one's own cultural outlook and expressions would have been seen as embarrassingly self-centred and unnecessary. The main thing we knew, as simple Christian people, was that we should aim to be kind, courteous and inoffensive towards everyone, no matter what their race or religion; and that's what we've tried to put into practice, despite some of the taunts we or our children have encountered through strangers in the street, from school-children, or from those whom I once blithely imagined might rent us a room, or a flat.]

A new dimension.

Both my fiancé and I, in our separate moments of free time, had spent fruitless hours looking for a furnished flat where we could make a home together: but to no avail, mostly because of blatant discrimination. I can't count the number of signs I read that said: "No Irish, Blacks or Asians," or variants on the theme. But just days before the wedding one of my fiancé's relations offered to rent us two rooms. I moved in at the last moment, to make sure that it was clean and tidy, and had curtains hanging, and that the gas-meter worked. Then, with a determined acceptance of the demands both of my husband's responsible career and of his commitment to his far-flung family, I made my marriage-vows wholeheartedly, grateful that a new road lay ahead.

As I gaily organised my new life, however, with God half 'on hold', as it were, I was blind to God's plans for my life. He, eternally patient and loving, was already guiding me towards the One Church for which baptism had prepared me: the Catholic Church which, in its full splendour and comprehensiveness, was quite 'foreign' to me then. The date of my wedding was July 6th: the very date on which St. Thomas More, Chancellor of England, had accepted death sooner than submit to his Monarch's wishes and betray the Catholic Church by denying St. Peter's successor, the Pope. But in 1963 I had never heard of "Saint" Thomas. He had been mentioned as just another politician who had fallen foul of a difficult master.

After our marriage, I was immensely happy, and was prepared for any sacrifice to be a good wife. I longed so much to have children that I was thrilled when I became pregnant - and was appalled by an early miscarriage. But I remained optimistic, and longed fervently to be a mother.

The griefs and insecurities of earlier days seemed to vanish into thin air, as I dashed off to work each day and planned a cooked meal each evening. Life was so full and joyful that there was a serious danger that I'd create a new but earthly idol, more demanding than the disapproving childhood God Whom I'd almost forgotten; and there was another danger, which was that without a firm and adult faith my joy would remain only superficial; and that's what happened, as I began to develop an unspoken but almost superstitious fear that no joy so true and undeserved could be left undisturbed for long.

That's why I half-waited for something to disturb my life, as hope and fear battled for first place in my heart. With only tattered shreds of faith in God, I couldn't see clearly. I didn't realise the truth: that in my wonderful new life I was building myself a castle to contain merely earthly joys, and that one glance in the direction of God would shake the fragile walls. Also, I'd been unaware of the power of the Sacrament of Marriage, through which Christ leads us to love our chosen spouse with more than natural affection: with supernatural Charity, which inevitably brings about change, as well as making possible our everlasting fulfilment.

I believe that it was God's interior 'prompting' that led me, within a month of my wedding, to ponder the meaning of love: to see another dimension: to want to be of one heart and mind with my husband, united, perhaps, in prayer. That Sunday morning, my husband was about to set off alone to the church which he attended faithfully every week. I decided to go, to keep him company and to share his 'interests'. His goal was an Anglican church not far from our bed-sitter. The traditional order of service was, of course, familiar; but apart from Christmas-time and weddings I hadn't attended a service of worship for about five years.

Spiritual gifts.

By the grace of God I began to turn my thoughts God-wards during that hour's worship each week, no longer a resentful fifteen-year-old craning her neck to look at someone's watch. I soon found that, despite my rebellion against His Christians and His Book, the Heavenly Father whose laws I'd despised and Whose guidance I had spurned, now still IS, and was quietly waiting for me to respond to His love.

It seems to me that because I went to church for the best of motives, and began to listen and pray with an honest and enquiring heart, I was at last able to receive the spiritual gifts which God had always wanted to give me. It was as if, on previous occasions, my irritation or cynicism had kept my heart imprisoned and had shut out the faith, hope and love which God longed to pour within.

Yet there were still questions. Since truth demanded that I say in prayer only what I truly believed, I stayed silent for a few weeks at various moments during our church service. In my mind, I gravely tested the words of all the prayers, as though 'holding them up' against my conscience. I don't mean that I sat in judgement on the formulae, only that I was content to begin again, and to study things like a child. This meant that I was soon joining in the words which I could wholeheartedly endorse. I left unsaid certain bits of the Creed, but only until I'd had time to think about each phrase, and then to pronounce it out loud in church with wholehearted and free consent and belief.

4 CONVERSION
(1963-1964)

MARRIAGE. CHRIST. ILLNESS.

A little lamp of faith.

Every day was spent in trying to be good and kind. Every new week was wreathed in prayer. Moment by moment, I became more peaceful and contented. None of us can be certain of why or how faith is given; I only knew that the little lamp of faith I'd once carried as a child hadn't been entirely lost. It had been battered, warped, 'half-emptied' and neglected. But it was real; and it was marvellously precious. By its light I was able to see clearly once again: able to judge my duties and priorities rightly for a moment at a time.

It was true that some of the questions of my teenage years were still unanswered; but the largest issue had resolved itself, in simplicity. Now that I was older, and was less easily swayed by anger and fear, I grasped for the first time the fundamental principles of the search for God. Now that I was praying once more, I could 'see' truth more clearly. I took my first steps in an adult, freely-chosen Christian life. If I summarise my motives, I can say that I had decided that since God existed, I would adore Him; and since I believed that the Christ of the Christian Creed revealed Him, I would make every effort to obey Christ's laws.

These few words can't explain my faith, but I decided not only to be 'good' but to be 'perfect'. With some sweet feelings and some conceit - for I was proud of my will-power - I set about my reform, for love of a God Whom I didn't know, but Who I had come to believe was All-powerful and Good, somewhat different from Him Whose image I'd feared in earlier years: now more a Father than a law-enforcer, although remote from me and extremely awesome and strange.

Throughout that time, I imagined that I was looking for God. I didn't realise that He - in His kindness - had been seeking me, and was drawing me on by His grace. When I turned to Him in prayer, whole-heartedly acknowledging my dependence on Him, it was through the grace of baptism - forgotten but now 'revived' - that He was waiting within my soul, ready to receive me in Love, through Christ. He knew that, for the moment, I was only slightly sorry for my past sins. I was too busy to be able to think much: out at work all day and cooking each night: not to mention a diary half-full of parties - and with occasional winter evenings spent keeping warm at the cinema after the gas meter had run out. But it was a real conversion. It wasn't very deep, but it was wholly sincere. It changed my whole attitude to life. My good intentions, I know, were accepted.

The Christian Way.

Every night and morning I prayed brief but fervent prayers; and I kept all the Commandments, fervently, for the first time in my adult life, in so far as I understood them at the time. I gave up everything that I believed was sinful. Quite astonished at the good things which, by the grace of God, I was now able to do, I was astonished, and humbled, too, by the ease with which I was able to overcome some evils.

In order to keep the Christian 'Sabbath', I attended Church every Sunday. I gave up swearing - I mean the careless and casual use of mild swear-words which is common amongst youngsters. Then, in order to honour my parents more - as God commanded in the Scriptures - I became more cheerful and helpful when I visited: trying to listen as well as to talk; and I tried to stop grumbling.

As soon as I made those new efforts I realised how many of our conversations, whether between relations or friends, consist of taking turns at listing complaints about God, the weather, an employer - or one's own family.

Amongst these sincere efforts to reform, and as I tried to make every aspect of my life pleasing to God, I found that weekly church-going was very encouraging. I listened carefully to the readings and sermons, and it was marvellous to feel that I genuinely 'belonged'; and now that I longed to be faithful and good, I sat down at home, occasionally, with an exercise book and a Bible, making notes about what I found in the Gospels. I had a vague, guilty feeling that I ought to be reading the Bible much more frequently, but I raced along month after month, genuinely busy at work all day, and busy cooking and sewing in the evenings. I prayed at home every day, on my knees in our little flat, and enjoyed the Scripture-readings in church. But if I found time to read the letters of St. Paul I would feel I'd neglected Genesis or Kings. The Book of Revelation mystified me; and since I was still repelled by archaic language the Acts of the Apostles sounded like tales from Shakespeare: extremely worthy but remote and irrelevant. The Bible still conjured up my old memories of God the avenging Law-maker.

Sweet feelings in prayer.

Prayer-times, however, were always rewarding, during those first few months after my conversion. Within a short time, I even began to have sweet feelings about God. I was surprised to feel His 'touch' on my shoulder whenever I knelt to pray to Him. This was only during the first few months of renewed prayer: in a time of ease and encouragement, and before the 'Dark Nights' of the soul which would follow. But today that joy has been restored, as the Father touches my head whenever I turn to Him in prayer and also shines His Glory within my soul; but thirty years ago I had no idea of all the adventures that the spiritual life would bring: both torments and blissful surprises. I was happy to pray simple prayers and to make efforts to be more charitable. I would have coped with martyrdom, I hoped, should it come; but I didn't anticipate the particular problems that faith would pose in ordinary life.

So great was my longing to learn more about God and goodness that I picked up a book for the first time in months. We had few possessions, little to read, and very little money, but I found several fascinating books in a second-hand shop, and "ploughed through" them with enormous interest. I hadn't guessed that the Christian faith had such an interesting history, and was almost dazzled by the riches spread before me, as one book led to another and began an unfolding of Christian faith for me in all sorts of areas: in aspects of theology, spirituality, art, liturgy - and even geography. But I didn't let anything distract me from my main goal, which was to find out precisely what Christians believed - so that I'd know precisely what to do in order to please God and become holy. I was obviously far from holy; but I believed firmly that God could change me.

The clear-sighted Anglican author, C. S. Lewis, drew me - through his wonderful combination of extraordinary word-pictures with remorseless logic - to a greater sense of shame at my past cynicism and rebellion. I admired his skilful depiction of ordinary temptations in "the Screwtape letters", and the blunt yet inspiring explanation of the Christian cause, in "Mere Christianity." His repeated message was that Christians must expect to suffer, to be despised and persecuted, and to meet with terrible choices as they try to serve God in an imperfect and dangerous world. This echoed - though in more modern tones - what I'd once read in Bunyan and Milton; and in my own life I've learned the truth of it. Yet I've also learned that the difficulties we usually dread are rarely the ones we're asked to face; and problems which we've never considered can come hurtling along unexpectedly.

Sick-leave.

It was during that first year of our marriage, when I was tremendously happy, that I became unwell, again. I say 'again,' because I'd experienced several months of weakness and pain, two years earlier. Now married, and working full-time, though no longer nursing, I was distressed to find myself struggling against weakness once more. No matter how great was my joy at home or at work, and my longing to be busy, I couldn't throw off the painful illness by will-power; and I had to take 'sick leave'.

Each day, after shopping, I'd crawl up the stairs to our first-floor bed-sitter. After walking a mere two hundred yards across Turnham Green to buy a few groceries or to return a library book, I battled simply to get home. Only twenty-one, I was happy and optimistic; but my legs felt like jelly. I imagined that the mysterious pain and weakness would soon disappear, because although the consultant who examined me suspected various obscure diseases, the clinical signs were normal, and blood tests proved normal too. I didn't know what to think; and the weakness persisted for over a year.

During that time, I stayed in the flat in London, strong enough to cook a meal but unable to walk very far. It was a struggle, each day, to do the bare minimum of work necessary to keep our little home clean and tidy, but of course that was the first reason why I had so much time to browse through so many books on the Christian faith. The other reason was because we were in an unfamiliar part of London. There were no relatives in that area, and few personal friends close by; and within a few months, my husband's duties at work kept him away for days at a time; and since I was ill and didn't drive, I was at home alone for much of the time.

Still 'new' to the Christian faith, I continued earnestly in my new prayer-routine and in reading good books, slowly working out how an adult Christian should behave. I wanted to be free of bad habits and selfishness, and to be patient about my wretched symptoms; but I longed to enjoy the busy life we'd planned; and I blithely assumed that Christ's command to each of His followers that he "TAKE UP HIS CROSS" (Mt 16:24) referred to great trials far in the future which I would meet with perfect trust. "If only I knew what was wrong", I thought, "I could get organised, and cope!" The doctors remained puzzled and unhelpful, and the painful absence from work continued; but during that time I continued to work and read and pray - and ponder.

Some people will doubtless assume that I brain-washed myself into Catholic belief by reading only a narrow selection of works, yet the truth is that - as my interest in the Christian faith expanded - so a devouring interest in the whole world of books and ideas was awakened in me for the first time in my life. Much of what I'd read at school had been resentfully accepted, then grudgingly appreciated. My mind was unable to 'detach' itself from the heart, which, as I have had to describe at length, was woebegone and self-pitying.

Novels, on every subject.

Now happy in marriage, despite health problems, I was reading each month not only C. S. Lewis's solemn ponderings and other Christian works but novels by the score on every conceivable subject. What I should have been doing at twelve or thirteen, I had begun nearly ten years later. I found myself wildly excited by each new author. Each new work I enjoyed was quickly followed by every work written by the same person - if I could find copies; and so I tasted everything from the heartache of "Precious Bane", through "Jane Eyre" to "King Solomon's mines", with little excursions to C.S. Lewis's "Perelandra" and "William Golding's "Free Fall". Agatha Christie filled in a few gaps between Simone de Beavoir and D.H. Lawrence, and even smaller gaps were filled with French and English poetry.

On a roller-coaster ride through whatever material I could unearth in paper-back, or second-hand, or find in the library, I searched out and read equal quantities of trash and good literature. I became more critical as time went by, when I learned to separate an author's thoughts from the structure and language in which he had clothed them. We had no television or record-player to distract me; so whenever my chores were done I continued my amazing journey: once depressed for a week by a picture of rural Ireland, as presented by Edna O'Brian, and then engrossed for an evening by Charles Dickens' 'Tale of Two Cities'.

But so loathe was I to tackle really weighty novels, having been forced to read Sir Walter Scott and Henry Thackeray at school, that I ignored most of the old English Classics, and the complete Russian corpus - right until my 'forties'. Only then - and more mellow - would I discover, for example, the delights and burdens of parliamentary life as described by Trollope.

Meanwhile, in my early twenties, I soared in delight at evocative descriptions in the 'Alexandrian Quartet' by Lawrence Durell, then returned to earth via John Braine's "kitchen-sink" dramas. Good story-tellers such as Jack London and John Buchan caused me a few pangs whenever I was tempted to neglect my chores in order to finish a final chapter, but I became more thoughtful as I grappled with stronger writers. Simone de Beavoir gave way to Germaine Greer, whose "Female Eunuch" caused my mind to hover - as it were - in great agitation as I tested her conclusions against the morals and precepts of the Christian religion newly-revealed to me by C. S. Lewis.

'Domestic servitude'?

Almost inevitably, within a few years I would find myself facing a fusillade of feminist ideas, as Jill Tweedie and her literary sisters filled bookshelves and newspaper columns with their tracts against patriarchal authority. But all through the years of reading, and despite the typed urgings of a dozen liberated women that I free myself from domestic servitude, I tried to do what I believed - and still believe - to be my duty. I cooked meals for the husband who returned exhausted from work; and I looked after children too. I moved daily from prayer books, to novels, to recipes in newspapers, and back again, trying to be conscientious and cheerful, whatever work I was doing - though I didn't always succeed.

One of the few large books I bought was a volume of recipes. I couldn't boil an egg, when I married; and after a few domestic disasters I overcame my scruples about buying brand-new things at the shops, and bought a cookery book. I still have it in my kitchen. It lies, much-used, amongst telephone directories, books of religious history and dictionaries and art magazines. With simple instructions to follow, my cooking improved overnight; and I count it a privilege, now, to have been able to do the simple things that guests and passers-by deserve, as well as family members: to have simple, tasty meals put before them, shared perhaps with neighbours' children as well as our own, with the telephone interrupting us with monotonous regularity, yet all the smells and interruptions and conversations forming part of the fabric of what many of us gratefully call 'home'.

When we began to move more frequently amongst professional people in non-religious circles, it was sometimes hard to resist the fashionable view that a woman's life spent caring in simple ways for other people was 'wasted'. Although I enthuse about motherhood, I must agree that not every woman has that vocation; but I know that children are so precious, and so vulnerable, that they deserve the best possible care. Only someone very well organised or with profoundly important reasons, surely, would entrust her youngsters to strangers, and permit them an enormous influence over her children in their formative years.

But before our children appeared, and when I was first weak and unwell, and no matter how much I read, the time seemed to pass by very slowly. It was a year when I'd expected to be dashing about to all sorts of social events. But I didn't realise how fortunate I was to be able to continue with so much reading, and to be able to carve out of my life great blocks of time for peaceful pondering. I can see clearly now that it was only in the silence and stillness to which I was led through physical weakness that I was brought to a place where I could reveal my true thoughts and my deepest longings to God in prayer.

[Time for prayer.

I might well have dashed about for many years - perhaps for the rest of my life - perpetually busy with personal, family and business projects. I might have allowed God to have a few minutes of my time at regular intervals. I might have hoped that His Will would fit in with my ideas and plans. Instead, I learned to value His Will as being something rather more important than my own ambitions. So I see it as a cause for great gratitude that I was able to spend so much time thinking about God: and not only thinking but praying. No matter how much effort I might have expended in a search for God using only my mind, I would have come no closer to Him. I know that by using our intellects we can recognise His presence in Creation; but I believe, too, that He can only be truly known and 'touched' - so to speak - not by thought but by Love, expressed supremely in prayer, although expressed also in loving service.

I can never thank Him enough for permitting me to be brought 'low' by illness, since it was because of my torment that I began to pray to Him sincerely, with real hope and a glimmering of love, seeking His help; and He answered me, because He is good.]

A cry for help.

Within a few weeks of my new commitment to church-going, and to prayer, an incident occurred in my spiritual life that changed my whole life. It caused my fervour for God to become a passion, and led me at last to a true repentance for my almost-Godless years.

When I'd been married for less than a year, and my husband was away at work, I left our bedsitter one weekend to visit my parents, because I'd grown lonely - and was still unwell much of the time. One night I sat up in bed in the small spare room, in terrible pain, wondering what on earth to do. I can remember the very moment at which I prepared to pray determinedly to God for help, in a child-like and trusting plea made out of sheer desperation; but I can remember, too, the very second at which I consciously decided to believe that He would respond and help me.

In a split-second of thought, it was as though I took hold of my faith and decided that since it was true, it would 'work'. In other words, I didn't know God very well but I decided to believe that He is really trustworthy; and in that trust, and also in my utter misery and pain, I earnestly called out to Jesus, pleading for help, believing that in some way He would answer. I was aware that I had faith, and therefore I genuinely expected a lessening of my pain or a moment's consolation; but I was quite unprepared for the staggering generosity of Christ's response to the confident act of faith I made, as I cried out: "Jesus! Help me!"

Straight away, and suddenly, Christ Himself was with me. He had responded, in Love. He came to me instantly. I didn't see Him with my bodily eyes, but with the eyes of my soul. I saw Him standing beside my bed. But how blazing was His Glory! How foul and dark I saw my own soul to be! All my pain was forgotten. I found it impossible to look at Christ; yet it was impossible to bear my own terrible darkness-of-soul, now revealed by His light. It was as though I stood before Him in a white dress which was badly marred by large stains. I saw this with the eyes of my soul - although I couldn't have explained how I 'saw'; and the sight was horrific.

There's no reason for me to exaggerate. It was as bad as I describe. If a feeble or a careless home-maker were to have skimped on the chores, or to have ignored for many years every daily domestic duty, you can imagine how appalled that person might be, were an extremely powerful searchlight to shine, suddenly, into every hidden corner of the kitchen. All dirt, mould, infestations and rotting woodwork would be plainly revealed, causing embarrassment or shame. It was in just the same way - though spiritually - that Christ suddenly revealed to me, merely by His presence, the real state of my soul, after my long neglect of Him and of the spiritual life.

Christ didn't reveal my state of soul in order to make me repent. He came to me, full of love, in answer to my prayer. But He is so dazzlingly glorious now that - inevitably - His radiance revealed, within my soul, every 'speck' of past unrepented sin and selfishness. Every scrap of twisted logic, every lame excuse and every arrogant thought was thoroughly exposed in the brilliant Light of His burning Glory; and so I turned away, appalled: repentant. I huddled against my pillow, stunned by the experience of His presence. Christ my God had responded to my faith with a greater Love than I could have dreamed of, although I felt it only as punishment.

A wordless communication.

Something else happened, on that astonishing occasion; it was something which I accepted as quite normal, since I believed that Christ could do anything. I'm trying to explain that - in an instant, and not for the first time - I received "Knowledge". All at once, and by the mere fact of His silent Presence and wordless communication, Christ taught me all that I needed to know at that moment about how to obey and serve Him. He taught me a great deal, in a way suited to my limited understanding, at a time before my discovery of the sure and detailed teaching of His visible and united Holy Catholic Church. He told me several things, and did so without using words, although I have 'translated' His soundless instructions into words, as He has now advised me to do so that I can share them with other people.

Christ told me, very gently:

> **Look! Here I am: You are calling for help, believing in Me, and I am here to help you. (T:10 #1)**
>
> **Look at Me, Jesus, Who stand before you. I am awesome and powerful, yet also beautiful and holy. (T:10 #2)**
>
> **See how My Divine Radiance blazes upon you continuously, just as you are. (T:10 #3)**
>
> **Gaze upon My Glory and My pure Light. It is because of your sincere prayer and My loving Will that I now reveal Myself as being so close to you. (T:10 #4)**
>
> **Consider the sins which are revealed - starkly and undisguised - in the brilliance of My Light, in prayer. I do not accuse you. Yet - seeing your sins so clearly, and seeing them as large stains on the beautiful 'garment' which is your soul - you are repelled by the sight of them, and you turn away in torment. (T:10 #5)**

Let this 'turning-away-from-sin' be a new beginning, a true conversion. (T:10 #6)

Confess your sins to the priest. (T:10 #7)

Be restored to Christian fellowship and worship me as you ought. (T:10 #8)

Believe in My nearness to you. I am not distant, but close-by. (T:10 #9)

Honour and serve Me, your God and Saviour. (T:10 #10)

Seek My Will. (T:10 #11)

Love and serve your neighbour, for My sake. (T:10 #12)

Follow the example of My Saints, of past times and present. (T:10 #13)

An understanding was given here of the importance of the Saints who are now in Heaven. Like many Christians, I didn't know that the Saints are alive, and joyful, and are longing to help us by their prayers. Then Christ showed me:-

Listen to My Wisdom in the Holy Scriptures. (T:10 #14)

Learn about faith in Me. (T:10 # 15)

Read and study, in order to find out how to please Me. (T:10 #16)

Jesus, friend and God.

Through this visit, Christ overturned all my old ideas about His remoteness from our lives. I was astonished to learn that Christ isn't a distant figure, but is close-at-hand, whether or not we can see Him; and the other thing I learned then, and have never forgotten, is that although He is awesome and powerful, He is also immensely beautiful and holy.

I've no idea for how long He was with me, but I do know that He taught me then by the very method and with the very Love that He has shown to me in recent years. The method was His own; it consisted of pure Knowledge, infused wordlessly, by His own choice, into a heart which was willingly turned towards Him in real trust, momentarily free of selfish desires.

If Christ once said, of those who believe in Him: "IF YOU REMAIN IN ME AND MY WORDS REMAIN IN YOU, YOU MAY ASK WHAT YOU WILL, AND YOU SHALL GET IT" (Jn 15:7), I ought not to have been astonished that I was helped. Certainly, I didn't receive what I'd expected; but I'd asked for "help", and Christ had given me the best possible help - Himself. Of course, I was so appalled at the revelation of my own sinful nature - clearly seen in His Light - that far from thinking His calm gaze a help or a privilege, I interpreted it as disapproval. Yet it was a greater help than I could have guessed, since it was through that visit, and with my consent, that I was hurtled onto a narrower road than I might otherwise have found.

The Christ Whom I met then - the only Christ - taught me nothing new, by which I mean, nothing that can't be learned through His Church and His People. But under "THE PREDETERMINED PLAN OF THE ONE WHO GUIDES ALL THINGS" (Ep 1:11) I was given an all-encompassing, burning lesson such as few persons receive, a lesson which helped me to keep on struggling to do the Will of God throughout the next thirty and more years. Yet I feel no pride in this. All I felt for a long time was horror that after such an astonishing favour I didn't love and serve Christ as He deserves.

In an instant, in the bright Light which Christ shed in this way upon all my past actions, Christ had shown me the horror of sin. Instinctively, and sadly, since I knew myself to be quite unfit to be with Him, I had turned away from His gaze, just as souls do, I believe, who see their sins clearly at the end of earthly life and who therefore long wholeheartedly for purification.

Eventually, I drifted off to sleep; but without a word being spoken, I'd been shown what to do. I treated it all quite matter-of-factly, though I could scarcely bear the shame within my soul. I supposed that Christ came, somehow, to everyone who believed God's message to Jeremiah: "CALL TO ME AND I WILL ANSWER YOU" (Jr 33:3). So I had once heard; and now it had happened: on February 1st, 1964.

[The need for repentance.

I couldn't have analysed it at the time; but I realised later on that God is gently waiting for our true acknowledgement of Him. He delights in responding to the merest whisper of a heart which turns to Him through Christ; yet His grace and power can be held at bay - so to speak - either by a soul's deliberate refusal to love and to do His Holy Will, or by a soul's reluctant and half-hearted attention. Isn't it astonishing that the Living God is sometimes grudgingly acknowledged for only a few minutes each week! God reveals himself most fully to hearts which are weak and sorrowful, not to hearts to full of platitudes and pious phrases, or indifference, or conceit.

There was more than one reason for this extraordinary intervention - apart from Christ's future plans for my life; I was happily praying and trying to be good, after years of irreligion; my efforts were sincere and energetic; yet I'd blithely turned towards God in prayer without a word of regret for my past neglect and ingratitude, and with little trace of remorse for the damage I'd done to myself or to others by my sins. It was almost as though by newly cultivating pious habits, I'd been doing God a favour; or, rather, I was like a friend who turns up on an old friend's doorstep without a word of explanation for not having written for years.

What I know now is that God doesn't want us to grovel or to go through agony for agony's sake. But unless we have some clear insight into past wrongs, and make contrite attempts to put wrongs right, we shan't have cleared away enough debris, as it were, in order to build a firm foundation for our new Christian life. Purification has to come before growth, otherwise we're like men who - for example - have been swindlers for many years, who suddenly decide to 'go straight' for very good reasons, yet who do so without lifting a finger to help the people they once deceived or bankrupted. God Who is Love forgives all our sins, but invites us to take part in repairing the damage inflicted by our selfish choices.]

Putting things right with God.

Next morning, I had no hesitation in simply doing what I thought Christ wanted, still not knowing how it had become so plain. Ashamed and frightened, but wholly repentant, and determined to do what I thought was necessary to 'put things right' with God, I plucked up courage and went to see our minister, alone. My heart thumping in grief and misery, I knocked on the door of his home.

When he saw my distress, and heard me ask him to hear my confession, he reminded me that I was free to go to any minister; but I couldn't wait another minute with that burden, and said so. He led me to the Church next door, to kneel in the sanctuary. There I confessed my sins, unloading them all onto his poor shoulders. Immediately, I felt freed from a huge weight. I knew little about Christ's Sacrifice for sin but I believed that Christ had paid the price for my release My faith was weak, and obscure and inarticulate; but nothing could have kept me, then, from reparation, penance, and thanksgiving.

The minister was a kind and a holy man. He didn't 'lecture' me. He said to me firmly that the angels in Heaven are more delighted with one repentant sinner than with ninety-nine who are saved, which only prolonged my weeping. But as he led me back towards the house he was quiet and calm. He made a cup of tea, and chatted for a while so that I could dry my tears and calm down. Then he waved me back to my parents' house, where I'd stayed overnight.

[Happy to answer questions.

What a marvel that I'd gone to someone so approachable! Truly, his whole life was dedicated to serving God and to loving and helping his neighbour.

If an ogre had blocked my way, I believe I'd have gone to see an ogre, I was so desperate to do what I thought right, in order to be worthy to receive Holy Communion. Had I been less determined, or even more timid than I was, a frowning face in the doorway might have kept me from my duty; yet Father Caunter had always welcomed us in our 'teens', happy to answer questions or to listen to our minor grumbles; so although at twenty-one I found myself appalled at the thought of revealing my sins, I didn't actually fear my spiritual guide.]

A more thorough conversion.

Back at home, with my mother, I explained to her where I'd been - but not why. I said nothing about the details of my "conversion". The word didn't even occur to me. In my state of soul then, fearful and insecure, lacking in confidence, and guided until recently more by my emotions than by firm principles, I felt that a sharing of my experience would provoke much teasing from my family, and I quailed at the prospect. Also, I thought it was a private matter.

Thanks to God alone, courage wasn't lacking; that gift had sustained me through the humiliation of confession. Having once become unsure about whether confession was really necessary, I now sought it, despite my shame, in order to be obedient to Christ's gentle instruction. I'm not saying that it was what the Catholic Church would call a sacramental Confession; but it was a preparation for that Sacrament, in that it was a devout compliance to the Scriptural advice that urges us: "CONFESS YOUR SINS TO ONE ANOTHER" (Jm 5:16). I had done my duty by confessing my sins in the only place I knew about, and therefore was rewarded; and the minister had acted as a true man of God: after all, we've been asked to "CARRY EACH OTHER'S TROUBLES" (Ga 6:2).

The first stage of conversion.

Whenever, in later years, I've been called upon to speak about God's work in my life, or about the process of conversion, I've found that I've had to correct the assumption that it was by an astonishing vision of Christ that I was converted, whereas, by the time He came to me so powerfully, the first stage of conversion was well underway. Of course, it was only God's prompting within my soul that had led me to worship in church, after my marriage, and to make wholly sincere efforts to please God in every aspect of life; and yet it was because I had already opened the 'door' to Christ in that way that He came to me when I called out to Him from my distress, and taught me what I needed to know about His love for me, and about the meaning of repentance.

Ordinary duties.

It didn't seem necessary to speak about everything to my parents. I instinctively felt that God's secret and personal dealings with the soul are sacred, not to be exposed casually to others nor to be revealed for the wrong reason, with the precious relationship treated merely as a subject for gossip. One ought not to discuss God carelessly, as one might sometimes casually discuss one's reactions to a particularly moving film or play. I could bravely defend my faith - and did so, on occasion - or discuss the concept of God; but it didn't seem right to treat lightly what was a serious matter: that I'd worshipped God in childhood, offended against His laws in adult life, and had been brought back to Him again.

When it seemed appropriate, I mentioned to friends and family that I'd begun to attend church regularly once more. However, there was no time that weekend to examine myself or to work out everything I ought to do or say. One thing was crystal-clear: that I must do the work which Providence had set before me. I mustn't neglect the duties of daily life. So I went straight back to our little rooms in London, to carry out the usual routine, and to think and pray as I worked.

I cooked, rested and cleaned with a hopeful outlook. I longed to be well, but I was already sure that God Whom I had - so late - decided to reverence and serve, would be honoured best by a patient fulfilment of my ordinary duties, pursued in sickness or in health, solely for love of Him.

So began a more earnest attempt to love God as well as I knew how, to love my neighbour, to avoid sin, to pray, and to forgive as I had been forgiven. I decided to accept, gladly, as a penance, every pain and sorrow that ever came to me, permitted by God; and I resolved to be always optimistic and cheerful.

As I prayed and worked and pondered in my new way of life, my heart ached horribly at the memory of past falls and failures; but I tried to look forward, and to move ahead 'in Christ.' It became plain that the whole point of the Christian life was to live for love, prompted by God, supported by Christ, and strengthened by the Holy Spirit - All known by faith alone. I gathered that love meant far more than cultivating 'niceness', and I made earnest resolutions about loving my neighbour for God's sake, whether or not I found that neighbour attractive or grateful.

Anglican blessings.

I'm bound to explain, at this point, before I say any more about 'The Church', that my whole purpose was to live and act as a good Christian - by the grace of Christ; and the only Christian life which I had ever experienced had been rooted in the Anglican Church; yet at no time in those early days - or at any stage - did I say to myself: "Yes. I embrace and accept all that the Church of England represents; and I wish that other people could be brought to see the truth of Anglicanism." Yet there was nothing but gratitude in my heart for the good things I'd found there, in what was the only Christian 'context' I knew: a context which was to be thoroughly explored and examined as the weeks went by, a context in which I was happy to pray, listen, and go to Communion, but one which I would eventually feel conscience-bound to leave, in order to become a Catholic.

By my parents' choice, I was an Anglican; so for as long as I was I considering their choice and my responsibilities, I continued to go to a weekly Communion service: sometimes with my husband and sometimes alone - or with my parents, on visits home; and I approached what we called "The Sacrament" with reverence, in great need of strength and wisdom. Each time I approached, I asked Christ to come to my heart and to help me. I believed He would do so, and therefore He did help me, because He is good. Week by week, my soul was nourished and made stronger, whatever was the precise way in which I received that help from Him.

What a grace it was that every Sunday morning my frail, humiliated soul was soothed and splinted, so to speak, propped up by the mellow and lovely words of the Order of Communion, as found in the "Book of Common Prayer." Knowing little about liturgy - so much more about repentance - I gave myself willingly to its support, making its words my own. I learned to recite, again, but from the heart, phrases such as those used in the 'prayer of humble access', for example: "We do not presume to approach this thy table, O Merciful Lord, trusting in our own righteousness, but in thy manifold and great Mercy". No longer did a few 'thees' and 'thous' distract me from the essence of the plea to a God of forgiveness and compassion.

[Useful and familiar phrases.

How fortunate I was, to have memorised already - through childhood Christian worship - the words of a great number of prayers which are central to the Christian faith. I knew the Creed and the Our Father, besides being familiar with acts of contrition, hymns of praise and of pleading, and grace before meals. And, for all my complaints about the impenetrable language of our Authorised Version of the Bible, I knew dozens of little pieces by heart, having absorbed them not just by sitting through our Eucharist, but from singing in "The Messiah," reading Christian magazines, and belonging to a family where religion was not just practised but was spoken about, matter-of-factly.

My parents had been quite free with their quotations amidst daily tasks: for example: "GOD LOVES A CHEERFUL GIVER" (2 Co 9:7), or, to a complaint that so-and-so did not 'deserve' his good fortune, or that life wasn't 'fair':"HE CAUSES HIS SUN TO RISE ON BAD MEN AS WELL AS GOOD" (Mt 5:45).]

Meditation.

Soon after my experience of Christ's presence, and my sincere confession, my husband and I moved to a different bed-sitter - and so to a different parish church. I was still alone and unwell much of the time, whilst my husband shouldered a crushing work-load and studied for exams, so I had a great deal of time in which to ponder, and make decisions. The foundations of my new life were very simple and plain. Knowing my own lack of generosity, I made very few rules for myself; but I clung rigidly to these, aware of their importance. I drew on childhood memories and on my reading so far, and continued to pray every night and morning, and to go to Holy Communion once a week. Our new church in Chiswick was yet another which was dedicated to St Michael.

I vowed that I'd pray every prayer with great love and reverence, and would examine my conscience, daily, in order to put wrong things right. Each month, I went to 'Confession', travelling some distance away, as most Anglican churches near our flat didn't advocate the practice.

It appals me now to think how gaily I took for granted some of the gifts given to me at that time. For example, not once did I experience any difficulty in prayer: I mean, in how to pray, or in how to meditate. Thinking about God came naturally to me. So easily had I been practising meditation, at intervals, every day for many months, that I was surprised at all the attention paid to it in books about prayer, where guidance was given on how to sit still or how to "compose a place" or how to hold onto and examine a valuable thought. Since then I've learned how difficult it can be for people with certain temperaments to sit and ruminate; and I suppose that they, at least, are grateful for detailed instructions. But for my part, I was able to meditate all day - partly because my chores were so simple and intellectually undemanding. It was easy to slip into 'pure prayer', sending my heart and desires Godwards, whenever I got down on my knees before God. Yet there were two further and greater reasons why I found prayer so easy, besides a determination to pray regularly and a lack of distractions. First, I was very reverent before God; and He has since shown me how much He delights in our reverent approaches; and, secondly, I was utterly determined to discover His Will for me, and to do it.

[Whatever God wants of us.

Experience has shown me, countless times, that we pray with the greatest ease and simplicity when - in our daily life - we're trying to do everything that God asks of us. And in those early days, before new problems caused me to hope for escape or for change, I gladly undertook everything I thought God wanted, no matter how difficult. At the same time, I was blind to many of my faults, and frequently uncharitable; but I refused Him nothing that He asked; and so prayer-time was an awesome but simple greeting of the God for whose sake I was always trying to behave with perfect charity, even if I was frequently unsuccessful.

This doesn't mean that certain 'desert patches' in our prayer-life are necessarily our fault or can be avoided; nor does it mean that a person who is 'enjoying prayer' is perfect! It means that if someone who professes to love God and who prays regularly is constantly refusing, in everyday life, to do God's plainly-evident Will, and isn't just 'falling' into sin through weakness or carelessness, he will find that progress in prayer becomes impossible. He will be simply incapable - because ungenerous and obstinate - of "looking God in the face", so to speak, in prayer-time, with any genuine desire to please Him, or with any gladness.]

Efforts to be 'good'.

The Commandments were foremost in my mind, when I thought about 'how to be good'. They were the foundations of my new attempt to love God and love my neighbour. I tried to practice what I prayed for in the Lord's prayer. Knowing, alas, that affection for and delight in others is not what Christians mean by love, although we include these as a further cause of thanks to God, I resolved to work whole-heartedly for the true welfare and joy of everyone I knew or met, determined to be kind and forgiving. I tried to control my temper and my tongue, counting on God's help. I vowed that I'd never be deceitful or selfish.

Grimly determined to be perfect, I decided, too, that I'd never avoid anyone I disliked, though I found myself praying frantically before going to see people I found 'trying'. I tried never to look bored, nor to argue unnecessarily. It would be thoroughly un-Christian, I saw, to rejoice in someone's misfortune; I could never say 'serve him right' - or be glad to see anyone suffer. There was a need for discipline, I saw, in child-care, and in school life or in wider society - but I could never be glad in a gloating way that anyone was suffering pain or punishment.

It became more evident that only by very positive efforts would I learn to accept other people's weaknesses and grow into the habit of making allowances for behaviour which seemed to be wrong. Meanwhile, I pursued God as determinedly as I had pursued pleasure, failing in many of my resolutions at one time or another, but learning much from the good books that came my way about Love: Divine Love, to be welcomed and then 'radiated' by every Christian even to the point of 'crucifixion'. It was plain that a weak person like myself has no hope of doing good things without God's help. I had to ask for the grace to love as Christ loves. I saw that I ought to go to the very limits, for the sake of others' welfare: yet for the good of their souls rather than the fulfilment of their earthly ambitions. I hardly dared to think about my own Salvation; that was something so mysterious, so undeserved and momentous, and even uncertain, that I would live in hope, I decided, living for love of Christ and of my 'neighbour' in what I had seen described as "the sacrament of the present moment."

Alas, I felt more exasperated than loving, when we were visiting relations one day. I saw very clearly just where any routine unselfishness would lead me. If I were perpetually leaping up to be helpful, and to do chores which others were grateful to relinquish, I'd be marked out for dreary and unpleasant tasks for evermore! People would be bound to take advantage of my generous attitude. Was it really the Will of God that we do things which others - perhaps selfishly - chose not to do? Should we be fools for God's sake?! My conscience told me that we must fulfil Christ's wish that "JUST AS I HAVE LOVED YOU, YOU ALSO MUST LOVE ONE ANOTHER. BY THIS LOVE YOU HAVE FOR ONE ANOTHER, EVERYONE WILL KNOW THAT YOU ARE MY DISCIPLES" (Jn 13:34).

God's Will for me.

While I was mulling over this problem, I came across another book by Thomas Merton. I had devoured "Elected Silence" and other autobiographical works, yet his later works irritated me. Cynically, I wondered how a monk dedicated to silence could write so much. But I thank God for some of his insights. A piece he wrote about the Will of God for each one of us lit up my soul and mind with its simplicity.

He said something like this: that at each moment, when we're trying to decide on a task to do or a course of action to follow, we ought to do whatever is demanded of us by charity, since Charity IS God: and Charity is therefore our best prompter or source of guidance.

Solid Christian teachings, with obvious daily duties, should provide us with inspiration for our moment to moment decisions about what to do next; but I could see that if someone needed help, and I had the time and energy to help, then I ought to do so for the love of God, whatever my personal feelings. He said nothing about the damage we can do by pandering to manipulative persons; but of course we must use our common-sense and prudence in all our decisions about how best to put love into practice in order to keep God's Commandments.

So I concluded that if I couldn't physically help someone I should at least pray for that person. If I were torn between conflicting needs, I ought to attend to the greater need, or to the need of the person who was bound most closely to me by duty, since it's God's Will that we value our Divinely-ordained relationships with family members; but I was bound to help close friends, especially. How much I could do for strangers in need depended on the circumstances; but preference should be given to the sick, the old, the very young and the despairing.

Whole books have been written, I'm sure, on the Will of God, and on the apparently conflicting duties in different areas of life. Yet through those few words I was enabled to set out more confidently on the path of Christian discipleship; and because I was agonising less frequently about what to do, I was able to concentrate on the way in which I did things, trying to do them less grudgingly. Supposedly adult, I was a mere infant in the practice of charity. However, God is so good that He didn't despise my goodwill. He rewarded me in all sorts of ways, amidst my blunders and misjudgements.

In every circumstance.

There were numerous problems in those early days, and moments when things were really out of proportion. Random thoughts took root, festered and caused me distress. For example, as I went about my work, thinking and praying, full of both fear and wonder, I was so amazed by the thought of God's holiness, and so fearful of displeasing Christ, that I half-wished I were a nun. I was tempted to become puritanical: to act as though God wants us to suffer, only, or takes delight in our pain. I worried about my use of make-up, and my interest in clothes.

These thoughts were the first stirrings of a true and good desire to stop fussing about inessentials and to give my life wholly to God. But thanks to the clear teaching I'd absorbed, I saw that Christians live their lives for God in every circumstance, especially in the holy state of marriage: a way of life witnessed and honoured by Christ during His life in Galilee.

What 'counts' is that we rely on God's grace to be faithful to whatever vocation He has offered us - through circumstance or through an almost audible 'call' - whether a call to marriage or a call to make the promise of celibacy in preparation for the priesthood, or a call to a religious order, or a call to an unspectacular and chaste single life, out in the world; and now that I was married and hoped to have children, I had more reason than many to thank God for His gifts, and to care for the people amongst whom I'd been placed by God's Providence, and by my free choice. I came to see that besides carefully reserving times for prayer, alone, in obedience to Christ, I could best prove my love for God by continuing faithfully in my normal way of life, trying to cultivate greater faith, hope and charity.

Regular study.

For the next two decades I scarcely ever recalled to mind the astonishing meeting with Christ in 1964, nor did it occur to me to mention it to the priest who eventually received me into the Catholic Church. As I said, I was sure that most people who prayed had met Christ. I supposed that if other Christians seemed less ashamed than myself it was because they had nothing to repent of. My heart ached when I thought of how badly I was serving Christ. But I wanted to go on trying to please Him despite my failures.

Realising that I was ignorant of many details of Christian belief and practice, I read many more books about Church, Christian life and Sacraments, knowing that I could no longer simply take for granted everything I'd been told as a child. It seemed important that I use time well, and that I study the essentials of the Christian faith. So, whenever I was forced to rest, and in between one chore and the next, or when my husband was at work, I learned about Church History, and about holiness: but I couldn't bring myself to finish a single book entitled "A life of Christ".

Each time I began such a work, I'd be disappointed to find that each new author portrayed Him as rather ethereal or worried, or hectoring. None of the descriptions of Christ matched up to the Christ Whom I'd glimpsed in Holy Scripture: the loving and loveable and passionate and Righteous One Who had blazed out His Glory on Mount Tabor (Mt 17:2), and had wept over Jerusalem (Lk 19:41): the very Christ Who, I matter-of-factly accepted, had stood beside me in my prayer. True, I'd been terrified, because His pure light had revealed my sinfulness; but I knew that - however else Christ might be portrayed - He ought not to be presented as hesitant or boring.

The Christian 'classics'.

Little by little, I was working my way through what are known as the Christian "classics". And since each writer on prayer invariably mentioned the works of whichever authors or writer-Saints had helped him or her to progress more rapidly in the spiritual life, I was led from one marvellous work to another. I'm sure I was drawn onward through the promptings of the Holy Spirit, but it was also through my reverent curiosity and my real thirst for knowledge about God's Will and about His Church.

From brief but illuminating lives of the Saints I was led to Saint Augustine's autobiographical "Confessions", and then to the minds and hearts of people as different from one another as William Law and Brother Lawrence. Yet the accounts of their spiritual lives were all for the same purpose: to bring other people to strive wholeheartedly to give Glory to God and to cherish and serve their neighbours.

The books I read weren't all helpful. It disturbed me to read in Thomas à Kempis' "Imitation of Christ" that we ought to flee from or despise everything and everyone on this earth in order to serve God perfectly. Knowing little about the true meaning of spiritual detachment, I was unable to enjoy that book, so determined had I become to love and cherish all my God-given relations, above all my new and beloved husband. It was in the "Imitation" or in a similar work that I was disturbed to see much emphasis on silence; but I came to see that what might be good advice for monks and nuns isn't necessarily good for Christians who live in the world. I read much criticism of worldly conversation: and I decided that such crudely-stated prohibitions are of little help to people who are trying to lead a normal family life, where words can be used like the healing oil of the scriptures.

[Frivolous talk, or soothing words?

Of course, the author of the "Imitation" was only emphasising the need for 'recollection' as a foundation for a life of prayer. 'Recollection' means: a calm and quiet state of mind, which should 'include' a peaceful conscience; and such a state is kept away or destroyed by someone who freely fills his head with gossip, frivolous talk about solemn things, fantasies, indecent thoughts or constant entertainment. Monks, nuns and married people - if they want to draw close to God - will find that mental discipline is even more essential than bodily penance. But families have an especial duty to support 'communion within', that is, to develop and strengthen loving bonds between members, with apt expressions of concern and affection.

What mother can fret about keeping silent for God's sake when her soothing words, quiet reminiscences, little stories or vigorous phrases of appreciation can weave a web which will bind together different members of a household, or soothe hurt feelings? A wise parent, by numberless little calming interjections can soothe members who are reluctant to maintain family bonds. How damaging would silence be, in such circumstances.

It's true that mothers and fathers would do well to make some sort of 'retreat' each year, in order to examine their hearts and minds, silent before God; yet we shouldn't be hasty in accepting monastic prescriptions about the spiritual life, when we have different routines, and our daily lives are intertwined with different duties and pastimes.]

A desire for holiness.

Thomas á Kempis was left behind when I discovered Saint Francis de Sales. What wonderful surprises occurred, amidst the stern reminders of duty offered by so many spiritual writers. Some of the books I'd discovered buttressed a new and exciting concept, which held that every "ordinary" Christian should be trying to work hard and to pray well, and to be kind and truthful towards his neighbour; yet the motivation for such efforts should be the desire to please God, principally by desiring to achieve union with God: even in this life. By 'union' was meant holiness, which is something very different from respectability.

Thanks to St. Francis de Sales' extremely helpful work - "An Introduction to the devout life" - it became clear to me that Christians should aim to be neither dull and impeccable super-citizens nor world-hating puritans, but should hope to live in the world whilst "KEEPING ONESELF UNCONTAMINATED BY THE WORLD" (Jm 1:27). Saint Francis hoped that the devout ladies to whom he was giving spiritual advice would be the best-dressed in any room, since he knew that even an attempt to dress smartly to honour one's hosts or one's husband was an act of charity. Such an act would of course be pleasing to God, since charity to others is the second great Commandment (Mk 12:31).

St. Francis also taught what others had explained in different books: that all ostentation in dress, in speech, or even in posture at prayer, is to be avoided. If it's pride which might lead us to draw attention to ourselves then we're as proud in flaunting wretched clothing, supposedly worn for the love of God, as in flaunting jewellery or fine garments. He wasn't criticising the wearing of a recognised uniform of a Religious Order, but only an unnecessary display of asceticism in lay-persons, in the guise of simplicity. He abhorred all the subtle ways by which we can signal to other people that we're very fervent and possess a spirit of penance. He knew that, unrecognised, these could lead us into the great danger of Phariseeism - "I THANK YOU, GOD, THAT I AM NOT GRASPING, UNJUST, ADULTEROUS LIKE THE REST OF MANKIND" (Lk 18:11): "I thank you that I don't wear bright colours or enjoy parties or appear cheerful"! He coaxed the reader into considering the essence of the Christian life, which is to imitate Christ Our Saviour.

If Christ Himself went to weddings (Jn 2:1-10), and drank wine and talked with friends, then we could do the same; but we must imitate His interior dispositions, too, growing more and more obedient to our Heavenly Father, and slipping away regularly to pray to Him, alone.

Practising true charity.

Saint Francis taught me a great deal about true love. He explained that it didn't involve parading our good works; we should never make other people feel small. We're obliged to hide our penitential practices; it's our duty to be pleasant and companionable, for the love of God. The more I read, the more astonished and delighted I was that someone known as a canonised Saint could sound so normal and even amusing. But I didn't digest the knowledge that this saint was not solely a Saint, but a Catholic priest.

As I tried to put his teaching into practice, I was touched to the heart at finding that a Saint could write so calmly and surely about everyday life. As I said, I had read St. Teresa's "Life", when I was still a school-girl; but St. Francis de Sales' advice was more to my taste, since he was really aware of many womens' concerns, such as husbands, or dress, or duty and parties, rather than convents and visions.

For several weeks, I continued to think about these things, and, eventually, it seemed wise to organise a brief period alone, away from the flat. I had a great deal to ponder, and I saw the danger of being continually immersed in the busy-ness of our fast-expanding social life. Following my mother's advice, I went away 'on retreat' for three days. I went alone, and attended no lectures. I'd been assured that a period of reading in a quiet atmosphere could lead one closer to God. It was true, I found. I spent three days, almost dazed with joy, in the guest-house of an Anglican convent, reading and praying, thinking and sleeping, relishing the silence and peace - and guiltily leaning out of the upstairs window, to enjoy a secret cigarette. I wandered through the lush gardens, full of thoughts about God. I remember sitting on the bench amongst the trees, inwardly exclaiming at my new peace of soul and my constant, silent delight.

Truly, in giving me such joy and faith, God was at work. These were His honeymoon days, which weren't to last for long. He was spoiling me because it was my first retreat: and as I've discovered in recent years, He always rewards us when we're generous and make efforts to spend time with Him.

In that uncomplicated time before my real trials began, I accepted gaily - and rightly - the truth that God loved me just as I was, there 'before' Him. I'd given up everything I believed was sinful, because I wanted to please Him: and as for the little faults which remained, He is very tolerant. As I prayed, I silently absorbed the truth about His Merciful Love. He didn't say: 'I will love you when you have stopped smoking, or when you are no longer self-indulgent.' I had come to believe that He is a true Father: "A GENTLE FATHER AND THE GOD OF ALL CONSOLATION" (2 Co 1:3); and I believed that He would gradually show me just how I needed to change, if I really wanted to be happy with Him forever; and indeed, I gave up smoking some years later, and never looked back - though there's always something more to conquer.

Faith in God's plans.

As soon as I adopted a regular routine of short but sincere prayers, with more fervent attempts to be patient and charitable, I found that prayer became the breath of Life for me: my spirit's breath, its very oxygen; and God led me on. There was all the time I could have desired for prayer. Even a reluctant and sick housewife can spend the day-time in pondering, and thinking intensely, wondering: "Who is God? What does Christ want of me - and how shall I serve Him? What should I do? What is the Church?" I didn't waste the time, despite my pains. I found, planted in my soul and strengthened by prayer, enormous faith in God. I had faith in His plans, in His guidance, and in the holiness of His Will, wherever it led.

Whenever I was alone at home, and was neither reading nor praying, I cooked and cleaned for as long as my weak legs allowed, completely puzzled by my illness, and humiliated and frustrated too, at times. But there was tremendous joy in our marriage, our little room, and our meals with friends, and in my new routine of quiet worship. Only by the grace of God did I begin to accept my limitations; but I thank Him for that sense of contentment.

[A noble instinct.

Many times since then, I've noticed that 'new' Christians, in particular, feel an urge to rush off to do something 'great' for Christ. It's a noble instinct which contains the seeds of true love, but it can be flawed by romanticism about the Christian life. None of us can hope to please God by disregarding our duties towards our relatives and friends. We can't run away from the real obligations of our present way of life. How important it is that all who feel an urge to dash off to help others should examine their true motives before making plans for a new, 'exciting' task. I've learned that the Catholic Church has been cautious, for example, about welcoming into monastic life people who would leave behind ageing parents or young brothers or sisters. Many good persons want to imitate the Apostles, who left everything in order to follow Christ; but He doesn't ask everyone to tear themselves bodily away from family and friends. He wants our hearts, above all. He wants us to love and help, for His sake, everyone for whom we're really responsible.]

Suffering.

Work and prayer continued, and meanwhile my illness persisted. I was sometimes sad and frightened, but I wasn't angry that I suffered. Life wasn't easy, nor was I brave. But illness was never an obstacle to faith, nor a reason for anger towards God. I had accepted sufferings in childhood for purely human reasons. In helplessness and ignorance one suffers in mute incomprehension. But when I became an adult and a Christian the reason for acceptance changed.

Faith told me that God was perfect, Just, Merciful and Good. I accepted these truths so completely that I had no 'problem' about pain itself. I supposed that if God our Father had permitted Christ to suffer so horrendously at the hands of sinful men, there must have been a reason for it. Who were we to demand, of our Saviour, that we be shown an easier road? If it were true - as I believed - that God is Perfect, and Infinite, whereas we have only finite minds, I saw that He must know everything - far more than we - including the reasons for our pains.

It's obvious that much of our human suffering arises from the cruelties which we inflict on one another; yet I reasoned that since the free will of all human beings is a gift from God, our freedom to hurt others or to do good is woven into the whole mystery which is earthly life. All other causes of pain were beyond my understanding; but faith told me that we shall understand in the end, when we reach Heaven. Until then, I believed, we need only trust that God will bring good out of evil, in His own way. It seemed like impertinence to question why the world hadn't been made to our specifications.

Others' sufferings caused me anguish, and I did what I could to help those who were in pain; and I was very keen to avoid unnecessary suffering. My nursing experience had given me a sense of realism about illness and death. Nevertheless, all the horrors I'd seen had confirmed my view that suffering is unavoidable in a normal human life in a sinful world. It could be alleviated to some degree; I saw that it's unrealistic to hope to live on earth without some experience of pain or sorrow. So, despite my surface distress and moments of sadness, I was content to believe in God's mysterious Love, and I felt secure in my spiritual honeymoon, for a few months more.

---

5 CLARIFICATION
(1964-1966)

THE CATHOLIC CHURCH. SAINTS. THE REFORMATION.

'Normal' Christian practice.

What shocks God has in store for those who want to be good! At first, in my half-turning towards Him, I was so fervent in my efforts to please Him that I was tempted to believe that I was rather virtuous. I began to think of myself as a 'successful' Christian who was cheerful and kind, and very devout in prayer. Full of pride at what I'd managed to do, I was forgetful that this small beginning was due entirely to God's grace. But God took me seriously. I wanted to be very holy, for His sake, and so I could be sure that I'd be shown the way: but I didn't know that I'd also be shown the chasm to be crossed - crossed by the grace of Christ empowering me and not by my ruthless 'will-power.'

Once I'd taken the first few steps, further problems arose. There were questions of ethics, morals and Church discipline to which I wanted answers, so I asked for advice. Friends and parents held the same attitude towards the Christian life, saying that we had the Bible, and prayer - and that in everything uncertain we should make up our own minds. Then I asked the local Rector if we should fast before receiving Holy Communion, or undertake some small penance during Lent. He said that everyone was entitled to do whatever he chose, since "the Church" - of England - didn't issue rigid guidelines any more.

My heart wasn't secretly longing for rules and regulations for their own sake. I was beginning to see how ignorant I was. Wanting wisdom, I longed to know what was 'normal' Christian practice, following tradition. What ought any Christian to do, in order to love and serve God perfectly? So whilst I dutifully but happily continued on my way, caring for my husband and my home, and praying like a child, I ventured new questions about other subjects. I was curious about them all, seeing it as my duty to know the teaching of the Church on all important topics, in case I should have to explain my beliefs to others, in detail. Besides, I was determined to be really saintly.

It was disturbing to see how much conflicting advice was put out by the different churches, as I considered a number of issues in a Christian light. Was it still true, I wondered - not fourteen but twenty-one - that Christ had founded a Church which had "broken into bits"? Whose answer ought a Christian to accept, on the subjects of divorce, contraception, or other moral issues? I noticed how many different opinions were proffered about very serious matters such as the care of the handicapped, born or unborn, and about many other topics. It seemed extraordinary to me that on subjects of such importance Christians could 'make up their own minds' or, in other words, do as they pleased. Surely Christ wouldn't have left us without guidance on difficult matters? How could He bear to see His Christians - once so firmly taught by Him about what was right and wrong - wandering around on earth, confused, if by our choices and our behaviour, as Christ had warned us, through the Scriptures, we're making our way towards either Heaven or Hell (Mt 7:21-23)?

[Exaggerated devotion?

It seems right to say here, in a short digression, and 'leaping ahead' once more to the faith and teaching which I've found in the Catholic Church, a few words about avoiding evil and doing good. How marvellous it is that good priests, and many parents too, now speak about aspects of the Faith in ways which encourage trust in God's goodness as well as faith in His judgements. It's marvellous to see good human friendships treated more with gladness than caution, and to hear as much about God's love for every person He has created as about the consequences of sin for the impenitent. Yet what a lot of dangerous advice has been handed out since the Second Vatican Council by some theologians and other thinkers who stress what they see as the 'formality and fear' in all pre-Conciliar education.

It has become fashionable to decry any talk of sin and punishment, as though present-day Catholics, unlike their ancestors, have no need of detailed guidance in the difficult paths of faith. We will lead mature and holy lives, we are assured, if only we cultivate a cheerful outlook and try to avoid the exaggerated devotions of the Saints, especially the Saints' unnecessary emphasis on obedience, on reparation for sin, and on suffering.

While it's true that no Christian ought to be looking inwards all the time, so obsessed with his journey to perfection that he rarely thinks about the needs of his neighbour, every Christian needs to be taught quite clearly about how to avoid sin, and how to be certain of pleasing Christ. So many modern Christians seem to be unwilling to speak about sanctity, preferring to speak about self-esteem. So little is heard about the life of purity and holiness through which we can be drawn into a wonderful "life-in-union" with Christ our Saviour, as we prepare for eternal enjoyment of His friendship in Heaven. For a teacher to minimise the dangers that a Christian is bound to meet in efforts to be faithful is surely as reckless as to send a trainee soldier to cross Dartmoor without a map or to climb the Jungfrau without a guide.

So here was the reason for my puzzlement in the 1960's; how was it possible that apparently responsible Christian leaders could contradict one another on matters which the Saints and writers in the Early Church had said would lead us either to Heaven or to damnation? Surely, goodwill is not enough; firm teaching is essential.

As I'll shortly describe, I came to see that the Catholic Church alone has been guaranteed the perpetual guidance of God specifically in this matter of teaching truths about faith and morals. This belief was set forth in the constant Tradition of the Church, and also in the Gospels, when Christ had said to Saint Peter: "I WILL GIVE YOU THE KEYS OF THE KINGDOM OF HEAVEN. WHATEVER YOU BIND ON EARTH SHALL BE CONSIDERED

BOUND IN HEAVEN" (Mt 16:19). Long centuries ago, in the early Church, the primacy of Saint Peter and the authority of the Apostles was widely acknowledged; and in our own times, I was to learn with gladness, faithful Catholics accord the same authority and dignity to the Apostles' successors: to the Pope, and to the Bishops who are in communion with him.]

The Roman Catholic Church.

Back in 1963 and 1964, and realising my ignorance, as I said, I continued to read, think and pray. Everything I learned through my studies led me to a greater awareness of the meaning of the holiness to which God calls us all. Still examining books about faith and about Church history, the better to understand and explain my own re-discovered faith, I soon encountered the Catholic Church of earlier centuries. Then I learned for the first time in my life, in such clarity, that the Church of the Apostles and Martyrs had not vanished, despite many centuries of upheaval and persecution. It had spread throughout the whole world, and still exists today. It is still guided by a Pope, and is still united in its faith and teachings.

But there was more to disturb me: facts about my own people and my own country. Even though I still read books written by English Protestant authors as well as by Catholics I learned facts which were new to me about the sixteenth-century Church in England and about the Monarchy. For the first time in my life it dawned on me that when the English monarchy had torn the English people away from Rome, it had done wrong. The Catholic Church today was neither divided nor impotent; it was still One and Holy - and had been so in Tudor times as well as in our own day; and nor was the Catholic Faith merely a folk memory in English minds. There existed a huge and holy family, with One Faith, still, and One Lord, and - what was most painful for me to discover - I was not within it. I was baptised, to be sure, but I didn't wholly belong to Christ's Body. I wasn't "in Communion" with the Catholic Church.

As I examined the consequences of English independence from Rome, I found that even Anglican authors confessed that "schism" was a regrettable state. They boldly protested, however, that the Church of four centuries ago had been so monstrously corrupt that the schism had been justified, but I couldn't see that this was right. Perhaps I didn't know much about the Reformation in England, I decided; but although I recognised that people in every age are corrupt - we are all weak - I couldn't believe that if Christ founded a Church which taught with His authority and offered His Sacraments, there would ever be a valid reason which could persuade one to leave it. I knew that the early Church, much admired by Anglicans, had experienced bitter grief from the sins and squabbles of its members. Yet none of the 'early' Saints had dared to defend dis-unity in "BELIEF AND PRACTICE" (1 Co 1:10), or schism; and Saints throughout the centuries had been aware of the dangers inherent in any separation from 'Rome'.

At the end of every avenue.

The implications of this thinking appalled me. Perhaps I'd misunderstood? I knew many good Anglicans; could they all be wrong on this matter, or had they never thought about it all, comfortable with the "Branch Theory" of Church development learned at Church and Sunday School? Or did this discovery prove me right in my certainty that Christ hadn't left His

Christians without guidance on earth? No matter what I read, nor how hard I thought, there was no avoiding what seemed like a brick wall at the end of every 'avenue' within my mind; and that 'wall' was the Roman Catholic Church, with a huge door set in it.

I peered into little 'roads' on each side, but found that each was a dusty cul-de-sac, without much light. I couldn't see how anyone could avoid knocking on that door to ask for admittance, but I was horrified at the unexpected discovery, and by the Code of Conduct which, I understood, each conscientious candidate would be bound to follow. By this I mean that my ideas of a Roman Catholic's daily prayers and practices were festooned, in my mind, with weird half-remembered phrases about penitential practices and strange devotions. The very words 'Catholic priest' almost made me shudder, so closely were they associated with tales about the treachery of certain Englishmen whose loyalty once lay with Spain as well as the Pope.

When I spoke about the problem, some people assured me that the Holy Spirit had guided all Christians through the ages, and that I ought not to worry myself about the different Churches, since it's sincerity that 'counts'.

I have learned since then, thank God, that God does indeed love sincere hearts; but I've learned, too, that one can do evil things sincerely, from ignorance or fear. I wanted to know what was true, so that I could please God in the best possible way. My question was: how can one tell whom the Holy Spirit is guiding, if one church said that such-and-such an activity was wrong, and another said that it was right? I had no longing for novelty or change, but only wanted to find out God's Will, from whoever knew It.

Anglican Bishops.

Continuing the search, I read widely, and sought out writers who might help me banish my confusion. I was sure that God didn't expect His People to be scattered amongst dozens of churches, but rather to be united in the One, Holy Church which He had founded upon the Apostles - who were headed by St. Peter. But the more I studied, the more astonished I became as I uncovered new facts about four centuries of Anglican history. Questions arose by the score, therefore, on major matters - and minor. How was the Queen head of the Anglican Church, when she wasn't a priest? I'd been told as a child that Bishops, priests and deacons formed a sacred Ministry, which was not only reformed but was also 'Catholic'. How strange was our history. Could the citizens of any country, I wondered, suddenly decide that the monarch and not an Archbishop was the Head of its church? What was the precise role of the Anglican bishops?

If the Queen had no authority, and was a mere figurehead, then what was the point of her title? Moreover, why were Anglican Bishops not chosen by her, but by her Prime Minister, who might be an atheist or a member of another denomination? I'd learned that it was his task to select a candidate from a list offered to him by churchmen who were bound to accept his decision. How strange this seemed.

I was to discover, later, that even Catholic Bishops in different centuries had been appointed by Catholic Kings, due to a policy of 'peace-making' which seemed wise at the time. But it seemed extraordinary that similar things were permitted in any Christian country in modern times, especially in the Anglican Church which, since it was English, I'd been led to believe was very sensibly organised.

Inconsistencies in our beliefs and our administration weren't the only problems I encountered, and I continued to ask for advice. Each clergyman I questioned about "the Sacrament" in our Holy Communion service had a different answer, when I asked only: "What is right? What is true?" Some said that our Eucharist was a pious memorial, designed to stimulate our faith as we ate bread and wine. Others claimed that Christ is Really Present with us, and that we consume "THE BODY AND BLOOD OF THE LORD," (1 Co 11:27) as explained in the New Testament.

Trying to be logical, I thought this latter answer seemed to be the truest, or Saint Paul wouldn't have had to issue his awful warning about "EATING AND DRINKING HIS OWN CONDEMNATION" (1 Co 11:29): but who was I to judge? I sought the teaching of "the Church" and found that my church taught several different things, despite the evidence that for more than a thousand years before the Reformation, the Real Presence of Christ in the Blessed Sacrament had been recognised and treasured throughout Christian Europe.

Obedience.

For my own welfare, and perhaps even for my own Salvation, there was yet another problem to be solved. If it were our solemn duty to know, love, and serve God in this world and in the next - as advised by the author of my Anglican catechism - then what, I wondered, was the best way of getting to know God? Was it through penance and sacrifice as well as through prayer, as all the Saints seemed to suggest. And if I ought to be obedient and good, then precisely to whom should I be obedient, when Bishops and priests of our church gave conflicting advice?

The author of almost every book which I'd read about sanctity or Saints had spoken of obedience and faithfulness. Life on earth seemed to be so complicated and so difficult, and God himself was described by Saints, Church leaders and theologians as so glorious, that it was surely important to know precisely how to please Him. The advice given in childhood - just to "follow the Bible" - seemed quite inadequate, when nearly three hundred Protestant churches had been 'born' because of squabbles about different interpretations of the Holy Scriptures. If God had inspired the biblical authors, surely someone could tell us what they really meant, and what were the essentials of the Christian way of life today? I was dismayed and astonished to hear one view after another which advocated a vague 'muddling-along'.

There arose a further cause for alarm. The people who seemed to have known and loved God best were the Saints - who were all Catholic. Could they all have been misguided about their loyalty to the Pope, which seemed to go hand-in-hand with their worship of Christ?

It became evident that if it were true that there was only One Church, guided by the successor to St. Peter, and that it contained not just sinners but amazing Saints, then I ought to find out more about it, and ask to be admitted. The alternative would be to accept what I'd been told as a child, that the Church had fallen apart - which sounded to me as though Christ had abandoned His People. I found that hard to believe.

'Roman fever'.

Twice weekly, I went to a Communion Service at our local Anglican Church, and, occasionally, as I have said, I went to a 'High' church about a mile further away which was called St. James' church. It had an extraordinary notice just inside the door, which read: "This is a Catholic Church". In smaller script, below, I read the explanation: that Anglo-Catholics consider themselves to be members of the Catholic Church, and that the Anglican Church is a part of the Catholic Church, thought not at present in communion with the Pope.

Naively thinking that an 'Anglo-Catholic' would be my best guide to the truth about Roman Catholicism, I consulted one of the clergymen there about my qualms, and was amazed by his advice. He merely laughed at my questions, saying kindly that I had a touch of "Roman fever; we all get it now and then!" He reminded me that his colleagues routinely used the Roman Missal, wore Roman vestments and followed the Roman calendar throughout the liturgical year; and so his advice was simple. "We've got all this", he beamed, waving his arm around the beautiful interior of the Church; and he added: "There's absolutely no need to go 'in'." I thanked him for his reassurance and went back to the flat.

For a few days I supposed that a trained minister must know more than someone like myself who had fewer qualifications. However, common-sense and logic couldn't be defeated so easily, and I realised what had happened. This kind man had probably assumed, because of my anxious manner, that I was hoping for a verbal salve which might soothe away my distress about what many Anglicans called 'The Roman problem.' But I'd been hoping for a few facts which would help me to see whether the claims of the Roman Catholic Church were as awesome as I thought they were - or had no good foundation; and instead of the information I'd expected, I'd received evidence that someone who labelled himself an 'Anglo-Catholic' might be no nearer to the Catholic faith than were his 'low-church' brothers and sisters. If, by private judgement, he had made a selection from the 'Roman' Church of the teachings and devotions which he himself judged to be true or attractive, whilst discarding the rest, he had sat in judgement on Christ's Church on earth. Although he couldn't see it, and despite the elements of Catholic devotion in his words and in his building, he was every bit as much a sincere 'Protestant' as the Evangelical Anglicans whose worship he wouldn't have seen as 'Catholic' like his; and that's why I felt disappointed.

Contradictory guidance.

How could it have been possible, I wondered once more, for the Father of Our Lord Jesus Christ to send His Son to earth for a few years, to inspire the Christian Church for a few years - and then to leave it alone for hundreds of years with only such basic 'tools' for faith and good behaviour as the much-disputed Bible and the Nicene Creed? Had God intended that each one of us should see his own interpretation of these sacred words as right? Was there no guidance, or only contradictory guidance, on every important Christian moral and disciplinary issue in modern life?

It seemed that very many Anglicans recognised - as had my mother, at an earlier stage - the continued existence of the Catholic Church, although saying that the "Romans" had gone "too far" or had "gone wrong". If pressed to state firmly what the "Christian Church" believed, they claimed that it had all broken asunder a long time ago, and that God no longer guides "The Church", but only guides individual Christians who, sad to say, disagree. The 'One Holy, Catholic and Apostolic' church which we proclaimed in our Creed was an ideal, not a reality; and if we all remained optimistic and hard-working, it might come together again. Some of you will realise that this is the view which is widely put about today by many Christians who are involved in Ecumenism.

Why were some 'Anglo-Catholics' so insistent that they were 'Catholic', I wondered, if there was no longer a Catholic Church, and when the Church of England had been described, in a not-long-ago Coronation, as the 'Protestant Reformed Religion' which had been established by law? And surely, if the Catholic Church existed still - the "Roman" Catholic Church - she herself must be the best judge of who was or wasn't a Catholic?

Doctrine, devotions and moral guidance.

It seemed that even people who disliked certain Catholic teachings and practices had enough respect for the Papal Office to be disappointed that the Popes had said for centuries that we Anglicans were deficient in doctrine, discipline, sacraments and true unity. It was as plain as the nose on my face that the 'Roman' church taught doctrines with which those outside her disagreed, approved devotions which they despised, and issued moral guidance which they ignored, or claimed was too harsh. Surely, she was plainly wrong - or plainly right. There was no such thing as the 'Via Media', once proposed by John Henry Newman, in his years as an Anglican minister, some years before he became a Catholic priest.

Having come to believe in Christ and in the Christian creeds, I also believed that One, Holy, Catholic and Apostolic Church had been founded at the time of the Apostles; and a church existed, I saw, which claimed that title, and which nothing had been able to destroy.

There came a moment when I realised that I'd find no wonderful answers from any Anglicans which would demolish the Roman claims. It seemed so obvious to me that Christ had intended to found a single church, and that a united and extraordinary Church existed which provided enough evidence for her own claim to be unique: the Catholic Church of the Fathers, the monks, the mystics, the Reformation martyrs - and of mothers and fathers, single persons, and also children: people of every sort, in past ages and today. This Church had brought sure Christian doctrine to every sort of culture and people, for two millennia; and she contained not just sinners, but Saints. It occurred to me then, that the "problem" which I'd taken to the Anglo-Catholic minister didn't exist. The only problem lay in admitting that since the one Church founded by Jesus Christ existed still, and was guided by God, the doctrines and devotion which she recommended must be true, and I should attempt to follow them.

English and Catholic.

As I've made plain in the Preface, and as I'll describe a little more fully in another chapter, I not only found the Catholic Church, but entered it: the One Church founded by Christ, and the one Body to which I could listen with complete confidence when she explains to us how to please God and how to worship Him. And I mention this here because I hope and pray that

Catholics will always see it as their duty - or even their delight - to share with other people the Good News about their Faith. I might well have grasped the truths of the Catholic Faith joyfully, and even at fifteen years old, had they been presented to me a little more plainly.

As I've just been struggling to explain, the truths of the Catholic Faith seemed immediately and wholly convincing when I discovered them at twenty-one; and nothing that I've read, heard or experienced in the decades since then have caused me to doubt those truths or to reject them. Yet I suppose there are usually two requirements for the successful acceptance of truth into our hearts, requirements which were lacking in my teens, when I was unhappy, and when, besides, I'd never met a single English Catholic. First, I mean that when someone's heart is soured by loneliness or anger he or she is more likely to greet truth, and the responsibilities which follow upon truth, with suspicion or resentment; and secondly, I believe that most people find it easier to make enquiries and to weigh evidence in the company of someone like themselves. St. Francis Xaxier found this to be true, when, in India, and then in Japan, he came to realise that the type of costume he chose to wear made a vast difference to whether or not he made conversions to Christ and to the Catholic Church; and this was not because people were converted for superficial reasons, but because some groups of less-than-perfect people were reluctant to listen to him because of what they saw as his outlandish appearance; and different cultures had different ideas about what clothing was acceptable.

It's plain to me now, that it was when I became a happy young adult that I was willing to look at Catholic propositions with an unprejudiced mind; and it was when I found modern English Catholics authors who spoke my cultural language that I was willing to believe the plain truth: that Catholicism isn't something 'foreign' - neither Irish nor Italian - but something for all peoples: even for the English, and even for a woman like myself who was young and ignorant but who was so fascinated by truth that she was willing, when she found truth, to venture along unfamiliar ways in order to grow as close as possible to God.

It was true that a puzzle had been solved. The whole problem had been one of authority: and since I'd found that the Catholic Church has a Divine commission to teach all people authoritatively, I realised that everyone who believes in God and in the teachings of His Church can have a sense of peace and security to be found nowhere else - and can have this even in the midst of the problems of earthly life. But I didn't feel much delight in finding the solution to my problem. On the contrary, my heart sank.

Every question was answered to my entire satisfaction. Everything I learned about the Catholic Faith, through my continued research, seemed to fit marvellously with all the other things I'd discovered. The Catholic Church provided a coherent doctrine which impressed me both in its depth and in its details; and yet I felt leaden, with a sort of normal human grief, as I saw where my simple faith would lead me. Any talk of membership of the Catholic Church was bound to jeopardise my earthly happiness which was so recent, and so fragile. My family would be shocked and puzzled. I would have to cope with mockery or worse.

Canonised Saints.

As I pondered about our country's Christian history, I half-wished that I could see it all differently, but everything seemed very clear. There remained no trace in my mind of the comforting myth of childhood, that each Christian body which interprets the Bible according to its own wishes is proclaiming the truth of God - even when Christian communities disagree. Wherever I looked, the answer was the same. One Church had been founded by Christ, and one Church was teaching the truth in all its fullness still - as that Church proclaims with astonishing assurance, still, in her Council documents and in her catechisms; and it was God Himself Who was showing me my duty, which was to enter that Church and to make it my home, until death and beyond.

The more I read, the more I found that everything which had puzzled me had fallen into place. Even Cyril Garbett's "Claims of the Church of England", which I bought because I half-wondered if it could persuade me to stay where I was, seemed illogical. There were good Anglicans and good Methodists, I saw, and brave 'Quakers'; but there was no firm common teaching about every important issue of faith and morals, and no Saints: at least, not in the sense in which Catholics used that word in speaking of the heroes and heroines of the Faith who had been canonised. Furthermore, the first Commandment is that we love God, which means putting His Will before anything or anyone else; so it seemed to me that if God had really founded a world-wide Church for our benefit, I had a duty to join it. Only by doing His Will in that way would I be led "TO THE COMPLETE TRUTH" (Jn 16:13). Only by finding Christ in the Sacraments which He had so marvellously provided for us would I learn to love my neighbour as he should be loved: with Divine charity in my heart and not by a merely human love, no matter how tender.

For the glory of the Father.

The whole process of realisation and discovery was so painful that although I did my chores as efficiently as possible, it was hard to keep my mind on my work. At one moment I'd be agonising about the future, and at the next I'd be wondering once more whether I was being wildly impertinent in thinking that I'd discovered something about faith and truth that many Anglicans didn't know: even my own parents. But I kept on thinking and reading, and was enormously heartened to read the stories of the Saints. I was so weak and ignorant and they were so brave and strong, it seemed; but our goals, I saw, were identical. Although I might still have been afraid to pronounce this out loud, I knew that I wanted to be able to live the rest of my life "in Christ" to the greatest possible degree, by the power of the Holy Spirit, and for the Glory of the Father.

It was intriguing that the Saints I read about were burning with love for Christ and were longing to do His Will, and yet they were all so different from one another: of every sort of temperament and aptitude. I'd never encountered people like that before, in the tales I'd read in earlier years.

It seems that in every century and in every sort of Christian community, and indeed, amongst people of other faiths, there have been extraordinarily good and devout persons: men and women who have sacrificed their reputations or their lives for the sake of their fellow human beings. I've always admired Mr Wilberforce, and Elizabeth Fry, and Bunyan, and David Livingstone and many more good people. Which of us can fail to admire the virtues of people of every nationality or faith, where generosity, peace and forgiveness are admired and practised? But from the evidence I've seen, I believe that only rarely is the staggering love of God and of neighbour - heroic holiness - to be seen in all its fullness outside the boundaries of the Catholic Faith.

Workers of miracles.

The Saints of every century resemble the Apostles, I discovered, in their fervour, their courage and their devotion to Christ: and in their horror at seeing risked or brought about any serious disunity within the Church, or any departure from the One Body, or any schism. They resemble the Apostles, too, I realised, in their working of miracles - right through the ages and even in our own century. It's true that a reputed worker of miracles isn't necessarily saintly, yet I was pleased to realise that God's work through special signs hadn't been just a special sort of help for an infant Church: help which was never to be given again after what I'd heard called "The Apostolic Age."

If God is unchanging, and ever-generous, and if He once worked miracles through Christ and through the members of the Early Church, surely it made more sense to believe that He still works miracles through His Saints, rather than that His marvellous assistance came to a sudden halt in one or two hundred A.D.? Every true Christian must admit that God is Almighty; and although I had no great curiosity about signs and wonders, and neither asked for them nor hoped for them in everyday life, I realised that a Church whose heroes and heroines resembled Christ in every way - in prayer, love, suffering and hope and also in miracles, for example - seemed to have provided compelling evidence for its own message and its own claims.

There were so many Saints to enthral me. I had known for a long time that the Early Church could boast of Saints of the stature of Saint Augustine, whose "Confessions" I had read, and Saint Jerome, who translated the Bible. Pictures of Saint Clare and of Saint Anthony are found in many non-Catholic books; but I was just discovering names which were entirely new to me. A whole young life-time had passed before I ever heard of Saint Ignatius Loyola - who founded the 'Jesuits' - or Saint Rose of Lima. Other Saints entirely unknown to a young Protestant woman like myself were Saint Francis Xavier, and Saint Aloysius Gonzaga. These, with many other Saints, had blossomed in the Catholic Church, and had worked miracles by the grace of God, although their lives had been hidden from those who had tried to convince me that the Apostolic 'age of miracles' had long since vanished.

A visit to a Catholic Church.

It's taken me such a long time to list my questions, and to describe the beginnings of this spiritual journey; yet the initial exploration didn't take very long. Only a few months passed between my renewed commitment to God in church worship and in private prayer, and the extraordinary experience of Christ's presence in my room. Then only a few more months went by, as I examined the claims of the Catholic Church and then decided that I was conscience-bound to ask for admittance. I was very much the same person, throughout that time: thrilled by all that was good about daily life, grimly determined about new things which seemed important, but also shy and inarticulate. My heart ached at the thought of causing misunderstandings or of being un-loved or judged. It was with great trepidation that I set out, one day, to visit the nearest Catholic Church, and to find out the name of the priest.

Who likes to think about change and destruction? Who wouldn't have felt some fear at risking all the joys which, at that time, made life worthwhile? The church was called by a strange title: "Our Lady of Grace, and St. Edward". I wondered what 'Grace' really meant. My heart was thumping as I turned the handle and peered inside. I opened the door and went in.

As soon as I'd tip-toed across the shiny floor to kneel down by a pew at the back, I felt terrified of being noticed or questioned. The church was dark and unfamiliar. It had fewer statues and paintings than there were in the Anglo-Catholic church of St. James, along the road; but I sensed a Presence in the tabernacle. I'd sensed that Presence in a convent-school chapel, and in France. I recognised Christ in the darkness.

When I'd prayed for a few moments, I set off for the bookshelves at the very back of the building. Hurriedly searching through the pamphlets in the 'Catholic Truth Society' stand, I was thrilled to see that some of them dealt plainly and logically with the sort of questions which occur to every new enquirer. Putting two or three of the booklets in my pocket, I went back to my shopping and my household tasks, already planning another visit. I hadn't an iota of doubt about Catholic teaching, now that I'd accepted that the Church had been founded by Christ, and is still guided by Him. I was determined to make arrangements to be admitted, so that I'd please Him, and so that I could receive Him in the Blessed Sacrament. All I wanted was that He keep leading me forward and show me how, and where, and when I could come in.

A joyful ordinary life.

Another week or two passed. But after further study, with further reflection on my way of life, I became newly-aware that although married life had made me happier than I'd ever been before, it was a brittle happiness which depended on one person.

I can explain my feelings better if I skip ahead a year or two: to a few weeks after the birth of a beloved first baby, when my husband and I were living in that same London flat. My mother had come to visit one afternoon, which was a great treat as she was still in full-time paid work, and I couldn't see her very often.

We'd talked about family, friends and faith. She was delighted to see me on the 'right track,' at last. Then, as we stood on the doorstep, saying our farewells, I told her - and I remember this clearly - that I was so happy that I didn't see how it could last. Shocked, she replied that that was heresy; and of course she was right to be on the lookout - in her own daughter - for foolish attitudes, perhaps for an un-Christian preoccupation with good luck or bad: combined with nervous gloom instead of Christian hope. Yet she was wrong, in that my blurted fear now sprang from realism, not superstition. I recognised that at that hour, in that week and that year, at only twenty-four years old, I already possessed everything 'earthly' that I'd ever wanted.

With a precious husband, precious child, little home, friends and family, and with a great deal of work to do, and the prospect of a lively family life ahead of me, I had so much joy that I hadn't a single, earthly ambition to fulfil. I was quite content with our various and real drawbacks and limitations; but it was faith that made me stand amazed at the marvel of an ordinary life full of marvellous joys; and it was faith that made me see that no purely earthly joy lasts for ever. Earthly life involves change and loss. So, even wrapped in faith, my very human heart felt, and expressed in private, an occasional shudder of fear that I might become dependent on what are transient joys. What my mother didn't yet realise, because we'd had so little time in which to talk, was that my intermittent fears were now underpinned by a firm belief in God's goodness and wisdom.

Since my conversion to Christ, I'd used St. Paul's words as my life-line in every sort of crisis: "BY TURNING EVERYTHING TO THEIR GOOD GOD CO-OPERATES WITH ALL THOSE WHO LOVE HIM" (Rm 8:28). I hoped that that belief would remain fixed forever in my heart and mind, whatever might await me.

Imagined disaster.

During those first weeks of exploration of the truths of the Faith, in 1963 to 1964, I found it difficult to imagine telling my husband or other family members that, after only a short time of trying to live the Christian faith as an adult, I'd realised that only in the Catholic Church could I find the fullness of what Christ wants to lavish upon us, to make us holy. Who was I to make pronouncements on religion? Who would believe that I was earnest and determined, when only a few years before I'd been a bit supercilious and argumentative about things to do with church and church-going? Even worse: how could I think of upsetting a husband who was kind, hard-working and dutiful, but who had imbibed in childhood, just as I had, the potion of prejudice against most people, things and places connected with Catholicism?

Never had I imagined that it might be because of the demands of God and His Church that my recent happiness might be snatched away. Of all possible imagined disasters, I hadn't considered that difficult choices between good and evil, God's Will or 'Loss of God', would suddenly arrive to cause me such torment. I was only twenty-one years old; and since I hadn't yet plucked up courage to find a priest to discuss the matter, I had no true guide in this dilemma except my own private mixture of prayer and logic, which guided my conscience.

Meanwhile, I found that all my sweetness and joy in practising the Christian faith was evaporating. The first ease in the daily spiritual routine had been replaced by struggle. I didn't understand what was happening, but my real training had begun. A clear, true spiritual life was developing within me, tested and proved by spiritual battles. The more I prayed for strength and guidance, the clearer became Christ's wishes. He gently nudged me towards the Way of truth, wordlessly inviting me to move forward, no matter how lonely I felt.

I saw that there was no way of avoiding anguish. Frightened but determined, I resolved to face facts; and in order to make sure that they were accurate, I went in search of a Catholic priest. It was the first time in my life that I'd been required to overcome my fears about their almost magical influence and terrible powers. Someone from the presbytery not far from our street kindly agreed to come to our flat to talk to us about the Catholic way of life.

What a good man he was, giving us his time and attention; but I was young, and anxious. My husband was uneasy at discussing daunting issues with a complete stranger, after a hard day at work. Also, the anti-Catholic indoctrination which I had received was mild, compared with certain views which he had unthinkingly absorbed. I can see that I ought not to have 'rushed' him about religion, at that stage, before we had discussed the matter very much, nor to have introduced him in such haste to Catholicism personified by so suddenly confronting him with a representative of the 'ruthless and authoritative' Body whose beliefs and traditions he thought strange and outrageously demanding. I had introduced him too soon, too suddenly. It wasn't kind, and it wasn't the right time. I had much to learn about prudence and even more to learn about patience and love. But the priest was very understanding, and was quite willing to discuss things again whenever we wanted to see him.

Attitudes to the Catholic Church.

Resolving to think clearly and to be thoroughly grounded in the facts, I continued to read, and to ask the advice of people I respected. But the people I knew well were, without exception, Anglicans. Each one belonged, it appeared, to one of several groups.

Those in the first group had never considered the claims of the Catholic Church. Many worshipped fervently, but without considering the claims or history of any other church or denomination. They accepted anomalies and confusion in their Anglican worship as readily as they accepted problems in any areas of life. They weren't historically-minded, anyway; and they had no doubts about their faith in Christ. He seemed very remote, sometimes, but they devotedly carried on trying to serve Him. They were saddened by the divisions in 'the Church', but thought it inevitable that human beings everywhere would disagree.

The second group, I found, consisted of those who were like my parents' circle in being utterly secure in their beliefs. They held the view that the Church of England was a purified continuation of the Catholic 'presence' in Britain. The claims of Rome, if considered, seemed laughable to them. They were utterly convinced that 'Rome' had 'gone wrong', long before the Reformation. They thought themselves to be tolerant and fair, and right. They spoke of 'Bloody Mary' and boasted of Cranmer's courage, but brushed aside all talk about the victims of Elizabeth the First. She was a heroine, to them. She had made Britain 'Great'. Besides, they believed that any historical study would show that Catholics had been unpatriotic, and "Jesuitical" and "wrong".

Some Anglicans, I learned, had studied the Roman claims in depth, but had found to their dismay that she made demands which they thought too bold or too difficult. They went away sadly, half-hoping she would change her laws or her moral code: but they lived like deserted lovers who couldn't keep away from the loved one's haunts and images and souvenirs. They admired Catholic devotions and Catholic Art. But they hadn't received the fullness of the gift of faith, through which we believe that difficult things can be faced and accomplished, not by great human qualities but by Christ's Divine power working within our frailty.

Later, I was to meet Christians who were indeed convinced that the Roman Church was the Church of Christ. Yet they didn't seek permission to enter. Many waited year after year in order to avoid displeasing family or friends, or half-hoping that Popes might change some of the teachings. They 'hovered' in uncertainty, longing to become Catholic but lacking the courage to change.

I saw that no-one could help me. The decision about whether I should be asked to be received had already been made - as soon as I'd discovered that I wasn't a Catholic. However, I couldn't take a different avenue without considering those whom my choices might affect; so I talked and waited, and prayed: all the time thinking about the details and implications, and wondering: where, when, and how could I belong to the Roman Catholic Church, fully "in Communion"?

Christian friends.

As the months went by in this way, I longed for the path to become clearer, but I continued to worship at the Anglican Church, grateful for what it truly gave me. I valued then, as I value now, the friendship of fellow-Christians. Through the communal worship, and through annual feasts, I was given lovely reminders of Christ's life and Christ's parables, with interesting sermons. I went to Communion frequently, blindly determined to look for Christ wherever He might be present - in whatever manner.

During that time, my illness disappeared. I took a job with a nearby firm, thrilled to be well and busy again, and still longing to have a child.

A young women in our office was a member of a very fervent Christian denomination. I hadn't known of this until a day came when religion was under discussion in the firm's canteen. Someone poured scorn on 'Christians' and said something silly about Christ; and the young woman didn't join in the general laughter. When the group had left, I asked if she belonged to a Church or a group - and she confided in me about her faith in Christ. I reflected, afterwards, that adherence to the Christian faith is as difficult in twentieth- century England, in some respects, as in ancient penal times. Few Christians can escape being mocked or persecuted to some degree.

As we talked about our belief in Christ, we didn't see ourselves as good persons in a wicked world; rather, we knew ourselves to be weak people who were trying to be good; and since we were rather young and very shy, we spoke about our faith in whispers over the lunch-table now and again. I kept silent about my "Church" queries, full of admiration for her love for Jesus. She wrestled with her own problems. Certain persons had chided her for being 'fanatical' about Christ. They considered 'religion' to be a private affair which shouldn't be pressed upon other people.

She and I consoled one another with a few words here and there, each uncritical of the other's community, simply glad that we were trying to love the same Lord; and then, within a year, I became friendly with a fervent Anglican of my own age who was married, and lived nearby with her husband and young baby. I was delighted to be able to enjoy her company and to exchange views about family life, fashion, work, poetry, dressmaking - and God.

After the birth of my first child I was to spend many happy hours with my new friend as we nursed babies together and attended mid-week services at our local Church. But before that way of life began I had a marvellous holiday with my husband, which bought me lavish and unexpected insights into the Catholic Faith and Catholic ideals.

Discovering the Saints.

The holiday plans were so urgently made because I was pregnant at last. We were both thrilled, but expected hard work ahead, and few holidays. That was why we borrowed my mother's 'mini'-car and seized what we saw as our last chance to wander, carefree, across Europe.

We began our leisurely drive through France and Italy four months before the baby was due. I had just handed in my notice at work, so I was thrilled by the chance to relax, and also to visit the towns I'd so recently learned about whilst re-discovering the Saints. My husband was delighted to visit any place at all that I suggested. He has a great interest in history, and enjoys sight-seeing.

During the journey, I came across all sorts of evidence that sanctity hadn't 'evaporated' at the Reformation. The impression I'd gained from history books at school that canonisations, pilgrimages, and all outward and joyous celebrations of holiness had nothing to do with modern times was firmly squashed. It seemed that there were Saints aplenty, here in our own times.

As we stopped at one shrine after another, and as I read pamphlets about each new heroine or hero, I learned about ordinary people made extraordinary by God. They had battled against evil within and without, determined to love God and their neighbour, whatever the cost. I knew that many good Christians had sought truth and loved God: Bunyan amongst them, and many more; but only Catholics had in their midst, guided by the truths taught by the Church, persons graced with the truly staggering, heroic sanctity of Christ, whether that holiness were evident in their lifetimes or quite unrecognised. Catholic Saints, I learned, influenced every age of history, sometimes by visible example and at other times by silent sacrifice.

During continued reading at home, I'd learned from books by Thomas Merton, Ronald Knox and others much more about the quest for truth and holiness. Through the "Confessions of St. Augustine" I'd seen that temptations and sacrifices are weighed and pondered by Christians in every age. I'd discovered more about the real meaning of Christian heroism, with each new brief biography I opened. But it was through visiting the shrines or former homes of several Saints, as I toured Europe, that I was made aware of the details of their daily lives, and so came to understand more about the ideals and activities which they valued above all else.

Daily duties and God's Will.

It seemed that the 'Saints' I so admired were mere mortals, upon whom God had lavished His own holiness as soon as they had given themselves unreservedly to Him in love and sacrifice. It was heartening to know that many of them had been terrible sinners, who had come to know Christ very simply and swiftly through penance, prayer, and obedience to His Will. Even better, I learned that 'God's Will' isn't a name to be applied to whatever someone grimly decides to do for God. It's a reality which can be seen and grasped in safe, sure ways: as we follow not only the Commandments but also the teachings and laws of the Church, and the sure guidance of the Pope. I saw that Christ shows out His Will for us, also, by the examples of His Saints. We can be sure of remaining on the "HARD ROAD" (Mt 7:14) of holiness if we're trying to fulfil our daily duties in ordinary life, with a sincere trust in God, and constant reliance on the graces of Christ, given supremely through the Sacraments. What a marvellous thing is the Catholic Faith, I saw, if everyone within it - whether truck-drivers, priests, surgeons or housewives, nuns or princesses - could follow the same Way.

Although the Saints were different from one another in background or temperament they had all passionately desired to do God's Will at every moment. They didn't reach perfection on earth, but attempted to be perfectly faithful and loving in major matters and minor, throughout every difficulty. They really trusted in God: in His Wisdom and Providence; and none of them was lacking in devotion to Christ in His Passion. But I also found out that most of them had become so simple and childlike that a bubbling joy and a lively sense of humour endeared them to their friends and brightened sad hearts around them.

One of the first comparatively-modern Saints I learned about was called St. Bernadette. She had led a short life dominated not by extraordinary phenomena but by countless chores and conversations and episodes of ill-health. The heroic child behind the pastel pictures had been canonised for her love of God and neighbour, in years of quiet endurance amidst her trials and pains, and not for the short series of visions she'd received as an illiterate fourteen-year old girl. She was glorified after death for her resemblance to Christ, not for indirectly founding a shrine for the world's pilgrims, at Lourdes, although I thank God today, with all my heart, that the Mother of God is honoured there.

Saint Thérèse of Lisieux.

After reading about St. Ignatius, St. Dominic and others, I was initially puzzled when I encountered the brief life and writings of St. Thérèse. Her life had been so different from my own. Her flowery language dismayed me. Then I learned that she had lived and died a mere eighty years ago, only a short distance from the town of Rouen which I'd explored as a child. She'd spent a few years in a convent in Lisieux, as a contemplative nun, and had died at the age of twenty-four. Her autobiography seemed peculiar, even as I grew more interested in the details of her way of life. The reverent books about her puzzled me, too. For example, she was praised for her "heroism" in enduring the "harsh Norman winters" and for eating whatever was put before her; yet everyone I'd known had shivered in unheated bedrooms. I myself had eaten what others had chosen to give me, at home or school or elsewhere, without thinking it to be unusual or brave. Yet, in my ignorance, I didn't understand that Thérèse hadn't been used to a "working-class" style of life. Some of her biographers were accustomed to servants and all sorts of luxuries and so were doubly appalled by what she had endured.

The style of the autobiography repelled me, mostly because I was unused to the reverent intimacy with which nineteenth-century Catholics spoke about Christ. In the Anglican circles of my youth, people who displayed evangelical fervour were regarded as being a bit juvenile and undisciplined, especially those who spoke about "Jesus" in an enthusiastic way. The names I'd been encouraged to use - as though for Someone a long way away - were: "Almighty God" and "Lord".

But curiosity led me through the unfamiliar phrases. Térèse's joyful acceptance of suffering was revealed. Her courage was of the same calibre as that of St. Bernadette, yet the tremendous determination shown by these young women, as well as by other Saints, arose not from pride or stoicism, but from their love for God. Their belief that they were able to offer "reparation" for sins, in union with Christ, through sufferings joyfully borne, was a new concept for me, and it took me by storm. Wariness about St. Thérèse began to turn to admiration.

A certain phrase by Saint Paul, in Holy Scripture, had until then failed to whet my curiosity. What had he meant by saying: "IT MAKES ME HAPPY TO SUFFER FOR YOU ... AND IN MY OWN BODY TO DO WHAT I CAN TO MAKE UP ALL THAT STILL HAS TO BE UNDERGONE BY CHRIST FOR THE SAKE OF HIS BODY, THE CHURCH" (Col 1:24)? The answer was given to me through the lives of the Saints. What a piercing, life-changing revelation it was, that if we voluntarily unite our own pains with those of Christ in His Passion, we can do His work. Such a work of love is invisible, effected only by faith; but its power can be tremendous, if we can persevere in offering that reparation to God not only for our own sins but for the sins of other people. I was thrilled to learn this. It meant that by every loving 'offering-up' of pain or distress, we can please Christ by our love, help Him in His Passion, offer reparation for our own sins, and help our neighbour towards his Eternal goal. It also meant that no pain or grief we bear need ever be 'wasted'.

Four special women.

During the holiday, we saw the streets which St Thérèse had known as a child; and then we visited the gaudy, glorious Basilica which had been built in her honour. It awed me, not by its size, but by the statement it could have made to me as it soared boldly above the town. It was as though it might have proclaimed on behalf of those who built it: "Christ lives! Christ sanctifies those who love Him faithfully. Believe us, all you who come here. Christ's Church still preaches, proclaims and cherishes sanctity, and still celebrates the wonderful lives of her Saints."

It was in the hope of learning more about the same subject that I searched a few streets in Paris hoping to find the chapel where St. Catherine Labouré had prayed. This modest woman had received instructions from the Blessed Virgin Mary; but Catherine's sanctity lay not in her visions but in heroic virtue practised through the years. I was unsuccessful in my search, but met with more success, however, further South in Paray-le-Monial. There, I became full of joy at seeing the little convent where St. Margaret Mary had prayed, when she was almost overwhelmed by what was powerfully revealed to her of the marvellous Love of the Sacred Heart of Jesus.

In Italy, during our second week away, we toured castles, gardens and Cathedrals, enjoying the sunshine and the meals. But the greatest thrill for me was in finding "old" Saints, and seeing them in a new light. Saint Catherine of Siena became real for me, in Siena, when I saw the steep steps that she'd climbed with her band of comrades, taking food to the poor. Then as we arrived in Assisi, I found not just a bird-lover or a jolly comrade but a Saint of such a towering sanctity that all the pretty stories in my mind were peeled away. The crypt where Saint Francis was buried had a holiness about it in the air: the holiness of a passionate man who'd been determined to follow Christ at any price, through derision and pain.

As I looked at the relics of Saint Clare, whose tomb was nearby, I thought how marvellous it must have been for the two Saints to have encouraged one another in holiness: for each to have been spurred on by the other's devotion to Christ. Saint Clare's blond curls were there on display. I was sure that she'd sacrificed them without a pang, as she ran away to lock herself in a monastery for prayer, so that she could serve Christ with the same burning intensity of love as that being demonstrated by Saint Francis.

I was thrilled that through their prayers and example, all of these Saints were somehow 'ours'; and there were so many more! I was rather timid about asking for their prayers, as I was timid about discussing Religion or Christ. But I became more sure that it wasn't odd to want to turn away from sin and to become holy. It seems that even in our modern, technologically 'white-hot' and atheistic century, the needs of the human spirit are unchanged. For the love of God, and the sake of Eternal Life, we all ought to do penance, to pray every day and to live entirely for Christ. I realised that this is a thoroughly Christian, a thoroughly Catholic notion: and so, over thirty years ago, I earnestly embraced it, determined to avoid the fate of those who are "ONLY LUKEWARM" (Rv 3:16).

In my youth, of course, I couldn't really imagine myself ever growing old or preparing to die. But I knew, nevertheless, that I wanted to be prepared for that inevitable time-of-departure, principally by learning how to please God in the intervening years. I became even more determined to spend every day of my life learning more about the Church, and about prayer, solely for the love of Christ.

At the end of our holiday, I was full of admiration for the Saints, and even more fervent in prayer. There were only a few weeks more in which I'd be able to pray and meditate, uninterrupted.

Motherhood.

Our first baby arrived, after several months of joyful anticipation and two days of anguish. But his presence was like a private miracle. We were overcome with wonder at his life, and at his delightful presence. Although we hoped that we'd love any child born to us we were entranced by his physical perfection.

I remember leaning over his cot in my hospital room, in an interval between visitors, in a daze of wonder that I should have been able to produce another human being. I had never imagined that motherhood meant this: this storm of joy, and sense of completion.

The 'storm' had other effects. At around that time I read a newspaper story about some far-off disaster; and for the first time - I mean with such a passionate empathy - I wept over the experiences of mothers and children who were suffering on the other side of the world. My hard and cynical heart was at last being stilled and softened because a helpless infant was now entirely dependent on me.

At home in our bed-sitter with the new baby, I was nervous for a day or two, but was thrilled to be a mother. I can't describe how much we loved the child. His daily care became my chief concern: my great joy. Even while I frantically worked out whether he was well-fed or hungry, warm or chilly, at any hour of the night or day in my new and very flexible routine, I was astounded to be a mother: to have my own precious child: for us to be a family.

During those first few months of motherhood, I persevered in prayer. Formal worship was limited to two hours a week, and prayer became a mere soul's glimpse of Christ between the kitchen and the bath. Later, I managed to spend one or two half-hours in prayer each day when the baby fell asleep; but during those early days I found that it wasn't difficult to keep my heart wholly turned towards God, even if in an exhausted, inarticulate way, between crises and bouts of anxiety. I simply ached with gratitude and wonder.

We were to be thrilled in just the same way at the birth of each one of our precious children; but meanwhile, we arranged for the first to be baptised. My former parish priest - who had 'heard' my confession - agreed to officiate at the nearby Anglican Church. It was an extremely happy celebration by a large collection of friends and relations; and my mother was especially joyful at seeing me with husband and child, apparently 'settled' at last and following in her very sensible domestic footsteps.

[Already at home.

It's been a great blessing that when I became a mother I was able to stay at home to look after the children, and so didn't miss the wonderful 'unfolding' of their personalities, with so many opportunities for us all to give joy and to receive it - even in the midst of everyday struggle and growth and misunderstanding. But there's another reason why I've been grateful for the support of my husband, and also grateful for the Church's encouragement to us that we care for our relations. I mean that if a married woman is already at home caring for several persons, it's possible that she'll welcome into her home further needy persons - whether in the 'shape' of a pregnancy or an ageing parent.

Apart from my four pregnancies there were to be several occasions on which I genuinely believed that I was pregnant, although perhaps I wasn't; and I'm only writing about this to explain that although, each time, I wondered how I'd cope, I knew that the event wouldn't point to a total change in my life-style; and so although I was sometimes very worried about pain or ill-health, I managed not to panic, but assumed that we'd manage somehow - with God's help. Panic, however, is more probably the reaction for women who are anxious to be out all day in paid work - which I realise is unavoidable for some needy people - or in any circumstance where a woman is encouraged to look upon her unborn baby as an enemy, rather than a gift.]

Catholic spirituality.

Amidst the care of a husband and child, the question of Church membership hadn't gone away, but had merely been postponed. The studies continued, even we moved to different homes in a different town. Whether I'd been cooking, playing or sewing, I found time to read. I was equally at home with a Catholic Truth Society pamphlet or with Cardinal Newman's "Grammar of Assent".

Fascinated by all I learned, I was thrilled to read Newman's works, which I'd come across before the baby was born. I learned an enormous amount from this clerical 'convert,' as I dashed next through his 'Apologia', joyful at hearing the details of a journey similar to my own. Yet he in no way swayed my mind, which was already 'made'. As I have said, I knew already that I ought to become a Catholic as soon as it were possible, though I half-imagined only Saints need apply. I felt a great longing, mixed with fear. Newman's gift to me, becoming more weighty as I read his "Development of Christian Doctrine", was this: he showed me that others had followed the same path, at great personal cost; and that was exactly the sort of reassurance I needed at that time. I was still amazed at my own impertinence at believing that I could recognise truth when others did not. I'd spent most of my life so far assuming that other people knew far more than I, and believing that my opinions were unimportant.

I didn't know a single Catholic - besides the priest I've mentioned - to whom I could turn for advice. The lovely Irish family were many miles away, and there were no Catholics, as far as I knew, amongst our acquaintances. In all my short life I'd never met an English "cradle" Catholic, and only one convert to Catholicism; and despite having heard about my own father's changes of allegiance - from the Society of Friends to the Church of England - I was vaguely of the opinion that most people usually remained faithful to the 'denomination' in which they were brought up, and that most people were untroubled by what were seen as minor differences of opinion between practising Christians.

Wise guides.

Thanks to Cardinal Newman, I was reassured that it's not humility that tempts anyone to say "Good people disagree with me, therefore I must be wrong". Truth alone counts. I too must pursue Truth and embrace it at any cost. Newman's works re-inforced my belief that we can't abdicate the use of our reason as we struggle to see where our loyalties lie; and when we've seen truth, we have to be brave and act upon it. My only query about his own journey towards recognition of the claims of the Church, was - why did it take him so long to recognise the Church, when he'd had years of study and conversation as an Anglican clergyman?

Now that I'd conceded that present-day advocates of the Anglican 'Branch' theory of Church development were well-meaning but wrong, I was relieved to discover that many others, besides myself, had come to this conclusion. Fr. Knox's "Spiritual Aenaeid" encouraged me, as did the books of Arnold Lunn, with Fr. Vernon Johnson's "One Faith, one Lord," and the 'lives' of various Saints; yet history wasn't enough for me during those difficult years. My soul as well as my mind needed greater nourishment: but I found a sort of soul-food in books also, in some measure. For example, Père de Caussade's letters on "Abandonment" of oneself to "Divine Providence" helped me to think more clearly about the meaning of trust in God. They gave a glimpse of a truly fervent and Catholic spirituality which increased my desire for sanctity; and that desire increased precisely because I had learned something about the essence of sanctity. I realised more clearly that Francis and Dominic, Catherine and Bernadette weren't spiritual athletes who bore excruciating trials through sheer will-power. They were flawed but loving persons who emptied themselves, so to speak, so that God's own holiness could pour within them and so could eventually illuminate, comfort and change other people as well.

Père de Caussade's aim in writing so many letters had been to urge various fervent nuns towards even greater generosity towards Christ. It seemed that great holiness, through union of the heart with Christ, demanded a constant and complete voluntary sacrifice of all one's ambitions so that one might fulfil the Will of God in every detail of life, that is, might fulfil Christ's ambitions. An explanation such as this was very different from the good-hearted but moderate advice offered to me by certain guides, to whom zealous professions of faith or devotion were seen as exaggerated and 'un-English'.

Thomas Merton's books helped me again. I ploughed through Herbert Van Zeller and C.S. Lewis. I tried to read works by Teilhard de Chardin, but thought some ideas unorthodox, so gave up, and continued with Mgr. Escriva, Dom Eugene Boylan, and - on a lighter note - Fr. Bernard Bassett. I bought most of my books in dusty second-hand shops where I browsed for a few minutes whilst the baby slept in the pram. I was still car-less and almost penniless: but was very happy in my family and my home, though not yet happy in my faith.

Some books seemed very strange to me: for example, the 'Cloud of Unknowing'. I didn't understand much about the spiritual life. I was content to struggle amongst the 'foothills', because I'd learned that it's not will-power but Divine grace which transforms some people into mystics or Saints. Yet I wasn't surprised or saddened by my ignorance. I felt like the woman who had been happy to approach Jesus through the crowd, saying to herself that she'd be helped: "IF I CAN TOUCH EVEN HIS CLOTHES" (Mk 5:28). I believed that Christ heard my simple prayers and offered a plain and simple way. In all my puzzlement, I knew that I must avoid sin, and love my neighbour for Christ's sake, and pray to God in ordinary ways but with the fervour of the Saints.

From town to town.

As I said earlier, I'd given up paid work just before our child was born, to be free to look after him full-time and to follow my husband wherever his job led him at each new promotion. We worked hard in various ways, but had a great deal of fun, and made new friends wherever we went. We were to move house five times in the first seven years of marriage; but it was exciting to explore new places and to create new homes. We were happy anywhere - in any bed-sitter, flat or house. There was still little money to spare for luxuries; but childhood had been the same, and we were content. I gladly sewed and painted, patched and hemmed, delighted by our way of life.

We set no great store in possessions. People mattered more than things. We were grateful for our gifts of second-hand furniture and old books, but had no television, vacuum cleaner or washing machine. Nearly all of my clothes were home-made, as were the curtains and covers - and toys and games.

Occasionally I bought a small object from a junk-shop for its sheer beauty, something I couldn't have made myself: a tarnished brass tray with an extraordinary design, and - on another occasion - a carved wooden box. I still made time to paint pictures, when our first child was asleep. But more hours were passed in washing nappies, cooking for relatives and friends, and happily walking miles each day for shopping, and for fresh air and fun. I didn't mind such simple tasks; and as I walked and pushed the pram, I prayed the Rosary, or chatted with the baby, or thought about God.

In England, long ago.

There was a great difference, I found, between cherishing a longing to belong to the Church, albeit a painful longing, and feeling a dreadful emptiness at not being able to "go in". This latter mood began to predominate, the more I examined the details of our English religious history. Several years earlier, at school, my friends and I had gasped with astonishment on hearing of the exploits of Henry the Eighth. Yet his life had seemed as remote and as irrelevant to our own lives as that of King Canute or Nell Gwynn. We saw them as bit-players in a bright but useless pageant put before us by teachers beguiled by myths about the "Golden Days". The study of history revealed quaint but useless facts, we thought at the time. We'd surely be better prepared for modern life if we studied more science or modern languages.

It was a Catholic author, Phillip Hughes, who suddenly opened my eyes by his plain recital of historical facts in his "History of the Reformation". Late one night, when I was sitting up in bed, reading, I was suddenly amazed to read the phrase: "The Mass was abolished". That was what had happened in England, long ago: something terrible, which, far from being irrelevant, was very significant, in the light of my 'faith-journey.'

What a lot I'd heard about the 'good' which was achieved by the Reformation, and by the Dissolution of the monasteries in England: so much about purification and reform, but almost nothing about the disastrous effects which followed the general retreat from Catholic doctrines and the ruination of Catholic sanctuaries and shrines. The more I read of the plain facts of the matter, the more horrified I became at what had been hidden from me through my ignorance and through a lop-sided presentation of our nation's history.

Nothing changed, in one sense. I'd known for three years that the Catholic Church hadn't "broken up" into small pieces centuries ago. I had longed for three years to 'go in'. Yet - this was the moment at which the longing became a compulsion. The bright facade of 'Anglo-Catholicism' swayed and collapsed; and I knew that I could no longer go to Communion in an Anglican Church, no matter how far off was my Reception. I realised that despite my reluctance to believe it, Cranmer's attractive Church was Cranmer's still. No matter how great was the devotion to Christ of the Anglicans I knew, nor how sincere had been the adoption in recent times of 'Catholic' clerical dress or Catholic ritual, nothing could obscure the fact that, in the sixteenth century, almost all of England's thousands of Catholic Churches had been desecrated, and therefore changed. And those changes in externals reflected various changes in doctrine, changes enforced in the sixteenth century by State power, as Monarchs usurped the teaching role of Catholic Bishops.

By order of the Monarch.

One of the important things I've learned in recent years, especially in studies and conversations to do with Ecumenism, is that we Christians who claim to love and respect one another in our different ecclesial communities ought not to blunder into the unnecessary use of what's called emotive language, or labelling; nor should we keep using phrases or names which make people feel uncomfortable or which resurrect past misunderstandings. We mustn't forget however, that there are serious differences of belief and practice between the Christian groups; and so it's for the sake of truth, in telling this story, that I feel bound to mention in plain language some of the things I learned in my twenties: things which had never been mentioned by the people who surrounded me then, and who had an unthinking prejudice against everything to do with Catholics. The impression which I'd received as a child was that Catholicism was so foolish a faith, and so unpopular, that the English People were glad to discard it; but I learned, however, in the 1960's - from reputable Catholic historians - that the decline of Catholicism in the Middle Ages hadn't been due to a popular movement, but had been caused by determined people with tremendous power to terrorise or punish devout Catholics who didn't want to see any change.

It became plain to me that by order of the Monarch, and almost all over England, churches had been vandalised. Statues had been ripped out of their niches. Paintings and stained glass, too, had been stolen or destroyed. But - worst of all - within a generation, not only had the Mass been re-written and changed, but even the very altars on which the Holy Sacrifice of the Mass had been offered for centuries had been dismantled and removed. So there seemed no question but that the Catholic faith in England was being practised today not by the descendants of those advocates of the new Communion Service in those sad, despoiled churches, but by Christians who are still loyal to the Pope.

I learned that true Catholics, for several generations, had risked their lives to ensure that the Holy Sacrifice was still celebrated in England, and that true Catholic teaching was passed on - whatever the penalties.

Imprisonment and death.

When I was young, it had never occurred to me to wonder why there were so few Catholics in England nowadays. I'd been entirely ignorant of the ways by which the Faith had been uprooted in the sixteenth and seventeenth centuries; and now at last I discovered a little about the recusant families, with their fines, imprisonments and deaths. I learned that for three centuries, before the building of Catholic institutions was made legal, again, in the early eighteen-hundreds, young men went abroad to train for the Catholic priesthood. I was full of admiration when I learned that, during penal times, those brave young future martyrs knew that arrest and torture were highly likely; yet they prepared for personal sacrifice by prayer and study, fervent in prayer to Christ and His Holy Mother and to the Angels and Saints. They relied, too, on the prayers of their friends and relatives - of earth or of Heaven - as they undertook hazardous journeys in order to bring the sacraments to Catholics who wouldn't give their allegiance to the new State church. So many good people sacrificed or risked their lives to preserve the Catholic Faith in England, especially the families who provided safe havens where Holy Mass could be celebrated and faithful people be strengthened. Then I learned, about our own times, that through the arrival in England of poor, persecuted Irish people - so pitied or despised by people I had known - the Faith in England had been marvellously enlivened and enriched, just when things looked extremely bleak.

Penal times had passed, it was true; but I gathered that some of the unfortunate developments of Tudor times had never been undone. In the twentieth-century, as in the seventeenth, the picture was similar: the picture of a State Church accorded tremendous privileges, whilst the Catholic Church which had been established here by Saint Augustine at the wish of the Pope, Saint Gregory, was still reviled as a church for foreigners. So the choice to be made by each English Christian, if he or she ever became aware of the issues, remained the same as the choice that people had faced in penal times. The penalties might be less severe, but each new 'convert' would experience some degree of mockery or alienation.

'With authority'.

By the grace of God, I now believed in everything which was taught by the Pope and by the other Catholic Bishops. Like Christ, they "SPOKE WITH AUTHORITY" (Lk 4:32). Although my enquiries about that authority, in childhood, had brought me only ridicule, I realised at last that the Faith of which I'd had a brief glimpse at a Catholic Primary School, and in an Irish home on our Council estate and also during several visits to the great Cathedral of Rouen, was the Faith which had flourished in England for a thousand years, before its official rejection in the sixteenth century. I wouldn't be un-English were I to become a Catholic The Faith was thoroughly rooted not only in my heart and soul but in my own country. Customs and beliefs which I'd heard described as mediaeval or superstitious were in fact wise and well-founded. They flourished all over the country, as well as all over the world.

What a great gift is faith in God and in His Church, and how I took it for granted, when I found it; and since I was ignorant in so many matters, I didn't know that there are differing degrees of faith, or, rather, that faith, hope and charity are given to the soul by God, according to our soul's capacity: our willingness to welcome those virtues; and I must admit that God gave me a tremendous faith in Him, although through no merit of mine. It was tremendous because He is generous, but also because I'd always loved truth and now had welcomed the light of truth when true faith was offered to me.

When I say that I'd always loved truth I mean, first, that as a little child I had delighted in the perpetual unfolding of reasonable, useful information from parents and teachers about the material world. Most of that information seemed to fit together in a remarkable way. For example. I thought it marvellous that prehistoric eruptions in the earth's crust had produced coal, and also diamonds, and that the coal was useful for cooking carrots which one could grow on the surface of our Earth's crust. Then again it seemed astonishing to me that our house was sheltered by huge and beautiful trees. They entranced me by the swishing of their leaves during storms and by the dappled patterns of their leaves on the pavement on hot summer days; and yet their trunks were made of a marvellous material which was of exactly the right consistency for the building of furniture. Remember: I was ankle deep in wood shavings whenever I watched my father build some new stool or household item in his workshop, so I was familiar with the marvellous properties of wood.

A marvellous mosaic.

What I'm trying to say is that when certain facts about our material world were verifiable and seemed admirable, I was ready to welcome them. When I originally learned, as a child, that diamonds 'grow' in the ground, or that tadpoles become frogs, or that a cut finger heals itself, I wasn't cynical or disbelieving about these marvels. So when I was confronted in adult life with even stranger facts which were being offered to me by a sensible and trustworthy person, facts which seemed to fit together as neatly as had the little pieces of the mosaic of the whole marvellous universe, I was happy to accept them; and it was this delight in the inter-related 'facts' of the material world that disposed me to accept interrelated truths about the supernatural world when I discovered that 'new' world through Christian prayer and teaching, and when I was offered the free gift of faith.

What I realise now is that God poured His gift of faith into my heart after my marriage, when I was happy and grateful, and was willing to pray, and to read about God, and therefore was no longer untrusting, bitter or cynical; or perhaps I should say: it was then that I discovered that God's faith, hope and charity were being offered to me, as always, but only then did I recognise and accept them. And, in wholeheartedly accepting faith, that is, believing in God, and in God revealed to the world by His Divine Son Jesus Christ, I longed, immediately, to find out even more about God.

I believed all that seemed to belong to the main 'body' of Christian truth as I was learning it at first, mainly from books; and I was never cynical, never thinking: "How little need I believe?" or: "What's the minimum that I must do to fulfil my Christian duties?" I know that it was because I was prepared to make sacrifices for my very rudimentary faith that it grew stronger; and at the same time my spiritual 'sight' grew so much clearer that I was able to recognise the plain truth - the full truths of the Faith - when they were first presented to me by faithful Catholic authors and by the priests to whom I eventually turned for advice.

So that's partly why nothing in the Church's teaching seemed illogical to me, or perverse, despite the criticisms I'd heard from non-Catholics. If one believed in the Divine origin of the Church, and in God's guidance of it even now, one could see how every teaching "fell into place". Each could be seen as part of an harmonious system of thought and belief which held within itself an explanation for, and an answer to, every human yearning and every apparent aspect of the Divine Will, as made known through Jesus Christ, through His Apostles, through the Sacred Tradition, and through the Sacred Scriptures which had emerged from the Apostolic era, sealed with Divine authority.

Through reading both Catholic and non-Catholic journals and newspapers I learned that many writers vehemently criticise not only Church discipline but the constant and unchanging teachings about faith or morals. But it isn't intellectual cowardice, I saw, which allows 'converts' to accept Catholic doctrines; it is humility which enables them to avoid saying: "I neither like nor understand this doctrine; therefore the teaching of the Church must be wrong." It is humility that causes wise enquirers to say to themselves: "If my mind is stumbling in its efforts to understand the sure and certain teaching of the Church, which is Christ's teaching, then my mind, evidently, is in need of more light. What more can I learn? May God guide me to see clearly".

A prayer for Truth.

At that difficult stage of my explorations, I prayed for help every day, but neither asked God to help me to stop thinking about disturbing questions nor to "make" me a Roman Catholic. I knew that life is full of pain and heartache, of one sort or another. What I wanted was truth, above all. So for those three or four years, I prayed a sincere prayer daily, in simple words which calmed me, as I said: "Oh God: show me my true place in your Holy Catholic Church."

My return to daily prayer was so recent that my mind still echoed with the accusations of non-believers who said that the whole business of prayer was 'auto-suggestion'. That was why I took special care to pray in very simple ways: with entirely sincere phrases.

It's possible that someone will wonder why Christ didn't teach me all about the Catholic Church, if, as I've explained, He had visited me when I'd prayed, and if He wanted me to serve Him and to do His Will. But I can say from experience, now, that He teaches us exactly what we need to be taught at a particular moment; and He rarely teaches what can be found through the normal 'channels' which He Himself, out of love for us, has established and upheld.

There was no need for special 'teaching' in prayer for what was so obvious: for what I'd indeed found out very quickly: that Christ had founded a holy and united Church, and that for reasons of history and ignorance, I wasn't a member of it, or, more accurately, wasn't in full Communion.

---

6 CONFIRMATION

(1968)

FULL COMMUNION. PRAYER.

Christ, tugging at my heart.

It's no exaggeration to say that I felt a pang of human terror as I studied and pondered. Horrified at the consequences of this train of thought, I saw ever more closely that the One Holy Catholic Church of the history books was the One Holy Church which exists today, which was vilified by people close to me yet was led by a Pope who preached with the authority first conferred upon Saint Peter, the first leader of Christ's Apostles.

Christ was tugging at my heart, urging me to follow Him, despite my anguish. He issued a fervent invitation which I could hardly bear to accept, but which I couldn't bear to ignore. He urged me, daily, in a wordless, insistent manner:-

> **Follow My inspiration and speak with a priest of My Church. Ask him to receive you into Communion so that I can teach, feed, sustain and comfort you in the best possible ways. (T:11 #12)**

At last I admitted that God indeed had shown me His Truth, through faith, reason, history and prayer, and through the uncomfortable, persistent "nudging" of a conscience which had recently become much more accurate and sensitive. I was entirely free to respond or to disobey, but, since my greatest desire was to please God, I found the address of the local Catholic Church, and made an appointment to see the priest: a different priest, since we'd moved a long way by then from our first bed-sitter.

It was from a sense of duty that I made my way, at around the same time, to the vicarage of our local Anglican church of St. John Chrysostom. For a few months since our arrival in Manchester, my husband and I had worshipped together each Sunday, with our baby tucked up in a pram at the end of our pew. How marvellous it would have been, in one sense, if I could have avoided the heartache of the coming years: caused by separate worship of the same Lord, with other problems. But what blessings would have eluded us: blessings not to be recognised for many more years, but now seen as astounding.

Still half-quaking at my own impertinence at believing that I was right and others were wrong on this question of Church and Papacy when I'd been such an unwilling Christian and so rebellious, I nevertheless held firm. How could I do otherwise? I saw that I wasn't the first or the last to see obedience to the Will of God as more important than the fulfilment of earthly hopes. Even if I were going to be condemned by other people, that wasn't a factor that had to be considered. All that was important - even more important than my duty to my dearest 'neighbour', my own husband - was my duty to God, Who made me so that I should love and serve Him above all. That was the first and greatest Commandment, which I had a duty to obey by entering the Church which His Son had established, even if this would mean disappointing other people: and even if it nearly broke my heart.

A search for guidance.

Finding the rectory, I explained to the minister as tactfully as I could that I believed I ought to become a Catholic. He expressed only dismay. Then I set off for St. Edward's, the local Catholic church. I'd made an appointment with the priest, who was a young man, and very gentle. I told him my story and asked him to help me to find my way in. He suggested that I see "the Jesuits" at their own church a mile further away. Perhaps he guessed that they would have had more experience than himself in receiving 'converts'. So once again I plucked up courage, determined to face another door and another stranger for the sake of accurate information and advice.

The Jesuit presbytery was vast, dark, and very frightening to me, but nothing could have kept me out. My visit evoked past experiences of being sent to see 'the Headmaster'. It was an even more momentous visit, but I knew my feelings were irrelevant, provided I was given hope, and truth. Someone was on duty at the door; then one of the priests took me to a side-room. I was asked to sit on a bench by a long polished table, and to recount my story again. The priest had received a brief phone-call from the Catholic parish priest; and when he asked me why I'd come to see him, I told him very swiftly about my search for knowledge about the Faith, about my 'discovery' of the Catholic Church, and the fears of my non-Catholic relations. He asked me what I'd read, and whether I prayed, and then asked me if I'd come back the following week. (Illustrations: No. 11)

When I returned, I half-expected to be questioned for weeks, or taught further, or sent elsewhere; after all, what did I know of the Church's methods and recommendations? Yet the priest wasted no time. Perhaps he was pleased with the amount of reading I had already done, or with the fact that I already believed in Christ and in all of the Church's teachings and was determined to be fervent and faithful. I had no idea what he'd do, and it wouldn't have occurred to me to ask him. But he suggested there was no reason why I shouldn't be received. He invited me - knowing that I'd discuss this with my husband - to "pick a date". Perhaps this was a wise pastoral decision by a priest who wanted to avoid friction in a sensitive family. Perhaps he'd decided that there was no need for me to attend the Presbytery for instruction when there was scarcely a facet of the faith left unexamined to any great degree. But I was delighted.

Astounded by the simplicity of the proposal, I was unable to bear a long wait until a major feast. It was mid-winter, wet and cold; so I chose "the Chair of St. Peter", which was less than two weeks hence. But I hid my disappointment at not finding a major feast 'to hand' - perhaps the Annunciation, or the Immaculate Conception of Our Lady. Not until twenty years later did I find out that February 22nd is the feast-day of that passionate 'convert', St. Margaret of

Cortona; and now that I understand more clearly the meaning of St. Peter's vocation I'm grateful for my connection with "the Chair of St. Peter," which gives me a small association with the responsibilities of the Holy Father. It's an incentive to become even more fervent in prayer for someone who often receives more mockery than thanks, as he does his gruelling work.

As I said earlier, I secretly felt that only Saints ought to enter the Church. It didn't occur to me that I might be welcome. I didn't realise, fully, that the Church exists for sinners. I just felt an enormous gratitude to God that someone timid and ignorant like myself should have finally been told that she'd be "let in."

God's ways.

I'd already decided that with God's help I would respect and obey all the Church's teachings and commands. There were aspects of her teachings which I didn't wholly understand, but I nevertheless believed in what she taught. The basic premise in which I placed my confidence was that the Holy Spirit is guiding this amazing institution which has been founded by Christ. No weaknesses in the Church's human members could blur my perception of that fact. Christ hadn't guided His people for five or ten centuries, only to give up. He teaches us constantly, I had learned, through the Pope, and through the other Catholic Bishops who believe and teach the same Faith in a united and visible community.

It seemed to me that obedience to the Church is, truly, obedience to God. It isn't an immature, lazy way of avoiding the use of one's own reason, but a free and loving act of submission - made through the Church - to the Author of our reason; and this submission is made for the sake of truth which is not against reason, but sublimely beyond it, in the Mind of God who sent His Christ to earth to help us.

In following the God who said "MY WAYS [ARE] NOT YOUR WAYS" (Is 55:8), I thought that it would be wrong and impertinent of me to say: "At the moment, not understanding everything, I shall be disobedient even whilst demanding that I be received!" I couldn't make conditions or excuses to the Church of Christ. I simply trusted that, in time, I'd come to understand everything I need to know.

What a terrible pity it is that even our intellect, which is such a great gift from our Creator, can be used by desperate people to look for reasons to disobey or to ignore the wise and wonderful laws which God has engraved in our very souls.

A fruitful conversation.

This is the point at which I should mention that when I first began to think about the meaning of 'Church', as an adult, I 'phoned my mother, who was always extremely busy, but who made time to meet me in London. She came accompanied by our Anglican parish priest. They were on a trip to Westminster, but stopped off to meet me for a coffee and to try to answer my questions about faith and duty.

If she was astonished at being consulted by a recently-teenaged and moody daughter about faith and the Catholic Church, she didn't show it. But neither she nor our minister had any neat solution about how we can be certain that we're doing right, when it seems as though the Lord is leading us to new places; nor could they tell me how to avoid disagreement with one's critics. So in the end we said our goodbyes, and she went back to her hectic routine.

That talk was more fruitful than I might have dreamed: although for my mother, rather than for myself. I believe that through that vigorous discussion with her, and with our Vicar, of their 'Anglo-Catholic' views - with my firm statement that I knew I was going to become a Roman Catholic, even if I didn't yet know when - she saw Reception as something possible for herself. Indeed I was astonished that only a year later - and before I myself was received - she 'phoned me to say that she was about to be received into 'full Communion' in her local Catholic Church in Little Chalfont. She wanted a private ceremony with no fuss, so didn't invite me to go.

The news was a complete surprise. During my childhood, I remembered, when she and my father had been members of the same Anglican Church, they had differed vehemently on various important topics. As I said, my mother had recommended private confession of sins to an Anglican minister, whereas my father claimed that it wasn't necessary. Yet each had given me the impression of being thoroughly at home within the Church of England. Never had I heard my mother express a desire to become a 'Roman Catholic'; indeed, she had proclaimed throughout my childhood that she was a true Catholic, though of the 'Anglo-Catholic' variety; and she had spoken with confidence of a union between the two 'Churches' becoming a reality in her life-time. She was convinced that the Apostolic succession had continued in the Church of England, and that Christ dwelt in our church in the Reserved Sacrament; and since these two beliefs were, in her opinion, the supreme signs of any Church's true Catholicity, she had mentioned no desire to benefit from the teachings or guidance of the Pope, although perhaps she hadn't been very frank with me. Perhaps she had spoken more freely with her contemporaries than with a child.

It was quite wonderful to know that she had entered the Catholic Church, after such a quiet and peculiar journey; but the fact remained that there was no hope of her being with me at my own Reception. She still worked full-time as a deputy head-teacher in an secondary school. Indeed, she was busier than ever, and was a long way from my new home in the North. She was rarely able to visit us, and I was quite unable to return home except for emergencies, as I catered to the demands of baby, husband and relatives, who couldn't be deserted. That's why I prepared to be received alone, unaware that two students - complete strangers, from the nearby University, would be called in by the priest to act as my 'sponsors'.

Reception into full Communion.

The day of my Reception at the Church of the Holy Name was a day of sheer loneliness and grief. We were now two hundred miles away from old ties. At the last moment, from a sense of duty, my husband came along to watch the brief and private ceremony; but I knew no local Catholic except the priest. I felt a bit nervous, yet at the same time I was thrilled at the thought of ending what seemed like a terrible fast. I longed to receive Christ in His Sacraments.

Quite soon after we'd arrived in the church, I was asked to step into the Confessional box to make a General Confession. This didn't upset me, now that I knew it was Christ Who was inviting me, through His Church, to be reconciled in this way. I was glad to be able to make a fresh start for the best of motives: not in order to pacify a parent but because my whole heart was burning with longing to become holy, for God's sake.

When my sins had been forgiven, I was provisionally baptised, and was questioned about my faith. Eventually - like a child - I was received, wholly, into Christ's family of Faith. At last, His sanctuary had become my home.

My mind was calm and my heart steady; but, soon after the Reception, my emotions were in turmoil, as I walked on through new trials and heart-aching pain. Pure faith had led me in. Christ alone wordlessly showed me the way. He gave me courage, and held me up, day after day, in His Spirit's calm, amazing power. I was sad that my Reception had made others sad, but I wrote a letter to my father - amongst others - trying to explain my situation.

Quite simply, I knew that my soul's salvation was at stake. I was convinced of the plain truth which I'd found in the Catholic catechism, and which sat squarely with my conscience: the truth which had been confirmed by the Fathers of the Second Vatican Council, who had stated quite clearly the importance of faith and Baptism and membership of the Catholic Church; and yet my main aim was not just to be Catholic but, through all that Christ offers in His One Holy Church, to become charitable and holy - and so to please Him.

Whatever you bind on earth.

It was precisely because I knew that I wasn't good or strong, that I longed for all the types of help the Church could offer me. I needed the sure Apostolic teaching offered through the successors of Saint Peter: the man told by Christ: "WHATEVER YOU BIND ON EARTH SHALL BE CONSIDERED BOUND IN HEAVEN; WHATEVER YOU LOOSE ON EARTH SHALL BE CONSIDERED LOOSED IN HEAVEN" (Mt 16:19). Above all, I needed Christ Himself, found most fully in the Church which He had founded. He had said through Holy Scripture: "LOVE THE LORD YOUR GOD WITH ALL YOUR HEART, WITH ALL YOUR SOUL, AND WITH ALL YOUR MIND" (Mt 22:37); and since faith told me that His Church was reliable, I wanted to grasp all the 'handholds' that Christ had placed in His Church. I needed the Food of the Sacraments to make my way up the 'Holy Mountain' described in the Scriptures. True, lasting joy was my supreme hope, rather than temporary pleasures.

That's what I tried to explain, though in plainer language, to people who were important to me: some face to face, and some by correspondence. Whatever they thought of my decision, I can say, over thirty years later, that despite failures and heartaches, any hopes I might have had have been fulfilled beyond every possible expectation. Great human joys have at times made me weep with gratitude; yet I had no idea that anyone could experience - on earth - the astonishing joys which Christ Himself has lavished upon me in recent years. His goodness and generosity are indescribable.

As for the moment when I entered the Catholic Church: the truth is that the only hope I had was that God would keep faithful to His Son and to the Catholic Church until the day I died. I lived so thoroughly in 'the present moment' that the family's future state - or the country's, or the Church's - was unimaginable. I was content to enter the Church and to leave everyone and everything in God's hands - although praying fervent daily prayers for everyone I knew. But it's wonderful for me, now, to be able to look back with gladness, because I can say wholeheartedly that, despite all my sins and failings, never for a single second of my life have I regretted having asked to be received into full Communion; on the contrary; my heart is yearning to be able to see many more searchers 'come in', to enjoy Christ's astonishing gifts: especially the Holy Sacrifice of the Mass: the Eucharistic Banquet.

First Holy Communion.

My new beginning as a Catholic Christian in those damp February days held not a shred of human enjoyment, but I believed that I'd done the right thing. I spent three days in numb, dark endurance, and then, when Sunday arrived, I set out alone to attend Mass at my nearest Catholic Church. It was at St. Edward's in Rusholme that I made my first Holy Communion. I had no more appointments with the Jesuit Father at the "Holy Name", so I thought I ought to worship near my home. There was neither fuss nor fan-fare for what is, spiritually, so staggering an occasion, and no friends or relatives; but an elderly neighbour, no doubt sent by Providence, called to me across the street, and asked if I was going to "St. Edward's"? She walked along with me, showed me where to sit in church, then disappeared, having done her duty.

Following the custom of the Church and the teaching of Holy Scripture, I veiled my head in the church, in the Presence of Christ in the Blessed Sacrament; and then I found a small space on one of the packed pews, and knelt down to pray.

The situation was far from ideal, in that I was a stranger to most of the congregation. But despite that and various other drawbacks, I found that, in my attendance as a Catholic at that normal Sunday Mass, every yearning of my heart towards God was more profoundly satisfied than I could have dreamed might be possible, even though I was a complete newcomer.

Church visits, so far, had been limited because of the baby's needs. Quick visits to the Blessed Sacrament had been my usual 'Catholic' worship until then. I had occasionally plucked up courage to attend Mass; but I always sat just inside the door, at the back, barely able to see but frightened of being noticed. The one place of worship where I'd felt really free to think and to wander was Westminster Cathedral, in London. There, I'd managed to feel less self-conscious. So many people of every size, class and colour were calmly and earnestly praying there, either kneeling or walking around, that I'd been happy to slip in amongst them for a lunchtime Mass, or to pay a visit to a wonderful shrine. There was so much to enjoy: Christ's own Presence in the Blessed Sacrament, above all. The peace was tangible, wherever I watched or prayed, whether before the High Altar or in a side chapel.

But on that first Sunday as a Catholic, I was awe-struck as I watched the Consecration. I kept quiet, because I didn't know the correct responses. All I could think was that I was a Catholic at last, happy to be on my knees in gratitude to God. I was thrilled that through His goodness my 'starvation' would soon be over. I longed to receive the Body and Blood of Christ. But I have to say something here about the Blessed Virgin Mary, who is the Mother of our Saviour, and was close to the Apostles in the early Church (Ac 1:14). What a true mother she is, and how good she was to me, on that day. What a welcome she gave me in the Church - although there was no noise to be heard. I had no spiritual 'light.' I suddenly 'learned' from Christ, as I waited to make my first Holy Communion and when my heart was still raw with grief at my various difficulties:

> **Believe in My Mother Mary. She is a real "flesh and blood" person who is now alive and close-at-hand, not a mere myth or symbol. (T:13A)**

Confirmation.

I hadn't the faintest idea what had happened. All I 'knew' was that Our Lady was present. The 'knowledge' was imageless, without feeling or thought or emotion; and I couldn't even think of analysing what had happened, since I knew that my duty was to pray, and to pay attention to the Holy Sacrifice. But the effect of the 'knowledge' was calming; and so I went up to receive Christ Himself that morning, at the heart of the strange crowd, with one ambition consuming me. I wanted to be able to love Christ, and to love every neighbour for His sake, perfectly, and to do His Will in everything until the end of my life.

How miserably I was going to fail. But how marvellously He was going to teach me: to teach me, first, that He loves me; and to teach me, as well, that His heart is touched more by humility and contrition than by self-purification and great achievements.

One ceremony was needed to confirm me in my new way of life, and that's why I went to Salford Cathedral a few weeks later. Once again, I went alone; but I was grateful I'd been able to get a lift across town for the ceremony of Confirmation. When I went inside the great doors I was told where to queue; and the Bishop prayed as he laid his hands on my head. I took the name of 'Mary', in honour of Our Lady, the Mother of God, before returning to my family.

I chose that name in her honour, again, several years later, when I had a baby daughter.

Opposition.

Trying to be tactful, I rarely spoke about my faith with people who thought me foolish. Perhaps my suspicion is true, that some "cradle" Catholics think that 'converts' exaggerate the amount of opposition they've faced in their struggles to enter the Catholic Church. But I've found from experience that Catholics in this country are rarely challenged face-to-face about their faith, unless they freely enter into a discussion with others about Church authority or about moral issues. I mean that the vast majority of "cradle" Catholics might have endured mild teasing or may have overheard unpleasant remarks, but few will know the true extent of the dislike stirred in many fellow-countrymen at any mention of Pope and Roman Catholic authority, or of monks and nuns, Jesuits, Inquisition, Mass, Confession or Saints: such a clutch of terrible words which can stir up to fury many who sincerely see themselves as pure, faithful servants of a Gospel uncorrupted by "Rome".

Alas, many converts, in their younger days, have hurled abuse, but out of earshot, at their Catholic neighbours; so they know at first-hand all the old scare-stories and hatreds and fears: relics of our national family quarrels over four hundred years ago. When they themselves enter the Catholic Church, they know only too well what opinions are held about them, or what stories will circulate. Unable to live in the happy ignorance of the cradle Catholic, they try to deal patiently with old friends and relatives who are convinced that any "convert" must have had a breakdown, or must have been "got at" by some Svengali-ish figure in the background, or - as was more believable in the days before certain misinterpretations of the directives of the Second Vatican Council led to a new 'stripping' of many churches - have foolishly given in to an aesthetic longing for candles, incense and liturgical drama. That's one of the reasons why I tried to be tactful and unobtrusive in my handful of new devotions.

At the time of my Reception, as in the present day, some of the externals of the Catholic religion were achingly precious, though as much for the graces brought through them, and for the traditions which they embodied, as for their beauty or novelty. But it would be unwise, I decided, to provoke annoyance in people who acted more from ignorance than from malice; so I was careful not to flaunt externals, nor to thrust my Faith uncharitably at people who were unsympathetic to all things Catholic. I left my rosary hidden in my pocket.

Apart from the tiniest possible statue of Our Blessed Lady, I did without holy pictures for a few years, though I put a crucifix in each of our new homes; and I made a private scrapbook of pictures of the Saints, adding the newly-discovered "Stations of the Cross": cut out from a Catholic Truth Society pamphlet.

True graces.

There were beautiful and worthwhile things in the Church of England that I was required to surrender, when I entered into full Communion with Rome; but in general I slipped peacefully and gratefully into the long-established patterns of worship and discipline which are familiar to practising Catholics.

I had no problems thinking about the Blessed Sacrament so newly-received, and then about the many wonderful 'Communions' I'd enjoyed as an Anglican, and for a simple reason. It was true that I wholeheartedly accepted the authority of the Catholic Church, and so I accepted her decisions about Anglican orders and ceremonies. I was genuinely happy to let her be my guide, since she knew far more than I, on the subject; but I was happy, of course, because I wasn't called require to say: "Christ didn't love me, whilst I was an Anglican; He didn't touch me with His grace, in a spiritual communion, when I offered fervent prayers to Him during our Communion Service." I knew then what I know now, which is that Our Lord is good; and when did Our Lord - Who is even now praying to the Father on our behalf, in Heaven - ever fail to respond to a sinful person who has repented and who longs to be close to Him? I'm sure that my sincere prayers were fruitful. I know that I experienced Christ's peace and support many, many times, as a member of the Church of England; and I thank Him for the graces He gave me amongst so many caring and cheerful people, no matter in what manner I received them.

'Be perfect.'

Wonderful graces were given to me, amidst all the difficulties of that time. From that day in February 1968, little moments of pure spiritual joy came to surprise me, in between the times of turmoil or struggle. The domestic routine went on in the same way, but, inside my soul, much had changed. Where, once, dread had lurked beneath my brittle pleasures, now true joy flowed beneath each day's surface sorrows and trials. For Christ's sake I wanted to be a Saint. I'd said as much, three or four years earlier, when we'd been quizzed about our plans and ambitions by a group of friends. Perhaps I had - and have - an "all or nothing" nature; but it didn't occur to me to be less ambitious. How could anyone deliberately aim for mediocrity in God's service?

Our friends had all laughed, of course. Who was I to be so bold; and besides, what modern woman prayed and did penance? - That's what they thought. But faith told me that God could achieve anything in me, if I'd consent, and would try to do His Will. What else could I aim for, I argued silently, when Christ had said to us through the Holy Scriptures: "BE PERFECT, JUST AS YOUR HEAVENLY FATHER IS PERFECT" (Mt 5:48)? He had also said: "NO-ONE CAN BE THE SLAVE OF TWO MASTERS" (Mt 6:24); but I can see that for a long time I half-hoped this might be possible.

Meanwhile, I bought a second-hand copy of "Our Lady's Psalter," entranced by the lovely readings. I soon realised that it was a simplified version of something called the Breviary, the prayers and readings of which are used world-wide by Catholic monks and nuns, and which, long ago, Archbishop Cranmer had elegantly if drastically edited to create the Anglicans' 'morning prayer' and 'evensong'.

Christ's Real Presence.

So great was my longing to copy the best habits of earlier converts such as Thomas Merton and others that I overcame my nervousness, entered a Catholic bookshop, and bought "A Shorter Breviary." Numerous holy writers described it as the "official" prayer of the Church, so I treasured it. I tucked between its pages a picture of the 'Holy Shroud,' which perhaps is the face of Jesus, and also a copy of the lovely prayer: "Soul of Christ, sanctify me". Thus, I was happily fed with a marvellous selection of prayers and psalms, whenever I used the Breviary at home. I allowed the Rosary to lead me into gospel meditations every day, as I pushed my sleeping baby in his pram.

The Sacraments made me grow and change in Christ's life and Christ's strength. I had little courage of my own, and less confidence, but I was thrilled - then as now - by the thought that we can find Jesus everywhere: not only in Heaven and in our hearts, but in the Blessed Sacrament. It was a constant source of wonder to me that we can go to greet Him in that way, wherever we travel. He can be found on all our altars throughout the country, indeed, throughout the whole world; isn't that a breath-taking thought, for everyone who believes? I was astonished, I suppose, that the churches weren't crammed at all hours with worshippers who were desperate to be near Him. As for myself, having a firm belief in Christ's Real Presence, and having already glimpsed something of Christ's Divine Glory, I would gladly have lain flat on the floor in worship in front of each tabernacle. I'd read so many dire warnings against 'singularity', however, that I restrained my impulses, and tried to pray in church just like everyone else.

"Arrow prayers" were useful during the busy patches of the day, as I learned to pray in simple phrases such as: "Jesus, I love you" - or "Into your hands, O Lord, I commend my spirit," or simply: "Jesus mercy: Mary - help!" and many more. I accepted, joyfully, all that the Church gives to those who understand her task, and who struggle in the midst of the world to lead a "supernatural" life. The Commandments of course, guided me, just as they had in the past four years; but I understood them more clearly, guided by the Teaching Church. Then I discovered, and tried to keep, the laws of the Church, which included supporting our 'pastors'. I took that to mean that we should support them by our respect and obedience as well as by prayer and by financial assistance.

A framework of prayer.

Day after day, I resolved to love God and my neighbour, to do good and to avoid evil, and to forgive as I was forgiven. Each day began, continued, and ended with prayer. I fasted when required, used holy water with reverence when entering or leaving a church and asked the Saints for their prayers. Christ's mother Mary - holier than any other 'mere' mortal - became my mother in the spiritual life.

Gradually, a framework of prayer and devotion was constructed which strengthened and held together my whole day, and every good thought and action. It wasn't a rigid framework, but it meant that I was firmly in touch with Christ at the very centre of my life, from hour to hour; so if daily life seemed very quiet and mundane at one moment and then hectic and demanding at the next, I rarely felt 'swept away' by change or distraction, since I had a basic spiritual routine; I had a firm 'place' on which to stand: a place in which I hoped to meet Christ and to grow in His friendship, whatever changes were occurring in domestic or national life.

I tried to follow Our Lord's advice by retiring to a 'secret room' before praying to the Father. I always tried to hide my devotions, and therefore prayed secretly in any quiet place in the house. Spiritual reading was best done in the kitchen, while a meal was cooking; and I prayed the rosary, silently, on my way to the shops - the beads hidden in my pocket. I didn't want to embarrass anyone by my devotions, because that's not how we love our neighbour. I knew that Christ spent a lot of time talking and being sociable: and yet whenever He wanted to pray, He didn't make a fuss, but slipped out early in the morning or late at night.

True devotion to Our Lady.

As I continued with my studies about the Catholic Faith I read that a certain priest once vowed never to preach a sermon without mentioning Christ's Holy Mother. I longed to imitate his devotion. Delighted though I was to find, in little pamphlets, simple examples of true devotion to our Blessed Lady, I felt sadly lacking in the sort of daughterly affection that was described in other books I read. I was quite loathe to "hurl myself on her motherly bosom in every affliction", never having been encouraged to fling myself at an earthly mother: who had proved her love in hidden ways. I loved "Our Lady" dearly. I was awed by her holiness. I prayed her Holy Rosary. But in order to honour her further and to prove my love, I resolved to imitate that holy priest's devotion. I decided that I would never kneel in prayer before Christ again, without honouring, too, the wonderful woman who bore Him, by asking for her prayers and for her help in all my difficulties.

A sign of the Holy Trinity.

The sign of the Cross became a weapon and a prayer in the fight against sin. It wasn't unfamiliar, but I now signed myself devoutly at the beginning and end of each prayer, in honour of the Most Holy Trinity, into Whose Life I wished - somehow - to enter fully, one day. How to love God? How to do the Will of His Son? These were the ever-pressing questions. There was always something more to learn.

Christ continued to encourage me in prayer. I didn't know how He taught me, but I knew that He had urged me:

> **Believe that I can achieve anything in you, if you will consent and will do My Will. (T:14)**

New Light on the Bible.

Very soon after my Reception, a wonderful thing happened; or, rather, I was amazed to realise one day that listening to Holy Scripture at Mass was one of the highlights of my week: I actually understood, not just the words, but the true meaning.

Now, one of the reasons for this was that a new translation was in use, in the Catholic Church. I particularly liked the letters of St. Paul. They now sounded to me as though he'd written them in Bristol or Newcastle, and had posted them to us in a hurry, urging us not to give in to modern trends, but to be faithful to Christ's teachings. At about the same time, I saw that my daily reading of the shorter Breviary - or office book - had made me know and love the Psalms.

It was true that I'd relished the Psalms as an Anglican chorister, but I'd paid more attention to the music than to the words; and, of course, the Gospel of my childhood was recited weekly in the melodious but, to me, impenetrable phrases of the Authorised Version of the Bible, which I found as repellent and mysterious as the Shakespeare plays which I was then being "force-fed" at school.

The second reason, I saw, for my new understanding of Holy Scripture was this: God had been acting like a dear mother to me. Knowing of my fears and phobias about the Bible, He had secretly and quietly and patiently led me first to one devotional practice, then to another - all Bible-based - thereby helping me to 'break up' the Bible into bite-sized chunks. I was astonished to see that I'd been steadily absorbing Holy Scripture, like a child helped by its mother to eat something strange: a little at a time. Or I was like a small child whose father has stooped to explain that what seems like a huge problem, in arithmetic, can be tackled through a series of small, easy calculations.

When I came to hear three excerpts from Holy Scripture whenever I attended Mass, and when I came to learn some of the Psalms by heart through regular recital of the Shorter Breviary, I became wholly enamoured of the Scriptures I'd once found boring or incomprehensible; and then I found that every meditation on Holy Scripture led, inevitably, to a moment or more of sincere prayer.

A vivid Bible story.

When I remember my early meditations on Holy Scripture I recognise that, amongst all the stories and parables I'd rediscovered, Jesus' story about "THE SHEEP AND THE GOATS" (Mt 25:31-46) had the greatest impact on me. I saw that none of us dare disregard His advice. I knew no prisoners except those trapped in the misery of their own despair - but that was an opportunity to start. I resolved to care, always, for anyone I met who was sick, hungry, lonely, or imprisoned, so far as was possible within the limitations of my way of life. Careful thought was needed, and prayer, in order to ascertain God's Will. It would be foolish to spend more time than I could afford with strangers, if I neglected my own family, given to me by God.

There was another problem. I found that no matter how long I spent in prayer, I rarely felt that I had prayed "enough". Whether "enough" to satisfy my own yearning for contact with God or "enough" to satisfy the wishes of my unseen but Almighty Father, I wasn't sure. But I knew I ought not to prolong my prayers if I could be listening to someone's troubles, or taking part in family fun. Somehow, I must work things out. But no day must pass, I vowed, without my kneeling down to praise God and to thank Him, and to pray for others, in my 'secret room'.

A spiritual revolution.

There was much joy in our little home while this spiritual revolution was taking place. All the normal, marvellous aspects of life with treasured companions on earth - with family and friends - were greeted and enjoyed. There were simple meals and impromptu parties. Introductions and outings interrupted all the hard work and the griefs. But they are the subject of a different story - or, rather, a simple silent memory, since it is prayer above all which must be analysed here, after these few words about its domestic setting.

Soon after my Reception we were able to buy a little house of our own. It was near St. Cuthbert's Church in Withington; so I asked for St. Cuthbert's prayers each week at Holy Mass, but asked his especial help one day when we went to visit relatives in Yorkshire. I was thrilled to be able to visit the grave of the Saint, in Durham Cathedral. Then I plunged back into my hum-drum but oddly satisfying routine. I was very happy to be looking after a happy toddler, cooking more adventurously for husband and friends as - briefly - our income and my courage grew, and shopping and sewing as usual. I didn't know a single person in that town, when we arrived: but every new friendship was treasured, and every bus journey to the town centre was an adventure.

On the spiritual front, a reverent participation in the Holy Mass became the high-light and goal of each week. It seemed to me that I wouldn't be honouring God with much sincerity if I failed to prepare for Holy Communion or if, on arriving at church, I failed to pray throughout the Holy Mysteries. So in order to please God I never stared at people's clothes, or looked around. Kneeling in prayer - with head veiled in accordance with our custom, as practised for centuries and recommended by St. Paul in Holy Scripture - I learned to concentrate, to listen, and to watch with awe, drawing nourishment from all the details of the Celebration, whether they were to my liking or not.

The books I'd read had told me that every sermon could be a source of information and encouragement, however superficially dull it might seem. Since I was determined to find 'nourishment' in church I soon found that every reading from Holy Scripture and every word of each prayer was a source of knowledge or of joy; and although I unashamedly preferred beauty to ugliness in painting or architecture, I knew that in one sense it didn't matter if the church were ornate or plain, warm or cold. I would have knelt in two feet of mud, I thought, for the privilege of being there before Christ as I prepared for Holy Communion. In my whole person I felt utterly fulfilled, even though - at the same time - I bore numerous private burdens.

I was received soon after the Second Vatican Council, so the Mass was celebrated more frequently in English than in Latin. It made no difference to me in what language it was celebrated, if it were what the Church decreed; but I was surprised - at twenty-five years old - to find myself grateful for the bit of Latin I'd learned at school during my five years of grudging attention. I could have memorised the Creed, I think, in any language, but it was a joy to understand the Latin prayers and commentaries which occasionally came my way.

[Holy places, and beauty.

Since I'm writing about 'externals', I feel obliged to explain, here, that although I was thrilled above all by the celebration of Holy Mass, and by the Real Presence of Christ in the tabernacle, I liked to worship in church for the material beauty, as well as the Liturgical prayer.

Of course, we can pray to God anywhere and everywhere. But when we step inside a church to celebrate the Holy Mysteries, a church which is truly a holy place, set aside for the worship of God by His Holy People, we are surely right to hope to see beauty within. How do we honour God, except by giving Him 'the best' - whether 'the best' of our love, time, energy and service, or the best work of our craftsmen and artists for the decoration of these wonderful places where Christ our God comes to be amongst us? It's true that each culture has its own ideal of beauty; but how sad it is that a dull sort of minimalism has caused many of our sanctuaries to be stripped almost bare, in recent decades, and that some churches have been made to resemble - at great expense - archetypal factory buildings or warehouses: not perhaps the ideal setting for what we hope is a foretaste of our participation in the Heavenly Banquet, in the presence of the Saints and the Holy Angels.

Apart from the honour due to God, and which can be achieved in some measure through beauty, we have a duty to the worshippers. What a lot we can learn through being 'immersed,' week by week, in a place which is decorated with some of the symbols of our

Faith: if someone has explained them to us. I'm thinking of the Monogram of Christ's name, and the early Christian "fish symbol" - as well as the Crucifix, with carvings of the Sacred Host and Chalice, or of the Instruments of the Passion, or of symbols of the Holy Trinity.

It's not just as teaching aids that paintings and carvings are to be recommended. Surely it's sensible to have the eye of a grieving adult or a bored child 'fall' in church upon things which are both beautiful and instructive. How many people think about the Holy Angels, for example, if they're never seen beautiful representations of these extraordinary beings? Surely, better an imagined Angelic face to inspire us to offer thanks for a real Angel, than no inspiration and inadequate prayers?

Furthermore, what great reminders we can have of our Heavenly heroes and heroines, in coloured statues, stained-glass windows and church embroideries.

I'm grateful that, despite aspects of my early indoctrination, I've had no misunderstandings about "graven images" in church or indeed, in my life. I've never thought it wrong to paint pictures of Our Lady and Christ. My view has been based on the traditional teaching of the Catholic Church - followed by some Anglicans too - that once God had given us on earth the "living image" of Himself, Christ our Lord, He wouldn't want to forbid the creation of the holy images which are produced by Christians to remind themselves of the Incarnate Saviour who is God's greatest 'Work of Art'. As Saint Paul writes, of Christ: "HE IS THE IMAGE OF THE UNSEEN GOD" (Col 1:15); and so more than one solemn Council of the Church has stated that veneration of holy images is a commendable practice in a devout Christian's life, since honour is being offered not to the stone or to the pigment, but to the person who is represented. Which of us would condemn another Christian for possessing family photographs, accusing him or her of idolatry?]

Priests, and Sacrifice.

As I moved from house to house during the first decade of marriage, and therefore from church to church, there was no shortage of things to ponder, practices to learn or unlearn, behaviour to emulate - or to ignore. So convinced was I that Catholics - with so many helps to their faith - must all be very saintly, that I was astonished if ever I met a member of the Church who mocked our rules or our teachings, or spoke flippantly about the Pope.

Within a short time, I realised that one might easily be tempted to complain about some of our priests, who have such a prominent role in the Liturgy and in our lives that their faults are as prominently displayed as their virtues. But who was I to criticise anyone who was trying to serve God?

I decided that such behaviour wouldn't only be ungracious, but entirely wrong. Every priest, surely, had made great sacrifices in order to serve God and to bring us the Sacraments. How sad it seemed that anyone should draw attention to personal weaknesses or foibles. How shocking, that anyone should grumble about their accents, their sermons, or their great age, or their youth. It seemed - and still seems - to indicate ingratitude to God, if we recognise that the lives of the majority are given as a free gift to God, so that we who are in such need of help can receive consolation, counsel - and Christ.

I was awed by their priestly work. I was full of admiration for the vast number of celibate priests who had given their lives to Christ, and who now lived out that sacrifice, united to Him in the service of His People. I was awed by the supreme Sacrifice which was offered through their actions: by which I mean Christ's Holy Sacrifice of the altar: usually known as the Holy Mass.

Christ's Offering of Himself.

The more I prayed at Mass with attention and devotion, the more I came to see and understand what I had read in books: that this wasn't a "Holy Communion" service where Christians gathered together in simple prayer, looking forward to an intimate moment with Jesus. It was all this, but was much more. It was a solemn re-enactment of what Christ did at the Last Supper, when He had said to His Apostles, on consecrating first the bread, and then the wine: "THIS IS MY BODY WHICH WILL BE GIVEN FOR YOU; DO THIS AS A MEMORIAL OF ME," and: "THIS CUP IS THE NEW COVENANT IN MY BLOOD WHICH WILL BE POURED OUT FOR YOU" (Lk 22:19-20); and as Christ acted thus, and spoke of the Sacrifice which He was to offer from the Cross on the following day, He was making it possible for His Apostles and for their successors throughout all time - our priests - to do those same things and so to make present His Sacred Blood and Blood: to make present, in fact, the whole living Christ: Body, Blood, soul and divinity: the Divine Person Who can never die again.

As I grew in understanding, I realised that we have far more to celebrate than Christ's Presence; it is through the sacramental and Real Presence of this Eternal Victim and Priest that we, as Christ's Church, can offer a living sacrifice to the Father: a living memorial of the unrepeatable and unique sacrifice of Calvary. Whenever that Sacrifice is re-presented through the Mass - the Holy Eucharist - and is offered by the Church to God, through the actions of the priest, whose Priesthood is a sharing in the Priesthood of Christ, we know that Christ the Priest and Victim, here on our altar, offers His perfect praise to God our Father, with perfect thanks, reparation and petitions. Furthermore, when our own prayers are united to Christ's own prayer and are offered to the Father, they are thereby made glorious, worthy, powerful and effective, as one perfect Offering ascends from upon this earth to the Most Holy Trinity in Heaven.

It became plain that the offering of the Holy Sacrifice of the Mass is the supreme event in the Church's life; and it became plain that although the reception of Holy Communion, if we are in a state of grace, is very important, it is the culmination of the Act of perfect worship rather than the central act of the Liturgy.

The more I grew in understanding of the Mass, the more awed and grateful I became. I understood more clearly, week by week, how Christ's offering of Himself in this Holy Mystery, when He is Really Present in our midst, is the reason for our reverence and for our joy. Just as our pains can be united with His sufferings on Calvary, so all our hopes can be united with His prayers, here, when He Who is risen and triumphant makes His Eternal Offering to the Father. As we kneel before the altar, we can offer all Christ's Merits to the Father in this true Sacrifice of praise and thanksgiving. Furthermore, the privilege of being able to receive Christ's Body and Blood - Christ Himself, in Holy Communion - isn't solely a private joy, but is the means by which Christ purifies and adorns our souls and welds us all together as One Body, in one Faith; and our Communion of Love includes ourselves and the Saints of Heaven - the whole Church of Earth and Heaven - and also the Holy Souls still undergoing purification.

Praying with love and conviction.

Quite probably I could write a hundred pages on the Mass, and not exhaust my enthusiasm. Through the grace of Christ, and, despite my sins and fears and trials, I haven't been bored at Mass even once during my whole life; and this has nothing to do with any sort of goodness, or with powers of concentration. It's all because of faith - given by God, and treasured. Now that I know, by faith, that Christ our Incarnate God comes to our altar, albeit in a sacramental manner, I can't help praying fervently right until the Consecration, as a preparation for His arrival. I can't help giving Him a fervent welcome; and I can't fail to thank and praise him after the Offering of His Holy Sacrifice, and in Holy Communion; and since the best way of doing all these things is by praying every prayer of the Mass with as much love and conviction as I can muster, I've tried to do so at every celebration I've attended ever since my Reception.

Of course, God is so good that He rewards our every effort by making our faith even stronger and by increasing our delight in His Presence; and that's why I dare to say that if we're praying all the time, I believe it's impossible to be bored. It's not for me to question anyone else about whether or not they pray throughout the Mass or whether they've been well-taught about the Sacraments, however - unless I'm speaking to people in private. But I hope it's a question that school-teachers and priests will feel able to ask of the pupils in their care.

Sacramental Confession.

When I was establishing a regular routine of prayer, as a practising Catholic, I was occasionally perplexed by people who complained of boredom or of boring priests; but I tried to concentrate more on my own faults than on others' faults, encouraged by the frequent practice of 'Confession'. I learned a great deal. The visits to the 'box' were painful for me and humiliating, but were the basis of a solid spiritual training as well as a marvellous source of grace.

I fell victim to scruples within a short while, but that was a recurrent symptom of a spiritual ailment which Christ alone could cure. I was so lonely in the practices of my new faith, and was so lacking in confidence anyway at that age, and I was and am so proud, that I sometimes went through torment deciding if a small failing were a dreadful sin. So this isn't a criticism of a 'system' which can bring not only forgiveness but self-knowledge but is a revelation of my own weakness and immaturity, coupled with a longing to be truly 'impeccable' for God. My faith was firm, but was overlaid with strange ideas about holiness. I half-believed that it was by will-power that I'd eventually become 'good'; and I secretly felt that God wouldn't really approve of me until that time arrived.

My faith in God was by then sincere and true, in the sense that I believed wholeheartedly that He loved me, that He forgave my sins, and that He would 'give' me Heaven; but I didn't yet 'feel' it in my heart and mind. No matter how genuine and firm was my faith, as I prayed, my emotions, in prayer, were those of a child called to give an account of her poor behaviour. In that sense, I still felt that God was a mysterious Law-enforcer Who was ready to banish me or punish me, the very second that I tripped or misbehaved.

That was why I was genuinely grateful for the regulations concerning fasting, and for firm teaching about duty and love and prayer. It wasn't the fault of the Church that I had to eradicate the fears arising from various unfortunate influences; and it's foolishness to suppose that if the teaching Church were to abolish all firm laws and regulations, Catholics generally would construct rules for themselves. We need discipline, and firm guidance. It's surely essential that we have 'handholds' for the times when the practice of our faith is difficult. If too much discipline is swept away, people can 'drown'. I believe that we only have to look at some recent trends to admit that 'personal choice' about prayer and penance can easily become 'no choice.' As Saint Paul said to Saint Timothy: "KEEP AS YOUR PATTERN THE SOUND TEACHING YOU HAVE HEARD FROM ME" (2 Tm 1:13).

Regular sacramental confession was both a blessing and an education in spite of my shame at having to look clearly at my many faults. A regular, brief and frank admittance of my failings seemed not dissimilar to what was required in a doctor's surgery. Although it was pride that made me reluctant to expose my soul and my weaknesses to a priest, I believed that the experience was worthwhile if I could be 'diagnosed' and healed. The Church seemed like a nice mother, who knows how hard it is to reveal one's inmost heart, so I was grateful for the anonymity permitted to us all, and for the fact that I was free to choose a confessor.

The privacy was comforting; and when I'd chosen the priest in whom I would confide, I was safe in the knowledge that he heard me in secrecy, and would give his life rather than reveal what had been said. This Reconciliation was a sacrament, above all, to be sought and valued whatever the cost. I was sure that my feelings of embarrassment would disappear when I'd learnt the meaning of humility; and meanwhile I accepted the whole process out of a longing to please Christ.

The beginning of liberation.

In all sorts of unexpected ways the discipline of the Church made things easier than they had been before. I no longer bothered to examine my moods or emotions before turning to God in prayer. For the love of God, I learned to develop a new attitude, whether I was approaching prayer-time or was seizing opportunities to help people in practical ways. I tackled everything in a spirit of penance and hope, trying to act solely for the love of God, whether I were 'in the right mood' to do good or not. I was determined that by grace and by acts of the will I would co-operate with God's grace, whether in prayer or in everyday work.

Warm feelings in my heart were undoubtedly pleasant, but they couldn't be taken as a measure of my commitment to God. I believed that the only means I have of knowing how much I really love Him is an honest assessment of whether I'm determined to do His Will. I knew that if it were His Will that I worship Him, and that I serve my neighbour, then in doing these things, whatever my passing mood, I could be confident of pleasing Him in some small way, through my union with His Son, My Saviour.

This realisation was marvellously liberating. It didn't mean that I could permit myself to become hard-hearted or cold. What it did for me was to free me from the need to "take my spiritual temperature," as someone has said, and from the need to rely on the feelings of fervour which some Christians seem to want to cultivate in themselves through the use of overpowering sermons and hymns. Which of us, anyway, could maintain our emotions at such a pitch, hour by hour, every week?

Perhaps a little bit more of Christ's wisdom had crept through to me as, day after day, I looked after a small toddler, and nursed him in little sicknesses - whatever my own state of mind or health. This doesn't mean that I was brave; it means that I was learning the true meaning of love, which is to wish the best possible things for another, and to try to bring them about, whether one's 'feelings' were warm, cool, perplexed or hectic. Love 'lay' in the will - or, rather, in the true and sincere intention of the will to put love into action, if it were possible; and of course, the best love desires not just to promote someone's physical well-being but also to help bring about true spiritual fulfilment in Eternal Life, in God.

It was in moving from sleepy toddler - at his bedtime - to God in prayer, that I learned more about the true meaning of love. I saw that both love of child and love of God were only proved by willing, prompt and devoted service, or - if one were sick or feeble, for example - by a longing to serve: no matter what one felt like.

It seemed that this was what Catholics meant when they said to me, later, "It's the intention that counts." They meant that God sees our good-will, even if we're yawning in His service, just as He sees our ill-will, sometimes, when we appear to be devout and 'respectable'. So by this acceptance of the state of my real emotions - fervent or sluggish - I was truly freed, and was able to concentrate on the more important aspect of a deepening relationship with Christ: on developing a determined willingness to act lovingly in every circumstance, and to do this for my own Salvation, but to do it also - in some mysterious way - for the greater Glory of God.

Interior battles.

Through studying the constant teaching of the Church and the examples given in the lives of the Saints, especially of the married ones such as Saint Elizabeth of Hungary, I learned much more about Divine Love: the possession of which, after all, is the point of all our endeavours. I attempted to "PRAY CONSTANTLY" (1 Th 5:17) in one way or another, beginning each morning by making the 'Morning Offering' to God of everything I would do that day. I struggled not simply to obey God's commands but almost to anticipate His wishes by being alert to ways of being more loving and forgiving than ever before. It seemed like a betrayal of His loving-kindness ever to grumble or to complain, whether in my mind or in my speech. Even the weather was a good training, as I learned to delight in what He either permitted or sent as I set off to do the shopping or to fetch the washing from the clothes-line.

The needs of my neighbour, I found, weren't served merely by good deeds and smiles. I struggled not to argue unnecessarily about unimportant things, nor to condemn others for not agreeing with my views. Led on by God, I became ruthless about gossip: determined never to betray others or their weaknesses at any time. But more and more, I realised that one's interior battles would go on endlessly. As one bad habit was recognised and fought, another revealed itself. The whole point of all this, I told myself countless times, was to love others as Christ loves them. In these particular circumstances, with this particular person - what would He do? What is His Will?

This was a new way of life, in the sense that at last I was trying to live for love. All the childhood years spent in trying to be good, through fear, had left me trying to do good for imperfect motives. There had been a certain sense of justice in the code we'd followed, which had urged us to do good and to obey the rules, or to prepare for punishment. It had been applied in an 'Old Testament' way, however: common in our culture and in that era.

In case anyone should think I'm denying the Biblical truths about reward and punishment, mercy and justice, I must explain that I have believed, throughout my life, in Heaven and in Hell. The Church simply teaches what Christ revealed to His followers on earth, and I believe in all its teachings, still. But in those early years of struggle in the Faith, I learned not to permit myself to agonise any more about the details. I was duty-bound to live in hope; and since I couldn't say: "This seems too terrible to be true, therefore the Church must be wrong", when God had spoken frequently on the subject through His prophets and Apostles but above all through His own Son, I decided to discipline myself. I tried to refrain from anguished thoughts about the subject of the After-life and to develop an attitude of trust.

Christ Himself was my only hope; and I believed that He Who had said "COME TO ME, ALL YOU WHO LABOUR AND ARE OVER BURDENED" (Mt 11:28) could surely be trusted to keep me in His care and in His Love, if my deepest and most constant intention was to please Him and to do His Will.

Christ's dual nature.

That belief in Christ had more substance, now that I'd learned just Who He Is. Through the Catholic Church, I learned to rejoice, boldly, in Christ's Divinity as well as in His humanity. I was no longer confused, as in the days when my teachers had spoken hesitantly about his status, some seeing Him as God walking this earth, but others saying that He was a mere mortal who was, somehow, wonderfully close to God. Whether I meditated on the Gospels or read articles about the Hypostatic Union, all was clearer now, and more encouraging. My belief in Christ's Divinity meant that I saw Him as a safe, sure guide. My belief in His humanity led me to marvel at His humility. I was awed that the Word-made-flesh had suffered so appallingly, yet willingly, for our sakes. The Christ of the Gospels became less frightening to me, as I began to notice the tender words He'd used to sinful humans beings, as well as the awful warnings He'd issued to the self-righteous and the self-satisfied.

How kind and protective He'd been towards a woman "WHO HAD A BAD NAME IN THE TOWN" (Lk 7:37), as the distraught woman had wept all over His feet, when He was at a dinner with friends. And what great joy He'd brought to Zacchaeus by His declaration that He was coming to dine with him (Lk 19:1-10). I'd never noticed these little stories before, in childhood days, when I'd only seemed to hear Christ's warnings about millstones around necks (Lk 17:2), or Hell (Mt 10:28): always convinced that I was one of those whom He was warning.

139

[Heaven and Hell.

In His great kindness, Christ has been teaching me, in recent years, something of the meaning of both Heaven and Hell; and - strange as this might seem - I've been comforted, but not because the Christ of my prayer has contradicted the Christ Who teaches us through His Church, but because He, the One Christ, has explained the meaning of free choice. He has shown me just how fervently and powerfully He is drawing people towards Himself: towards joy. Yet He has shown me the fierce determination with which some people resist His call, turn their backs on His Will, despise the laws which He has devised for our happiness, and even try to draw other people towards sin and evil; and He has also shown me that since I believe that He, our God and Saviour, is the Source of all Eternal Good, I can also believe that people who refuse to have anything to do with Him and who persist even until death in a real rejection of Goodness, are freely moving away from joy: freely and determinedly choosing to live without those things which would have made them happy forever. They are freely rejecting the Vision of God, the Company of the Saints and the Angels, with Light, peace, order and beauty and every virtue; and we can be certain that whoever rejects the things of Heaven necessarily experiences Hell - even if none of us knows about Heaven or Hell in great detail.

But this knowledge has brought me hope, rather than gloom, since I believe that if I rely on Christ's Love, and remain determined to stay close to Him until I die, I shall never for a single moment be freely choosing to walk in another direction, away from Heaven, and happiness, and peace. In other words, I can boldly say, as I live in friendship with Christ, that just as He is now mine, as I live "in Communion" with Him, so Heaven is mine, now , "in" Him and in His friendship - so long as I persevere to the end.]

The 'Jesus Prayer'.

To return to the days when I'd just discovered a horde of Catholic Saints, and was delighted to study the lives and habits of people who loved Jesus, I discovered the "Jesus prayer", which seems to be better known amongst Christians of the Orthodox Churches than amongst Catholics. It's become more popular in recent years, but I'm overjoyed that I read about it in the years when it was little-known in England. The regular use of a simple phrase in frequent prayer was just the sort of devotion that suited my daily life as I cared for a small baby. It was so easy to pray, in the silence of my heart, a prayer based on one of Jesus' Gospel stories (Lk 18:9-14), as I said: "Lord Jesus Christ, Son of the Living God, have mercy on me, a sinner". I could pray these words whether I was leaning over the dirty dishes in the sink or striding out behind the pram; and since the words encapsulated both my faith in God and in His saving work, and my own need of help, I was able to recite it with fervour.

I prayed it from the heart, without trying to adjust my breathing in the way that numerous prayer-guides recommend. What is certain is that it brought Jesus' name and Jesus' own Self to me day by day throughout the years, until the day came, imperceptibly, when the Name was engraved in my heart and mind as an unceasing prayer. But having said all that, I know that my soul was nourished supremely by the Liturgy, and by Holy Communion.

The glorious cycle of feasts which was presented to us through the Holy Mass, between one

Advent and the next, brought before me the incidents of Jesus' life on earth, and the Mysteries of God. Easter was a glorious celebration of my true hope, and Christmas was a time of extraordinary thanksgiving. As in my Anglican days, it was the feast of the Most Holy Trinity which brought me to worship almost breathless with awe. Yet I was nearly overwhelmed with joy when I was able, publicly, to celebrate feasts which were 'new' to me, such as Our Blessed Lady's Immaculate Conception, and the feast of her Assumption into Heaven.

Praying with words and without.

From the moment of my Reception, I resolved not to swerve from my private and well-established spiritual routine. I made the "Morning Offering" fervently, downstairs, before anyone else awoke, praising God and thanking Him for everything good in my life, and repenting of any wrong I'd done. Name by name, I prayed for family and friends, whether they were well, sick, dying or departed, and committed everything and everyone to God's care. I did the same each evening, just as I'd done as an Anglican; and I prayed at other times, if I were free.

I soon found that, apart from the Breviary, books of other persons' prayers were of no use to me except as subjects for meditation. I could 'pray' old classics when I was tired or in pain, but, more and more, the words became impossible to say. All the beliefs expressed in them were acceptable to me; I could think about them for a long time, with joy; but to say them to God, in private, was to distract myself from Him. It was as though the words 'got in the way' of a true moment of communion. The vehicle of communication was distorting and so hindering a more secret and subtle communication which is the spirit-to-Spirit loving exchange between the soul and God. I knew that if I persisted in using words at times when it seemed as though God was urging me to pray without them, I'd be acting like a typist who wants to communicate with someone else in the same room, and who insists on tapping out her requests and who demands written answers, instead of using the swifter, plainer ways of exchanging ideas.

Through all my reading, I'd absorbed the traditional advice about meditation and prayer, by which we're urged to place ourselves in the presence of God and to think about His attributes, or else to read a story from the Gospels which will inspire us to make fervent resolutions which we can offer to God. All the reliable Catholic authors described how sensible it is to take up a book and meditate for a few minutes when you can't seem to pray any longer. But despite my best efforts, I found that I was quite incapable of plodding through such procedures. My free and whole-hearted act of turning my attention to God in order to please Him led my soul almost skipping - as it were - from one stage to the next, or rather, led me to telescope several stages into one single act of yearning-for-God which almost consumed me; and it was God, I know, Who was guiding me.

To the edge of a 'precipice'.

Within a few weeks of my Reception I was led to what seemed to be a 'precipice' in prayer - within my soul. I can remember the room where I prayed then, and the fear I felt. I was unsure of what was happening; I was in an extraordinary state of prayer which I experienced

141

as a 'being-held-in-God's-peace', although I was convinced at the same time that God was making a wordless request of me, there in the silence.

In the marrow of my bones, as we say, I knew that He was calling me. He was inviting me to meet Him; but the Way was stranger than I'd dreamed. It seemed as though He wanted me to abandon the security of thoughts and concepts and words; and yet I understood that this request only involved the present moment. I wasn't being asked to give up my daily prayers of intercession. I was being urged to trust in God in prayer: to surrender control to Him in prayer just as I tried, daily, to surrender my will to Him amidst earthly activities. He wanted me to make a free offering of my soul to Him, so that He could bring me close to him; but as He guided me in those first few weeks through the beginnings of contemplation, I felt more terror than gratitude.

On that first occasion of knowing that I was being drawn by Him, I was astonished. I remember kneeling alone, with not a sound in my mind or soul. I felt as if I were perched on a lip of rock over a vast precipice. As I knelt before God, my heart was half-seized with horror at the strangeness of meeting Him Who is Other. I couldn't cope with such naked prayer for very long; but I didn't give up. I tried to meet God in silence, in that extraordinary way, for a few minutes each afternoon.

Launched into 'Nothingness'.

As my courage grew, I learned how to turn my soul 'towards' Him, in spiritual darkness. I learned that He was teaching me about the spiritual life and about Himself, even though His teaching was soundless. Here below are a few of those first instructions: a few of the wordless yet detailed gifts which I was astonished to be receiving. You can see that I've 'translated' that advice into words, as Christ has recently suggested; and this is what He told me, in the Spring of 1968:-

> **Turn to Me in trusting prayer. Speak to Me when you wake, and before you go to sleep; but kneel and pray, at least once a day, in a quiet place, so that I can lead you into the immense depths of My Divine Life. (T:15 #1)**

> **Accept My invitation to you. I want you to enter into My very Being. Every person who prays receives that invitation, and only in humble prayer do you hear it clearly. (T:15 #2)**

> **Ponder what you experience in prayer. Until you prayed, you were quite ignorant of My true and mysterious grandeur and majesty. I, Your holy and invisible God, am calling you to wholehearted abandonment to My Will. (T:15 #3)**

> **Don't let fear keep you from 'plunging' within My Life, through prayer. (T:15 #4)**

142

Be prepared to lose your life through trusting in Me. (T:15 #5)

Turn your heart and attention towards the deep darkness within yourself. (T:15 #6)

Aim your soul's attention towards Me, your Lord, Who am hidden within your soul's darkness. Only in Me will you find perfect joy and fulfilment. (T:15 #7)

Pray with words or without, whatever seems best. But if you use words - like tools or building blocks - at particular times of sorrow, praise, thanksgiving or petition, try to give your heart to Me in silent prayer at some other time each day. (T:15 #8)

Leap over the 'precipice' within your soul. **You can know Me and please Me. Yet you must learn to live by faith, and to trust Me as I lead you into a strange new way of living. (T:15 #9)**

Launch yourself, within your soul, into 'Nothingness', in order to respond to My prompting, in prayer. (T:15 #10)

Abandon entirely, for periods of silent prayer, the security of thoughts, concepts and words. But keep your heart's intention or desire firmly 'aimed' towards Me, in your soul's darkness. "Aim" your heart by a simple, determined act of your unseeing but steadfast will. (T:15 #11)

Look upon words as useful but clumsy tools with which you frequently construct good prayers to Me, prayers in which you express your praise, thanks and sorrow-for-sin, and in which you plead for help for yourself and others. (T:15 #12) Continue to pray in your usual, faithful way. But if My Holy Spirit fills your heart, calling you to silent contemplation, leave behind all speech and speculation. (T:15 #13)

The prayer of silence.

Through the strength of that strange and wordless 'teaching', which seemed to have little resemblance to anything I'd read about in books, I clung to words, as if to tools or building-blocks, at particular times of praise or thanksgiving, and when pleading specifically for mercy or for help; but I gave myself to the new type of prayer once or twice every day, living entirely by faith, and longing to know God and to please Him. Each time I went to my room I remained for much of the time entirely without words, on my knees before God, as my heart was led from yearning to awe - and then to terror - as I began to encounter in an entirely spiritual way God's invisible and intangible but real holiness.

The "Our Father" was central to my life, as were the "Hail Mary", the "Divine praises" and the Nicence Creed; but it became quite impossible to say them at these moments. Whenever I went away to a room, alone, to adore God through Christ, asking that the love of the Holy Spirit would fill my heart, I found that words became impossible to pronounce. I was 'held' by God; and I discovered that I could very easily remain like that for ten or twenty minutes, in pure prayer, without a thought in my mind. Yet I didn't realise what a gift it was. I 'practised' it every day, almost taking it for granted, genuinely supposing that every Catholic prayed in this way. I was limited only by the pressure of work, or by discontent. I mean that the least selfishness on my part would leave me unable to 'settle' in prayer in the same way. Despite all that I'd learned from books, nothing had prepared me for the ease with which this "prayer of silence" took place within my soul. I had no name for it. It wasn't 'mysticism', I was sure. After all, I'd been so wicked; and I was a 'beginner' in prayer. But if ever I heard or read a complaint that prayer was boring, I was genuinely amazed.

How could anyone find God boring, I wondered, when we could be in contact with Him - obscurely - in this way? For as long as prayer lasted each day I felt not stirrings of human joy but an unfamiliar yet real peace within my heart. I was surprised to find that all fear evaporated, and that I was held at rest, nearly every day, in utter contentment.

That sense of peace only lasted for as long as I knelt in silence in my strange prayer of attention to God as apparent Nothingness. Whenever I stood up to go about my work again, my head became full of the usual flurry of thoughts and ideas and worries. It would be a life-time's work, I thought, to train myself to be calm and recollected; but I made a start. Asking for the grace of God, I disciplined my mind for His sake as rigorously as I'd disciplined my feelings and my heart. I knew by then, from experience, that God in fact woos our hearts. I knew, too, that lack of generosity on our part can't stop Him loving us, but that it can stop our 'contact' in prayer. In my naiveté I assumed that everyone who claimed that prayer was boring had been willing to make the sacrifices and commitments which I had made so far.

Choices postponed.

It became evident to me later on that many Catholics "coast along" much as I had done in my teenage, Anglican years. At first I regarded this with disbelief, thinking that surely Catholics had encountered fewer difficulties than I had. Besides coping with my own selfishness at one stage or another I'd had to 'cope' with doctrinal confusion. In time, however, I saw that everyone has to face the same choices at some point in life, from whatever point we start. Each one of us needs to ask: "Do I believe in God? Do I believe in Jesus Christ? If I do, shall I show my trust and humility by kneeling to pray to God? Shall I love and serve Him, trying to keep His commandments because I love Him, or shall I insist on my own will being done?"

Many Catholics postpone the choice, it seems, muddling along quietly, praying briefly now and again, half-hoping that Christ will make fewer demands on them than on their spiritual ancestors, and remaining fearful all the time and far from contented. But even this way of life was faith in practice, I saw. People might not seem to be passionately interested in God, but many are surely held in grace, faithful to the Sacraments, living lives far different from the lives of those who have turned and walked away. Anyway, I dared not judge, since God alone understands the trials or fears which plague different people. Only He knows the "SECRETS OF MANKIND" (Ro 2:16), just as He has always known my private thoughts and miseries.

[Posture and reverence in prayer.

Having just said that I daren't judge anyone, I feel bound to mention something about posture in prayer, and about a reverent attitude towards God, in order to encourage anyone who worries about being thought 'old-fashioned' because, for example, he or she still kneels to pray. I'm not discussing the problem of someone who is utterly determined to go against a reverent community spirit; this is mainly about private prayer, though also about informal prayer-groups and various bodies such as R.C.I.A. groups.

I've read of Bishops and priests who bewail the lack of reverence in prayer, in church, amongst some of the younger generation. Indeed, it saddens me when I see it, but I'm scarcely surprised, because I know that some of it has arisen from the attitude encouraged in the past two or three decades by some teachers and parents and by various persons in authority. The attitude which has been fostered is that which a young adult perhaps holds as he lolls on his bean-bag, reflecting that since God's Love for him is unending - which it is - and since it is infinitely great - which it is - then God doesn't mind whether the young man kneels upright to pray, or lies in an armchair with his feet up. What does his posture matter if he's making a sincere prayer from the heart?

Alert and attentive.

It was C. S. Lewis, I'm sure, who once told a story of someone who asked: could he smoke a pipe whilst saying his prayers? The 'correct' Christian answer was that if a man is smoking, it's a good thing if he prays as well, whereas if a man has decided to pray, it's not a good thing for him suddenly to light up a pipe. Likewise, perhaps, with what I must call the 'bean-bag' problem. Surely, if young students have been sitting comfortably in armchairs and on bean-bags whilst discussing the Church and prayer and God, it's a good thing that they decide to pray, and that they do so exactly where they are. But the reverse shouldn't be encouraged.

If people express a longing to pray, they should be steered, I believe, towards a chapel or an oratory, or should be encouraged - where the room is large enough - to kneel or perhaps to stand beside their arm-chairs, in order to be alert and attentive before God; and I write this not from some peevish longing to see people made uncomfortable in prayer, but to see people realise that God is awesome and majestic as well as loving. At the very least, an especial sort of courtesy is due to the Holy Trinity whenever we pray - although of course we can be sure that God delights in our merest whisper of sincere prayer from whatever situation we're in. It's important that we try to avoid the lukewarmness of soul which is described in the Book of Revelation.

It was two or three years ago that Our Lord confirmed by a vision - (in T:1922) - what I had always known by faith as a Catholic adult. He led me - in prayer - towards the invisible and Eternal Godhead; but what I saw before me, by the eyes of my soul, was a wall of fire: a vast sheet of flame which stretched high above us, and which also reached far below the edge of an Abyss which hid most of its Glory; and the point of this vision was, first, to give me Christ's consoling reminder that it is with Him, at the end of my life, and in His love, that I can hope to enter the Fire of Love which is the Godhead, and Heaven. But, secondly, Our Lord was teaching me that although the Godhead is truly Infinite Love, it is also Infinite holiness; and only those who have been thoroughly purified can hope to enter into the Father's heart in utter peace and gladness.

Entering pure Holiness.

Any imperfect creature who enters that pure Holiness necessarily experiences pain - hence the experience of purification known as Purgatory. Furthermore, Christ has shown me that this is as true of our prayer-time as of our meeting with God at the time of our death. Since God is Infinite holiness, and is therefore worthy of awe, adoration and self-sacrifice as well as love, delight and admiration and gratitude, we must surely pray to Him in as reverent a manner as possible; and if we do so we shall not only come to know Him, we shall allow Him to draw us even closer to Him and to make us His close friends. He can't do this, Christ has shown me, for people who are so lacking in love for Him that they don't think He's worthy of a little heart-felt praise and reverent devotion and who think that by lolling in a chair for times of worship they honour Him. I know from experience that God the Father is swifter to teach me, and also grants my prayers in more extravagant ways, if I've taken the trouble to kneel down before asking for His help or making special intercessions.

From what we're told by numerous observers, today, many people are ignorant about reverence in prayer, through no fault of their own. I wonder if they've been so lop-sidely instructed about God's great Love for them that they have heard very little about His transcendence. The need for Reconciliation for all who have turned their backs on God is sometimes barely mentioned; so perhaps it's not surprising that many people are unhappy at Mass, bored by prayer, and outwardly lacking in reverence. Perhaps they've never been taught that God is utterly mad with love for them and yet at the same time is so glorious and holy that He is Infinitely worthy of respect and honour as well as of child-like trust and confidence.

How surprising is it that a careless approach is commonplace towards the reception of Christ our God in the Eucharist, for example, if, for a whole generation, people have been encouraged to keep busy with good works for their neighbour, but have rarely been encouraged by teachers or persons in authority in matters which are even more important, such as how to show sincere and loving homage to God by acts of reverent worship and by penance and mortification.

By this, I mean bowing, kneeling and prostration, with a reverent use of the Sign of the Cross, and with the practice of self-denial, with some fasting, and with something else. Surely everyone should have an attitude towards Christ in the Blessed Sacrament at least as reverent as that recorded in the Scriptures about the attitude of devout persons who approached Christ and who knelt down.]

7 PURGATION

(1968-1980)

THE NIGHT OF FAITH. CHILDREN. FEMINISM.

Spiritual infancy.

Day by day, after my Reception, I continued with my efforts to love God and my neighbour. By the grace of God I did God's Will for no other reason than that it was His. There was nothing I wouldn't do for Him, I thought, even there in spiritual loneliness without any close human guide except for the priest whose homily I listened to once a week.

Stern lessons awaited me, however; I had no idea just how ignorant I was: nor how blind I was to my need for greater honesty, courage, humility, and faith. The faith I held was a pure, great gift: strong, but not strong enough. I'd been content to battle onwards each day, struggling to leave the future in God's hands; and this was a good way to live; but once we begin to see ourselves as brave or well-behaved, there arises the terrible danger of pride. In spiritual infancy, I didn't know that my faith was still very feeble; nor did I realise that temptations wouldn't cease, but would become progressively more subtle and dangerous.

The 'night' of faith.

For a little while longer I was busy but content. I didn't know the meaning of defeat or despair. But terrible times lay ahead; and it would be only by descending to the depths of pain that I would come to see the depths of my own self-love, and would be able to ask more sincerely for God's love and mercy, genuinely knowing my need of both.

Never in my life as a Catholic have I doubted God's goodness, or doubted the teachings of His Church - although not everything has been easy to understand. I've never doubted that God cares for me. Faith has told me so, even if my feelings have been in turmoil. But one day, some months after my reception, I realised that I'd became encased in spiritual darkness. Life "in" God was no longer effortless and joyful. It was time for the first of many purifications. God was at work within my soul, and - by His Will, in order to strengthen and test me - He withdrew all the secret sweetness and delight that I'd found in prayer, and hid Himself. I believed in Him with every fibre of my being. I wanted nothing but to do His Will. But, suddenly, prayer became a torment, a chore, and it seemed to me as though God were a thousand miles away.

A 'night' of faith had descended. I didn't know this at the time, because I'd only heard the phrase once or twice, and it wouldn't have occurred to me, anyway, to pin such a solemn title onto the day-by-day spiritual darkness which I was experiencing. It was a sense of loss which I knew had nothing to do with willing alienation from God through sin, but which was just as terrifying.

In the core of my being, I knew that it didn't matter what I felt, as long as I was making every effort to please God by doing His Will; and yet the darkness kept growing even deeper. Having felt at first that nothing I did ever pleased God, I next had the constant feeling that, whatever I did, I was damned. I didn't believe this, since faith was still active; but that's what I felt within my soul.

There was no reason for that fear. It was a temptation, I was sure; so I went on in pure faith alone, trying to be 'good'. I prayed every day at home at the usual times, sending 'arrow' prayers into the darkness: making acts of faith, hope and love, and dashing to Mass and Holy Communion weekly, which was all that I could manage, though I was desperate to receive Christ.

Domestic turmoil.

In the same year, a change occurred in my domestic world, where the care of infants overlaid every waking thought.

It seemed to me that some burdens laid upon me, and some things demanded of me by charity, were so difficult, so crushing, and so overwhelming in my ordinary life that only Christ's love in my heart made me do them, although I was hardly a picture of perfect joy and patience. I became immersed in a sea of activities which left me with barely enough time to clean my teeth, it seemed: still less, to kneel down in prayer for a reasonable length of time each day.

Our house was in turmoil at all hours from the day that an extremely sick relative came to our home, to be nursed. I did the best I could for about a year, by which time she seemed to have recovered. It was a year spent chasing around at top speed to keep up with the daily schedule. My first child was then a two-year-old toddler who had to be fitted very lovingly into a sick-bed routine. I had hours of cooking to do for patient and visitors, and a part to play in a still-hectic social life; but I was glad to have been able to cope.

Alas, my poor mother-in-law's illness returned after a few months away from us. She was at death's door, and extremely under-nourished, when I was asked to care for her again; and by that time I had a ten-week old new baby in my arms.

A mixture of pity, love and duty led me to agree. I remember that it was on Good Friday that I was asked to help out once more, and I dared not refuse. I'd just been to Mass, where our meditation was about how lonely Christ had been in His suffering. I was ashamed of wishing that I could avoid further work: ashamed of worrying about how I'd cope. Despite the fact that I was up at all hours nursing a second cherished child as well as the first, my longing to be kind and selfless urged me on.

Heavy burdens.

While I rushed from our patient to the new baby, with a toddler at my heels, and cooked huge meals and looked after visitors, my husband bore his own heavy burdens. He was "on call" day and night. Whenever we weren't out at official gatherings, he had to study for examinations, able to snatch only a few moments to comfort his mother in her ever-increasing pain.

After I'd coped for a few desperate days or weeks, we arranged that a nurse would help me; but even with her kindly assistance, I was working for sixteen hours a day at top speed, growing more and more puzzled that life was so unremittingly grim. I worked for seven days a week, all year round, and was tired. It never once occurred to me, however, that I deserved a few hours or days of "free time". No religious book within my reach had ever suggested such a thing, nor had my upbringing encouraged it. Besides, we had no extra helpers, no relatives or close friends nearby, and no spare cash.

Once or twice, I was able to dash 'down South' on the train, to see my parents. But day after day in my usual routine at home, whenever the babies were asleep, I knelt down in private, begging God to help me to go on. The work itself didn't make me resentful, rather, the fact that it was continuous, and that some health problems had returned, and that there was no end in sight. I couldn't even communicate very well with my mother-in-law, since she spoke hardly any English. By learning a few sentences of Chinese, I was able to ask about her symptoms or discuss her food; but she was in tremendous pain, and although she was very brave and stoical there was little jolly sick-room banter.

A further cause of discomfort was that, like many other families, we had little heating. I was warm in one room, but most of my work had to be done elsewhere; so I used to stand in the single-storey kitchen every day, clad in my usual clothes, but with jumpers added, and Wellington boots, all set to wash the sheets and nappies by hand. It was literally freezing in there. Then I juggled the babies' feeding times to ensure that we reached the shops each day to buy fresh food for our patient.

We were out in all weathers, the pram piled high with supplies, because of the concerned visitors who appeared every night and the dozen callers who shared our meals at weekends. Apart from doing the usual chores, I was cooking for about four hours a day. I still didn't drive, nor did I know of any play-groups for toddlers nearby. Even if I'd known, I wouldn't have had time to take my eldest child along. Every minute of almost every day was spent in hard physical work of one sort of another, and I was nearly always tired and in pain, and - except for the summer-time - cold. The latest news on the medical front was that I had a spine problem for which the only remedy was regular exercise.

Little crucifixions.

I'm aware that most of the human race has probably lived and died in far worse conditions than anything I've ever known; and I'm saying this because the difficult things I've mentioned aren't so much reasons for self-pity, although I'm not guiltless, but rather are markers on the journey I've made: markers for the story that Christ wants me to tell. He doesn't want me to refuse His request because I've never been captured in a war or spent years in prison. He wants me to say just a little about what I did find painful in what I know are privileged circumstances; and He wants me to do this in order to bring hope not just to those who suffer in extraordinary ways, but to those who suffer from the little crucifixions of daily life, whether from secret crosses which only Christ can see, or from the burden of monotony, exhaustion or loneliness - or from the knowledge of one's own frailty. That's why I'm not ashamed to continue with my reminiscences. I hope and pray that someone will learn from my mistakes: or, even better, will be encouraged to turn to the Saviour whose friendship is worth every sacrifice, and whose tenderness is incomparable.

Christ wants me to say, through these pages: "Never turn away from Him. Never cease to believe that He helps you whenever you call. No matter what you're enduring, He can help you in the darkness. Have faith. Persevere."

Eagerness to please.

What battles I fought with myself. Self-pity was barely held at bay, during those busy years when I was hardly aware of what was happening outside my own front door. I enjoyed an occasional cup of coffee in another kitchen. Our neighbours were kind: and were almost as busy as ourselves. We grew very fond of them; but there was no time to develop many long-lasting friendships.

I found that the more I did, for love, and the more effectively I did everything, then the more I transformed myself into an ever-willing work-horse; yet I couldn't overcome my eagerness to please. As I cooked huge meals, carried trays up and downstairs with a baby under one arm - the first at my heels - and changed sheets, I steeled my will and fed on Christ for survival. I gulped Sacraments at Mass once a week. I couldn't have put a name to a single face at the Catholic Church during those first two years. I went there each Sunday for an hour's fervent prayer, as my husband looked after the family; then I dashed home to get on with my work.

Any outings in the evening were with my husband's professional colleagues, or involved meeting people once - then only seeing them annually at the same type of event. One kind woman invited me to her sewing classes, but it was impossible to attend regularly; I was amazed to meet someone who had so many hours of leisure each day that she found time to pursue several hobbies, when I myself had no time to paint, of course, and battled with myself about the meaning of 'Art'. It seemed obvious to me that people mattered more than 'things', however precious. A needy person in my home was more deserving of attention than a canvas and easel. It pained me, however, to be unable to use this talent. Being deprived of time in which to sketch and paint was as painful for me as if, for example, I'd been told that I could never again open my mouth to sing.

It was to please Christ as well as the family that I made sure I always sounded happy and cheerful, but it was becoming a struggle. I was on my knees before God two or three times a day in prayer - however briefly - to pay the homage He deserved, and to beg for the grace to keep going: utterly determined to do my duty and to put family care before what is sometimes called 'self-fulfilment'.

Occasionally, I found myself longing to be able to study, and to have more stimulating topics

150

of conversation than the childrens' new words or the price of beef. Later - and after the birth of our third child, our daughter - I was made more dissatisfied through reading feminist tracts in magazines; and I made enquiries about teacher-education courses and Art Degree possibilities. As I shall tell, another sick relative then came to stay, so I did what I believed to be right. I accepted my domestic commitments, and made efforts to look upon my day, with its apparent trivia, as Christ would look upon it: with gladness.

[Repetitive work.

Quite obviously, some women who would like to stay at home are forced out to work, to put food into little stomachs, and therefore can't look after their own children all day. Other women go to work joyfully because they know their children are being looked after by loving friends or relations. But I know that some ambitious women look upon children as a nuisance, and would be horrified at the prospect of caring for their own children full-time; and so, as I look back, I'm glad about the choice I made.

It was a privilege to be able to stay in the home with children and other relatives, teaching and cooking daily. Those tasks, with all the washing and cleaning, were sometimes tedious and tiring and repetitive. But faith told me that lasting joy stems from our doing the Will of God for the love of God, whatever sort of task He wants us to do; and I believe it's generally better for children if they can be close to a loving parent - in the early years, especially, but also through the 'teenage' years.

It's true that God delights in seeing us develop our talents, if circumstances permit; yet we ought to look very carefully at our true motives if ever we hope to leave our mundane duties for the chance of finding something outwardly more exciting; and, as I was to learn, nothing is mundane if it's done in union with Christ, in order to please Him and to help souls.]

Common-sense changes.

When I'd adapted my prayer-routine to my rearranged domestic pattern, I saw that the changes which were taking place in my little kitchen at that time reflected the changes which were taking place in the whole of my life.

The shelves had become so cluttered with new food-stuffs, as I regularly cooked special food for my mother-in-law and for our other relations that there wasn't enough space for the items I'd once used daily, but now rarely needed. A rearrangement of my kitchen was essential. It was only common-sense to stock up with ingredients which were genuinely useful, whether I liked them or not, and to discard the items which I could use only rarely in my new way of life. Likewise, in the spiritual life, it made sense to cling to a prayer-routine which could flourish amidst all sorts of duties and distractions, and to discard whatever devotions were attractive but which were time-consuming, or - by their fulfilment - selfish.

Through the hard thinking which made me focus on what was essential in the spiritual life, and what was peripheral, I saw that morning and night prayers were very important. Going to

Mass was essential - even if it could only be once a week. Regular Confession was important, and helpful: such a wonderful source of grace. Praying the Rosary was important, too, but not as something which shackled me to a grim routine, but as the free offering of a decade of sincere prayers, here and there, whenever I had a rare few moments alone with neither toddler nor patient to attend to.

As for the Breviary, the same commonsense rule applied. I wasn't bound to it by a vow; so I read two or three of the 'hours' each day, in that time of my life, and offered to God as a sacrifice my constant busyness with the washing and feeding of weak bodies rather than with the prayer-times for which my heart yearned.

Chores and agitations.

Alas, I can't describe how tired I was in the most difficult days of being nurse and mother; and despite my real longing to please God and to help others, I was tempted to feel sorry for myself, and so I felt not only exhausted but selfish and guilty. Natural timidity kept me silent; but as my work-load increased I became more scrupulous and afraid. I endured each day's frantic activities and never-ending physical load in complete spiritual darkness. Outwardly, I was busy, friendly, and talkative, but my prayer-times were passed without a sliver of 'light'.

Later, illness would drag me down, but for the moment I didn't complain. All that I'd read had led me to believe that God is to be loved and served for His own sake, not for 'consolations' or for sweet experiences, so I went doggedly on, always exhausted and still without joy in prayer. I can see now that although I genuinely acted from charity, at the same time I was too proud to admit defeat, and too cowardly to decline the extra tasks proposed to me; and I suppose that if I'd been more confident I would have asked friends or relatives for more help. It astonishes me to realise, now, that from the time of the birth of our first child, I didn't have a day off, entirely by myself, for several years.

We went on holiday with the children occasionally. As many mothers know, a holiday with two or three babies or toddlers in a cold, cramped chalet, near a rain-sodden beach, provides a change of scenery, for which to be grateful; but all the usual chores and agitations take place in unfamiliar and difficult surroundings. It was a rush for me to get away, then a rush to go back home to relieve the kind relative who had coped with Grandma for a few days.

Another patient.

We were all very sad when she died. She had been the focus of our attention for a long time, and we loved her dearly. But we were glad her suffering had ended; and we began a new way of life.

There was a respite for me of about three or four months, in which my husband's job promotion took us to another town. We rented a house at Luton at first; then we managed to buy a home of our own in Harpenden, within reach of my own parents and my brother and sister. It was less than a mile from a Catholic Church, which was dedicated to Our Lady of Lourdes. But I seemed to be leading a roller-coaster of a life, in my late twenties. Joy and a sense of adventure swept me along after each new difficulty, but my optimism was dented every few months. I'd hoped to make plans for our family life, having all sorts of outings and projects in mind. Then I heard that another relative was severely disabled and needed to come to stay. Once again the daily routine became hectic as I cooked for the enlarged family - and for the devoted visitors who flocked along again.

My father-in-law was a cheerful, grateful soul; and I was determined to make him comfortable. I struggled up and down stairs umpteen times a day, completely drained of energy, with two toddlers to look after and hordes to entertain throughout evenings and weekends. I remember looking at my neighbours in the summer-time, amazed that people with young children could spend leisurely hours in their back gardens or go to evening classes. There were many joys in my life, but at the same time it was full of suffering. Dashing round my home, I thought hard thoughts about duty and obedience; but I believed - and still believe with every particle of my soul - that God's Will is to be loved and obeyed, through whatever apparent chaos it might lead us.

After six months of our care, and after intensive physiotherapy, our patient went home. Then, when I'd enjoyed my third pregnancy and had a baby daughter he suddenly came back again, having suffered another stroke. The children were six years, and four years, and nine months old, and I was almost submerged in chores and conversations and 'broken' nights.

For a very brief interval after his second departure, I relished the new freedom to go out and about with the children, and greatly enjoyed my family and friends. Then, suddenly, the strange illness of my own returned. Life seemed full of disastrous surprises. I wasn't merely tired. My legs were weak and I found it difficult to stand for long, whether standing were required in the kitchen or out at parties. Worse, every scrap of energy was used for doing the bare essentials. Having made strenuous efforts to do a bit of serious study, by learning some Hebrew at evening classes in term-time when the children were small, I was weaker now, and our social life took precedence.

Ambitions postponed.

We needed baby-sitters for so many official engagements that, even if I'd had the energy, I couldn't have found more sitters if I'd had regular engagements of my own. Apart from Sunday Mass, it was impossible to commit myself to regular meetings of any sort, whether to classes, prayer-groups or committees. This is not a complaint, however, but a plain description of the way things were. I was happy to be a housewife, and I accepted that few mothers have opportunities to go out and about. It's true that the long years spent with young children can make some of us impatient; but I was willing to accept that until the children were older I should base my life more on love than on efficiency: although both are good.

Even if I'd been constantly full of energy, I think I'd have recognised that anything which demanded a commitment to other people would have to be postponed for a few years. I could rush in and out of an evening class, or even not attend if the children were ill, whereas any serious and long-term commitment to our church's social or pastoral life would take up far more time. One task would lead to another, as proved to be the case later on, and there'd be a danger that my obvious duties which deserved first place would be carelessly brushed aside. For example I'd already found that everything had to be 'dropped' if a relative was unwell. It seemed unwise to keep dashing out at bath-time and bed time when life was so unsettled, so I decided that pleasurable meetings or discussion groups on prayer would have to wait until life were more 'settled'.

Besides these considerations, there were physical limits. My tedious and wretched illness persisted. I'd had remissions, but none very recently; and when our baby daughter was only three, it was difficult for me even to sit upright to read to the children at bedtime, or to host dinner parties while they slept. I simply ached to lie down and rest; and if I did, I ached still. Meanwhile, the work had to be done, or the children would have been unwashed and unfed.

After a particularly long spell of illness, and after a three-week wait for a bed, I was admitted to hospital for tests. I entered, grateful for my mother's help, because she'd now retired, and had offered to look after the children. But by the time I was examined my symptoms had disappeared. The tests were negative; I was sent home, but eventually the weakness came back again.

It would have been helpful to have had a diagnosis; yet I can see that what I needed - well or ill - was an occasional day of peace and quiet and rest, in order to think and pray, and to quieten my rushing thoughts. But for various reasons this was far too difficult to organise. I continued to look after children and visitors without question, astounded that life should be so hard, but determined to plod on, trying to serve God and my neighbour.

Illness again, and work.

About seven years after my Reception into the Church all sweetness or 'consolation' was like a distant dream. Even with all my faults, I was as fervent and as faithful as on the day I'd been received; but even the memory of the joy which I'd once experienced in prayer had gone. I shouldered each day's workload determined not to fail in love, but I'd never really understood Christ's command that we love our neighbour as ourself. I should have been bolder about making a few sensible arrangements in order to rest a bit more during each new episode of weakness. But I lacked confidence. All the shyness and self-blame of childhood was with me still, and held me back. I was so anxious to appear perfect that I rarely mentioned my own needs, and rarely refused even unreasonable requests. Besides: I'd been told that there was nothing major 'wrong' with me, so I dared not appear to be pampering myself; and since conscience demanded that I expend energy on essential tasks there was little strength left for hobbies or for other personal interests.

In my early 'thirties', by elaborate planning, I managed to attend two evening courses: one class each week in term-time, for two years. In two hours of leisure-time snatched from the chores, I studied Art, and also the Classical Hebrew I mentioned. I was thrilled by everything I learned. I even began to paint once again, late at night; and somehow to read about Christ and the Church - between the cooker and the bath. However, these efforts left me even more exhausted.

Each day was busy, and each evening was becoming busier still, as I cooked meals for ten or twenty visitors, or for fifty now and then. Besides all this, there were other trials. Daily work and prayer-work were pursued in darkness, over-shadowed by my fear of the God of my imagination: the hard task-master of my childhood days. He was still unapproachable, fearsome and vengeful, I felt. Faith told me that God loved me, but I didn't know what that meant. It seemed as though He was hidden behind an infinitely-high wall.

Christ, in the Blessed Sacrament.

As I look at what I've just written, I feel impelled to add that it was the whole Mystery of the Godhead which seemed unapproachable and impenetrable. It was God the Father, Whom we sometimes address in liturgical prayer as 'Almighty God', Who seemed to me to be more Critic than Friend, or rather, more Absence than 'ground of my being.' I didn't stop believing in His goodness; but I had neither a mind full of wonder at His gifts nor a heart full of warmth at the thought of His love. It was as though a blanket had been thrown over me to keep me in darkness - perhaps as a cover is laid over certain plants by a gardener, to assist growth and to give protection from various dangers; but whatever was happening, it hadn't the 'feel' of something caring, but of something isolating and painful. I had one never-failing cause for wonder, however, in that darkness, by which I mean the Real Presence of Christ in the Blessed Sacrament, in church.

God the Father seemed remote, as I said. I didn't know much about the Holy Spirit, although I believed that He was alive and active in my soul to some degree, since it was He, surely, Who was urging me to avoid sin and pursue virtue. But I knew that God the Son, My Incarnate Saviour, was sacramentally Present in the tabernacle - and of course in the Sacred Host which I received in Holy Communion; and He was my life-line: most truly my Way, as Holy Scripture says. Brief visits to Christ, whenever I popped into church during a shopping trip, never failed to help me. I didn't have any sweet feelings as I knelt before the sanctuary; but I believed so strongly in Christ's Presence that I made acts of faith in Him and asked for His help, and so of course I was silently rewarded: not because I'd 'earned' a reward but because He never fails to reward even our feeblest efforts to be faithful; and that reward seemed to consist of a stronger determination to persevere on the Way to Heaven.

Quite a few people I've met recently have told me how much they've been helped by having a spiritual director. Every book on prayer suggests that it's sensible to have a personal guide; but I was living in a busy home, not a monastery, and had no leisure-time to search for someone 'special' to take an interest in me. The parish priest, I knew, led the Church in our town. Canon Terence Keenan was a warm-hearted and faithful pastor who had visited me in hospital, and always enquired about the family; and he was my regular Confessor. I was sure that I'd ask his advice if I had a particular problem; but I knew that he'd have no marvellous new answer if I posed this question: "How do I love God and my neighbour when I'm ill and in pain?" I thought I knew the answer, which consisted of following Christ's example. I just wanted to survive and to keep going without complaints or self-pity.

There were three other questions I never asked of God - or of His representatives: "Where is God? Why should we suffer? Why should this trial happen to me?" The commitment which I'd made to God several years before precluded such questions. Since faith told me that God is good, it would have seemed like sheer impertinence to question anything that He permitted. But it was a terrible struggle just to keep putting one foot in front of the other.

In spiritual darkness.

In the darkness of the night of faith, I cherished my family, ran a busy household and supported other people in their trials. The strange illness persisted. I grew weaker still, yet tried to be 'good'. Cultivating patience, I battled to be kind and forgiving, praying and reading every day to nurture my faith. I don't mean that I was good; far from it: but only that my whole longing was to please God and therefore to be kind - despite my many failures. So of course I dashed to the Sacraments, and helped my neighbours, worked for 'Charities' and visited the sick. I tried to be a "good" wife and mother. I hoped to make everything seem jolly or peaceful on a surface level, though I didn't always succeed. I experienced much of each year, on another level, as a lonely journey through private torment; but I'm immensely grateful that, with hand on heart, I can echo other Christians who say that "Jesus saved me": and in more than one sense. He certainly saved me from despair.

More than anything else, it was the truths which Christ had given to me through His Church and through faith which kept me going. Never for a second did I doubt the existence of God or the teachings of the Church, even though it can be hard to remain faithful. And if ever temptations insinuated themselves into the forefront of my mind I'd always make a firm act of faith and then press on with my work.

I'm writing this principally to help those who are tempted to argue with the tempter. We're right to explore the reasons for our faith, I know, and to examine our teachings in detail. But there are some sorts of fruitless enquiry which are better ignored than pursued. The phrase is surely right which says that 'he who would sup with the devil should use a long spoon' - whatever recipe the evil one has cooked up especially to suit our palate in difficult times.

A useful framework.

My own children saved me, in another sense. I mean that although it's impossible for anyone to have much rest when little children need attention I was grateful for the framework which a conscientious mother must keep firmly in place if she hopes to build a happy home. It kept me active and anchored. With a day that was founded on chores, conversations and school-visits, I had a basic routine which was flexible enough to allow for crises and yet was firm enough to 'lean' on when I was almost too tired to think. I managed to keep going.

Perhaps it's wise to mention, here, that the underlying reason for my intermittent episodes of weakness was that I have a mild form of Multiple Sclerosis. I suspected as much, at the time; but the clinical tests were negative in the early years; and I was so devastated at being judged as inadequate rather than unwell when I'd made huge efforts to be sociable and active that I was eventually frightened to go near a hospital. Only after a very lengthy bout of weakness, and an M.R.I. scan, in the nineteen-eighties, did I learn that, besides the other problems, I'd had 'M.S.', undiagnosed, for twenty-five years.

I still feel mildly ashamed of mentioning this, so strong is the influence of earlier days when we were told that to display one's feelings or one's soul to other people was unnecessary, and to speak about one's health was not only unnecessary but vulgar. As someone before me must have pointed out, the world wouldn't even have heard the Christian message if Christ's friends hadn't been 'vulgar' enough to describe their own weaknesses and setbacks and also to say what they'd seen and believed: and how they'd felt when they heard the Good News that "ALL WHO BELIEVE IN JESUS WILL HAVE THEIR SINS FORGIVEN THROUGH HIS NAME" (Ac 10:43).

Little children.

It's been part of this task to mention that the early years of motherhood were physically gruelling; but I never ceased to delight in the children as persons, even when I was temporarily irritated or impatient. There was tremendous joy in being with them, holding conversations, teaching, teasing, having expeditions, going to paddle in the River Lea in summer - or showing them how to play chess. I made a picture-board with chess pieces on it, and with arrows which indicated the various possible moves.

By turns, the children cheered, puzzled, annoyed or delighted me. It was hard to keep the peace, with three. I wasn't always patient; yet there have been great joys in being a mother. The children were and are so loveable. I'm overwhelmed even now, to think that apart from the brief times when we tip-toed amongst the heartaches of their adolescent lives, the children have been a constant source of happiness. They have brought us nothing but delight and gentle companionship since they reached adulthood.

There was never a moment when I didn't love them, although I was very strict with them about important things such as honesty, sharing and caring, and keeping one's promises. They were affectionate and funny, as they are today. Despite the squabbles and disagreements they were extremely kind.

For my part, I tried to be kind, reasonable and trustworthy. I didn't always succeed; but I never ceased to be grateful for their lives and for their different personalities and gifts. I praised and rewarded them for every evident effort to be good, and answered every question truthfully on every subject. When they were small, and still willing, therefore, to listen to a parent, I taught them informally and according to each one's capacity, about the existence of God and Heaven, and about the Catholic Church.

Outings and adventures.

In those early years, when I had enough energy to do more than just encourage the children in their activities, we moved contentedly from work to play and then to work again, chatting and explaining throughout the household tasks. We were rarely bored; we did the chores together, made castles out of cardboard, chanted nursery rhymes, and explored the garden for flower specimens, and watched the insects, too. From the garden I gathered the privet leaves on which I fed the stick-insects which we kept for three years.

The garden always needed attention; but when the weather was good, we weeded the borders together, and then fed the fantail pigeons which were our legacy from the previous owners of the house. We sometimes excavated flowerbeds to make exciting roadways for the boys' toy cars; and there was a small plastic paddling pool permanently in the garden, for use on hot days. I could drive, at last, and took the children to catch 'tiddlers' in a shallow river nearby.

We had outings to the zoo, and to the Natural History Museum, sometimes accompanied by several friends; and I continued to take my three little ones to visit Christ in the Blessed Sacrament, whenever I had the energy and they were willing.

I tried to ration the amount of television the children watched, not to frustrate them, but to entice them towards other things. We made papier-mâché puppets to use at parties, and we painted together - using vivid colours and large brushes. I made models of the fairy stories which they knew by heart and taught them how to make models of their own. We decorated a tree and a Crib, at home every Christmas. My attempts to wait until Advent were defeated because the children came home from school in mid-December, thrilled by the parties and decorations they'd already enjoyed, and wanting to decorate our home immediately. I gave in, because it seemed unkind not to continue the celebration of Christmas which the school had fostered.

We had another tradition which had begun in babyhood. It was to last for many years. It was very simple - but almost sacred. I read each child a story, in bed at night. It was a way of loving them, entertaining yet calming them, and it brought us very close no matter how busy each day had been. When I grew ill and even busier - with Grandpa - and as they all grew older, the custom had to end. However, it had been valuable: as precious as all the things we'd done together, whether making preparations for a birthday party, or talking about life and God whilst the children sat in bubbly water in the bath. I can hardly bear to think about the mistakes I made in their upbringing - or about my bad example - but I think they knew that they were loved.

An awesome responsibility.

What an awesome responsibility God entrusts to us, in parenthood. My husband and I had been well-taught by our parents about the precious gift of children. We cherished each one even before birth, awed at being allowed to create new life: longing to see each child as the time came for delivery. Their extreme helplessness caused me to love and care for them as well as I knew how; but the gradual revelation of their longing for love and their thirst for knowledge, as they developed year by year, made me as concerned for their souls as for their little bodies.

As soon as they were old enough to be sitting up, in a safe place outside, in the back garden, in summer, they marvelled even before they could walk at nature's variety and colour and change. I taught them all I knew about its Creator, and about Jesus on earth. I used simple words and analogies to explain what God wants of us; so they learned kindness, and reverence for all the good things that He's created, but especially consideration for other human beings. They came to see that in our inmost hearts, it's easy to idolise self. By living in a real community - of family - they became aware of the needs of other people.

Life-long marriage.

We were never surprised by the childrens' natural curiosity about their own lives, and about birth and death, and society, and family life. I tried to answer their questions as they arose, with honesty, but in language which was appropriate for their age and understanding. It was wonderful to be able to state a number of other things too, with great conviction: things to do with faith or courtesy; but when I didn't know the answers, I told them so, and explained that they should be patient with me because I'd never been a mother before - and was learning 'as I went along.' But they were reassured by firm statements about important things.

When the whole family was in the car one day, returning home from a trip to London, perhaps, the children happened to be discussing other parents; and one of the boys said: 'Mummy, would you ever divorce Daddy?" My firm "No, of course not!" - was echoed by an equally firm declaration from my husband about the importance of life-long loyalty, and keeping our vows; and that little exchange perhaps gave the children some security, amidst the normal ups and downs of family life and amidst the chaos of a society where so many spouses are abandoned.

There's so much that's easy about child-care, if we're willing to be loving, and willing to make sacrifices; and yet there are such enormous risks taken with little hearts, minds and bodies that it seems astonishing to me that God can allow us all to look after children, and even to let us make mistakes. That's how much He trusts us; and I tried in my turn to trust my own children at one stage after another - letting them make decisions, even letting them make a few mistakes or be hurt, as they stepped out, moved forward, observed, and drew conclusions: perhaps different from mine.

By the love which God put into my heart for these children, He enabled me not only to care for them, but also to keep on praying that He'd bring them entirely to the knowledge of His Love. I was even keener for them to become holy than for them to be physically well; yet I was well aware of my own weaknesses; and so I prayed fervently that He would veil my bad example. How can a mother try to shield her children from every harm, yet allow them to be damaged by her own failures? I believe that God answered me by putting such love into their hearts that they've forgiven if not forgotten whatever faults of mine might have grieved them.

A sense of isolation.

During the busiest of those years, we had loads of friends living nearby, and more than a dozen children in the same road. There was little traffic at any time of the year; and I used to find myself preparing 'tea' each day for twelve friends - or none. The children were safe and happy in any of the houses in the street. It was a real community, and we were grateful for all the loving friendships and simple gatherings: full of joy, as we shared the small dreams of everyday life, and passed around warmth and sympathy as well as chicken pox or 'flu'.

All of this was thrilling when I was well; but I was weak and in pain for weeks or months at a time, and couldn't walk a long way. It was a relief to have no proof of serious illness - yet I felt humiliated by my constant weakness. It hadn't depressed me - so far. I loved the life we led; but I found myself, in my early thirties, reduced to walks of a few hundred yards. Although the children were lively and adventurous, and we were full of plans and ideas, I hadn't the strength to stand up for long, and grew impatient. I still cooked large meals, and welcomed family and friends, twenty or thirty at a time, yet all that I'd done so easily with youthful energy now demanded extraordinary stamina; and I was far from old.

Term-time was bearable, since I could rest, but the long school holidays eventually brought me low; and physical exhaustion was accompanied by a sort of heartache since, even with all the conversation and companionship of that place and era, I was still lonely, and felt isolated even amidst good friends. I treasured the warmth and kindness of our neighbours: but although I had shared meals, conversations and parties, I'd been unable to share my faith.

Throughout my first ten years of Catholic life, there had been little human encouragement: few Catholic friends. It was due to circumstance, despite my weekly attendance at the local Catholic Church. Since we weren't formally involved in Catholic education, although I taught the children what I could, I met no Catholic parents or teachers day by day; so I wasn't fully involved in the Catholic Community. I had no opportunities for retreats, pilgrimages, or special celebrations - and few conversations about the Church, or the Council; and although I knew that this situation was far from ideal, I believed that it had to be regarded simply as a further trial. Faith told me that God is at work in every circumstance, even where there's limited access to all the good things available in a lively Church community.

Dangers avoided.

It might be worth suggesting, however, that by God's Providential care, I was isolated not only from the good Catholic company which might have consoled me but also from some of the faithless and disobedient urgings which were so prevalent in the nineteen-seventies and eighties.

It had already been made harder for me to cling firmly to the constant teachings of the Church as I'd seen those sure teachings scorned by well-known Catholic writers. I'd found that faithful Catholic teachers - the Holy Father amongst them - were routinely being dismissed as old-fashioned, authoritarian, patriarchal - or plain savage - for having restated what were the plain truths of the Catholic Faith: beliefs which were deemed unnecessarily difficult for modern enlightened men and women and plainly irrelevant to modern Catholic life.

I was spared the talks by extreme feminist teachers - whether Sisters or others - who spoke with exasperated pity of people who still practised "Pre-conciliar" devotions and clung to "Pre-conciliar" doctrine: as though the great Fathers of the Church, with the Ecumenical Councils before 'Vatican Two', with all of the Saints who had preached about Heaven and Hell and repentance and forgiveness rather than, primarily, about self-esteem and self-fulfilment, were so remote and "Pre-conciliar" as to be of little use to Catholics at the end of the twentieth century.

It seemed to be as though, until my faith grew stronger, God kept me safe from the sort of influences which would have left me confused. If I'd been more exposed to dissenting voices I might have wondered if I needed to know all about the different 'levels' of consent which can be given to different sorts of statements made by the Magisterium, before I could decide whether or not to try to obey the Church on plain moral issues. I might have been urged, as many are urged today, to look upon an encyclical such as 'Humanae Vitae' - which was greeted with shocked surprise in 1968 - as if it were the personal and erratic opinion of a foolish old man, instead of the authoritative teaching of the Church on married love: teaching which, at its heart, echoed and clarified much of what I'd read in Pope Pius XI's "Casti Connubii" when I was exploring aspects of the Faith in the nineteen-sixties.

The Church's constant teaching.

Perhaps I'd come to believe that I can't be an active and faithful Catholic unless I'm busy with a Ministry, or on the Parish Council; and it's not good-hearted service which I'm questioning here, but only the frantic 'activism' that's evident wherever people won't accept that God can call us to fulfil His Will in quiet, hidden and prayerful ways. I might have come to believe that we're incapable of sharing the Faith with friends and neighbours unless we have a degree. I might have thought the following of Christ to be a complicated business, when, in truth, the Faith handed on since the time of the Apostles is, in its essence, simple enough for any willing child to understand: any child, or any child-like adult, who wants to know: "What is the Church's constant teaching on this subject, or the Holy Father's teaching on this new problem; and how can I please Christ best? What is my plain duty towards God and my neighbour?" And a true 'child' of God relies on Christ's grace to obey those teachings and to fulfil that duty, rather than to search for reasons to bewail the plain truth and even to persuade others to join in the protest which is peculiarly labelled "loyal dissent."

Dogma and discipline.

There were so many facets of Catholic life and teaching being held up for criticism, or even for ridicule, that I count myself fortunate that through regular prayer and the reading of good books, I was strengthened in my resolve to ask the best possible questions about every matter which was being discussed in the Catholic press and was supposedly a matter of 'dispute' and 'controversy'. I learned to ask: "What is the constant teaching of the Church in this matter? What are the Holy Father and the Bishops recommending to us? What has been the constant practice and witness of the Saints?" I was well aware of the difference between the authoritative moral teachings of the Church - which cannot be changed - and what we call the 'discipline' of the Church, which can in theory be changed even if it seems not to be the Will of God in a particular era that change occur; so I would never have aligned myself with someone who would elevate custom to dogma; nor had I any yearning for a mythical 'golden age' of Catholicism.

My only yearning was to be a faithful, twentieth-century Catholic, obedient in what was important, and thoughtful and generous-hearted about very minor matters which were not unreasonably the subject of discussion within the Church.

What acres of dismissive newsprint have been put before us, however, on those matters of faith and morals which have long-ago been recognised, defined and taught, and which so badly need defending, today. What scorn has been poured upon matters plainly understood and explained through both Holy Scripture and the Sacred Tradition.

Voices worth hearing.

Whenever I was tempted to allow myself to be flattened beneath the tidal wave of verbal abuse or jovial mockery which was pouring weekly even from Catholic publications upon everything seen as 'pre-Conciliar' or old-fashioned, I used to think about the many Saints whose life-stories I'd read, and I'd ask myself this question: "Whose voices are worth listening to? Who encourages us most surely to follow the Way of Christ: the Way of the Saviour Who tells us to take up our cross, daily, and yet Who promised that "I AM GOING NOW TO PREPARE A PLACE FOR YOU" (Jn 14:2) - in Heaven? Is it those whom the Church holds up as role-models for us: the Saints who are very different individuals, firm-willed and fiery-hearted, yet who were humble and obedient, light-hearted and joyful - and who were burning with love for God and neighbour even while they spoke frankly about their sinfulness, and did penance, and urged others to do the same? Or is it those fervent but misguided persons today who speak contemptuously about penance, never mention sin, repentance or sacrifice, see obedience as demeaning, consider the Saints of past times to have been unbalanced, promote personal fulfilment through the satisfaction of worldly longings, and dismiss as retrograde or unhealthy any expression of longing for holiness - or for Heaven?"

Orthodox reading material.

Probably it was because of the isolation I experienced in 'cultural' aspects of Catholicism that another danger was avoided, which might have endangered not my faith but this special task. I mean that my work was wholly focused upon the needs of family and friends and needy neighbours; and my continuing personal study of things to do with faith was focused mainly on what was orthodox reading material - since I couldn't go out and about as someone without children might have done; and so I was entirely ignorant of the fact that very many persons, both in this country and elsewhere, are busily writing about their visions or their supposed visions, attracting attention - whether deliberately, or through the inevitable chatter which accompanies anything unusual in human life. Consequently, I wasn't tempted to compare myself with anyone else, nor to imagine a role for myself that wasn't of Our Lord's devising. I had no desire except to keep on trying to find out Our Lord's Will for me from one moment to the next, and to receive the grace to do it.

For all of these reasons, I thank God for the path along which He has led me. A broad, attractive road might have led me to dangerous places, whereas the rocky, narrow and lonely road upon which Christ led me took me swiftly through a sort of mountain-pass: on a short route to another stage of the journey.

One family.

There were dangers in that isolation, of course. The Church herself recommends that converts be thoroughly 'inculturated': that they see themselves as precious members of a large family, with a place and a role in the Catholic Church in or near their local community. Hope flourishes in a good Catholic congregation, and faint hearts can be made bolder and stronger. But none of us who has been a bit isolated - apart from regular prayer and weekly Mass-going - can blame that isolation for faults and failures which stem from our own weak human nature. If there is frequent and fervent 'encouragement-in-faith' available, it may well encourage people to remain on a 'narrow road' for a time. It would have been a blessing for me to have been fully involved in a good Catholic community; yet difficult decisions would have faced me just the same. No amount of community fervour can obviate the need for each individual to decide on his or her priorities, before God, in a particular way of life. Temptations and trials in this life are inevitable, and each one of us stands alone, at some point, choosing to follow either God or 'man', and perhaps torn between Divine law and human preferences: between saintly ambitions and diverse temptations.

[Symbols of the Faith.

Having said that it's not possible for some Catholics to be active in parish social life, I must almost contradict myself by begging everyone to be persistent in looking for ways of being thoroughly 'in Communion' with fellow-Catholics. I want to urge people who have met opposition to their faith to make a stronger commitment to Christ and to His Church at the very earliest opportunity, to be braver about proclaiming that they are Catholic, and to be less apologetic about displaying symbols of the Catholic Faith wherever it seems appropriate. We ought not to set out to discomfort others; yet if we're so cautious that we remain invisible in a supposedly-Christian country, who will believe that the Catholic Faith is not merely practiced to some degree, but loved?

Who will believe that Christ and His Holy Mother are supremely important to us, if we won't bear a little mockery at displaying statues in our homes, or a picture of the Sacred Heart of Jesus? Is it through tact, or cowardice or unbelief that so few homes possess a crucifix or a holy water stoup?

How I wish I could put a Catechism into every Catholic home, as well as a crucifix, and a statue or picture of Our Blessed Lady, as well as a Bible and the "Lives of the Saints." What an enormous quantity of scorn has been poured upon what's been called the 'ghetto culture' of earlier Catholic communities. Wouldn't it be wonderful, now, if each one of us were as loyal, as brave and as grateful for our Faith as many of those who have lived before us. How wrong it is to scorn or to ignore people who don't share our Faith; but how wrong it is, too, to be anxious to minimise its importance in our lives as we converse with other people. How tempting it can be to make it sound more 'palatable', and to forget that the Christ Who promised "A PEACE THE WORLD CANNOT GIVE" (Jn 14:27) also said that loyalty to Him would set "A MAN AGAINST HIS FATHER, A DAUGHTER AGAINST HER MOTHER"(Mt 10:35).

Surely everyone who follows Christ ought to "SINCERELY PREFER GOOD TO EVIL" (Rm 12:9) in ways which will help the voice of Good to speak louder. Can't we all collect, as far as circumstances allow, good Catholic newspapers, books, pamphlets and videos as encouraging material for ourselves and for our families and neighbours, as an 'antidote' to the publications which call themselves 'Catholic' yet which regularly denounce Church teaching, and as a source of information for interested friends?

Now that I'm writing about culture, I'm duty-bound to suggest that many Catholics in 'inter-church' families aren't aware of the dangers which arise from a fairly casual abandonment of the cultural 'casing' in which Catholic Faith has been nurtured. I mean that although many 'mixed marriages' between practising Christians have resulted in homes with an unusual breadth of hospitality and tolerance, dangers lie in wait where a shamefaced and wholesale abandonment by the Catholic spouse of sacramentals and of little reminders of Catholic culture leads little by little to the ghastly idea that truths of the Faith, on which Salvation depends, can be cast aside with as little distress: for the sake of a false harmony.]

Weakness and pain.

If I return now to the long weary story of my increasingly poor health and my spiritual struggles, it's to describe the point at which I finally learned to put my entire trust in God and to stop worrying about life, health, opinions, hopes and future; and that 'point' of utter surrender to Him came in my late 'thirties', but only when I'd learned from bitter experience that I can't do anything by my own strength.

By the time I was thirty-four years old, I could go a hundred metres to the corner shop and back. Long rambles with the children were a thing of the past. There wasn't much time for reading, yet a quick glimpse at a line from a good spiritual author used to remind me that God is as delighted by our faithfulness in little things as in great deeds. In between outings to the supermarket and the school, I'd try to put my feet up for a few minutes, to open a trustworthy book.

Baron von Hugel was a great help for a while. I liked his simple advice in his "Letters to a niece" that she patiently pack and unpack, and pack and unpack, on holiday, if that were the Will of God. So for a long time, I washed and cooked and cleaned - and sat down - and started again, with as much grace as I could muster. I believed against all the evidence that perseverance counted for more than impressive projects. But when eventually every single day was passed in weakness and exhaustion, and it became a struggle to do simple chores, I became worn down by pain. There was no prospect of relief or rest. Even though my mind clung to God all the time, my heart was torn more and more by grief and fear. It wasn't mere tiredness which I felt, which every mother expects, but real weakness in my limbs.

I remember when the children were nine, seven and three, and still needed careful supervision and encouragement. I nearly wept with exhaustion by lunchtime. The house was full of demanding people and I had many hours more work to do. It's impossible to sit and rest when caring for young children, but without frequent rests, I couldn't do all the chores. Yet if I rested, the washing stayed unwashed and the children squabbled and grew sad. It was also painful to sit upright throughout evening engagements but I felt obliged to try.

Becoming sad and moody, I veered from optimism to anger, yet tried to look at the situation with different eyes. How would I myself react to a person who was always 'ailing', and whose medical tests showed nothing strange at all? It was bound to perplex and irritate people, and I became irritable too. I was brave in some ways, yet behaved very badly in others. I thanked God for good friends and a kind G.P.

Though tempted to self-pity, as I said, I still managed to sound fairly cheerful: and a firm commitment to my prayer-times kept me going. As usual, I went to Mass and to Confession, and looked forward to the strength always gained in Holy Communion. I knelt at home to pray two or three times a day, wherever in the house I could find a quiet corner if the children were occupied elsewhere. Of course I prayed for healing, but the greatest pain was caused by my failure to accept the unexpected. I disliked my inefficiency, and was grieved by the attitude of good people who were puzzled by my weakness.

Invisible trials.

Two or three years more passed by in what seemed like an inhuman routine. I had no doubts about God's existence, or about His care; but prayers by myself in the kitchen, early each morning, became battles for hope, and self-control. I worried about being seen as a weak-willed and neglectful mother; and because of pride, I disliked being pitied. Then I grieved that I couldn't do all that I'd done in the past - I: who was so lively and sociable, always ready to go to a party or a dance, or to paint until two in the morning if I had exciting work to finish. There was no end to the fuel for the fire of self-pity. I fought on in shame and confusion, still believing in God, and still praying to have equal measures of charity and courage in my heart, yet in a mood now approaching despair. Furthermore, in becoming self-pitying and sad because of ill-health and spiritual loneliness, I was tempted to cast a sour eye at every area of life: even to question the necessity of doing what others call unwaged mundane work.

Once, briefly, I was tempted by discontent to think that the sort of feminism which was being preached by bold and angry women writers through the newspaper columns of the nineteen-seventies might provide an alternative wisdom. I was urged, as so many other women were being urged, to see myself as trapped by an ogre called 'domesticity'. I was urged to see the men in my life, whether they were relatives, priests, or doctors, as willing conspirators in a centuries-old policy of keeping women in the "slavery" of patriarchal systems of government: both ecclesiastical and secular. No male escaped criticism. It's a marvel that I had good friends: 'housewives' who had a balanced outlook and who could remind me, as I've reminded others since, of the privileges of womanhood, and of the extraordinary importance of good child-care: in the child's own home, if possible, and by his or her own mother. No beginning in life can rival a stable and warm family atmosphere.

[Secular doctrines.

How sad it is that so many women have been seduced, in the twentieth century, by the more extreme doctrines of the "womens' movement." Whenever clever propagandists in any revolution hold out the hope of power to angry workers, there's a chance of success: unless some core value, or person or ideal or truth is judged worthy of being defended at any cost. How many women have managed to stand firm for a life-time, in defence of motherhood, and marriage and faith? I can't tell. But which woman, busy with demanding toddlers and a busy husband, hasn't begun to long for more glamorous tasks to do, or more appreciation? Which of us hasn't felt a surge of longing to echo the call so frequently heard in modern-day books, magazines and television shows: "I demand respect; I insist that you value me and make me feel important, and not pity me for doing unskilled, undervalued and repetitive work."

Who can deny that it can be humiliating or tiresome to be patronised at social gatherings by those who assume that full-time housewives are dreary creatures with low intelligence and little conversation? Who can deny that many men have taken advantage of superior physical strength, economic power or better education or that the gifts and labours of many women are taken for granted? In a sinful world, we can hardly be surprised: though we ought not to condone evil. But I learned - to my sadness, more than twenty years ago - that the most voluble apostles of feminism were beginning to pour scorn on Christian family life. They were so keen to encourage women to use their skills in paid work - even as astronauts or foot-soldiers - that they portrayed women who were kept busy in the home with children, traditional skills and quiet routines as being spineless or defeatist. The normal husband-wife relationship was depicted by some ardent feminists as being a state on a par with slavery.

No-one mentioned, it seemed, the life-long 'servitude' to industry of men with bills to pay. Few writers mentioned the need for calm, stable homes where calm, stable children might grow up without seeing themselves as obstacles to their mothers' 'self-fulfilment'. How easy it is for us to absorb, as if by osmosis, the interpretations and insinuations which arrive in our houses and hearts through the un-Christian opinions of newscasters, for example, or through particular plays or films. How greatly we need regular prayer, clear thought and doctrinally-sound sources of information to offset the barrage of faithless opinions which are put forward on every subject.

What extraordinary recommendations about charity and faithfulness Christ makes to anguished human beings: and how impossible, without God's grace. Yet what a marvel, that Christ Himself - and thousands of His Saints - have greeted trials and darkness with patience and fortitude, free of hatred and resentment. How important it is that Christian men and women try to resist current un-Christian advice that we adopt a utilitarian approach, for example, to human life, as new plans emerge for the destruction of the sick unborn, and even for the chronically ill or for the aged. How important it is that we don't give in to current secular opinion on numerous important moral issues; and, in the matter of marriage and motherhood, how important it is that Christian wives and mothers remain faithful to the duties of their state and refuse to look upon simple work as 'demeaning'. What does it matter if they're seen as foolish because they don't keep demanding respect? It's true that women who endure real injustice deserve practical help, where this is possible, as well as sympathy, yet I believe that no angry woman's scorn for men or for patriarchy echoes the Gospel message, in which Christ asks us follow His example of meekness and humility.]

Fear of failure.

Amongst the house-wives I knew was a friend who had four youngsters. She wasn't a church-goer. She had, and has, a genuine and passionate concern for truth and justice, as well as a generous helping of common-sense. She ruminated quite casually over a cup of coffee one day on the great privilege which we both enjoyed, of being able to stay at home peacefully, and without fear of starvation, in order to look after our children and to create a welcoming place of growth and safety. Her wise words helped to anchor me; and I've treasured the wisdom and warmth and wit of all my house-wife friends; but words couldn't keep me going when I'd quite run out of energy and was almost overwhelmed by pain. My legs remained weak, and I was crushed beneath the weight of innumerable chores.

Now, this wasn't what God wanted - or, rather, each of the activities was good, but I had to learn that He's not a Hero to be impressed by a list of tremendous deeds. He wants our hearts, entirely, knowing that deeds will follow; but these will be calm deeds, well-chosen deeds, fulfilled in a way which accords with His Will. Whether my achievements were seen or unseen, many or few, those carried out with great love and peacefulness for God's sake would be the ones He would cherish. So long as I was swept along by my emotions, or driven by others, or was full of my own ambitions - which had crept in, unnoticed, as we'd moved from one place to another - and as long as I was secretly longing for human approval, or success, all I did would be wasted, in God's eyes. I'd imagined that I was living for love; but I was still living in fear: fear of failure, fear of not getting or keeping what I wanted, fear of being un-loved or mocked, fear of making mistakes, and fear that in serving God I might lose all that I secretly hoped to keep.

[Tempted to refuse the Cross.

God is so good: even as He allows us to be tested. It's only through sufferings and trials that we're forced to decide, in our inmost hearts, whether or not to give Him first place in our lives, and so to move swiftly towards the true peace and joy that only He can give. This means, as I know from experience, that we can either 'wave away' our trust in Him, our faith fading, as we blame Him or others for our plight, or we can doggedly keep believing, and grow in trust: sure in our hearts that the God who made us will bring us safely through all earthly distress.

This is the test which all sincere Christians must face - not once, but many times. Each one of us will have to stand on a little Calvary, where we shall be asked to accept the Cross, and will be tempted to refuse it.]

Trying to cope.

There came a time when, for various reasons, I saw myself as unloved, overworked, sick and alone. Too tired to do everything I felt I ought to do, I hardly knew what to tackle next. 'Cutting corners' and trying to cope, I felt that I'd been judged and found wanting. I didn't trust enough in God, and found myself longing for a way out. One sin led to another as I tried to see where God's Will lay in the apparently conflicting demands made upon me.

For the whole time that there was no clinical evidence of disease, I know I was seen as merely tired and inadequate - despite my enjoyment of different interests and my determination to do as much as I could. I was seen as someone who didn't enjoy her life and who therefore developed symptoms, when it was the other way around. The symptoms were so painful to me that life was almost unendurable. I felt as though I were a coal-miner suffering from pneumonia who was trying to wield a shovel with his usual gusto. There were invisible trials, too, besides pain, but this isn't the place to list them.

Just when I thought I couldn't cope for much longer the demands on me seemed to increase. I gave in to temptations from within and without and was appalled at myself. Yet I clung to the Sacraments and never fully turned away from God in my heart. I longed to love and serve Him, even in exhaustion and grief, but I was attempting, from duty and fear, to do work which would have taxed even the fittest wife or mother. My misery increased.

What a catalogue of woes! Alas, it was made worse because I was worrying about six different goals, when Christ said that "FEW ARE NEEDED, INDEED ONLY ONE" (Lk

10:41), for the perfect service of God and for the perfect fulfilment of His Will. Lacking confidence, fearful of appearing weak, living in dread of neglecting the children, I shied away from what I might face if I lived in utter truth and simplicity, becoming honest and forthright before everyone, admitting my weaknesses but living at every moment in a way consistent with my most heart-felt yearnings.

Christ in 'the depths'.

The war within me was ceaseless, and I came to see with great clarity that the service of God with a pure and honest heart would mean the renunciation of all human hopes and ambitions - however valuable they seemed. All my hope would have to lie in God, and in His care and in His plans, no matter what anyone might think.

Only one friend at that time had any inkling of what I underwent. I said very little to her, and nothing at all to others. Throughout those years I appeared outwardly cheerful, and it wasn't simply a deceitful mask. Since I never gave up daily prayer and had never decided to abandon God I still thought it wicked to cast a blight on other people by appearing gloomy in God's service, and I thought it wrong to burden others with my woes.

Only God's strength in prayer gave me the faith to beg the 'impossible' daily, and to continue to believe that I'd be rescued from the darkness of the "pit" in which I saw myself imprisoned. Faith alone took me from one day to the next (T:18). It seemed as though I was caught between one unhappiness and another; and I couldn't choose. I sought to avoid becoming bitter, or growing ungrateful. I still believed that everything good in my life gave me a genuine reason for thanks to God; and I never ceased to be grateful for the sacraments: for Mass with Holy Communion, and for Confession, even though it seemed, at times, as though there was an invisible, palpable barrier in front of me whenever I approached our church to enter it. I had to force myself to push past it, in order to go to Mass; and I can say now, from experience, that it was yet another temptation to give up prayer, and to give up hope in God.

Life became even more difficult. Coping with some injustices and many temptations, all the time ill and in pain, I was near despair. I was a failure in more than one sense; I wished I could always appear patient and serene; and since I couldn't, I was horribly ashamed of setting a bad example.

Thanks to God's grace alone, I never lost hope. I struggled to be faithful in the darkness, not realising that Christ was waiting in the depths of my heart, ready to hold me and bring comfort, whenever I would freely put my trust in Him.

A blessing in disguise.

Once again in my life, a disaster happened, but one for which I would later be grateful, as so much good came through it that I was helped to move forward with new vigour, wholly determined to put God first in everything.

One evening at twilight when I was dashing out in the car to buy some food, my car crashed into a stationary vehicle. I hadn't seen it. No-one was hurt, thank God. But I was shocked and anxious, for good reason. I was arrested and was locked in a cell for an hour, although, to tell the truth, I was shocked to realise, when I was invited to come out, that I was reluctant to leave. If someone had said that I had to stay there for a week, I'd have been relieved. It would have meant that I could rest for a week, instead of going back to my constant round of exhausting activities, with the incessant 'phone calls and the late nights. That was how tired I felt. Then within a few weeks I was banned from driving for a year.

It was hardly something I could boast about; and it was inconvenient in several ways; but what a blessing in disguise. But for the first time in years I wasn't able to ferry three children and friends several times daily in the holidays from A to B. No longer was I able, weak and unwell, to shift large boxes of groceries in and out of shops, car and house at frequent intervals. Nor could I visit the distant sick, exhibit my paintings, or go to the innumerable social events where my presence required transport. But I had a great deal of time for thinking and for prayer.

Out of the sense of disgrace and disaster, peace emerged, although it was peace in the midst of humiliation and a sense of failure. I hadn't a shred of self-satisfaction left about the least of my gifts or achievements. I had great faith in God, however, and went on blindly putting one foot in front of the other, to do my daily chores, and to go regularly to Mass, Holy Communion, and Confession.

A gentler routine.

As the months went by in a far-gentler routine, I began to 'see' everything more clearly, in God's own Light. It shone brightly upon every thought and desire in my heart That's why a new life began for me: a new life of the soul, as soon as I'd decided at last to put all my trust in God, forever. On what was one of the worst and most humiliating days of my life I began my new life in God. One terrible day - or, rather, on a day more terrible than most - I came to realise the extent of my sinfulness. I fell to my knees in prayer in some far corner of the house, overwhelmed with the God-given sight of my frailty, and thoroughly contrite.

This was the moment in which my hopes of being saintly were entirely shattered. I don't mean that I no longer wanted to become holy: quite the contrary; but I was so humbled and humiliated by the realisation of my sinfulness that the last vestiges of my early notions of sanctity were shattered: of sanctity being something to do with will-power and self-control. I hadn't managed to learn that sanctity consists of God's own pure and beautiful holiness pouring through the contrite heart of someone who believes in Him, repents, and is willing to accept His gifts. It's true that every faithful Christian hopes to control his foolish impulses, fears, and riotous emotions; but humility is the key to holiness. It opens up a 'channel' through which God can send down the torrent of His own grace and glory, to work a wonderful transformation.

From the moment of this new conversion I could suddenly 'see' clearly: 'see' life, and life's duties, and persons, through God's eyes. Then I looked carefully at my whole life, in His inner light. Finally, I dared to consider what might be the worst that I'd be required to face, were I to follow God's way at every second. In a strange burning prayer of complete trust and abandonment, I asked God for His help in making choices.

Taught, in a mysterious way.

Suddenly I was taught by God within my heart's darkness, in a silent, mysterious way; yet it was only because I was willing, at last, to listen to His least whisper. He steered me, very gently, towards simplicity and holiness, telling me:-

> **Follow My inspiration. In order to serve Me with a pure and honest heart you must renounce all human hopes and ambitions, no matter how valuable they seem to be. (T:18 #1)**

> **Consider your sinfulness and My tremendous holiness. How deep is the 'chasm' which is inhabited by everyone who is estranged from Me, or who hopes to ignore My Will. (T:18 #2)**

> **Recognise the truth: that you have no hope but in Me, Jesus Christ, your Lord. (T:18 #3)**

> **Put your trust in Me. I love you! I Who am God-made-man am 'waiting' for you in every circumstance, waiting to touch you in any sort of grief, remorse or loneliness, whether you have brought them upon yourself or have suffered at the hands of others. (T:18 #4)**

> **Do your duty towards Me before anyone or anything else. Love Me and love your neighbour, and keep My Commandments, no matter what the cost. (T:18 #5)**

> **Love your true neighbours; love those whom I call you to love and serve, close by, in daily activities, as you fulfil your ordinary duties. (T:18 #6)**

> **Don't try to serve two 'masters'. Commitment to Me and to My Holy Will comes first, even if this should bring you further humiliations and loneliness. (T:18 #7)**

> **Examine your heart's true desires, which determine your behaviour. Don't expect to serve Me and also to be a great success with others. You cannot always follow Me, 'The Crucified', and enjoy a good reputation on earth. (T:18 #8)**

> **Abandon hopes of pleasure, respect or sympathy, if you wish to serve Me. Accept whatever joys I choose to give to you, as I guide you from minute to minute. (T:18 #9)**

Thank Me for having loved, guided and sustained you throughout so many burdens, broken dreams and causes for shame. (T:18 #10)

Turn to Me, with all your failings. *I will bring you towards perfection in the measure in which I become your only true desire and goal.* **(T:18 #11)**

Look into your heart to see whether or not you love Me. You will know that you truly love Me when you see that your heart is no longer 'divided' by conflicting desires. (T:18 #12)

Give Me your whole-hearted loyalty. (T:18 #13)

On wings of faith.

A great deal of teaching was 'given' swiftly in prayer, without a sound being heard. I absorbed it all. I knew it was Christ. I knew He loved me, but felt nothing but shame. I was determined to follow His instructions, though I felt broken-hearted, recognising His goodness, and my frailty; and so I asked again for His strength and for His virtues. Then I found that I was being 'taught' once again. Christ told me very gently, in my soul's centre:

Turn to Me, whatever burdens or griefs you carry. I know all your battles, and I see the trials and cruelties you suffer. But I don't ask you to bear more than I bore (T:19 #1)

Believe in My power. Have faith in Me. At the right moment, in an instant, *I can lift you up and carry you on wings of faith,* **so making things easier than you had ever dared hope was possible. (T:19 #2)**

With utter trust, I believed everything Christ told me. All at once, He had shown me my sins, forgiven me, and brought me hope and comfort.

For many years, my fearful heart had been thinking: "Christ will love me when I'm perfect", but that wasn't the Christian creed. I knew at last that "HE LOVED US FIRST" (1 Jn 4:19). He was willing to bring me towards Himself, because He loves me, and by His power: but only if I gave Him my whole-hearted permission: such is His respect for us and for our real freedom. He helped me to see that my heart had been divided for about ten years. It was true that I'd tried to do His Will and to obey His Laws, and to love those whom He'd put close to me. But at the same time I'd set limits to the depths of my self-offering.

The bottom of the 'pit'.

On that Sunday evening, as I sat and prayed before God in great sorrow, silently considering my way of life at the bottom of that particular "pit", I realised that few situations on earth last indefinitely. I needn't assume that every detail of my life was going to remain the same. Opinions change, and circumstances alter. I knew that I had to re-assess my priorities as a Christian. I must become wholly devoted to Christ, Who said: "SET YOUR HEARTS ON HIS KINGDOM FIRST, AND ON HIS RIGHTEOUSNESS" (Mt 6:33). I must love God and do His Will, and love my neighbour and love myself, whether healthy or unwell, labelled or undiagnosed, feeling happy or depressed.

It was overwhelmingly plain that I had to make a firmer commitment to God, even if my choice should bring problems. Christ had never left me alone, indeed, had pursued me. I'd been held up by Him through exhaustion, burdens and broken dreams, and through shame at all my failings, too. It was He Who enabled me to pray a true prayer that day, as I knelt in my house, repentant, when everyone else was out.

By the grace of God alone, and in a single moment, I made a new beginning. I untangled several guidelines which would lead me up to a more God-centred if very feeble life.

For the rest of my life.

On that painful but wonderful day of grace, nearly twenty years ago, I decided with all the power of my heart that I would turn to God in every circumstance. I wouldn't hesitate. I would choose Him as He had chosen me, and would serve Him alone. With Christ's help, I would love my neighbour as Christ had loved me, that is - at any cost, wholeheartedly, until death. I would live for Christ, and would do His Will at every moment rather than my own. I would bear sickness patiently, for love of Him, and would shoulder all misunderstanding and pity. I would ask for the grace to serve Him whatever the cost - for evermore. I decided that I would live entirely for Him, even if this spiritual darkness were to continue, unrelieved, for the rest of my life. Indeed, that's what I really expected.

What other people thought of me didn't matter any more. I was determined that I wouldn't compromise. I wouldn't be half-hearted in God's service. I would do what was right, and nothing else. I would never, ever again, willingly or deliberately offend God, or go against His love or against His laws, in the least degree. Those were my fervent resolutions: not to be perfectly fulfilled in future years, but never, so far, deliberately to be set aside: thanks to His goodness.

Everything I've described was worked out in an instant; and I thank God for accompanying me there. The choices were stark but very clear. I begged Christ to give me faith, courage and love; and suddenly, I found that He gave me everything I needed. He gave me a new strength.

[A contrite soul.

How I long to be able to convince other people that repentance before God is the key to the 'gateway' of the soul: to the 'door' through which God can pour within us not only the peace which He longs to share, but also the sweetness and delight which can't be found except in Him.

It's so sad to think that people who insist that they're too mature or enlightened to wallow in 'guilt feelings' and who claim that the Church is wrong to encourage sorrow-for-sin and reparation, are keeping joy at a distance. They're not only mistaken, but are depriving themselves of the extraordinary joys which God loves to give to every "BROKEN SPIRIT" (Ps 51:17) who has responded to the urgent plea which Christ made in His public ministry, when He said: "REPENT, FOR THE KINGDOM OF HEAVEN IS CLOSE AT HAND" (Mt 3:2).

By repentance, we might experience temporary distress and humiliation, at least at the beginning of our spiritual journey when the destruction of pride within us is felt as pain; yet repentance is the key to peace, the gateway to the Kingdom within the soul. Without repentance, we are 'locked out' from God's Bliss; but through it, we can find true friendship with our amazing, consoling God.

Reconciliation and Bliss.

Looking back now, I marvel at how patiently Christ had 'waited' for the moment when - quite freely - I'd choose to make true friendship with Him the most important goal of my life. In prayer, He continued His instructions. He advised me, with infinite gentleness:

> **Turn to Me promptly, in every struggle to be free from sins and failings. (T:21 #1)**

> **Trust in Me. I can transform you. All I want is your goodwill and your sincere if pitiful efforts. (T:21 #2)**

> **Admit your weaknesses to Me. When you have struggled against them for a while, and have therefore turned to Me wholeheartedly, I Myself - by My power - will complete your transformation. (T:21 #3)**

> **Give your wholehearted permission to Me, so that I can help you. My respect for you - as for everyone - is too great to allow Me to 'bully' you. (T:21 #4)**

> **Confess your sins. Be reconciled. In this way you co-operate with Me and prove your devotion. (T:21 #5)**

The very next weekend, I went to church earlier than usual. After pacing up and down, inside and outside for many long minutes, agonising not only over the revelation of my sins, but over the question of what had been sinful, and what hadn't, I was given the grace to make a more thorough-than-usual confession. I was reconciled and forgiven. It was a painful operation, but I shall never forget its after-effects.

Before I even had a chance to pray for the priests who, for the love of Christ, listen to the terrible things we have to tell, I was suddenly and for the first time nearly overcome with supernatural Bliss.

173

A bright banner, on a battlefield.

Christ was with me, though unheard and unseen. I was utterly light and joyous in His presence. It was as though my soul was illumined, soaring in its new freedom, as I walked outside in unexpected and purely child-like delight. It would have been impossible to kneel in church any longer, nor could I have gone home in such radiance without evoking comments. In an effort to postpone the moment of re-immersion into my busy and noisy routine, I walked with Christ along the pavements and past the shops, out in the fresh air, yearning to stay like that for a long time.

Now I knew that Christ had loved me all the time. Now I knew that He had forgiven every single sin. It was as though He held up my soul for one day, like a bright banner, triumphant at the working of His Grace in me. That's what I learned, in an instant of astonishing union.

Christ explained to me, with infinite kindness, as I stood there on the pavement:-

> **Think about My joy! Forgiveness of your sins brings joy, light and peace not only to you, but to Me, your Saviour; I am made joyful by every repentance and conversion. (T:21 #6)**

> **See how I delight in your co-operation. I am triumphant at the working of My grace in you, as you bravely follow My loving inspirations and do My Will. (T:21 #7)**

> **Look, upwards! See what I see. *Your soul now shines like a bright banner,* held aloft as if on a battlefield where Good struggles against evil. I am triumphant that you have turned to me and are letting Me reign in your daily life. (T:21 #8) (WC:21)**

Individual souls.

For a minute or two I walked on a little further, my soul still engulfed in light and joy. I came to a local fun-fair where people were pushing and twisting past one another amongst the crowd. I saw a tired man who was carrying a child; then I noticed his sad face - and then one more nearby. For the first time in quite this way, I saw all the faces - the persons - just as Christ sees them, with His eyes, as people surged around the stalls. Then Christ reminded me that although I am unique, and tremendously precious to Him, and reconciled, I have in common with the rest of mankind a degree of loneliness, with struggle and apprehension too, at times. I was suddenly taught, by Christ, with astonishing sureness and clarity, that I should be as compassionate to other people as Christ had been towards me. He explained to me:

> **Look upon others as if with My eyes. Try to be loving, patient and sympathetic. *Each individual soul is known to Me. Each heart suffers alone,* bearing his own particular burdens. (T:30 #1)**

174

Remember that it's because of My humanity that you have a special obligation. *Each person demands your love, because of My humanity and My Holy Passion. Each person created by Me is part of My flesh and blood.* Also - if I love each person so much that I suffered for him, how can you fail to recognise each one's importance? How can you fail to love him for My sake? (T:30 #2)

Never fail in charity. *To hurt another person is to hurt Me, and is therefore to hurt yourself too,* since you and I now live united to one another by grace, as well as by our humanity. (T:30 #3)

The keys to the treasury.

I didn't know it at the time, but that experience was a gift from Christ which He, my God and Saviour, was 'enabled' to give to me only because of my gift to Him that very day: I mean, the gift of love and contrition. By confessing my sins to the priest, in the Sacrament of penance, in utter determination never to offend God again, I'd unlocked the door to many special graces.

How I long to bring other people towards Reconciliation, now that I know how lavishly God wants to shower His gifts upon us: grace upon grace, pure hope and pure Love: astonishing rewards for our feeble attempts to please Him. (T:17). What depths, yet what clutter there is within our souls; and what a small place I had reserved for Christ, Who longed to be my whole Life! What silly trinkets I had longed for, when the keys of the whole "treasury" could be mine - if only I would turn away from the trashy and the fake, and from the hollow stones of success, pride or popularity, which the world sees as 'treasure.'

175

HOPE:

THROUGH GOD THE HOLY SPIRIT
OUR GUIDE AND CONSOLER

"Everyone moved by the Spirit is a son of God. The spirit you received is not the spirit of slaves bringing fear into your lives again; it is the spirit of sons, and it makes us cry out, 'Abba, Father!' The Spirit himself and our spirit bear united witness that we are children of God. And if we are children we are heirs as well: heirs of God and coheirs with Christ, sharing his sufferings so as to share his glory.

I think that what we suffer in this life can never be compared to the glory, as yet unrevealed, which is waiting for us ... From the beginning till now the entire creation, as we know, has been groaning in one great act of giving birth; and not only creation, but all of us who possess the first-fruits of the Spirit, we too groan inwardly as we wait for our bodies to be set free. For we must be content to hope that we shall be saved ...

The Spirit too comes to help us in our weakness. For when we cannot choose words in order to pray properly, the Spirit himself expresses our plea in a way that could never be put into words, and God who knows everything in our hearts knows perfectly well what he means, and that the pleas of the saints expressed by the Spirit are according to the mind of God.

We know that by turning everything to their good God cooperates with all those who love him, with all those that he has called according to his purpose..." (Rm 8:14-32)

8 ILLUMINATION

(1980-1984)

DUTY. SIMPLICITY. KNOWLEDGE-IN-PRAYER.

Wounded by His work.

Christ gave me one day of brief bliss and deep grace. It was a little taste of a Heavenly way of life - similar to that which I enjoy today: a firm promise of joy which could be called a Betrothal. But after such a singular day of reconciliation the work of God went on. By the promptings of grace, and the help of prayer, I went contentedly about my work in darkness again; but it was a healing darkness given by a merciful Father. It was like a blanket or a bandage which held me quiet and still until some of the inner wounds had begun to heal.

During the process, I suffered agonies from my memories, and came to see the various ways in which pride and cowardice had combined with fear and self-pity to keep me in a spiritual pit of desolation. But the ascent to joy was underway.

For many months after this new, true conversion, I walked around in torment. I was outwardly carefree, but was inwardly pierced by a shame so intense that I could scarcely bear it. I could hardly go on. It was a tremendous grace, though quite unrecognised at the time. My soul was so fiercely scorched by the pure dark grace of God as it burned within me that, at times, when I was doing my shopping, I nearly groaned out loud in the street.

In His Love for me, God appeared merciless as He burned away impurities in order to pour His Purity into my soul; and even though I saw myself and all my past actions in that dreadful Light, I found that the more I emptied myself of all desire except the desire to do His Will alone, the more He filled me with His Presence and gave me strength. He upheld me in my daily tasks as I stumbled from one chore to the next, burning in a sort of grief, wounded by His work, and dying within at the knowledge of His Holiness, and of my sins (T:22).

[God's burning light.

Not one word of what I've written about God's burning grace in prayer is an exaggeration of my pain. Writers might tell us that humility comes from meditation on our frailty, or from acceptance of humiliations for the love of God. But they say, too, that humility is a gift from God, and this is true. Yet it's a gift which can be received only by those who are prepared to die to themselves, as Christ taught; and God alone can uphold the one who permits Him to uncover the soul, naked, in His pure Light, as the soul accepts - for the love of God - the death of its long-cherished illusions about its own self, and also accepts the death of its many foolish ambitions. The torment is indescribable, and one is tempted to turn away. Yet - we can't fail to continue, if we truly long to know and love God, since He alone can make us fit to see Him, despite the terrible cost. Faith and hope and love, given freely by God, persuade us to go on.]

Spiritual Light.

Praying regularly, despite the pain of it, I suddenly found numerous aspects of my life laid bare by Christ, as He 'held up' in my soul and mind everything of importance to me, and pierced it through by the sharp ray of His Truth. He showed me, down to the smallest details, what He wanted of me; and I know that He only taught me in this way because at last I'd given my free consent to His Will being done henceforward in every detail of my life. As I knelt, day by day, before Him, I was given clear but soundless instructions: the first to be given to me in a new era of true 'Communion'. I was shown that the path to Heaven is very simple and straightforward. He taught me:-

Go to the Sacraments. Keep all My Commandments and the Laws of My Church. (T:22 #1)

Be faithful to private prayer. (T:22 #2)

Do all your work for My sake. (T:22 #3)

Take a short break each year, and thank Me for the leisure in which I enable you to think and pray more deeply. (T:22 #4)

Suffer whatever I permit, without complaints. (T:22 #5)

Then Christ reminded me of my importance, in His sight, and encouraged me further:-

Pray to Me in all your needs, however trivial or embarrassing. Nothing is trivial to Me, if it concerns you. (T:22 #6)

Remain completely trustful from day to day. (T:22 #7)

Love others for My sake, with your whole heart, leaving all problems in My hands. (T:22 #8)

Put all of your problems into My hands. Take reasonable steps to try to solve your problems, but leave the results to Me. (T:22 #9)

> **Accept every possibility as part of My plan for your life - if I should permit it to occur. Strive to preserve life and health, obedient to My Will; but accept with equal calm either failure or success, health or sickness, or life or death. (T:22 #10)**

> **Love and serve others as well as you can. (T:22 #11)**

Then Christ reminded me that the whole point of our efforts is that we become Christ-like. So He urged me:-

> **Bear patiently any complaints about you. (T:22 #12)**

> **Pray for people who criticise or annoy or ignore you. Love them. Don't be perturbed by their judgements. (T:22 #13)**

Pain and peace, side by side.

Prayer continued in darkness, but it was sometimes lit by great shafts of spiritual light. It wasn't the Light we associate with bodily sight, but was something spiritual like a swift blade of lightening - or like the awesome, brief and far-above illumination which is seen at sea, when a ship in distress has sent up a flare. Yet this 'light' was invisible. I can't explain it; but I experienced it. I knew it was from God. It 'contained' within itself both wisdom and majesty, and then it was gone before I recognised what had happened. All of the early 'teachings' which I'm quoting came to me soundlessly, as if in the wake of the mysterious wave of spiritual light: yet everything was 'given' in a split-second, as a gift, in the new calm of my contrite but painful prayers.

Pain and peace hovered side by side. I was tormented by regrets which interrupted my prayers and made my hours of mundane work almost unendurable; but I tried to turn my mind away from wishful thinking, and learned, with God's help, to walk through the pain. I knew that at each new stage of the spiritual life, even if we're unaware of 'stages', we have to begin again, like a baby taking its first steps. We're more likely to reach our goal if we have a determined heart, and rely on Christ for courage.

Having learned through grace that there are truly "SO MANY THINGS" (Lk 10:41) which aren't worth worrying about, I simply endured from day to day, saying to myself about God, in the words of Holy Scripture: "LET HIM KILL ME IF HE WILL; I HAVE NO OTHER HOPE THAN TO JUSTIFY MY CONDUCT IN HIS EYES" (Jb 13:15). I asked Christ never to let me fall away, but to teach me to trust, and to love. I begged Him never to let me push Him to the margins of my life; and because of my sincere prayers, and His grace, I began to do nothing but what I thought He wanted. All that He permitted, through the circumstances of daily life, I accepted. I learned to speak out when required, in certain circumstances, in order to uphold truth or justice, but I looked for no reward except the knowledge that I did His Will, without complaint, in an unremarkable domestic routine (T:23)

Faith told me that I was forgiven, though I felt nothing but shame. Faith told me that Christ loved me but I felt absolutely nothing at all of this wonderful love: I only believed. Faith alone told me to thank Him and serve Him day after day, as well as I could, whether or not I had any evidence of His involvement in my life: so deep was my usual spiritual darkness; but I was no longer disconcerted in the way I was before. In the depths of my heart and conscience I was utterly at peace: utterly determined to have no ambition other than to allow God to do what He wants with my life.

Teachings in prayer.

Once, I had read: "WHATEVER YOU EAT, WHATEVER YOU DRINK, WHATEVER YOU DO AT ALL, DO IT FOR THE GLORY OF GOD" (1 Co 10:31). So, I decided, the smallest of my new efforts wouldn't be wasted. I could work a little, pray and suffer a little, cook meals, act patiently, hold back a complaint or forgive a hurt - all for the love of God. All of these small things would be accepted by God, in His service, in reparation for sins, and in intercession for the needs of the world and the Church. It was what Saint Thérèse had taught me many years before, yet it wasn't until now that I believed wholeheartedly in the worth of small, secret sacrifices. I was at last convinced, however, that God sees everything we do for Him and that He rewards us for every kindness, whether something practical done for a neighbour or a charitable thought. More and more confidently, I began to offer Him my small, daily tasks, and to trust in His Providence. Every chore was done to please Christ - and also to help the family. But Christ was first on my list.

For Christ, I endured every unavoidable problem in silence. To Him, in His Passion, I offered every weary walk upstairs, every burdensome trip to the front door and every 'phone call that disturbed my sleep. Such tiny things: but so precious in His eyes. I know this, by faith, but I know it too because He has told me so; and the more I did for Him, because of my love for Him, the closer He drew me to Himself in prayer. My over-riding aim was to please Him, and He continued to teach me. I even began to enjoy walking quietly along my lonely footpath, freed from concern about very many things which had once distressed me.

Wisdom, in prayer.

Month by month, and now that I'd placed all my trust in God once again, as I said, I found that I was receiving a sort of wisdom in prayer: received with no effort, and still without words, but extraordinarily clear; and it was wonderful to notice that Christ taught me as much about hope and joy as about sin. He showed me that the point of all our efforts is to respond to His invitation and to become His friends. He told me, to my astonishment:

> **Let your faith convince you that all occasions of humble, sorrowful prayer are worthwhile. (T:23 #1)**

> **Remember that I rejoice more in one poor, pitiful, small but holy desire to please Me, than in any number of grand projects which are set in motion by self-glorifying ambition. This is true of both secular and 'religious' works. (T:23 #2)**

> **Learn to love Me, willingly, with your heart as well as with**

your mind and will. You can do this by withdrawing your heart from all My 'rivals', by which I mean from everything and everyone who tempts you to steer your hope and your loyalty away from Me. By such mortifications, you will prove your love for Me, strengthen your faith, and enjoy a more peaceful heart. (T:24 #1)

Make your way towards true joy - the joy which comes from loving obedience to Me - by aiming to serve and please Me more than any other person. (T:24 #2)

Give up all sin and foolishness. Substitute loving friendship with Me for grim duty! You cannot be happy in My service if your heart is torn between two masters, or two courses of action. (T:24 #3)

Utterly determined to love, work and pray wholeheartedly, whatever it should cost me, I began to grow accustomed God's new and wordless help. I had no idea what was happening. For a long time, I hadn't appreciated the fact that God 'cannot' generally give His help to persons who - whether carelessly or fearfully - fails to look straight towards Him. Truly, God has given us free-will; and until this new conversion I'd been incapable of receiving further Knowledge from Him in prayer.

Patterns of behaviour.

At last, I'd put everything into the hands of God: life, health, reputation, future: all I had to give Him. My only hope was the true hope which He gave me in the darkness of prayer: a hope in which I believed, but which I didn't feel. The past was gone, the future was His; the present moment was all-important. Here alone could I prove my love. It was so simple. My heart was in a strange way liberated, even amidst continuing miseries. Christ guided me in the darkness more clearly than ever before. His Will slowly became my joy as well as my duty. Rarely, in future, would I be perplexed about what I ought to do; I'd need courage and trust to do what was now so plainly, and daily, revealed to me: revealed so fully because I was at last choosing to look constantly in Christ's 'direction'. I knew that even there in the darkness of prayer, I was gazing at Him face-to-face.

With a new awareness of my many faults came a new realisation of how certain events of my early life had left me fearful about the repercussions if I failed to please everyone. That was partly why my personal, independent decision to enter the Catholic Church had demanded so much courage; and that was why each new decision cost me all my strength, as I shook with fear at the thought of disobeying God, but was just as afraid of displeasing anyone else.

Meanwhile, I continued to examine every facet of daily life, to fulfil Christ's silent request, as He drew me towards Himself. I went about my work in darkness, still, but I was willing to let Christ lead me. I was content to accept both outward and inward changes for His sake, and to walk silently wherever He wanted me to go in the spiritual life and for as long as He permitted. Amidst all the difficulties, I struggled to think clearly, and to consider everything before God, in silent prayer.

Horribly aware that I wasn't a good example, and nearly overcome with shame, I saw that my longings for the welfare and Salvation of other people were simply a further 'problem' to be handed over, trustingly, to God. At each celebration of the Holy Mass I offered the whole of my wretched life to Him, asking Him to change it, and to use it for His work and His Glory. And in going about my shopping and my chores, I smiled and thanked anyone who advised me to try a special remedy or to take more exercise. I had to please God, above all; and I clung to that Commandment, determined not to worry about anyone's opinion. Although I longed to make other people happy, I was no longer anxious to placate them. I relied on Christ, who showed me where my duty lay.

Plain duties.

My first duty, as ever, lay in looking after the family as well as I could. But if I were ill, I learned, I must see that as God's 'problem'. He knows my needs. He expects me to ask for help, and therefore I should expect help - and meanwhile I should do what was physically possible.

With what energy I had, I played with the children, prepared meals, washed clothes and tried to keep the house clean. Unable to do more than that, I stopped feeling ashamed. I even decided to find someone to help with the cleaning: and three wonderful woman - each at a different time of my life - have helped to keep our house 'ship-shape'. God knew all about my physical weakness and my problems; I was sure that He'd see me through it all somehow; and indeed, that's what has happened. It seems so wonderful to me, now, that we can look back, occasionally, to discover that God's help was greater than we could have dreamed. We can see how wise He is, and how limited are our desires. There I was, begging Him for strength, but He gave me a different gift: the one I really needed. I'd asked for strength and He had given me trust, without which steady spiritual advance is impossible.

My new campaign went on: of taking practical steps to ease spiritual problems. For example, when it seemed that books would have to be relied upon for words of encouragement about the Catholic Faith, due to a continuing dearth of Catholic friends, I put a bookshelf in the kitchen, so that I could read a few pages whenever I was tempted to be sad or fearful. I was determined to thank God for every good experience in my life, and to avoid complaints and self-pity. It became clear that I ought to leave my reputation entirely in God's hands, and to stop worrying about whether other people thought me idle or ill.

One of the lessons I learned was that true trust in God meant relying on His help for one single second, hour and day at a time, even if I was exhausted or apparently unsuccessful. I knew that I had to avoid all speculation about my state of health. Common-sense told me that I might get better again, in which case I'd be grateful. However, if my health grew worse, I would have to assume that God would help me to cope.

At my every unspoken thought about personal fulfilment, the words of Christ arose in my mind; He'd given a warning that each of His followers should "RENOUNCE HIMSELF AND TAKE UP HIS CROSS" (Mt 16:24). So I realised that since God Himself - the Divine Son of God, Christ our Saviour - had been willing to walk upon this earth and to accept death in torment, for our sakes, it was my duty to ask for the courage to imitate Him in my small, ordinary way. I couldn't hope for special comfort and respect, when Christ was content to accept whatever came His way: whether praise, or spittle and mockery. As Holy Scripture says: "A SERVANT IS NOT GREATER THAN HIS MASTER" (Jn 15:20).

The right road.

It all sounds so simple; and I sometimes failed in my resolutions; but I was astonished to find that several years passed in this way, with an increasingly-steady spiritual 'health', and with occasional remissions in my mysterious illness. I changed my priorities as new needs arose but I felt I was on the right road.

Something that was enormously helpful was the short break I organised each year in obedience to Christ's wordless suggestion: a brief stay, alone, in a quiet place in a different town, with time for prayer and thought, and daily Mass. It seemed such an extravagance; but every family member was having trips away, from around that time. Plans were always in the air for one conference or another - or for an extended school trip; and people in every sort of paid job have some sort of change each year, I persuaded myself. Most housewives, surely, would benefit from a short retreat.

The three or four-day respite which I planned annually, from then on, and at Christ's prompting, was enough to refresh my soul for a whole year. Our social life was so hectic, and the domestic routine so busy, that the mere appearance on my horizon of that oasis of peace, for decades to come, made everything seem so much easier; and it was made possible by the kindness of my husband, who agreed to look after the children.

Month by month, my inner contentment grew. Some things which had seemed important couldn't be fitted into my new way of life, but it didn't seem to matter very much. It simply wasn't possible to paint much for a while; but I matter-of-factly painted when I could, with great concentration. When I was doing other tasks I forgot about my own hopes or modified my ambitions.

Since I know that it's when we die that we'll see things clearly, I longed to be ready to answer Our Lord's question without fear. I don't think He'll ask me: "How many pictures did you paint?" - though of course if life allows we can use the talents that He's given us; but He says He will say to those on His right-hand: "I WAS HUNGRY AND YOU GAVE ME FOOD ... NAKED AND YOU CLOTHED ME" (Mt 25:35). It seemed to me that He meant that I should feed my hungry family, and visit my neighbours, and clothe my children and my sick relatives: activities far more important than any sort of hobby or worldly ambition.

There was the question about having to make time for rests; but since rest was essential, I rested whenever it was convenient, not making a 'song and dance' about the need, but making the most of every quiet moment. I abandoned my efforts to please everyone, everywhere. With some qualms I became more straightforward, learning to be more prudent, sometimes saying 'no' when friends or family suggested extra tasks, although I was thrilled to be able to organise anything from dinner parties to carnival floats in the two or three periods of time in which the illness went into remission.

During this gruelling period of mixed contrition and reassessment, I grew ashamed on realising how easily, almost unawares, one can slip into some of the despairing little ploys of the sick: the sad frown or drooping shoulders announcing one's pain to the world. I ruthlessly excised them; yet the opposite tendency had to be avoided: the brave glare, daring the questioner impudently to mention one's health; rather, I just had just to forget about cultivating impressions or opinions, and learned to "act natural" amidst my embarrassment, aiming to cope with enquiries in a frank and graceful way whilst being more anxious to listen than to be heard.

Greater contentment.

We went away on numerous family outings, throughout the nineteen-seventies and eighties, as hard work was interspersed with parties and holidays. I was always exhausted, but managed the essentials in a calmer way, although aware of how tiresome I could be as a weary family member. My memories were almost insupportable, but, at times, I could look calmly at the present and the future. I resolved not to worry, and so I made the general plans that any mother ought to make, whilst striving to remain 'flexible'.

Christ was my rock: Christ in the Mass, in the Blessed Sacrament, in Holy Communion, and in the tabernacle. It was because of God-given commitments that I could rarely go to Mass more than once a week; but occasionally I was free to attend a late-morning Mass on Thursdays, which fortified me even more.

It was a new experience for me to have an utterly quiet conscience, and I became more content, aware of an almost unchanging peace in my soul, which rarely left me. I could scarcely feel it during trials and temptations but quite soon it persisted throughout each day. We still led a busy life, but I learned how to be more honest with everyone, gently declining invitations to undertake this extra task or that, and not quite so full of pride - hoping to impress others with my 'talent' and 'generosity'. I went backwards and forwards to the doctor, whenever it was necessary, but I stopped thinking about a diagnosis - or the lack of it.

At last, I'd come to believe that God our Creator cares for us more tremendously than we can begin to understand; and He can keep us going through every sort of anguish. It's when our hearts are perpetually agitated through lack of trust in Him, or are cluttered with selfish ambitions and desires that we fail to notice His helps or can't accept them.

Establishing priorities.

The task continued. The darkness persisted. But occasionally, even the apparently impenetrable blackness of my soul in prayer was pierced by the sudden and amazing Light of Truth. The peculiar and wordless guidance by God - which I described a little earlier, about Christian duties and love of one's neighbour - made me look at life with a clarity which I'd never experienced before.

Examining anew, by God's 'Light', all my acts and attitudes, all my works, hopes, goals and intentions, and even my thoughts and phrases, I leaned on Christ as I cut and pruned, and established our priorities in life, since I was now adamant that His aims and mine would be the same. I left the future in His hands, though, to tell the truth, it's possible that if I'd known what spiritual sufferings still lay ahead, I might have given up the idea of achieving union with God in earthly life. To have seen all future suffering clearly would have been the same as having to gaze all-at-once upon the pains of Purgatory, whilst being invited to enter in order to reach perfection, and God, and Heaven. And yet everything which God permits us to endure can contribute to our eventual joy and to His Glory.

For one minute and one day at a time I walked with Him by faith, and lived with Him, and did His Will wherever it led. There were failures, but none too serious. He never let me down. I noticed with astonishment - now that I'd given my whole life to Christ, so late, and so very reluctantly - He refused me nothing that I asked (T:23-34).

I really loved Christ at last; and for His sake I ignored all that tempted me, dumbly bearing burdens and suffering "wounds" which I can hardly bear to think about; but I had this relief: by uniting them to the Wounds I made Christ bear, mine seemed very small, as long as I continued faithfully in my dark and peculiar prayer, day by day, and clung to the Sacraments in faith and love; and the teachings went on.

Christ began to teach me about the heart of the Christian Faith: about His own nature: about love. He showed me what's involved in the struggle to be Christ-like. He explained to me, emphatically:

> **Always love and comfort other persons, in every circumstance, whatever impression they might give by their words or actions. If you who are so blind and weak have longed for understanding and leniency, you ought to be lenient with others. (T:26 #1)**

One goal.

Imperceptible changes were taking place: things I didn't recognise until much later; but life began to seem very simple. I was content to be able to make new efforts to put Christ's commands into practice; and I discovered that the constant heart-ache of sorrow-for-sin was eventually accompanied by a constant conviction of being 'on the right track', with very little dithering about tasks, duties or goals. Every effort was totally devoted to the one goal: to please God and to love His Will. All lesser goals seemed to fit with greater ease into my life's new pattern. Suffering was part of that pattern, I realised: but Christ had been showing me how to suffer: to suffer in union with Him, and not to waste these various bodily or mental torments, but to make them fruitful. That was why, through all the years of pain still to come, I sat with Christ in Gethsemane, my heart and mind united to His, day after day, as I learned to bear my pains and humiliations with His agony, and, with Him, to make one willing act of Reparation and Love.

Other sufferings had to be endured. Not all were brought about by my own stupidity or my own flawed nature. Besides the illness, and other problems, I was suddenly bereaved.

One summer, at the end of a holiday abroad, I returned to England with the family to find notes all over the house, left by anxious neighbours. On phoning my parents' home, I was told that my father had been seriously ill for a week, and had just died. I hadn't been able to say goodbye. Comforted solely by the hope that we'd meet again one day, in Heaven, I tried to comfort others, especially the children, to whom he'd been a lovely Grandfather. It was wonderful to see how my mother's faith upheld her. For two years more she remained vigorously independent and active; and meanwhile, I pressed on with my usual occupations.

[Achieving good, even in darkness.

It seems very important that I stress, at this point in the story, that none of the miseries and struggles of the past few years had been 'wasted'; and I say this with confidence - in order to help those who doubt that any good can come from their own struggles - not just because I know it by faith but because, several years later, Christ confirmed it. He told me, to my astonishment, that He was delighted by every effort I'd made to please Him, even amidst my mistakes and hesitations. He said that He was pleased with me for every good thing done out of love for Him and for every wrong thing avoided. (T:1187)

That's why I'm bursting to say to every spiritual brother and sister who is wondering if our battles are worthwhile: "Don't despair. Don't give up. Although you don't perhaps realise it, it's at this very moment, as you're plodding along in spiritual darkness and yet are still battling to remain faithful for a minute at a time that you're proving the depth of your faith and love. It's right now that Christ is doing great work through your faith and perseverance. Right now, and for as long as you hang on to Christ, even in darkness, your soul is actively being purified, your faith, hope and love are being strengthened, and the precious people in your heart are being helped, whatever you see or don't see. The Church on earth is made stronger, through your life and love, the souls of Purgatory are helped, and the Saints and Angels are given greater cause for joy. Christ delights in your love, the Holy Spirit sees that His work in you is fruitful, and the Father of Light and Glory - your Heavenly Father - is glorified, and draws you more surely towards Himself so that you can one day share His Bliss and Glory. On that day, these torments will seem like a dream - or will be seen as mere pebbles over which you once stumbled, briefly, on your journey to Heaven!"

I want to say to every spiritual friend: " I'm speaking from the heart about these things because I know from experience that they're true. I haven't yet reached Heaven, but I've 'reached' the Father, "in Christ", through Christ's merits; and He has shown me much about our trials and their true significance. It's because He loves us so tremendously that He draws such a great good from our 'bad' times as well as from the good, if we only trust in Him and endure, until the time when He chooses to give us consolation."

Undergoing temptations.

To everyone who is undergoing temptations which make him feel humiliated or ashamed I want to say: "Keep fighting. Ask for help in prayer. It's by these struggles that you're proving your love and growing in virtue. And even if you 'fall', don't despair. Keep on going to Confession. When you're reconciled, you are shining with God's grace, even if you can't see it; and He loves to come to good-hearted and purified souls at Holy Mass, in Holy Communion. That's one of His rewards - as well as being a spiritual food and strength for us. But He has even greater rewards in store for you if only you'll persevere."]

Un-Christian views.

The new 'Rule of Life' which had emerged was very flexible, and changed with my needs. But as circumstances changed, I saw that some things must remain the same, whatever the cost. Prayer, as ever, was supremely important, three times a day, at home or away. Holy Mass, as I said, was the source of all my strength. I went as frequently as I could to Mass and Holy Communion. Each year seemed to bring greater peace and patience. I had a thousand reasons for gratitude, and tried to make every aspect of life thoroughly 'in tune' with God's wishes.

Much time in the past had been wasted, I saw, reading silly novels and magazines. It was true that they were entertaining and took my mind off my problems and pains; but many of them promoted amoral or un-Christian views. It had been sheer self-indulgence to read so many. It was pride that had me confident that I could read whatever I chose, without being influenced to some degree. By such carelessness I'd filled my mind with rubbish and endangered my faith.

I owned a book, in those days, which I had bought myself, had read at least three times and was tempted to read again. In some ways it was a magnificent book, written with skill and passion, and full of fascinating anecdotes about women's lives. But one day I realised that if I continued to read forceful and angry works by women who advocated 'liberation' from male 'aggression' I'd become bitter and angry, and would lose all trust in God and in His Providential care of us. I wasn't uncertain about truth or falsehood. I feared the book's influence as one fears being swept into a hot-headed mob in the street. A passionate hatred surged through some of those stories; and it was directed not at the real source of pain in many women's lives, which is sin - but only at men. I found that in many of the books I read, half the human race was condemned by feminists outright, and collectively, as responsible for the sufferings of women of every era.

It wasn't enough for the authors to denounce a few injustices and then to unfold the history of real improvements in the status of women who have been ill-treated in various ways. Certain relentless denunciations of men and of male-dominated institutions were so vehement, and stirred up such a violent sympathy in my heart, that I realised I was being tempted by the ploys of clever propagandists to leave aside not only a long-held Christian point-of-view, but every sort of sensible analysis of mens' hopes, marriage itself or the state of modern society.

In attractive pieces of writing which were truly so witty and skilful that the 'core message' was prettily disguised, various columnists and authors were tempting me to look at life through a different 'eye' and to ask not: 'What is God's Will for His people on earth, and God's Will for me, and how can I know it?" Rather, they encouraged women to demand: "Why should I suffer; why should I make sacrifices or stifle my dreams, or forgive other people when they marginalise or hurt me?"

All my years of listening and reading had taught me, through the Church - and especially through the Saints - that it's through self-sacrifice, rather than through self-love that Christian women in families can do most good for the whole human race. I saw that while some injustices can't be condoned, indeed ought to be strongly opposed, many real, dispiriting and long-term evils can surely be borne by Christians with God's help - in order to avoid all the terrible tragedies which can come through 'self-assertion'. I began to be appalled that so many families are destroyed so that one member should feel happier.

[Christian self-abnegation.

It seemed quite evident to me that no-one should concentrate, primarily, on his or her own 'self-fulfilment', I mean, in the worldly sense of ensuring at all costs that one's natural skills and aptitudes are appreciated and used, whilst still claiming to be seeking, primarily, the Will of God.

In every age, we can see that God sometimes calls people - for His own good reasons - to endure loneliness, or to make some great sacrifice, or even to accept martyrdom. Although reasonable efforts should be made to secure fair treatment for oneself as well as others in the interests of justice, Christians have always been invited to imitate the self-abnegation which Christ practised during his life on earth; and that's why it's so sad to see that many women have split their families, egged on by fervent critics of 'domestic slavery' in marriage. Children have had to grow up with divided loyalties. Some mothers even rid themselves of unborn babies, with permission from people in authority. What wonderful ideals and persons have been sacrificed on the altars newly-raised to the cry of womens' 'freedom'.

How dangerous it can be when an author's superficially attractive but un-Christian ideas are freely imbibed by a naive or over-confident Christian who wants to be educated or entertained. Truly, careless reading or 'viewing' of many things can damage hearts and minds, and stealthily encourage the worm of rebellion or of secret rage or envy: or whatever we might carry hidden within us, not yet "Christianised".

For these reasons, and others, I never again picked up reading material which provoked but which didn't help me. Also, I avoided becoming fruitlessly agitated about abuses or problems in areas of the world where I couldn't become involved in practical ways; instead, I wrote letters about them, and lifted up to God in prayer all the people being hurt. In that way my heart and soul and mind were involved, but my practical energies were used for the good causes to be found within the obvious duties of daily life.

How easily we can be tempted to misdirect our efforts, supposedly in God's service: to overlook the small injustices which it's our duty to correct close-at-hand, and, instead, to rage ineffectually about tragedies which are best handed over to the power of God, for remedy, through fervent sacrifices and through prayer.]

Favourite authors.

When I was still struggling to cope with the daily physical load, but was more at peace, and was less anxious to escape into a fictional world, I turned to books which would teach and encourage me in every circumstance. I read something 'spiritual' every day for at least half-an-hour, and ended each episode with a brief prayer - even if this meant that I had to set the alarm and go downstairs far earlier than anyone else. It gave me time to ponder, and to put things 'in perspective'. No matter what difficulties might arise in the day ahead, I'd find that one or two useful phrases from my reading would come to mind, just when they were needed.

Good books were like steel for my will, or like true friends urging me not to fall. Whenever I wondered how I'd cope with certain things, or whenever I was tempted to become scrupulous and fearful again, a few paragraphs of de Caussade or some other favourite author set me free from worry. I was reminded to keep my thoughts on the "HEAVENLY THINGS" (Col 3:2) which I ought to pursue at any cost. These authors, too, had walked through the "NARROW GATE" (Mt 7:13) long before me, in order to find Eternal life.

Heartening influences.

Every good Catholic writer reminded me of our need to use our God-given intelligence as well as our faith. It was encouraging to read accounts by people of different centuries, and especially of the present day, of how they had re-organised their lives, even in little ways, in order to leave enough time for prayer and silent reflection. It was heartening, too, to hear what other people said about the Mercy of God, and about God's loving influence upon their souls, no matter how reluctantly or painfully they had served Him nor how frequently they had given in to despondence or sin. I re-read works by the Abbot, Dom John Chapman, and by Cardinal Newman. I 'discovered' the Abbé de Tourville, and I clung to him for sustenance when memories or scruples threatened to pull me down. Once again, St. Francis de Sales helped me to think more carefully about the Christian life. Gerard Manley Hopkins' description of his "Hero" inspired me.

"The Great Divorce" by C. S. Lewis was fascinating; I still admired much of his work. But I realised that his heavy emphasis on doom and punishment was bad for me. His Creator seemed closer to my old "Headmaster" God than to the Father in Heaven whom we praised at Mass; so I left C. S. Lewis behind, to re-read Ronald Knox, more profitably, since I learned more about the teaching Church, and about Eucharistic devotion, and Saints, for example.

Biographies still fascinated me, and poetry, and films; but some of them left lingering after-tastes which were a danger to my faith. The desire for them grew less when my appreciation of what is truly good in life increased: by which I mean simple kindness and loyalty, patience in all our small duties, and happy moments with family and neighbours; and as I was reading, I found more new 'friends' amongst the Saints, some of whom had seemed fierce and frightening when I was twenty-one and was amazed by their asceticism. I grew to love the Curé of Ars, and St. Bernard - through his sermons - and St. Dominic. I was much encouraged by stories of modern Christian heroines: all different but all full of faith and love: Corrie Ten Boom, Mother Teresa, and then someone who had died in the month that I was born: Edith Stein, also known as Sister Teresa of the Cross.

For the first time, I read "Orthodoxy" and "The Everlasting Man", by G. K. Chesterton, and marvelled at the clarity with which he explained the Christian way of life. I was full of wonder at his inspired word-pictures and analogies. F. J. Sheed - in "Theology and Sanity" - was more 'technical' in his approach to the Faith, but like Chesterton was accurate and straightforward.

Within a few years I'd discover a whole host of 'new' authors, some of whom I'd never heard of until then because they were rarely mentioned by some of the post-Vatican-II writers who wished that the Church were less 'dogmatic' or 'old-fashioned'. Books by Fr. Tanquerey and Fr. Garrigou-Lagrange figured prominently in second-hand book lists, so I read a few chunks of "The Spiritual Life" and other works with tremendous joy, before discovering Dom Columba Marmion whose "Christ the Life of the Soul" went straight to the top of my list. Then along came other good works which persuaded me that there was still solid 'meat' to be found in Catholic bookshops and catalogues, amongst some of the watery dishes on offer.

Unorthodox works.

But my reading wasn't confined to Catholic authors; I was encouraged and taught, for example, by the wisdom of Gonville Ffrench-Beytagh and others, touched to read of their love for Jesus, and their passionate involvement in the great adventure of the spiritual life. I explored a number of further works, too, by present-day Catholic authors, but two problems held me back from great amounts of reading, first, the eye problems which accompanied my illness, and then the sadness which threatened to engulf me every time I opened a new book, looking for nourishment, only to be astonished that yet another Catholic author, in widely-published writings, was attacking the Church.

There seemed to be no limits to which some persons wouldn't go in print, in their criticisms of Church discipline and Church teachings and even in mockery of the present Holy Father.

Many of them claimed that their opinions were consistent with what they called "post-Vatican-Two-theology". However, having familiarised myself with the documents of that Council, and having absorbed and respected the Council's recommendations, I knew that none of the Council Fathers had newly-enshrined in our Faith any fundamental changes to our doctrines or moral code; nor had they expected the promotion of true 'renewal' in Church life to be made an excuse for disobedience.

It was a treat to find that Bishop Restieaux had authorised a re-print of his wonderful sermons about the Catholic Faith. I was fortunate to be able to buy several copies, to share them with friends. Cardinal Hume had written a new introduction. At around the same time, an American woman called Ann Ball wrote two volumes of the lives of "Modern Saints" - lavishly illustrated with photographs.

As I turned more frequently to both new and old "Lives of the Saints" - many women amongst them - I was comforted to read their stories. Most of these people had been full of love, not full of hatred of men or of institutions. They didn't pour scorn upon the Bishops and priests in their day; nor did they express dismay that the Church should ceaselessly and unhesitatingly state what was right and what was wrong. They were grateful to God for His care of them in the midst of life's trials. Many canonised saints had denounced injustice, but the fuel for the fire in their hearts wasn't scorn but a love of truth. That was why I became bolder in asking for their prayers: asking for help in all sorts of situations; and I began to ask the help of the holy Angels, more frequently, just like generations of Christians before me, overcoming my slight feelings of embarrassment.

Prayer and duty.

I never missed my daily prayer-time before God, even if I had to kneel at the side of the bath, which was sometimes the only peaceful spot in the whole house, due to our lively family and social life. Hordes of the childrens' friends used to drop in, the excited voices interwoven with noises from the television, perhaps with someone's lawnmower roaring outside, whilst trains thundered through the nearby cutting every ten minutes. Also, every meal, every peaceful moment, or visit from friends or relatives was interrupted by telephone calls from anxious patients or hospital staff.

Absorbed as I was in domestic tasks, and filling in the 'gaps' with prayer, there was no time to be bored. Letter-writing was squeezed into gaps between 'school-runs', and visits to sick friends and to healthy relatives. I was interested in very many other things, - in history, art, and gardening. My husband's job was so demanding, and my health so poor, and the needs of relatives so great, that I didn't go to a major gallery for several years, but I satisfied my curiosity with books. By visiting the Blessed Sacrament whenever I went out shopping, I never failed to receive greater hope and strength; and when I was well I took part in little art exhibitions on the village common.

[Mundane, dutiful work.

It seems plain to me now that although God would like us to develop our talents if circumstances permit we ought to look very carefully at our true motives. We're surely wrong if, for selfish reasons, we exchange mundane, dutiful work for something outwardly more "heroic." For example, someone who spends all day in gruelling fund-raising work for 'Charities' or who passes each day in back-breaking work for the needy, but for his or her own glory or satisfaction, is doing work which is quite unrewarded by God. And the work of the many who, noticed or unseen, quietly tend the sick or clean lavatories, or queue weekly for someone else's pension, and who do such things for the love of God and neighbour give joy to Christ and to all his Saints and Angels, as He has shown me.]

Beloved children.

Despite my never-ending longing to tell the world about Christ's love for us all, I spent years struggling to live with my shame at having served Him so badly. My hopes about bringing other people into His Church seemed very fragile. If I was asked about my faith, I stoutly defended it, as always, but I was convinced that if only Catholics led holy lives and were more articulate about their faith, many more people would come into the Church; and I wished that I myself were fit to tell other people just Who could be found in the sanctuary, in the Blessed Sacrament. I was sure that crowds would be flocking up the road to church, struggling for the chance to be near our Blessed Lord, like the crowds in Galilee - if only people would realise the astonishing truth about His Real Presence.

Although I was lacking in confidence, I wasn't afraid to admit that God had gradually brought me to a truer understanding of his Will. He yearns to see us obey Him not as slaves who pander to the whims of a tyrant, but as beloved children of a Father Who alone knows what will make us truly happy and content. I realised that what God wanted for me was that I live faithfully in His Love, in my weakness, unconcerned about the approval of others, willingly accepting blame or criticism, but quietly and lovingly doing what I saw to be essential for the fulfilment of my duties. He wanted me to entrust to His Providence all that I could not - need not - actually do. That is why the new road, in one sense, was easy; I had only to be loving and forgiving, as I slowly worked out where God's Will lay in each single moment, amidst the details of ordinary life.

My main regret was that my love for God and my readiness for sacrifice had grown so slowly and so grudgingly that I'd waited until near-despair before being persuaded to give my whole life to Him - and my whole heart. I hadn't leapt unhesitatingly into His Love, but had waited until I'd lost all other means of support. But how thankful I was for faith in Him. I had great faith in His love and His mercy, even though I lacked other virtues; so I carried on, expecting to struggle in the same way for the rest of my life. Nothing mattered but to try to love God, and for His sake to love other people: especially those with whom He brought me into contact from day to day.

I still had to fight my fears, weaknesses and scruples. I had no idea how I'd 'get through' the next day or year; but for the first time, my will belonged wholly to God - through the Christ Whom I couldn't hear, see, feel or touch. I hoped I'd remain grateful, forever, for the sacraments and for opportunities for penance. I accepted the darkness in peace.

The Will of God.

The beginnings of a true resurrection were lived out in very simple ways. I worked, I rested, I was ill, I was well again: I learned to say "Fiat". That was the word from the Gospel by which Christ's Holy Mother had consented to the Will of God being done. "Fiat", or "LET WHAT YOU HAVE SAID BE DONE TO ME" (1 Co 15:57) and "Deo Gratias," which means "LET US THANK GOD" (Lk 1:38) became my most frequent prayers.

The family grew more independent, and the work-load eased for a while: "Deo Gratias". My closest friend moved away: "Fiat", again. Some things gave me joy, some things saddened me, but by God's grace I recognised God's Will in everything, and was content. I came to the stage when I could even be glad that through these experiences I'd begun to learn about trusting God. How could I have been brought to trust Him, if I hadn't turned to Him in desperation, appalled by my own weakness: desolate and fearful?

What a great gift is faith: a gift I'd been given, undeserved. But there was no gladness in it, for many years. I had no sweet words to say to God in prayer. I sat or knelt at Mass as usual, saying, "O God, I want to love You," which was the truth; and even though I didn't know this, my faith was being strengthened by every little prayer and every little effort.

Lourdes.

Within two or three years of that new resolution, I happened to be with my family, on holiday in France; and we stopped in Lourdes for twenty-four hours, to enable me to pray at the shrine of Our Lady, and to let our children see the famous torch-light procession. I remember standing at the edge of Rosary Square before the main procession began, leaning on my stick, and watching a procession of wheelchairs race through the large crowd. Well-trained brancardiers held us back from danger until all the carriages had flown by; and I felt so unwell - and so lonely there, as the only Catholic in the family - that I prayed a fervent prayer to Our Lady, begging her to help me. Never could I have imagined what good things she could bring about through her prayers and God's grace - and my mustard-seed of faith.

Within twenty years I'd find myself praying at almost exactly the same spot, yet this time surrounded by grown-up children each of whom had freely chosen to become a Catholic in adult life - and with the elder son newly-ordained. Furthermore, there stood beside me the husband who was preparing to be received into full Communion: and who indeed was received and confirmed in Harpenden at our Easter Vigil in 1998. So I hope and pray that other people will believe that Our Lord and Our Lady can help them, and that it's worth persevering in prayer. God is so good; and the results will astonish us, if only we don't give in, and give up.

That's one of the reasons why I now thank God for those dark, safe years: but 'safe' only because I put Christ first in everything, at last: not 'safe' because of any special feelings of comfort. Faith did its work and told me that Christ loved me, but I felt as though I'd been abandoned. I couldn't escape seeing my sins in memory, day by day, as I prayed in spiritual darkness to the invisible God.

God's purifying Fire.

For several years, and for my own good, Christ led me along in utter blackness as I clung to Him in desperation, feeling lost, with dangers at each side. I made frequent acts of faith, hope, and love. The first two years were spent in 'fire' and in darkness, by which I mean: in a state in which I endured the experience of God's purifying fire as it burned within my repentant soul. The remainder were spent in pure 'darkness' which was occasionally - and suddenly, briefly, puzzlingly - lit by an extraordinary Light.

There were human woes and misunderstandings; and these were no minor things, but severe trials, hard to bear when it seemed as though God Himself were silent. I was in pain, and suffered weakness in my legs for months at a time. It seemed as though I was a 'failure' in almost every way. I had failed in my work and in my ambitions - even in my supposedly good aims. No longer could I see myself as an excellent wife and mother, welcoming friends with boundless energy, and being gay and hospitable to strangers. Ever more clearly, I was able to look back and recognise my obvious mistakes. Formerly, I saw, I had tried to be heroic, but sometimes for the wrong reasons.

In my attempts to please God I had undertaken tasks which He hadn't wished me to do, and had made misguided attempts to please others: sometimes through fear, and sometimes from a desire for peace or for popularity. Persevering in tormented prayer, I encountered my true nature, day by day, as I prayed before the face of God, no longer flinching at the sights He revealed within my conscience and my heart, but accepting them all as God-given glimpses of Truth.

Then a marvellous process began, or, rather, continued - but far more surely. It became evident that the more I uncovered my soul for God, then the more I learned - wordlessly - about His ways. The true, great, marvellous conversation of prayer was at last underway. It was utterly mysterious and extremely dark and frightening. It was also a silent conversation, one which God rarely undertakes with a soul who refuses to look steadfastly in His direction, in awe, and with some semblance of regret and humility. I remained quite blind to a great a number of faults, but more and more frequently, in prayer, my intention was pure, by which I mean that it was set on pleasing God and not myself.

As ever, I wanted to please God solely because He Is: because He is God, and so 'deserves' our obedience. It didn't occur to me to try to do good primarily in order to be rewarded or to go to Heaven; yet I can say from experience that I've been helped to avoid doing greater evil, at various times of my life, because of the Church's constant reminder of Christ's own warning: that evil is punished.

The door opens.

One day in 1980, having prepared me by suffering, God took pity on me. He knew that I loved Him. I had faith and longing, though without much understanding. He knew that my whole desire was to please Him. He knew that I had no ambition except to do His Will until the moment of death; and that is why, within our dark prayer of silence, a new life unfolded.

Something now happened within me, deep within prayer. Now that I'd spent many years in prayer and penance, and after many years of kneeling in spiritual darkness, I made a discovery. Christ had moved the clutter that had held tight the 'door' of my soul. I was able to open the door in prayer, to let Him in. What was happening was wholly spiritual, but it was experienced as even more 'real' than real ordinary life.

A terrible light shone around when Christ came at last to my soul's centre. Many foul things were to be revealed: depths of junk, and spiritual and emotional horrors, impossible for me to move alone. But Christ kept me free from all anxiety about this. Whether I knelt before Him in church or at home, I was taught by Him, wordlessly, to carry on in His way, and to serve Him faithfully for a single minute at a time; and He gave me the courage to let Him continue with His work, as His burning light scoured the interior of my soul in a way never experienced before. Christ taught me, in my soul's silence:

> **Be glad that your faithful preparation is showing results. After many years of prayer, penance and reparation, you have removed the 'junk' and clutter and wrapping - as if layer by layer - from the interior of your soul, revealing, at last: a 'door'. In only a moment, I your Lord, can remove whatever has been holding it tightly shut. (T:25 #1)**

> **Give me permission to enter your soul, in prayer. I can remove every remaining obstacle. I can enable you to *open the door of the soul*, and you can invite Me to enter. (T:25 #2)**

196

Recognise the gift which I have given to you. Only after many years of faithfully reciting your words of praise and thanksgiving, sorrow and petition were you privileged to open the "door of the soul", to *let My light shine through.* By your obedience to My wishes in regular and dutiful prayer you were giving Me 'permission' to act within your life and soul. (T:25 #3)

Don't be upset by 'bad' feelings in prayer. My Light is bound to reveal all sorts of 'junk' within your soul - junk which it is impossible for you to move alone. Bear the pain which must accompany the beginnings of humility. (T:25 #4)

Avoid all anxiety during the 'scouring' which I am doing, and which is your soul's purification. (T:25 #5)

Carry on in My way, for one minute at a time. (T:25 #6)

Open the interior 'door' of your soul every time you pray, whatever the cost. *It is opened by contrition and by a true longing for union* with Me. (T:25 #7)

Deliverance.

Christ gave me the strength to bear my shame each time that I knelt down in prayer. I was racked by mixed feelings of hope and regret, but was learning to show Him my whole heart, and then to move forward in a prayer of pure faith and supernatural love. I was full of fear and reverence towards Him, but since my only desire was to please Him whatever the cost, even if it should cost me everything, I'd been released from a servile terror.

Life went on its usual pattern; work, prayer, leisure, work, prayer, reading - work! To and fro, Christ led me in the darkness: to the various persons whom He'd put in my care, and then back to Him in prayer. It was as though I sat with Him in fire and darkness day after day, not really knowing what was going on: but I trusted Him with my entire life, at last, hoping that because He'd led me through so many dangers He wouldn't suddenly give up His work.

As the strange, silent 'teachings' continued I had no idea what was happening; but my only aims were to please Christ, to pray regularly and sincerely and to be cheerful in fulfilling my duties. Christ taught me something about 'aiming' one's heart and soul towards Him unerringly, in prayer. He explained how our burning feelings of guilt and shame should be accepted as by-products of the process of spiritual purification. He advised me:

Keep on praying. It is through your prayer that I can change and strengthen you. (T:28 #1)

Meet Me in the most secret 'place' within your soul. Whenever you pray, turn your heart and mind towards your soul's dark 'centre'. (T:28 #2)

Throw away your 'armour' in prayer - all your hesitations, excuses, and self-justifications. *Sit* patiently *with Me in* what seems like *both fire and darkness,* as My purifying Light does it work within your soul. (T:28 #3)

Again and again, in prayer, *let Me burn away the clutter within your soul, so that My Light can shine here more brightly.* (T:28 #4)

Accept and endure all burning shame in prayer, since - with a desire to please Me - it serves as a penance for past sins. It is a proof that I am at work in your soul. (T:28 #5)

Ignore all fantasies and images in prayer. Peer deeper into your soul's interior darkness as though reaching out your heart and mind to Me, within. (T:29 #1)

A warm heart.

On another occasion, Christ showed me how to deal with distracting images. He told me:-

Recognise idols, within your soul, when you come to prayer, whether they are constant or fluctuating, grotesque or attractive. Ignore them. (T:29 #2)

Permit Me, though I am invisible to you, to 'steer' you within our soul's darkness. *Look beyond images, monster-Gods or phantoms into My own universe in your heart, where I, Christ your God, reign. (T:29 #3)*

Look upon your soul as the Kingdom *where* We - *the Holy Three, One God - reign in Light.* (T:29 #4)

It amazed me again to realise that God, our Infinitely Holy Creator, not only loves us but always awaits us. Whenever we demand His time, His love or His presence, He is here! We never fail to find Him. There is no place where He 'is not' - and He never keeps us waiting, but listens to us with love whenever we turn to Him. I was reminded that it's faith that assures us of God's love and concern, whether we sense His presence or not. Feelings come and go, but God's love is real and everlasting, and our faith in that love is increased further at every occasion on which we turn to God in naked trust. (T:29)

As I prayed one day, in my usual darkness, trying to reject all images and sensations for the sake of Truth who is God, my heart was warmed when He made His presence felt for the first time in about ten years. He knew then, as He knows now, that I expected no extraordinary consolations. I had no ambition other than to do His Will; and so this experience of His presence was a pure gift: pure kindness, and pure grace. Though I think He could scarcely have bound my will to Him more tightly, He at last bound my heart, which became entirely His.

I thank God for the darkness of those years, in which Christ enabled me, quietly, to grow braver and stronger. I thank Him, too, for my ignorance of all that was to be put before me. Had I known in advance of the trials and torments I'd face in trying to be loyal to Him, I'm not sure I'd have had the courage to begin the journey. How wise He is. He knows how much we can bear during our training, and gives us strength at each moment; and so I thank Him profoundly for having given me the grace to persevere in prayer, and so to retain a degree of hope in my heart that some sort of joy and fulfilment awaited me.

Household changes.

Daily life continued very full and busy as usual, in the early nineteen-eighties, but became much more joyful, even amidst family crises.

About two years after my father's death, my mother became unwell. Her treatment was unsuccessful, so she agreed to come and live with me and my husband and children. She was much comforted by relatives and old friends, and found this was a happy time, in many ways. She had gladly laid down the burden of work and house-keeping, and had been able to renew her acquaintance with several grand-children. She sat in an easy chair out in our garden for a few hours each day throughout that long warm summer, all her plans completely surrendered. We had moved to a different house by then, and had plenty of room for her, and for all her visitors.

She gave her whole life cheerfully back to God, helped by the tender care of our doctor and by the Sacraments received from our parish priest when he visited every day or two. Our dear Canon Keenan was by now very old and somewhat disabled, but continued to make his usual cheerful and loving sick-visits.

Far from being dismayed by our household changes, I was delighted to be able to look after my mother. All my thoughts, over the years, on work and duty and suffering had led me to see the Christian life as one of service and self-sacrifice, yet with these untainted, I hoped, by a martyred air. I mean that I'd learned something about prudence, and had developed a bit of common-sense in arranging my own activities; so instead of blindly charging into another anguished sick-bed routine, I resolved to care for my mother as wholly-heartedly and as cheerfully as possible - but at the same time I arranged a corner of the house where I could paint undisturbed in the occasional hour or two that I could spare from her company or from other occupations. I'd long given up any remaining ambition of taking up serious study: for example, of doing what is called a distance-learning degree. I'd decided that it was impossible to make that sort of commitment if I might find it necessary, instead, to welcome a new guest; and that's why I'd concentrated on a more modest ambition, such as developing as a painter who specialised in flowers and still-life. That sort of work was possible to organise at home; and when I eventually became a founder-member of a Botanical Art Society, I was able to exhibit in London every summer.

My mother had always enjoyed my paintings and had encouraged me to do more. So her delight in what she saw as my recent and unexpected artistic 'success' was communicated to all her friends. She took great pleasure in telling them all that her daughter had even exhibited at the Royal Academy; and she took pleasure, too, in sharing some of her own story with a 'new' priest. Canon Keenan had at last retired - and then died suddenly, to my great sadness. But he'd been replaced by a very kind and dutiful priest called Canon Maurice O'Leary.

We were able to care for my mother until she died, grateful for that precious opportunity. Once again, faith enabled me to entrust a departed soul to God. I hoped and prayed for her eternal joy, and for our reunion one day in Heaven; and I asked Our Blessed Lady to be both my spiritual and my earthly mother.

A Catholic child.

During the next few years other relatives died, and also friends of our own age. Life's pattern no longer surprised me since experience had proved to me that all our plans and activities are interspersed by unforeseen joys or griefs. I had learned that it's wiser not to cling to anything on this earth - neither persons nor things. It's easier and wiser to accept whatever God gives us at the present moment, and to accept that the people we love are entrusted to us only for a short while. Then it becomes easier - with His help - to remain accepting and trusting when, inevitably, things or persons are taken away, whether by robberies, or by 'misfortunes', or by death - which, for those who trust in the merits and promises of Christ, is only a temporary parting.

But what great joys were given, amidst the sorrows! About a year after my mother's death, our eldest 'child' - a son who was nineteen and was about to set off for university - told us that he'd asked to be received into the Catholic Church. I hadn't expected a joy as great as that, having learned to live in the present moment, and not to worry about my own future or anyone else's. I was overwhelmed with gratitude to God. It was a tremendous privilege to go to Mass and Communion with one of my own children, in his end-of-term holidays.

Another cause for personal celebration was that from about 1984 or 1985 the times of Masses at the local church were changed, and I was able to go there daily, when the family's breakfast was eaten and cleared away; and that's why I began to meditate, each evening, on the daily readings of the Mass. I was too weary to continue to read the Breviary as well, and it seemed sensible to alter my routine; so I swapped the Breviary for a Daily Missal, treasuring the Church's choices in the three readings from Holy Scripture each day, even if I was less than enthusiastic about recent translations of Psalms and prayers. I wasn't disturbed by the loss of archaisms but by the occasional lack of accuracy.

Jerusalem and Galilee.

Little problems were briefly swamped, soon afterwards, by yet another tremendous joy. The people and events of the Scriptures were to be seen in a new light after a marvellous trip to "the Holy Land", as I still called it, from habit. I seized a wonderful opportunity, and flew to Tel Aviv airport in the spring of 1985. So fervent had been my longing to visit Israel one day that I'd even prepared to some extent by learning Hebrew at evening class, as I mentioned, when I'd taken weekly lessons from a Rabbi, with a dozen other enthusiasts. I can't describe my joy at being in what was Christ's own country, amongst His people; and I wept on seeing the coast from the aircraft. I visited and prayed at every possible shrine, touching my crucifix to those ancient stones.

Based not far from the centre of Jerusalem, I took coach tours, daily, to the places where Jesus had lived or walked or suffered during the life we've read about in the Holy Gospels. It's not worth trying to share my impression of the whole trip when thousands before me have written about those sacred places; so I'll content myself with mentioning little pleasures.

It was thrilling to discover Bethany, where Christ could count on a welcome from special friends. Then when I travelled North, to gaze at the hills surrounding His home town of Nazareth, it was marvellous to know that His eyes had seen those very sights, since the hills don't change even if buildings fall down or people disagree about the authenticity of the holy places. In just a few days, the marvellous childhood words such as 'Galilee', 'Wilderness', 'the Jordan', 'Jericho' and 'Jerusalem' all came alive in my mind in a new way, no longer 'festooned' with shreds of inaccurate associations, of the sort which I'd gathered since the age of three. My faith didn't change, although I recognise that Providence helps us in all sorts of ways, especially through our acts of devotion when we're on pilgrimage; I mean that the images and historical facts which can feed or sharpen our faith became more truthful and effective.

Amongst personal highlights was a moment of prayer in the church in the garden of Gethsemane, seeing the great stone where Christ might have lain weeping with fear. I learned something more about His great love for us. And I was awe-struck on approaching another great rock: the stone of sacrifice sited within a mosque on Temple Mount. What an ancient site, and how holy! I was awe-struck to be so near the spot where Abraham had stood in obedience to God, and near which Isaiah had trembled, knowing himself to be unworthy to be in God's presence. I would have liked to have stayed there silently for the whole day, but the crowd pressed round chattering, and I knew the tour-guide would be waiting.

New authors.

Once back in England, involved in the usual hectic routine, I made time for further encouraging spiritual reading. New authors helped me to keep my resolutions. Yet, despite my determination to be 'broad-minded', since works by Christians of different loyalties were all interesting, I found that there was no substitute for 'solid' Catholic nourishment. The documents of Vatican II were most enlightening. But I tried to keep an historical 'balance' by reading a certain amount about the early Councils, the great Church fathers, and also about the Council of Trent, the teachings of which are still valid, as the Church tells us, no matter how much they might be criticised or ignored by some modern theologians.

But several modern writers were helpful, such as William Johnston and Sheila Cassidy. Thomas Merton's work led me towards Catherine De Hoeck Doherty. Then I discovered Fr. Aidan Nichols' "Looking at the Liturgy" and Cardinal Ratzinger's "Church, Ecumenism and Politics," when at last I'd found some reliable Catholic booksellers and publishers. Certain other authors, praised by friends and reviewers, seemed sentimental or unsound; but it had been useful to read widely and to find out what different Christians - even different Catholics - believed. As ever, in new books or pamphlets, there were 'new' Saints or holy persons to discover. St. John of the Cross caught me by his humility and Matt Talbot touched my heart by his total self-giving. So many of them strengthened me by their prayers.

For some time I'd been helped, too, by modern translations of Holy Scripture. It was a marvellous experience to read the letters of St. Paul in each new modern version. They sounded as though he'd written them only a week ago.

Greater peace.

Prayer-times became almost as peaceful as the times spent with a book. I still knelt in prayer in faith mingled with fear. But as my trust grew, nourished by frequent Communion, the fears lessened and joy crept in from time to time, accompanied by greater hope; and as I went on in darkness, I began to discern a new pattern to my life. I was free from scruples most of the time, and free from concern about my health - or lack of it. Christ had taught me to repent of my failings, but never to dwell on minor things. By interior self-laceration my heart had been kept anxious, bleeding from the wounds of memory. Acts of trust and firm resolutions lead me closer to Christ: closer to His peace.

But if ever I made foolish choices, not from weakness but from selfishness, the peace disappeared and I was left in torment - something different from mere guilty feelings; it was a terrible spiritual pain. I've experienced this on only two occasions in the past few years, and about faults which can't remotely be called serious; and I hope and pray that I may never, ever, offend Christ again. When He has taught someone about His Will, by personal instruction, He is very strict about any deliberate little betrayal. He would overlook such things in the life of someone who is genuinely good-hearted but not in the life of someone who is acting selfishly even after having been privileged to receive extra 'coaching' from Our Lord. He wants to see real change and self-sacrifice, not self-indulgence.

Christ had always been as lavish with encouragement, however, as with necessary rebukes; and He's also known about every difficulty and every cause for sorrow. He alone knew that I'd lived in an interior night for so many years - in pain, still, and struggling; but He alone could see ahead; He could see the wonderful gifts which He was longing to shower upon me more and more lavishly as I went through successive spiritual purifications.

Pierced by 'Knowledge'.

All I expected was that I'd carry on in darkness for the rest of my life; but I was astonished and puzzled to find that the usual gloom of my prayer was pierced, occasionally, by an extraordinary, invisible Light. Every few weeks - then every few days - when I was praying at Holy Mass, I'd find that my soul had been 'pierced' by 'Knowledge', and that in a split second I'd learned something marvellous about God, about Christ and His Church, or about grace, prayer, and souls. I learned nothing new, but many truths already learned through worship or through books and sermons were wonderfully given anew or illuminated. The 'occurrences' were always unexpected, brief and astounding: totally new and strange. Never had I anticipated anything like this happening in my everyday spiritual life.

All that I'd ever read had warned me to mistrust strange 'feelings', although these weren't 'feelings' - but "happenings" which disappeared as quickly as they came. I tried to ignore the knowledge and the 'events', and to pray as I'd always prayed. It had never occurred to me to hope for special gifts: someone like me! Also, every authoritative Catholic writer had warned the reader to flee anything unusual experienced in prayer.

In my ignorance, I didn't realise how or why I was being taught. But Christ had brought me to a new way of life where He Himself was teaching me about the life of grace. It was totally unexpected; I'd hoped for nothing more than to have enough grace simply to endure. But every few weeks - then more frequently - when I was praying after Holy Communion, in darkness, I'd find that Christ had suddenly illuminated my soul with His soundless wisdom.

I confessed my sins and made acts of faith, hope and love. I adored God in darkness, and knelt in a numb silence after Mass. The daily routine was the same; it consisted of self-offering, and the 'Jesus Prayer,' with morning and night prayers, all prayed in faith alone as year followed year. I combined them with secret penance and with regular attendance at Holy Mass, as I said, and Reconciliation. Meanwhile, I told no-one about the teachings. Whom could I tell, and why? But I eventually realised that each gift of 'knowledge' clarified in a marvellous way the truths of God and of His Church. I felt secure, because although I hadn't looked for such experiences they seemed to have increased my faith and fervour, and caused the Scriptures themselves to come alive in a new and wholly beneficial way. That's why I dared to believe that they came from God and not from an evil source. Who but God, I reasoned, could cause me - by this extraordinary means - to love obscurity, to consent to being ignored or misunderstood, and to grow more patient in my pain?

It seemed to me, at last, that I'd be very ill-mannered if I ignored what God was choosing to do for me; so after Holy Communion one day I solemnly and briefly thanked Him for what I'd learned. He knew that I wanted nothing except His grace and strength so that I could keep walking on in darkness, if darkness should be what He permitted. He knew that my faith and hope weren't dependent on extraordinary experiences in prayer.

It was the right thing to do, though I continued to pray that Christ would preserve me from all evil and self-deception. Meanwhile, He continued to give me this sort of 'knowledge' in one brief unexpected moment after another. Each time, I learned more in a split second about Christ and His mercies than I could have learned from reading and thinking for years and years.

A plateau on the Mountain.

Now that I was clinging to Christ through thick and thin, He began to encourage me in a more vigorous way. For example, He showed me an image in prayer: of myself, standing on a hill-side high above a great plain; and then He astonished me by explaining:-

> **Learn to see life so far as a long journey which you have made with Me. Though you couldn't see Me, I was beside you all the time. (T:31 #1)**

Turn to Me in prayer, and - whilst you are kneeling here
before me - consider the details of your daily life. This is
how you can see each day's incidents and problems most
clearly. (T:31 #2)

*Look back, as if to gaze upon a 'wide plain' below, to see all
the events and trials of your life in a new light, which is My
Light. See the battles which you have fought for Me and the
triumphs which you have won!* (T:31 #3)

Don't be afraid that I'm going to remind you of your sins
and failures. In My sight, nothing of them can be seen. By
confession and forgiveness they have been taken away for
ever. (T:31 #4)

Aspects of Goodness.

It was still only by naked faith in God that I believed in His love for me, and in the forgiveness
that I'd received in the Sacrament of Reconciliation; so this teaching certainly consoled me.
But there was more to learn. I wasn't going to be allowed to slacken my efforts.

Christ reminded me once again of the importance of my loving my neighbours and also of
seeing Divine goodness in them. He explained this one day by means of a vision, when I was
praying at Mass. I was shown an image, in prayer.

I saw the faces of a few people I knew, appearing, indistinct, in a great ray of light which
seemed to come from God, from far above. I stood in prayer, near the left side of the church,
beneath a window; and as I prayed, I suddenly found that Christ had explained to me:

Be grateful for every good and loving quality which you see
or experience or sense in the people you meet. All goodness
is from Me. It is a gift. Every aspect of goodness is a gift
from me. (T:32A #1)

Ponder the marvel of it: that every good person's good act,
gesture, word or thought or expression reflects some aspect
of My Almighty, extraordinary Goodness. (T:32A #2)

Thus He encouraged me to be more thoughtful and observant as I lived and worked amongst
all sorts of different people and continued with my efforts to love everyone for Christ's sake.

The illuminative way.

It wasn't to be until much later on that the 'teachings' which suddenly appeared within my
soul in prayer ceased to surprise me, or rather, were recognised as comprising a normal part of

the spiritual life. I was going to be shown by Christ that He has lavished His teachings upon me in such abundance for a specific purpose, which is that I share them with the whole Church, through my paintings and writings, as a reminder and an encouragement of important truths of the Faith. But I believe that all who persevere in prayer and try to be loyal to Christ and His Will, no matter what it cost them, will be 'taught' by Him in some manner, in what's known as the Illuminative Way; and as I look back to those early 'teachings' and notice the way in which Christ taught me, by a wonderful interweaving of truths, as He gave me detailed instruction in the teachings of His own Church and also tactful advice about personal concerns, I am touched to the heart by this evidence of His goodness.

As personal concerns decrease.

Just in case there are readers who prefer not to see this narrative interrupted more and more frequently by 'teachings', I'll better explain that the number of such excerpts must increase in the second half of this book.

Since I'm writing this story of the 'journey' of the soul at Christ's request, and since a main characteristic of any journey towards Him is that personal concerns decrease as there arises within the soul a longing to see Christ's Will fulfilled, I must let Christ's words replace my own, to a large extent - or, rather, I must let the teachings of the Three Persons of the Holy Trinity replace my comments and opinions. In this way, I hope to show out not just the several stages of the journey, and not just which topics are most important in Christ's eyes, but, most importantly, the way in which Christ has led me to the Father.

As I include further excerpts from these teachings, I must suppose that most readers will notice the somewhat stilted language in which I've 'clothed' the teachings. It was Christ Who invited me to translate His silent teachings into words, as well as to record His own 'given' words, when He had chosen to use them. Yet I was so appalled at being involved in such work for God in spite of my unfitness that I could barely bring myself to write. Inevitably, the language of my early 'translations' reflects more of the crippling awe which I felt in the presence of Christ than His own true simplicity and beauty. But anyone who perseveres and examines the language of later teachings might believe that it corresponds more closely with Christ's tender, gentle and unhurried way of explaining things - whether points of theology or expressions of delight in my efforts to please Him.

A cry on Calvary.

Right at the beginning of what was to become an unending stream of 'teachings', I was given a powerful reminder of my debt to Christ; and this was necessary, I'm sure, in order to place all of the 'teachings' on a very firm foundation. The humility which Christ has always tried to foster within my soul is not only vital for a truly-Christian way of life but is absolutely essential for someone whom He has called to a way of contemplation and reparation. So that's why He startled me one Palm Sunday as I was listening intently to the solemn reading from Holy Scripture in which Our Lord's Passion is described: about how "THEY CRUCIFIED HIM THERE AND THE TWO CRIMINALS ALSO" (Lk 23:33).

As I stood in the crowded church that morning I suddenly saw and heard in my soul, though not with my eyes or ears, Our Lord's terrible cry on Calvary; and I was silently instructed:-

> **Listen to My cry of agony as I hang on the Cross; I - the Lord of Heaven and earth - have been punished as a criminal (T:32B #1)**

> **Try to comfort Me in My Passion, by your compassion. I Who am God and man suffered tremendous torments for you - and for each one of you, not merely for 'mankind' - on account of your sins. (T:32B #2)**

> **Spend time sitting prayerfully with Me in Gethsemane, or in any place where I suffered for your sakes. This comforts Me, and also helps you to persevere. (T:32B #3)**

> **Offer your pains and sorrows to Me, in reparation for sins, and as a proof of your devotion. (T:32B #4)**

I never forgot that cry. Christ's Passion became, for me, something recognised as being very closely connected with my life: with my 'status' as a child of God, and with the security and hope which have been brought to me in the Christian way of life.

Then, very soon afterwards, I was given a teaching, or a 'vision', which brought me not only information but consolation.

Joyful news.

Every new 'teaching' puzzled and astonished me, but what I was shown next, with extraordinary clarity, was something I'd never in a hundred years have expected to see; I'm speaking about the state of soul of a person who had died; and it was only as I was praying to God the Father in the Name of Christ that this was suddenly shown to me, by His choice. I had always prayed fervent prayers for departed souls, ever since I'd become a Catholic, but I'd always been content, then, to leave them in God's hands and never to be impatient thinking what had become of these people, but only to pray for each one in case "THOUGH HE IS SAVED HIMSELF, IT WILL BE AS ONE WHO HAS GONE THROUGH FIRE" (1 Co 3:15). It's so sad that some desperate people try to achieve knowledge about the dead by dangerous means. But what Christ chose to show me, to my astonishment, was the sight of a very good person who had died and who was now rising upwards to Heaven in great happiness and glory. I was much comforted, because the man who was now looking so young and carefree was my own beloved father, who had died only a month earlier (T:35) and whose purification had evidently been very brief.

'Purity-of-Knowledge'.

Christ gave me numerous other teachings which of course I can't possibly include within this book. These frequent "piercings" of Knowledge were extremely puzzling, as I said earlier; but the puzzlement was slight in the sense that I'd spent many years in simple work and worship. As a busy mother who had been further restricted by physical weakness, I had seen years pass by in apparent spiritual stagnation while other people managed to attend retreats, conferences, discussions or prayer-groups; and although I didn't resent this, I came to see, later on, that because of my isolation I had little idea of what other people experienced in prayer. So the 'knowledge' was a total surprise to me, unsought, unexpected, and puzzling: a mild mystery which I assumed would probably cease in the near future. I was content with whatever Christ chose to give me in prayer, or to withhold.

It was true that during the past few years I'd learned through books, sermons and pictures that holy people in every era have been disturbed by visions and peculiar phenomena. But I knew only too well how sinful I am, and so I never labelled any of my 'happenings' as 'visions'. I thought of them as a strange sort of prayer which God arranged in me for His own secret purposes; and the teachings I received bore no similarity to the multi-coloured apparitions which I supposed the Saints had seen before their bodily eyes.

It was true that when I'd prayed to Christ for help many years before, He had appeared to the eyes of my soul; but that wasn't an 'apparition,' as I understood the word. He hadn't been a phantom whom I could have chased away, but had really been present to my soul, somehow. I'd accepted it as a normal, though disturbing, spiritual 'happening', which was due entirely to His kindness. Hadn't the Scriptures said that the Lord promises that "THEY WILL CALL ON MY NAME AND I SHALL LISTEN" (Zc 13:9)?

In recent years I hadn't thought much about it, living in a darkness of soul which had grown familiar, even though it was terrible to bear. I lived fully in the present moment, not in memories, and wouldn't have dared to demand either light or relief from God. I was quite incapable of looking back joyfully at any earlier spiritual experience.

But one thing I did notice was that the 'Knowledge' was utterly "pure" in a particular way; and since I want to explain about 'purity-of-Knowledge' I must first explain something about memory, or rather about my personal manner of recalling things to mind, whether thoughts, events, or writings.

Information with no 'style'.

It's probably true that I've always taken for granted the fact that I have what's called a photographic memory, by which I can recall to mind various facts or events, whilst also remembering where it was that I read or absorbed a certain piece of information, and even the size and colour of the book in which I had read it. This aptitude had proved very useful when I was doing history exams at school.

But now, for example, were I to recall a paragraph written by C. S. Lewis, on Purgatory, I'd know that the words were his. The concept would be put across to me in his distinctive style. A different style would be noted if ever I recalled Abbot Marmion's wonderful phrases about "Christ in His mysteries", or Fr. Knox's comments about the Eucharist in his book the "Window in the Wall". Yet, the pure 'Knowledge' given in prayer was word-less and immediate. There was no visible or audible 'vehicle' bringing it to me. It had no 'style' except its own marvellous fullness and purity. I hadn't 'recalled' it from an historic source. Every scrap of such 'knowledge' was a total surprise to me: unsought, puzzling and mildly mysterious. It would go away one day, I supposed; and meanwhile, I was genuinely content to welcome my soul's interior darkness for as long as God willed that I should remain in it. I accepted that agony as a penance, since faith told me that I had only one task of importance to do; I was to cling to God at the centre of my soul as I worked to be loving and patient for His sake. I was to get up repentant but confident whenever, in my weakness, I failed to love others as perfectly as Christ loves me.

Work, and dark prayer.

As I tried to trust in God in the darkness, and to avoid sin and to find the courage to do His Will, my heart was secure. All the moments of 'Knowledge' were so pure, so sudden, and so utterly unsought, that my fear lessened. These were the truths of the Gospel: truths which urged me towards nothing else but love and endurance and sacrifice for the love of Christ. I knew the weakness of fallen human nature. I knew that we can deceive ourselves; but I also knew that, thanks to the grace of Christ, I could at last see very clearly. I wasn't deceived; neither was I agitated or depressed. Besides, I didn't think that any delusion could bring not merely brief 'imagined' joy, or patience or calm, but the pure Knowledge which only comes with faith and which, like faith, too, is a pure gift from God. Of course, knowledge is mediated through one's own self with one's limitations and inadequacies; and all Knowledge is useless, without love.

Year by year, and throughout each new day, amidst parties, meal-times, supermarket trips and various visits, my mind, when not occupied with normal work, became full of amazed awe at the Glory of God, or saturated with pain at the knowledge of my sinfulness. But since I still had no idea how or why I was being taught in prayer, I continued my work and prayer as usual, trying to be faithful to Christ no matter what I suffered. Most of the time, I worked and knelt and prayed in utter 'interior' darkness, just as I had for the previous decade and more.

I yearned for everyone to be able to know and love Christ; but what I asked of God most sincerely was the grace to be able to love Him, and - for His sake - to make other people happy from day to day. My occasional failures no longer surprised me. I was appalled by my weaknesses, but I'd begun to understand what Saint Paul wrote, about Christ's assurance that: "MY GRACE IS ENOUGH FOR YOU; MY POWER IS AT ITS BEST IN WEAKNESS" (2 Co 12:9). I'd been taught in prayer simply to do my best, and to leave the results in God's hands.

---

9 UNION
(1984-1987)

CHRIST'S LOVE. JOY. TEACHINGS.

A daughter of the Church.

Each dark morning, after my new conversion, and with winter approaching, I began to find a strange comfort and strength in those broken-hearted prayers in the kitchen, before anyone else awoke. I grew accustomed to the darkness of those years - the strange, safe darkness. Christ gave me courage, and the sure hope that I was on the right path. He never ceased to encourage me to believe in His Love, and in our friendship.

One great day at Mass, I was praying as usual; and for a moment I wondered how I dare go to Holy Communion. It was true that I'd been reconciled; but my life had been so sinful and my weakness so profound that I was astonished, again, at my faith in daring to approach the One who is so Pure and Holy. Straightaway, at that moment, Our Lord showed me that I can walk confidently towards Him. He astonished me by showing me a vivid image of myself walking up to receive Him in Holy Communion: walking up the central aisle in church, wearing a long gold cloak; and then He explained to me, forcefully:-

> **Believe in My work in you. Don't worry. It is I Who have led you to a new repentance and to Reconciliation, and so have prepared you again for Holy Communion. (T:33 #1)**

> **Recognise your dignity. *You are a daughter of the Church, reconciled and forgiven. By My work in you and through My Merits, entirely, you are now more fit than the greatest princess to approach Me, the King of Glory, at the altar.* (T:33 #2)**

> **See how generous am I, Who have clothed you in the beautiful 'garment' which is the Life of Grace. *You wear a long, gold cloak, through My generosity. What dignity you have, as you approach Me, worthy to receive My Holy Body and My Precious Blood!* (T:33 #3) (WC:33)**

Influencing other souls.

Christ wanted me to realise that my efforts to please Him were going to be fruitful for other souls besides my own. He reminded me one day after Holy Communion:-

> **Respond to Our call. We Who draw you towards the altar, the Most Holy Trinity, are 'at work', to save you. The Father 'calls' you; My Holy Spirit 'propels' you to turn towards Me, Jesus Christ; and I unite you to Myself as if in One Offering from the altar, during the Holy Sacrifice of the Mass. (T:37 #2)**

> **Reach out determinedly, in prayer, despite trials. We, the Most Holy Trinity, truly draw on and attract, enfold and guide the faithful and courageous soul; and by a like power, that soul pulls along in her 'wake', in a life of prayer, all who belong to her in some degree, though of course they are all free to resist Our grace and influence. (T:37 #3)**

It's because prayer is so important that Christ reminded me very gently why we should all pray in church - and elsewhere - with great reverence:-

> **Think about Me, your Lord, Whose Sacrifice is offered before you.** *It is not fitting, during the awesome offering of Myself on the altar, that you worship with minds and hearts alone. If you who are so weak are careless with your bodies, or lazy or untidy in your communal gestures, you are led to be careless and distracted in your minds. Thus, you might fail to pay Me the honour and holy worship which are due to My Majesty.* **(T:36A #2)**

Then He urged me to persevere in intercession and always to pray with great confidence in His goodness. He showed me an image of the whole globe of the Earth suspended in space; and the globe was wrapped in a sheet which represented prayer. Christ then taught me:-

> **Persevere in intercession. As you kneel and pray in My Name,** *your prayer 'wraps up' the whole earth, as if a vast sheet, and enfolds it.* **(T:39 #1) (WC:39)**

> **Believe in the power of prayer "in Christ".** *There is no part of the earth which is not touched and enfolded by grace, when, by prayer, you beg Me to touch it and to help the people who live there.* **(T:39 #2)**

> **Make requests of Me for others, whilst accepting mankind's real freedom.** *Others may refuse the graces brought near to them by those who have prayed for them.* **(T:39 #3)**

Reaching towards God.

Day by day, and more and more frequently, God poured secretly, into my inmost soul, knowledge of Himself, of the most Holy Trinity, of Creation, of sin, and of mankind and its redemption through Jesus Christ. He taught me, in a manner sometimes unknown to me and always 'unfelt', about the Church, about prayer, about union with Christ - but above all about Love: about Christ's Love for us, and about the power of the prayers which we pray in His Name to the Father; and each time I received one of these teachings, my soul became more confident and hopeful. As I said earlier, there was no question of my wanting or seeking 'experiences'. Christ, more than anyone, knew my heart. If I had been swamped beneath a deluge of fierce emotions or colourful images I would have fought or fled them, but this wasn't what was happening.

It was true that some of the teachings were being given to me as images which were accompanied by 'Knowledge' or understanding. But most of the occurrences in prayer were imageless; and each arrived unexpectedly - yet always within prayer - at the point where my heart was at peace, and was totally devoted to reaching towards God in the darkness of faith, in penitence and worship.

Everything I learned from God within that darkness was suddenly and unavoidably received. In a swift and secret manner, the knowledge pierced my soul and left its mark. Each experience was so brief and unexpected that it had finished before I could even react to it or think; and only the 'knowledge' remained. That's why, in the midst of my slight puzzlement, I was content to know that I'd been hoping or searching for nothing except to know what was God's Will for me at each moment: whether in prayer or 'out' of it.

All my will was centred, now, on trusting in Christ in each new earthly joy or grief, and in doing His Will as perfectly as possible - by relying on His power. It seemed to me that only one grief would be utterly unbearable: the sorrow of failing to respond to His love, after learning so vividly what He'd suffered and done for us all. All other miseries and disappointments are minor, seen in this way. There's nothing which isn't foreseen, understood and encompassed by God; nor need we allow anyone or anything to take us away from His care: that's what I'd learned, even though I was still in pain, and still had hardships and turmoil to bear; I was still weak and sometimes afraid. But I'd found from experience that nothing serious could defeat me, as long as I kept on turning to God in constant prayer.

Centred on Christ.

All of my struggles were 'beneath the surface' of my life. Outwardly things seemed the same. We worked and travelled, and entertained friends. I nursed my own mother, as I mentioned, and cared for the children day by day, as usual. Attendance at Holy Mass was - is - my greatest source of strength. Prayer at home was pursued in private, although I didn't always kneel, but sometimes sat. I'd been well and strong for short periods, but eventually the weakness became permanent.

Through every episode of pain and every hospital visit, the old 'classics' helped me. The psalms, the rosary and my crucifix all held me up; and when it was difficult to go on, the

"Lord's Prayer" and the Creed were like jewels in the dark, and fulfilled my need to offer words of fervent praise to God when I felt almost too tired to pray. The Divine Praises were like a ladder leading to peace, although I still found that silence was my best prayer. But when I was tired beyond belief, the "Jesus Prayer" almost said itself in my mind, and I was led further on in trust and hope and love. I can never thank God enough for my faith in Him, which enabled me to face each new day. It was above all through the belief that I'd be pleasing Him if I remained faithful to my various duties that I was enabled to get up and start again each day, and to make the 'morning offering' with a sincere heart.

Meanwhile the 'teachings' continued; and despite my determination to ignore all I learned, and not to dwell on the 'occurrences', I found that they interrupted my usual darkness more and more frequently, as I knelt in church, at Holy Mass.

Dumb endurance.

Resolutely pressing on with my work, puzzled by the 'teachings', I learned how to live in the 'present moment.' For a long time I continued to take no notice; I really tried to ignore the "knowledge", the events, and continued to pray as I'd always prayed. I repented of my sins, made fervent petitions, and knelt in dumb endurance throughout the Mass. I would sooner have died than 'miss Mass', unless kept away by illness or by duty. Faith told me that it was the source of all my strength, and experience proved to me that Christ, at the heart of the Mass, is an infallible source of peace.

In the darkness, spurred on by all that I learned at Mass, I lived only by faith. I mean that even my attendance at that Holy Sacrifice was itself a sacrifice in that I rarely felt a spark of inspiration or joy. I went to church, I prayed, I listened to the words of Scripture, and adored Christ, blindly, in Holy Communion; but I still lived in spiritual darkness, still fighting against feelings of shame and fear. Even in my prayers at home I found no tangible comfort or joy - nor did I expect any. It no longer mattered very much to me what I felt, as long as I knew that my prayers were sincere, and that in everyday life I was still trying to please Christ and to be faithful to my duties.

Daily, I prayed in simple words about my sorrow for sin, my gratitude to God for His gifts, and about the needs of my family and friends - and of the Church. Daily, I adored God in darkness, certain, however, that He accepted my homage; and week by week the teachings continued. I assumed, vaguely, that one day I would find myself praying as before: not only lonely and in darkness, but quite baffled as well; but it didn't matter to me what happened, as long as I could be faithful to prayer and to God's Will.

Our parish priest until 1984, the year my mother died, was the generous-hearted Canon Keenan whom I've already mentioned. But it didn't occur to me for years to ask a priest about the teachings. I felt quite unworthy to speak to a priest about anything, even about prayer; and I really thought that this might be a passing 'phase'. I had no desire to draw attention to myself; nor did I think that one ought to chat casually about God's secret gifts, unless there were a pressing reason.

As I'll explain further on, I sought advice a few years later, by which time Canon O'Leary had been with us for a few years; and I wasn't merely reassured but was told that the teachings were a "gift from God". I can't begin to describe my awe and gratitude; but at the time of which I'm speaking, I was frightened as well as puzzled, afraid that the "occurrences" would be seen as a sign of 'emotionalism' or 'neurosis': a sign that I was a weak, foolish woman who 'imagined' her pains and weaknesses. But I thanked God for enabling me to continue. I calmly and quietly did the essential tasks for my family whilst my physical weakness increased but the 'teachings' went on. As I shall explain, they continue still.

Learning patience and trust.

Daily work became gradually less gruelling, when I was no longer coping with small children but with young adults, who were extremely kind. New problems arose when some tasks were evidently beyond my strength; but nothing made me depressed, thanks to Christ. The only things which made me really appalled and ashamed, later on, were the two or three occasions when Christ Himself rebuked me about some sort of selfishness or self-indulgence.

Unseen and unheard, until future occasions in prayer, Christ taught me to be patient and trusting, and to bring all my problems to Him. He taught me to work as He wished me to work. But He never left me for long without encouragement, even though that encouragement was known only through faith, at that stage. There was no pleasure in it.

A different way ahead.

The spiritual life is such a mysterious thing. Although I was unaware of this, all the occurrences of both pain and light were being given to me in preparation for a very different way ahead. I was being given glimpses, in darkness, of many things which would become even clearer when at last I'd been brought to real union with Christ.

In prayer-times, in between family meals and meetings, the teachings continued. Sometimes I walked home after Mass stunned by what I'd unexpectedly seen.

Eventually I noticed that all the Knowledge from Christ in prayer gave me something besides hope and understanding. I received greater courage to do what I thought He wanted, in the life of our church community. That was why I began to attend routine meetings of the Parish Council. Besides, the children were more independent. I had no extraordinary motive, beyond duty; but I had a little more leisure time and thought I could quite contentedly talk of either gutters or liturgies, taking my turn at a necessary task. Then I was asked to be the Catholic representative on the Council of Churches in our town, and so I attended many more meetings, and came to feel as though I really belonged in this community, of Christians together, living for love, cherishing one another through work, prayer and conversation.

I relied on Christ to bring some good out of my attendance at inter-church gatherings and to help me to be crystal-clear and truthful as I wrote numerous minutes and reports. I realised that the trust which He inspired brought wonderful rewards to me as I was set free from anxiety about results, in any field.

213

Council Documents.

It seems Providential to me that in the nineteen-eighties, in my efforts to be scrupulously fair and accurate in discussions with fellow-Christians, I was conscience-bound to turn to the documents of the Second Vatican Council which deal with the Church, and with Ecumenism, and Mission; and as I let one document lead me to study another, I was thrilled to see plainly explained all the great Catholic doctrines and recommendations which I'd already known and admired for so long, and which I'd promoted - as best I could - in the previous twenty years. But that delight came not because I'd been provided with some sort of armour in which to protect myself in ecumenical discussions. Rather, it was a delight in seeing stated as central to the Faith the wonderful Church teachings which had been labelled by discontented Catholics as peripheral or old-fashioned.

As I'd been reading and pondering, through two decades as a Catholic, I had never wavered in belief. I had stated plainly to any enquirer just what it is that is central to the Faith, and what are matters of discipline or custom - and how 'custom' means a different thing from 'the Tradition'. The perpetual drip-drip of criticism of Catholic teaching, however, which is encountered by anyone who reads 'across the spectrum' of Catholic journalism, can have a demoralising effect; and so I was re-invigorated by the discovery that no Council document recommended the 'loyal dissent' which some Catholics so loudly promote today. No document recommended 'indiscriminate' worship with other Christians, nor the sort of 'multi-faith' worship which for the sake of false peace ignores the existence and the Mediation of Christ. Many documents had been widely misquoted, in the sense of a different perspective being given to a particular subject by the omission from the quotation of certain phrases which, in the original document, had helped to provide a balanced view.

Selective quotation.

The damage done by the use of selective quotation of Council documents by Catholic critics of Catholic doctrine was evident in the ecumenical field. It's true that the Church documents state that we can recognise 'seeds' of goodness in other cultures and other faiths: and we're all invited to promote whatever good is found in other faiths. But I had never heard quoted by any apostle of a false harmony the 'balancing' paragraph which I found in the Constitution of the Church: in chapter two of "Lumen Gentium." The Council Fathers explain that Salvation is indeed possible for those who, through no fault of their own, don't know the gospel of Christ or His Church, yet who sincerely seek God and try to do His Will as it's made known to them through their consciences; yet the Fathers also explain that people are more often deceived by the evil one, which is why the Church is still continuing with her missionary work and still hopes that the entire world will become One People in Christ, the Head, for the Glory of God the Father.

How very different is the ringing proclamation of the Council document from the bland statements of those who have been urging us towards the 'indifferentism' so widespread today. It was heartening for me to see such evidence that the aims of the Church of God - of the One, true Church, and not of those of its voluble members who defy her authority or mock her teachings - remain the same in every era, even though re-statements and clarifications of her eternal truths are appropriate for different times and places.

Seductive ideas.

There was something which saddened me, however, as I became more involved in Eucumenical work. I'm referring to my discovery that a number of the Christians with whom I discussed faith, prayer and morals at various official meetings or Lent-groups appeared astonished if I said that "Yes, I do believe in the teachings of the Church, and I have great respect for the Holy Father."

Of course, I'm stating this so bluntly in order to point out that these good people had gained the impression from the media, and even from the Catholic press, that the 'normal' Catholic finds the Church old-fashioned and its teachings foolish. It was blithely supposed that I believe the Pope to be misguided, that I choose to steer an individual course in moral matters and am delighted by every opportunity to move away from the 'authoritarian, paternalistic and guilt-inducing' doctrines and practices of past centuries. That's why much of my time was spent explaining that the Church's teaching never alters, on matters of faith and morals, and that many of us believe in that teaching still, no matter how difficult it might be to put into practice, and no matter how loudly and critically it's discussed by some who wish it could be changed.

It was by this gradual process of study, discussion, reflection and report-writing that I came to see just how subtle are the temptations put before faithful Catholics today by many discontented Church members - and just how seductive these ideas can prove for people who have never studied the Faith carefully or for those who prefer to drift comfortably into the arms of one group or another which holds out an apparently easier and less abrasive way of being Catholic and Christian.

Emerging from darkness.

As I write this account of how I studied our Faith as best I could, in ordinary ways, and then of how I learned to accept and to treasure Christ's teachings in prayer, which so marvellously 'replicate' in a different idiom much of what I've learned through the Catholic Church, I must recall a handful of events of the last few years: years in which the daily rhythm of prayer and 'teachings', of simple work, rests and conversations was quiet and steady. Good news as well as sad was woven into a simple pattern as I wrote, painted and prayed - and frequently just lay quietly at home waiting for some energy to return.

The events of which I write have all happened in the years since late 1985, when Christ showed me that the worst part of the spiritual journey had ended. He lifted me from darkness to glory; and I'm yearning to tell other people to keep trusting in Him, no matter how great their present darkness. There's no one like Him: no greater friend. I want to shout out, almost - hand on heart - that He's worth any sacrifice. I've found from experience, especially in these past few years, that our tiniest efforts to please God or to love our neighbour are staggeringly rewarded, despite our dreadful mistakes; and that's why I'm planning to write in the last few chapters about the astonishingly joyful life to be experienced at the 'heart' of the Holy Trinity. Meanwhile, I believe that Christ wants me to share further details about the long journey, for the sake of those who follow the same path .

So many pages in this book speak about union-in-darkness, pain and fear. But Christ cannot leave in darkness those whose main desire to please Him and serve Him and who have abandoned everything which might cast a shadow on their path towards Him.

It was in 1985, on the eleventh of December, that Christ came to me, utterly unexpected, to draw back the curtains on my long and lonely night, and to lift me up by the power of His Spirit into the warmth of an eternal and unshakeable union with Him. All of this is what He explained to me, later on.

Christ Himself came to my soul, visibly, for the first time, and in the same way, since my 'conversion' about twenty years earlier. But this time His radiant presence brought me not torment but bliss; and now I dare to hope that the darkness has been taken away forever, through His indescribable kindness. It was a day which another writer might have chosen to call the day of his or her spiritual 'marriage'. I see it as the day on which Christ lifted me wholly into a very close friendship. It's true that each of us is made an adopted and true child of God by Baptism; yet Christ has told me that of those of us who survive beyond earthly childhood very few are making every possible effort to remain close to Him; and of those who neglect or betray Him, very few make wholehearted efforts to be fully restored to His friendship and also to be made ready for Heaven.

A new temptation.

It was on a dull day in December that Christ came to me, transformed me, and stayed close to me, all day and ever after; and now I'll tell how it happened.

It was at a time when I could say at last, by God's grace, that Christ had first place in my life. For more than a year after my mother's death in 1984, I'd 'plodded along' determinedly in the usual way. I did the chores, prayed, read, and went regularly to Mass and to the sacraments; I also cooked meals for hordes of friends, painted works for galleries and fulfilled individual commissions. But I wanted nothing more than to be allowed to battle from day to day to love God, and to make others happy for His sake. If I failed, I was no longer surprised. I did my best and left the results in His hands. During 1985 - for the whole of that year - I had worked and prayed in utter 'darkness', just as I had for very many years, though wholly determined at last to love and serve Christ whatever it cost me. But one evening, in the midst of all sorts of afflictions, I was tempted to lose hope, and was tempted to love and serve God less than perfectly, and to make conditions and demands. But I said my prayers as usual, and went to sleep.

The next morning was hectic, with the usual chores and interruptions; but then I dashed to the station, to go to London to do some much-needed Christmas shopping; and as I sat on the train that morning, and thought about my life, I began to pray in silence, in a moment of profound sorrow. I felt entirely without hope except for the hope I held in the darkness of faith. There was a feeling almost of horror in my heart at the thought of saying 'yes' once again to God's commands. Then I paused for a split-second in order to remind myself of my very reason for living. There was a real danger that because of frequent illness, with other problems, I could plunge into the depths of self-pity. Clear-headed and very determined, I willed, with all my will and heart, to see, again, the true meaning of abandonment to God and the true meaning of love.

Freely entering a tomb.

Christ said that "IF A MAN SERVES ME, HE MUST FOLLOW ME" (Jn 12:26); and now that I'd seen once again that real love is about perfect self-giving, I was led to make a firm decision, for the love of God, with all the strength of my soul. I resolved to love - to keep on acting only, and utterly, for the love of Christ - even if what I considered the worst should happen, by which I meant the death of all my hopes and desires. I was even willing to forgo all natural or supernatural happiness for the rest of my life, if that had been what God Willed for me. As I sat there on the train, praying in silence, oblivious for once to the people around me, I gave my entire life to Christ once again.

It was just as though I was entering a tomb: a place of burial for every private hope or dream. By an act of the will, I closed the door behind me, or, rather, I rolled the stone across the doorway. I made a sincere and whole-hearted self-offering, in voluntary sacrifice, so that Christ would reign supreme in my life; and as I prayed, my feelings remained normal human feelings of grief and near-despair.

So familiar was I with suffering that I'd almost forgotten about the promise of Resurrection. So weak was the virtue of hope, in me, that I was almost deaf to Christ's promise that all who make sacrifices for His sake will receive, even in this life, "GIFTS FOR YOU: A FULL MEASURE, PRESSED DOWN, SHAKEN TOGETHER, AND RUNNING OVER" (Lk 6:38).

A resurrection.

What a marvellous day that was when, finally, I made God truly Sovereign in my life, and determined to do His Will even "to death": to the death of every dream and personal plan. Only by His grace did I do it, but I've been extravagantly rewarded. In giving my life to Christ yet again, I arrived at the moment of what I can only call my spiritual resurrection. Christ powerfully demonstrated to me the truth to which I'd clung for many years in the darkness of faith: the truth that God's glorious Love for us infinitely surpasses human love, and obliterates every sorrow and heartache.

As soon as I'd said that new and whole-hearted 'Yes' to God, and to His Will, I suddenly, astoundingly, and quite unexpectedly, saw Jesus. In the very moment that I saw Him blindly, with my soul's eyes, dazzled, I was lifted to His Glory, and was united with Him in Heaven's bliss and joy and light. In the wonder of reaching up and seeing myself loved by Christ, every memory, fear and pain was left far behind.

We were beyond time and place, and beyond thought too: beyond every earthly limitation. I was entirely His in unimagined and perfect happiness and peace; and although I say that His light dazzled me, rather, He Himself was the light. He was so brilliant that I couldn't see His features clearly at any time. I hope He's saving that joy for me in Heaven; but in that pure Light, love, understanding and knowledge where Christ held me I knew Him and recognised Him. I knew Him better than I know myself. I saw that He delights in me, and loves everything about me. He showed me that He loves me better than I love myself.

At last I understood the fact that God 'is' Love. I was astonished to find that the living, radiant Christ Who is so precious to me, was now familiar, and at the same time glorious, as the Son of God must be glorious. Furthermore - and I could have died for joy on seeing this - He was full of admiration for me, and tender, almost beyond belief: and to someone who'd been so reluctant to love Him as He deserves. I experienced then more pure bliss, joy and celebration than in my entire life. The mere memory of it, now, brings me almost more joy than I can bear. But it wasn't just a time of personal spiritual fulfilment; it became a feast, or a festival of praise and thanks with the holy and blessed Company of Heaven who in their happiness shared my joy.

Living in Christ's friendship.

Although I couldn't fully appreciate at the time the magnitude of Christ's generosity, my life was transformed, then, all at once, and forever. At the same time, Christ taught me about that transformation. Soundlessly, and with great gentleness He showed me the new state to which He'd brought me. He even referred to my determination to serve Him faithfully. He told me:-

> **Here I am! Rise up with Me to Glory! Rejoice in your self-conquest and self-sacrifice. You and I are now united in heart and longing. (T:43 #4)**

> **Accept these moments of Glory. I, Christ, am the Light which now illumines your soul. I am the Light in Whose radiance My holy Saints are living and rejoicing, even now as they greet you! (T:43 #5)**

> **Accept this new joy which is My perpetual gift to you. Where I am, there is also Love, understanding, knowledge, innocence, friendship, fearlessness and joy! (T:43 #6)**

> **Live in hope, in My friendship. With My Saints, I live in unutterable bliss and celebration. Now you can see why anyone, believing in this bliss, would be willing to endure even a thousand difficult life-times in order to be made worthy of Heaven! (T:43 #7)**

> **See how I Myself love, reward and praise one who has suffered for love of Me. My Saints add their tender greetings to mine. Heaven's rewards are unimaginably wonderful and heart-warming. (T:43 #8)**

Then the conversation continued. Christ's Light and Christ's presence still held me secure. I remained in His bliss for about half an hour: half an hour spent in Heaven; that's what I knew then, and believe now, though it would have been quite impossible for me to write that in my first brief reminiscences. I hadn't spoken to anyone about Christ's gifts to me in prayer; and my mind was struggling to cope with two apparently conflicting truths: first, the truth that Christ had taken me to Heaven; yet, secondly: the truth that I'm not fit to be there. That's why I first wrote, of my meeting with Christ on that extraordinary day: "I do not know where." I couldn't have done otherwise, until I'd spoken to someone who had the wisdom of authority, someone who could confirm that my 'teachings' and experiences could be 'accepted'. Only then did I find the courage to say: in print and out loud: 'I'm not fit to receive such joy and such gifts. But the fact that I did receive them only proves God's goodness, and proves His love for me, someone weak and sinful.'

Living in Union.

After about half-an-hour I emerged from that overwhelming rapture to find that the train had arrived at St. Pancras Station. Christ didn't leave me. When I returned from where He'd taken me, I took the tube-train to Oxford Circus; then I walked where I'd planned to walk, still marvelling at His presence and at my unbelievable joy. Who would concentrate on shopping with the Prince of Peace at her side? I hardly dare to say this, but it's important, and true: Christ was with me in that way, that day in London, for half the length of that part of Oxford Street, as I tried to do my shopping, then failed and gave up the attempt.

A mere glance at Him, there in the street, was guidance, knowledge and peace; but I couldn't think about what to buy during our wordless conversation. I was almost struck witless by the knowledge of His love for me; so I decided to go home, and then to shop for Christmas presents on the following day. My heart was stunned all day long by His presence, by His joy in me, and by my heart and mind's unceasing bliss.

Falling in love.

If it hadn't been for this personal revelation, I might never have come to realise that our love isn't just 'owed' to God, but is something which utterly delights Him. I could hardly have conceived of the notion that I, such a weak and weary admirer of Christ, could not only serve him but could touch His Heart, and could give Him so much joy. So I plucked up courage, then, to ask Him, silently, about all sorts of things, and about people too, by a glance and by a mere look. He gave me many answers, tenderly. It was quite extraordinary, as though we were communicating in a soul-to-soul manner in pure knowledge and love.

Time flowed by. All care and effort were gone. For several hours Christ was entirely present to me in this way; and He taught me clearly, at the same time, that He'd like to see me more confident about His Love. He explained with infinite tenderness:-

> **Believe in My immeasurable love for you. I love you truly, here, now, just as you are, even before you are perfect. *I love you in your weakness,* just as I love all sinners. Yet I long to see every one of you delivered from sin and made happy. (T:43 #9)**

> **Be glad that you make Me happy! Even the love of someone like yourself can give joy to Me, Who am thrilled by your efforts to be loving. I delight in you. (T:43 #10)**

> **Have faith in Me and in My Holy Church. Continue to be**

> obedient in everything which I ask of you through My
> Church. Understanding comes later. It grows according to
> your advancement in love. (T:43 #11)

That day was the first of all the new days spent with Christ, with Him beside me, before me, and continuously here. There's no way I can thank Him enough for His love, except by living for love, until I die. All my cares and resentments had gone in an instant. What could now frighten or defeat me in future, with the powerful help of a Saviour Whom I knew, by experience as well as by faith, to be a loving, tender and constant Companion?

That was the day when - in the purest sense - I "fell in love" with Christ. That was the time from which my every new effort to please Christ and to serve Him would stem not just from faith, as it fuelled the whole aim of my will, but also from the deepest yearning of my human heart, which had been so profoundly moved by His tenderness and by His evident affection.

A souvenir.

After a few hours I was able to concentrate, for Christ's sake, on loving tasks for the family: but all the while with such joy and fervour that all tasks seemed the same. I was amazed to find that everything I'd previously found tedious or boring had become easy to do. All chores were simply opportunities of serving my holy Friend, or of loving my neighbour for His sake, whether I was preparing for a birthday party or mending socks. I had years of pain ahead of me; but I found myself going joyfully from one thing to another with a lightness of heart which astounded me; and, all the time, it was as though Christ held me in His peace. He encouraged me to be faithful in everything, and taught me to live in greater trust. He taught me not to worry, but to turn to Him in every need, and in every sorrow.

The experience of Christ's kindness on my journey to London had so stunned and reassured me that I became determined to mark the event in some concrete way, even in secret. I imagined that nothing so precious might ever happen to me again.

I hadn't the faintest idea of what plans Christ had in store for my life, nor any inkling that the joys which lay ahead would make that day seem less like a 'summit' of the spiritual life than like the top of a peak in the foothills, from which my willing soul would eventually be led to Himalayan heights: and not only 'by' Christ but "in" Him, and wholly within the Holy Trinity. But meanwhile, I vowed to myself that if all that should happen to me from then on was that I grew old, disabled and toothless, I would leave some mark behind at which I could point one day, saying perhaps to my children: "That was the date. That was when I learned the real extent of Divine love for poor sinful people."

At a local jewellers, I chose a thin gold ring to mark the event. I didn't tell anyone about it, for years. It had a bark-like pattern on it, which reminded me of the wood of Christ's Cross; and I arranged to have engraved, within it, "11.12.85" and also: the signs "A and Ω". I wear it now, as well as my wedding ring.

The Alpha and Omega Day.

The gift of joy which was lavished upon me on that December day has been like a secret current running through my heart, ever since. The last thirteen years have brought new and unexpected trials, yet that joy has continued to flow in my life almost continuously. It seems to me to be one of the greatest proofs, for me, of Christ's visits and graces; and it's a joy so great that it nearly breaks my heart by its strength each time I go to Holy Communion.

Since no-one could live on earth, and walk and talk, or work, when preoccupied with such company and such bliss, Christ's presence became less strongly felt, though still with me. He arranged this, in His mercy, for the sake of all the work I still have to do, and for the sake of all the good people I love and with whom I share my life.

I've named that day, to myself, the Alpha and Omega Day; and I've celebrated it gratefully as a feast on the eleventh of every month, and also on the anniversary each year, by having a Mass offered in thanksgiving. I'm almost lost for words to describe my present state of joy, but this is what I've found: Christ is with me, unseen but present here, all the time. I continue to do my work and to pray in ordinary ways, but His Knowledge and His gifts have been poured upon me almost unceasingly ever since the day of our true union.

Christ has remained with me since that day, although, as I've explained, His presence has become unbearable to me whenever I've done wrong. Yet even such warnings seem to be blessings by which Christ, for His own purposes, teaches me more about the life of grace. So I can genuinely thank Him for his severity as much as for His kindness. I've learned so much from both. As for the joy He brings now: if anyone should say that the words spoken to me were imagined, or that His 'teachings' were a delusion, I can only reply that I myself believe in His teachings and have done my first duty by writing them down; and something else which I'm happy to declare to anyone, now, is that Christ chooses "WHAT IS WEAK BY HUMAN RECKONING; THOSE WHOM THE WORLD THINKS COMMON AND CONTEMPTIBLE" (1 Co 1:27-28), as St. Paul says, to show and prove His goodness and His power for the sake of the faith of people who don't know about His love. He has certainly chosen "WHAT IS WEAK" in this case; but I'm thrilled by His friendship, and I long to please Him by encouraging others to go to Him, to love and to be loved, and so to arrive at a degree of peace and security which I'm sure is unknown elsewhere.

Christ's life now mine.

What I find quite extraordinary now is that since I gave Christ my whole life - every aspect of it and every dream - He has given me His. As I freely gave my consent to His Will being worked in me, so He now reigns more truly over my will, my memory, and my understanding. He wants to make them entirely His. That's why He's been purifying them, as He's shown me, by the fire of His love, so that there's no aspect of my life or my being that isn't being offered for His use and service until my life's end.

There's nothing on this earth, now, which I prefer to His presence; I mean that such leisure-time distractions as television or certain social events are quite simply distractions from His presence: from His holy companionship: His own precious self in this sanctuary of the soul. The earthly joys which we can share with other people remain real joys which can be enjoyed with gratitude to God, and also for the sake of God and of our neighbour; but I can say with passionate conviction that there's no music, sound, sight or touch more sweet and beautiful than the silent, invisible but real presence of Christ within the soul.

In spite of all that I've just said about joy, it's true that there's has been one occasion, which I'll mention later on, when Christ left me apparently alone in torment for a whole week; I was as if suspended over an abyss of desolation. Only in that way, I was to understand, could I learn true humility. By that powerful teaching, Christ reminded me that everything good that I've ever received is from Him, and that I'm nothing without Him; yet even that teaching was a work of love. It's because He loves me that He wants to make me fit to do His work - and also fit to go to Heaven, when He calls me.

A desire to make Christ known.

Otherwise, Christ is here with me; and I'm lost for words with which to thank Him. I hardly dare to say this, but my whole desire is to make Him known and loved. The opportunities have seemed pitifully few, until recent times; and everything is held back, it seems, by my weakness and bad example. Yet I trust Him entirely now; and I leave this wretched life and these feeble efforts in His hands.

Since that day in 1985, I've seen more and more clearly how Christ rewards me for every loving choice, as He rewards love by Love; and He includes in His gift a pure joy in the mere sound of His name. I hear 'Jesus', or say it, and can hardly bear the joy which the sound, the thought, or the presence bring to my heart: such a pang as I never expected to feel again, when I was merely enduring from day to day, sustained in a longing for Divine love by dry faith alone. When I recite the Creed, today, I can scarcely manage a few phrases without being half-enraptured by the Glory each phrase suggests.

In the months after this union, when I was wondering how Christ our Lord, Who is so bright and beautiful and holy, should do such things for a person like myself, I thought of St. Paul's warnings about "AN ANGEL OF LIGHT" (2 Co 11:14). But since I knew, by then, that in the midst of even greater trials and afflictions than ever before I still wanted nothing except to do God's Will, whatever the cost, I was reassured.

It didn't seem possible that anyone evil could have given me not just peace and joy in prayer but such an increased determination to do good. I was also encouraged later, as I've said, by the judgement of my parish priest.

From about that time it became almost overwhelming to listen to the Scripture readings in church: to hear in the Gospels the words used by the very Christ Who, in His goodness, had revealed Himself to me. It's as though I'd once received letters from a distant relative whose character and speech had only been filtered through stories or news reports. If I were to meet that relative: if I travelled to his home, talked with him and heard his voice, how much more joy and knowledge would his letters give me, once I was at home again, reading what he wrote, with a true acquaintance at last established.

Friendship with Christ.

To return to the 'story' of the 'Teachings': three years went by, yet Christ continued to teach me in the manner I've described; and it's usually been in Holy Communion that He has taught me something more about Himself, and about grace, prayer and souls.

Many of the earlier teachings, as I've described them, sound very simple; but neither words nor pictures can describe the glory, the fullness, or the simplicity of the sublime things which I've learned by God's power. I've rarely used my imagination in prayer, but I couldn't have begun to 'imagine' all that I've been taught and shown during the past fifteen years.

For example, when I was praying at Mass one day, Christ reminded me about the astonishing power of the prayers that we offer, through our union with Him, to our Heavenly Father. I was astonished to learn:-

> **Remember to Whom you address your prayers: *to the Most High God, in My Name:* the Name of *Jesus. You who are united with Me by love and obedience offer your prayers with My authority and love.* I am truly your Champion and your Intercessor. (T:51B #1)**

> **Pray with confidence, whenever you pray in My Name: the Name of Jesus Christ. It is as though every prayer you make is vouched for by Me. It is as if I stand beside you, saying to the Father - as though to a King - "Accept the message of this person, my own friend, as though it were issuing from My own lips." (T:51B #2)**

> **Pray in spirit and in truth, through Me - Jesus Christ your Lord. How, then, can you not be heard? Try to stay close to Me, and so be closer to the Light which pours around Me from Heaven. (T:51B #3)**

Loyalty to Christ's Mother.

Soon afterwards, on another day at Mass, Christ suddenly explained to me something about the importance of His holy Mother, Mary. I didn't understand how I 'saw', but I saw her standing beside Him, in Heaven, and I heard Christ explain to me:-

> **Look towards My Glory in prayer and see the gentle woman who now stands beside Me. Don't be afraid to *love* her whom *you rightly call the "Mother of God". How precious is My Holy Mother. How tremendous is My Love for her who lives with Me now in Heaven. How vivacious is My Mother, in her joy and beauty: how full of love and happiness.* (T:53 #1)**

> **Thank My Mother for all that she has done for you. *How***

greatly she has suffered so that I, the Word, might be revealed to the world. (T:53 #2)

Love My Mother, and thank her for giving Me to you by My Spirit's power. How loyal you should be, ever-grateful for her devotion and concern. (T:53 #3)

Defend My Mother. *How loyally you ought to defend her against those who - through ignorance - think they please Me by ignoring her, My dearest creature.* (T:53 #4)

The Father's Glory and splendour.

On another day, I was astonished to be taught something more about our Heavenly Father Who is the goal of all our strivings. Christ taught me, in an extraordinary, soundless and also sightless 'vision' of the Father's Glory:-

Consider the Glory and Splendour of the Father, the Source of all joy, Who "Is" in His bliss - in life and union and Love - the sublime heart of the Most Holy Trinity. (T:55B #3)

Believe, of the Father, that He exists *"in"* **the blissful embrace of** *Word and Spirit, which is to say, in a perfect and joyful state-of-union with Myself, the Divine Word, and with My holy and Divine Spirit: three Persons yet One Lord.* (T:55B #4)

Believe, of the Father that *He "Is": is the Source of all that is created. He is Glorious beyond your imaginings.* (T:55B #5)

Believe, of God your Father, that *He "Is", holding in His embrace the Hosts of Heaven: the Saints and Holy Angels who worship and adore Him. He is holding in His heart, in bliss, all who have been 'freed' to live in His Love and who are now united in love with one another:* **faithful departed souls who have been "freed", through death, to live with Him eternally.** *He is the Father of all, the Source of all beauty. He is My Father, Father of Me, the Holy Son Whom, through tenderness, He sent to redeem you and with Whom He is united in the unfathomable love of the Holy Spirit.* (T:55B #6)

The Holy Trinity.

Then one evening when I was kneeling in prayer at home, I was also shown by Christ - about our new stage of prayer and the work of the Most Holy Trinity:-

Follow My inspirations and come to prayer whenever I 'call' you by an interior prompting. (T:56 #1)

Believe in Our Love and work: the work of the Most Holy Trinity. We act within your life on earth. You cannot see the end of the journey, but it is I, Jesus, Who hold you all the while, in your 'travelling'; it is My Spirit Who fills your heart, whilst you and I, together, go gently towards the Father, Who is nevertheless ever-present in your life and ever-welcoming. (T:56 #2)

Be glad that you are not trying to make a spiritual journey alone. You need Me, your Guide, your sure Way and your powerful Intercessor. (T:56 #3)

Persevere in prayer and sacrifice. Turn to Me in every circumstance. I invite you to pray, and also to throw yourself into My "river" of grace in every temptation, weakness, or trial. My Life within you is like *a river of light in which you will "bathe" one day.* You will be completely submerged in that 'river' of grace when you live with Me in perfect union. (T:57)

A window into time.

Even though Christ gave me hope and consolation, He vigorously reminded me of the cost of my redemption. It was at Mass one day that He revealed to me the 'sight' of His Crucifixion. It was during the Consecration. Christ showed me what seemed to be a "window into time" which was set high in the wall, beyond our priest. Through that 'window', in the centre of the circle, I saw Christ our Lord hanging on the Cross.

Christ was suffering in agony: helpless in the cold dark air. The dark sky behind Him reflected the pain of that terrible Sacrifice, made once for us, so long ago, and made present for our sakes today, through the Holy Sacrifice of the Mass. Then Christ taught Me:-

Be confident about what you profess. I, your God, really entered into time, and into earthly existence. I really was crucified, and I died on the Cross to save you from sin and from eternal death. (T:59 #1)

Make my Holy Sacrifice your own. Through your participation in the Holy Mass, where My once-for-all Sacrifice is made present, you benefit from its power. I love you so much that I died for you; and through our Communion, you can become more like Me, your Saviour. (T:59 #2)

Imitate Me, your Saviour. *What really counts in your*

ordinary life is love and tenderness and simplicity. (T:59 #3)

Strive to live in pure love of Me and of your neighbour, day after day. *All the "understandings" of the years* - given during prayer - *are gifts from Me, your merciful Lord, for My own purposes, and you can take no pride in them at all.* (T:59 #4)

Don't be despondent. *You should accept My gifts with joy.* Accept, like a child, the pure and holy gifts and graces which I Myself shower upon you, especially in Holy Communion. (T:59 #5)

Reason for hope.

Christ alone knew just how lonely and hesitant I sometimes felt, on my strange new path; and that's why, one day in prayer, He showed me a simple image which was accompanied by very encouraging words. Christ showed me an image of a small figure, vigorous and determined, who was leaping into God's life of prayer, utterly trusting, arms outstretched, expecting gifts and blessings. Then He explained to me:-

Always believe in My Love for you, and in My nearness. For as long as you live on earth, you can live in hope, and you are invited to make the free decision to serve Me, and to avoid being entirely and eternally separated from Me. (T:65 #1)

Be confident that, throughout your life, *you live and breathe and exist "in" Me,* your God. *Whether you are holy with My holiness, or selfish, you "fall" into My embrace with every movement of your hearts. 'Up' or 'down', in hope or sin, and whatever you choose, now, you are surrounded by Me still.* (T:65 #2)

But whatever discoveries I was making in my friendship with Christ, I wasn't to be allowed to forget the supreme importance of charity. Christ taught me about the best way of loving my fellow-Christians, and other neighbours. One day at Holy Mass I was shown the power of prayer, by which I mean intercessory prayer for others. Christ showed me a glimpse of the Saints in Heaven, in Glory: and He explained to me:-

Never forget that although I am hidden at present, you are present before My Glory whenever you turn to Me in prayer. (T:67 #1)

Learn to pray as if you are standing *in this vast "Hall of Light", in Our Presence: the Presence of the Most Holy Trinity. In prayer, you need only lift your friends into*

226

Our Light, by a word, a thought, or a pang, and they are
helped and renewed by your intercession, if they do not
shut it out. **(T:67 #2)**

Christ taught me, also, about how to deal with supposedly-controversial matters, whenever I encountered opposition to His teaching - to His Church's teaching - in magazines or conversation. He explained that my task is simply to believe, love, pray and hope, in the way that Faith teaches me to believe, love and hope. He told me:-

Don't waste time or endanger your soul by listening to opinions or by entertaining thoughts which contradict the teaching of My Church. (T:69 #1)

Keep to what is important. Obedience is important, vague curiosity is not. (T:69 #2)

The Sign of the Cross.

On another day, Christ reminded me of one of the ways in which I could bind myself even closer to Him, if I took more care with my prayers. He urged me:-

Use the sign of the Cross both to begin and to end your prayers. It is a sign of your life "in Christ", and is a devout and holy prayer to Us: to the Three Persons of the Most Holy Trinity. It is like a firm rope which binds you to Us in every task or every danger. (T:75 #3)

Then He encouraged me to be content to accept the fact that I'm a weak person who needs much help. He advised me how to approach Him now that I longed to be able to change. He urged me:-

Be a 'beggar' before Me in prayer. Leave behind your
achievements, props and self-satisfaction. **(T:78 #1)**

Trust in My kindness. It is when you have nothing to offer to the Father but My merits and My Love that I can change you and use you. (T:78 #2)

Rejoice that you have greater cause to be hopeful when you are weak and in pain, and yet trust in Me still, than when you have something to boast about. It is when self-love and conceit are flowing away from you that I am most truly with you, surround you with My peace. (T:78 #3)

Every gentle rebuke, however, was followed by words of immense encouragement. Christ told me:-

Be content with lowly tasks or even with loneliness. It is in

'hidden' hearts that I am now powerfully at work, in apparent darkness. *Through My power, something secret and magnificent is being done in your life* - for your good and for My Glory. It arises from your faith and humility. (T:78 #4)

Don't worry if you see no apparent results in this life. My Love is at work in you, through faith, trust and love. I know everything; and I 'see', already, all the good things which 'are' being accomplished, later on, through your present secret sacrifices. (T:78 #5)

Join in formal worship as well as you can, but never be anxious if you are tired or ill and therefore inattentive or distracted. I listen with unimaginable Love and understanding to all your sincere prayers. I am always 'waiting' in patience, throughout your wavering prayers and distractions. (T:79)

Christ: the Bridge to Heaven.

The subjects on which Christ chose to teach me astonished me. Once, when I was at Holy Mass on the anniversary of my mother's death, I was shown an extraordinarily-powerful image in prayer: of Christ crucified, with His arms held out to make a bridge across the Abyss in which He was standing. I could see thousands of people walking from one side to the other. Then He told me:-

Turn to Me, in order to find Heaven. *I, Jesus, am the 'bridge' between earth and Heaven. Through Me alone can you pass into the holiness of Heaven.* I am the "bridge" over the Abyss which separates mankind from God. You can cross the Abyss in safety only if you join My People, who stream across as One Body. (T:81 #1)

Don't worry about faithful people who have died and who have come to Me, that is, don't worry about whether you can hurt them. They are quite beyond the reach of any hurtful conversation. None of your memories or thoughts can upset them now. But pray for their deliverance from purification. (T:81 #2)

Look upon Me as the 'channel' through Whom your thoughts and words can 'flow' to the departed, as you offer your prayers to the Father "through Christ our Lord." Only good thoughts and prayers can 'flow' through Me, the Good Christ, when you pray in My Name. (T:81 #3)

Unite every humiliation and suffering to Mine, in My
Passion. By your union with Me, our sacrifice is One, both
in your heart-felt private prayer, and at the altar. (T:83 #1)

Consider the power of your union with Me. Through it,
everyone you care for and pray for is drawn into My
prayer. *Just as you, through Me, gather others into the
Father's Light and Love so they in their turn will gather one
another.* (T:83 #2)

Strengthen My Church. It is by your prayers for others
that the Church is made even stronger. By your
intercessions, you and your brothers and sisters lift one
another into My Light. *My Divine 'Light' on earth is
increased* by your fellowship, and *the 'circle' of love is
stronger*: One Body, growing stronger. (T:83 #3)

Strengthen fellow-members of My Church in the best way,
which is by helping them to grow in faith and in love. (T:83
#4)

An altar, in my soul.

In November of the same year, on the feast of the dedication of the Cathedral Church of Rome
- St John Lateran - Christ astonished me in Holy Communion by appearing to the eyes of my
soul. At the same time He announced His purpose and my new vocation. That day, after
Holy Communion, Christ appeared in my soul in glory, showing me an image of a stone altar,
around which beautiful flowers had been scattered. Then He explained that He Himself had
placed this altar at the centre of my soul. He told me:-

Try to do My Will in the best possible way, which is by
sacrificing your own will. (T:88 #1)

Make your life into a continual sacrifice of praise of Me. I
deserve your free submission. (T:88 #2)

Dedicate your life to Me. *"In you, I have set myself an altar,
and nothing shall dislodge it."* My plan for your life is being
fulfilled, step by step, as you live wholly committed to the
fulfilment of My wishes. Despite all your faults, I know
that you love Me above all things, and I have accepted all
your penances and sacrifices. (T:88 #3)

Rejoice at whatever I permit to happen in your life.
*Continue on the path of obedience to My Will, until your
life's end, for your good, and for the good of My Church, and
for My Glory.* (T:88 #4)

> Let go of all selfish desires. *Your life must be a continual*
> *sacrifice of praise, in the sacrifice of your own will so that*
> *My Will may be done.* (T:88 #5)

The profoundest implications of this declaration were hidden from me, only to be revealed in the future; but although such a solemn announcement puzzled me, the formality and grace with which Christ had spoken to me on this occasion showed me with what careful attention He deals with each soul. As we greet Him with reverence, so He honours our dignity: such is His love for us all and His admiration for those who endure all sorts of things for love of Him.

Christ's Glory in our souls.

For the whole of that day, Christ remained with me, more 'present' than was usual. He continued to teach me about the life of holiness and grace, by showing me an image in which He was seen standing, glorious, close behind a certain person, holding her hand, and showing her where to walk; yet He was letting her take the first steps forward. I saw that Christ's Glory is so powerful that it shines even 'through' His special friends; and He explained to me:-

> **Stay close to Me; I am a sure guide for everyone who**
> **wishes to please the Father and to do His Will. (T:90 #1)**

> **Realise that you are free. I allow you real freedom in which**
> **to make your choices. I have not created the human race as**
> **a race of robots. (T:90 #2)**

> **Co-operate with My work of grace within your soul. I not**
> **only accompany and help one whom I love and who loves**
> **Me. I make everything within you pure and clear and**
> **gradually 'transparent', so that, more and more, you and I**
> **will look at everything together as one. (T:90 #3)**

> **Consider the 'fruit' of your union with Me. When you**
> **have learned to do everything in union with Me, My Glory**
> **will shine out from your feeble life, words and actions.**
> **(WC:90) (T:90 #4)**

Christ reassured me one day, after Holy Communion:-

> **Permit Me to work within your soul. It is by your prayers**
> **and sacrifices that you invite Me to set to work.** *I am*
> *brushing aside the rubble and untidiness of selfishness within*
> *this 'room' which is your soul,* **as I make a home for Myself**
> **within, now that I am welcomed. (T:91A #1)**

> *Abandon all fuss and worry.* **I can eradicate your**
> **uncharitable habits and opinions; but I will do so gently,**
> **from moment to moment, as** *you and I sort things out*

together, as I help you to do good and to avoid evil. (T:91A #2)

'Facets' of Divine Life.

Throughout 1986 I was still amazed at the goodness shown to me by Christ. Yet I couldn't understand why He was showing such extraordinary kindness to someone like me. The more I ignored all that happened in prayer, determined only to do my duty and to work faithfully for love of Him, the more He sought to reassure me that He was leading me on a noble and truthful way; and He showed me something else about the way in which I was being 'taught':-

> **Accept whatever I give to you, in prayer. I Who am Truth cannot mislead you. I Who am Wisdom deal with human souls wisely. (T:91B #1)**

> **Don't confuse My gifts with My Being. Anything which you 'see' in prayer is only a 'facet' of My Divine Life, like a flash of light thrown from the side of a sparkling diamond. Such 'flashes of light' may be revealed to a devout soul, during prayer, if such is My Will. (T:91B #2)**

> **Realise that, in the course of your true and humble prayer, nothing is ever revealed to your soul through your own decision or yearning. These special gifts which I offer to your soul are offered only because of My sovereign Will. Yet you would not receive them, had you not already 'opened' your heart to Me. (T:91B #3)**

> **Accept My all-holy Will. No-one but I can choose what 'facet' of My Life will be revealed in prayer. Nothing which I show of My Life can be 'grasped'. Each glimpse is shown for a moment, in prayer, according to My Will. Yet none of the 'facets' of My Life "is" Myself, Who am briefly, inadequately and mysteriously 'reflected' across the Abyss which separates My Divine Nature from your frail human nature. (T:91B #4)**

But Christ explained, too, that He - the God/Man, our Saviour - is very close to us; and we ought to turn to Him in every need, since His Love for us is unchanging. Furthermore, He explained something which almost completely banished by fears about ever losing His friendship. He said to me, very tenderly:-

> **Trust in My Love for you. *I never leave you.* It doesn't matter where you go or what you do, I will be there with you at every moment. (T:95 #1)**

> ***You must never fail to trust in Me.* I cannot possibly 'leave'**

anyone who - by every effort - tries to stay close to Me. Yet, people are free to leave Me. (T:95 #2)

Remember that *"I was with you all the time"*, *today, at every moment of the day.* *I Whom you love and serve have made you My own;* *"nor shall I let you go."* *You are now totally Mine.* *You now belong to Me, and I will allow nothing and no-one to take you from My Heart or from My service.* **(T:96)**

Christ, speaking to me.

As you can see from the use of 'speech-marks' in the paragraph above, it was at around this time that Christ began to speak to me, within my soul, in a new and remarkable manner. I couldn't adequately express my gratitude to Him not just for His words, but for the peace and joy which He was bringing, daily, as well as for all the other blessings of my life. As the days went by it seemed plain to me that the vivid expressions of truth and love which God gave me in prayer were so abundant and so marvellous, that they weren't meant to help just myself, but others too who were struggling to be faithful.

Over and over again, I had found how pure and delicate were the 'occurrences' of Knowledge. They were neither moods nor emotions. Over twenty years had passed since the day when I had first called out to Christ with firm faith, and He had come to my side: and in all that time I'd neither spoken about nor written anything about His dealings with me. For about six years, now, He had been teaching me not only through His Church in the usual ways but also by pure Knowledge; and it was because both Church and prayer-time provided me with the very same truths of the Faith that my confidence increased. I can't remember the date of it; but I decided one day that I ought to follow my inner prompting and to write down a few words about each of the 'teachings'. I bought a small black notebook, and in one afternoon, without a pause, I noted over seventy graces or teachings which were still extraordinarily clear in my mind.

From that day on, I made brief notes on all of Christ's teachings, if not on the same day, then usually in the week when they were given. But I was very self-conscious, and so jotted only a line or two, even on momentous subjects. All I wanted was enough to jog my memory. I had no idea where this was all leading, nor any inkling of my future task; but I was happy that every detail of the teachings remained clear in my mind, and could be recalled when I eventually decided to write at length on the different subjects.

I wanted to be obedient, and so far as I could tell, my writing didn't displease Christ. He continued to encourage me and to show me His care and concern; and since He had been so strict about my deliberate faults, I felt sure that He would have corrected me if I'd been mistaken in making that record; yet it wasn't because of kind words spoken to me in prayer that I came to trust in His guidance, but because He guided me so frequently in accordance with the teachings of His Church. I mean that anyone who had taught me things which contradicted our beliefs would quite obviously not have been Christ.

A fruitful union.

It was a source of wonder to me, that day after day, in this new state, there was no longer any need to reach "outwards" to find Christ. He filled every day with His peace, within and around me. Also, He gave me new courage to face further, unexpected trials.

But they weren't pointless trials, Christ explained, as He told me:-

> **Accept your privileged state. Since I am truly with you, nowadays, and since, by your free choice you are truly 'with' Me, *I will live through you for others.* Your union with Me will be fruitful. (T:92 #1)**

> **Persevere in your soul's work. The more you empty yourself of sin, selfishness and earthly desires, the more will others - on seeing you and your actions - see, instead, My action, My love and My tenderness. The more successfully you banish your preoccupations, the more 'transparent' shall you become for Me. You will shine with My Presence! (T:92 #2)**

> **Don't hesitate now, just because you have been so sinful. I not only pardon and heal you but permit you to bring My grace to others! (T:92 #3)**

10 PURIFICATION

(1987-1989)

VIOLENCE. ILLNESS. THE ABYSS.

Forceful reassurance.

As the implications of my task grew plainer, I was so worried about my faults and weaknesses that Christ taught me the simple meaning of trust in His care. He gave me forceful reassurance, as He urged me:-

> **Have no doubts about My Love for you, nor about the special union of Myself with you - with you who are now transformed. Only I could have given you such perfect joy, not only for a day, but at every moment for the past year - and amidst real sufferings. (T:93 #1)**

> **Follow Me wherever I lead you, no matter how strange the path. I will continue to guide and uphold you. (T:93 #2)**

> **Fix your soul's gaze on Me in prayer. I never 'try' you beyond your strength. But you must ask for the graces which I long to pour upon you! (T:94 #1)**

> **Rely on Me for the graces which you need in order to do the work which I Myself have put before you. I am bound to help you! (T:94 #2)**

Then Christ explained - about my requests for help:-

> **Ask Me for virtues; but be bold, and *ask for all the virtues*. *The virtues are not to be wished for separately*. It is useless to long for patience, for example, if you are unwilling to receive all of the other virtues. (T:99 #1)**

> **Look upon the virtues as being like a number of coloured rays, all emerging from a 'White Light' which is the source. I am like a glowing white light; I am the Source of all the virtues. (T:99 #2)**

> **Don't be confused by your self-examination. You may see yourself as more in need of an increase of one virtue rather than another.** *But all the virtues are with you, and are part of My presence in you,* **even though your obvious faults may be distorting your perception of the state of your soul.** (T:99 #3)

> **See how much cause you have for hope.** *Wherever I am, there are My virtues, poured out on you in a way that perfects your present nature with My grace.* (T:99 #4)

Christ reassured me that He understands every difficulty which stems from illness. He told me:-

> **Don't struggle to praise Me with elaborate greetings. Don't tire yourself - when because of illness you are flagging - by thinking about how to greet Me worthily. You can rest here, quietly, in loving prayer, united with Me before the Father.** (T:100)

Then Christ said to me, on the 6th February 1987:-

> **Be confident and joyful about your life in My loving service. You have been begging Me to help you, and now that you try to love Me at every moment, you can be sure that, from now on,** *"you are no beggar, but My daughter!"* (T:103 #1)

Ignorance about the task.

Perhaps this is the point at which I should give a reminder that for every moment of consolation in Christ's presence, as the teachings continued, I experienced a thousand moments of silent recollection mixed up with times of puzzlement or shame. The whole direction of my life was changing to an astonishing degree; and it's easy, now, to forget how much 'in the dark' I was about Christ's plans for me. I didn't know, in 1987, that He had been training me for the whole of my life - despite my terrible hesitations and falls - for the huge task which today involves not only myself but most of my family.

Since I was so ignorant about many things, I had no idea, at first, of why I was being taught in prayer; nor did I know that the 'teachings' would continue. I didn't know, when I wrote the "First Version", that Christ would urge me to produce further versions which in their different ways have reproduced His messages and instructions more fully, and have also made me, through this repetition, ever more familiar with them. The details, phrases, images, words and concepts which Christ has been pouring upon me so lavishly have been absorbed more thoroughly by my heart and mind at every re-writing of them in a different style or format; and it's now marvellous for me to realise that this 'familiarity', thus re-inforced, is part of Christ's plan. He knows that I've sometimes been so busy writing down His teachings, in between domestic tasks, other work and friends' visits, that I haven't even had time to let them 'sink in'. Not until days or months later, therefore, have I been able to 'step back' and appreciate His extraordinary kindness and so of course thank Him in a more worthy fashion. I didn't know, when I was first writing the teachings, that I'd be asked to share them with other people, that I'd produce oil paintings of some of the more important images, that I would one day write little essays based on what I'd learned from the teachings - for example, about the Most Holy Trinity or the Holy Mass - or that I'd 'end up' with half a roomful of writings and pictures. This very week I've been trying to put them in some sort of order, or rather, to catalogue and label them more efficiently, to help people after my death.

But Christ is so kind and so wise that He's been gradually enlightening me about His plans and wishes, showing me just as much as I need to know from year to year: though much more in recent times, since we're now true friends, as He has explained.

Several levels of teaching.

Throughout the late 1980's, Christ continued to enlighten me, by giving me a series of extraordinary teachings, interspersed with minor teachings of a personal nature; and it seems to me now that Christ was building yet another 'platform' on which to begin the next stage of a 'building' of teachings which would one day form a complete catechesis; and He was giving me nothing new, but only a reminder, in a contemporary form, of what His Church already tells us is important.

I wrote 'another' platform, because it was as though the foundation had been laid at my Baptism in 1942. The first level had been built in 1957, when I was told, by silent 'knowledge,' that my true home lies elsewhere. The second level had been laid in 1964 when Christ brought me to repent of my sins; and the third level was constructed in 1968, as I was received into full Communion, was confirmed, made my first Holy Communion, and then was marvellously taught how to leap into the depths of God, in prayer. The fourth level had consisted of the basic teachings given throughout the 1980's about recollection, love of neighbour, intercession, Christ's Passion - and the Church and the Holy Mass: as recorded in the pamphlet "An Introduction" and also in the Blue Book of "Instructions from Christ." But it was as though the fifth level was achieved through union with Christ as described in T.43. The sixth level began with the Holy Family vision which I'm about to describe in the next chapter; and for the construction of that new level it seemed as though Christ brought me with lavish generosity to a greater understanding of some of the marvels of the Catholic Faith.

He 'showed' me, in this way, the work of the Holy Trinity (T:314), the magnificence of the Holy Sacrifice of the Mass (T:369), the power of Our Lady's prayers (T:465), the welcome which is given in Heaven to those who resemble Christ (T:496), the unique and important role of Our Blessed Lady (T:735), the significance of our knowledge that "God is Love" (T:771), our true Communion with the Angels and Saints - including Saint Joseph (T:896). The perpetual Presence amongst us of Christ in the Blessed Sacrament (T:928) - and the meaning of sacrifice (in T:1003A). These are the teachings which I shall write about in the next four chapters. But there was a special reason for this extraordinary collection of teachings on some of the truths of the Catholic Faith - besides providing a reminder for people in the Church.

It was as though Christ was showing me that these things are all true, and important; yet even more important are the deeper truths for which these are a preparation, by which I mean things of an seventh level, things such as the power of the Holy Spirit at work at the Consecration (T:1360), the Sacred Tradition (T:1386), the New Covenant of Christ's Blood (T:1613), the Immaculate Conception (T:1734A), the work of priests (in T:1770), the heart of the Liturgy (T:1804), and Christ's work of Substitution (T:1829); and this more 'obscure' series of teachings, interspersed as usual with 'minor' teachings, culminated in an experience of meeting the Father (T:1941).

The Father Himself taught me, to my astonished delight, at what I shall call the eighth level, about his Love for us, and the meaning of Union; and in that way I was shown something about the supreme purpose of Christ's whole plan for my life, which is to cause the Father to be 'seen' anew, discussed, admired, praised and glorified.

For the Glory of the Father.

Since it's to the Father that Christ leads us, since it's to the Father that the Church prays as one body, since it's from the Father that Christ has been given to us, and since it's to the Father that Glory is given because of all the wonders which He has worked for us, the truths He has taught us and the Saints He has sanctified for us, so it's to the Father that Christ has been leading me steadily in prayer; and He has been doing this so that, at what I now call the 'ninth level' of this building, I can receive many, many teachings not solely about the spiritual life or about the Church but from and about the Father Who 'lies' beyond and beneath everything good that we believe. Therefore I've been taught about the Father's beauty, about His Love and His nature, and also about the work and life of the Holy Trinity: Father, Son and Holy Spirit - and about the meaning of "Life-in-God," either on earth or in Heaven; and I shall write much more about these subjects towards the end of this book, as you'll have guessed from the 'Contents' page.

Perhaps the 'tenth level' will be dying and death: and the Eternal Union for which I yearn; but it's as though I feel a spiritual vertigo, as I describe all this at last, and see it in black and white. These are the things which have been happening in my life for many years, by God's choice and not by any plan of mine, but only at my puzzled consent. Yet now that I see everything so plainly I'm beginning to be over-awed, again, by God's astonishing goodness and by His kindness to me; yet I shan't waste more paper by saying again that I'm not fit to do the work. I'm awed, also, by God's great Love for the Church which is in such dire need of both encouragement and instruction, even through a work as flawed as this; I mean flawed in grammar and presentation, not in truths expressed; and meanwhile, I hope and pray that God will keep me fervent and faithful, whatever happens.

Strict correction.

How little room there is for boredom in a vigorous spiritual life! I mean that every word of thanks to me from Christ, in a moment of delight in prayer, has been tempered by a warning about my faults - just as every severe comment has been balanced by an expression of tenderness which has nearly broken my heart. That was how Christ trained me, at that stage of my life, to put Him and His interests first, at all times; and it was only necessary because I have so many faults.

On several occasions, I've been made painfully aware of Christ's displeasure at my faults. Yet it's only because He wants to bring me real fulfilment and happiness that He's gone to such lengths to make me whole-hearted in His service. He's spared no effect to prepare me for the task which I was born to undertake. It's been through His strict correction as well as His extraordinary kindness that I've learned how to please Him best. As part of my training, Christ showed me, more than once, that He was offended by my priorities.

I remember a day when I'd found an exciting new novel, and became so enthralled that only I did the bare essentials of my household duties, and sat in a chair reading for the rest of the time. I was even anxious to avoid conversations in order to bury my head in my book. But, when Christ's scorching light shone in my soul, it left me aghast with shame; and at the same time Christ taught me, in an instant of scorching prayer:-

> **Don't repay Me, a generous Lord, by greed and discontent. Whatever you do that 'blots Me out' entirely from your life is quite unacceptable, as when you sometimes, briefly, try to ignore Me in order to fulfil your own plans or longings. (T:63 #2)**

> **Be recollected. I alone should be the ultimate object of your thoughts, attentions and desires. All the good things which I permit you to enjoy should be enjoyed through and with Me, but not 'instead of' Me. (T:63 #3)**

> **Be grateful for the good things which are appropriate for your way of life, and which I permit you to enjoy. But don't fill your whole mind and soul with ceaseless words and music. How can you hope to grow close to Me in prayer if you fill every spare minute with songs and novels and therefore ignore My silent and loving presence? (T:63 #4)**

Self-indulgent ways.

No-one should think that I'm suggesting that novels are evil. I suppose that good novels are an art-form, equivalent to good plays, operas or films. I only mean that Christ didn't want me to read them in my own particular circumstances, at that stage of my life. He showed me that to be self-indulgent in certain ways was quite unacceptable; yet time lavished in apparent idleness with relatives and friends never displeases Him: quite the contrary, since He wants us to show our love for one another; and generosity with our time is a great proof of love.

Christ was teaching me that by burying myself for long periods in novels, I was running away from reality. That's why He asked me, at around the same time, to do without perpetual background music on the radio or cassette player. Music and conversation were to be valued -

and enjoyed with friends at home or at occasional concerts; but, as with books, it was a question of priorities. How could I "PRAY CONSTANTLY" (1 Th 5:17) and always be alert enough to recognise Christ's Will and His guidance, if I were deliberately distracting myself for long hours with someone else's ideas and melodies? I understood that my attention to His wishes would be more sincere and profound, if I'd accept His invitation to turn away even from legitimate distractions. So I made the sacrifice which He was inviting me to make; and, in return, He drew me closer to Himself and taught me to love silence.

I wasn't forbidden occasional concerts, since music is truly His gift. But He was teaching me that the Giver - adored in silence, by faith - is more precious than any of His gifts; and how could Christ 'teach' me, if my heart and mind were full of different voices, preferred to His?

It was at about this time that He showed me further behaviour which isn't appropriate for one of His friends. I say 'at about this time,' because I'd become so determined to please Him that He had begun to show me in detail not only what was sinful in my life - every uncharitable word or resentful thought - but what was merely foolish or unnecessary. He had chosen not to show me these things earlier, when I might have been crushed at seeing His displeasure. But now that my love for Him was stronger, I was allowed to understand, for example, that it was better if I didn't wear much jewellery. I should stop dying my hair, and also wear more modest clothing.

Attention to externals.

Little by little, Christ steered me towards the sort of quiet attention to externals that would result in a more harmonious way of living: if in every aspect I tried to reflect His joy, simplicity, modesty and truth. I can hardly bear to write this, when I'm so ashamed of the way I've lived much of my life, but this is what Our Lord wants me to say; and I hope it will help people who are dithering about His wishes. There's nothing wrong - indeed, everything right - with lovely clothing or necessary ornamentation; I've already written about the dangers of being puritanical. But Christ made it quite plain to me that in a number of little ways I had vainly or thoughtlessly compromised with current secular attitudes; and He showed me that I would please Him enormously by being faithful to His Will even in these minor matters.

Christ's tenderness.

Whenever I sincerely tried to correct my faults, discipline was swiftly replaced by tenderness; and when, one day, I was worried about the direction of my life, and about the 'teachings', besides being full of memories of past sins, Christ stood beside me in prayer, gentle and consoling. He said to me:-

> **Don't worry about your experiences in prayer.** *"Haven't I shown you enough"!"* **Since that which you learn is genuinely good - is in accordance with the Faith as taught by My Holy Church and believed by Saints - you can remind Yourself that all good things come from Me, your Savour, Who am Truth and goodness. (T:243 #1)**

Don't be afraid. You do well to be cautious, but, truly, it is My Spirit Who teaches you good things about Me. Someone like yourself who is content to pray in order to please Me and who does not run after new experiences, and who longs only to live according to My Will, is unlikely to be deceived during prayer. (T:243 #2)

This was a wonderful consolation.

A Robbery.

Within a year or so, real trials came upon me. It was on March 11th, 1988, that my slowly-increasing trust in Christ was thoroughly tested. Yet each year, I suppose, I invariably find that I have some new reason for making a vigorous renewal of my commitment to Christ's way of patience and sacrifice. Towards evening on that particular day I answered a knock at the back door, and was horrified to be seized there by two armed men, and to be pushed down onto my kitchen floor. My child was taken to another room, but, mercifully, she was left unharmed; I was warned and threatened, and then, for half-an-hour, was dragged at knife-point around my house in the search for valuables.

As I said earlier, everyone on earth must live at the mercy of people who choose to do evil, just as other people suffer when we ourselves act uncharitably. Yet trials are certainly more frequent when the enemy of Christ - as Holy Scripture tells us - is at work in the world trying to draw away from God those who are weak yet who want to be faithful and trusting.

Although I shook with terror, I relied on Christ's power, which enabled me to speak quietly as I replied to the intruder's questions. I prayed the 'Jesus' prayer silently, over and over again; and Christ kept me calm and helped me to be polite to the masked man, who finally apologised as he and his companion left with our few treasures. I say 'few' because we'd been burgled once before, at home, and I'd also been robbed in a London street.

I thanked God for His goodness, finally aware that we were safe, though frightened. Nevertheless, I'd learned several lessons about greed and fear and trust. So, first, I resolved not to collect things which I didn't need. I wouldn't plan 'bigger barns', nor would I permit my possessions to be a source of temptation to others. I was given one little gift, anyway. A pendant with a 'Nativity' scene on it was dropped, unnoticed, by one of the men as we left an upstairs room to search the rooms below. I didn't find it until late that evening, but I thanked Our Lord for the souvenir.

Through mentioning all these details I'm trying to say why the whole episode affected us immensely, probably for the rest of our lives. All that makes an earthly person feel carefree and invulnerable was to be lost for a while. But the gains were immeasurable as we learned to look to God for the sort of security that really counts. I don't mean that I didn't hope to prevent the same thing from happening again. On the contrary, I did everything that was reasonable to make our home secure; and I was so frightened, for a while, of being attacked again, that every trip to the back door with a basketful of washing, or every return to the house after a trip to the shops, ended in a moment of terror as I approached our porch, half-expecting to see someone else crouched down there, ready to seize me.

It isn't appropriate, here, for me to speak about my daughter's reactions. Her life is her own; it's not for me to write her story; and so I'll say no more than this: I was amazed by her courage; and I've been deeply touched by the way in which she comforted and encouraged me, as indeed I tried to comfort and encourage her, during those dreadful months immediately afterwards.

Although it's true that I've never again been surprised at meeting earthly problems, at the same time I've never been more sure that if we can remain determinedly 'fastened' to God in our hearts by faith and by prayer, He can help us to endure whatever might happen. In one sense, every difficulty we meet can be seen as a test. We'll be tempted to fail in trust towards God, perhaps asking why we should suffer so much; or we might even be tempted to congratulate ourselves on our courage and forbearance, forgetting that God Himself gives us the grace to endure. "I WILL NOT EVEN PASS JUDGEMENT ON MYSELF" (1 Co 4:3) as St. Paul says. But I'm just so grateful to God for the grace to have kept on praying.

Fear and weakness.

Although it was all over, I remained terrified for months, whether sitting at home half-expecting to be attacked again, or walking past the shops and almost cowering when young men in jeans and 'trainers' walked by. I didn't waste time feeling guilty about my feelings; I already knew how weak and human I am, so I concentrated on working out practical measures to lessen my fear. Christ, I knew, didn't condemn human emotions; indeed, He'd been terrified Himself. More clearly than ever, I understood something of His feelings in Gethesemane: probably shaking with terror, though determined to persevere; and although I can't deny that I hope never to be attacked again, yet neither can I deny that I'm glad to have had a little glimpse of what Christ suffered - and of what He still suffers, in a way, in the lives of those of His children whose lives are so much harder than mine. It made me less dismissive of the fears and weaknesses of other people, and more ready to praise the tiniest efforts towards what is good or brave which are made by people who live in horrible circumstances.

Strangely, it was my turn to be 'reader' at Holy Mass, on the very day after the robbery. I read from the pulpit some words of Holy Scripture about how God permits us to suffer; yet it is "HE WHO SOOTHES THE SORE" (Jb 5:18). Then Christ taught me, when I was praying:-

Cling to Me in My Passion, in your distress, when a terrible experience leaves you in turmoil. (T:201)

It wasn't God who had hurt us. He'd allowed the men to use their free-will; and I had no excuse to be bitter, when on so many occasions I myself had made selfish choices.

Of course, I thanked God for the strength which enabled me to go about normally; but I felt safe nowhere, except in church, until I'd undergone a Providential aversion 'therapy'. I mean that I was confined to the house by illness for the whole month of June; and it was only because I was 'forced' in that way to spend many hours in my kitchen and sitting-room, although still jumping up whenever I heard a strange noise outside, half-convinced that I'd see further intruders, that I learned to be at peace there once again. I was helped, as my health improved, by a regular cycle of quiet occupations: by prayer, housework and sleep; and meanwhile, the 'teachings' went on.

"Shaped and tested by suffering."

One day, in prayer, Christ showed me:-

> **Believe that your sufferings and trials can be fruitful. (T:209 #1)**

> **Bear your burdens bravely.** *It is good to bear all things patiently - even temptations - for My sake and for the Glory of the Father.* **(T:209 #2)**

> **Take comfort from the knowledge that your sufferings will be fruitful.** *The more you grow like Me in love, shaped and tested by suffering, the more you can stay close to Me, holding My wounded hands, pleading with Me before the Father.* **Many people will benefit from the prayers which you offer, prayers which are united to mine. (T:209 #3)**

I was reminded through the Scriptures that: "UNLESS A GRAIN OF WHEAT FALLS ON THE GROUND AND DIES" (Jn 12:24) there will be no growth and no harvest. But one day at Holy Mass, after these words of Scripture had been read: "GOD LOVED THE WORLD SO MUCH" (Jn 3:16), I was astonished to be reassured by Christ, in my soul:-

> **Believe in My Love for all people - for** *"you too!"* **My Love is personal and tender, yet I wish to 'form' you and make you beautiful, and this is achieved through trials and storms. (T:202).**

A happy routine.

During the next three months, I was led to make more profoundly self-emptying resolutions, as Christ taught me even more about true love and true hope. I went to daily Mass and tried to put into practice everything that He'd taught me in Church.

I worked hard when I could, and rested when I couldn't work any more. Everything I did was very ordinary, but I didn't mind. I looked after the family and tried to help friends and acquaintances in little ways. I cooked, shopped, painted, cleaned and sewed. I wrote letters, and visited sick friends in hospital and clung to Christ in every pain, thanking God for all my beloved friends and family members and praying for each one every day. The needs of the world expanded, it seemed, before my eyes; so my daily intercessions included even more people, known and unknown, living and departed; and all the prayers were woven into the minutes and hours of my hum-drum but happy routine.

All the time, too, I asked Christ to help me in my acceptance of everything I found difficult to bear. I begged him to bring some sort sweet 'fruit' out of my life; and so He continued to 'hollow out' my soul and my aching heart, in prayer. I asked Him to destroy my selfish desires, and to help me to create a better home for Him within my soul; so He kept me low and quiet in His company. He gave me everything I needed, through His own power, and through the words of His priest in the Sacrament of Reconciliation.

In past years I'd gone to 'Confession' every month or two, before major feasts; but now I realised how silly it is to neglect such a marvellous source of grace and advice. Since then, I've attended more frequently in the certainty of receiving help from God, but also as an act of humility which pleases Him - as He has delightedly shown me. But I rarely thought about rewards or punishments. I hoped for Heaven one day for the sheer bliss of seeing God at last. My heart's main hope was that I'd serve him faithfully in little ways, and that He wouldn't allow me to be deceived. When I told Christ of my fears, He said that He'd chosen me so that, united with Him, I'll "BEAR FRUIT IN PLENTY" (Jn 15:5).

Throughout these months, Christ showed me not only His own great love for me, but also the love which the Angels and Saints have for us; and He brought them to comfort me in my weariness at Holy Mass (T:161).

Very close to Christ.

Christ continued to teach me, more by pure knowledge than by words; yet whenever He spoke within my soul I was tremendously comforted and strengthened. I was urged to love my neighbour, to trust in God in every circumstance, to accept with gratitude all the gifts which come to me through Christ, and to remain always aware that His grace is not earned. Christ reassured me about the value of prayer, as He explained to me:-

> **'Touch' Me in My Holy Sacrifice by uniting yourself with My Offering, with My intentions and with My own Self in Holy Communion. When you 'touch' Me, you touch, also, something of joy of Heaven, and you approach the depth and the breadth of My Divine Glory. (T:191 #4)**

> **Never let the plain sight of your sinfulness keep away from Me.** *As you kneel before Me in prayer, in all your weakness, conscious of your faults, you are like a beggar in rags before Me, Who am sinless. Yet, I love you, in your rags!* **I love you truly, with great warmth, tenderness and affection! (T:192)**

> **Reach out in prayer, through Me, to those who have died.** *It is through and "in" Me that you find the dear faithful departed, since they now live with Me. All their loving thoughts towards you, and all your prayers for them, find a channel in Me, Jesus, Who have brought together earth and Heaven.* **(T:193 #1)**

244

> Think about your nearness to Me. How thin is the 'veil of Unknowing' which separates earth from Heaven. (T:193 #2)

Heavenly Friends.

Even in difficult times, when it was becoming harder for me to get out and about, and to see my friends, Christ didn't leave me alone, and lonely. One day at Mass, after Communion, I was thinking about how amazing is Jesus' Sacrifice, and was considering my own reluctance in sacrifice; and suddenly I learned:-

> Have faith in Me. I have given you many loving helpers. You are assisted and encouraged not only by Myself but by the whole court of Heaven: the Saints and the Holy Angels. (T:234 #1)

> Believe in your Heavenly friends. The Saints and the Holy Angels are full of compassion and tenderness for you who have not yet reached the end of your struggles to be faithful. Listen to their encouraging words: "We all want to help you along." (T:234 #2)

> Let Me *bring sweet fruit out of your 'emptiness'. It is true that you have much suffering to bear, but by this 'hallowing', I make a home* for Myself within your heart. (T:236)

> Notice how lavishly I reward all your sincere little efforts to please Me, especially when you have been to 'Reconciliation' and Holy Communion. Truly, I reward you lavishly in the presence of My Saints and Holy Angels, even if you are not always aware of My generosity. (T:260)

> Believe in My great Love for you. *"You must believe that all the time."* Your faith in Me ought to be constant and ever-increasing, since, here and always, My Love for you is real, tender, and reliable. (T:261)

> Don't let frailty hold you back from service. *"Love people"*, for My sake. Every small, good act or thought or prayer is valuable. When faithfully done, such things are better than greater tasks badly done, and better than foolish unfilled dreams of tremendous acts. (T:262 #1)

Christ forbade me to worry. He rewarded me for my acceptance, for His sake, of the little pains and humiliations which I suffered because of ill-health. He led me, again, to offer my whole life to Him, for His work. He gave me an interior joy so great, however, that it seemed to me as though the joy which He has promised us - in the Gospels - was mine: "A HUNDRED FOLD" (Mt 13:8), not just through spiritual delights, but through 'earthly' blessings. My husband and I spent a wonderful evening with our children, on July 6th of that year, celebrating our silver wedding, grateful for all that we'd been given, especially for the children: and grateful too for all that we'd endured and achieved together with the help of God.

The Holy Family.

Then came a marked change in the 'type' of certain teachings. During the summer of 1988, Christ taught me about Himself at Mass, for the first time - at this stage of my life - not simply by pure wordless "Knowledge", but by an appearance before the eyes of my soul.

One weekend in the summer, we went away, as a family, to attend a wedding in another town; and when the celebrations were over and we'd stayed at a local hotel, I was offered a lift to the local Catholic Church. I didn't want to miss Mass, anyway, but this was a special day; I'm sure it was the Vigil of the Assumption, rather than the feast itself; and I've loved Our Lady more and more, since I became a Catholic, and have given special thanks on her feasts.

I entered the church as I enter any church - looking for the holy water stoop. I blessed myself with the Sign of the Cross. Then I reflected on the lives of the martyrs who had lived and worshipped nearby in penal times. I made my way to a vacant place on one of the benches.

Having learned to pray anywhere, at any time, I wasn't distracted by the strange church or by the unfamiliar faces; and Holy Mass was celebrated with great reverence. When I was praying, after Communion, Christ came to my soul in the usual way, but this time He lifted my soul not to joyous darkness, but to Glory. He held my spirit there, high in His peace and joy, as I gazed at Him Who is "THE RADIANT LIGHT OF GOD'S GLORY" (Hb 1:3). I saw Him quite clearly, with my soul's eyes, but - just as when I saw Him in 1964 - His Holy Face was too dazzling to see. I was amazed to see His Mother Mary by His side; and Saint Joseph was beside her - all three of them standing before me, though some distance away. Christ immediately taught me:-

> **Draw close to Me in prayer, and close to My Mother and St. Joseph, who are greeting you. (T:275 #1)**

> **Rejoice that My radiance no longer causes you pain. (T:275 #2)**

> **Be joyful. I, your Saviour, have much to teach you, and so I welcome you, now revealing to you a glimpse of the Glory of Heaven, where I live with Mary My Mother, and also with Saint Joseph. Each one of us, each member of the 'Holy Family', is radiant, beautiful and joyful. (T:275 #3)**

> **Rejoice in the privileges which you can enjoy during prayer. I wish you to share our joy and Glory. (T:275 #4)**

> **Make sure that My holy Mother occupies an important**

place in your life. *"When you look at Mary, you see Me."*
Every one of the true and good spiritual characteristics or
virtues which has been noted in My holy Mother is also
true of Me, her Divine son. (T:275 #5)

Turn to My Mother. *She can be loved and imitated. She
gives you comfort.* (T:275 #6)

Rely on My Mother. *She and I both long for your joy.*
(T:275 #7)

Remember that *I come from My Mother. No mother can be
more tender than I!* (T:275 #8)

*Have faith in Me, and trust in My Mother, Mary. United
with Me, she comforts you, and she prays all your prayers,
that is,* she offers your good prayers through Me to the
Father. (T:275 #9)

Marvel at *the glory* and power *which I have given to My
Mother and to Saint Joseph. Marvel at the wonder of
intercession - My Mother's intercession, and Saint Joseph's,
and yours!* I have given tremendous power to those who
pray for others. (T:275 #10)

Beneath the surface.

At the very next moment, all-at-once, Christ taught me something more about what should be
our attitude to prayer in everyday life:-

*You must pray even in your weakness; that is of no account
to Me when I listen to your prayers.* (T:275 #11)

Be confident, in prayer. *You glide trustingly in the depths of
My Love,* during your prayers and pleadings. (T:276 #1)

Be confident about My care of you. (T:276 #2)

Wait patiently, in times of trouble. Learn to live within My
embrace, through prayer. Let me wholly enfold you. *Glide
and turn with ease, in My 'waters', and rest in Me, just like
swimmers beneath the surface of the ocean, during surface
storms.* (T:276 #3)

Put your trust in Me. As you face the various trials and
upheavals of your life, I have every sympathy for the
agitated thoughts and emotions which I know you cannot
entirely control. (T:276 #4)

> Trust in your Holy Angel, who accompanies you
> everywhere. (T:277 #1)

> Offer a continual sacrifice of praise to the Father,
> everywhere, your pains united with My sufferings, in loving
> intercession for everyone in your heart. (T:277 #2)

Then I left the church at the end of the celebration, almost overwhelmed by Christ's beauty and kindness.

Learning to trust.

Ever-grateful for what I'd been shown, I still told no-one about such a 'teaching'; I had no idea why Christ should show me these things, but I was happy to believe that He had good reasons of His own, and so I tried to put into practice what He taught me, which, as I said, was nothing new. It was a loving reminder of the blessedly simple ways of life urged upon us by Christ's Church and Christ's Gospel. Constantly, in His teachings, Christ urged me to be both realistic and trusting. He assured me that although it's my vocation to share in His sufferings and so to help other souls, His courage and patience are mine, if I ask for them.

It was during a holiday, as I travelling from place to place, in the summer of 1988, always exhausted, that I was helped by Christ's presence, and was assured that He had a definite plan for my life. After Holy Communion one day, as I battled amidst various torments, I was shown by Christ:-

> Put your entire trust in Me, even though I might keep your
> soul in quietness, or in ignorance of My plans, until your
> spiritual training is completed. (T:278 #7)

But something about my vocation was revealed with great clarity, at the end of 1988. I was shown, by Christ, at Holy Mass one day:-

> Look upon all your sufferings as a sharing in My
> crucifixion - as you freely make reparation for your sins
> and for the sins of others. (T:302A #2)

> Make every effort to be brave, and to suffer patiently, in
> imitation of Myself. I love you deeply, and I look tenderly
> upon you, full of admiration for your virtues. I stand
> beside you, upholding you in your sufferings. (T:302A #3)

> *"Don't worry, Lizzie,"* about your temptations and
> torments, when your will is fixed wholeheartedly on trying
> to please Me. *"You're so much a part of Me that nothing
> can separate us."* (T:302B #1)

Then right at the beginning of 1989, when I'd made my New Year resolutions, I was comforted by Christ once more, as He told me:-

> **Don't be ashamed of revealing all your silly faults to Me. I**
> **use even sinful people for My work. Yet, I love you, and I**
> **work in and through your weaknesses. (T:303)**

Made fit to praise the Father.

Christ reminded me of how privileged we are, to be able to live in union with Him, and to be able to offer worthy praise, through Him, to the Father. He told me:-

> **Treasure the Holy Sacrifice, and thank Me for My work in**
> **your life, as I prepare you to take part in the Holy**
> **Mysteries. Whether the congregation be large or small -**
> **and even with all your faults and failings -** *you are hallowed*
> *and made fit to praise the Father through Me, and to*
> *intercede for others.* **(T:312 #2)**
>
> **Be more generous towards Me. (T:312 #3)**
>
> **Imitate My Mother, whose surrender to grace, at the**
> **message of the Angel, was immediate and spontaneous, like**
> **a natural breath from her pure and undivided heart.**
> **(T:312 #4)**
>
> **Stay quietly 'beside' Me, throughout each day, in order to**
> **grow in resemblance to Me.** *The more you resemble Me in*
> *sacrifice and in purity and in conformity to the Will of God*
> *our Father, throughout all suffering, and the more you stay*
> *quietly with Me in work and in prayer, one with Me in mind*
> *and heart and prayer, then the more fully will the Father use*
> *you for His Glory and for the comfort of your neighbours*
> *and the cause of Truth.* **(T:314)**

I didn't really understand what Christ meant, but I believed Him.

Always before me.

As the months went by, and as I learned to live in greater trust and obedience, Christ taught me much more about prayer and about union with Him in this life. Yet the more frequently He taught me about His wishes, the more frequently I was obliged to struggle against my weaknesses for His sake, and to be brave and uncomplaining! I know that although nothing in my power could have made the 'teachings' occur in prayer, they wouldn't have continued if I hadn't attempted to follow Christ's advice. He couldn't have led me in this strange way towards "THE CITY OF OUR GOD, THE HOLY MOUNTAIN" (Ps 48:1) if I hadn't continued to put one foot firmly after another on the pathway which was being revealed to me

- lit by Christ's radiance in prayer. This isn't to say, however, that I was satisfied with my efforts; but I tried to please Christ, and I tried to accept whatever sufferings God permitted me to undergo; but when I wasn't at rest with Him in prayer, I felt that "I HAVE MY SIN CONSTANTLY IN MIND" (Ps 51:3). I was ashamed of how little I did for God, Who has done so much for us.

I wanted to walk every step of the way with Him, wherever He might lead me, since Scripture said: "YOU THEREFORE MUST BE HOLY BECAUSE I AM HOLY" (Lv 11:45), and I couldn't ignore that command. I was aghast at my sinfulness, but hoped that somehow, Christ would deal with it.

Devotion to Our Lady.

When I was busy with very simple chores, I used to puzzle over the purpose of the 'teachings'; but one thing in particular surprised me, as the 'teachings' continued: I mean, I was astonished by the prominent place which Our Blessed Lady seemed to hold in her Son's 'thoughts'.

It must have been partly because of my Protestant upbringing that my automatic instinct, for many years, was to suppose that the role of Our Blessed Lady in a Christian life was important, but was in danger of being over-stated; yet here was Christ explaining again and again, in prayer, the great importance of His Holy Mother and the details of her ever-continuing work and example. I say 'again and again' because much more was explained to me than has been appropriate to record in this autobiographical prologue to the books of His teachings.

It was around that time, before the "Holy Family" teaching, I think, not afterwards, that I regretted my timidity about paying honour to Our Blessed Lady. I quite deliberately and confidently added a new phrase to the offering I make to the Father in prayer each morning. I was unsure of the complete meaning of the phrase, but I knew that it was important. I added the words to those which I'd used for about twenty years. Daily, I had begun my prayer: "Abba, Father, I offer You all my thoughts, words, actions and sufferings this day ..." but now I added: "through the most pure heart of Mary" - which was a phrase used by Popes and Saints for centuries; and then I continued as usual: "for the intentions of the Sacred Heart of Jesus in Heaven; and I beseech You never to let me offend You, but faithfully to love and serve You and to do Your Holy Will in everything, from this moment onwards until the moment of my death."

This little change, coupled with a more frequent praying of the Holy Rosary, later on, and with daily wearing of Our Lady's 'scapular', helped to bring me closer to my Heavenly Mother; and the adoption of these few practices helped me to 'tune' my heart and body more closely to ancient Catholic culture. Faith is only half-formed, I believe, if it rules only mind and conversation. I'm not suggesting that everyone should follow the same devotions, just hoping that Catholics everywhere, especially adult converts, can be less awkward and embarrassed about taking on some traditional pious practices which honour Our Blessed Lady and which therefore delight Christ, her son, and which make us spiritually stronger, and therefore more joyful.

Those who are crushed in spirit.

At this point in the 'story', it seems unfair of me to mention my physical weakness yet again; however, it's part of the whole pattern of my life, and an essential component of my story; so I must tell how late in 1988, I was asked to enter hospital once more, because of recurrent illness.

My weakness had grown more serious; so I plucked up courage and packed my bag again, prepared for more humiliation but ready for the family's sake to risk an answer. The children were now nearly adult. They were delightful company and very tolerant of my weaknesses, yet puzzled by my nameless difficulties and limitations.

Sitting on my hospital bed, preparing to be prodded and questioned again, I took a few notes from my handbag; I'd photocopied the Church's choice of Holy Scripture for that day, so I was reminded that we can say, about health and about life itself: "YAHWEH GAVE, YAHWEH HAS TAKEN BACK" (Jb 1:21). Then Jesus encouraged me to put my entire trust in Him, as I waited to undergo a series of tests. For the first time, instead of endlessly thinking of my fears, I was able to say wholeheartedly to God: "All these tests are in Your hands. I've been impatient, but I trust You now. If something definite is diagnosed, I shall thank you for clearing up the mystery; however, if I'm regarded with bafflement again, I shall thank You still, for all You've done." I hoped I was ready to welcome anything He allowed: health or sickness, indifference or understanding. By His grace, I could say, at last:- "I want only what You want. Show me the way: only Your way!"

Surrounded at every moment by other patients and busy staff, I adored Christ in silence, thanked Him for all His blessings, and gave everything back to Him, to be used as He Willed:- life, heart, mind, soul and body, memory and will, for His Glory. I said "Fiat" to the waiting: "Fiat" to anything He decreed. Whatever the results might be, I knew that "HE HELPS THOSE WHOSE SPIRIT IS CRUSHED" (Ps 34:18). So I resolved: "O Jesus, I will bring you to others. I will see You in them. I will make Your presence known. I will love You and show Your love to others."

I was forty-fix years old, and for over half of that time I had thought to myself: "If only I knew what was wrong!" Twenty-five years of 'not knowing' had enabled me to live at last from day to day, content to aim at kindness rather than efficiency, although it was a dreadful thing to know that one's problems made life difficult for other people. I trusted in God that I'd continue to muddle through; and I trusted Him with My entire future, as well.

A diagnosis.

The Consultant who came to see me was a kindly man who had delivered bad news before, to many others. He told me briskly that I have a mild Multiple Sclerosis. He was to tell us later that I'd suffered from it for twenty-five years. He said that the expert who had dismissed my symptoms over ten years ago had been wrong; "They often say that to people with M.S."

Feeling so ill at that time, I was almost numb on hearing the news. I was neither upset nor surprised, but, rather, released from fear - although not from future trials. I saw clearly that yesterday I'd been unwell, and that today I was unwell in just the same way; so nothing, in that sense, had changed. But this doctor had given me what I'd once longed for: understanding, and justification in other people's eyes. But through the grace of Christ, I'd come to value Christ's opinion above all, and I'd stopped worrying - most of the time. I saw that the diagnosis was Christ's choice for me, and His gift, whatever happened next. It would bring sadness to others, but I hoped the sadness would give way to relief. Perhaps we'd all be able to cope with illness, if it could be faced and accepted, and if we could all encourage one another at home, no longer puzzled by my 'decline'.

Once out of hospital, I was able to attend Mass again. I offered myself - life, body, soul and strength - in union with Christ in His Holy Sacrifice. Through the priest, I was given the graces of the Sacrament of the Sick. I'd asked my parish priest for this wonderful help, and so he anointed me with holy oils as we prayed that God's Will would be fulfilled in me.

Wholehearted acceptance.

One day soon afterwards, back in my usual domestic routine, I experienced real helplessness in the street, when I was shopping. I found myself unable to walk far, and unable to do the work I usually do. I asked Christ in prayer to show me what to do in my powerlessness, and to show me how to do it. Then I was inspired to unite my weakness with His own helplessness on the Cross; and immediately, I knew what was to be attempted. I knew that Christ was encouraging me towards a repeated and wholehearted acceptance of my physical weakness. Prompted in this way, I resolved to want only what Christ wants for me, at each moment of my life, and to do gladly only what He permits, at every moment. Then I resolved never to regret not doing the things I can't do. I resolved to accept and to absorb my very helplessness, and to thank God for having an opportunity to show my love for Him by trying to be patient in every circumstance and by accepting His Will for me.

I knew that my small sacrifices could comfort Christ in His Passion since God isn't bound by time. I prayed that this union of our wills might be the cause of His Will being done in others, though only through the merits of His Sacrifice. Then Christ poured out His courage and peace on me, as He urged me:

> **Do My Will fervently and frequently, simply for love of Me.
> You will find that, more frequently, I will do what you
> want. (T:305 #8)**

Speculation discouraged.

Occasionally, having more time to think, and astounded by the implications, I half-wondered if the 'teachings', or, at least, the 'visions', would inevitably be attributed to my illness: whether that was what other people would believe, if ever I were to speak about what I'd been shown in prayer. Yet why should anyone doubt me, I wondered, if it was only within a disciplined prayer-life that I was 'taught?' How could I make sensible judgements about a catalogue of subjects relating to several areas of life, and pass a driving test, and study Hebrew, if my mind were weak or unstable? I couldn't deny my many failings; but surely all sorts of people wouldn't be turning to me regularly for comfort and advice, I wondered, if I was fanatical or unbalanced?

Still sure that other people would one day look for explanations, I wondered if someone would see the 'teachings' - perhaps - as peculiar 'surfacings' of things from my memory-store; yet what was 'surfacing' included aspects of our faith which were previously unknown to me; and they were beautifully 'presented', quite unlike the way in which snippets of past reading can sometimes emerge from the depths of our minds, emerging festooned with half-remembered thoughts and emotions from another era.

Besides, I wondered, why should I worry if I were considered to be a victim of delusions if everything I was learning in prayer was thoroughly orthodox? What reason could there be - apart from God's 'intervention' - for my receiving, in prayer, what I can only describe as 'chunks' of theology?

None of these queries is an attempt to prove the origin of the 'teachings', but they give a glimpse, perhaps, of the sort of thoughts I couldn't entirely control. Although my inner conviction at every single stage of the spiritual life was that the teachings and visions had come to me from God, my acceptance was uncomfortable in the way in which other information can be painful. Anyone who has ever been shocked to hear that an acquaintance has died, yet who irrationally thinks: 'That can't be true; I was speaking to him only this morning', will understand my discomfort. I knew that I was being taught by God; I also knew that I'm not a good person; and yet something - snippets of what I'd read - told me that God only teaches good people, not a failure like myself, whose mind was more full of remorseful thoughts than of praises of God's goodness.

All of these speculations were firmly discouraged by Christ, Who wouldn't permit me to continue with any sort of dissection. He was very strict about this. Of course, my faith in His wisdom and power wasn't as strong as later on; and I wasn't aware of how wonderfully He can put our minds at rest - whether my own mind, or the minds, for example, of those in authority who are now having to 'weigh and judge' me. But I'm utterly sure that there's no-one wiser or kinder than He is; and I leave my life and work and reputation in His hands. He can do what He likes with them, as long as He gives me the grace to remain faithful.

Christ made it plain that I was to carry on peacefully, trusting in Him in every little difficulty. He also explained, as I've hinted, that if I made various sacrifices for His sake - music and novels were only the start of a new 'reformation' - and if I managed without inessential day-time medicines, I could be very attentive to Him in prayer. Every pain could be united to His sufferings, to draw down graces upon myself and upon other people. Of course, I was supposed to save life or limb with such blessings as antibiotics, but I learned that any remedy which banishes pain must be treated with caution. Our poor little prayers offered in sickness are tremendously valuable; but nothing is more precious in ordinary times than to be alert before Christ, attentive to His presence and also alert to the 'stirrings' of His Holy Spirit.

Together, looking towards Heaven.

Throughout the following year - 1989 - the training continued, as did the "teachings". One day at Holy Mass, Christ began to urge me, more fervently:-

Reach up to the Invisible Father and intercede for others. Every prayer made in My Name is welcomed by the Father. (T:317 #2)

Obey My inspiration, and remain within your soul, close to Me, in My Passion. Turn to Me, your loving Saviour: to "Jesus Wounded". Unite your prayers to Mine. Together, we can look towards Heaven, and you can offer our pleas to the Father on behalf of others (T:317 #3)

Believe in your adoption. You really are a "child of God". *The more surely I am present on earth in you,* **and the** *more fully you really live on earth "in Me", then* **the more surely** *is Heaven joined to earth* **- by My power - as if** *by a column of Light.* **Thus, within your soul,** *I pray continuously to the Father.* **(T:317 #4)**

A total offering.

Despite my best efforts, that winter, I found it very hard just to get up every day to do the bare essentials; and so I was prompted, in prayer, to turn to Christ more fervently than ever before and to say: "I offer everything: every moment, every action and pain: my whole self, to be used however You wish." I begged Him to permit me to stay faithful and peaceful in His company, even though I'm so weak and inadequate. I resolved to remain in my soul - as it were - with "Jesus wounded", pleading for help for other people, minute by minute, although I'm aware that our prayers are effective only because of the Merits of the Precious Blood which Christ has poured out for us: poured out for everyone who is close to my heart, indeed for the world.

Then Christ taught me, delightedly, in Holy Communion:-

Reflect on the joy and privilege which is yours as you take part in the Holy Mass. *You are a member of My Church, in her holy worship, praying with Me for the whole world.* **(T:312 #1)**

Rejoice in your friendship with Me. I delight in your efforts, as you prepare to take part in My Church's worship. All who take part can be made worthy to take part by confessing their sins and by leading a new life in Me, despite all remaining weaknesses and imperfections. (T:317 #6)

Rejoice in your dignity. *Consider the majesty of those who are called to take part in My holy worship at Mass. You reflect My own majesty and dignity as you stand, glorious with Me,* **your frailty clothed in gold. (T:317 #7)**

254

For the remainder of the day I plunged into my normal work. Then I rested, and worked again, having learned by then, by God's grace, how to remain for longer and longer periods of time quite without speculation about God's plans and God's 'teachings', but truly content to do my work, for His sake, in each 'present moment'. I had no inkling of the joy in store.

Enfolded by the Holy Trinity.

I was determined not to complain, but to be patient, and to be grateful for all the good things in my life, and for the friendship of Christ, above all. So that day passed in its usual fashion; by the evening I'd forgotten about my 'offering' because I'd been concentrating on my work. I eventually sat down in an armchair, glad to be at rest, reading a book. All the members of my family were away, or out.

When I was sitting in peace in my home, - at about quarter past nine - Christ suddenly appeared to my heart - though without sight or sound; and just as swiftly, and with a power that astonished me, He led my soul upwards into the very Life and presence of the Most Holy Trinity; and there, He showed me, as He held me in incomparable peace and radiance:-

> **Rejoice that you live "in God", wholly united to Us in heart, mind, and intentions, and now gathered up into the warming and enlightening movements of Our Love: the love of The Three Divine Persons. In Us, the Holy Trinity, you are assured of love, grace and safety. To live "in God" is to be 'saturated' with Our peace, and to be saturated also with knowledge from Us, within the Light in which We live: the Light in which We contemplate Our own Being. (T:318 #1)**

Then I was taught, very suddenly and wordlessly, about God's own Being. I was shown:-

> **Learn something about Our Divine Life.** *God the Father holds all, in existence, and all lies within His Love. I, Jesus, am your sweetest friend and lover. My Spirit continually holds and soothes and strengthens you.* **(T:318 #2)**

> **Be comforted by Our merciful care of you.** *God the Father cools the burning pain of the two 'spears' - which are shame and fear - so that although they still pierce you as wounds and nails, they are softened by His kindness. They will check your pride, even though in your pride, weakness and silliness you are wrapped in Our care, and loved.* **(T:318 #3)**

> **Submit joyfully to My wishes.** *It is My loving Will that you stretch out your hand, as many do, across the Abyss between yourself and your beloved other-Christians, that is, between yourself and your spiritual brothers and sisters who are not in communion with My Holy Catholic Church. You must welcome them with joy. The Abyss is very deep, but not wide.*

255

and they can step over. (T:318 #4)

In the Light of the Holy Trinity.

Here, I realised that the formal teaching had ended, yet God still 'held' me. It was as though He was offering me an invitation to take part in a real conversation between friends: between a weak woman and her God. I was awe-struck, but joyful, and was so wholly at peace in that state that it was just as when a child is resting on its parent's lap, confident of having its questions answered. Then I remembered all the people whom I carry in my heart. I named and held and 'established' each one in the Light of the most Holy Trinity.

In the presence of the Father, I made a new resolution, and told Him that from now on I was determined to live and wait and rest in Him, without thinking about effects or results or the opinions of others, and unconcerned about my own helplessness. From moment to moment I would live with Him and in Him, doing whatever He wants, for the sake of His People and for the glory of His Name.

I prayed to the most Holy Trinity: "I abandon all rushing, all anxieties, and all straining and speeches, and even the sort of interior, verbal self-laceration by which I've kept reminding myself of causes for shame. Just as I am, so will I rest in You, as You are, held here by Your grace, and loved."

Then I thanked and praised the Father for Christ's faithfulness and mercy; and I resolved to accept others and to be merciful to everyone.

I was able to say: "Most Holy Father, I accept Your love, Your forgiveness, your medicines and mercies and friendships - all the days and joys and pains and wounds of prayer, and all the dancing delights of the spiritual life - and the times of peaceful waiting too. May I only live and die in You."

I prayed that - whether I always remember the goodness of God, or forget - I'd be able to leave aside all useless speculation, in order to trust and to persevere.

I prayed that, by God's grace, I'd stay hopeful whenever I fall, pausing briefly to let Him look at me and heal me. I resolved that I'd move on 'in Him,' with confidence.

I prayed that I'd be able to convey to others the peace which had been given by God to me.

Jesus: my whole life.

The whole experience affected me profoundly. Awe and joy were intermingled in my heart. The embrace of this prayer lasted for less than an hour, but the peace given then has rarely left me; nor has the thought of the goodness of God, even in recent unimaginable trials. From that day onwards I no longer hesitated in admitting to myself that, at last, truly, Christ was my whole life and my whole desire, and that I had found in Him everything I'd ever hoped for or needed. Hour by hour each day Christ patiently revealed His Will for me, through my normal duties, through the teaching of the Church, through the Holy Scriptures, and through prayer, as usual: sometimes by His own words and instructions, so long as I worked and prayed solely for love of Him.

However, through experience, I found that the least unfaithfulness on my part left me in darkness: I don't mean the faults or failings into which we fall despite all our efforts. But the smallest movement of pride in my heart for any of Christ's gifts, or the merest flicker of hope that He'd lead me in extraordinary ways, and I'd be left in darkness for my own good, thus being purified in my desires and trained to work and pray solely for the glory of God, in obedience.

Christ's words and visits continued. His teachings and His gifts were always unexpected, unasked, sudden, and usually delightful, as I learned through Him to hope for nothing but the grace to seek and do His Will in everything, in darkness or in Light, day by day, motivated solely by love for Him. And He didn't allow me to become engrossed in my work or in His 'teachings', but gave me many instructions about looking outwards as well as inwards. He emphasised my obligation to love my neighbour, and told me:-

> **Reflect on My Sacrifice of Calvary. My Precious Blood was poured out - brimming over - and was spilt for you. My life ebbed away so that I could give you Eternal Life. (T:365 #2)**

> **Imitate My true self-giving. True sacrifice involves self-giving even to the last breath in your body. (T:365 #1)**

The Holy Sacrifice of the Mass.

It was only a few weeks later, in 1989, that Christ began to teach me much more about the Holy Sacrifice of the Mass: not solely reminding me about its importance, but explaining in what special ways it is supremely valuable.

One day, at Holy Mass, at the Sanctus, Christ taught me something more about the joys of being "in Communion" with other people in the Church. He told me:-

> **See how closely you are united with other people who love Me. *You who belong to Me are wrapped and encircled in My Spirit of Love, in one Sacrifice of praise to the Father, at Holy Mass.* (T:359)**

Christ gave me enough time to 'digest' the wonder of this 'Communion of Saints.' Then, shortly afterwards, in Holy Week, when I was praying at Mass, I thanked God the Father for everything that He's done for us through Jesus; and I adored Christ, Who was Really Present; then I was suddenly overwhelmed with 'Knowledge'; and the whole teaching was about the God-man Who is "THE SACRIFICE THAT TAKES OUR SINS AWAY" (1 Jn 2:2) because His Blood was shed for us on the Cross.

The splendour of Christ's Divinity.

By God's great kindness, and with piercing clarity, I learned many dazzling truths about Christ's One Holy Sacrifice. In an instant of prayer, Christ taught me all of these things:-

> **Never doubt what My Holy Church teaches about Me, in that** *I am truly, gloriously Present on the altar, after the Consecration, in all the splendour of My Divinity and power and Light and beauty and energy.* **(T:366 #3)**

> **Live as if you could be "another Christ" on earth.** *Those who suffer for love and who are most like Me, Christ, in their self-giving, are most easily able to 'leap up' to stay with Me in love and in prayer. They and I so resemble one another that, through Me, they are drawn to the Father more easily than others who do not resemble Me so closely.* **(T:366 #4)**

> **Believe in My Love, and in the power of My Holy Sacrifice. (T:366 #5)**

> **Rejoice at the marvel of My Offering.** *All who are present at My Sacrifice,* **united in faith and joy within My Holy Church,** *are gathered up by My Spirit and are joined to Me, their risen Lord. They are made a part of this glorious Offering and union* **- an Offering to the Father and a union with Him through Me, Jesus -** *the splendour of which cannot be imagined or described.* **(T:366 #6)**

At the same time, I was given a reminder which was directed not at myself, but at other Christians. I was told:-

> **Let all who are not "in Communion" be patient.** *All who are not yet members of My Holy Church, or who are not yet united with her in faith and worship, yet who would take a handful of this Glory* **- by going to Holy Communion - must be patient, and should** *ask Me to bring them into the unity of My holy family* **- by which I mean** *My holy People.* **(T:366 #7)**

> **Be joyful. During the Holy Sacrifice, you can be sure of being in My Presence.** *I, Christ, am Present in the splendour of My humanity and My Divinity,* **and the Sacrifice which I offer is perfect.** *The love and joy of this holy Offering and acceptance is complete and blissful.* **You can believe that God gives to God, in this Holy Sacrifice, perfect honour and perfect Love, in a bond of perfect joy. (T:366 #9)**

A true sacrifice.

As I was being taught in this way, I could see a light before me on the altar, a blazing white fire - though seeing it with the eyes of my soul; and Christ was explaining the meaning, all in one instant. He told me:-

> **Consider the meaning of sacrifice. You see before you, during the Holy Mass, an altar, a holy Sacrifice, and a Victim.** *The "white fire" of sacrifice is consuming the Victim,* **which is to say: the pure, perfect, fiery and Divine Love of the Father "consumes" Me, Jesus, Victim, in our bond of perfect Love. (T:366 #10)**

> **Never doubt that what My Church teaches you about your faith is true:** *My Offering in the Holy Mass is a true Sacrifice,* **and is accepted by the Father as an offering for your sins. (T:366 #11)**

> **Rejoice in My Love for you and in the power of My Sacrifice.** *The radiance of My glorious Offering falls upon all, whether living, still, on earth, or departed "in Christ".* **All of My people, living and departed, can benefit from the offering of My Holy Sacrifice. (T:366 #12)**

I was shown all this in a split-second. It was nothing but what the Church has taught about how the Sacrifice of the Mass bring enormous benefits both to the living and to the 'dead'; yet the truth of it all had been made plain to me in a startling yet glorious way; and I grew even more grateful for what Christ had done for us when He first instituted the Holy Sacrifice of the Mass, at the Last Supper, and so provided us with a living memorial of His Passion and Resurrection.

All the 'wounded'.

The 'teachings' continued, week after week. I was instructed further about the life of grace within the soul. One day at Holy Mass, Christ taught me:-

> **Cling to Me, the "broken Christ", in all your weaknesses. The Father, in accepting My Sacrifice, also accepts all who belong to Me and who live in love, united by My Spirit. The Father is 'conquered' by humility. (T:379 #1)**

> **Accept your soul's 'wounds', out of love for Me. You can be sure that I hold all the 'wounded' in My embrace. (T:379 #2)**

> **Say to Me: 'Your Will be done', and so unite your**

acceptance to My own acceptance of the Will of the Father. (T:379 #3)

Accept from the Father all that He Wills, whether life or death, pain or joy, cruel delays or moments of comfort. All your faithful prayers and sacrifices can be united to My prayer, to become One prayer which can be offered for the Glory of the Holy Trinity and for the benefit of My Church and of the world. (T:379 #4)

After such encouragement, I was able to offer every pang I felt to the Father, in union with Christ's own sufferings: such was the offering which Christ so frequently encouraged me to make. Then, soon afterwards, in Holy Communion, I learned even more about the union of our wills with the Will of God, in all circumstances. Christ showed me something more about the soul. He urged me:-

Follow My Spirit Who leads you into silent adoration of the Father's Glory. (T:460 #2)

Look upon your soul's centre as a "place" which is vaster than any place you can see around you. *Within the "interior universe" We, the Most Holy Trinity, may be adored and worshipped.* (T:461 #1)

Rejoice at the marvellous work which I have been working within you. *The soul* which is full of My Life *is a 'place' on earth where I am First and Last, and have been enthroned and adored* by one who consents to do My Will, and who permits Me to reign in every detail of life. (T:461 #2)

Harmony.

All the while, as the teachings continued and my friendship with Christ grew closer, the every-day events of family and village life kept me outwardly busy. But the various aspects of life all seem to 'fit', at last, as my prayer overflowed into my work and guided me in conversation, and as the various friendships and relationships of a busy life were all being pulled into my prayers before the Blessed Sacrament.

There was a new unity in my life. It was a gift from Christ, which was, at the same time, the cause and the effect of the peace within my soul. It didn't usually matter to me any more, in my 'heart of hearts' - although I sometimes wavered - whether I were busy or resting, attending a dinner or writing a letter, or being praised or overlooked. It was God's Will that I longed to know, whether it brought difficulties or consolations; and there's so much extra help for us all when we've discovered and really believe in everything that the Church can give us, or, rather, in everything that Christ is willing to give us through His Church: so many sacraments and sacramentals, with His own Presence in the tabernacle - and the help of an army of Saints and holy Angels: and the loving-kindness of His own beloved Mother.

Blessings, through Our Lady's prayers.

One day, during Holy Mass, as I praised God for Mary our Mother, for Jesus, and for Mary's prayers, I was suddenly shown that Christ was pleased with my devotion. He told me several things which increased my confidence. He reminded me:-

> **Ask Me for the prayer of *My Holy Mother Mary*. She** *scatters grace like rain,* **at the very moment that you ask Me for her prayers. (T:465 #1)**

> **Have confidence in My Mother. She does My Will now, as ever, and since it is in My Will that she help you, you can be sure that** *through her you are showered with blessings on earth.* **(T:465 #2)**

> **Turn to me ever more frequently.** *You are changed into 'other Christs',* **the** *more you are united with Me in heart and will.* **As you grow in grace and in sanctity, you remain yourselves.** *You retain all that is good and distinct about yourselves, but you are made 'whole', and 'willing'* **- that is, willing and ready to serve Me in any good way. (T:465 #3)**

Christ even increased my hope that I'll enter Heaven in the end. He urged me:-

> **Be hopeful about Heaven. Through your whole-hearted striving to love and to know Me - and** *if you become like Me - then must Heaven 'open' for you, and, "clothed" in Me, you shall enter the true home where you belong.* **(T:465 #4)**

> **Put your trust in Me. My Mercy to sinners is greater than you could possibly imagine. (T:465 #5)**

After such teachings as this, my longing to please Christ increased. I longed to act as lovingly towards everyone as Christ acts towards me. For example, as Christ had recommended, I tried to learn a little more about how to listen to others. I wanted to chatter a bit less about my own affairs and concerns and to follow the good example of a priest I knew; and I saw that a loving heart is more inclined to listen to others' troubles than to speak about itself.

As long as we're seeking to 'entertain' others, or to show off in subtle ways, or to score points, or to insist on being 'right' - we're not usually listening or loving; and so we're not doing Christ's work. There's a place for reasoned argument, I know; but in my usual daily conversations it was sympathy that was needed more than arguments or lectures.

A deeper spiritual 'night'.

The teaching continued; and even as they were being given to me, Christ simultaneously hollowed out my heart to receive them. I mean that He never ceased to train me in the practice of the virtues: sometimes stern with me and at other times all tender encouragement, like a good parent. Although I didn't know it then, He was preparing me for an awesome task, and so was determinedly teaching me the true meaning of humility, without which any work supposedly done for God is a waste of time and does no lasting good.

That is why, towards the end of the same year, Christ led me to look more clearly at the whole of my earlier life. He purified my soul more severely than ever before, through a re-kindling of memories. He permitted such torment only for my own good; but once the new trial had begun, I didn't know how I'd survive it.

Suspended over the Abyss.

If anyone should say that what I'm about to describe stemmed only from my imagination or from a normal but prolonged bout of anxiety, I can only warn him or her that "IT IS A DREADFUL THING TO FALL INTO THE HANDS OF THE LIVING GOD" (Heb 10:31). All of our shabby thoughts and acts and habits and grudges burst into flame within us when - by our free consent to Him in sincere prayer - we permit this great Lord to shine His Holy Light into every corner of our soul. And that burning Light causes the greatest pain in the one whose depths have been hidden in darkness longest; and the torment of our gazing at those depths when at last they're revealed, with no hope of shadow or concealment, can only be borne by someone who is utterly determined, blindly, to obey God, since it seems as though there's no end in sight, and no hope of relief.

It happened that when I was alone one day, I was suddenly swamped with terrible memories and fears, and - once again - with scruples. I had hoped to make a brief retreat which would bring some peace to my busy mind and rest to my soul. But instead, I found that day after day was spent in torment, as I remained clutching blindly to what seemed like the very thinnest thread of hope. I prayed to God at every moment in naked faith, in deepest night, whilst half-remembered, half-denied causes of shame and remorse were revealed at last to the eyes of my soul in an utterly clear and relentless light.

I felt as though I were damned.

Knowing that there was no hope of enduring the pain, except by trusting - utterly defeated - in the Blood of Christ, I went to find a priest; and then, in great sadness and darkness, I was more thoroughly Reconciled.

I reminded myself that penitents throughout the ages had been loved and forgiven by Christ, but nothing made me feel better. I made acts of faith hour by hour, resolving to stay really 'low' and grateful, and resolving never, ever, to offend God again. I vowed that I would never forget His mercy towards me, and that I'd never look down on other people.

For several days more, my soul was confined in a prison of utter distress and loneliness. I had to make acts of faith in order to force myself to go to Holy Communion, nearly overwhelmed by a temptation to despair of having received Christ's forgiveness. Aware of my own nothingness, and aware also of the power and unseen Majesty of the God Who had brought me into existence and Whom I had once offended, I had never in my whole life known such complete and relentless desolation.

A gulf between mankind and the Godhead.

After a few more days, the teachings began again. Wordlessly, Christ taught me about His Sovereignty, speaking more as a Father than a Brother. He showed me how important it is that I recognise my utter dependence on His graces and that I live in perpetual gratitude and humility. He told me:-

> **See how helpless you are, without Me. There exists a great gulf between mankind and the Godhead, a gulf which is like a wide, deep and steep-sided Abyss which is so dark and so infinitely deep that you cannot see the bottom. (T:472 #1)**

> **Remember the meaning of Salvation, which is Life in Me. Unless a soul lives in Me, it is lost. If pride, rebellion or self-sufficiency predominate in someone's heart, that person is doomed. (T:472 #6)**

> **See how every good thing stems from Me: life, hope and Salvation. (T:472 #7)**

Reasons for humility.

Although I didn't know it, this purification was a preparation for great joys ahead. For the moment, however, it was only naked faith that took me towards Christ in the Sacrament, and kept me 'glued' to Him each day, in hope of being able to carry on. It was a great blessing that I found the courage to ask for advice; and so I was encouraged to say to God: "If You wish me to go through this Desolation, then I accept it." I did accept it; and then I found that a pain accepted is, mercifully, a pain lessened.

Once, briefly, Christ came to me, appearing to my soul's eyes as a King. There, during the Holy Mass, He explained to me why He was letting me see myself - by an image - sitting at His feet as a penitent. He was reminding me that I would be grievously sinful were I to nourish the least scrap of pride or conceit about His gifts, when He had rescued me from the death-of-soul of former years. Even then, He hadn't finished His work.

Each time I went to Holy Communion, Christ reminded me of the great debt which He has paid to save sinners. He told me:-

> **Be glad that you can live in the truth of the knowledge of your weakness and dependence. *It is true that you are dust, yet you are made, loved and sought out by Us: by the Three Divine Persons who dwell in Glory: One God.* (T:474 #2)**

> **Never forget the reason for your present joy and continued hope. *It is through Me, your Saviour, that you are re-born, ennobled and lifted into Light; yet you have been redeemed at a terrible price.* (T:474 #3)**

> Consider My life's end. I, *Jesus,* died *in torment, crucified and raised up* before scornful witnesses. *This was the consummation of My earthly life. How can you who follow Me hope to receive earthly glory and popularity?* (T:474 #5)

> Understand the reason for earthly power. *The Father above permits earthly thrones not that you might struggle for power and position, but that you might see in them a glimpse of the true Throne and the true Majesty of His Kingdom, where I reign.* (T:474 #6)

> Honour the Mother who bore Me. Lowly and unknown, she was given by Me a tremendous dignity, and she is now given great honour and glory in High Heaven, where - full of grace - she lives in My Light. (T:474 #7)

The price of our sanctification.

Then one day, Christ showed me, in Holy Communion:-

> Think about My life: the life of your beloved Saviour, Who hung upon the Cross in agony, to save you. (T:474 #4)

> Don't begin to think that you can 'save' yourself. Great effort is needed in the spiritual life, but you are saved from sin and eternal death, and made holy, not by will-power but through My Precious Blood which was poured out for you on Calvary. *This is the price of your sanctification: Myself, Crucified.* (T:475 #3)

Christ was obviously determined that I should be 'rooted' in humility; and so I stumbled on through each day's chores and conversations, determined to endure whatever He allowed me to undergo.

An Abyss of desolation.

For a further week or more Christ left me helplessly suspended over an abyss of desolation which words can't describe. But one day He took pity on me and encouraged me to look upwards, towards Heaven. Suddenly, within our usual prayer, His teachings recommenced. Christ led me once more into His radiant Light, in Holy Communion, restoring my former joy. Truly, "OUR GOD IS A CONSUMING FIRE" (Heb 12:29); yet He knows what we can bear, for the good of our souls, and perhaps, of the souls of other people; and He gave me what I really longed for, after those terrible days and hours. He gave me peace. Past, present and future were now laid out before Him, seen in His Light. The very "attics and cellars" of my soul had been sorted out and scoured. I saw that there's nothing good in me which He hasn't given to me. I also saw that to take pride in anything good I might see in myself would be sheer madness, like a lie, or like a theft from the Source of all good.

Vowing, more fervently than ever, that I would allow nothing to take me even an iota away from Christ, I longed more surely than at any time in my life to fulfil the all-important aim of any daughter of the Church: for the love of Christ, to believe, to hope, to trust, to love, to work and to pray.

Christ can't leave us, however, without good advice, and comfort. Within a few hours of hearing me make new resolutions, Christ taught me how to pray well from the 'depths' of a new humility. He advised me:-

> **Don't be anxious, in your weakness. You can pray well in Holy Communion by offering My praise from within your soul. You have nothing good of your own to offer the Father; but because of your faith in Me, which brought you here to receive Me, you can be confident that I am the "All" that you now have, the "Everything" of goodness, Really Present here, Whom you can offer to the Father, for His Glory. (T:477 #1)**

> **Don't dwell upon your unworthiness, in prayer. It is through your humility - especially after purification - that I delight in leading you into Our 'heart': the Heart of the Holy Trinity, in prayer. (T:477 #2)**

> **Follow wherever I lead you, in prayer, even if such prayer is wordless, incomprehensible and apparently fruitless. (T:477 #3)**

> **Surrender to Me completely, in order to be made fruitful. If you 'give' Me every day and every moment to be used entirely as I wish, you will live to make Me known and loved - as you so greatly desire. (T:478)**

To my surprise, further teachings followed. What I didn't know was that I was being trained not only for Heaven, as is every Christian who tries to co-operate with God's grace, but also for a new task which I couldn't have foreseen: the task of encouraging others. But I had to learn how to do so without the least scrap of pride in my soul as I spoke up about Christ's teachings and about prayer.

---

11 CONSOLATION
(1989-1990)

MASS PAINTINGS. WRITINGS. OUR LADY.

The gate of Heaven.

Throughout every new difficulty, in 1989, Christ provided me with reassurance. In Holy Communion one day, I was shown some of the reasons why we all ought to thank God for the tasks and trials which makes us stronger. Christ spoke to me very clearly, as He revealed the wonderful sight of Himself, with His Mother Mary, standing in Glory at the very edge of Heaven. He told me:-

> **Look towards Me in your living and in your dying!** *I am*
> *the Way to the Father*, **in life and in death. At the "edge" of**
> **Heaven, I await all the people who, after death, approach**
> **Me in the presence of My Saints and My holy Angels. My**
> **Holy Mother stands next to Me. (T:496 #1)**

> **Think about the moment when at last you will hope to see**
> **Me, Jesus:**

> > *I, the Crucified, wait at the Gate of Heaven,*
> > *   looking for those*
> > *who bear the marks of the Cross,*
> > *who resemble Me,*
> > *who have borne all things for Me,*
> > *who are weary from My service,*
> > *who have loved all poor and wounded ones*
> > *for My sake,*
> > *who have given no thought to their own glory,*
> > *but longed only for Mine,*
> > *who have kept on through criticism and humiliation,*
> > *their hearts aching like Mine*
> > *for the world's pain, not for their own.*
> > *I know My own. They resemble Me. (T:496 #2)*

Then Christ reassured me:-

> Don't worry about appearing shame-faced, weary and with head bowed, when at last you stand before Me, your Saviour. Truly, you will have good cause to be hopeful if you are weary from My service, obediently holding out your wounded hands to Me, your Wounded Lord. *I know My own. They resemble Me.* It is when people resemble Me that they are fit for Heaven. (T:496 #3)

Sweeping away distractions.

Not all of the teachings were so worthy and chastening. Some were given to my soul by Christ in sheer celebration and joy. One day, He reminded me:-

> Remember that I am at work in your soul, in Holy Communion. I am radiant and beautiful, Really Present and active. I am preparing your soul for the work which we can do together. I am sweeping away distractions so that you and I can rest here together in silent love and worship, for the Glory of the Father. (T:509 #1)

Then soon afterwards, when I was at Mass on the feast of the Immaculate Conception, I was shown a further glorious sight which consoled me.

Saint Anne, with an Immaculate child.

It was on the 8th of December, 1989, when I was praying my routine but fervent prayers, at the Consecration, that I was astonished to see, with the eyes of my soul, that Saint Anne stood before me in Glory, her head encircled by a halo. She was youthful and radiant. Her arms were held protectively in front of her body, since a gleaming circle of light indicated the presence of a child in her womb. Then Christ explained to me:-

> Praise Me for Saint Anne, in whose womb was conceived Mary, *the "Immaculate One" - like a host - from whom would come My Sacred Body.* Everything of My human nature was received by Me from My Immaculate Mother Mary who, as I now show you, was 'immaculate' at her conception. (T:519)

I was amazed at Christ's generosity in coming to me on Our Lady's feast-day to explain in such detail what a special person she is, and why she had been worthy to become His Mother: Mother of our Divine Saviour.

As I was to discover, this was simply one more in a long procession of teachings - over many years - about Our Lady's special privileges and virtues; and so I became even more grateful for what God and Our Lady have done for us all.

Painting, and colour theory.

In all the conversations and joyful gatherings of that year, with family and friends, I found it difficult not to tell anyone what I had 'seen' with my soul's eyes in prayer; but I knew it wasn't yet time to tell the whole 'story'. I spoke freely about the truths of the faith - however they had been learned - whenever it was appropriate; but I said nothing about the origin of the images which I'd recently begun to incorporate into a series of 'prayer paintings'.

At last, by my late 'forties', I had become established as a painter: a founder-member of the Society of Botanical Artists; and I'd regularly exhibited in London galleries. My artistic aims were simple. I enjoyed using paint to reproduce things which were beautiful or interesting. That's why I had illustrated a book, and had painted designs for greetings cards. However, by the late nineteen-eighties I was no longer strong enough to control a fine water-colour brush for the length of time which it took me to produce my usual work. Many of my "still-lifes" had taken me sixteen or seventeen hours to complete. Now I found I was exhausted after sitting upright for even an hour. So I took up oils for the first time in about fifteen years, and, using a large brush or a painting knife, enlarged and brought to life some of the tiny landscapes sketched during past holidays. In the same period I made a systematic study of colour harmony, followed Johannes Itten's theory; and this was all fitted around household tasks, conversations and social events, with periods of rest, and attendance at daily Mass; and I continued with the jottings in my notebooks.

Then, in my art-work, a strange thing happened. Since I couldn't produce my usual professional work, I made an exploratory leap in my painterly thoughts and practice that I wouldn't otherwise have had the time to make. The freedom given to me because I was no longer producing my usual work for the London gallery led to the creation of a whole body of new work, entirely different; and the images on my new canvasses - on board, to be strictly accurate - came not from nature but from my own soul. Until I began to do this work in 1988 I had never before composed a painting 'about' prayer.

The 'Mass Paintings.'

A series of work which would in future be known as 'the Mass Paintings' began unintentionally one day when I wondered if I could paint a particular 'resting place' which I had experienced in quiet prayer. As I was explaining earlier, the constant darkness of prayer had gradually been relieved by a distant 'light'. I began to paint what would later be called the *"KYRIE"*. Through colour, I tried to convey something about that 'light', and to indicate my sense of shame before the holiness of God. The darkness of the soul is contrasted with what I perceived as the distant Glory towards which we travel, throughout our life in Christ. I purposely chose certain colours to convey my sense of awe.

I added several small figures, who stand, humbled, before the tremendous Light of Glory. They are obeying God's command that they "HUMBLE THEMSELVES, AND PRAY AND SEEK MY PRESENCE" (2 Ch 7:14), even as they tremble with a holy fear at the thought of approaching God. They're aware of His Purity, and of their own sinfulness; yet they believe firmly that He is "TENDER AND COMPASSIONATE" (Ps 103:8). They represent all believers.

When the painting was finished, I called it *"KYRIE"*, as I said, or 'Lord, have mercy'. Then I realised that it not only summed up my feelings about private prayer at that time, but expressed something else. It seemed to illustrate the point at the beginning of the Holy Mass when we remember Whom we adore, and we plead for mercy and peace. That's why the *"GLORIA"* - 'Glory be to God' - (3) next came to mind, as a moment of great importance; so I began a second "Mass" painting. However, this time, it was different; all gloom and fear had disappeared. The worshipper bows with joyous reverence amidst Light and Radiance. He isn't grovelling before God; rather, he instinctively and gladly imitates the loving reverence of the Saints who worship in Heaven. So this was an 'expressionist' painting, with a simple, imagined figure, and intense colour; and thus it was that the Series began. I decided to complete and to offer - through board and paint - what composers bring to us all by their unique arrangements of simple notes.

My intention was to indicate something of the splendour and majesty and power of the Mass, and the marvel of the Presence of Christ amongst His People; but since I believed I was busy with a simple painting project I allowed one of the first designs to be used as a book-cover; one of the intuitive, 'expressionist' compositions. It wasn't until I'd completed five of these oils that it occurred to me that I could do more than express the feelings in my heart and soul; I could utilise and 'amplify' the God-given images from prayer.

Through Him, with Him, and in Him .....

After the *"KYRIE"* and the *"GLORIA"*, I moved on to the *"INTROIT,"* or 'Entry to the Sanctuary' (1) and then the *"DEO GRATIAS"*, or 'Thanks be to God' - (20). But then I painted the *"CREDO"* (Creed - (5)) and the *"HOC EST"* (This is my Body (9)), in which, for the first time, I incorporated an image once given to me within prayer. But the 'centrepiece' of the series was an image which Christ had once given to me, at the *"PER IPSUM"* (- 'Through Him, with Him, in Him ....') Christ is seen robed as a priest. He stands facing the Invisible Father, arms wide in adoration; and it had been at the summit of our offering of the Holy Sacrifice in church, one day, that Christ had shown me this image, and had taught me:-

> **Allow Me to draw you steadily towards Heaven. Be solemn but joyful. I am here before you. I am wearing My priestly garment which is decorated with the Sacred Sign of the Cross. Thus robed, *I offer My Holy Sacrifice on your behalf*. I look upwards in love to the Father, and *you* - who love Me - *are the 'jewels' on My robe, you who make the Offering with Me*. (T:535 #2)**

One by one, new aspects of the Eucharistic Celebration seemed to me to be essential to the whole concept of a Series of Mass Paintings. Eventually, I found that I'd painted eighteen pictures, covering the most significant moments of the Holy Sacrifice of the Mass; and those first eighteen pictures were exhibited publicly in Holy Week, 1990, in the local Anglican Church, by invitation of the Rector, Neil Collings. He hoped that his parishioners would use them as focal points for their meditations. Later, I produced two further paintings.

Pictures, for meditation.

Two years had gone by, as I'd worked in this way. I had cooked and sewed, attended meetings, and chatted with family and friends; and I'd been to daily Mass and Communion. So the pictures were done amidst life's usual occupations. The painting was a true part of my normal life, as was the faith which inspired the work and the Sacrament which gave me strength.

In the Spring of 1991 it seemed clear to me that the twenty pictures shouldn't be tampered with any more. It was tempting to add further images - of the "Sign of Peace", perhaps, or of the "Breaking of Bread". However, my task wasn't to produce a sort of catechism-in-pictures, or a child's picture book. This equivalent of a musical "Mass" had to stand just as it was. I hoped to produce other series on different aspects of prayer, later on, using the images which Our Lord had given me, but I knew, at last, that the 'Mass pictures' should be circulated to encourage fellow-Catholics in their worship. I wrote the first edition of a little leaflet about the paintings and the Holy Sacrifice, so that each set of photographs would be better understood.

Several hundred sets of photographs were printed within a few months after Holy Week that year. They were circulated amongst friends who, in their turn, passed them on to other people. Numerous enquirers wrote to me asking for 'sets' of their own; and then one day a religious teacher wrote, asking if 'slides' were available. Soon afterwards, a theologian-teacher and a priest made the same request. The pictures were used as study-aids, and were chosen as a starting-point for meditation in retreats. They seemed to appeal to different people for a variety of reasons.

I was told that sets had been framed and hung in a place of quiet prayer, or pasted in books to be carried about and studied. I was pleased that they were helping to give people a deeper understanding of the Mass. The slides were used in schools and lecture halls, and I was told that they stimulated a more trusting yet still-reverent attitude to prayer.

It seems important to say that I'd always been a 'realist' in painting, and I remained one, still. While some of the pictures were composed as expressions of my feelings during Holy Mass, combined with a 'real' view of the priest or congregation, the others are all 'real' in the sense that they portray - if inadequately - what really happens in our sanctuary during the celebration of the Holy Sacrifice: things which Christ has 'really' shown me, although not through my bodily sight, but to the eyes of my soul.

Christ's plans.

Little of my earlier work seemed important to me, once I'd completed the 'Mass' series. Much that I'd done before it seemed to have been a preparation - almost, an apprenticeship - for work that I couldn't have foreseen when I was struggling with both paints and prayer, two decades earlier. The last few of the "Mass Paintings" had been intriguing for me to compose. It was exciting to be able to convey some of the truths of our Faith in paint: doing so in an everyday medium, and without drawing attention to myself; and that was the reason, of course, why I suddenly withdrew from all my usual commercial ventures, to concentrate on providing to others, freely, the images which Christ had so generously given to me in prayer.

All twenty of the paintings were soon to be exhibited in a side-chapel at Westminster Cathedral, and then elsewhere, but simply with a view to encouraging people in their faith. There was no question of putting them on sale. By then I'd gladly given up all my ambitions, and would have been happy to lend the pictures anonymously, or even to stop painting, if that had been God's Will. However, it became plain that - although the time wasn't yet ripe - Christ wanted a real, visible person to speak boldly to other people about the Mass, indeed, about the whole Faith. He made it plain to me, in prayer, that although some people teach by preaching sermons, and some teach about the Mass by saying Mass, my job was to paint and to write, and at a later date, to speak boldly about what I'd seen in prayer.

As Christ began to lead me into my unexpected and more prominent role, He showed me that no lay-person with a job to do for Him should do strange new work without being in step with the Church. He made it plain that I shouldn't undertake anything extraordinary without seeking the advice of the parish priest, who is my spiritual superior in certain matters, even though I'm not formally 'tied' to him by vows, like a religious who is bound to his Superior. That's why I began to keep my parish priest informed as each stage of my new journey was unfolded. I was prepared to be obedient in anything which might affect our parish; and meanwhile, Christ continued to teach me.

Through His instructions in prayer, and by His grace and kindness, Christ increased my courage, and helped me to bear both interior and exterior trials. He explained that it wasn't enough for me just to circulate the "Mass Paintings". It was no use my hoping to lead a quiet life, circulating religious art-work, trying to spread the Gospel as an anonymous artist and housewife. He had a special role for me, if I'd overcome my sense of unworthiness in order to speak out about the supernatural, and to proclaim out loud what I'd seen and understood.

There was no reluctance on my part about sharing good news about Christ - but only about whether I was a suitable person. Now that the whole series of paintings was complete, I was longing to say to others: "Come and see what God, in His Mercy, has gradually revealed to me about the Glory of His Holy Sacrifice: revealed through faith and also through the Church, and also through prayer, in daily worship." I say this because I didn't think an atheist could have painted these pictures with quite the same fervour.

I longed to be able to confide in close friends and relatives about the development of the series. It had been conceived as an art project, and was one still, to most minds. But I couldn't answer my friends' queries about 'light in prayer' without speaking of the 'Teachings'; and I didn't like to let them assume that I'm inventive, or have an extraordinary imagination, when that isn't the case. But I had to wait until the right time. Christ had a plan, and it was my duty to work and to speak at precisely the times which He was going to indicate to me - and not before.

'In step' with the Church.

Throughout the last few years God has lavished many gifts upon me; but I've been especially thrilled by His gifts of faith to my family. In January 1990 another great joy was given when my younger son was received into the Church, and was confirmed, and received Holy Communion for the first time. I was more grateful than ever that Christ was very evidently at work in the people I love so much; and I was shown, at Mass, that everyone who responds to His love truly lives in Him, becomes alive in His life, and so can rejoice at being brought 'with and through Him' into the Father's arms.

Meanwhile, as my faith seemed to grow stronger and my joy increased I became physically weaker. I could no longer stand for very long, but of course I hoped to go on with my work if it were possible. By using an electric wheelchair I was able to continue with the shopping and also take myself to Church each day, to Holy Mass. I was given new energy, too, since by sitting down as I toured the shops I was sufficien'ly rested to prepare simple meals at home. Also - whilst at the shops - I could listen to anyone who stopped to chat with me. I no longer felt my legs fail half-way through a conversation, nor did I look at queues in despair, as in the past. Amidst some remaining trials, though, Christ came to my soul in great gladness and continued to encourage and enlighten me.

At around that time, during the Mass, Christ's words to me became so clear that I felt I couldn't continue on my strange path any further, unadvised. None of us follows the Christian way of life alone; and I had to be sure about the "teachings": sure of walking in step with the Catholic Church in my home town, and therefore in step with the whole Communion of the Catholic Church.

Although my heart knew the truth of what I'd been shown by Christ for many years, I couldn't be at peace without submitting myself to the judgement of the parish priest - who represented the Catholic Church. So, when I'd prayed for help and had asked others for their prayers, though without explaining why, I plucked up courage to make an appointment and to speak of what I'd experienced. A further reason was that I felt sure I didn't have many more years to live.

The real essence of all the 'teachings' was already being passed on, in conversation with children and friends whenever we discussed the 'spiritual life', although I didn't say why I was so confident about our beliefs, and I'd told none of my friends about having being taught in this way. But I didn't want to mislead anyone, nor to be misled in whatever time I had left to me; so I kept my appointment at the presbytery, to ask our priest for advice.

Asking for advice.

I'd been to see Canon O'Leary before on several occasions, to ask him about topics of importance to me in my working out of God's Will. Then I confided that I'd recently been asking myself what I'd feel I'd neglected if - say - I were told that I hadn't long to live. I knew without a shadow of doubt that I'd wish I'd sought advice on what was now the only thing which disturbed my peace of soul: something which, until quite recently, I hadn't mentioned to anyone.

Part of the 'problem', I explained, was that I seemed to be teaching a lot nowadays, teaching all sorts of people in ways which he wouldn't have known about; and everything I say, advise or think or paint or draw nowadays is based entirely on what I know: but most of what I know about God has been taught to me, by God, in prayer, in the past few years.

What I'd learned was nothing new: nothing which isn't already taught by the Catholic Church; but if I were wrong about this, I'd be in danger of misleading others, and I didn't want to take that risk without consulting a priest. I said that I didn't want to take up more of his time with the story of my life, but I needed to say something about the earlier years: about how at twenty-one, my renewed faith in God's existence had caused me to turn back to Him; and I'd come to know Christ - a little - in prayer. I had a passion for prayer.

Here, I didn't take up Father O'Leary's time explaining just how I knew Christ 'a little'. I didn't mention the experience of sinfulness before Christ, in prayer, in 1964; but I said that I'd become a Catholic, and had spent the next ten years trying to do what many Catholics do: trying to keep the Commandments and the laws of the Church, to do good, to pray, to be a good Christian and to find out about what God wanted. At the end of that time, life was difficult - dreadful in all sorts of ways. Through ill health and misunderstanding, overwork and different things I was brought near despair. Prayer was pure darkness; but in utter misery I kept going to confession and Communion; and in the end, I came to a decision. I would never, ever, deliberately offend God again, in the least degree; and I would keep going, for Jesus' sake, trying to love God and my neighbour, and to do my duty in every area of life, no matter what the cost.

I explained that I'd made that vow about ten years before, and that prayer had continued in pure darkness for five more years. I had walked around in torment for three years, as if walking through fire, almost overcome with shame at my sins. I didn't feel as though I loved God, and could only pray "O God, I want to love You," which was the truth, at the time, in my heart. Yet there came great moments of light. I found that every few weeks - and later on, even more frequently - God would quite unexpectedly and suddenly teach me something in prayer: something about Himself, or about things to do with Him. I received a totally pure knowledge in which I learned and understood more in a split second than I could have learned from books, or from thinking for years and years.

It seemed so amazing - so mysterious, and so frightening. Who was I to be taught in a special way? At first I tried to ignore it all - putting the remembrance of these things aside in my mind. I hoped that, working, praying and trusting always in Christ's teaching, and trying to do His Will alone, I couldn't go badly wrong.

In the end, it seemed to me that if God were truly teaching me, it would be tremendously rude to ignore Him and not to give thanks; so, one day at Mass, I had thanked Him; and it seemed to be 'all right'.

Occurrences of 'Knowledge'.

I went on to explain that in the brief occurrences of 'Knowledge' in prayer I had learned much more about God Himself: about His Glory, about the most Holy Trinity, and about Our Lord, and what He's done for us. I said that I'd also learned about prayer and 'how it works' - and many other things which had seemed too stupendous to 'belong' to me. I said that I knew I'd absorbed it all; and it became part of my faith as I lived and prayed and struggled and encouraged others, from day to day.

All of these things were truths of the Catholic Faith which I had believed in for many years;

but so many things were now not only believed, but made amazingly vivid and clear.

I explained that after about six years of living in this way - in total darkness in prayer, except for the momentary teachings - my life, generally, was even more difficult, and I was still struggling with awful problems, living entirely in Faith. I had led a dreadful life in many ways, but didn't deliberately offend God at all, any more. I had no human hope - only the hope that comes through faith; and my feelings about life's difficulties were feelings of near-despair; and so it was almost with horror, in 1985, I said, that I'd decided to go on, for Jesus' sake, and to keep on loving God and my neighbour for the rest of my life. But suddenly, quite unexpectedly, Jesus was with me.

Here, I offered to tell the priest more details if he asked, but I said that Jesus had been with me ever since, except for three occasions, when whether He was absent or whether His Presence was too terrible to bear I could hardly tell. The first occasion was when I'd spent two days reading a novel, except for doing essential tasks. The second was when I'd spent too much money on myself. The third, I reminded him, had been when I'd come to ask his advice a few weeks previously, when Jesus had left me 'suspended' in utter desolation for a week: to teach me humility.

I explained that I'd never doubted that this Person was Christ, although I'd had qualms about my own power to judge. However, I'd eventually decided that since this Person was encouraging me in prayer only to be loving and more thoughtful towards others, and less selfish, and since He made me quite willing to be 'stepped over' or ignored, and since I wanted only to love God and to do His Will, and to love my neighbour for His sake, then I thought that what was happening was good, and was therefore from God; and so I'd carried on in my usual routine, working and praying, finding that Christ is with me constantly, teaching me as before; and I, in my turn, teach others.

Then I told the priest that I had only one ambition, but that it might sound terribly bold. I said that I long to see God, and to see Our Lord clearly. I had led a dreadful life, but God is so amazing that I trust him now, entirely, and I only want to do His Will.

It seemed important to say that I had no worries, apart from the reason for my visit. Whether I lived or died, were healthy or well, praised or misunderstood, I'd given myself totally to God a year ago: giving my whole self, my life, my death - and even my worries about my family.

All my ambitions had gone, except to love God. I'd entrusted all my family to Him, including Mary my daughter. I had no worries about her, having asked Our Lord to look after her; so I was happy to spend the rest of my life trying from minute to minute to do God's Will; and although it was true that I'd had more trials and sufferings recently than ever before, yet I'd never been so happy in my entire life - apart from this question: was it all right to accept it all? Did he understand? What did he think?

Gifts from God.

As I waited for an answer, I was quite content. I'd put my trust in God, and in the priest as His representative: as the voice of Church authority in our town. I was so ignorant about what I'd mentioned that I really had no idea what our priest would say. I half-expected that he'd tell me to do what I'd tried to do, anyway, for several years: to ignore the 'teachings' and to get on with my work. But he was a theologian as well as a parish priest, and he recognised what had been happening.

To my immense relief, He answered that it was quite all right: that these teachings were gifts from God - Who gave gifts to some, he said. though not to others. I ought to thank God for them.

He said quite matter-of-factly that I could accept them; and when I said I felt I must write about some of these things, he suggested that perhaps Providence would make use of any writing I might undertake, but there was no cause for concern. Then Father reminded me that for as long as we're on this earth, we're still able to 'grow', meaning: to grow in charity and understanding.

Freed from fear.

Although greatly encouraged by his words, and by his calm acceptance of what had been happening to me, I was puzzled why he was so sure about it; I'd expected questions, or even doubt. But I was overwhelmed with gratitude that in this way, and through God's Church, I'd been set free from fear. I decided to rejoice in God's gifts, and to use the Knowledge for God's Glory, in whatever way might seem appropriate. Indeed, in the years to come I was guided very surely in prayer about the precise ways in which I ought to share the teachings with other people without neglecting any of my usual duties.

After that reassurance I became even more content to grow weaker and to fade quietly away into decline or even death, if that were what God Willed. Pains or misunderstandings or other trials remained painful on the surface, because I was - and am - still weak and human. But even they were a delight in another sense, since God had permitted them, and He had been encouraging me to welcome every manifestation of His Will.

Each opportunity to imitate Christ in His patience, if accepted with love, could enable me to make reparation for sin, through Christ's merits. It could draw grace upon myself, upon those I love, upon the Church and upon the world; this was traditional Catholic teaching, and was also what I'd learned in prayer. Nothing in my life - no event or experience - need be wasted.

So, in this way, and through His Church, God delivered me from my quandary. I gave Him thanks through Jesus, in the Holy Spirit, for all His graces. There were never-ending struggles, however, despite my good intentions; and one day in Holy Communion, as I timidly complained to Christ: "I'm so weak," He suddenly taught and consoled me, saying:-

> **Be glad that you are weak!** *"That is why I came"* **- came to earth for your sake in My holy Incarnation and come lovingly to you now in Holy Communion. (T:631)**

'Write the vision down'.

Many months later, I was shown by Christ that I must begin my new work, which consisted of writing down almost all of His 'teachings-in-prayer', solely in obedience to Him, for the Glory of the Father. For Christ's sake, I was ready to reveal these things when the time was ripe, despite my timidity. I had come to see that - despite my apparent uselessness - others might one day benefit from what I was doing. I hoped that others would be comforted, and would turn to God more swiftly than I had done.

Wanting to make a good start, and to be able to concentrate, I arranged to go away for about three days; and there in my room, alone, I asked our Holy Mother Mary and all the Saints and Angels to pray for me; then I set about my new task in silence. First I made small brush-and-ink pictures of the images I've mentioned, which Christ had given to me in prayer from time to time to illustrate what He'd taught me about prayer and the spiritual life. Then I began to write a full account of every important 'teaching', most of which had been given to me in prayer through pure Knowledge, unaccompanied by any sound, image or sensation. I did this, because I'd been instructed by God (T:632) on 11th August, 1990, at Holy Mass:- "Write the vision down" - which was a Scriptural phrase which I find slightly altered today, when I read in my Bible: "WRITE THIS ACTION DOWN IN A BOOK TO KEEP THE MEMORY OF IT" (Ex 17:14). It was made plain, however, that the writings were to be put aside until Christ gave me further instructions; and of course, He did so - but not until the Spring of 1992.

The first draft of a prologue.

When I'd completed that 'First Version,' based upon my notebook jottings, I began to write what was the first draft of this 'Prologue', that is, the story of my up-bringing as a Christian, with my memories of conversion and adult commitment; and I did so as a response to a further un-spoken request from Christ, Who made His Will clear to me in every area of life. As I wrote, I decided that because Christ's 'teachings' hadn't been given to an automaton, but had been given freely to a free human being, and had sometimes been given in response to decisions and vows which I had made in particular circumstances, I ought to explain precisely when and where the teachings had occurred in my ordinary, everyday life. I knew instinctively that I must write about Christian faith and struggles rather than about the external details of my routine.

Christ made it plain that although He was pleased with the work, I was to write my story up to that date and then put it on one side for a few years. It wasn't the right time at which to share it, but there was something else. Christ knew something that I hadn't yet realised, which was that if I were to look at the 'Prologue' occasionally over a number of years I'd be able to see things in better perspective; I'd also be able to soften my judgements of people and events. Christ's intention in leading me forward in this way was to enable me, in time, to look at persons and events - and even at my own life's problems and mistakes - as if through His eyes. But it was also to spare me being overwhelmed with work today, in 1998, when it's been a struggle to write the final 'up-to-date' section of this book, and when I'm glad that so much of the 'ground-work' was done when I had more energy.

[Life at many levels.

Perhaps it seems from these reminiscences that I've been pre-occupied with my own soul at every moment of every day - but that hasn't been so. Each one of us lives out a life at many levels; and throughout the events which I'm trying to describe in order to be obedient to Christ I was happily involved in the physical, outward aspects of life on earth throughout each busy day, and with the changing emotions of a normal, "multi-occupation" life.

As I've indicated in a sketchy sort of way, no year has passed without my being fully involved with family, friends, church community, visitors, neighbours, work and social life. I haven't written about these aspects of my life because I haven't been asked to do so. The only reason for my writing at all is because Christ has instructed me to do so.

Books could be written, by any one of us, about numerous events in family or village life; but it isn't appropriate, here, when I ought to be writing above all about prayer, to speak about family life, meals, hobbies or holidays: or about achingly-funny outings or conversations, or heart-breakingly-joyful birthday treats. If I put in all the fun, and all the times of quiet contentment, too, this book would be a thousand pages long. But it's not my task to speak of these things. That's another story.]

Several subjects.

Besides writing out the 'teachings' during the past few years, and composing a 'Prologue', and writing reports on ecumenical work, with long letters to various friends and acquaintances, I was busy in the early 1990's with other writings. From that time until now, Christ has been urging me to write on one further topic or another: a few pages here and there on subjects of His choosing. It's as if I'll have no peace unless I leave my other work - or my rest - to go and write down what I know, about whatever matter He has silently mentioned: whether the Holy Trinity or Marriage. And the facility I sometimes have in expressing ideas, and the unending stream of 'Light' on various topics is such that I know I've 'only' God to thank for these things, although it's true to say that I hardly dared to write, at first. I was still wondering: 'How can I believe that anyone would want to read what I say?'

But in my heart I did believe that the writings would be valuable, even though it's obvious that I'm not a scholar, and I didn't know when they'd be used. At that stage, when I pondered the growing pile of writings in a box which were ready to be typed one day, there was no publisher on the horizon, nor had I any idea that Christ would ask me to make arrangements to have my work privately printed. That's something I'd never have thought of doing, anyway, without His direct invitation.

Christ's foreknowledge.

One of the pieces I wrote when I was less busy than today was on the subject I mentioned: the Holy Trinity; and it thrills me to realise that Christ urged me to write it, then, just as He'd urged me, even earlier, to write a piece about prayer-categories, because He knew by His Divine foreknowledge that these would be just right later on as chapters of this very book; and thus He 'provided' me with two chapters just when I was in need of them but just when I'd have found it a struggle to sit down and concentrate for long enough on topics of such importance! His goodness is indescribable.

A reminder of my frailty.

During those first few weeks of writing out the teachings I sometimes wondered if I should be spending every spare minute in that way; but Christ reassured me, in Holy Communion. It was clear that I had to persevere in the work, even though I didn't understand how or where it would be used. So I continued to draw, paint and write down nearly all that Christ had shown me, offering Him every thought and word and work, so that His Glory might shine out even through my weakness. I was ashamed of my poor writing and bad grammar; but as I worked, I was astonished to hear Christ speak to me about the faith and hope that He'd seen in my heart as I'd tried to serve Him throughout the years. He's full of tenderness towards us all, especially in these days when we're condemned in some quarters for being "religious"; and He's full of sympathy for us about our physical problems, too.

Just when I was finding that I had to rest after even a short period of standing, Christ spoke to me with astonishing impact through the Holy Scriptures. He told me that I can say, about His teachings and my frailty:- "WE ARE ONLY THE EARTHENWARE JARS THAT HOLD THIS TREASURE, TO MAKE IT CLEAR THAT SUCH AN OVERWHELMING POWER COMES FROM GOD AND NOT FROM US" (2 Co 4:7) and then: "ALWAYS ... WE CARRY WITH US IN OUR BODY THE DEATH OF JESUS, SO THAT THE LIFE OF JESUS, TOO, MAY ALWAYS BE SEEN IN OUR BODY" (2 Co 4:10).

So, at appropriate times and in various ways, Christ either reminded me of my frailty, in order to foster humility, or gave me marvellous encouragement.

Words from the Father.

Throughout 1990, Christ was preparing me, as always, for the fulfilment of this special work, but He was also preparing me for further stages of the spiritual journey: for a closer relationship with God the Father.

On the 11th of October, 1990, when I was praying before a Requiem Mass, I was so determined to please God by praying 'well' that I asked God our Father to teach me the very best way of praying. I was astonished to be suddenly instructed that the best way is:-

"... by the sacrifice of your own will." (T:689 #1)

I sat in the pew for several long minutes, stunned by the impact of that phrase. Although I'd heard Christ speaking to me on a number of occasions, this was the very first time, as far as I can remember, on which I heard words spoken in my soul by the Father: by the same God, but by another Divine Person of the Holy Trinity - by God our Heavenly Father.

Kneeling alone at the front of the church, near the old organ-loft, I was almost overwhelmed at the mere fact of receiving such a teaching from Heaven; and I was amazed at the wisdom of that reply to my simple question - and at how different the answer was from one that I might have expected to hear. I mean that I'd asked about faith or approach or method, in prayer; yet the Father had shown me what's really important: our attitude: or, rather, our humility, sincerity and purity-of-heart.

At the very same time, Christ explained to me, wordlessly:-

> **Hope to resemble Me in self-abnegation. If, like Me, you prefer the Father's Will to your own, you will find that your prayers - united to My prayers - will be more glorious and effective. (T:689 #2)**

Teachings such as this left me with mixed feelings of awe and puzzlement. I could see more clearly, however, that an increasing amount of special work for Christ would only be effective if it were accompanied by a corresponding growth in trust, with a fervent longing for holiness.

A modern woman.

As I continued with my writing, it felt very odd to be covering pages by the dozen with descriptions of Christ's teachings. I was extremely self-conscious and ill-at-ease. After all, I was a modern woman. What would people think, when they learned more about my peculiar task - or, worse, about my life, and my daily routine. How would I cope? Although I didn't know it, glorious help was on the way.

Daily life continued in pain and struggle, but I kept on writing; and then I prayed at Holy Mass one day more fervently than usual: for myself, for the Church and the world. The Word said in Holy Scripture: "LISTEN, DAUGHTER, PAY CAREFUL ATTENTION: ... DRESSED IN BROCADES, THE KING'S DAUGHTER IS LED IN TO THE KING" (Ps 45: 10-14) and also "YOUR ANCESTORS WILL BE REPLACED BY SONS" (Ps 45:16). Then, Christ taught me something of the beauty of our friendship and of the purpose of my training. He told me that this reading described the spiritual gifts in which He was clothing me; and He continued:-

> **Never despair. I have great plans for those who remain faithful. (T:733 #1)**

> **Put your trust in Me, amidst all your weaknesses. Out of the struggles and labours which you have endured for My sake, I am bringing spiritual children. (T:733 #2)**

A new resolution.

At that same celebration, after Holy Communion, when I was truly repentant that I didn't try at all times and at all costs to do the Will of God perfectly, I made new resolutions. I vowed to love God with all my heart, and to love my neighbour as fully as Christ loves me. I resolved to give myself fully to the one goal or task that Christ wants me to undertake at each moment, and to avoid, vigorously, all weakness, haste, vanity or fear. Then, after Mass, I worked and prayed as usual until the evening.

As a total and awesome surprise, I was about to receive a visit from Our Blessed Lady; and I'm mentioning this here, in order to tell you how kind she is, and how kind is Our Lord, Who asked her to come to me. He has explained to me, recently, that I myself wasn't worthy of such a privilege; but He allowed it because of His Love for me and because of my need.

He could see how terrified I was at the thought of being drawn from obscurity to prominence as His teachings became more widely known; and if there was one person who could help me by a woman-to-woman conversation, it would be His own sweet Mother; so that's what happened; He brought her to visit me, and, after a long time, I was reassured, and was made more content with my task and with the implications of the whole Divinely-conceived project.

Now I'll tell how it happened: one evening when my husband was out, and the children, too, were away at different events.

A visit from Our Lady.

On a Thursday evening towards the end of 1990 - on November 22nd, when I was alone in my room - I decided to say my night prayers early. It was only eight o'clock; but after prayer to the most Holy Trinity, I recited the Hail Mary as usual, but for the love of God and of her, only, as I was exhausted. Then, suddenly, as I sat there in the armchair, I saw our Lady within my soul.

I hardly dared to believe that my Holy Mother - Mary - was truly beside me, as I prayed; but I saw her with me, as Jesus began to explain about her in His usual way, as if Mind to mind. I've put His silent teachings into words, below, as usual; and as I said earlier, the words in italics are His very own. Christ taught me, as I sat awe-struck before Heaven's Glory:-

> **Look towards My Holy Mother, who has come to join you as you greet her devotedly in prayer. (T:735 #1)**

> **Revere My Mother Mary. See *how great is her dignity. Her holiness surpasses that of all other mere creatures.* Her glory is dazzling. (T:735 #2)**

> **See, before the eyes of your soul, the vastness of Space, in which the earth shines like a little jewel! Notice the small figure who stands alone, poised ready to receive an outpouring of Divine grace. This is My holy Mother, the Virgin Mary. *I poured My Spirit on her, from Heaven, and made her fruitful.* Thus, she conceived Me in her womb. (WC:735) (T:735 #3)**

Mary: "Mother of God".

Here I begged my Holy Angel to deliver me from deceit or illusion or danger, and I made the sign of the Cross with holy water, yet Our Lady was still present to my soul's eyes; and Christ permitted me to understand even more. By a simple image, and with a soundless implanting of knowledge within my soul, Christ taught me, about His Incarnation:-

> **See, before the eyes of your soul, how a stream of grace poured out through Heaven's gates, to tumble downwards, to enfold this Holy Virgin. Because of her immaculate soul and pure heart, and her great love and obedience, the bright grace of Heaven came to a dark earth.** *Thus did I take flesh of Mary, and enter your world, through the power of My Spirit. She was made fruitful for the sake of the whole world.* **(WC + OIL:736) (T:736 #1)**

> **Rejoice that this great gift of the Father was lavished upon the world for every era.** *He worked this marvel so that Divine grace would* **always** *pour out* **through Me, Jesus, the Son of God, and through My Holy Mother. (T:736 #2)**

> **Turn to your Heavenly Mother.** *"Mother of God", you rightly call her! I your Lord came from her, took flesh and blood from her, was subject to her and was taught by her.* **She who 'formed' Me in My earthly life can help you in every circumstance. (T:736 #3)**

There, at that very moment, what had been a glorious 'teaching' about Our Blessed Lady and her magnificent role was transformed into a visit. I still saw her only with the 'eyes of the soul': yet from then on she was really with me in my room, beside my chair - and for the reason which I'd be shown later, as I told you.

All I could think about was my unfitness to be there before someone so holy. Yet I didn't leap up, or kneel, or say special prayers. It wasn't required of me, I knew. I wasn't well; and besides, my whole heart and mind were so stunned by what I was being given, that it didn't occur to me to do anything of my choosing. I knew that if God wanted to teach me, I ought to listen rather than talk. Everyone in the family was out somewhere, as I said. The house was silent; and because I wasn't worried about being disturbed, I gave all my attention to God and Our Lady for as long as I was being 'taught'.

When there was a pause in the 'teachings', it seemed as though Our Lady was waiting patiently beside me, inviting me to speak if I chose. So - still sitting in the armchair, astounded by Our Lady's presence, and by her holiness - I dared to speak to her about my unworthiness: telling her about my sins. But she didn't mind. She knew that I was sorry, and that I'd been reconciled. I even began to make requests of her, at last, knowing that she can do wonderful things for those who trust her; so I asked her to arrange that even my failures would somehow be used, by their good effects, for the Glory of God. I know that He can work wonders for people who really trust in Him, and can even bring good out of evil.

Mary: "the wise Virgin".

Suddenly, Christ began to teach me once more, by infused knowledge; and this is what He told me:-

> **Honour My Mother. This Holy Virgin is like the "wise virgin" of the gospel story. (T:737 #1)**

> **Look upon this Holy Virgin, who stands before you, dazzlingly beautiful - a lamp in her hand - her head veiled, her clothing brilliantly white. She is the purest of all 'mere' creatures, totally dedicated to My service and ever-alert to please Me. (T:737 #2)**

> **Give all your attention to My holy Mother as I teach you about her and encourage you to trust her. (WC:738) (T:738)**

> **Follow My inspiration and speak to My Mother even about sinful and stupid things, even as you consider her great holiness and your worthiness. Just like Me, she is tender, just, and understanding. (T:739 #1)**

> **Imitate My Mother by sharing her concern for others. Speak to her about everyone dear to you (T:739 #2)**

> **See what special care My Mother gives to one who has been named in her honour and entrusted to her care! (T:739 #3)**

It was so wonderful to be there. I was awe-struck, horrified at my unworthiness, and yet immensely joyful: dazzled by her radiance and beauty, convinced of her kindness. I was able to speak about stupid and sinful things without a trace of embarrassment because I knew she'd be just and understanding.

Since I couldn't possibly experience such joy without gaining a share - as it were - for the people I love, I instinctively prayed: "Mary, Mother, here are my four dear ones, one by one before you;" and I was suddenly shown, by a vision, something of her motherly concern for us all. One, she watched gently. One danced, it seemed, before her in their mutual joy. Another was cherished by her; I learned that she can rely on his loyalty, especially. Then I saw that she carried in her arms the child whom I'd named in her honour, many years before.

After a little while longer, the vision of my family faded away, and I saw that Our Lady was standing very close to me. She was still dazzlingly bright, but I began to see her more clearly. Until then, I'd hardly dared to raise my eyes to look at her.   But now that I'd grown a little used to her radiance, and felt a little less ashamed, I could see that her head was veiled. In fact, she was clothed from head to foot in dazzling white garments. She was looking straight towards me; and she held her left hand up level with her shoulder, although I couldn't see that shoulder because she was holding up a little lamp which was casting its rays all round for about half a metre. Then Christ was silent again, as He allowed me to see that Our Lady, who put her trust in God at every moment, is truly like one of the wise Bridesmaids of His Gospel who "WENT TO MEET THE BRIDEGROOM" (Mt 25:1). Christ made it plain that His Mother can be entitled: 'The Wise Virgin'.

An extraordinary privilege.

I was left in silence, untaught for a while. Christ stood aside, unseen, leaving me free to speak and free to learn more. I had no idea what would happen next, and my heart was thumping with a mixture of awe and fear. Fervently wishing to know and serve Our Lady much better, I told her that I longed to see her clearly just as I hoped to see her face of my beloved Christ; yet I was happy to wait, I said, if it be His Will that I wait all my life, until Heaven. I was still determined, as ever, not to look for special consolations in prayer, preferring truth above all.

Straight away, through the Will of God and her great generosity, Our Blessed Lady showed me her holy face, which is so like Christ's. I was utterly amazed at that brief but detailed glimpse of her. My heart was almost overwhelmed with a mixture of bliss and astonishment. I had no idea why this was all happening, or where it would lead me. Then Christ showed me:-

> **Put your trust in My Mother, Mary. Like Me, she is full of love, good, gentle and calming.** *She is like Me in so many ways.* **Consider her astonishing beauty, modesty, and serenity. (T:740)**

The experience was wholly unexpected. As I realised later, it was such an extraordinary privilege. For perhaps half-an-hour I'd been rooted to the spot in Our Lady's presence, attentive to every word and instruction, almost overwhelmed by my unworthiness and her dignity, and remorseful to be able to look at her properly. I felt like a bashful twelve-year-old before her graceful figure.

A real woman.

My surroundings were forgotten. Our Lady was gazing at me steadily, very tenderly. For a few moments, I saw her lovely features clearly. Her veiled head was framed against what seemed like a dark blue circle, like a halo.

She had the grace and serenity of a happy fifty-year-old, but looked only about twenty-five or thirty, depending on her expression: gently smiling or thoughtful. I noticed that she had a high forehead, beautiful eyes - with straight dark lashes and slightly curved eyebrows. Her nose was long and slim, not tip-tilted, and her mouth pretty and with rounded lips: feminine but not doll-like. Her cheeks were gently rounded, and she had a little rounded chin. She was utterly lovely, though not in the sense of glamorous; and every attempt of mine to draw and paint her has been quite inadequate. She was perfectly feminine, without any sort of 'sparkle' or posing. I think she might have been about five foot five; and she was slender, but not slim. Although she was as simple as a child, she was a real woman; and I can't describe how honoured I felt to be there in her presence. Who wouldn't have been overcome before the holiness of the one especially chosen to be the Mother of God?

She gazed at me steadily, eyes quiet and gentle, dark eyes in a serene and beautiful face, and with a look that was serious but not solemn, but was ready to smile.

If anyone should wonder how I can describe her face in such detail, they can remember that I've painted many, many portraits. I'm used to letting my eyes 'run over' faces, marking each feature: remembering the height of the brows or the slant of an ear. But of course, the details I'm now mentioning were only noted because of God's goodness, which caused Him to offer me those few moments when I saw Christ's wonderful Mother so close to me, and so patient and gentle.

How can I describe her? She had an oval face, and a slim neck. I could see her black hair parted, beneath a plain white veil which fell down on each side of her face to cover her shoulders. She wore a plain white dress with a round neckline. I saw no frills or jewels. I was so absorbed in her holy face that I noticed nothing below about shoulder-level, and have no idea how she held her hands after that first holding-up of the lamp. But she was quite beautiful, and - more important - she was utterly 'full-of-love': simply good and trustworthy and calming.

Several times before, in prayer, I'd glimpsed Our Blessed Lady, but usually as she stood at Christ's side, in Heaven. Never before had I seen her face so clearly. Never before had she stood beside me in my room; and never yet had I heard her speaking.

Waiting for me.

After a while spent, captivated, gazing in silence at our Lady's beautiful face, I suddenly realised how long I'd spent in prayer. It seemed as if Our Lady had distanced herself slightly, simply to leave me free to think or to turn away.

Twice, I turned away and looked around my room to reassure myself that although I was being honoured with an extraordinary visit, everything else about the moment was normal. I mean that I confirmed that even though Christ was drawing me up time and time again into His extraordinary bliss and Knowledge, I was sitting in my usual place, in my room, and - except for the few moments when I was wholly 'lifted up' in spirit to be given a teaching about Our Lady's role, for example (T:736) - I was able to look around and to reflect rationally about the marvels of our Faith and the holiness of my visitor; and this reassured me.

Each time I turned back to her, Our Blessed Lady was still there waiting for me. Having known her for so many years only by faith, in spiritual darkness, I now saw her in an extraordinary way: still by faith, but with faith illumined for a moment by God's freely-given Light; and I gazed upon her continuously.

Still feeling some remnant of fear, and some astonishment at my own 'impudence' at believing that Our Lady would dream of coming to someone like me, I made the sign of the Cross again, using holy water, knowing that if it were really Our Lady, she wouldn't be insulted. I asked my guardian Angel, once again, to keep me in true prayer and to help me to avoid anything evil: I meant evil persons or evil thoughts.

Gratitude for Christ and for His Mother.

But my courage grew, and Our Lady still stood before me; and, because I longed to be more worthy of her and her Son, I asked her quite spontaneously: "Show me how to love you". It didn't really occur to me that she'd answer. I often ask questions of God in prayer, knowing from long experience that many of His answers are given as clearly through events as through words; so I was astonished to receive an answer. I was astonished to hear Our Lady reply, straight away, and quite clearly, in an almost childlike and matter-of-fact way, as though simply stating truth, without apology: "No-one who truly loves Christ can fail to love me".

I realised that this observation was for other people besides myself; it was part of a declaration of truth, not just part of a personal conversation; and by the way, her voice was lovely. She sounded just like anyone I meet around here, yet very simple and calm. Then Christ took part once again. Invisible and silent, He taught me more about Our Lady, and told me:-

> **See how My Mother looks upon all her children. Her gaze is not limited to Heaven. She understands the hearts of all who try to serve Me, her Divine son. She sees the actions of all who oppose Me. (WC + OIL:741) (T:741 #1)**

> **Encourage other people to honour My holy Mother. Tell them what you discovered so many years ago: that you can all 'prove' your love for Me by loving the holy Mother whom I Myself revere.** *One who truly loves Me is therefore full of praise for the Motherhood of Mary, and is full of gratitude to her for her joyful consent to her holy task, whereas one who does not love Mary proves by that stance that he does not truly love Me, Jesus, or he would be grateful to her for giving him, by Divine grace, so great a Redeemer as Myself.* **(T:741 #4)**

> **Follow My inspiration, and confidently ask the prayer of My Holy Mother, as she stands before you. (WC:742) (T:742)**

A private litany.

These teachings were 'new' to me only in their phrasing. In essence, I learned nothing that the Church hasn't taught us before; and since the manner in which the 'teaching' was being given to me was familiar, I began to gain confidence and to stop worrying about being deceived.

Apart from my inner conviction that the beautiful woman was Our Blessed Lady, and was good, I was by now content to trust that the God to Whom I pray continuously for help wouldn't keep me with an impostor; and I was sure that nothing evil could have urged me to feel so grateful to God and to Our Lady; so, less timidly, and at peace, I stayed in prayer with this Queen and true Mother. Then, not wishing to keep such extraordinary peace and joy just for myself, I asked her prayers for the world and for the Church.

When I had prayed enough to satisfy my conscience, I sat peacefully before her for a long time in quiet wonder and admiration. I asked her, over and over, but gently and at peace: "Mother Mary, pray for me." It was like a private litany, prayed with extraordinary joy, there in her visible presence.

When a great deal of time had passed I started to grow tired; and then I began to wonder if I'd remember everything I'd been shown; so I asked Our Lady if she minded if I turn away to write. I was happy to be obedient to whatever she said: but she didn't mind whether I wrote or not: it wasn't important. This was explained very graciously, but without words. So when I'd looked around desperately, not wanting to leave Our Lady for long, I found a piece of paper; and there in her presence I made hurried notes about the 'teachings' of the past hour or so, already stunned by the implications of her visit.

Our Lady's kindness.

When I'd finished scribbling, I hurried turned to Our Lady again. I'd suddenly realised that I'd asked her prayers for the living, but not for the departed. I was prompted by Christ:-

> **Ask the prayers of My Mother for the faithful departed.**
> **Her prayers are powerful and effective. (T:743 #1)**

Ashamed of my neglect, I looked up at Our Lady again and asked: "Mother Mary: please help my own mother" - and it was God Who reassured me, through Our Lady, that my mother is now in Heaven.

Then I was urged, in prayer:-

> **Ask My Mother to help you to be faithful in your ordinary**
> **daily duties - to be a good mother. (T:743 #2)**

I asked Our Lady: "May be a good mother"; and I sat still with her for a long time, in bliss, just looking at her in my heart, confident that she would help me by her prayers.

For most of the time it seemed as if Our Lady were almost passive and serene, quietly waiting; I mean, waiting with delight in case God should choose to explain something further to me about her role, and waiting at times - with marvellous charity - for me to ask the questions which I think she half-expected. Or she simply waited, utterly content and kind, whilst I sat stunned with joy in prayer before her. What graciousness and self-giving.

Throughout this time, Christ waited, unseen. He didn't intrude or interrupt her conversation; and I was amazed, still, by Our Lady: astonished that we two women could walk side by side, it seemed, as I entrusted others to her care.

Then I was taught by Christ, in the presence of Our Lady:

> **Admit your sinfulness and imperfection beside the purity of**
> **My Holy Mother and Myself. Accept that *you are as a***
> ***crippled or disfigured one, wounded by sin, beside her purity.***

> **Yet even one so pure and great as she despises no-one who is in need of help. (T:745 #1)**

> **See how kind and gracious is My Mother, content to wait, to listen and to pray, as I wish, and now walking beside you as you entrust others to her care. (T:744)**

> **Imitate My Mother's generosity.** Just as she listens tenderly to your words, and patiently helps you, *so must you walk in great charity with others; you must* always be patient and tender with other people, and must *always remain aware of your unworthiness to serve them. You must count it a privilege to be able to do so.* **(T:745 #3)**

Whoever imagines that Christ was cruel, in speaking so frankly about sin and imperfection should be aware that we're all marred and marked by what Christians call 'Original Sin' as well as by personal failings - except, of course, Christ and The Blessed Virgin Mary; and so Christ's words about sin were chosen not to humiliate me, but rather to emphasise the beauty of the purity-of-soul of His Immaculate Mother.

The reason for the visit.

Next, for the third time, I paused again, asking the help of my Guardian Angel. I made the Sign of the Cross with holy water again. I was still wondering: 'Who am I, so wretched a sinner, to talk with the purest, most Holy Lady of all?' Yet Christ continued - for His own purposes - to teach me more about His Holy Mother, in pure Knowledge, with silent words. I learned:-

> **Don't worry about your sinfulness. Love Me and accept My gifts.** *My graciousness, and My Mother's, are greater than you can imagine.* **It is because of our love for you that My Holy Mother has come here to reassure and comfort you, as you press on with your difficult task. The teachings which you receive from Me will serve a great purpose. (T:747 #1)**

Ordinary duty.

When that 'teaching' ended, I plucked up courage and looked up at the clock, not sure whether a few minutes or a whole evening had passed by. I had learned so much and was beginning to worry about people coming back. Then I saw that it was nearly nine o'clock. Nearly a whole hour had been spent with Our Lady.

After thanking Almighty God whole-heartedly for this blessing, I thanked Our Lady, saying: "Mother, you know my heart - my hesitations and feelings ..." - I was aware that my duty lay not in praying for any longer, but in doing my work. I asked, trustingly, if she would please let me know if I were wrong to leave her to do the 'chores'; but I was astonished to learn, immediately:-

> **Don't be afraid to reveal your heart's true thoughts to My Mother, even your longing to please Me by leaving her to do the washing up, since it is your duty. She wants you to be obedient to Me, and it is My Will that you look after your family's needs. Listen to what she is saying: "I am not going to leave you!" (T:746 #3)**

I left my studio and went into the kitchen. And as I did so, and as I put on my apron, I half-expected to find that Our Lady had gone; I was so puzzled, and so amazed that she should come to someone like me. Yet I did believe it. What else could I believe in the presence of someone so holy and so close to Christ?

Filling the kitchen bowl, I started washing the dishes, and I concentrated on my work. I knew it wouldn't be kind to welcome back the family to a messy kitchen, just because I might have hoped to prolong the joy of my prayer with Our Lady. They were due to return very soon. As I worked, my heart still stunned and awed by the experience, and my mind still thinking of her, I was suddenly taught, by pure knowledge from God:-

> **Trust that I am at work in your prayer.** *You are taught Heavenly things according to your capacity - capacity of heart, mind, health, or yearning, and according to your need, such as for your consolation or in preparation for some task ahead.* **(T:746 #2)**

> **Don't be despondent about your sinfulness. My Mother is delighted by a heart which - with soul, mind and strength - is dedicated entirely to My service. She scarcely sees little failings in love, and little weaknesses, in one who lives for My Glory and for the good of souls. (T:747)**

A conversation, and a kiss.

It amazed me that I was being taught in this way about God's dealings with the soul, and about prayer. It was usually in church that God taught me this sort of thing; but I saw the truth of what I'd been told; and when I was still standing there, leaning against my sink, terribly moved by God's goodness, yet determined to live only in crystal-clear honesty with Our Lady, as I already tried to do with Our Lord, I decided to speak. I decided that if I didn't confide in someone as wonderful as Our Lady, I'd waste an opportunity; and that's why I determinedly said to her then, standing in my kitchen, "Mary, Mother, see this weakness", daring to show her how faint-hearted and fearful I was about the consequences of speaking out even more widely about Christ's intervention in my life and about His teachings-in-prayer. I knew she'd be willing to listen to anything and everything, as she'd done earlier. Then, suddenly, I was shown, by Christ:-

> **Follow My inspiration and reveal every facet of your heart and life to the gaze of My Holy Mother. Like Me, she is**

utterly trustworthy, and understanding. (WC:748) (T:748)

Don't worry about upsetting My Mother, who, like Myself, is quite unshockable. She is delighted by your trust and by your longing to be truthful. (T:749 #1)

Trust in My Mother. She sees you as you really are: her child, and her Son's close relation. She is reassuring you, again: "I am not going to leave you!" (T:749 #2)

Listen to the advice of the best possible Mother, who is insisting: "Elizabeth! Do not worry!" With the help of both My Mother and Myself, you can peacefully set out to do My Will from hour to hour and day to day, released from the fear which has overshadowed you. (WC:749) (T:749 #3)

As I turned away from my sink, I stood, head bowed, in front of Our Blessed Lady, showing her my heart; and she leaned over to comfort me. She treated me as her true child; she kissed me on the forehead; and how like a true mother she was, when she spoke to me: using this child's proper name!

After my work I was utterly exhausted. I couldn't sit up straight any longer, because of my illness, or stay awake to listen to her further; but I knew that she understood my weakness. I went off to bed eventually, my heart full of gratitude. I was determined to honour her more reverently for the rest of my life.

I resolved, too, to pray and work in her honour, especially on the 22nd of each month, out of love for her and for the Glory of Christ her son, just as I already celebrate the 11th of each month in memory of His kindness on what I call the 'Alpha and Omega' Day.

Extraordinary steps to help me.

Anyone who reads the first volume of the 'Teachings-in-prayer' will see explained once again the reason for this particular visit. The knowledge which had been given to me, by God, in Our Blessed Lady's presence, of the pouring-out of grace and Divine Life at the Incarnation, was a small part of the whole series of 'Teachings'; but the personal, extraordinary kindness of Our Lady on that occasion was given to encourage me in my task of writing and explaining the teachings. God knew that at times I'd been almost paralysed with fear at the thought of the questions I might be asked and the friends who might desert me, and also the ridicule I might have to bear if, in our modern world - though every age is 'modern' to itself - I made myself conspicuous, in obedience to God, by truthfully claiming to have received 'teachings' in prayer.

I know I keep stressing my unworthiness; but Christ Himself showed me how true this is, when He explained, later on, that my task alone was worthy of Our Lady's visit, which hadn't occurred because of any merit of mine. Christ has explained not once but many times just how important it is that the 'teachings' are recorded and - at a time decided by Him - poured out, through His Church, to help His struggling People and also many others. That's why He and His wonderful Mother have been willing to take extraordinary steps to keep me going during the past few years. He has also explained that the knowledge of Our Lady's kindness to me would affect other people so much that it would 'soften' many hearts, and so prepare those hearts in the way that seedbeds are prepared, so that they'd be ready to receive a lavish 'planting' within them of the other teachings which He'd been giving to me in prayer.

It makes me very happy to be writing this account of the visit. I yearn to tell people about Our Blessed Lady's goodness and beauty. But sometimes I feel ashamed, when I think about her visit, because what excuse have I, now, at ever failing to love, after being offered such a Heavenly example of loving concern? And what excuse have I, ever to stop being joyful, when Christ has promised me that He'll let nothing and nobody take me away from Him? The goodness and tenderness of Our Lord and Our Lady is indescribable.

12 INSTRUCTION
(1990-1991)

GOD IS LOVE. SAINTS. THE BLESSED SACRAMENT.

"God is Love".

As I reflected on the goodness of Our Blessed Lady, I made more resolutions! I hoped that I too would always be kind to anyone poor or sick or lonely, and that I'd never judge or dismiss anyone at all. I resolved always to speak and act in true love and compassion - by the grace of Christ - out of gratitude to Christ Who has taken pity on me in my needs. I'd at last given up every notion of somehow keeping my own life 'to myself': and that's why, about two weeks later, in Holy Communion, I found that I could say to Christ in prayer, and with my whole heart: "All I am, I give to You". I was led to say this, peacefully, over and over again; but I expected nothing but the grace to carry on with my duties, living in hope, grateful for whatever simple gifts and graces Christ might to choose to give me - or withhold.

On the following day, at the Vigil Mass of the Feast of the Immaculate Conception of Our Lady, I prayed with new fervour after the Consecration, offering all my pains to Christ in union with His pain, in reparation for the suffering of His Passion. I offered Him, again, my whole life in sacrifice, and then suddenly, God's own words were given to me. Speaking of Himself, with devastating force and clarity, God the Holy Trinity pierced my prayers by His truth. The eyes of my soul were dazzled by His majesty and Glory, as Christ taught me:-

> **Accept My reassurance and comfort, as you open your heart to Me in prayer. All that you have learned and believed about Me is true. Listen to your Heavenly Father Who is now teaching you - as if in words of fire, and about Our nature - that:**
>
> > *"God is Love.*
> > *He is."*
>
> **You are right to believe that We are surrounding and upholding everything - and every being - which We have created. (T:770 #4)**

Thus Christ confirmed much of what His Church has already taught us about His nature, His power, and our freedom. Then I was powerfully taught, about the Godhead:-

293

Understand Love's meaning: My entire nature consists of Love, and therefore "includes" generosity, mercy, justice, faithfulness, and every good, with unchanging delight in all that is good. (T:770 #6)

Understand the difference between Creator and created. I, your God, am 'Being' Itself. I have not been created. I had no 'beginning', but am eternal, whereas all that I have made - visible or invisible, in or around the earth and in the whole of Creation - exists only because I am keeping it in existence. (T:770 #7)

Understand that, from the depth of My goodness, I have created only good things, and have also created good beings who - in their real freedom - may refuse to do or to be good. (T:770 #8)

Understand that just as I Who am Love 'cannot' - because of My loving nature - create anything evil, so too I 'cannot' reject any being whom I have created for a loving relationship with Me. I Who am Love cannot be unloving; however, others may reject Me. (T:770 #9)

Consider the importance of the right use of your free-will. Consider My goodness in permitting My creatures such freedom. Beings who freely turn their backs on goodness and who thereby turn away from Me, the Source of all goodness, are thus demonstrating their aversion to "Life-in-God". My 'enforced' presence - should such a thing happen - would bring only torment. (T:770 #10)

"Jesus is Love."

When those initial statements were 'poured' within my soul, it was with such magnificence and glory that I wouldn't have been surprised to have heard trumpets prefacing each phrase. Then, when I was aware that I'd received this marvellous knowledge, but before I'd had time to reflect upon it, I was suddenly shown that Jesus was standing before me, dazzling in the radiance of His holiness. It was as though Christ stood at the heart of a blazing furnace; and as I gazed at Him, I was told:-

Listen to your Heavenly Father, as He proclaims about Me:

"Jesus is Love!"

Don't be afraid to declare, boldly, that I, Jesus Christ the Divine Son, have the same nature as the Father and am therefore rightly to be seen as equal in majesty. (T:771 #3)

Then Christ taught me about our attitude towards Him. I understood that many people who try to look towards Christ in prayer or at death are forced to look away, so unbearable is His brightness; and at the same time, I was taught:-

> Consider the meaning of Divine perfection: *I, Jesus, am burning with a blazing purity.* I am glowing with a terrible, awesome Love, in Glory now. No longer earthly, I no longer wait for death to claim Me, and My Sacred Body is incorruptible. I have died and am Risen. I am transformed and risen to Heaven. I am burning with the Divine Life and Holiness which - through prayer and the Sacraments - I can share with you in order to make you holy with My holiness, and pure, and wholly transformed. (T:771 #4)

> Consider the reason for spiritual pain, shame and guilt: *All that is not Love blazes at My touch. I, Jesus, now triumphant in Heaven, am all Truth, Love, Beauty, Purity and Power.* No-one who loves secrecy, selfishness, disobedience and darkness can bear to experience My presence, nor My generosity, beauty, holiness and majesty. The radiant Light of My Glory is unbearable for those who are unwilling to look upon Me, or who are unprepared: by which I mean, who have not yet undergone purification - whether during earthly life or after death. (T:771 #5)

> Be joyful, knowing that between Myself and the soul which lives in a true communion with Me, the "veil" which separates Heavenly beings from earthly, is very thin. *If you love totally, I, Jesus, am therefore "yours" to offer to the Father, you and I together pleading for others, asking for anything - as prompted by My Holy Spirit. The 'door' will be opened by the Father, for the sake of Myself, Whom He loves and Who am yours!* (T:771 #6)

Then Christ showed me:-

> Understand the meaning of prayer 'in Christ' which is prayer that conforms to the desires of My Heart. See, therefore, why no-one can offer to the Father, in My Name, a plea for something which is evil, impure or foolish. Such 'prayers' cannot be called true prayers. (T:771 #7)

> Realise that the Father's response to particular petitions depends on your generosity in loving and serving Me, His Divine Son. All that the Father gives to you is given for the sake of Me, His Son, Who died for you and Who have made you My beloved friend. (T:771 #8)

A single plea from a single Christ.

Next, Christ explained to me the reason why I should be confident and joyful as I dedicated myself more and more determinedly to the sort of prayer into which He had been leading me. Christ showed me, by an image, that whenever I pray in His name to the Father it's as though we're praying together to the Father, offering a single prayer to Him. Christ explained to me:-

> **Consider the marvel of prayer made in union with Me, Jesus - and the power of such prayer. When you cling to Me and try to please Me, your prayers and Mine are utterly united. It is just as though you and I stand praying before the Father, Whose Light shines down from Heaven upon us both; and since you stand in front of Me, so closely imitating My stance - standing reverently in prayer - and since you resemble Me so closely, by a sincere love of the Father's Will, your words and intentions could well have sprung from My own lips. So the Invisible Father in Heaven 'sees' only a single plea from a 'single Christ', and answers your prayer for the sake of Me, the Saviour, as I pray - with you - before Him. (T:772)**

I can't describe the impact of this teaching, which I had learned in one way, of course, through Christ's Church; but never before I had understood it with quite so much clarity and joy. I wanted to share the news of the richness of it all, and of God's goodness to me, but I knew that I ought to wait until the appropriate time.

Every day, I was free to tell other people, in one way or another: "God is pure love; God's love for you, and for everyone on earth, is tremendous"; but I couldn't yet talk about my experience. It was one more gift which must be quietly pondered and absorbed, and written down; but I returned home from church that day resolving that my whole life would be a thank-offering for all of Christ's blessings and graces.

The Saints: jostling to help us.

As time passed it seems as though my resolutions almost made themselves. There was no end of the trials of life, generally, but I lived in peace and contentment for a while, full of gratitude for new friendships, for opportunities for painting, and other joys; and week by week, I was taught more about prayer.

About six or seven weeks after the visit from Our Lady, I learned more about the Holy Mass. Christ showed me the power of the Holy Offering which He makes on our behalf. Then, on the same day, when Mass had finished and I was praying alone, Christ brought my spirit, in prayer, into the presence of His Saints, at the 'edge' of Heaven. I think it was to encourage my faith in the unity of the whole Church in Christ's praise to the Father.

In Holy Communion, that day, I had spoken my usual words of gratitude to Christ; and later, I'd asked all the Angels and Saints for their help in my struggles; and I suddenly found that Christ was teaching me about these wonderful friends in Heaven. He explained to me, all in one moment:-

> **Turn towards My Saints in Heaven, and ask for their
> prayers. Don't struggle alone.** *You honour them by your
> request. My Saints 'jostle' for the privilege of helping you* **or
> of helping anyone.** (WC + OIL:812A) (T:812 #2)

> **Consider the life of My Saints in Heaven.** *My Saints are full
> of love, and are full of longing to help you because they are
> so completely full of My own Love!* **They are full of grace
> and joy, dazzling in their glory.** (T:812 #2)

> **Remember to thank and honour My Saints. Each one is
> gladdened by the joy given to any and every other Saint.
> They are delighted when you confide in them, pleased when
> you ask for assistance, have every sympathy for you in your
> struggles and understand your temptations.** (T:812 #3)

> **Don't be tempted to think that any of My Saints is too
> 'grand' to help you. Each one has the gratitude of a little
> child, in the face of My astounding Love.** (T:812 #4)

Before the eyes of my soul, and in the radiant Light of prayer, I could see the Saints in Heaven, above me. I was astonished to see St. Thérèse of Lisieux. In pure Knowledge and love she responded to my heart's request, and came to stand at the centre of the group. I saw that she loves us dearly; all the Saints shared in her joy at being greeted so fervently by someone on earth.

When I prayed to Saint Teresa of Avila, she turned towards me, very loving and motherly and wise. Then I asked St. Thomas More to help me; and he smiled at me, and I realised that this wonderful man understands our problems.

St. Dominic was with me next - grave and gentle in his humility and his love for Christ.

Then I was encouraged, by Christ:-

> **Ask the help of many more Heavenly friends, especially of
> My holy Mother, the Queen of Saints.** *How great is her love
> for you. She honours you by her prayers.* (T:812 #5)

I realised that I hadn't asked for our Holy Mother's help, so I did so, ashamed of having waited for so long. I watched her walk to the centre of the crowd; and Christ showed me:-

> **See how My Saints draw back in honour and reverence
> when My holy Mother stands amongst them. They admire
> the beauty and simplicity of this Most Holy Virgin, through
> whom mankind was given its Saviour: Myself.** (T:812 #6)

There was Our Lady standing at the centre of a huge crowd of radiant and joyful people.

Then I asked St. Maria Goretti for help. I saw that St. Maria is loved much, by others, in her wisdom and innocence.

It was possible to use my will in order to communicate, wordlessly, with the Saints, and to reflect on the goodness of God who was permitting me to be so close to them; but at the same time I was held up in bliss.

St. Mary Magdalene stood before me, next. She is honoured by everyone in Heaven; and she is beautiful - and at peace in her sanctity, and very dignified.

St. Paul seemed to be almost embarrassed at our love and veneration, although I feel sure there can't be any real embarrassment in Heaven. He would have given a thousand lives for his beloved Christ. St. Peter was full of humility - awed, I felt, that Christ had chosen a man like him.

Then I saw dear St. Joseph, whom I'd seen once before because Christ is so generous and kind. I asked him to pray for me, a sinner - then suddenly realised that I had to leave the church. It was going to be locked for the rest of the day; and nearly everyone had gone; so I thanked all the Saints, and Christ as well, and then left the Church and made my way home.

All the way home, I was full of the peace given to me by Christ, and full of joy having seen the wonderful Saints whom I hadn't hoped to see in this life - only in the next. I asked Christ to help me to benefit from their prayers and from their example. I asked Him to bring me to join Him one day, to meet the Saintly "WITNESSES IN A GREAT CLOUD ON EVERY SIDE OF US" (Heb 12:1), and to be united with them in the praise of the Most Holy Trinity, in Heaven.

Christ: A devoted 'parent.'

I didn't reflect on these things as much as I might have hoped because all the writing that I'd done in obedience to Christ at that time had stirred up a whole host of memories, which became distractions.

I tried to brush them aside, gently, knowing that we're not blamed for little things we can't avoid. When I spoke about this turmoil to Christ in Holy Communion, and ask Him to help me, I was reassured by His loving Presence; and He led me swiftly into His silent and unknowing praise. This was, by now, the pattern of almost every Communion, although I tried not to take good things for granted. I was determined to live for love alone - not for sweetness here 'below' - and to follow Christ blindly.

The following weeks were full of the usual tasks and joys: writing, friendships, household jobs, family conversation, and attendance at daily Mass. One day, when I was flagging, I was shown by Christ that it didn't matter if, through illness, I could hardly concentrate during the Mass. He told me:-

Be confident, in your humility. I love you, and I

understand that some of My 'children' are sick, weary, or despondent; I invite you to *"come and sit here."* *Rest quietly, as if in a place by My feet.* (T:857 #1)

Be like a little child who sits beside her devoted parent. *I pray for all of you* who are too weary to utter even a single word or pious thought! I delight in your loving desires, and in your desire to pray, even when you can scarcely begin! (T:857 #2)

One single 'Hail Mary'.

One Saturday, a few weeks later on, when I'd been to Confession, I made my way to the Lady chapel for a few minutes of quiet prayer. There, I continued to make acts of faith in Christ's love for me. I was nearly overwhelmed with weariness and work. I dutifully said a "Hail Mary" as I paused before the Blessed Sacrament, thinking of Christ's love for us and thinking of Our Lady's love for us, too, and praying for those I love. Then suddenly, I was shown:-

Believe in the tremendous value of your prayers: prayers which are made in My Name and with My power. (T:859 #1)

Be confident that the effect of a good prayer is real and immediate, even if unseen and unrecognised. Think about the prayer which you recite so frequently:

"Hail Mary, full of grace.
Blessed art thou amongst women,
and blessed is the fruit of thy womb, Jesus.

Holy Mary, Mother of God,
pray for us sinners,
now, and at the hour of our death."

I assure you that *one single "Hail Mary"* - *said for someone's welfare* - *is like a drink* which has been *poured into a chalice for someone's refreshment.* By a single 'Hail Mary' you can help, to some degree, each person you meet, or hear about, who is in need of help. (T:859 #2)

By this single teaching I was helped to look outwards rather than inwards and to give more frequent and sure help to all sorts of people.

Submitting my work for appraisal.

One day in March 1991 when I'd been writing for many months besides doing my usual work, I learned from Christ that it was time for me to explain things again. So put the whole 'work' into God's hands and asked for God's help. I arranged to see our parish priest once more, in order to explain that I was obliged to publish an account of most of what Christ had taught me, since I'd found that these things aren't for me alone, but are a gift, through me, to His Church. Our priest replied that he would try to find someone to advise me.

For the next four weeks, I spent every spare minute finishing the writings, and trying to accept, gladly, all the normal daily duties and visits, and interruptions. No special work is worthwhile if it means neglecting everyday duties, and so failing in love; and I wasn't lacking in encouragement to do good, as Christ told me:-

> **Prove your love for me, whilst you still live on earth, by faithfully fulfilling little duties as well as large! If you have letters which need answering, letters buried deep in your handbag, *"love means clearing out your handbag!"* You fail in charity if you neglect your friends or relations. (T:893 #2)**

Then Christ showed me, at Holy Mass, the beauty of His worship, and encouraged me to trust in Him entirely. He spoke about all sorts of things, during prayer: about life's huge problems as well as about little duties. It was when I felt very ill one day that He even told me:-

> **Don't be afraid. One who truly loves Me need not fear death, because My Love will then be experienced in all its fullness of joy. No earthly joy, nor any love, can compare with My Love, as experienced by the soul who loves Me and who is loved by Me. (T:893 #1)**

There was yet further encouragement.

Saint Joseph.

On the twenty-fifth of April, 1991, I had finished writing an account of all of the teachings in prayer which I'd received up to that time. In the evening, when I'd resolved to pray the "Stations" for love of Christ, despite late activities and exhaustion, I prayed my "night" prayers also. When I had said the 'Hail Mary' as usual, and finished my prayers with the sign of the Cross, I decided to ask St. Joseph for his prayers. I was thinking, briefly, that I ought not to 'neglect' someone whom Our Lady loves so much. It doesn't take much energy to say: "Saint Joseph, please pray for me, a sinner."

At the very instant that I turned my heart towards him, Saint Joseph was present before my soul's eyes; I was astonished. Christ, unseen at first, was with us, wordlessly teaching me:-

> **Turn your gaze to St. Joseph, who is here before you. See how magnificently I am responding even to a tiny prayer.**

We are delighted that - because of your belief in his virtues and your desire to please My Mother Mary - you turned to him in prayer and asked for his help. (T:896 #1)

Reflect upon the marvellous qualities of St. Joseph, who acted as a good father to Me, his beloved foster-son, when I lived upon earth. (T:896 #2)

Ask for St. Joseph's prayers. Show towards him, now, the tremendous love, respect and admiration which I showed towards him during his life on earth and which I now display towards him in Heaven. (T:896 #3)

Consider St. Joseph's virtues. He is so noble, fatherly and kind that My Mother Mary was fortunate to be entrusted to such a man - though he was fortunate to be married to someone as loving and holy as she. (T:896 #4)

Don't look upon St. Joseph as the bumbling old man of some caricatures: someone foolish and graceless married to an ethereal being and wholly unworthy of her. My Mother is a real woman - and very warm-hearted, yet dignified and very holy; and St. Joseph is worthy of her love. He, too, is a loving person; he is a man of great stature, though very sweet and tender. I gave him all the qualities which were needed for his highly responsible task. (T:896 #5)

Be confident. Remain happily in St. Joseph's presence, for as long as you are able. Your friends in Heaven are delighted by the prayers and greetings of those who love them and - more important to them - who love and serve Me. (T:896 #9)

Not Christ's 'natural' father.

At this point I asked Our Lord: "Jesus - don't let me be misguided", thinking: "Who am I to pray a simple prayer and to receive such a gift?" But He replied to me immediately:-

Turn to St. Joseph for help. *"How can you be misguided by My Father?!"* He loves you, as he loves all who love Me and My holy Mother. He loves you and he prays for you. (T:896 #6)

Realise that he whom I chose to act as father-on-earth to Me the Christ-child is one whom you can trust. With great esteem, I call St. Joseph "Father," because he acted as a very good father to Me in loving and caring for Me on earth, although he was not My 'natural' father. (T:896 #7)

301

Even as He was speaking, Christ suddenly appeared to me. I saw Him standing quite close to Saint Joseph. Christ was making a lovely gesture: holding out his hand towards him, thus encouraging me to look closely at the beloved foster father who stood, all the while, head bowed in humility besides his God.

For a few minutes of awe and bliss and wonder, I sat quietly in their presence - too unwell to kneel. Then I made the sign of the Cross with holy water, still amazed that I should be so honoured, but hoping that Our Lord wouldn't permit me to be deceived in the very centre of my soul, where He dwells. He knows how I long only for Love and Truth. After some time, when I'd sat silently in prayer in their company, I explained to St. Joseph that Jesus would tell him that I'm weak, and can't sit up for very long. St. Joseph smiled and blessed me; but I was amazed to notice that he didn't leave me. With true charity, he waited for me to leave him; and although I could hardly bear to tear myself away, I didn't want to fall asleep in front of him. So I left that silent prayer, and began to prepare to go to bed, my heart full of gratitude to God for His kindness and full of love for Our Lord and St. Joseph.

The next day, I pressed on with my household work and my writing as usual.

Hard work: and extra helpers.

When I wrote a little further back that I had "finished the writings", I meant that I'd reached the stage where I was able to take a good look at the three piles of paper in front of me. I had a Prologue which led up to 1985, and also a Narrative (1985-1991), as well as the Teachings and the paintings. I photocopied the most important sections to produce a "Summary" - of which a tidier version would later be printed as: "Teachings-in-prayer: an Introduction." Then I handed the work to my parish priest. I didn't know who would assess it, or when I'd receive an opinion on it; and I quaked at the thought of laying myself open to criticism or mockery.

I was less worried about my parish priest having to read my writings. He was always straightforward and courteous with me. I was still self-conscious, however, and horribly aware of my spiritual and literary failings; so I was both touched and astonished when my parish priest sought me out on the day after I'd handed in my work to him, and asked me: "What, exactly, is the message?"

As I've said somewhere else, I was still 'in the dark' about much of Christ's purpose for the teachings. But I wrote a letter to our priest next day, trying to explain what I'd learned so far. It will be easier if I reproduce some of that letter, below. I told him that I was almost as puzzled as he was about the purpose of the teachings; and I continued (T:910):-

" ... I said, a few weeks ago, that I could see no further than one step ahead, whilst I was busy writing all that I had been taught in prayer. That was true, then, as Christ kept me in darkness so that I could finish one part of my work.

The next task was to hand over to you (and thus to the Church) the revelation about Christ, Our Lady, Holy Mass, Love, the Saints and St. Joseph. I have done this, in part, by giving to you the 'Summary' to read or to share; I have no idea what you are supposed to do, but my only hope and security has been in trying to be obedient to Christ at each new and extraordinary step - I'm sorry if 'all this' causes you problems.

This morning, you mentioned someone who delivered a message. In that instance, God chose someone young and innocent who could quite guilelessly say to her parish priest - "I have seen Our Lady ... she asks for prayer and penance." That was how God, in that century, used one of His creatures for His eternal purpose: His Glory and the sanctification of souls.

I hardly dare to write this, but I think I have been led to offer you a message for the same purposes, but led in a different way, to meet the needs of our own time. The method is 'back-to-front', in this sense:-

Christ has trained me by suffering, for over twenty years, and throughout that time He has been teaching me His Knowledge. So: the 'message' I have written down about Himself and His Holy Mother and His Holy Sacrifice and His Saints is marvellous, and it should be published; although there is nothing new here, as I said, but I think it is an encouragement to people in the Church, that God, Christ, Our Lady, the Saints, the whole Church (living and departed), the Sacraments, Prayer, Penance, and Reparation through patience in suffering, are important today, AS EVER. (I did not choose what I was taught - nor how much I was taught. I suppose that some 'messages' are brief, and some are longer. That is Our Lord's decision, not mine. All I can do is repeat the message, through you, to the Church.)

However, there is another 'aspect' to the message.

Each part of the major 'teachings' was given (I see now) in response to a loving and costly sacrifice on my part - prompted and sustained by grace alone.

I dare to think that my task, now, is not only to reveal the 'messages' or 'teachings' for their own sake: as aspects of the One Revelation given through Christ and His Apostles. Their publication, I think, will reveal, too, the graces of Christ IN and THROUGH my own wretched life; that is why I have written at length (in obedience) about my life, conversion, repentance and sickness and daily life.

So: that is the second message which God wishes to give through these revelations, through me, a sinner: "Here is grace at work in one who is weak, and inadequate. Here is Christ teaching a soul to be faithful to God, to be obedient to His Church; for the sake of Christ learning to accept sufferings with patience, trusting in grace and being nourished by the Sacraments. Listen to her. She speaks the Truth."

I am, I dare to say, one of His 'little ones': a sinner, un-learned, poor - in the sense of being dependent on others' generosity - female, a lay-person, married, and sick: the "RUBBISH OF THIS WORLD" (cf. 1 Co 5:15).

Yet even as I (at last) gladly and freely accepted my status and my sufferings, for the love of God (by His grace) Christ was teaching me about Himself, and adorning' me (- rubbish -) so that others might one day listen to me speaking about faith, obedience, prayer, hope and Heaven - about all the things which He has taught me. The 'major' teachings are my 'introduction' - for His purposes. (I have not been 'used', briefly, and then 'put behind a door' like a broom, but have been behind the 'door' for nearly three decades as an adult, being prepared for the time when I must direct others towards God, through Christ and His Church, and using His teachings and images. Ours is a visual age; that is why the "Mass Paintings" seem to me to be important. I shall gladly do whatever you say, but if I am permitted to say: 'This is what Christ has shown me', many more persons will benefit.

Whether I should teach by direct speech or by writing, I have no idea, since I am very feeble, and do not know whether I shall live for another week or another decade.

I could be tempted to groan at the thought of being questioned or pestered, mocked or scrutinised, but I do not dwell much on the future. I am simply trying to do the Will of God from one day to the next, trusting that Our Lord will prop me up and help me to persevere; I really have no courage but Him. Meanwhile, my youngest child was eighteen years old last month; that means that my long-lasting, immediate responsibility for 'children' has ended, (though not my love). I shall, perhaps, be 'free' to do a different work. Right now, I have to say: "I have seen the Lord!" Should you or your superiors tell me that I am merely silly or deluded, then I hope that Christ will be satisfied with my obedience in speaking to you; I hope I shall quietly carry on as usual, cooking meals and going to Mass, and writing.

On the other hand, should you believe everything that I have written, then I hope that I will be given the grace to follow your advice, whatever it is, and wherever it leads me.

... I think I have left out as much as I have included, in all the writing I have done in the past few months. Much is private and personal, but the 'pieces' which I have included are meant to point others towards the beauty and grace of Christ, not towards myself.

Anyway, I have explained many more things about prayer and writing in the large version which, perhaps, someone will have to 'plough' through, at some stage ..."

One step at a time.

It was a year before I heard anything more about my writings. But throughout that year the 'teachings' continued, and I continued to write them down for future use, knowing that this was what Christ wanted me to do.

One day at Holy Mass, Christ gave me further encouragement, by telling me:-

> **Make generous acts of trust in Me. (T:912B #1)**

> **Walk with Me through each 'present moment'. Walk one step at a time, neither dwelling on the past - since you are repentant and reconciled - nor peering anxiously ahead. I long to see you living peacefully - all the time - in complete rest. (T:912B #2)**

> **Never think that I am 'absent', as you complete your earthly journey. I am pleased to see you happy and patient as you do My work, and to see you believing in My**

presence, even though you cannot see Me. It is as though *I stand on one side of the 'veil'* which divides Heaven from earth. You are in My presence and you are loved by Me, although we are not yet completely united for all eternity. (T:912B #3)

Heavenly friends to assist us.

On another day, as my courage flagged, I went to Confession, and then prayed for a while in church. There, before the Blessed Sacrament, I said to Christ: "Lord - I have You alone to help me!" I meant: "See how weak and how lonely I am in my struggles, with such strange work to do." Then I suddenly saw Christ within my soul, as He gaily indicated that His beloved Mother was present, with all the Angels and Saints who long to help us. He explained to me, wordlessly:-

> Rejoice that I care for you deeply, care so much that I give you innumerable extra helpers! I entrust you joyfully to the care of My holy Mother, and to all the Saints and holy Angels who long to help you. (T:915 #1)

> Don't think of yourself as alone or lonely. *You have many holy friends and helpers*; a great number of Heavenly friends can assist you, as they can assist all my friends. (T:915 #2)

> Confide in My Saints and holy Angels. Ask your heavenly friends to pray for all who are dear to you and in need. Name them one by one. You can be sure that your holy friends are leaning forward, eager to hear about even more beloved persons whom they might have the joy and privilege of helping by their prayers. (T:915 #3)

When I said: "There are more in my heart" - meaning that there were many more people for whom I wanted to pray, but I couldn't remember all their names, I heard this tender reassurance:-

> Be secure in the knowledge that My holy Company respects your 'privacy-of-soul'. Yet be glad that everyone whose problems you have unveiled before Me, so that I can help, is therefore 'known' by the Saints who live "in" Me. *All whom you have at some time - however briefly - brought before Me, are now known by the Saints to be in need of prayer,* which is thereafter given gladly, lavishly and lovingly. My Saints are reassuring you about your beloved people: "We know all about them" and about their needs. (T:915 #4)

> "Weave" the melody of your frequent prayers into the

blessed harmony which is the prayer of My Holy Church. How like a great symphony is the love and prayer of My whole Church of earth and Heaven, as the prayer of each member is touched and intermingled with the prayers of My Saints and My Holy Angels, My holy Mother and Myself. (T:915 #5)

Intercession, and 'Unknowing' prayer.

It seems as though there's no end to the 'treasure' that we can find through Christ. When I was going to the shops one day, and was silently offering a little prayer for someone I met on the way, Christ suddenly showed me His delight in my effort. There in the street, He taught me, in one swift moment:-

Turn to Me in order to receive gifts which you can give to others. It is as though I walk beside you, laden with gifts; and whenever you ask Me to reward, help or support someone I invite you to plunge your hands into the pile of "jewels" which I am carrying, and to draw out presents of faith, hope and love for the people you meet, as well as special helps for people with special problems. I delight in answering the prayers of My friends; therefore, since you turn to Me on behalf of others, and since I understand every human heart, I see clearly exactly what sort of help is needed. (T:909)

On another day, in church, He explained something more about a different type of prayer:-

Follow My call in prayer, whenever - through My Spirit's urging - I invite you to follow the path of contemplation. (T:913 #1)

Give instant obedience to My prompting; this is how you can move silently towards the invisible Light of My 'unknowing' praise. I 'point' to the Father and I lift the soul into 'unknowing' silent and sightless worship; I 'work' My praise and My Will within the soul who has consented to leave behind all words and preoccupations. (T:913 #2)

Christ is my praise.

On another occasion, I was given answers to questions which I hadn't even asked; yet most probably the answers were to be remembered for other people. In that moment, at Holy Mass, I was taught once again that Jesus Himself, at Holy Mass, is our prayer to the Father. I was instructed:-

306

Allow Me to work within your soul. I will lavish My gifts upon you. *"I furnish you with all you need,"* **as you try to serve Me and do My Will. (T:911A #1)**

Understand the infinite value of My Worship, as I come to your midst at the Consecration, during My Holy Sacrifice of the Mass, to make My infinitely worthy Offering to the Father. Turn with Me to the Father, in prayer, and consider:

> *- Would you give praise to Him?*
> *Here I am, Jesus, Myself, praising the Father.*
> *- Would you give thanks to Him?*
> *I, Jesus, am your means of thanksgiving, your Offering.*
> *- Would you offer reparation to Him?*
> *Here I am: Jesus, your Sacrifice.*
> *- Would you plead with the Father, in intercession?*
> *I, Jesus, plead with you: does the Father refuse Me?!*
> *(T:921 #2)*

Unite to My Act and words and Offering at the Holy Mass each of your little acts and words of love for the Father or your little acts of sorrow-for-sin. Your offerings, when united to My infinitely-worthy Offering, are perfect, and are accepted by the Father. (T:921 #3)

Approach the Father with great gratitude for His goodness, in that you are the children of such a King, and the sisters and brothers of so sweet a brother as Myself. See how little it matters that you are poor, feeble or sinful, as you stand before the altar, preparing for the Holy Mysteries. Through a contrite heart, and through My prayer, you can offer a prayer of infinite power and glory from within your frailty. (T:921 #4)

This was an enormous encouragement to me whenever I was tempted to become despondent; but of course it didn't mean that we should give up the struggle against sin and discouragement.

The promise of Baptism fulfilled.

Only a few days later, on the feast of the Immaculate Heart of Mary, Christ spoke to me about His Divine Life within my own heart and soul: about how that life is active and fruitful. He was rewarding me for a vigorous act of faith in His Love; and He taught me:-

Continue to be fervent in prayer, turning to Me for faith and strength. I delight in your trust. (T:925 #1)

Be grateful for the union with Myself which you now enjoy: a true union, even here on earth, a union in which - even amidst real sufferings - you receive ceaseless joy. (T:925 #2)

Be at peace, in My Love!

> *What a steady prayer has been*
> *My own prayer, as I have prayed*
> *in your heart,*
> *through our union, from baptism.*
> *What a Fire of consuming prayer*
> *now pours to the Father*
> *from your union with Me in Communion,*
> *as you say: "Here is Jesus",*
> *trusting in My perfect praise.*
> *Thus, the promise of baptism is fulfilled*
> *when the spark of faith becomes*
> *a burning torch to lighten the darkness. (T:925 #3)*

Christ, in the tabernacle.

On the 15th June, when I had spent several hours persevering with my simple chores, and had interspersed the tasks and moments of rest with prayers of acceptance of God's Will, I 'offered-up' my pains and weaknesses to God the Father in union with Christ's pains. I said 'Fiat' again, on my way to the evening Mass. I meant 'Yes', again, to all of Christ's plans for my life, whether to silence, suffering, and obscurity, or to anything else He might permit, as long as He'd keep me close to Him, and would allow me to do His Holy Will.

He is so generous to those who give up all their desires for love of Him! As I greeted Christ in the Blessed Sacrament, before Mass began, prepared to list my pleas and to name everyone who is specially dear to me, I found that He wouldn't permit me to continue speaking.

I was astonished to see Him standing near the tabernacle, His arm outstretched in prayer, and His whole being radiant with Glory, as a group of reverent Angels stood around Him in adoration. Then Christ told me, very lovingly:-

> **Adore Me in the Blessed Sacrament. Direct the eyes of your soul towards Me; I am Really Present in the Tabernacle. My holy Angels surround Me; they stand silently in adoration. (T:928 #2)**

Awe-struck, I adored Christ. I gave my heart and my life to Him, again. Then I asked the Angels to teach me how to love and serve Him; and suddenly, I heard them say, as one voice within my soul, as clear as a child's voice: "Do as we do," which meant: look towards Christ, always, yearning to serve and to please Him, poised to do His Holy Will in the least manner, out of pure love for the Saviour whose face was too dazzling to see.

Immediately, I prayed "Jesus, don't let me be deceived in this holy place", frightened of being led astray, even there in His sanctuary. But as I continued to adore Christ, yearning only to do His Will and to stay in His Truth, He showed me, by an image within the soul:-

> **Put your trust in Me. I Who stand before you - clothed in white and dazzling in My Glory - bear the Wounds which prove My Love for you, Wounds on the pierced feet which are visible below My dazzling robe. (T:928 #4)**

> **Look towards Me; I await you at the tabernacle. Stay close to Me. (T:928 #5)**

> **Have faith in My power. Even here amidst the usual bustle and muttering in the Church before the Holy Mass begins, and as you kneel at my feet, I am praying to the Father on your behalf. (T:928 #6)**

> **Accept the fact that - a frail human being - you seem to be in darkness, below the Light of My Divine Radiance. Truly, by yourself *you are small and powerless, but this is not a cause for worry, since My arms reach out to the Glory which you cannot see, in an image of the Eternal Prayer to which all your prayers are united, through My Merits and your union with Me. (T:928 #7) (WC: 928)***

Then the bell rang and Holy Mass began. I vowed that I'd rather forget everything that Christ had shown me than be distracted during the Holy Mysteries; and by His grace I was able to pray the usual prayers, disregarding His wonderful teaching until afterwards, when I recorded a few details in order to obey His instructions. But I was given a further 'teaching', in Holy Communion, when Christ told me:-

> **Prepare your soul for further contemplation by understanding the path upon which I sometimes lead you. First, you turn to Me, and welcome me, then you wait in silence for My Will to be made plain. Next, you follow My Spirit to "unknowing" praise, and so you permit My praise to be yours, in utter emptiness and self-offering. (T:928 #8)**

> **See how little you need be troubled by the thought of your real frailty. Your faith in Me is all-important; and you can rejoice to know that My praise, when offered from within your contrite soul, is a torrent - unimpeded - which rises to the Father! (T:928 #9)**

The Cross, in ordinary life.

Month after month, as I worked and prayed and rested, Christ taught me about prayer and weakness and suffering - but as much for the sake of all the people who would read my work later on as for my own sake. On July 26th, 1991, He taught me:-

> **Rejoice in your weakness. You who are sick are tremendously loved by Me. Your worship is enormously precious, in My eyes. This is because** *in your frailty, you trust in My prayer and My Offering.* **It is also because - even in frailty and suffering -** *you have faith in the goodness of Me as Father. How you are loved!* **(T:959)**

> **Follow My inspirations in prayer. Reflect on My Passion. I look lovingly and tenderly upon one who shows devotion to My terrible sufferings and who - through following the "Stations of the Cross" - accompanies Me in My journey to the place of crucifixion. (T:960 #1)**

> **Let your compassion drive you to action. All your little sufferings can be united with My torments. They can be "offered" in reparation for your sins, for the good of My Holy Church, and to save souls from sin and damnation. (T:960 #2)**

> **Ponder the reality of the life of faith: that tremendously significant events in your spiritual life have taken place amidst dreary surroundings, with few or no witnesses, and with only faith leading you on. This was true of Me during My life on earth. (T:961 #1)**

> **Don't imagine that My earthly life was glamorous or easy. Think about the noise which you can hear nearby during the offering of My Holy Sacrifice: the noise, outside the church, of the local school-children playing. Their shouts and calls are like the everyday noise, bustle and shouting which I heard as I hung on the Cross in agony, dying, redeeming Mankind, whilst passers-by gossiped, and rushed about their business. (T:961 #2)**

I'd never been able to stand in a busy street or a market place, since that day, without remembering that our Redemption was won amidst similar crowds of hagglers - by Someone Who was dying in agony only a few yards from the indifferent pedestrians and shoppers.

13 A REVELATION

(1991-1993)

CHRIST'S PLANS. A BOOKLET. THE FATHER'S LOVE.

Preparing to meet the Father.

As I begin this paragraph, the date is August 6th 1998: the feast of the Transfiguration; and I've just been awed and consoled once again in prayer by the Glory which was poured within my soul today, in Holy Communion, and which is Heaven's daily gift to me, now that Christ has led me to the Father; and it has just occurred to me that I should give a brief summary of the ways in which Christ has taught me about Himself and about the life of grace, and then I can move forward to describe the stages of my journey to the Father.

It seems best to reproduce, in the paragraph below, the descriptions of prayer which God prompted me to record in 1993 and which I copied and sent to Father Edwards so that he'd have a better understanding of the 'Teachings' which he was checking from year to year. I'm reproducing the exact words I used because the whole piece reflects not only what I'd learned, but also what I still hadn't achieved at that time; I mean that I was still writing with some timidity. I'm not suggesting that we ought not to be humble and cautious if we're given extraordinary tasks by God; I'm noticing how obvious it is that I still lacked a happy and carefree confidence in His Love and in His loving purpose for my life. It was as though I was 'on the edge of my chair,' still anxious about my experiences, and still fearful that by the least carelessness I'd displease Him.

What I copied and sent to Father Edwards was this piece called "Extraordinary Prayer:"

"What follows is a brief explanation of the different ways by which (in my experience only) pure knowledge is imparted to the soul by God - in prayer. But first I must mention that many of God's dealings with the soul are so secret and marvellous that we see or understand very little of them. Also, His Holiness is so sublime, and so unimaginable and pure, that none of us can see Him in this life.

The best prayer - the most pure and holy praise of all - is that which He works within us, secretly, through the power of the Holy Spirit in our union with Christ. This secret, silent prayer of love takes place unseen in the soul which has been purified by God. He chooses when to unite the soul with Himself in this marvellous way: a way which is so pure and so secret that we cannot sense, see, hear, taste or touch anything! We do not know what is happening; God praises God in our soul whilst the mind, the imagination and the memory

311

circle - as it were - below. The will strains towards God with all its might, (but peacefully) and He, unseen, unknown, gives His gift of prayer-in-union as and when He wills.

So - all that is felt, sensed or seen in prayer is not a 'grasping' of God. He, in his tenderness, sometimes permits these 'touches' for His own purposes or for our sake. I have written much more fully on this subject elsewhere. But it seems to me that - admitting the superiority of unsensed, unknowing, pure prayer of union - the 'occurrences' which I have noticed in prayer are of a certain order of purity and grace.

In descending order, I would list these types of prayer in the following way:-

1. "Knowledge".

First and most holy, is the unexpected, pure, sudden, instantaneous and wordless KNOWLEDGE of God or of His attributes, given in prayer, usually after Holy Communion, though sometimes at other times during the Mass, and particularly at and after the Consecration. When God wills, He unites me entirely with Him by knowledge, with no consciousness on my part of thoughts or memory or will or imagination. He has utterly enfolded my soul to give me His pure gift. Just as suddenly, I am released (back) into ordinary prayer, and (if distracted) am aware of what I have just learned; I then try not to think about it but to continue in prayer, as before.

As I will tell, I wrote down nothing of this during the first few years but I found later that (if I chose) I could spend hours writing down all that I had learned in that brief instant of teaching. When Providence demands that I write on one subject or another, learned in this way (prayer, perhaps, or intercession, or Holy Mass) I find that I can write about Catholic doctrine and teachings at great length.

I have hardly dared to write this, but it is true - although how, God only knows! I might have read much in books, but I could not remember it all; or if I had - I would be unable to see the connections between one thing and another, or be unable to explain with such conviction and ease all that in truth, I do know, thanks to Him.

2. "Knowledge" with Translation.

Sometimes the wordless and pure, sudden, brief knowledge is almost simultaneously 'translated' (in the same state of body and soul) into an image in my soul. The image is not conjured up by me - in fact, I can do nothing but receive - (I do not know what I am doing). It is a pure gift - for me, and, perhaps, for others later on.

3. The Same - at length.

Sometimes these gifts of 'knowledge' and 'translation' are of greater length, continuing for five minutes or an hour, and might be received when I am not totally enfolded by God, but am still conscious of my body (although my heart leans towards God in prayer). I would ignore mere images, but when I am taught in this way, I can rest in God, wordlessly accepting what is silently being revealed, when it immediately is gone.

4. Prayer of Felt Union - with "Knowledge".

Sometimes, Christ's felt presence (after Communion) saturates my soul so entirely that it detaches me from all that my body would experience as I kneel or sit in prayer in the church. In this state I might receive knowledge with or without a "translation". He makes me completely absorbed in Him, or in the most Holy Trinity, but I never faint or fall or lose consciousness: any person could (can) attract my attention. It can last for up to thirty minutes, in this way. It is entirely His gift, 'unknown'.

5. Prayer in Union - but alert.

Sometimes in prayer outside the time of "Communion", Christ absorbs my soul in this way. I can still hear conversation around me but am undisturbed. I am free, too, to become less absorbed in Christ, in order to give the correct responses during Mass, since that is my solemn duty when I am at worship during the Holy Sacrifice.

6. "Knowledge" with Words.

Sometimes in prayer, when I am 'saturated' or 'absorbed' in Christ entirely, Christ speaks to me, within my soul. He speaks clearly but not 'out loud' - others cannot hear. The words have in no way been conjured up in my imagination. (I know that this is possible, but if it happens the words are very different). Christ's own words to me are always quite unexpectedly and quite suddenly heard in my soul with great clarity - and, usually, are brief; they always bring great joy, and explain much more to me than such simple phrases might ordinarily suggest. Hearing His words is like receiving pure knowledge, too. I immediately receive great knowledge, with the words - which I could write about at great length, even years later on.

7. "Knowledge" with a Given Image.

Sometimes in prayer, although aware of all around me, I see an image of great importance, with the eyes of my soul. This means that it has not come from my imagination; it is not like those images which we can move about at will - as when we select and alter visual memories in some though-processes or meditations. This image is seen within the soul clearly, unchosen, suddenly appearing, and still. It lasts for a longer time than the images of the "Knowledge-Translation", and knowledge accompanies it. I might think that it is a gift which can be contemplated later, or communicated to others for their encouragement in faith, but because my first duty is to pray, especially at Mass, and not to be distracted by any image, I turn away from it, if I can.

8. "Knowledge" with a Living Image.

Sometimes in prayer, Christ Himself has appeared to the eyes of my soul, alive and moving though dazzling in His glory; He wordlessly gives me knowledge, or encouragement. Sometimes, too, He is here with His Holy Mother; He is nearly always accompanied by angels, and sometimes by saints too. I am absorbed but not wholly enfolded and am free to turn away. If I turn away to think about His appearance, He leaves. If I turn away, however, to praise God in the Mass, or to do something kind for a neighbour at Mass, He remains there in my soul waiting for me to return.

9. The Same - at length.

Sometimes, whilst praying or working or reading at home, or elsewhere, I have become aware of the felt presence of the enfolding love of the most Holy Trinity or of our Lord Himself, or of the most Holy Spirit, or I have seen within my soul Christ or Our Lady or the Saints, wordlessly present (occasionally speaking) here in my soul in peace and glory. This is always sudden and unexpected; it usually brings knowledge too, and sometimes continues for minutes or hours. I am always, at these times, free to stop my work or my reading in order to pay attention, and to give myself up to love, in prayer. These are not mere images or distractions, but are - in some way - the persons to whom I usually pray - or so I conclude, when I am urged towards love and unselfishness.

10. The Same.

Occasionally, Christ teaches me more and more, entirely without words, whilst our thoughts move to one another in an exchange of pure love and knowledge. I am conscious but uplifted and am free to turn away, either (because I'm) distracted, or (because I'm) turning away to fulfil some duty as Christ looks on in love.

11. The Same.

Very rarely, in the state of prayer just described, have I been gently urged to ask questions, concerned for those I love; I have been led to hold up each dear one to Christ or to His Holy Mother, and have been answered with pure knowledge, spirit to spirit, and with gentle gestures. Sometimes Christ teaches me with words; He is present within my soul, sometimes seen and sometimes unseen.

12. Guardian Angel.

My angel walks with me and guards me. I do not see Him with my eyes, but sometimes glimpse 'him' with the eyes of my soul, or feel his presence. Sometimes, through Knowledge, I am made aware of his response to my prayers, requests or actions, and witness His gestures of reverence or of celebration! Sometimes, with my soul's eyes, I see many angels at Mass.

13. Our Lady.

Wherever Christ our Lord is, there too is His holy Mother even when I do not see her. This will be explained later, in the detailed writings.

14. "Knowledge" with my own image.

Sometimes when I have received knowledge about something without any 'translation', my mind has immediately provided an image, and I am aware that this image (alone) comes from my imagination. It is to be ignored, since worship is so important, but I am permitted to recall it later on, since Our Lord prompted my imagination to clothe - as it were - His knowledge, for my encouragement and the encouragement of others.

314

15. Memory.

In these writings, when I recall some great grace or moment or action or decision, I have noted '(M)' for memory - meaning that the picture painted of that occasion is of what I recall with my memory of everyday life at the time.

'(U)' denotes understanding; that is: not a mere insight into something from thought or meditation, but a sudden gift of understanding, similar to knowledge, though not as extraordinary in its intensity or purity. It is more like a sunrise in the soul, with regard to something told, than like the narrow, blinding, piercing beam of pure Knowledge to the soul, unknown, in prayer. However, it is a gift. It is quite different from the experience of light 'dawning' in one's intellect, in thought.

16. Scripture.

'(S)' denotes the words of Holy Scripture used by God our Father or by Christ Himself to teach me something in particular about God, or about my soul, or to instruct, command, rebuke or encourage me - all this with great impact and immediacy, quite unlike hearing other parts of Scripture read aloud. These phrases are directed to me with clarity and power, and I understand far more than the simple words suggest, but not by thought or by imagination, but by grace.

I must add that all the numbers given above (1-16) are given only to help the reader to follow my thoughts during these few pages.

The different types and stages of prayer are described more fully in a separate work, and there (in "Prayer-in-Union" which includes the aptly-named "Categories") I have listed these stages and have labelled and numbered them more succinctly."

Words from the Father.

I suppose it was in 1991 that I began to walk along the final stretch of my journey to meet the Father; and every year since then has been outwardly busy but has brought increasing joy and peace to my soul. It's with amazement and gratitude that I now look back, and see how thoroughly Christ had prepared me to receive - from His Infinite goodness - occasional brief teachings from the Father.

It was on July 27th in 1991 that Christ reminded me, of Himself, (in T:963) that "THE FATHER AND I ARE ONE" (Jn 10:30). At the same time Christ taught me how to rest 'in Christ,' by the Spirit's power, in the Father's presence, in prayer; and He assured me that by such a prayerful repose in the height of contemplation I am brought as close to the Father as it is possible to be, in earthly life. This reminder of the Oneness of the Godhead - the Trinity in Unity - was Christ's way of holding me firm in that belief just as I was about to receive far more frequent teachings in prayer specifically from the Father's 'heart' rather than from Christ's own lips.

A new 'stance' in prayer.

It was in August 1991 (see T:971) that we were all reminded at church, in the Holy Scriptures, that: "YOUR SONS WILL ALL BE TAUGHT BY YAHWEH" (Is 54:13); and Christ urged me, in the same month (in T:975) to be like a true child with Him, in simplicity and trust, as I prayed and received teachings in prayer almost daily. Furthermore, I was shown (in T:977) how to stand before the Father in unutterable peace, and how to pray Christ's prayer of trust, sacrifice and obedience. Then, two days later, on August 19th, Christ spoke to me as I began my daily intercessions (T:978). He urged me: "*Ask the Father.*"

Christ was leading me to adopt a new 'stance' in prayer: urging me to look 'past' Him to the Invisible Father. Christ wanted me to be perpetually aware, first, that it is only through Him, my Saviour, that I have been brought to a wonderful state of friendship with God in prayer and conversation. He wanted me never to forget that it was by His Passion that my spiritual journey towards Heaven was taking place; but, secondly, He wanted me to go through Him, with Him and "in" Him to the heart of the Godhead both in daily prayer and in everyday life: to dwell in the heart of the Holy Trinity at every moment.

This doesn't mean that Christ didn't want to see me pray to Himself any more. He was encouraging me, rather, to live out fully, in prayer, our belief in the Holy Trinity, a belief by this time regularly confirmed for me as I prayed, though confirmed only by spiritual means, and still through faith. Christ was training and teaching me how to co-operate very gracefully and yet intelligently with the promptings in prayer of His Holy Spirit, so that it would be as if I were always standing at the 'centre' of Divine Life.

Prayer from within God's 'heart'.

Some time later on, Christ explained this more fully by showing me (in T:2513B), that when we look at God as if from 'outside' we are like persons who gaze at a circle as if from far away; we see 'only' a unity. Then He explained that if we pray to God by praying wholly "in" Him - which means praying to the Father, but praying while dwelling wholly at the heart of Divine Life through Christ, and in the Holy Spirit's power - it is as though we stand to pray at the centre of a circle; and we cannot therefore 'see' the whole of the circle, but rather whatever is "in front" of us. When we pray to God from within God's heart, therefore, we don't usually describe our prayer as a meeting or conversation simply with 'God'; rather, we identify which of the Three Divine Persons is communicating with us at a particular moment.

I didn't understand all that at the time. I mean that I had no idea that one could 'meet' the Father in this life in the way which was going to be revealed to me later on. But I was content to follow Christ in prayer as usual, knowing that nothing that I was learning was against Catholic teaching; and I continued to send all my writings for unofficial approval, year by year, to the same Jesuit Father. By his kind response to my first set of writings, with his assurance that, in his opinion, God had 'intervened,' and that my work was orthodox and ought to be published, he had made me very happy; and the knowledge of his kindness helped to lessen my nervousness whenever I took another package of writings to the post-office, to send them off to him for checking.

The nervousness I mention was due to the realisation, when I'd stood with my hand up to the letterbox with one of the earlier packages, that there was no turning back. My life could never remain the same, once I'd consented to let some of my work and therefore my life be weighed and examined outside the small circle which is our family circle and our parish. I once experienced a few moments of sheer terror, before making yet another act of trust in God and in His Will for my life; then I posted the parcel and continued with my shopping.

A little 'death'.

In one way or another, Christ rewarded me for every act of trust; and more and more, I was able to feel confident of Christ's love for me. I showed Him every thought of my mind and every movement of my heart. That's why, on 16th September in 1991, when I was trying not to slacken in fervour, and was longing to do Christ's Holy Will in everything, I went to Holy Mass; and as the Word said in Scripture: "WE CARRY WITH US IN OUR BODY THE DEATH OF JESUS" (2 Co 4:10), I showed Christ a little death which, by His grace, I had freely accepted for love of Him. I offered it in union with His Holy Sacrifice; and at the very moment that I showed Christ the struggle, and the 'wound', I suddenly heard within my soul:-

> **Never regret the struggle and pain of your self-offering to Me, as you try to obey Me by accepting each little death to self, and as you unite your offering to My Sacrifice of the altar.** *"This is the highest kind of love."* **(T:994A #1)**

My heart ached at receiving such consolation; but Christ continued to teach me. He told me:-

> **Rejoice, amidst your trials.** *Take comfort from My showing you that this type of love - of honouring, by sacrifice, My known Will, in love and obedience - most resembles My love for mankind. (T:994A #2)*

As I began to think about how the sacrifices I'd made had been outweighed by my many failings, Christ told me:-

> **Consider the simple reason why one as weak and sinful as yourself should have been led to such a loving union with Me:** *"it was through your surrender!"* **When you willingly agreed to make a great sacrifice, solely in order to please Me,** *such an utter gift of your will to Me - inspired by My Spirit - was the channel by which I was 'enabled' to pour My grace upon and through you. Such is My goodness and generosity. (T:994A #3)*

A warning about complacency.

On another day at Holy Mass, when I showed Christ - with ever more honesty - every one of my heart's secrets and all my true thoughts, He rewarded me again with Unknowing Union. He showed me a little later:-

> Be glad that you can follow in My footsteps. Through sacrifice, you imitate Me. I did My work alone, in pain, and lonely, but determined above all to carry on in obedience to the Father and to be faithful to the end. (T:999 #2)

Then one day, at Holy Mass, I heard the words from the book of Job, in Holy Scripture: "I HAVE BEEN HOLDING FORTH ON MATTERS I CANNOT UNDERSTAND, ON MARVELS BEYOND ME AND MY KNOWLEDGE" (Jb 42:3) ..... "AND IN DUST AND ASHES I REPENT" (Jb 42:6). I was awe-struck, once more, thinking about God's goodness and my failings.

Then when I reflected that these words were as true now as in 1964, Christ comforted me, and accepted all the hopes and prayers and people that I entrusted to Him. He led me deeper into humility, and taught me:-

> Never forget the time when you were almost entirely ignorant of My Church and of My real wishes. It is I Who have brought you to your present joy and security; you are entirely dependent on My Love and on My graces, and so you ought never to grow complacent. (T:997)

But since He always wants to see me cheerful and grateful, He told me:-

> Rejoice in your union with Me, as I lift you up towards Heaven and 'towards' the Father. *With what* an intimate and *true union you can present My Sacrifice to the Father, the more you resemble Me in the wounds and sacrifices of love.* (T:1000 #1)

Words from the Father.

At the end of September 1991 (in T:1003) the Father taught me with startling clarity about the essence of the self-offering which He invites us all to make; and He did so by holding up Christ's Passion before me, as a teacher holds up a story-book before a child, to illustrate an important message. Through showing me Christ's wounds, the Father showed me the meaning of discipleship; and this happened on a day when I was in danger of becoming despondent, and was struggling just to 'keep going.'

This happened on 28th September, when I'd been to Mass in the morning, and was still battling with temptations from within and without. I was strengthened and comforted by some words from Holy Scripture: "I WILL BE A WALL OF FIRE FOR HER ALL ROUND HER, AND I WILL BE HER GLORY IN THE MIDST OF HER" (Zc 2:9). Then I found myself struggling again during the evening Mass.

As I prayed to the Father about my weakness and sinfulness, I said to Him:- "Abba - I offer You Christ our sacrifice, our reparation". Then I was suddenly shown a vivid image in prayer;

it was the sight of Christ at the time of His scourging; and at the same time Christ Himself taught me:-

> **Understand the worth of My suffering and sacrifice, through which reparation was made for the sins of mankind; but don't imagine that My torments were - in themselves - somehow satisfying for the Father to behold. Listen to the Father, as He assures you:**
>
> *It is Love that counts."*
>
> *My supreme and utter sacrifice of Myself, in Love, is what redeemed you.* **It was because of Love that I came to earth to save you. It was because of Love that, during My life on earth, I willingly travelled wherever the Father led Me, in order to speak Truth, even accepting mockery, arrest, and trial, rather than be disobedient. I even bared My back for the scourging, before going on to be crucified. (T:1003 #1)**
>
> **Consider how horribly I suffered, during the scourging. Listen to the Father speaking, as He shows - by an image - the terrible wounds which were inflicted upon Me:**
>
> *"It was sin did this."*
>
> **Understand, therefore, that your Heavenly Father does not devise tortures for His beloved people, although He inspires brave and loving people to make sacrifices on behalf of others. So you can profess that** *God Willed the Sacrifice, yet men caused My Blood to flow.* **(WC+ OIL: 1003)   (T:1003 #2)**

"God Willed the Sacrifice".

Here, I was astonished at the richness of the teaching: and also at the fact that, as well as Christ, the Father had spoken to me yet again; and as I was shown the image of Christ's naked and wounded back, and saw it bleeding from the scourging, I understood more deeply than ever that sinful people like ourselves were the cause of Christ's pain.

This is such a great Mystery that I hardly dare to write anything else; yet: truly, Christ showed me:-

> **Believe in the Father's Wisdom. The Sacrifice which was offered by Me, His Divine Son, on behalf of mankind, is a great Mystery; yet you can be sure that the** *Father's Will "encompasses" all that He permits* **to happen** *on this earth, or has ever permitted.* **The Father - the Righteous One - is not pleased by wounds and pain and suffering, although, in**

the mysterious and holy Sacrifice which was My Passion and Death, they were "necessary". Yet the Father permits them, and He delights in the love and obedience and thanksgiving which have been offered by Myself and by My Saints, even amidst our torments. (T:1003 #3)

Look upon the subject of My holy Passion as something sacred. You have read in Holy Scripture that no-one unworthy ought to venture onto especially holy places; so, My sufferings can be seen as *holy ground* on which only a prayerful friend of Mine might venture. My Passion is so holy and awesome that no-one ought to speak of it lightly, cynically or carelessly. (T:1003 #4)

Encourage others to look upon My Passion with reverence, since there - you can tell them - *"God was suffering for sinful men";* and all who turn towards Me ought to 'look' upon My suffering and repent of their sins, or keep silent. (T:1003 #5)

An uplifting reminder.

How grateful I was, to have been led to a deeper understanding of Christ's Passion; and how kind is Christ. Every such 'teaching' which might have unnerved me or made me sombre has been 'balanced', it seems, by something very uplifting. Christ told me one day, soon afterwards, for example:-

Believe in My Love for you. *"I love you all the time!"* I'm glad that you have learned to confide in Me; your trust is well-founded, since I never change. I Who loved you many years ago - as you well know - love you just as much today; and you are right to trust in Me and in My Almighty power. (T:1016 #1)

Persevere, quietly, with the task which I have entrusted to you, and remain unconcerned about the outcome. Everything which frightens you can be overcome or endured by My enduring grace. (T:1016 #2)

Infallible prayer.

Within a short time - on All Soul's Day, November 2nd, 1991 - as I rested peacefully in prayer, in Christ's own praise, in Holy Communion, I offered to the Father Christ's own perpetual praise, and trusted in Christ's merits; and then I was suddenly reminded of why I can be so confident in prayer. Christ told me:-

Aim to live in unceasing union with Me, so that My prayer

and yours will be 'One Prayer' to the Father. (T:1020 #1)

Offer My Holy Sacrifice of the Mass as the most powerful prayer for every good intention. There, at the altar, I offer My Divine Praise, My infinite thanks, My perfect reparation and My perfect pleas. (T:1020 #3)

Understand something about the perfection of your worship, during the Holy Mysteries; that perfection is due entirely to Myself, Jesus Christ your God and Saviour, Who am Really Present before you. (T:1020 #4)

Proclaim, joyfully, that which the Father is teaching you about My holy Sacrifice of Cross and altar:

> *"Jesus' prayer is the best prayer.*
> *Jesus' prayer is infallible.*
> *His praise is perfect,*
> *His reparation is infinite,*
> *His thanksgiving cannot be surpassed,*
> *His pleas cannot be refused." (T:1020 #5)*

Remember that during the offering of the Holy Sacrifice I ask the Father - on behalf of you My brothers and sisters - for many gifts, all of which are granted. So the best and most effective prayer for an earthly friend is for My Holy Sacrifice to be offered for that person's intentions; and the best and most powerful prayer for a departed soul - 'best' because it is prayed by Myself - is My Holy Sacrifice, offered as a plea for pardon and Salvation. (T:1020 #7)

The 'Source' of Divine Love.

It was wonderful for me to see, day by day, that Christ was as keen to comfort my heart with tenderness as to feed my mind with Truth.

One day in Communion, wordlessly, He explained that I must never think that He doesn't love me. It may be that His presence seems obscured sometimes by the noises and distractions which arise from work or ill-health, or from times of turmoil. Yet: here He is - Who loves me in all circumstances.

Christ spoke to me on the Vigil of the Feast of Christ the King, at Holy Mass. I had been truly Reconciled, in preparation for the Sacrament of the Sick; and in the midst of my trials and heart-ache I found that Christ came to me in Holy Communion and showed me:-

Entrust your whole life to Me, and make especial efforts to be trusting in Holy Communion. *"Now that I am here, is there anything to worry about?!"* **There is no situation on**

earth where I am not ultimately "in control", even though I
have granted you free-will. There is no-one - whose welfare
concerns you - who is not known by Me. There is no-one
on earth whose opinion should cause you to fear, when you
are trying to do My Holy Will from moment to moment,
obedient to My Holy Church. It is My opinion which
'counts'! (T:1028 #1)

Let Me guide and reassure you. *In longing for, and loving
wholeheartedly, My Divine Will, you are most surely open to
the action of My grace and are most surely led along the path
to Life.* (T:1028 #2)

I knew by then that the "WAY OF LIFE" (Ac 2:28) was the path to the Father which was
unrolling before me.

Three Persons, teaching.

Towards the end of 1991 it was beginning to seem almost 'normal' that I was taught in prayer
- albeit very briefly - by the Father as well as by the 'Son', my Saviour.

The Father spoke to me briefly, again, on 26th November (in T:1030) when I showed Him
how sorry I was for my failings; but this time He spoke my name, saying *"Elizabeth ..."*. He
reassured me that I live in His Love, and explained that my sins had vanished from His sight. I
was astounded by His tenderness; and also puzzled. Although in the same month (in T:1034)
Christ Himself still taught me about a great number of topics from week to week, it was the
Father Who spoke to me in answer to one of my questions about prayer; and each time He
spoke I was nearly struck dumb with awe and gratitude, and with a sort of aching
compunction because He is so pure and holy, and because He was kind enough to speak to
someone like me.

Of course, when I say that He 'spoke' to me, I don't meant that I heard a human voice, but
that He gave me spiritual 'Knowledge' as ever, but sometimes in the form of 'Knowledge-
given-as-implanted-soundless-words, in short statements which pierced my soul by their purity
and charity.

But as I said, I almost grew used to His teachings in the sense that they became more and
more 'inter-woven' with Christ's own teachings, and then - more and more evidently - with
the clear illuminations and instructions of the Holy Spirit. In this way, the Three Divine
Persons were leading me into an extraordinary way of prayer and life which has both
developed and continued right until now. But at the end of 1991 I still hadn't 'met' the Father
in the way that I'll try to describe after this necessary preamble. I still had much to learn; and
Christ continued with His preparations. He inspired me, daily, to new efforts to conquer my
faults and to grow in humility and charity; and for every effort, He rewarded me. The more I
trusted in His Mercy and love, the greater were His exclamations of delight in my 'progress';
and then He began to reward me by revealing His Glory to me in Holy Communion: not once,
but (as in T:1037) at frequent intervals: whenever I had made special efforts or sacrifices for

His sake; and every moment of bliss encouraged me to turn more swiftly to Christ in every difficulty.

A secret 'alchemy'.

One night, for example, when I was a bit despondent, I turned to Christ in prayer; I was suddenly urged by Him:-

> **Show your wounded heart to Me. I, too, suffered on earth; and in wounded hearts** *I work a secret "alchemy" of Divine Love.* **Whenever - prompted by Myself - you turn to Me** and *you offer freely the pain and hurt of a heart which has been wounded for love* **of Me,** *then this accepted pain is the cause of the 'wound'* **which is therefore made within your soul, a wound** *through which the 'gold of grace' is poured out for others!* **(T:1042 #1)**

In order to encourage Hope, I was shown something wonderful a few weeks later, at Holy Mass; it was after the Consecration, and as the Precious Blood of Christ was held up for our veneration. Christ told me:-

> **Persevere in reverent prayer, during the Holy Sacrifice of the Mass.**
>
> *My plea to the Father, now,*
> *in My One Sacrifice of the Cross,*
> *which is made present here before you today,*
> *sustains My Holy Church in this generation,*
> *draws grace upon those who love Me, and*
> *changes the hearts of sinners.* **(T:1064 #1)**
>
> **Approach the sanctuary with awe and wonder. Revere the holy altar where My holy Sacrifice is offered, and adore Me - your Saviour. I gave My life for you.** *I sacrificed Myself for you, from Love.* **(T:1064 #2)**

With such encouragement as this, I grew more confident about trusting the Lord Who so frequently showed me His wishes.

The 'fruit' of penance and sacrifice.

In March, 1992, Christ began to reveal my task more clearly than ever before, through a further series of 'teachings'. It was partly because I'd boldly shown Him, one evening, the true yearning of my heart: that even someone like myself longs to give Him glory and to make Him known and loved, and longs to see His Holy Mother and St. Joseph honoured and loved even more than at present.

323

I'd been wondering if my small "way of the cross" were to continue in much the same way; and as I asked Christ to help me whatever might happen next, I was suddenly taught a great deal, as Christ told me:-

> Co-operate with My Will; your soul is like a seed which, planted 'underground' in a darkness and loneliness which is permitted by Myself, is softening, changing, growing and 'splitting', as a preparation for growth and harvest; and through enduring this time of darkness you can learn patience and obedience. (T:1074 #2)

> Remember the purpose of your soul's purification, which is to make your soul fruitful. Your soul is like a plant from which a shoot has been emerging - and now many shoots appear; the whole 'plant' continues to burst upwards with life, until the branches fall sideways, bent under the weight of the abundance of 'fruit'. Thus, by the "fruit" which is My work within your life, I am proving that your loving sacrifices have been worthwhile. (T:1074 #3)

> Have faith that even now I am drawing up the great results which spring from the love which you have shown for Me during your penances and sufferings. Your renewed and vigorous spiritual life is like a burst of Light, like the light which springs from an indoor firework which - when lit - produces much light and growth. From so small a device, extraordinary results are brought about during its own destruction; and that "destruction" is like your self-immolation through penance and sacrifice. (T:1074 #4)

> Consider how - in the natural world - a burst of lava flows from a volcanic mountain after many years of only tiny subterranean movements; the steady flow of fiery light is the product of many earlier and unnoticed 'fires'. So it is with the faithful soul; tremendous results or 'movements' take place because of earlier penances and purifications. (T:1074 #5)

> Consider your own life, into which I am lavishly pouring My Light and My instructions, during prayer. The purifications and sufferings which you have patiently accepted are now leading to fruition. By My Will, *that 'dying' of those silent years now produces this "fruit"*: My "teachings". (T:1074 #6)

A white booklet.

Very soon after Christ had given me that teaching about the 'fruit' of the past few years, He

324

showed me precisely how I could share it with other people. One day while I was resting at home, I was shown in astonishing simplicity what to do with my writings in order to fulfil Christ's Will for me.

In an instant, I was shown that the 'teachings' could be printed and then given out to friends, who in their turn would pass them on to be read by others; thus, the 'teachings' would be spread around in much the same way as the 'Mass paintings'.

Furthermore, Christ gave me very specific instructions, in a moment of prayer. He asked me to circulate, privately, a small, plain white booklet which should contain a selection of the major teachings, in a slightly simplified form. At that stage, it was to have no illustrations. They would appear in a book, later on. But it ought to have a few introductory words about faith in Christ and trust in His Church - written by myself or by someone else. I was made to understand that illustrations shouldn't yet be placed within the text. It would have proved too complicated at that stage to try to select and print them.

Because I was nervous about relying on my own judgement in such matters, I sought advice before circulating my teachings, although, privately, I immediately began to re-arrange and prepare the writings according to Our Lord's wishes. I bore in mind the words of Holy Scripture: "FOLLOW RIGHT TO THE END OF THE WAY THAT I MARK OUT FOR YOU ... THEY HAVE NOT PAID ATTENTION; THEY HAVE GROWN STUBBORN AND BEHAVED WORSE THAN THEIR ANCESTORS", and, in another place: "COME IN: LET US BOW, PROSTRATE OURSELVES, AND KNEEL IN FRONT OF YAHWEH OUR MAKER" (Ps 95:6).

Then Christ revealed to me that many souls in the Church today are in danger. He urged me to keep working to save souls, telling me:-

> **Speak to other people about friendship with Me. (T:1087A #7)**

> **Follow My instructions faithfully. Your primary task is to encourage people of your own country to be true to the Catholic Faith, first planted here many centuries ago. Many members of My Church in England are unfaithful to the Faith which they have received from their martyred ancestors, and are blithely endangering their souls. (T:1087A #10)**

> **Encourage fellow-Christians in prayer; invite them to adore Me, and to pray with the profound reverence which you all owe Me. (T:1087A #11)**

"An Introduction".

A kind friend offered to type my brief summary of the 'teachings'; and when her work was finished and when that first edition of the booklet had been printed, I began to distribute copies to any friend or acquaintance who expressed an interest. Each copy of "Teachings-in-prayer: an introduction" was prefaced by a few pages about conversion and about prayer in daily life.

Christ had explained that although I shrank from publicity I ought to put my name to the book, since I am a witness to His Love; and my future work would consist above all in speaking about what I have seen and learned in prayer. Then He urged me to go back to my priest, once again, to explain about the little book, since it might cause 'ripples' in the Church; and although there was no strict need for me to seek approval from the authorities about communicating privately with friends and acquaintances, courtesy demanded that I mention this new project: a project planned by Christ, to encourage His People to be faithful to prayer, and to Him.

As I had to explain to different people, later on, the 'teachings-in-prayer' can be seen as containing something for everyone, even though they're very personal.

The general advice about prayer is for everyone, that is, the advice about repentance, reverence, and putting God first, and about making time for prayer - and remaining faithful.

The instructions about the Church are for everyone, since Christ's wish is that everyone hears His Good News about the forgiveness of sins, and that they freely come into the Church - into the Catholic Church, with its Sacred Tradition, and the Holy Scriptures, and the lavish gifts in the Sacraments, and also the guidance of the Holy Father and of the other Bishops, and many more good things.

Quite a number of the 'instructions' were just for me, at first, since they are about my job of writing, and sharing the teachings. But they are for other people indirectly. Christ wants people to know that - even if we feel a bit cowardly - it's always best to trust in Him and do what He wants. We don't usually see where we're 'going', but it's important to try to follow His plans and not our own; and He can help everyone to do this, just as He has helped someone as tired and timorous as myself to undertake this peculiar task.

A 'normal' life.

In case it seems that there was nothing happening in my life except frequent prayer-times, I must say that very little of what I describe about the visions and teachings was evident to anyone else, as I carried on with my usual cooking and shopping. Conversations and hospital visits were mixed in with the writing and painting, and all the normal things of domestic life, with minor crises and all sorts of delights; and some of those delights were wholly unexpected. It seems to me now that, in the early 1990s, the changes in both domestic life and in prayer heralded a period of fruition - although I didn't know it then. I'm astonished to realise just how many good things arrived all at once.

As Christ continued to teach me at Mass every day or two, He kept introducing wholly unexpected joys and challenges into my life. For example, it was when I'd spent a few weeks at the beginning of 1992 writing the first draft of this 'Prologue', in order to be obedient to Christ, that my elder son suddenly announced that he thought he was being called to be a Catholic priest. I could hardly contain my joy at the knowledge that he was even considering that vocation. Then, at the beginning of April of the same year, twenty of my "Mass Paintings" were exhibited - though not for sale, of course - in a side chapel in Westminster Cathedral, in Holy Week, to encourage people in their meditations. Then when I was at home one evening, enjoying a bit of peace, and praying as well, I was astonished to be shown by Christ that no part of my life must be seen as wasted. He assured me that even the 'difficult' years had been worthwhile, and He showed me, in an instant, the quiet gathering-together which was now taking place of all the strands of my life. He explained to me:-

> **Never look upon any part of your past life as 'wasted'. You have been following a lengthy path, coming upwards towards Me - as if in a spiral. But the progress is constantly 'upwards'. (WC:1079B) (T:1079B #1)**

> **Recall the path along which I have led you, through all events, circumstances, triumphs and set-backs. I was never absent, but was always present, in bad times as much as in good. (T:1079B #2)**

> **Notice how everything which has happened in your life - and this includes the apparently unimportant or puzzling things as well as the good - has contributed to shaping and fitting you for the task which I now wish you to do. Even recent restrictions and renunciations are helping you to concentrate on your work and on My Will! (T:1079B #3)**

> **Be sure that just as I have led you throughout your past life, I can and will lead you through the rest of your life. (T:1079B #4)**

> **Remember the trials and failures from which I have delivered you. All that you have undergone in past years has prepared you for your present efforts to fulfil My Will for you. You have seen for yourself that I have drawn good out of every evil, since I cannot be 'defeated'. (T:1079B #5)**

At the same time, Christ urged me:-

> **Don't keep your joy and gratitude to yourself. My gifts are to be shared. Share My teachings with friends and family. As your courage grows, you can say to others - through the written word and through conversation: 'I have seen the Lord,' and then: 'Repent, and believe the Gospel!' (T:1079B #6)**

> **Don't be afraid. You can tell that My grace is definitely at work in you when you continue in very quiet but steady work for Me, despite many difficulties. (T:1080 #1)**

> **Be grateful for the "hiddenness" in which you work. You**

are safer in ignorance of all the things which - by My grace - are being done through you and your work than if you were aware of what is really happening. Your present solitude leaves you less exposed to temptations to pride. (T:1080 #2)

Be glad to accept insults for the sake of My Gospel. (T:1080 #3)

Comfort yourself, if anyone thinks you misguided or mad, by remembering that *"that is what they said about Me!"* (T:1080 #4)

The distribution of booklets.

Whenever I was out and about in the village, and whenever it seemed appropriate, I continued to speak to one person or another about prayer, and God, and offered a free booklet. As I mentioned earlier, my parish priest had managed to find a Jesuit priest who was willing to examine my work, in order to reassure him about its orthodoxy. After a year-long wait, we had been reassured about the 'teachings'; and that's why I had no qualms about offering newly-printed booklets not only to relations and to distant friends but also to my fellow-parishioners.

Some people were interested. Others made no comment; and some never spoke to me again, though whether from fear, awe or embarrassment Our Lord didn't at that time allow me to know. I didn't ask for comments; I just did what I thought I ought to do, sometimes feeling a fool but knowing that that wasn't important. I 'offered up' every humiliating encounter. I knew that if God had given me a special task to do, He would grant my prayers; He would give me the grace to persevere, and to fulfil His Will for my life.

There was no special feeling in my heart or mind that I was busy with a privileged task. This book-sharing was one more job on my list of jobs to do, in the sense that I did it as well as I could, and then carried on with something more urgent. I didn't have much time to reflect upon it, because of my normal chores; and besides, Christ had shown me very little about its full significance - and for very good reasons, which He explained later on. He told me, three or four years later, that the lengthy period of time He'd allowed to pass by as I initiated conversations about the books, and had several more books printed, was so that I'd be able to shed my crippling self-consciousness, so that I'd have further time to grow in humility, and so that there would be an astonishing amount of work ready and available later on, and all at once, for the "great outpouring" which He was arranging should take place at exactly the right time.

Later that month, I gave my first-ever talk on prayer, to a local group. I spoke for far too long, because I was so nervous; but it was wonderful to be able to encourage a few more people in things I know to be important.

Then, just as I was painfully accepting what seemed like a 'deafening silence' from many of those who had accepted booklets from me about Christ's teachings, I was very much comforted (in T:1128) by another extraordinary visit from Our Lady: not a little glimpse of her, with a little teaching, as has occurred in prayer from time to time, but another special visit; and it wasn't even in England, but in Spain, when I was on holiday with my husband, on a pilgrimage to the shrine of St. James, in Santiago de Compostella. It was on 26th May 1992 that Our Lady astonished me by her tenderness, by her patient listening, by her holy courtesy, and by the way in which she encouraged me to keep silent about difficulties, and to keep on being willing to suffer and to pray so that God's Will would be accomplished. Yet I shouldn't have been surprised, since she's just like her son - always gentle and loving.

In August of that year, when I'd spent a lot of time putting together another collection of teachings and paintings to show to our priest, as well as doing the usual work, I was praying fervent prayers at the Requiem Mass of a parishioner, although I was tired. But Christ said to me, in Holy Communion: *"Thankyou for all you do for Me, Lizzie!"* and I felt so ashamed, once again, that Our Saviour is so grateful and courteous, when I've been so reluctant to do difficult things for Him (T:1172).

Yearning to serve Christ.

It seems strange and wonderful to me, now that I can see how everything has happened for my benefit and for the progress of this work at what has been obviously 'the right time'. In September 1992 I had just celebrated my fiftieth birthday. My youngest child was about to go away to University. Life was hectic but fulfilling - even though the whole matter of my 'being taught' was beginning to change my life and the life of the family not only inwardly but also outwardly, as more than one room became submerged beneath piles of papers, box-files and prayer-paintings. And it was at that most-perfect-possible moment that Christ began to show me in greater depth the meaning of life-in-God, and therefore made me yearn with all my heart to live to serve Him. I yearned to be able see Him and to be with Him forever. The desire began to consume me. This was the approximate time at which I began to approach prayer-times not with a dry sort of hope but with joy and yearning: not just with the knowledge that by sincere prayer I would please the Holy Trinity, but with a longing to be drawn yet again and again into the 'heart' of God.

That's one of the reasons why, later on, when the church was re-opened for about ten hours each day, I began to go to church for a short while every afternoon, when possible, as well as to Mass in the mornings. I was praying all day, of course, in one way or another; but the extra commitment brought extra inner strength and joy, and also - Christ taught me - greater help to others: and all the time, in the nineteen-nineties, in order to please Christ, and to do my plain duty, I've been switching my mind from Christ's Glory, to a new recipe for chicken, and back to His teachings - and then to the time of a dental appointment, as I've learned to 'mesh' gracefully together every aspect of my life and every hope of my soul.

Yearning to give Christ glory.

It was in the autumn of that very busy and joyful year that Christ steered, or rather, 'drew' me in prayer through two further purifications, as an immediate preparation for a way of life at the heart of the Holy Trinity.

On the second of September 1992, we heard at Mass, in Holy Scripture: "HAPPY THE NATION WHOSE GOD IS YAHWEH, THE PEOPLE HE HAS CHOSEN" (Ps 33:12). I was so grateful for this reminder of my current state of joy, that I greeted Christ fervently in Holy Communion, repentant of every distraction and weakness. But He led me into what had now become my one perpetual prayer: a plea to be able to glorify the Father and Christ His Son, with a plea for sanctity: and then a plea for conversions, so that others - with myself, I hope - will be brought to the Heavenly Kingdom. I also prayed that Christ's Holy Mother will be venerated, and Glory given to the Most Holy Spirit Whose power is at work as our hearts are changed and sanctified; and it was because of these fervent desires and because the best moment had arrived for Christ's purpose, that Christ came to my soul in Holy Communion on the following day, approaching me almost as 'Fire': as my Lord and God, in the purity and power of His Divinity (T:1178)

A strange feeling of dread overcame me, as I considered my sinfulness and my many failings. I was suddenly made aware, by the goodness of God, that I was about to step up to a new stage in the spiritual life; yet it was made plain - all at once - that this stage would not be achieved without my free consent.

A living flame of Christ's Love.

The nature of the change wasn't shown to me. All in a split second I was being invited by God to consent yet again to His plan for my life and for my soul; and that consent had to be given in naked faith.

Always, it seems, this is God's way with the soul who trusts in Him and whom He encourages to trust in Him even more. He asks for a further demonstration of trust - and then magnificently rewards the soul for that trust; and the soul, having made such an act, has of course advanced closer to God's heart and has become stronger; and that's what happened in 1992 , when I gave my silent consent to His Will, but when I also whispered to Christ - Who is always so just and kind - "Lord, have pity!"

Even as I spoke, I 'saw' that Christ was 'enveloping' me in His fiery Glory. I can describe this in no other way; and in that extraordinary meeting, He changed me, and also showed me that what Holy Scripture describes is true of His nature and of His work, that: " ... OUR GOD IS A CONSUMING FIRE" (Hb 12:29); and at the same time He explained to me:-

> **Have courage, and respond to My Will for you as I reveal your true vocation. Surrender to Me, Jesus, as I prepare you for your task. See how, enveloping you wholly, *I approach your soul, almost as Fire*, as *I make you a living flame of My Love*, a 'flame' which is *now reaching up in praise, perpetually consuming within itself all that is unworthy, on fire as a lamp before the Father and a Light for others.* (T:1178 #2)**
>
> **Offer perpetual praise to the Father, and help others, by My grace and power. *That is the life which you may now lead, if you are 'fire' from My Fire*, and if you are *burning***

in adoration at every moment. (T:1178 #3)

Ponder the marvel of real union with Me. *By the soul's existence in this holy state it gives Glory to Me at every moment -* **even in a silent, steady and simple routine in which nothing momentous is done, and which appears to be insignificant.** (T:1178 #4)

Don't be perturbed by fading health, diminishing strength, or general physical decline. *The interior of the soul* **which belongs wholly to Me** *is wholly flame, burning upwards, full of life and movement,* **even though the frail body which 'surrounds' the soul should weaken.** (WC:1178) (T:1178 #5)

Be ready to 'fade away' into My silent embrace, as all earthly and bodily things are abandoned. (T:1178 #6)

With the Mind of Christ.

In some way that I didn't understand, Christ had changed my soul, which was now burning with praise for Him. Then, soon afterwards, Christ opened my eyes to some of the effects of our union and His graces.

One week-day in September, I paid a visit to the shrine of Saint Alban, to ask for his prayers; and Christ comforted me through His teachings about the Angels who guard the shrine (T:1186 #2) and then about the way in which His close friends gaze upon ancient sites - or new projects. Then when I'd finished my visit, and was outside the church, walking towards my car, I thought about the sad history of Saint Alban's Abbey, about the shortness of life, and about my own brief residence in this area and this era; then Christ suddenly recommenced His teaching.

He reassured me, with astonishing clarity, that my way of surveying and 'weighing' various persons and institutions conforms very closely to His own. Christ reassured me about the close degree of union with Him which I now enjoyed, telling me:-

Notice how much more surely and steadily you are being led to look upon everything with My Mind! I give this gift to those who live in a true union with Me. Everything upon which you gaze, whether persons, communities, histories and traditions, problems, tasks, trials and joys, and places and claims and duties, can be seen as with My Mind. Furthermore, not only can they be seen; they can be probed, weighed and 'touched' as if with My understanding gaze. It is as though I am looking 'through' you, with My loving concern and My truthful analysis; and all this is for the cause of truth, and for a true understanding of the meaning of life on earth; it is

therefore also for the good of souls and for the Glory of the
Father. (T:1186 #4)

eceived as an embrace.

It seemed such a pity I hadn't always seen things as Christ sees them; but Christ nearly broke
my heart for joy, only a week later, as He reassured me even about the 'bad' times, by saying:-

> Never regret your past penances, trials and sacrifices.
> Never bewail a single moment of the contrition and
> repentance in which you struggled during many years of
> darkness. I love you, and I have always delighted in your
> love for Me. *Everything you have offered to Me* - every tear
> and every act of love - *has been received by Me as an
> embrace.* Your sorrowful embrace has been like the
> embrace of the weeping woman in the Gospel story. *"You
> did this to Me,"* through your great efforts to make
> amends; and you have touched My Heart! (T:1187 #1)

> You must believe - even of the 'difficult' times - that I have
> delighted in every good thing you have done for Me and in
> every wrong thing avoided, even in times when you
> received from Me no apparent glimmer of Light, nor any
> apparent response. (T:1187 #2)

> Never doubt that there is a good reason for My apparent
> 'distance' from the soul at certain times. A soul which has
> turned away from me can feel such a 'distance'; yet I
> permit a similar perception to linger within the soul of one
> who consents to undergo a spiritual training. (T:1187 #3)

> Remember that I am always at work, teaching and
> sanctifying My friends. By My Will, I can 'bury' someone
> in a dark night of ignorance and blindness, until that soul -
> with faith strengthened by My merciful care and training -
> has been prepared to come out into the Light of My
> comfort, and is at last enabled to bear the joy which I wish
> to lavish upon her soul in Holy Communion. (T:1187 #4)

A lingering ambition.

Gradually, I became used to the thought of having to claim that I am "LIVING IN THE
LIGHT" (1 Jn 2:10); but my hesitation wasn't due to any shame at proclaiming the plain
teachings of the Church, or announcing my faith in Christ - as I'd done whenever necessary for
many years, even though I hadn't set a good example. The reluctance I was now fighting had
arisen for two reasons: first, that in a secular culture - and amongst Catholics who had been

affected by that culture - I met considerable embarrassment when some people realised that I was inviting them to read about the supernatural and about visions of Christ.

In my heart of hearts, I sympathised with them, because I'd probably have run a mile if someone had come to me a few years ago not simply with a story of conversion but also with information about messages from Christ. I'm such a cynic at heart - though nowadays desperately keen not to sit in judgement on anyone. I could cope with embarrassment, however; but what I found difficult was coping with the feelings of rejection when certain persons avoided me, or when they greeted me and conversed with me but never again mentioned my work: either afraid that I'd given them evidence of dementia, or so perplexed that they preferred to ignore the subject - or, a few of them, so awed at God's work that they couldn't hold a normal conversation. Whatever the reason for their being ill-at-ease, it meant that some friendships were ship-wrecked and others made difficult; and although I continued to "offer up" all the distress, my heart ached, and I felt very lonely, even in the midst of kind people and a busy routine. When it was a struggle to go on, and whenever I wept, I did so in private; and meanwhile I found it immensely difficult, also, to explain about the teachings to the different members of my close family.

The study of Theology.

There was what I can call a negative aspect of the physical process of writing that caused me a few heart-pangs; I'm referring to the fact that I was to be so busy writing for several years to come - indeed, until the present day - that there wasn't a minute in which to fulfil what had remained a lingering hope in my heart - that I'd be able to study, by post, for a Theology degree.

It's rather strange, I suppose, even to think of being disappointed at not gaining a certificate in Theology when the Word Incarnate was teaching me; but that's how silly I've been - as I've shown Him in prayer, now that I no longer hide anything from Him. He knows how my heart had still yearned to do something which would meet with approval from my peers.

In itself, study is a 'neutral' thing; its value is surely dependent on whether we really ought to be studying: on whether it's the Will of God for us at a particular time. There's more than one sort of danger in being ambitious in this way The Church has always warned us against unbridled curiosity; and it's surely a sad thing if anyone studies solely for peer-group acclamation or for eventual worldly glory; so I knew that I could please God best and also do what was best for my own soul by avoiding that sort of self-indulgence, and by agreeing, instead, to spend all my spare time doing work that it was wise to have inspected by priests, and that was rejected or never spoken about by certain acquaintances and friends. But that's why Christ urged me so often in the 'teachings' - as you can see even in Volumes Three and Four - to surrender every remaining ambition; and that's also why He has rewarded me so lavishly.

Christ knows that weak people find it difficult to make sacrifices for His sake. He delights in the love which drives us to make them, whatever our feelings; and He has never failed to encourage me to look upon it as a privilege that I'm allowed to follow in His footsteps. For example, it was on 19th September 1992, that Christ urged me, in prayer:-

Follow My inspiration and surrender your entire life to Me, whatever might happen. (T:1188 #1)

Be joyful about My choice for you. *It is a cause for joy, to be led by me along My 'Way of Suffering'.* **It is a privilege to be able to walk where I walked, and to be as if hand-in-hand with Me, Jesus, Who was delivered from death! (T:1188 #2)**

Yet I'm ashamed that I was even thinking about my assorted problems. On that very day, my elder son was packing, ready to go to Seminary in Rome; and the thought that he might have a vocation to the Sacred Priesthood never failed to thrill me.

Entering the Fire.

When I had learned to be bolder in speaking to various people about God's goodness and also to be bolder about confiding every thought and longing of my heart to God in prayer, I was led by Christ in Glory before the Father to confide my remaining fears to Him (T:1194); and the Father rewarded me for every frank confession of weakness. Two days later, therefore, on October 10th 1992, Christ filled my soul with His burning Glory once again: with a spiritual Fire; and there, in the Father's sight, Christ invited me to step wholly into that Fire, so that I could be further purified by God's own action. Christ taught me, as a kind parent speaks when leading a young adult to develop a new maturity:-

Co-operate fully in your purification. I can achieve this within you, very simply, in prayer, when, through My grace, you display all your failings. Thus, of your own free will, you 'open' your soul to the Father, and by your contrition you invite Him to 'scour' the interior of your soul; and this is how - by the power of His Glory - your Heavenly Father 'burns' away and so banishes your failings. (T:1189 #2)

Prepare to plunge into My purifying prayer of union. It is My Divine Love which is the purifying Fire which - through this Holy Communion - I am inviting you to enter. One who would be close to Me must bravely step towards Me - so bright and glorious - and towards My Divine 'furnace' which is My vast, warm and all-enveloping, pure and fiery Love. (WC:1195) (T:1195 #1)

Leave the 'safety' of your self-centred prayer. Gaze towards Me as if from the edge of a cliff; by a free act of your will, resolve to step fully into the 'flames' which you see around you. If you wish to co-operate in this purifying prayer of union, you need only - bravely - wait in silence and ignorance *as My perfect Glory does its work in you, and*

throws its splendour Heavenwards in praise of the Father.
(T:1195 #2)

Understand that there is no way in which anyone can hope to purify himself solely by his own power. In prayer, just as after death, *it is My own true Glory which burns away all dross and imperfection. Nothing can exist in this 'Fire' except whatever is true, eternal, pure, proven and strong.* (T:1195 #3)

Notice, more clearly now, that your good but self-chosen penances have been only a preparation for the true purification which comes from Me. Through My presence within the soul, sins are burnt up and destroyed, if you give your permission. (T:1195 #4)

Let nothing remain in your heart which might hinder My work within you. It is My Will that nothing remains in your heart and soul *which is not part* of *the Work of Glory*. No thought, longing, action, hope, joy or memory should remain in your heart except those which spur you on, in the One Way which is My Way, in union with My Most Holy Spirit. (T:1195 #5)

True Communion.

Nothing could have been achieved without God's invitation and my cooperation: but five days later, when the major purifications had been completed, Christ led me to the heart of the Holy Trinity. He shared with me His own Understanding of life in a true Communion. It was at Mass, at the 'Per Ipsum', that He showed me the astonishing consequences of a meeting between a purified soul and her Saviour. He lifted me entirely into His Light, and taught me:-

Rejoice in your privilege; listen to My teaching; be glad to share that which I now reveal to you about your reverent and Holy Communion:

Communion in God, "in Christ", resembles
the Love of God for God, in God,
flowing in the Heart of God
in Eternity,
in utter purity and majesty and simplicity.

This simple and everlasting Love in Heaven
is a three-fold Love of Father,
Son and Holy Spirit; and when
you touch your Heavenly Father
and enter His Life,
through Me, Jesus,

in the Holy Communion which is yours on earth,
the Love is the same Love,
The Persons are the same,
but you are now 'drawn in' by adoption.
The moment is the same,
since Love has no end or beginning.
The Bliss is the same bliss,
though muted, here,
lest you be destroyed by joy.
Yet, because of all these,
you can truly say:
'Heaven is here;
I taste Heaven, in Christ!'
(T:1199 #3)

Christ's own Action.

Such teachings as that - about Holy Communion - provided me with fuel for ever more fervent prayer; and it seemed as though Christ was now longing to bring me to a very much greater understanding of the intertwining of our hearts and lives, and of the 'interweaving' of our prayers. He showed me much more about the Holy Mass, and about my 'part' in His prayer to the Father, through our union. He urged me:-

Treasure the Holy Mass. There is nothing on earth more magnificent or fruitful, nor more worthy of awe and gratitude than the Holy Sacrifice of the Mass, which is My own Action. (T:1218 #3)

Ponder the marvellous Offering which is yours to offer; *all the Glory which I have possessed from all ages is offered to the Father, in My One Holy Sacrifice of the Cross,* the very Sacrifice which is now being offered *on the altar.* (T:1218 #4)

Consider how perfect and powerful and worthy of the Father is My glorious Sacrifice of the altar; and see, therefore, that you need not worry about the right words, the right phrase or the right manner in prayer, provided that your intention is true. You can prove your good intention by your reverent thoughts and behaviour, but - more important for you to know - *My praise is perfect and glorious,* and *My praise is yours, if you are Mine!* (T:1218 #5)

Don't let little failings make you downcast; there's no need for you to search around within your soul for special gifts worthy of being offered to the Father, in an attempt to prove your love and your sincerity. *I, Jesus, am the most*

336

pure, holy, and precious Offering that you could make to your Heavenly Father; and I am yours to offer at every Mass, or at every moment in which you voluntarily unite your heart and your thoughts with My Holy Sacrifice. (T:1222)

Consider the marvel of the powerful and holy Sacrifice in which you share. My Love of the Father is tremendous, and that Love is expressed powerfully during My eternal offering of Myself in the Holy Sacrifice - and forever.

My prayer to the Father is
like a wall of flame,
Love matching the Father's Love,
Fire meeting Fire,
My Will: One with the Father's Will,
My prayer: the same as His:
One Fire, in which you share,
purified.
(WC + OIL:1223A) (T:1223A)

Extra gifts.

As I wrote down Christ's marvellous teachings and pressed ahead with my task, I had no proof that wonderful results would one day be achieved through my peculiar work. I had faith, and hope, and a conviction that Christ was guiding me; but every now and then a further encouraging gift from God was suddenly presented to me and to the family.

For example, my youngest child - my daughter - announced one day that she, too, was planning to be received into full Communion; and when, on the day after her happy celebration, I was unable to go to Holy Mass yet was full of amazed thanksgiving that my daughter had been received and confirmed at last, I turned to Christ to make my evening prayers, asking Him to be with me in a Spiritual Communion. (T:1240)

He not only came to my soul in that special way, but was with me very powerfully even before I had finished speaking. He was delighted at my gladness. Straightaway, He taught me how much He delights in my love; and so I can say that I've been rewarded in a thousand different ways for every little sacrifice I've ever made in order to please Him.

By the Son, in the Spirit, to the Father.

My daughter was received into the Church in mid-December 1992; and it was in the few weeks before and after that event that the life and work of the Most Holy Trinity was more astonishingly revealed to me.

The Father's loving self-revelation through Christ Our Lord was made plain in a wonderful way (in T:1244). Something of the Holy Spirit's holiness and beauty was shown to me, and also His manner of guiding us (in T:1249); and it was in the New Year, on January 23rd 1993, that the Father made known to me His acceptance of my offering, by which I mean my earlier dedication to Him of the whole of the rest of my life. My heart was pierced, in prayer, and was set on 'fire' by Love. Here below, is a necessarily lengthy account of how this all came about.

As if through a window.

It was on the 19th of December of that year that Christ brought me to the Father and revealed Him to me more closely than ever before. During the Mass, at the Sanctus, when I had spoken to Christ once more in sorrow for sin, with heart-felt thanks, too, for wonderful gifts, I was suddenly shown, as if by pure Knowledge and Understanding reinforced by an image, that the Father had decided to reveal Himself to me, at Christ's request; and yet even that was only the beginning of the 'revealing' that has now continued for several years.

How can I put such sublime things into language? Yet I have to try. Already, I've spent very many pages describing conversations with Christ Our Lord and visits from Our Lady - with descriptions of some of the Heavenly companions who help us on our journey; but nothing I've mentioned so far - except the joys of the 'Alpha and Omega Day' - had been as heart-achingly precious and significant as the 'meeting' with the Father which I must now try to describe.

I was sitting in church, wholly surrendered to God in prayer, as our priest prayed at the altar; then, all-at-once, in a wonderful way, Christ taught me:-

> **Live in perpetual gratitude for My goodness towards you. You have good cause to be confident in faith, since there is no situation from which I cannot draw blessings upon you. (T:1244 #1)**

> *Consider the Father's Love* for you; **He is always longing to pour out His gifts upon His children on earth. From Him has come the joy which is now yours. The Father's Love is over-flowing, warm, generous and tender; and from the bliss of His being -** *from His perpetual 'newness' and youth and Beauty* **- He** *delights in giving you good things, good news, and spiritual joy.* **From His generosity spring all the gifts which delight you - such as the friendship of Myself your Divine Redeemer and of your Heavenly Mother, and the spiritual progress of your family. (T:1244 #2)**

> **Turn to Me, Jesus, true God and also true man, Who now appear before you as if silhouetted against the Light of Heaven's Glory. (T:1244 #3)**

At this moment there appeared to the eyes of my soul an image of a beam of Light which shone down from the height of Heaven; and where the beam ended at the earth's surface, it changed shape. The straight sides of that bright beam were seen to be man-shaped; and the bright light within that outline of a figure represented - I learned by a soundless gift from God - the Divinity of Christ: the Glory of the Son of God, now made incarnate.

Christ reveals the Father.

By this image and this 'knowledge' I was also shown that Christ has the same nature as the Father, although Christ is a distinct Person: One of Three Divine Persons. I was made to understand in what way Christ can be said to have 'revealed' the Father to Mankind. Christ taught me:-

> **Look at Me, Jesus, to learn about the Divine nature and attributes which were revealed through Me during My life on earth. (T:1244 #4)**

> **Believe in Me, Jesus Christ your Lord, Who have come 'out' from the Almighty, unseen Father. I have come out from Him Who is pure, mysterious and powerful, and Who is a furnace of Love, inextinguishable; I, your Saviour, came from Him, and I have the same Divine nature. (T:1244 #5)**

> **Believe in Me, Jesus, Who took flesh from Mary and lived amongst you. I am true God, on fire with Divine Love. No impurity exists in Me, your glorious Redeemer. Only through Me has God been fully revealed; *I, alone, have given 'shape' to Divine Light*, in My human nature. (WC:1244A) (T:1244 #6)**

Christ, at work in our lives.

There was more. Christ explained about the Father's nature, which 'consists' of utter Bliss and joy, constant and Eternal. He told me:-

> **Learn about the Father. Let Me show you, as you open your heart, in prayer:**

> *Delight is!*
> *Joy is!*
> *He is*
> *like Me,* **Jesus.**
> *His Love is the same as My Love;*
> *He gives you Myself,* **His Divine Son,**
> *through Whom He is revealed;*
> *His Light shines through Me,*
> *and I 'touch' you for the Father;*
> **I touch you now, even here.**

339

I am already at work in your life,
in the Love of the Father.

I give you free gifts, in prayer, gifts from Him; but
remember:
humility opens the 'door'. (T:1244 #7)

Make every effort to draw even closer to Us: to Father, Son
and Holy Spirit. Open the 'door' of your soul, in prayer.
(T:1244 #8)

Bend "low" in humility, near the little door of Truth within
your soul so that you are poised to see if the door 'opens' to
release upon you a further torrent of graces. By humility,
be ready to receive gifts from Me in prayer; if you are
upright in pride, you cannot see the 'door' of the soul - and
so cannot receive all the gifts that I wish to give you.
(T:1244 #9)

There in the church, as I was praying, it was as if a window had opened in the sky above me,
in a spiritual night; I saw, too, that Christ was standing very close to me: and I was shown
how Christ is the image of the Father. It was explained to me, by pure knowledge, that
through His humanity, Christ was 'sent' as if from that window like a pure beam of Light.
Christ was sent to us by the Father to show us what the Father is like; yet Christ is also - and
at the same time - the Word of God "embodied" and thus made visible for our Salvation and
delight.

Then I saw with rapturous delight that God the Father had appeared at that window.
Furthermore, He Who gazed through that window was gazing at me with infinite tenderness;
and I saw that He looked like Christ.

But, Oh! - The heart-stopping tenderness of God: Father and Son. I couldn't 'see' the Spirit
Who was guiding and enlarging my understanding; but Christ reassured me:-

Consider what a marvel and a Mystery is the Father's Love.
Believe in the Father's Love.
Look upwards in prayer, as I, your Saviour, reveal Him.
Look upwards, as if into the darkness
of a night sky, where *a window opens,*
and *a curtain is drawn aside for a moment*
so that the Father might gaze on you,
and you on Him.
He is gazing joyfully upon you; He delights in you!
Oh! What indescribable consolation for your soul:
His face is the same as My face, and
His Love is the same as that which I, Jesus,
have shown to you.
His Love - the same as Mine - is fervent,
never-ending, transforming, and heart-warming.

Share His delight. He delights in you, His beloved!
He is gazing towards you,
gazing - as if from the height of Heaven -
with a look of unspeakable tenderness.
(WC:1244B) (T:1244 #10)

What a gift this was! But I don't mean that I learned anything new about God the Father: nothing new to me or to the Church. I mean that I was shown with heart-breaking clarity just what I was shown by Christ on the Alpha and Omega day. I was shown by the Father how deeply I am loved; and so life could never be the same, after that; for if you not only believe that God loves you, but know it - and delight in it - you couldn't be unhappy, even if the whole world were to think you a fool.

The Holy Spirit's gift.

What a long time I've taken just to reach a description of that part of the recent road where, as if by an image, I was shown the Father's Love. But His new work for me had only just begun. He had purified me by His power, in prayer. He had even shown me how He had achieved that purification - and I'm only writing this because He wants me to describe His work. I wouldn't dare to write that as a personal opinion, since I see so many faults and weaknesses. But He next taught me about the work of the Holy Spirit (T:1249), and did so with astonishing power.

It was when I had confided in Christ one day, in prayer; and then I'd decided, from gratitude, to say the 'Divine Praises' with greater fervour, and so I began the prayer. I said:-

"Blessed be God.
Blessed be His Holy Name.
Blessed be Jesus Christ, true God and true man.
Blessed be the Name of Jesus.
Blessed be His Most Sacred Heart.
Blessed be His Most Precious Blood.
Blessed be Jesus in the Most Holy Sacrament of the altar.
Blessed be the Holy Spirit, the Paraclete."

But when I said the phrase: "Blessed be the Holy Spirit, the Paraclete," I was astounded to be shown how this same Spirit was at work. Christ taught me, all in one moment:-

Offer heart-felt adoration to My Most Holy Spirit, Who is
all Holiness and Beauty: loving and powerful, gracious and
glorious. Here, whilst you honour Me by your reverence as
you recite "The Divine Praises", you can 'see' that *My Holy*
Spirit now 'accompanies' you in prayer from one phrase to
***the next,* as a music-master might guide a child in the**
reading of a melody. *It is My Holy Spirit Who enables you*
***to believe what you are saying, and* Who - through your**
belief - *has brought you to prayer.* (T:1249 #4)

341

By this extraordinary knowledge, Christ made plain to me that throughout my life on earth, as I live and work and pray in order to please Him, His Holy Spirit is overshadowing me, or rather, is hovering, as it were, in perpetual loving attendance, encouragement and supervision. This is true for everyone who believes in Christ and tries to serve Him; and so it's a cause for gratitude; but it must be a cause for humility, also, since - as was made so plain - we would be quite unable to do good things without the Holy Spirit's guidance and power; and by 'good things' I mean even a word of praise to the Father.

Christ taught me:-

> Realise that *without this gift from My Holy Spirit, you would not* - could not - *believe in the truth on your lips* as you continue the Divine praises, saying:
>
> **"Blessed be the great Mother of God, Mary most Holy,**
> **Blessed be her Holy and Immaculate Conception," and:**
> **"Blessed be her glorious Assumption." (T:1249 #5)**
>
> Rejoice in the faith which you have received from My Spirit. You are right to pray:
>
> **"Blessed be the name of Mary, Virgin and Mother.**
> **Blessed be St. Joseph, her spouse most chaste.**
> **Blessed be God in His Angels and in His Saints."**
> **(T:1249 #6)**

Pierced to the heart.

In successive waves, it seemed, in prayer, Christ continued to give me first encouragement, then warning, then instruction - and then another invitation to move closer to Heaven; and that's what happened when, in the New Year - on 23rd January 1993 - God the Father made me His own, in an astonishing way; and now I have to write about it - although it doesn't matter to me any more what anyone thinks of me. What I know and say unashamedly at last is the truth: that God the Holy Spirit led me into Christ's Church, long ago, and has continued to guide and to teach me; God the Son reconciled me with Himself, and made me entirely His own in December 1985; and God the Father accepted my sacrifices and praised me for my devotion, in January 1993, when He sealed our union; and it happened in this way (as is mentioned in T:1263 - as described at the end of the Blue Book.)

One morning at home, I was all alone and in pain. I prayed my usual prayers, and asked Our Lord to help me to cope with each new trial. I begged Him to increase my faith, and said to Him: "Let me live in perpetual repentance. Let me remember to thank You for the gift of faith. Let me not worry about what others might say - about the work You've given me to do. Let me imitate You, O Christ, when You set out for the Synagogue."

But as I prayed in this way, and made my Morning Offering - " I offer You all my thoughts, words, actions and sufferings this day ..." - I received a spiritual blow to the heart which left me almost unable to move: unable to articulate another word in prayer, though my heart remained wholly devoted to God. Indeed, God had seized my heart and attention. By His grace and action I had been pierced to the heart: suddenly made more thoroughly united to Jesus in wounds, and in pain, and in abandonment to God's Will. I had 'thrown away' my own life and ambitions for the Father's Glory, in ways that no-one knows about; and at that very moment I was taught that my offering had not been rejected.

This is what I learned from Christ at the same moment:-

> **Follow the inspirations of My Holy Spirit; it is He Who draws you into a real and intimate union with Me, from which springs your continued and repeated surrender to Me, in a daily self-offering. Renew your offering. (T:1263 #1)**

> **Accept this great gift from the Father, here, as you make your morning offering; you are now pierced to the heart - by His grace and His action - as a sign of His Love for you, and as a sign of your union with Me, Jesus your loving Saviour. Accept these wounds, through which you and I are more closely united. By this great privilege, our union is sealed. Every sacrifice that you have placed on the 'altar' of your heart has been worthwhile. As the Father now tells you:**

> > **_"The offering has been accepted"._**
> **(T:1263 #2)**

The consummation of the Sacrifice.

Then Christ urged me:-

> **Rejoice that every aspect of your life which you have given to Me has been made holy. _The consummation_ of the sacrifice _began_ last year, _when the Flame_ of My purifying Love wholly _overtook you._ (T:1263 #3)**

> **Prepare for further suffering. _From today, this living sacrifice of self_ - offered in union with My Sacrifice - _will 'burn' more brightly._ By this, I mean that your sufferings will be more intense, and, also, will be noticed by others. (T:1263 #4)**

> **Be glad that, because of your sufferings, you resemble Me so closely; _all during this 'burning'_ - which is constant self-offering - _'heat' and 'light' are being given out;_ and this 'heat' is My consoling prayer, within your life, and this 'Light' is My wisdom, in your soul; and this 'heat and**

Light' now flow outwards to others, *for My Glory, for the salvation of souls and for the good of My Church.* (T:1263 #5)

Look upon this moment as a moment of great grace. The flames of My Divine Fire are now warming your heart; see this as My gift to you, before you continue your difficult journey. Recall the words which I used about your soul and My teachings: that your soul is like a jar which is slowly being filled with precious drops of wisdom from Heaven; realise that, *now, the 'jar' can be broken, for the ointment of grace to pour out upon a wounded Church.* By this I mean that you will become even frailer and more feeble, as hard work and ill-health take their toll; however, through your slow 'dying', in imitation of Myself, the Father is being glorified and My Church is being renewed. (T:1263 #6)

Bear your 'dying' with great patience, in imitation of Me; thus, as My teachings are circulated, your work will be fruitful. (T:1263 #7)

Thank Me for the gift of faith; live in perpetual repentance; don't worry about what others might say about you, but patiently explain My friendship with you, and My longing to save you all. (T:1263 #8)

Like a simple child.

Then Christ reminded me:-

Obey My inspirations. (T:1263 #9)

Always be loving. (T:1263 #10)

Don't look back, but accept your weaknesses and do My Will in simplicity. (T:1263 #11)

Speak as a 'child of God,' and fulfil the unique task which I have given to you alone. (T:1263 #12)

Turn to Me more and more frequently from love as well as from need; I delight in revealing more about Myself to hearts which are eager to know Me; I love to welcome a fervent soul to share in My Life and therefore to share in My knowledge of Myself. *"Come and see."* (T:1264 #1)

Christ our Mediator.

Next, Christ instructed me:-

> **Remember the cause of your close 'connection' with Me:**
> *Through the merits of My Sacrifice*
> *My Divine Life can now penetrate*
> *every aspect of your humanity.*
> *Through My suffering,*
> *I broke down the barrier*
> *between Divine Life and human,*
> *bridged the 'chasm' between My Life and yours, and*
> *entered into your suffering.* **(T:1264 #2)**

> **Consider the consequences of My Sacrifice on your behalf:**
> *You are raised up - through My grace - to My Glory.*
> *You are made divine-by-grace: divinised.*
> *You are made My children, by adoption.* **(T:1264 #3)**

> **Consider your dignity as My children:**
> *At the summit of the Holy Sacrifice of the Mass,*
> *I lead you - My children -*
> *into the Glory of My self-offering,*
> *hand-in-hand,*
> **united with Me before the Father. (T:1264 #4)**

For the renewal of the Church.

Only three days after the Father had sealed our union in that astonishing new way, I was in church on the feast of Saints Timothy and Titus, on 26th January 1993 (T:1265). I was told in Holy Scripture that: "I AM REMINDING YOU TO FAN INTO A FLAME THE GIFT THAT GOD GAVE YOU WHEN I LAID MY HANDS ON YOU ... SO YOU ARE NEVER TO BE ASHAMED OF WITNESSING TO THE LORD" (2 Tm 6:8).

By the grace of Christ, I was encouraged to go on with my task, hoping to see many more people grow in hope and love and faith.

I wanted nothing but to do His Will from day to day for the rest of my life. My perpetual prayer was for a greatly increased love of God and of my neighbour, for the renewal of His Church, the salvation of souls - and for final perseverance: all for the Glory of the Most Holy Trinity and for the honour of Our Blessed Lady and St Joseph and all the Angels and Saints. Despite my hesitation and embarrassment, I was longing to speak to many more people, to say that friendship with Christ is worth any sacrifice.

---

14 OPPOSITION
(1993-1994)

A TIME OF TESTING. EVIL. THE FATHER'S WORDS.

The soul's journey.

When I began this spiritual autobiography, I was asked to put it on one side, as I said earlier, until the right time came for it to be used. It's now about three years since I last made additions to the story of the beginnings of my spiritual journey. Some of that story was shared through "The Introduction": which was the small white pamphlet I had printed, at Christ's request. But I was content to leave most of the spiritual autobiography unseen: a box full of paper in a corner of my room. Today, however, God the Father has shown me that the time has arrived to share the whole story, and He has encouraged me to write a few more pages, to bring it up-to-date. When I asked Him in prayer, only two or three weeks ago, whether He really wanted me to enlarge the book in this way, He said immediately: "*It is the end of the journey.*" What this meant was that it wouldn't be right if I just told people about the difficulties and heart-aches of the early stages of the soul's journey towards Heaven and yet failed to describe something of the bliss and glory which are experienced near the end.

He has shown me how important it is that I be simple and childlike, so that I can explain to everyone who reads this book that no friend can ever be found who is as loving and faithful as Christ. His friendship brings joys and consolations more sweet, astonishing and profound than anyone has ever imagined. I must say more emphatically than ever before that there can be no life as fulfilled and as joyful as a life in which God the Holy Trinity is Creator, Inspiration and Beloved; and nothing can be more worthwhile than to grow in the love and knowledge of God and His Will. That's how we can please God during our earthly life, and yet also prepare for life in our future home in Heaven, at God's 'Heart', in Eternal Glory.

It's precisely because God is 'on fire' with love for us, and yearns to see us choose to move towards Him and towards true happiness that He has given me this extraordinary task to do; and it's a task of such complexity that it was through God's goodness that I was left in ignorance of its full significance for many, many years - until about the time that I finished writing, a few pages ago. But since then, it's as though the Lord has drawn together all the 'threads' in my life, to weave a bright ribbon for me to inspect; and now I can thank and praise Him for the pattern I can see - a pattern I couldn't see earlier because it wasn't Christ's Will.

347

Training for the task.

When I'd finished writing the early 'Introduction' to Christ's teachings, and was busy distributing the first copies, Christ continued to teach me. It seemed to me that the teachings which I'd described in the booklet were enough for Christ's immediate purposes. I still didn't know more than a few details of His plan, except that, however this is achieved, Christ's Will is always directed towards the Glory of the Father, and the good of souls. I could have written many more pages about Christ's kindness.

It's true that He frequently asks us to take up our cross and follow Him, and to bear sufferings patiently, like Him; yet I've found that Christ gives us peace - even in the midst of our trials.

Ideally, we ought to serve God simply because He is God and not for rewards; but for many years I've longed to be able to tell people who despair of ever being happy or at peace that the grace of Christ can change every willing human heart, and therefore every situation. I haven't learned until recently, however, that it's part of Christ's plan that I shall have opportunities in which to speak and teach about Him, on a scale which I would never have dreamed might be possible. Indeed, I couldn't have known that, because it wasn't Christ's Will for me then. He was still training me for my future task, and was doing so partly through His own instructions, and partly through the inspiration which He had given to my parish priest: to the priest who had advised me that the teachings were a gift from God.

A severe test.

When I was beginning to grow accustomed to the teachings, and quite soon after I'd obeyed Christ by speaking to our priest about Our Lady's visit, I was made to undergo a time of trial. My wise and holy parish priest decided to test me, severely; and he did so for a period of about two years - but without telling me, of course. I know that this is true, partly from the circumstances in which the testing ceased. But all I knew at first was that after years of good-humoured conversations with him, and meals shared with him and the family at home, I suddenly found myself totally ignored, unless charity demanded that he speak to me to convey information at a Council meeting, or that he listen when I arranged to have a Mass offered for a special intention, in which case he'd be very courteous.

Only by God's grace was I sure that Canon O'Leary was acting to help me: to steer me firmly away from the danger of becoming proud about having seen Our Blessed Lady and about being 'taught' in prayer. It was all for the good of my soul, and so I continued with my efforts to be cheerful and courteous. I'm even grateful for what I learned, since it taught me once more not to lean on anyone except God, and not to hope for encouragement or consolation, unless God Wills it. It taught me to be wholly unconcerned by reactions to my presence or to my work. It taught me, also, to be more courageous, since, throughout that whole episode, I was sent back to our priest time after time, by Christ, to tell him something else that Christ had told me.

Christ wanted me to obey Him in this way whether my messages or statements were welcomed or not - and they never were. It was made 'worse', in fact, and yet even more profitable for my soul, because almost all of the messages were about Christ's gifts to me. It was as though Christ wouldn't allow me to relish any new spiritual gift from Him, or to endure a particular spiritual danger, unless, at around the time it occurred, I was obedient in going to our priest to describe it.

Speaking about Christ's gifts.

Some of the things I mentioned to Father O'Leary were private. I can say, however, that I was sent to tell him that Christ was going to use me to help His Church. It was very embarrassing to have to make such a claim when I was so obviously inadequate, but that was before I came to trust in Christ much more and also to have confidence in His training. Then I was also invited to tell our priest about Our Lady's visit to me - and then to describe how Christ shows me about the departed souls for whose welfare I pray sincerely: about their true state, whether joy or pain.

On a later occasion, Christ asked me to mention that it was in obedience to Christ's wishes that I'd re-adopted the custom of covering my hair in church, in accordance with Scripture and the Church's tradition. Wearing a scarf again was one of the most difficult things that Christ had asked me to do, because it made me conspicuous. It is true that Saint Paul wrote to the Corinthians: "ASK YOURSELVES IF IT IS FITTING FOR A WOMAN TO PRAY TO GOD WITHOUT A VEIL ...?" (1 Co 11:13) and also "TO ANYONE WHO MIGHT STILL WANT TO ARGUE: IT IS NOT THE CUSTOM WITH US, NOR IN THE CHURCHES OF THE LORD" (1 Co 11:16); and yet I knew that various people would think me foolish or old-fashioned. But although it's not a matter of good or evil, but a matter, rather, of how to pay God the greatest possible reverence in prayer - as He has told me - I was determined to obey; and it was Christ's wish that I speak to our priest about His wishes so that the priest would know that I wasn't trying to cause division or to strike a pose, but only to do Christ's Will; and Christ overwhelmed me with rewards for my obedience in speaking.

One of the other things I was required to mention - for what reason only Christ knows - was an assault by the evil one which I'd suffered in my kitchen. But Christ showed me that through my obedience to Him in these difficult matters I was keeping thoroughly "in touch" with the Church authority about His work in my life and about the opposition I endured; yet I was also proving to the priest that I was willing to be docile and to accept humiliation for Christ's sake. And I was humiliated; but I knew it was doing me good.

Then one day Christ asked me to tell our priest about a gift I'd received quite a long time earlier: a gift of knowing the intentions of human hearts. In order to be obedient, I explained to our priest that Christ wanted me to explain that although I can't read everyone's thoughts, I am shown by God in which 'direction' each person's true intention lies. That was the best way of describing such unsought, invisible and intangible 'knowledge'. But from the day that I explained this to our priest, he ceased his testing. He knew that it was pointless to continue, if I knew what he was doing, and why.

From then on, he was always joyful and smiling with me, even ready to tease me about little things: so very different, and so heart-warming, though I'd always known he was acting for the eternal good of my soul. He didn't feel free to say out loud that he believed in the whole project; but he respected the writings enough to advise me to apply to the Diocesan censor for an 'Imprimatur'. I found out, soon afterwards, that this isn't given to private pamphlets, but only to works sent in by a publisher; but it was good to know that Canon O'Leary wasn't unhappy about the books; and when he'd retired, later on, he always answered "Yes," when I asked him if he'd like a copy of each new volume.

I'm only writing about these things now because he has died, and so I can tell some of his story. It's Christ wish that I do so, anyway; and it was by Christ's kindness that I was shown, only one day after Canon O'Leary's peaceful death, that he had arrived in Heaven, at the foot of the steps which lead to the throne of our Heavenly Father (T:2320).

When I look back to that difficult time, I can remember a day when I was thinking about Christ's teachings and was puzzling over the reason I receive so many. I remembered Our Lady's visits, as well; and I asked myself why, since I was so weighed down by God's gifts, I wasn't more joyful and light-hearted; and the answer which eluded me was that I was still undergoing radical spiritual purifications: both 'exterior' testing by human beings, and spiritual opposition.

Meeting evil.

The evil spiritual assault which I suffered at home and which Christ asked me to mention to my priest is something which at first - like the teachings-in-prayer, until I understood their purpose - I preferred not to mention. I'd tried never to pay much attention to spiritual evil. I mean that I'd never talked much about Satan or about his tactics against God's People. As the Apostle says: "LET YOUR THOUGHTS BE ON HEAVENLY THINGS" (Col 3:2). But he also says that people who try to do good are certain to be attacked - whether by violence, sickness or temptation, or by disappointments of various kinds, or even by the sort of naked evil which I've endured.

It seems wise, however, to seize this opportunity to urge anyone who reads this: "Never, never, never 'dabble' in evil. Never do wrong, by which you perhaps align yourself with dark forces; and never take risks by 'flirting' with evil supposedly for fun, perhaps by using ouija boards, fortune-telling cards or lucky charms."

I thank God for having kept me away from such dangers. I thank God I had simple and sensible parents who deplored even any mention of such things in our presence. How sad it is that even many Catholics are deeply affected today by what other people are seen to do - whether through T.V. shows or through the habits of favourite 'stars'. That's why I say with some passion: "Avoid evil with all your power; and never copy anything un-Christian."

The 'tactics' which I've mentioned above became more evident as my work began to reach its fulfilment, and as one member after another of the family decided to enter the Catholic Church.

It seems right to mention these things as an introduction to a page or two on the reality of spiritual danger; but I must proclaim that I've never gone through life on the look-out for evil or danger, nor have I attributed any happening to a strange source if there was the least possibility of a natural explanation. But having said that, I must also say that I've recognised evil at work in recent years in just the ways that I've recognised good: by God's Will and

350

through His understanding. And God has hidden from me - He has told me - the worst of the knowledge of evil, whilst showing me that various phenomena were designed to frighten me: to make me agitated and untrusting so that I'd neither complete this work nor cling entirely to God. Yet, through God's goodness, none of these things could 'shift' me. Neither by assault, scrapings, bangings and sudden noises, nor by a silent evil presence have I been deterred from trying to do my plain duty; though I've only coped so far by God's grace and by prayer.

Repulsive sights.

Another of the evil one's tactics has been to conjure up before my mind - whenever I've tried to rest for a while - fearsome images of disgusting and repulsive sights, things quite impossible to drive away. So I advise anyone who suffers such assaults to do what I've learned to do, which is not to fight, but simply to turn one's thoughts and heart away, towards God. If that seems to be impossible, it's best to get up for a while and to pray with a book - and, of course, always to use the Sign of the Cross, and Jesus' Name, and holy water.

In case anyone should ask, I've never drawn or painted such sights. First, I've hoped to forget them; and secondly, it seems to me that artistic skills are best used for increasing the beauty to be found in the world, and not for reproducing ugliness and decay. But the mention of this subject, too, gives me the chance to say to anyone who will listen: "Never do evil. Never associate yourself with evil activities. Think about spending eternity with creatures whose perpetual state is in cruelty, rebellion, spite, pain, ugliness, darkness, anger and loss: then do all in your power to find God, and to make Light and goodness your 'medium'."

It's not going to worry me if anyone says that I've imagined every cause for distress. So many Christians today are ready to proclaim that there's no 'real' Heaven or Hell, reward or punishment - and certainly no devil. And my words probably won't change their minds, or the minds of those who have already decided that because of all the visions I've described I'm untrustworthy or demented. But I'm writing this for the few who are utterly determined to believe in God and His Church, and to persevere in His service. They will meet troubles and danger; but if they hold tight to the Person and the Name of Jesus, and call for help, too, to His Mother Mary, they will find that no evil presence can defeat them. And I say this because I've met naked evil, and have survived: but only because of Jesus, of Whom Saint Paul wrote: "GOD RAISED HIM HIGH AND GAVE HIM THE NAME WHICH IS ABOVE ALL OTHER NAMES SO THAT ALL BEINGS IN THE HEAVENS, ON EARTH AND IN THE UNDERWORLD, SHOULD BEND THE KNEE AT THE NAME OF JESUS AND THAT EVERY TONGUE SHOULD ACCLAIM JESUS CHRIST AS LORD, TO THE GLORY OF GOD THE FATHER" (Ph 2:9-11).

The evil one.

What I'm about to describe can be seen as much as a temptation as a spiritual attack, I suppose: a temptation to despair of God's help, and to abandon my determination to stay close to Him. I can state quite firmly that the experience, in all its horror, was the worst-ever experience of my life; so although I've understated it from beginning to end, please don't read the next three pages if you're a nervous person. But from beginning to end of it, in my heart and soul, I was adamant that with God's help I'd stand firm. I've decided to describe it, despite my reluctance, because in pondering what happened, it seems that what I felt is the nearest I've been able to understand with my heart - rather than with my analytical mind - something of what Our Lord experienced during His time on earth, in this matter of evil assaults or temptations; and so I'm sure it will be useful to certain persons.

There's no comparison, of course, between a merely sinful woman, and the God-man of the Gospels; yet there is a similarity between a baptised and reconciled Catholic and the Lord to Whom she is united by all sorts of bonds - supremely, love - in an everyday and day-long communion. That's why I dare to describe what happened, and to ponder Christ's own life on earth - thinking particularly about the 'reverberations' we feel as emotions are disturbed by external forces, yet our hearts cling to God.

The presence of evil.

During a time when I was being tested in all sorts of ways - it was on February 17th 1994 - I was alone at home one evening. In general and particular terms I was pressing ahead well with this work for Our Lord through the 'Booklet' distribution, and by continued writing down and painting of His teachings and images. The priest who so kindly checked my writings had written encouragingly of my work; and my parish priest - as I also said - had reassured me that I could accept the teachings. I had never for a second doubted their Source; but it was good to be reassured that I wasn't doing anything I shouldn't. And I was utterly determined to keep on with this work for Our Lord, until I 'dropped', if that were His Will. With my whole heart and mind I was determined to please Christ, no matter how many friends I lost, nor how peculiar it seemed to various persons, and despite the constant problems of everyday life, from broken machinery to health problems, from burglaries to plumbing disasters - and with constant visitors, and the usual duties. I don't meant that I was good, but that I was so utterly grateful to God for life and love and faith that nothing - I was determined - would stop me from loving and doing His Will.

Looking back, it was as though I was about to undergo a 'test' or a temptation which was to be worse than anything before it: and I haven't even mentioned the 'internal' temptations which, if succumbed to, can spoil work such as this, such as self-satisfaction, or irritation at people who oppose the work, and so on. But on that February evening, I was sitting in my kitchen chair, resting between one chore and the next, when I was suddenly and wholly unexpectedly confronted, to my utter horror, with the presence of evil; and I knew that the evil one was in front of me, with all his power and malice and his 'delight' in causing fear; and he was wholly invisible.

There was nothing for my eyes to see or my ears to hear, yet his presence was so overpowering that it felt as though I was almost enveloped in him, and yet he remained external, entirely, as every scrap of my heart and mind and being was as if recoiling with terror at meeting such naked hatred.

Naked hatred.

Now, the purpose of this piece is to give a warning about some of the dangers of the spiritual life, and also to say with conviction that no evil can conquer us, if we're 'armed' by Christ's power, and keep on praying in His Name for courage and endurance; and so I'll just say what struck me, especially: then I'll try to reach some sort of conclusion.

This assault of evil was wholly from outside myself. I don't have a scrap of doubt about that. Before it, I was happy and had been busy; and although the sudden presence of evil was so strong, the power of Christ remained so strong in me, through prayer, that the 'heart' of myself, if I can describe it thus, was held firm and inviolate. I remained untouched throughout the experience: as if 'walled around' by my steely will, and by grace.

The evil presence, as I said, was invisible and intangible; and yet I know that - all during that time - there was something more than a presence. There was being presented to my imagination, from 'outside', and in order to terrify me, an image which was of the most revolting, malevolent and terrifying face and figure that I had ever set eyes on; and the evil one was trying to use this image to frighten me further. The horror I experienced at this presence, at this malice, and at this image, was worse than anything I've experienced in my entire life: even worse than when I was pushed to my kitchen floor and threatened ten years ago, by a knife-wielding intruder: worse than any episode of fear. I know that it was an assault by someone who, from sheer malice, wished to spoil my enjoyment of some aspect of God's work in my life, even if he couldn't actually stop the whole project. The experience of evil was also a temptation - and wholly external - to make me despair of God's power.

The Holy Names, and the Cross.

There wasn't even a split-second in which, interiorly, I had the least intention of not continuing to trust in God, even in the midst of such a ferocious assault. There wasn't a single moment in which I was unsure that God would help me to endure this episode as - I am sure - He will help me to continue with the work. But, nevertheless, I had to 'fight', as it were, at every second for an hour, to maintain what I can only call 'composure' during that time: to fight against the need to shriek with terror, and instead, to continue to pray desperately for help. I did this by a fervent recitation of the Rosary which, as usual, was near-at-hand, and with heart-felt cries to 'Jesus!' and 'Mary' - and to the Holy Trinity, with frequent signs of the Cross, and kissing of the Crucifix. Although I believed with all my heart that, with God, I could win, I had to fight, as it were, to stay upright in the face of such malice and also to remain hopeful that the experience would come to an end.

One of the worst things about naked terror, whether brought about through meeting 'naked' evil, or through facing evil armed attackers, is that you don't know when the terror will end. That's almost the worst thing about it - and what makes people long for death, I believe, as perhaps being better than continuing terror. It was an experience, then, of feeling that I was about to be crushed or annihilated by the evil force, although I knew by faith that Christ's power was greater and that I needed only to keep trusting in Him. So, the evil was wholly external; and there was a little area in my true self or soul into which evil couldn't enter, it seemed, and "in" which I prayed fervently and confidently to God for strength, even though my emotions were reverberating from the assault. My imagination was being presented with an image which I didn't want to accept, and my spiritual senses recognised and recoiled from the almost-all-enveloping presence of 'pure' evil. Yet at the end of that time, the evil being suddenly abandoned the attack and disappeared.

The spiritual assault had lasted for an hour. It has never happened since, in quite the same manner, for which I'm profoundly grateful; in fact, I so dreaded a recurrence that I became more sensible and regular about my use of the Rosary and of holy water. I arranged to be invested with the Scapular; and, thus armed, I was even able to cast off my fear - for which I thank God, Our Lady and St. Michael - and others.

[Guardian Angels.

It seems hardly right to spend so much time writing about spiritual danger without also saying a few words about a special sort of help. I've already said so much about Our Lord, and about the prayers of Our Blessed Lady and the other Saints; but I haven't said much about the Holy Angels who not only serve God, but who give us tremendous assistance. I suppose I've been confident that many readers will come across the teachings from Our Lord about Angelic help and about prayer, teachings which can be found in the volumes I've already had printed. But I'm bound to say that if every Christian paid regular attention to his or her Guardian Angel, by which I mean through courteous greetings and through regular prayer, each person would find the spiritual life made easier and more joyful.

How many Christians today believe that God has provided an Angelic Companion and helper for each one of us, as Our Lord indicated, and as His Church still teaches? It's true that this is a help known only through faith; yet we greet, know and converse with Our Lord and the Saints of Heaven 'only' through our faith and God's goodness. I'm not in the least implying that we ought to be drawn, by a foolish curiosity, into peculiar by-ways to do with spiritual matters. It's just that God has provided so many marvellous helps for us for our day-to-day Christian living; yet some of what we can call the 'basics' are routinely neglected by a great number of Christians, as they themselves admit; and I say this not to condemn anyone, but to say how sad it is for us to see such helps passed by. It's almost as though we can see a stretch of rough water where swimmers are in danger of drowning. We see people call out for help, and at the same time we have to watch them as they ignore the life-belts, ropes, and other aids thrown out from a boat to help them. They continue thrashing at the water as before, because they've been conditioned by what they've seen in films: let us say, to expect a helicopter to appear every time they're in difficulties; and so they ignore the small but life-saving props which are lying around.

That's what Christians are like, surely, who grumble about trying to be faithful to God and who complain about their duties but who never reach out to 'pick up' the life-lines which He has provided for their guidance or rescue. They don't realise that the tiniest prayer, made with faith to God or to one of God's friends, can save them from danger.

Saints and Angels: our powerful friends.

By every good act we perform in order to please God - even a little act of trust - and by every sincere prayer we make, whether to God Himself or to His Saints or Angels, we enable God to make our faith stronger, and allow Him to give us powerful assistance: whether through an obvious intervention, or by light for the soul, or strength in the will. I hope and pray that many people will open their spiritual eyes, so to speak, to accept with faith the wonderful news that we have a Saintly family in Heaven urging us on to holiness; and by 'family' I mean the Church. I hope and pray that they'll realise that we have many Saintly and Angelic helpers close by us who are willing to assist us in every difficulty, if only we'll ask for help. These helpers resemble God not only in their charity, but in their respect for our freedom; and although there's much that they do for us that we don't know about, but will find out in Heaven one day, God Willing, it's as though they are waiting quietly for our requests for even more effective help.

A mere few words can bring that help immediately, if we have faith, and if we're willing to turn to them to say, perhaps: "Most Holy Angel, please give me your special help in this difficult task", or: "Saint Joseph, please take charge of the household today," or "Immaculate Mother, please pray for me."

It's very simple.]

Truths of the Catholic Faith.

It's only recently, when the purifications which I mentioned earlier have almost been completed, as Christ has shown me, that I can see what He's done for me. Only since that time of testing has Christ woven freely into His 'teachings-in-prayer' the numerous and very detailed explanations about the reasons for my prolonged training, and about the ultimate aim of the whole work; and He has continued to teach me on the usual subjects, although has somewhat perturbed me by the 'depth' of some aspects of those subjects. That's why my descriptions of the truths of our Faith haven't all been achieved with the same degree of ease.

One of the 'teachings-in-prayer' that I wrote down three years ago caused me a few heart-pangs, but not because I found it fearsome in its subject matter nor because I was inaccurate in the expression of the subject, which is the Holy Mass. Rather, it was because I found myself writing confidently about something which - until I received that 'teaching' in prayer, - I knew very little; and so I've sometimes found myself hovering, since that time, on the very edge of fear, since, unless I go to outside sources, I no longer have anything in my mind against which I can 'check' the truth of what I'm writing. It feels as though I'm walking on a high-wire, an inch from disaster, and yet, I do believe that everything I'm writing conforms to - merely 'illuminates' - that which the Church is teaching today. I don't in fact look up 'sources', but rely on a kind priest, as I said, to check my work for mistakes. Every new twinge of concern has made me resolve to carry on courageously and to ask in prayer for continued guidance, and for trust and humility.

Living Truth, within the soul.

When I talk about 'checking' truth in my mind, so far, I mean that until recently I've had no fear at all that anything I write about God might be against Church teaching. I wouldn't set down in writing anything which I believed was against our teaching. But, besides, I've routinely evaluated every word I write by a swift, intuitive act in which I 'hold up' my own words - as when someone holds a faint piece of hand-writing against the light from a window - against the living Truth which I believe fills my heart and mind and soul; and this 'living

Truth' consists of all that I know of our Faith, but faith's details as made known to me on two levels.

I can check my own phrases by weighing them against everything I've remembered from 'external' sources. Only God has given me the gift of faith by which I'm enabled to believe what the Church teaches, but the 'concrete' facts of faith and its doctrines have been culled throughout my adult life from many sources: Church catechisms, Catholic authors, Popes, Council documents and homilies, and through the prayers, pleas and readings of the Liturgy, the words of Holy Scripture - and the Church's interpretation of those words - and through good Christian friends and the advice of priests. This jumbled list, alas, is not necessarily given in the right order; but the whole body of sources provides - with details of tradition, and the writings of the Fathers of the Church, and the witness of the Saints - a good 'picture' of what it is that Christ has done for us, and the ways in which He wants to see us cooperate with Him so that we can glorify the Father through Him in the Spirit's power, help our neighbour and be made ready to enter Heaven.

So, if I were to be shown things during 'teachings-in-prayer' which were not according to the 'mind' of the Church, as I have understood it - for example, if I should be taught that Jesus didn't die on the Cross - I would try not to 'listen'. I'd assume that the 'teaching' was in fact a temptation from an evil source, or perhaps a day-dream. I wouldn't write it down, since I have no interest in recording untruths; and anyway this never seems to happen - I mean, I never learn in prayer things which are against Holy Scripture or Tradition.

Now, that's only the first 'level' against which I can check the teachings. I can also 'check' them against what I know of God from life, prayer, and experience.

A 'pattern,' within my soul.

I have to be bold, and say that God - in His teaching of me over a number of years - has shown me, all-at-once, and also in separate 'bursts' of explanation, something of what-He-is-like; and in learning from and of Him, the Source of Knowledge, I have therefore necessarily learned not only 'what-He-is-like' but 'what-His-Son-is-like,' and His Mother, and His Church, and His Saints.

So I can say, despite recent fears having surfaced, that "God-within-me" is like a 'pattern' against which, intuitively, I have been holding up every thought and query which arises from my heart, intellect, imagination, memory, or will. I hold up everything in 'God's-light-within-me'; and I evaluate every teaching in order to affirm or discard it, to refine or refuse it, or to write it down gratefully or try to forget it. So, throughout recent years, as I've been writing about God, Church, prayer and Salvation, I've been able to say, confidently, about every piece of writing that I've have done: this is the very truth which is explained to me by Church sources, or by God Himself, even if the 'setting', or analogy or parable, should be novel.

I mentioned 'hovering on the edge of fear' because some of the very lengthy 'teachings' which I've received in past years go 'beyond' all that I've learned from books, Liturgy and conversation. In my heart, I'm quite certain that everything I write is 'good' doctrine; but at this new 'level' I no longer have anything 'concrete' in my memory, imagination or 'working' intellect against which I can 'check' it: I mean, 'checking' it by memory. I have 'only' God within - by which I mean God-as-known-by-me - as the 'pattern' against which I 'test' the truth of every phrase I write. And that's why I've been glad to know that all my written work is checked by someone else. I'm happy that someone learned is able to reassure me that I haven't been misled.

Although I've always been quite satisfied with what I've learned from Popes, Church sources, Councils and Catechisms, I've led a 'sheltered life' in the sense that I'm not an academic who has been able to exchange views or read 'exploratory' theology. I'm not 'au fait' with modern theologians' diverse, adventurous or perhaps risky ways of explaining eternal truths in twentieth-century idiom. So I'm perhaps more 'alone,' humanly-speaking, than many others who write about God.

I can sum up the reason for my caution by explaining that as I've recorded some of the things which I've recently been taught in prayer, I find that I write about things which I don't already know - in such detail. So I've had to 'take a deep breath' and ask advice before carrying on. But no-one is as thoughtful as Christ. All the time that I've been translating His teachings into words, He's been weaving encouraging and personal teachings amongst what I think of as 'chunks' of theology.

Continual encouragement.

Month after month, Christ has explained even more about His tremendous Love for me - and for everyone; and He's continued to encourage and delight me by bringing His holy Mother to visit me on especially-significant occasions. So that's why I'm glad to be able to obey Christ by writing a few chapters on a handful of further topics which are like the threads I've mentioned: strands woven by Christ into the 'ribbon' of my life: woven not just for my sake but for the sake of many others who long to know about the hope which Christ brings.

Boasting about Christ's Love.

In order to fulfil Christ's wishes I must write something in the next few chapters about Christ's very clear instructions about what books to have printed, whom to visit for advice, and when to act on His behalf. I must write something about my own role in this huge task - a role which Christ has unveiled for me, now that He has trained me sufficiently for me to be able to bear the 'knowledge' and the 'weight' of it. I must mention some of the gifts which Christ has showered upon me: not to boast about them, but to boast about Christ's Love, and to say that it's ours - yours - whenever we open our hearts to Him. I must tell about the stages of prayer through which Christ has led me in these past years, as He has drawn me up to the Father, and so has 'immersed' me in this Love. I must weave amongst Christ's own teachings some of the extraordinary teachings of God the Father which have astonished me more than anything in recent years; and that's because, when He began to teach me, I didn't even know that it was possible to converse with Him in the way with which I've become familiar - through His Infinite kindness and through the Name of Christ and the power of the Holy Spirit Who 'lifts' my soul into prayer.

I must speak - as if from the house-tops - about what Christ is really like, and also about the peace which I've found in Christ: "A PEACE THE WORLD CANNOT GIVE" (Jn 14:27), and which Christ has given to me; and then I must speak about the life of incomparable bliss at the heart of the Holy Trinity. All of these topics are mentioned in the following few chapters.

Images to share.

The booklets of teachings which I began to offer to friends and relations from about 1992 were received with all sorts of reactions, as I think I mentioned. But Christ rewarded me for my efforts, even as some people reacted enthusiastically on meeting such encouragement-in-faith, and others never spoke to me again, being unable to cope happily with a friend who spoke about Christ and visions. I found it very distressing; but I 'offered up' every humiliation, and continued with my efforts. I tried to speak according to each person's capacity, either using a few words about prayer, or giving a lengthy explanation. At the same time I offered free photographs of my paintings of some of Christ's images about prayer and the Mass. I'd composed a caption for each picture, so that it would be understood, and could be used for meditation or catechesis; and the pictures proved to be more popular than the books, for various reasons.

Pictures are so immediate: easy to assimilate and with enjoyable colours - and in an age when comparatively few people read books. I began to see why Christ in His wisdom had given me so many images to share: glimpses of holy things and holy people for twentieth-century searchers who were used to cinemas and videos, picture-adverts and pictorial street-signs, and many of whom rarely approached a whole page of text.

Prayer-pictures.

Most of my friends are familiar with my vividly-coloured oil paintings of Christ's prayer-images; but it seems right to add a few points here about the huge series of monochrome watercolour sketches which I began in 1992.

It was only when I'd seen how many people had been led to meditate on the 'Holy Sacrifice', and only after I'd obeyed Christ by recording all the "teachings" for a possible future use that I came to realise the significance of the images which had been given to me in prayer; and I realised my plain duty. Yet as I hesitantly began to record in brush and ink all of the images given so far, I instinctively trimmed or altered or repositioned each image within the rectangular frame before me, as would any artist who is accustomed to making an artistically-acceptable picture from a very simple initial concept or image.

It was true that each new work was a valid design; yet I would soon have to start all over again, in order to forget about 'design', and to record with great simplicity, and accurately, and therefore in monochrome, exactly what I'd been shown in prayer, with no embroidery or sophistication. I realised that I ought not to 'develop' or use any further 'prayer-pictures' before I had painted a precise record of what had been given to me by Christ our Lord, for His own good reasons. I would have to paint hundreds of small, faithful images, each of which would have to be labelled and categorised and, when copied, placed within the typed 'teachings'. Only watercolour would convey the delicate and luminous quality of the God-given 'images', although, sad to say, many of the pictures are so clumsy and of such poor quality that only the barest inkling of the true, marvellous images is conveyed. For three or four months in nineteen-ninety-two, however, I worked very fast to complete the project. Despite my being rather 'ham-fisted', I consoled myself with the knowledge that the images were at least 'down', almost exactly as they'd been given to me. Most of them lacked detail, but most were full of light and glory.

None of them was in colour; and I know that this has puzzled some people. Certainly, in a handful of 'teachings' I've said, for example: "Christ stood before the altar wearing a priestly robe adorned with a Cross in red." But on such an occasion, the Glory of Christ was glimpsed as I've described above; and it's been solely "by knowledge", according to God's Will, that the redness of the Cross has been made plain to me, not by the soul's sight.

Images of Light-and-Glory.

It seems to me - after reflection - that there's a particular reason for the absence of colour in the 'visions'. I believe that the colours which so beautify our natural world and gladden our hearts, which so powerfully stir our emotions and which can be used to indicate gloom or decay are a gift of God, on earth. But it seems to me that they have no place in prayer, which, if truly supernatural, is so far above natural beauty and so peaceful that it has nothing to do with the changeability of human emotions. That is my experience; and that, I believe, is why the images given or permitted by God in some of the 'teachings-in-prayer' are full of light or light-and-Glory only. There's no need for any stirring-of-emotion, since God's truth and invisible Beauty give the heart and soul, even here on earth, in the fullness of contemplative prayer, almost more joy than can be borne; but I'd better explain why, in more recent years, I've persisted in making vividly-coloured oil paintings which are based on some of the most striking or significant of the prayer-images.

Even though most of the facts about prayer and the spiritual life which Christ wants to explain through the 'teachings' are explained best, and with great simplicity, through monochrome works, I've come to realise that there's also a place for colour in this whole project. It's because all the prayer-images have now been captured in their simplicity and can be seen by anyone who needs to understand them that I'm now 'free' to launch out into more vivid ways of sharing those images and truths with other people; and I've come to see that in our world today, in which vivid images play such an important part in advertising and entertainment, I can use colour for a good purpose.

Through making large colourful oil paintings I can harness, fuel or stir emotions. Through the beauty of colour I can prepare hearts to receive the teaching which is 'embodied' in each painting. It's true that emotions can't cause faith to be given, but they can warm cold hearts, perhaps, and make them responsive to paintings. Even people who don't read religious books - or who rarely read anything - can be given a glimpse of prayer, and of Glory, as they look at a colourful painting of the Holy Sacrifice of the altar; and now that almost every prayer-image is routinely recorded in watercolour, first, there's no possibility of confusion about what Christ has shown me. Anyone who, today, sees one of the vivid oil paintings and who then learns that they are based on 'given-images' can now say: "What did the artist actually see. Show me;" and the watercolour is available to show how simple was the initial image which has later been put over more powerfully in oils.

While I'm writing about a body of art-work, I should say that it's because I can't allow there to be any doubt about what Our Lord has given to me in prayer, nor any doubt that I try to share freely with other people the good things He has revealed to me, that I've given up all my commercial art-work. That era of my life is over. It's my privilege now to record all the images and teachings, and to speak about them during whatever time is left to me. That, as well as looking after my family through my usual domestic duties, is my present task, though my work may change in the future. Whatever God Wills, I hope I do it.

A huge correspondence.

Christ is so kind that He didn't show me all-at-once that He'd be asking me to produce several books, and hundreds more pictures, nor that I'd be required to speak to a far greater number of people than I'd expected. I didn't know what a huge correspondence I'd be undertaking on the subjects of Faith, books and teachings; nor did I foresee that I'd be invited by Christ to send these books to my bishops and to the Holy Father. Christ introduced me little by little to what is a huge task; but at every stage He gave me an understanding of what to do, with the courage to do it, and with a reminder to 'offer up' whatever suffering was involved; and it was He Who provided heartening and consoling assistance from some wonderful people who appeared on the scene just as their help and kindness were sorely needed.

It's not possible to mention them all; but I'd be wrong if I didn't speak about the generosity of my husband. Without it, there would have been no books printed; and so I thank God and him for his kindness.

Spiritual topics.

It is probably evident now, after thirteen chapters, that the subjects on which Christ has chosen to teach me - whether with images nor without - have all been to do with life on earth, Life-in-Christ, prayer, Church, Eternal life or death, God's nature and God's purposes, and related subjects. Each topic has been introduced by Christ in prayer, and then re-introduced at some stage, as He has led me to a deeper understanding of spiritual matters - and has given me a few surprises. I mean that I've been surprised, though I shouldn't have been, to discover how personal and tender is His love for me - as it is for everyone. I was surprised to find out how extremely important Our Blessed Lady is, not 'just' as the Mother of God, or as a role model, but as someone intimately involved, now and for all time, with Christ's work of Salvation.

Here's a list of some of the topics on which Christ has been teaching me since the major series of topics which I've already described in chapters nine to fourteen of this book, and in the booklet called: "An Introduction". I'm putting this here just to show how comprehensive has been His course of instruction.

I've been taught by Christ in prayer, for example, about the Sacred Priesthood (T:1285 and 1554), the Blessed Sacrament (T:1304), the Holy Mass (many times, including T:1309, 1470 and 1740C), the Church (T:1327B), Ordination (T:1331 and 1336B), Our Lady (T:1349A and 1459), the Atonement (T:1351), the Love of God (T:1354), Transubstantiation (T:1360), Purgatory (T:1366), the Sacred Tradition (T:1386), Christ's Passion (T:1405), our spiritual training (T:1422), Heaven and Hell (T:1438), duty (T:1445), intimacy with God (T:1508), penance (T:1542), prayer-in-Christ (T:1548), work and gender (T:1554), faith (T:1578B), Christ as a Bishop (T:1618), the New Covenant (T:1613), spiritual friendships (T:1614), full Communion (T:1615), Judgement (T:1623), sacred space (T:1630), Holy Scripture (T:1635), intercession (T:1660), time and Eternity (T:1668 #4), Calvary's Offering (T:1668 #12), shrines (T:1680), prayer for the Departed (T:1695), sharing God's nature (T:1706), priestly celibacy (T:1716), our Immaculate Saviour (T:1744A), one Doctrine (T:1734B-1, human-Divine co-operation (T:1794), the heart of the liturgy (T:1804), Marriage (T:1813), Substitution (T:1829 #4), Sundays and holy days (T:1857), the Sacrament of the Sick (T:1893), martyrs (T:1895 #3), children of God (T:1905), irreverence (T:1920), Reconciliation (T:1924), the 'Our Father' (T:1926), devotions (T:1930), chastity (T:1940), the Father's Love (T:1941), Benediction (T:1943), the Saints (T:2011), mediation (T:2017), unborn children (T:2025B), Baptism (T:2028), the tabernacle (T:2035), how to 'console' Christ (T:2055), ways of teaching (T:2093), the meaning of the Mass (T:2095), Creation (T:2120), Exposition (T:2138), joy in God (T:2162), Life in God (T:2169), Novena petitions (T:2176), the purpose of Holy Communion (T:2198), Salvation (T:2200A), the Redeeming Sacrifice T:2203), sinful priests (T:2220), no Way but Christ (T:2230A), the heart of the Godhead (T:2244B), the unprepared (T:2249), spiritual friendships (T:2286B), conception and birth (T:2348), priests who resemble Christ (T:2354), and holy love in Marriage (T:2382).

It seems a bit extravagant to have listed so many subjects here; but it will give a good impression, I hope, of the generosity of Christ Who has chosen this way, in a time of special need, to remind His People of the richness and the depth of the Catholic Faith. Yet these are only a few of the subjects covered. There are many more.

A thorough training.

But what was the real point of all these teachings and all this work? Christ had told me very little, until then. His plan was to give me a thorough training in obedience before allowing me to know His plans. I'd imagined that the teachings would encourage some people in their faith, even if others reacted as I might well have done if our roles had been reversed. I'd probably have been uninterested in private revelations, though I would have looked at some of the paintings.

From about 1995, however, Christ began to explain much more about His plans; and at first I was appalled. When I'd just finished writing Volume Two of His teachings, He showed me that He's offering through this work not just reminders about prayer and the sacraments and the Church, and all these others things; He's also providing a picture of the whole progression of the spiritual life: a sort of template of the spiritual life - from conversion to the transforming union. Of course, He showed me that although it's necessary that I try to write about the spiritual life, in order to be obedient to Him, the important thing is to 'live it out', that is, to live out what I'm writing: to put these things into practice in everyday life, amidst the chores and the apple crumble, as I cook, shop, and go to Mass.

It made me happier, however, to hear further reasons for the whole plan of sharing the 'Teachings'; and they astonished me, although they fitted in so marvellously with what I could plainly recognise as my weaknesses and my ignorance of Theology that I was even more admiring of Christ, Who provides help for people in every situation. I mean that He showed me the needs of the Church in our particular era, and also showed me how His work in my life would help to restore confidence in the eternal truths of the Catholic Faith. He showed me that He's going to achieve this precisely because I'm so weak, sinful and handicapped. He wants to show proud people who refuse to accept the plain teachings of His Church that faith is more important than scholarship, although both are important, and that obedience to God's Will as proclaimed by the Church is more important than the holding of an important position in Church or society.

Christ wants to prove, especially to priests and religious who won't teach the plain truths of the Catholic Faith, as well as to lay people, that if He can't rely on His appointed teachers to proclaim the Faith with the unashamed gladness and fervour with which it has been proclaimed in past times, He can teach an ignorant woman, in prayer, what is important in the Christian life and what is not; and He can enable her to share His wisdom with His 'little ones' in this era so that they aren't left unconsoled and unfed.

Christ's explanation.

My own boldness is astonishing me, as I write in so much detail about this task, and my role; but I'm only writing because Christ has shown me the truth, and because He's trained me not to think about what people will say when they've read my work. But I can provide a better understanding of the whole work if I explain that in recent times, day by day, Christ has been showing me all sorts of details about my past and future work, drawing my family towards the Church, and delivering me from a multitude of fears. He has warmed my heart by new friendships, consoled me most powerfully for every loss, hurt or danger and has also led me to new heights of prayer. He has even brought me to meet the Father: the Father of Light and Glory: "A GENTLE FATHER AND THE GOD OF ALL CONSOLATION" (2 Co 1:3); and since the Father is Love, and is the Source of Love, He therefore delights in greeting even a weak and sinful person when she has come to meet Him in the company of Christ, helped and changed by the Holy Spirit; and I claim to have achieved such a glorious, interim goal only because Christ has explained to me in great detail what He's been doing for my soul in the past two or three years.

There are quite a few things I must write about, therefore, for those who want to know a little about 'life-in-union,' as discovered and enjoyed by someone who has been astonished at every new stage by the immensity of God's love for a creature. Christ never fails to remind me that good results come about through faith and self-sacrifice; and yet He showers upon me so many wonderful gifts that I'd be ashamed to complain of any hardship. For example, I was inundated with blessings at the start of 1993.

On February 22nd that year, I celebrated twenty-five years as a Catholic; and at last I was living in a state of delight at God's goodness to me rather than of sorrow at how badly I've served Him. My elder son was at Seminary in Rome. On 14th May, our parish priest blessed the painting I'd just finished: a likeness of Our Lady, from memory. It's the picture which is entitled: "Our Lady of Harpenden." I had managed to do many more oils, all 'prayer paintings'; and I'd given up all commercial work, for various reasons; but every spare minute was spent on the writings and paintings, after family and church commitments and in between chores and meetings with friends and new visitors; and all the while, in prayer, amidst such joyful and fulfilling activities, the teachings flowed from my soul like a river.

Then Christ urged me, on 18th July:-

> **Give up every remaining private or selfish longing. The less there is of yourself - of your own plans and ambitions - mixed up in your efforts to do My Will, then the more firmly can My Will and My grace be given full space and first place in the 'Great Outpouring' later on, when you act as a channel for My grace to others. (T:1332B)**

True lovers, equal.

In August 1993, as I thought about all the work I had to do, I turned with Christ to the Father, and renewed my offering by saying: "Here is the rest of my life, for You - whatever might happen ..." and the Father lifted me into His joy. Then, on August 8th, as I revealed my whole heart and soul to Christ once more, He overwhelmed me with delight, and taught me that since true lovers are equal He has given me gifts which have made me worthy of union with Him. He urged me to be confident in His Love. Then He explained to me:-

> **Realise what a great grace it is that I have led you to reveal every thought, desire and anxiety to Me in prayer. To be able to confide in Me is a sign of great trust. Realise, further, that:**
>
> *Love is reciprocal.*
> *True lovers are bound to be equal,* **and therefore**
> *when you share your thoughts and desires* **and anxieties**
> **with Me**
> **in sincere trust and friendship,**
> *revealing and giving so much of yourself,*
> *I do the same for you:*
> *from My Godhead to your humanity!*
>
> **Consider My great Love for you.**
> **Such is My tenderness towards My friends, and**
> **so great is My desire**
> **to draw you all into ever-more intimate friendship,**
> **that I lavish my gifts upon you.**
> *Almost like a blood transfusion*
> *by which life or the properties needed for life are given,*
> **a great gift is given to you in Holy Communion,**
> **a gift by which the Divine Life within you is strengthened.**
>
> **My gift to you in Holy Communion is My very Self, and so**
> *I give to the soul just what is needed*
> *for the union of the soul with Myself*

> *in an equality of love!*
> *I give to the soul -* as if adorning you with Divine gifts -
> *Love, knowledge,* Divine *Life, and beatitude,*
> *thus making your soul equal to Myself*
> *in Love, intimacy,* eternal *Life, and bliss.*
> *(T:1341 #2)*

Ready to meet rejection.

What a marvel it is, that God exists, and that God loves, and, furthermore, that we who are so weak, cowardly or fearful are the objects of that astounding Love! What astonishing gifts have been held out to us because of God's Self-revelation in Christ; and how deeply my heart was touched whenever Christ described the graces with which He wants to adorn us. Yet these reminders of God's Love, and these numerous teachings, weren't just for myself; and as I continued to distribute my booklets about some of the earlier teachings, I was reminded by Christ that I was going to meet with different reactions to my writings. He warned me, in order to help me:-

> **Be prepared for mixed reactions, as you offer other people the 'Light' which is My teaching.** *Some will 'bathe' in the Light, rejoicing. Some will declare the Light too bright to endure -* **or will secretly think so - and so will not accept your friendship or teaching.** *Others will claim to be so repelled by your weaknesses -* **thoroughly revealed in this Light -** *that they will say that they are unable to accept what you say* **about Me, and about My Church, and about the spiritual life. (T:1342)**

God's tender and forgiving love.

A few weeks later, when I was repenting of some of these weaknesses, I turned to the Holy Spirit, at the end of the Sunday Mass, and asked Him to give me a more loving heart. He answered not by suddenly banishing my every remaining prejudice or grudge, nor by suddenly making me immune to cowardly or resentful thoughts, but by overwhelming me with His own Love, and so giving me the supreme example of love. I mean that as soon as I'd opened my heart to Him through my sincere request, He said to me, with neither image nor sound, but with Infinite Majesty and purity: *"I am the measure."* At the same time He overwhelmed my heart and soul with His tender and forgiving love, in a demonstration of the sort of consoling and encouraging love that He wants to see me show towards other people.

How pitiful is my love, I saw, when compared with the Divine Love which helps and sustains me at every moment.

Very much more information and encouragement was given to me in that single and simple teaching (T:1354); but what I tried to take to heart, as I reflected on these things later on, was the vivid reminder from the Holy Spirit that true love, in its extraordinary kindness, always wants to see the other person blessed with the gifts of God and almost weeps for sadness at the dangers which people face. True love does all in its power - whilst respecting everyone's freedom - to keep souls from sin; and yet does so by encouraging goodness in each person, place and circumstance. Someone who does this can be sure that he is imitating Christ, of Whom we can say: "HE DOES NOT BREAK THE CRUSHED REED, NOR QUENCH THE WAVERING FLAME" (Is 42:3).

Sharing good news.

It was because I was yearning to be able to tell people about God's patience and kindness that I once again overcame my nervousness about speaking in public. I'd been invited to give a talk about the "Mass Paintings" to several hundred Eucharistic Ministers; and that's why I visited York for two or three days in October. The day conference at which I spoke was held in the University building, and the twenty paintings were simultaneously being displayed at the Bar Convent Museum.

Christ showed me, in prayer, about a fortnight later, how important is the task He's given me to do, and how glad He is that I thank Him for all the helps He has given me (T:1358). But then He led me - shortly afterwards - to the Father in prayer; and I was given a vigorous but loving reminder that nothing I do or say is worthwhile unless it is done 'in Christ'. Only because of Christ does my work have any merit, in the Father's sight. But the knowledge helped to steer me not towards despondency but towards humility, or truth: which is the 'rock' of the Gospel story in which "THE SENSIBLE MAN ... BUILT HIS HOUSE ON ROCK" (Mt 7:24). This is what I was taught, as Christ lifted me up in prayer, and brought me to the Father in a marvellous way, so that I could be taught at greater length than ever before. I was amazed and delighted to be shown by Christ:-

Be grateful that you have been led to see how profound is your spiritual poverty, and how great is your need of My Divine graces. It is through your acceptance of Truth, and through the sincere and contrite prayers which you have offered in My Name that you are close to your Heavenly Father, who has something to teach you:

HOW TRUE IT IS
THAT YOU COME TO ME WITH EMPTY HANDS,
THAT YOU HAVE NOTHING TO OFFER
TO ME
EXCEPT CHRIST MY SON, AND THE MERITS OF HIS SACRIFICE.
"That is what I wanted you to learn,"
SO THAT, LIKE A CHILD,
YOU CAN LIVE AT LAST IN THE TRUTH!
IT IS WHEN YOU KNOW THE TRUTH ABOUT YOURSELF
THAT YOU CAN HOPE FOR TRUE HAPPINESS.
HOW FOOLISH ARE THOSE
WHO TRY TO RELY ON NATURAL GIFTS
TO DO MY WORK.

(T:1359 #1)

NEVER RELY ON YOUR OWN ABILITIES:
ON ABUNDANT WORKS, OR ON FLUENT SPEECH OR CHARM,
OR ON ANY OTHER GIFTS.
You can rely, only, on the Merits of Christ:
on the graces which He has won for you
and which He chooses to give to you
moment by moment.
ACCEPT THE TRUTH:
It is only through His graces
that you are enabled to help other people,
though I can use you, out of 'need',
USING YOU
as a good Carpenter uses a rusty implement.
IN THIS 'NEED' OF HELP
I MEAN ONLY
THAT IT IS MY WISH THAT MY WORK IS ADVANCED
THROUGH THE CO-OPERATION OF MY FRIENDS.
YET HOW FEW ARE WILLING TO ASSIST ME.
INDEED, HOW FEW ARE ABLE TO ASSIST ME.
HOW CAN ANYONE WHO LACKS FAITH
'HELP' ME, HIS GOD?

(T:1359 #2)

PERSEVERE IN PRAYER.
DON'T BE AFRAID,
BUT REMEMBER:
Only because of Christ's Wounds and Christ's pleas
do I, your Father, grant your poor prayers.
CHRIST, ALONE, IS WORTHY OF BEING HEARD,
AND YOU,
IF YOU BELONG TO HIM.

(T:1359 #3)

THINK ABOUT YOUR DAILY LIFE:
ABOUT THE GIFTS WHICH I HAVE GIVEN TO YOU,
AND ABOUT YOUR VOCATION.
PUT YOUR TRUST IN ME,
BUT REMEMBER:
YOU HAVE NOTHING OF YOUR 'OWN'.
Only through the graces
won by Christ's suffering on the Cross
do I, your Father, 'grace' you sufficiently
to do My Work on earth.

(T:1359 #4)

Reassurance, and Hope.

Throughout the autumn of 1993, I was immensely encouraged by these words from the Father

366

about the fact that I was doing His work in distributing books of 'teachings'. I had never had any doubts about this; but it was a great comfort for me to hear confirmed verbally in prayer what, until then, I had usually learned in wordless instructions; and so I became less cowardly about approaching people with my 'good news' about God's love for us and about His longing to see us made happy in the way which He knows is worthwhile, and sure.

When winter arrived, I had managed to produce many more oil paintings of the prayer-images. The teachings continued to flow, in prayer. I was taught about the work of the Holy Spirit, Who can change our hearts, and Who, daily, changes the bread and wine that we bring to the altar (T:1360); and this so inspired me that I offered my life to God once more; and the Father reassured me, in prayer, that it's through the abandonment of our own ambitions, and through true union with Him, "in" Christ, that we can find the greatest-possible joy.

Prayer as Purgatory.

Early in November, I was touched to the heart to be given, by an astonishing teaching, a deeper appreciation of God's goodness and of our need of purification.

It was when I had renewed my love and repentance before the Father that I was suddenly, and wonderfully, taught more about purification, and about how willing and contrite souls can hope to undergo Purgatory even during earthly life; but this news was given as a reason for hope, not for fear.

First, Christ showed me what had been happening within my soul; and then the Father intervened to teach me, as the Holy Spirit shone His Light of Understanding within me. In this way, I was marvellously taught by Christ:-

> **Be glad that - long ago and many more times since - you
> have been brought to repentance. You have seen what joy
> it has brought you, through My grace working within you,
> and your humility. (T:1366 #1)**
>
> **Be grateful for the purifications through which I have been
> leading you for so many years. Only through your
> contrition have you been enabled to walk the path of
> purification. (T:1366 #2)**
>
> **Look upon your purification - a 'scouring' which has been
> worked through remorse, penance, spiritual darkness and
> the sufferings of earthly life - as a priceless gift. Through
> this scouring, I have been preparing you for Heaven; and
> through the peace and the trust which have arisen within
> your soul, you have begun to pray to your Heavenly Father
> - in My Name - with increasing confidence and gratitude.
> Listen, as He reassures you that your trials have been
> worthwhile:**

HERE I AM
TEACHING YOU.
DON'T BE AFRAID.
REPENTANCE HAS LED YOU TO JOY,
BUT FOR YOUR GREATER JOY,
I AM SHOWING YOU THE PURPOSE OF PURIFICATION,
FOR THE SOULS OF ALL WHO HUMBLY ACCEPT THE PAIN
OF SEEING THEIR SINFULNESS.

True repentance is like this:
WHEN YOU REPENT SINCERELY,
AND WHEN YOU PERSEVERE IN PRAYER,
BRAVELY BEARING YOUR SHAME,
AND PRAYING IN THE NAME OF MY SON,
JESUS,
it is as though - VOLUNTARILY - *you approach Me,*
your God, your Father,
walking towards Me
- YOUR SOUL *'naked'* -
through the Fire of My Glory.

Yet as you approach Me, repenting,
naked in that Fire,
yet strong in the Life of Christ,
all sin bursts into flame.
Yet the 'Fire' does not touch your flesh;
and when your sins are at last consumed
you shall be like a child in My presence:
pure, newly-born, unashamed, naked and innocent;
and I will clothe you for the Wedding Feast.
THUS
in this life, and in prayer
some are invited - YOU AMONGST THEM - *to walk*
through their Purgatory.
(WC:1366) (T:1366 #3)

Perfect love, expressed in sacrifice.

Christ's love is so fervent that He didn't let me dwell for long on the subjects of sin and purification. He reassured me that He had especially chosen me for this work, even with all my failings, telling me:-

Be grateful for your task, without worrying about not being worthy of this work. It is true that you are not worthy; nevertheless I have chosen you, with all your faults. (T:1370 #1)

Accept My Will, in simplicity. Share My teachings. Let

nothing deter you from this task.

"It is your task.
I gave it to you
not because of your worthiness
but as My choice.
Others have other tasks.
This is yours!
I clothe you and adorn you for the task.
I make you fit.
I train you, and give you the gifts you need.
You are poor,
but I give you all you need
to bring riches to others." (T:1370 #2)

A declaration of love.

No-one is as tender as Christ, as He encourages us to believe in Him. Christ startled me at the Consecration one day, by speaking from above the altar to remind me just how profound is His love for me - and for everyone else for whose sake for He died a terrible death; and as I looked up and saw Christ hanging on the Cross, I heard Him call to me:-

Look up, at the time of the Consecration. Gaze upon the Sacred Host, as I Myself am calling out to you, saying: *"This is My Body!"* I am here before you. You are present to the One Holy Sacrifice which I offered on Calvary; and I am Really Present with you - here at the altar - pleading on your behalf to the Father. (T:1376 #6)

Look up, to see Me hanging on the Cross as My Blood was poured out for you. You have touched My Heart by your repentance and devotion; and although I am wounding your heart by speaking of My Love for you, I want you to listen, and to understand the reason:

"This is My Body!
this is what true Love means:
being wholly given up for you.
Not content with giving you
words of Love, from Heaven,
for you, I gave up My Body,
giving it
   not in ploughing fields like a family man
   proving his love by toil,
giving it
   not in sexual love, but
giving it

369

wholly, most perfectly,
in Sacrifice,
allowing others to take My life.
I did this for you, to pay your debt.
See how much I love you!
May this be a cause for joy
and not for sadness."
(WC + OIL: 1376) (T:1376 #6)

At the same time, Christ explained to me:-

> **Consider the work of the prophets who prepared the world**
> **for My holy Incarnation. It was through them that I sent**
> ***'words of love from Heaven':* words of pleading, reminder,**
> **promise, warning and anticipation. Their work was the**
> **prelude to the main theme of My action, which was My**
> **revelation of My Love for you: shown out through My**
> **Birth, Life, Death, Resurrection and Ascension. (T:1376 #7)**

> **Remind yourself that I cherish My friends. From Love, I**
> **gave My life in sacrifice and suffering, to save you. You**
> **can be sure - of the Passion which I suffered on your behalf**
> **- that *"I would have done it a thousand times, Lizzie,"* for**
> **you and for all of My precious brothers and sisters. (T:1377**
> **#1)**

> **Never forget how deeply I long to save you. (T:1377 #2)**

My heart ached for joy at this declaration of love. Indeed, after every teaching as fervent and reassuring as this one, my love for Christ grew stronger - and began to change in another way. I loved Him at last with my heart and feelings, as well as with my mind and soul. I mean that I had loved Him by faith, for many years: but with my soul and mind as much occupied with a concept - the idea of a Saviour - as with the real God-man Himself. But now I knew and loved Him primarily as a Person - albeit an Incarnate Divine Person through Whom I hoped to find salvation; and so every word of love I offered Him, and every sacrifice and act of witness, was made a thousand times easier and more joyful.

Prayer at every moment.

It was after Christmas, that same year, when we had all been thinking gratefully about Christ's love for us, and about His family life, that Christ showed me something else about faith, and its development - and more about how He Himself is our means of offering unceasing prayers of praise and thanks to the Father. On the feast of St. John the Evangelist, Christ urged me:-

> **Be grateful for the gifts which you have so far taken for**
> **granted. A small shoot of faith was planted in your soul in**
> **childhood. It was rooted in the 'rich soil' of a devout**

**family life, and in Christian worship, and in the words of
the Holy Scriptures. (T:1384 #1)**

**Continue to unite your prayers and sacrifices with Mine, as
you offer My Sacrifice to the Father. Say: 'Father, here is
Jesus' perfect prayer.' But don't imagine that you can
pray well only in church! Listen to your Father's teaching:**

OFFER CONFIDENT PRAYERS IN THE NAME OF MY SON: THE NAME OF JESUS.
You are not limited to the daily Offering at the altar.
You can make the same prayer at each moment of the day,
AS YOU LIVE "IN CHRIST," YOUR HEART TURNED TOWARDS ME.

You are not always before the altar
where the Holy Sacrifice is offered, yet
Christ's intention is always the same, **and**
He Who is now in Heaven - Jesus your Saviour -
pleads eternally before Me; AND
SINCE YOU AND HE ARE ONE IN LOVE,
by your union with Him, FROM BAPTISM,
His prayer is yours,
and can be offered
in its fullness and Divine power
at every moment of your life
by a little movement of your heart!
(T:1384 #2)

The Three Great Flames.

After that reminder of my utter dependence on Christ and on His Sacrifice, Christ Himself
showed me the goal towards which He had been leading me: He explained how I had allowed
Him to draw me, even during earthly life, into the heart of the Godhead.

On the first day of the New Year - 1994 - Christ lifted up my soul in prayer, to show me an
image of a small figure which was being enfolded by three great flames - and these represented
the Three Divine Persons; and Christ taught me that He delighted in my new abandonment to
His plans. He explained very gently:-

Rejoice in your security. *You who are willing to do My Will*
and not your own **are walking along a path which leads
towards eternal Life with Us - with the Most Holy Trinity -
in Heaven. Yet even during your life on earth you are
wrapped in Our Love. (T:1385 #2)**

Believe that even now you *are led by Me, Jesus, you are*
directed by My Spirit, and you walk towards the Father. **It is
as if your footsteps have led you - on your path to Heaven -
to step into the centre of a great Light which stretches**

across the ground in front of you; and that Light has risen up to enfold you; you can see that the single great Light consists of three huge flames, which, intertwined, hold you within their warm and peaceful embrace. *At every instant, you live at the Heart of the Holy Three - One God -* Who almost carry you, it seems, as you walk towards Heaven. We Three Divine Persons are like three great flames of Love; yet We are One Fire, in Whose unchanging Light you already live, even before you reach Heaven's perfection. (WC:1385A) (T:1385 #3)

Consider the wonder of Our union, the unity of the Most Holy Trinity. Truly, you share Our Life: the life of the Father Who waits before you, the life of Myself, Jesus your Lord and daily Companion, and the life of My Holy Spirit Who leads you onwards; and you have learned that none of Us Three Divine Persons lacks anything, yet None is ever 'without' the Others. Each perfect and Divine Person can be seen as wholly flame and wholly fire. Yet We Three, together, are One Flame or One Fire in which three 'flames' are distinct yet united. This One Fire of Love - Our Godhead - is simple yet three-fold. It is - I am - bright, pure, perfect and everlasting: One God, unrivalled. (WC:1385B) (T:1385 #4)

Continued teachings.

When I received that teaching about the Three Divine Persons, less than a year remained of the time in which, whilst I was being taught, I seemed to be as if 'below the cloud' which separates earth from Heaven. At the end of 1994, I was lifted up to the cloud in prayer, as if on Christ's outstretched hand, to begin a new way of life as if at the heart of the Holy Trinity.

During that year, Christ had shown me how sad it is (in T:1404) that when human life is given so that can be used for God - and for eternal fulfilment in God - so few persons do much except spend most of that God-given time in pursuing their own ambitions. He told me (T:1405) how few persons are prepared to make fools of themselves before others, in order to speak Gospel truths; and yet how extraordinary, blissful and fulfilling is friendship with the Father, for those who trust in Him and who are willing to turn to Him with sincere and loving hearts.

It was deeply moving for me to be shown by the Father, in prayer one day, that His Love for us is so great that it's as though He counts Himself honoured by even a moment's love and attention (T:1406). At the same time I was shown an image of a devout person being lifted up in contemplation towards the Father's outstretched arms - and therefore towards Heaven's Glory.

In prayer, I learned about the importance of a vigorous spiritual training for all who wish to please God (T:1422). Christ taught me more about Heaven and Hell (in T:1438), about duty

(T:1445), and about the peace and harmony which is experienced in each truly Holy Communion (T:1457); and that peace was being given to me ever more frequently in prayer, as well as at the reception of the sacraments; and that peace was enormously increased one evening in July, 1994, when Our Blessed Lady came to me again and taught me more about her role.

Our Lady's role.

On 24th July I was alone at home, waiting for my husband and children to return from an outing. I prayed my evening prayers as usual, but added fervent thanks to Our Lady for her kindness to me throughout the years - especially for her heartening visit of four years earlier. Then, with tears of gratitude and also tears for myself as I thought about my various difficulties and as I hovered on the brink of self-pity once more, I asked her: "Be a mother to me!" Straightaway she was with me, insisting: "I am your Mother!;" and as she comforted me by these reassuring words, her son Christ instantly explained the meaning. He taught me:-

> **Listen carefully to Mary, as she explains to you, gently, that her Motherhood of you is not a special privilege to be given on request, but is something wonderful which is already true for you; and as you now learn, she wants you to know that "If Jesus, by His humanity, is a brother to everyone, then the mother of Jesus is Mother of every person: to all!" (T:1459 #2)**

> **Ask My Mother's help in trying to serve Me ever more faithfully. Your trust in her is not misplaced. She is delighted that you turn to her, that you reveal your faults to her so frankly, and that you honour her by praying the Rosary. (T:1459 #3)**

> **Consider the wonderful results of regular prayer to Me and to My Mother, combined with contrition, and honesty. It is as though a pit has been prepared within your hollowed-out soul, a pit like those which workmen prepare in order to construct a firm foundation for a new building. In your soul, our 'building' can now begin! (T:1459 #4)**

> **Be glad that through your sufferings you have allowed Me to build a firm 'foundation' within your soul: so firm that it is like the 'rock' of the Gospel story; and the house built upon that rock was not swept away when floods came. I want you to remain firm amidst storms of temptations, and that is why it is important that you - and others - prepare your souls thoroughly by co-operation with My Will, and by prayer and contrition. (T:1459 #5)**

> **Turn to My Mother in times of great need, as well as amidst everyday joys and irritations. She is always**

> motherly and tender, waiting patiently to help you. Turn to
> her with each new thought and worry; none of your
> problems wearies her. She delights in helping her children,
> and that is why I asked you, long ago, to trust this beloved
> Mother, whom you call your 'Dear Lady'! (T:1459 #6)

> Notice the resemblance between My Mother and Myself.
> Although we are physically alike, I am speaking now about
> our attitudes. Just as I, your Lord, don't force anyone to
> welcome Me or to serve Me, but wait for an invitation to
> share in your lives and your sorrows, so My holy Mother
> too respects your freedom. (T:1459 #7)

> Consider what blessings you have drawn upon yourself
> today, through inviting My Mother to share more fully in
> your life and in your momentary sadness. (T:1459 #8)

Through ignorance of Our Lady.

Then Christ consoled me, saying:-

> Don't be ashamed that in past years you were tongue-tied
> before My Mother, feeling unfit to confide in her about
> various matters. Some of you who were brought up
> without knowing of her motherly love have nevertheless
> begun to know her; you honour her sincerely, praying to
> her, doing good things for her, defending her, and making
> sacrifices in her honour, to please Me. But you have done
> so as if from afar. You have been keeping My Mother at a
> distance not just in awe but through an ignorance and a
> lack of trust such as is sometimes found outside My
> Church. (T:1459 #9)

Comfort, from her presence.

It was true that my devotion to Our Lady had been dutiful rather than warm and trusting.
How well Christ knows our hearts; but how marvellously He can change them, in an instant.
It was by His mercy that I was suddenly shown an image of Our Lady, an image which
explained very clearly that the amount of help we receive in prayer depends upon our
willingness to approach the Heavenly friends who can help us. Christ showed me:-

> Ponder the image before you, in which you see My Mother
> acting as a true mother caring for two young children. You
> can see that one little boy has buried his head against her
> side; his face is hidden in her garments; he is tugging at her
> clothes, angry and rebellious and noisy; yet at the same
> time he trusts this Mother enough to stay close to her in his

misery, and therefore he derives comfort from her presence. However, the other little boy - you can see - is standing a few feet away from this tender Mother who is reaching out her hand to help him. But although he longs for help, and turns his face towards her sadly, he is too unbending or proud to run to her, and so he is not much helped. (WC:1459B) (T:1459 #10)

Run to Mary as anyone would run to a good mother. You will be comforted! (T:1459 #11)

See how important it is that you know My Mother well, and that you are truly grateful for her love. It is only now that you have been made ready to speak about her as she deserves. We want you to share with others the knowledge of her love, but we want you to speak not just with awe that she has come to you, encouraging you, but also with joy. Speak joyfully about that which now thrills you: that My Mother helps you all so sweetly because she cares for you so deeply! Don't be ashamed to speak of the bliss which you experience in her presence. (T:1459 #12)

Faith is needed.

Throughout the whole of 1994 I continued with my work, greatly helped by the kindness of Christ and His Mother. The prayers and teachings were woven into the usual meals, outings, bouts of illness, and days and weeks of writing. I was now overjoyed to be doing the work I was doing. It was difficult in some ways, but I was beginning to conquer my embarrassment at speaking about what Christ had been teaching me; and of course, I felt this initial embarrassment because I didn't think I was fit to do the work. Surely He could have chosen someone who'd been less rebellious?

But Christ showed me clearly that other people can be helped by seeing how much He can do in the life and soul of someone weak who finds it hard to be good. Then, on August 17th , Christ made a little more plain what He had been doing in my life. He urged me:-

Accept and delight in the knowledge which is now streaming towards you from within My Mind, to dispel your mind's former blindness. You can see, at last:

How great am I, Christ your God.
How kind am I
        Who stoop to you, My frail creature,
        Who stoop to you with such a gift,
        the gift of My 'teachings'.
How tremendous is the work which
        I am doing through you!

How many thousands will be helped!
How feeble and silly you have been
    during your efforts to speak
    about My teachings; yet
    how magnificent is My Love.
How glorious is My willingness to feed your soul
    both with Sacraments and "Teachings."
How few are willing to make efforts
    to be fit to receive My wisdom,
    to receive such 'teachings', in prayer.
How great a privilege is this intimacy!
How comfortable and stable is the union
    of your soul with Myself, a union
    sometimes even taken-for-granted!
How little faith there is in the world;
    and since faith is needed
    for this task,
    I use you.
How many assaults of evil,
    of temptation and illness
    - more evil than you are aware of -
    have been unleashed against you
    to deflect you from this work. (T:1467B #2)

Let this revelation encourage you
    to persevere
    through every trial which awaits you.
    I cannot fail to help you to complete this work,
    since it is Mine. (T:1467B #3)

Causes for joy.

During the month which followed that encouraging teaching, Christ taught me about the "ROYAL PRIESTHOOD" (1 P 2:9) to which I belong, as do all who live to serve Him (T:1469). He taught me more about the Holy Sacrifice of the Mass (in T:1470), and about His Mother Mary's role in our spiritual formation (in T:1489); and during that same year, I had further special reasons for rejoicing. The first was seeing the publication of the new "Catechism of the Catholic Church," which had been requested by the world's Catholic Bishops. It proved to be a marvellous reference work, with clear and unambiguous teaching on everything we need to know about our Faith. It included numerous topics on which some people wrongly claim that there is uncertainty within the Church, whereas the uncertainty lies in the hearts and minds of those who don't yet understand the teachings or who refuse to believe that they are true - or that the Church has the authority from God to proclaim certain things as true.

The book was greeted with cries of delight from fervent Catholics everywhere, as well as with the not-unexpected criticisms which grace every document sent out by the Holy Father and the other Bishops.

The comparatively minor reason for celebration was that I had a small statue of Our Lady installed outside our home: on the terrace near my back door. Our parish priest came to bless it; and when I thanked Our Lady for having made all this possible, she told me: "It is I who thank you." She is delighted whenever we do anything to honour her, and this is because she knows that it makes Our Lord happy to see her loved and revered (T:1471).

Speaking with the Father.

When almost a year had passed with wonderful spiritual treats mixed in with the usual difficulties, combined with hard work and ever more joyful and fruitful times of prayer, I was led into a lengthy conversation with the Father, Who astonished me by explaining how and why I have been 'taught' in prayer - and why I can be confident of spending Eternity with Him, if I live for love until I die.

Since that awesome day in November 1994 the Father has spoken to me at length on many occasions, in the communications of contemplative prayer. Most of these teachings are recorded in the several volumes of 'Teachings-in-prayer,' and so there's no need for me to reproduce very many here. I've already quoted a few of the Father's shorter teachings; but I've placed at the beginning of the next chapter the whole of this first lengthy teaching (T:1508), because it seemed to set a pattern for the many hours of dialogue with the Father which I've been privileged to enjoy in the past few years. Also, this will show several other reasons why I want to weep with gratitude that God is so good to us.

First, the Father responded to my heart's questions. Secondly, in His infinite courtesy, He let me 'guide' some of the conversation, yet took the lead very gently when He had some important information to give me; and thirdly, and most amazing to me, He shared His wisdom, in this way, to someone who has served Him so badly. Yet that's what He is like: utterly 'overcome', I can now say boldly, by people who are contrite and who trust Him. If only I could show people how infinitely sweet and consoling is the love expressed by this powerful, awesome and yet tender Father of ours Who has 'stooped' to us from Heaven, and Whom we can know through our union with Christ!

---

15 CONVERSATIONS
(1994)

A DIALOGUE. THE TASK. SPIRITUAL GIFTS.

Writing to my friends.

When I was sitting at my kitchen table on 26th November 1994, writing letters and greetings cards, I was grateful to God for the many friends to whom I was sending news and good wishes; and as I turned my heart to Christ, He led me to the Father and showed me:-

> **Follow My inspiration and pray for your friends, as you write letters and greetings cards. Turn to the Father, in your longing to be united in Heaven one day with these beloved people. Pray, in My Name, that they will be given the gift of faith in Me. Listen to your Heavenly Father, Who delights in your prayer, and Who now reminds you of My earthly origin:**

Here, to my astonishment, the Father vigorously yet soundlessly taught me:-

> ***Christ, the "Son of God", was born of the Jewish People.***
> YOUR DIVINE SAVIOUR
> WAS MADE INCARNATE THROUGH AN EARTHLY MOTHER.
> THROUGH YOUR UNION WITH ME IN PRAYER,
> AND THROUGH THE IMAGE WHICH I PLACE BEFORE YOU
> YOUR GLANCE CAN EMBRACE
> THE EARTHLY PEOPLE
> FROM WHOM SHE SPRANG:
> FROM WHOM CHRIST MY SON
> RECEIVED HIS HUMAN NATURE.
>
> LET ME SHOW YOU A RIVER, FLOWING:
> A 'RIVER' OF PEOPLE
> FROM ANCIENT AGES TO THE PRESENT DAY.
> SEE THE DARKNESS
> FROM WHICH EMERGED THIS PEOPLE, LONG AGO,
> OBEDIENT AND TRUSTING.
> SEE THE THOUSANDS OF FAITHFUL PEOPLE:

379

ANCESTORS OF YOUR SAVIOUR.

(T:1506 #1)

OPEN YOUR EYES TO THE WONDER OF CHRIST'S BIRTH.
HEAVEN'S LIGHT SHONE UPON EARTH, THROUGH HIM,
TO BRIGHTEN THE DARKNESS
WHICH STILL SHROUDED HUMAN HEARTS AND MINDS.
YOU SEE BEFORE YOU
A SPOTLIGHT, WHICH SHINES UPON THE 'RIVER':
UPON ONE GREAT SECTION: UPON THE FACES
CLOSEST TO YOU.
THOUSANDS OF PEOPLE ARE REVEALED, THUS, MORE CLEARLY,
THEIR FACES SHINING WITH HEAVENLY LIGHT;
AND THIS IS THE MEANING:
You who worship Christ
are direct spiritual descendants
OF THIS GREAT PEOPLE,
A PRECIOUS PEOPLE, CHOSEN BY ME, THEIR GOD,
YOUR FATHER,
AND GUIDED IN MY WAYS.
OPEN YOUR HEART TO MY TEACHING.
REMEMBER THE WAY
TO THE GREATEST POSSIBLE INTIMACY
WITH ME, YOUR FATHER:
they are most truly My People
who are united to Me
now.
People are most closely united to Me
when united to Me "in" Jesus Christ,
Whose Light shines on earth
with a clarity and power unseen elsewhere.
(WC + OIL:1508A) (T:1508 #2)

Life-in-union.

At this point, I was still sitting in my chair, too ill to kneel down, but almost overwhelmed by the Father's invisible yet wholly-enveloping Majesty. So I begged Him to show me how to please Him. I asked: 'Give me everything I need to do Your Will!' And the answer I received was exactly as I recite, below, except that, as before, I have 'translated' the Father's real but mostly-wordless teaching into my own language.

The Father told me, with awesome majesty yet infinite gentleness:-

DON'T BE AFRAID,
MY DAUGHTER.
YOU ARE CLOSELY UNITED TO ME, YOUR HEAVENLY FATHER.
I DELIGHT IN YOUR TRUST
AS YOU TURN TO ME, OPEN-HEARTED,

PRAYING IN THE NAME OF CHRIST,
REVEALING YOUR FEARS
ABOUT PRAYER, ABOUT BEING 'TAUGHT',
ABOUT YOUR WORK OF RECORDING THESE TEACHINGS, AND
ABOUT YOUR UTTER INABILITY TO DO MY WILL
UNLESS I ASSIST YOU.

DON'T BE AFRAID.
IT IS CHRIST MY SON WHO HOLDS YOU
CLOSE TO ME
WHO 'HIDE' MY DIVINE MAJESTY
- IT SEEMS -
BEHIND A VAST BANK OF CLOUD.
IT IS CHRIST WHO HOLDS YOU AS IF ON HIS OUTSTRETCHED HAND
AS YOU REACH UP TO GREET ME,
IN PRAYER.

(T:1508 #3)

Trust and humility.

Here, the Father consoled me, saying:-

DON'T BE AFRAID,
MY CHILD.
LISTEN TO MY TEACHING.
YOU PLEASE ME
BY YOUR LOVE FOR YOUR FRIENDS.
YOU PLEASE ME
WHENEVER YOU TRUST IN MY LOVE,
WHENEVER YOU REACH UPWARDS IN PRAYER,
WHENEVER YOU OPEN YOUR HEART TO ME,
WHENEVER YOU REVEAL YOUR WEAKNESS,
WHENEVER YOU YEARN TO DO MY WILL:
WHENEVER YOU FEED UPON TRUTH.

SUCH CLOSENESS
TO ME
YOUR HEAVENLY FATHER
IS MADE POSSIBLE
ONLY THROUGH JESUS, MY SON:
THROUGH HIS WORK WITHIN YOUR SOUL.

BY HIS POWER AND THROUGH YOUR TRUST IN HIM
HE HAS LIFTED YOU INTO MY PRESENCE.
IN THIS TRUE UNION,
YOU ARE A PRIVILEGED CHILD.

TRULY,

CHRIST IS THE WAY TO ME.
TRULY,
He brought you to Me, your Father.
HE BROUGHT YOU INTO THIS WAY OF LIFE:
THIS LIFE-IN-UNION.

(T:1508 #4)

A lengthy training.

Then the Father told me something which will warn others, through me, about the perils which are faced by those who receive great gifts from Him, and who then grow ungrateful or careless. He told me:-

DON'T BE AFRAID.
THOSE WHO ENVY YOU
OR WHO LONG FOR GREAT TASKS
SHOULD CONSIDER MY WISHES
AND THE LENGTHY TRAINING
WHICH HAS PREPARED YOU FOR SUCH INTIMACY.
THEY SHOULD CONSIDER, ALSO,
what a great fall, from such a height,
SHOULD ANYONE TURN AWAY, AND STUMBLE,
CARELESS OF LOSING LIFE AND LIGHT.

BE AT PEACE.
YOU ARE RESTING SECURELY IN MY LOVE.
I AM WARNING THOSE
WHO FLEE THE SACRIFICES,
AND WHO REPEL THE LOVE REQUIRED FOR 'LIFE-IN-UNION'.

YOU CAN REJOICE!
REJOICE IN YOUR SAVIOUR'S LOVE
AND IN HIS FRIENDSHIP,
AND IN THIS BRIGHT BLISS AND GLORY.

(T:1508 #5)

God's unceasing goodwill.

Then the Father explained how He and I can be perpetually united in prayer. He reminded me:-

DON'T BE AFRAID.
LISTEN TO MY TEACHING, THEN
RESPOND FROM THE DEPTHS OF YOUR HEART.
THROUGH MY SON, JESUS,
YOU ARE HELD WITHIN MY LIFE.
TREASURE THIS HOUR,

THESE PRIVILEGED MOMENTS
OF UNION, COMMUNION AND CONVERSATION
WITH ME
YOUR HEAVENLY FATHER
WHOSE MAJESTY IS INFINITE, UNFATHOMABLE.

DON'T BE AFRAID.
LET US CONTINUE IN PRAYER.
EXPRESS YOUR LONGING TO SERVE ME WELL.
My goodwill is unceasing.
I am always helping you to serve Me well
in whatever task I have set before you.
FURTHERMORE,
I never stop teaching you,
SINCE I NEVER WITHDRAW MY LOVING CARE
FROM YOU
THOUGH YOU ARE FREE
TO WITHDRAW YOUR LOVE AND ATTENTION
FROM ME.

(T:1508 #6)

CONSIDER YOUR WAY OF LIFE:
THIS CONSTANT COMMUNICATION WITH ME,
YOUR FATHER.
IT IS AS IF A 'CHANNEL' EXISTS
BETWEEN EVERY SOUL WHICH IS UNITED TO ME "IN CHRIST",
AND MY HEART.
THIS 'CHANNEL TO THE FATHER'S HEART'
IS OPENED BY PRAYER.
THIS IS A CHANNEL THROUGH WHICH COMES
ALL GRACE, LIGHT, TEACHING, WISDOM
AND JOY.
I NEVER 'CLOSE' THIS CHANNEL.
MY GIFTS POUR OUT LAVISHLY UPON
ONE WHO TURNS TO ME,
ONE WHOSE HEART IS 'OPEN' TO RECEIVE ME,
ONE WHOSE HEART IS 'OPEN' TO MY INFLUENCE,
ONE WHOLLY READY FOR MY PERPETUAL TEACHING.

THIS 'CHANNEL' TO MY HEART
- A CHANNEL OPENED BY PRAYER -
RESEMBLES THE BRIGHT 'CORRIDOR'
WHICH I REVEALED TO YOU:
A CORRIDOR THROUGH WHICH YOU TRAVEL
AFTER DEATH,
WHEN YOU CARRY ONLY YOUR OWN HEART:
A HEART FULL
- IT IS TO BE HOPED -

OF MY DIVINE LIFE AND LIGHT.

(T:1508 #7)

Prayers for the departed.

As the Father taught me about Divine Life, and about death, I was so aware both of the profundity and the length of this 'teaching' that I bowed down before Him, and silently and trustingly explained my intention; then I began to write down everything I could remember about the previous half-hour's conversation.

As I wrote, I suddenly remembered that two of our parishioners had died recently; and so I turned to the Father again, and asked Him to have mercy on them. In reply, He not only showed me how much He delights in each trusting prayer, but how it is that our prayers are answered. He taught me:-

DON'T BE AFRAID.
YOU PLEASE ME
AS YOU TRUST IN ME,
AS YOU RECORD MY TEACHING, AND
AS YOU PRAY FOR YOUR FRIENDS,
SO THAT THEY TOO MIGHT KNOW
THE LIGHT AND THE JOY WHICH ARE YOURS
AS YOU REST IN MY EMBRACE.

SEE HOW POWERFUL IS THE PRAYER WHICH YOU PRAY,
AS YOU PRAY FOR THE DYING
IN THE NAME OF MY SON,
JESUS.
MY HOLY SPIRIT PROMPTS YOU TO PRAY.
HIS PRESENCE IS ACTIVE, WITHIN YOU.
HE PRAYS, WITHIN YOU,
IN A SWIFT AND POWERFUL GUST OF GRACE
- LIKE THE WIND -
WHICH NOW STREAMS THROUGH YOUR HEART
IN FERVENT INTERCESSION.

IT IS WHEN A SOUL HAS BEEN EMPTIED: MADE 'HOLLOW'
- TO CONTAIN MY DIVINE GRACE -
THAT ALL HER PRAYERS ARE GRANTED.
ONE WHO CO-OPERATES WITH MY GRACE
IS MADE 'HOLLOW' THROUGH SINCERE AND FERVENT PRAYERS,
WITH PENANCES, AND ACTS OF CHARITY.

Through a 'hollowed' soul, the Holy Spirit 'breathes.'
He breathes His Will to Me, the Father
Who cannot refuse the wish of My Holy Spirit,
A WISH *made in the Name of My Son.*
(WC:1508C) (T:1508 #8)

Our free consent.

When I wondered why more people aren't made joyful by prayer, and by union with the Father, I was astonished to receive an answer. The Father explained to me:-

DELIGHT IN OUR UNION.
DON'T BE AFRAID THAT OTHERS ARE NEGLECTED.
I NEGLECT NO-ONE.
RATHER,
I DO NOT FORCE MY LOVE, GIFTS OR RESPONSIBILITIES
UPON THEM.
I DO NOT FORCE THEM TO DO CHRIST-LIKE WORK.
THOSE WHO LOVE ME, HOWEVER, CO-OPERATE WITH ME.

ONE WHO LOVES ME WILL TURN TO ME.
AT MY INVITATION
HE WILL LIFT UP HIS SOUL TOWARDS ME
LIKE A CHICK WHICH OPENS ITS BEAK
TO ITS MOTHER.
THUS, HE WILL RECEIVE SPIRITUAL FOOD.

(T:1508 #9)

God's concern for our welfare.

Here, I thanked the Father for His teaching. I was still wondering how it was that He was teaching me at such length - and yet He had told me once before (in T:1221) that His teachings would become fewer, but greater. Then, as I waited and wondered, like a child, still awe-struck by His kindness, and by the fact that I could ask Him things and be confident of an answer, I was suddenly told:-

DON'T BE AFRAID.
IT IS TRUE THAT I NEVER CEASE TO TEACH YOU.
IT IS TRUE THAT, THROUGH OUR UNION,
THESE 'TEACHINGS' GROW WEIGHTIER AND GREATER.
REMEMBER, HOWEVER, MY CONSTANT CARE FOR YOU.
AM I NOT MERCIFUL,
WHENEVER YOU ARE SUFFERING,
IN TURMOIL OR IN PAIN,
OR BUSY AT HOME, OR TRAVELLING?
THEN, THE TEACHINGS ARE FEWER,
SINCE IT TIRES YOU TO LEARN, WRITE AND PONDER.
SUCH IS MY CONCERN FOR YOUR WELFARE.

DON'T BE AFRAID OF THIS GIFT.
TRULY, THESE TEACHINGS ARE A PRECIOUS GIFT
FROM ME, YOUR HEAVENLY FATHER.
AS YOU HAVE LEARNED,
it is quite beyond your power

to lift yourselves up to true Union
and understanding.

The Holy Spirit lifts you.

(T:1508 #10)

TREASURE YOUR PRIVILEGE.
INTIMATE UNION
WITH ME, YOUR HEAVENLY FATHER,
IS SOMETHING GIVEN ONLY WHEN I WILL,
AS I WILL;
AND SINCE I AM MERCIFUL AS WELL AS GENEROUS
I LIFT YOU UP IN THIS WAY
ONLY FOR AS LONG AS YOU CAN BEAR IT,
SINCE
SUCH PROLONGED JOY, UNION AND INSTRUCTION
AND THEREFORE
PROLONGED WITHDRAWAL FROM EARTHLY ACTIVITY
TAX YOUR STRENGTH.
YOU CAN BE SURE
THAT *I your Lord* AND CREATOR
- SINCE I LOVE YOU -
DEAL TENDERLY WITH YOU, MY FRAIL CHILDREN.

Like a good mother,
I give to each child what is best for it
- WHETHER 'ORDINARY' GRACES OR EXTRAORDINARY -
best for its unique needs.

(T:1508 #11)

Even beyond death.

Perhaps I haven't yet said that during the whole of this dialogue, the Father's presence gave me incomparable joy, as well as inspiring feelings of awe and gratitude; and my praise became so heart-felt and confident that I told Him how good He is; and I said that since I couldn't seize Him with my hands, to stay close to Him forever, I was now 'seizing' Him with my heart; and here I offered my heart and my hopes to Him, wholly - only to be astonished at His response. God the Father 'spoke' to me, soundlessly, and gave me a promise - and an explanation. He urged me:-

DON'T BE AFRAID.
I, YOUR FATHER, DELIGHT IN YOUR LOVE AND PRAISE,
HERE IN OUR UNION:
A UNION WHICH SHALL NOT END
IF YOU ARE FAITHFUL.
YOU CAN HOPE TO BE WITH ME FOREVER.

THOUGH YOU CANNOT GRASP ME NOW,
YOU CAN HOPE FOR EVENTUAL INSEPARABLE UNION.

YOU CAN HOPE TO BE BOUND TO ME
- BOUND BY YOUR HEART'S YEARNING -
EVEN BEYOND DEATH.

If your heart and My 'Heart'
are of the same 'material',
which is Love,
then,
being the same, and BEING AT LAST *brought together "on fire,"*
AFTER DEATH
- AS IF FUSED, IN LOVE -
we cannot be torn apart.
Nothing can separate us.
"You will be with Me forever,"
and your body will be restored,
in Glory.

WHO COULD HOPE FOR A GREATER JOY:
A MORE GLORIOUS AND LOVING UNION
AND FULFILMENT?

(T:1508 #12)

A 'blank sheet'.

Then I said to the Father that I was giving Him once more, not only my heart, but my evening and my whole life to Him - as a 'blank sheet' for His work; and the Father responded by showing me why He teaches some people in prayer, but not others. He told me:-

DON'T BE AFRAID.
YOU PLEASE ME BY YOUR GRATITUDE.
YOU HONOUR ME BY YOUR GIFT:
BY THE GIFT OF YOUR HEART, OF YOUR TIME,
AND OF YOUR WHOLE LIFE,
GIVEN FOR MY PLANS, MY ACTION, AND MY GLORY,
AS A 'BLANK SHEET' FOR MY WORK,
AND FOR MY MESSAGE
TO OTHERS.

(T:1508 #13)

DON'T BE AFRAID.
UNDERSTAND SOMETHING MORE
ABOUT MY GENEROSITY
AND ABOUT MY LOVE FOR YOU.
All good things come from My Divine Love.
I 'long', perpetually, to share My Life and Love
with you.
IT IS TRUE THAT BY MY DIVINE WILL
I GIVE PARTICULAR GIFTS TO SOME BUT NOT TO OTHERS.

AS YOU YOURSELF - AMAZED - HAVE DISCOVERED,
those who live in a true union
WITH ME, IN CHRIST, AND WITH THE HOLY SPIRIT
are taught,
since knowledge and Love 'go together'.

AS YOU HAVE COME TO REALISE,
had you given up your own will, sooner
or more frequently,
you would have learned more
THROUGH MY 'TEACHINGS-IN-PRAYER'.
YET DON'T BE DESPONDENT.
I DO NOT REBUKE YOU. I GIVE YOU A GIFT:
A GIFT OF INSTRUCTION IN THE LIFE OF PRAYER.
YOU KNOW THAT AN EARTHLY TEACHER MIGHT EXPLAIN
TO A CO-OPERATIVE CHILD
THAT SOME CHILDREN HAVE DIFFICULTY IN LEARNING
WHEREAS OTHERS ARE EXTRAORDINARILY CLEVER.
A TEACHER MIGHT EXPLAIN, ALSO,
THAT ALTHOUGH EACH CHILD DIFFERS FROM THE NEXT
EACH ONE IS CHERISHED BY THE TEACHER;
IT IS WITH A SIMILAR FRANKNESS AND TENDERNESS
THAT I, YOUR HEAVENLY FATHER,
EXPLAIN SOMETHING FURTHER TO YOU
ABOUT CO-OPERATION WITH HEAVEN'S WAYS.

(T:1508 #14)

SEE HOW IMPORTANT ARE FAITH AND LOVE
AND SURRENDER.
IT IS TRUE THAT THESE TEACHINGS ARE FEWER
THAN WAS POSSIBLE
BECAUSE OF YOUR LACK OF GENEROSITY;
YET YOU ARE CONTRITE AND TRUSTING,
OBEDIENT TO MY WILL,
AND THEREFORE I TEACH YOU.
Some others learn nothing
because they do not give up their own will.
They will not open their hearts to Me,
their Heavenly Father,
so do not let My Light shine within.
I cannot teach them.
They will not permit it,
EVEN THOUGH I AM OVERFLOWING WITH LOVE,
OFFERING PEACE TO THEM,
WITH GAIETY AND JOY.

MY PRECIOUS, PURE, EVERLASTING GIFTS ARE OFTEN SPURNED,
UNRECOGNISED.

(T:1508 #15)

The Divine touch, in prayer.

When I renewed my offering of my heart to the Father, I was almost overwhelmed by the gift of His Bliss, and by the weight of the Glory of which He had chosen to unveil just a little. I say 'a little,' because a mere human being can't bear such a gift without Divine help. Then the Father explained that the gifts I had just received were not going to be snatched away from me. He reassured me:-

> DON'T BE AFRAID.
> YOU CANNOT YET GRASP ME,
> YET: SEIZE THE JOY WHICH
> - THROUGH MY SON, YOUR SAVIOUR -
> I OFFER YOU.
> BATHE IN THE LIGHT OF THIS JOY,
> WHICH IS OUR GIFT TO YOUR WILLING HEART.
>
> JOY AND RADIANCE AND WISDOM AND PEACE
> BELONG TO THE STATE OF LIFE WHICH IS YOURS,
> WITHIN OUR HEART: THE HEART OF THE HOLY TRINITY.
> TREASURE ALL OF MY GIFTS AND GRACES.
> ONLY BY MY GRACE DO YOU BEAR MY DIVINE TOUCH, IN PRAYER.
> ONLY BY MY GRACE CAN YOU CONVEY IN WORDS, FOR OTHERS,
> A GLIMPSE OF MY LOVE, AND OF MY POWER AND GLORY.

(T:1508 #16)

If I could have paid attention, I would have been taught even more; but at this point an hour had passed, and I was unable to continue either to sit upright, or to keep my heart and mind held 'up' to the Father in prayer. So I made the Sign of the Cross, aware that He was still loving and sustaining me; and I asked to be able to live out the whole of the rest of my life as a thank-offering to the Most Holy Trinity.

God's love for me.

It's been an unending cause for wonder that God has taught me so much about His loving nature - and about His personal love for me: a love in which I had always believed, as one believes in a dogma, but which, for so many years, I had misunderstood.

In the early years, I had a certain picture of God's love which I couldn't seem to escape. I saw that love as creating, embracing and sustaining the whole of mankind; and yet I seemed to feel that it was too vast or too diffuse a love to be concerned with a feeble and pessimistic soul like myself. I couldn't have imagined that God gazes upon me - as He's told me (in T:1941) with the sort of blissful delight with which I first gazed upon each new-born child.

My first dark dry faith in God's love for me was unswerving; indeed, it's precisely because of that faith - however 'dark' - that I managed to cling to Him, through prayer, in every new difficulty, and also to turn back to Him after every moment of weakness or shame. Yet the thought of that love didn't warm my heart, for many years. I couldn't really imagine what it meant: that His Love for us is infinite, fervent, unflagging and merciful. These truths of the Faith were wholly acceptable to my mind; and yet my heart and soul were too grey and faintly-lit to be able to delight in such knowledge - until they were warmed by God's love, and expanded. Then at last they could contain the belief that I'm precious in His sight, and that He takes a personal interest in everything I think, do and say; and it's that knowledge - that belief - that has made prayer such a delight in recent years, and every day so full of joy.

It's because of my gratitude for this realisation, and for God's love, that I feel bound to give a further reminder about the part we must play in developing a close friendship with God. I mean that most prayerful people realise that our prayerful union with God can be harmed by carelessness or rebellion in things to do with faith or morals - though God's love for us never diminishes and His forgiveness is lavished unceasingly upon all who, repentant, approach Him. Yet that prayerful union can also be thwarted or damaged by carelessness or irreverence in prayer - or by any attitude which involves forgetfulness of Who God is and who and what we are.

Approaching fruition.

More and more clearly, in 1994, I was shown by God that His teachings about prayer, as well as about related topics, would serve a great purpose; and so I became less anxious about new aspects of my work, and more confident that whenever I set out to do something for Christ's sake, He would ensure its success. Then, on the first Sunday of Advent, we heard, in Holy Scripture: - "SEE, THE DAYS ARE COMING - IT IS YAHWEH WHO SPEAKS - WHEN I AM GOING TO FULFIL THE PROMISE I MADE" (Jr 33:14).

It seemed to me as though those words applied to the way in which the Father was bringing His work in my life towards fruition. In the very next week, my work of child-care was over, in the strictest sense, when my youngest child graduated from University. I had just received the Sacrament of the Sick and therefore was given a new strength; and we were about to make a mini-pilgrimage to Aylesford Priory, where my intention was to ask the Saints who are honoured there to pray for the success of the work. I had no idea of the great joys which lay ahead of me: so many wonderful teachings, new friendships, extra tasks and surprising encouragements. But there was a comparatively minor but very painful sacrifice that was required of me before Our Lord could tell me that I was ready for the main part of the work; and it was wholly unexpected. It's what I mentioned in the last chapter, about veiling my hair in church: hardly a sacrifice, if compared with bearing physical pain or hunger for the sake of the Gospel. But it was a question of bearing a little humiliation out of obedience to Christ; and humiliations can be harder to bear than physical sufferings, for those of us who are proud.

A mark of respect.

It was on a January day, in 1995, that Christ made it clear to me - by a wordless request - that He would like to see me show greater reverence towards Him during the Holy Mass. He invited me to take up the practice which I had adopted when I'd first been received into full Communion, but had since discarded, as had many women in this part of the world who also thought it an insignificant matter. But, as I mentioned briefly in Chapter fourteen, I was shown by Christ that I would please Him if I were to act in obedience to our custom and to Holy Scripture. I could please Him, He explained, if I would cover my hair in church, during the Liturgy - and in any church or room where He is Present in the Blessed Sacrament.

Never would I have dreamed that He would make such a request of me. It seemed such a minor thing, but I was appalled at the thought of having to make myself conspicuous in that way. I longed to obey Christ, yet wondered if this were essential for reverent worship; also, I guessed that I'd be labelled by some other people as a traditionalist or an attention-seeker, when my whole yearning at Mass was to keep my heart and thoughts fixed on God, and on the needs of the Church and the world.

But Christ showed me a number of reasons why I should conquer my pride and do as He wished. Above all, He explained, He wanted me to be willing to *pay as much honour* to Him *exteriorly as interiorly*. Those were His words.

My heart sank, however, so I turned to the Father, "in Christ," in prayer. I longed for reassurance. I'd started to worry about whether I'd be encouraging factions in the Church. But I heard in my soul seven words from the Father which startled me and clarified the matter. The Father said: *"If you honour Me, who is divided?"* (T:1530A). What He meant was that divisions are caused not by faithful persons who try to be obedient to custom and to Holy Scripture but by the uncharity of their critics.

That is why, from the 3rd of January 1995, I have covered my hair in church. I felt so conspicuous and humiliated on that first day that I spoke to Christ about it in Holy Communion. To have to look different from others seemed such a little thing, I knew; but Christ replied to me straight away, by saying: *"Such a great thing, is obedience!"*

[A simple type of head-covering.

By the way, I've chosen to wear a black lace 'mantilla' scarf once again, rather than a patterned head-square or a hat, only because it's more convenient. It saves me from the need to keep choosing some different form of head-covering. Mantillas are worn all around the world where women are not ashamed to show reverence before God in the traditional manner; and besides, a mantilla is fairly cool in summer and warm in winter - and doesn't constrict the wearer's throat during singing: very mundane reasons for a choice which I know some mistakenly see as provocative or ostentatious.]

An act of faith.

How I long for many more thousands of people - or hundreds of thousands - to know the joy which can come through faith, and through attempts to be obedient to Our Lord's wishes. For example, I was enormously encouraged by a 'teaching' one April evening in 1995. I'd been praying 'the Creed', in church - trying to do so with a little more gratitude and fervour than usual; and suddenly, Christ showed me how the Father delights in our acts of faith, and how it is through faith that Heaven's 'door' is opened to us. Christ told me:-

Look upon your sincere prayers as a very worthwhile activity. Don't be worried because you are sometimes a little bit hurried or absent-minded. It is your sincerity of heart which is important. (T:1570 #1)

Believe that I treasure your prayers; for example, I am pleased whenever you pray 'the Creed' sincerely, as when you began 'the Rosary' just now, at home. Your Heavenly Father is delighted to respond to your fervent prayer. See what He now teaches you about faith and about single-minded persistence:

HERE I AM
FAR ABOVE YOU.
THE DOOR TO HEAVEN IS OPEN.
YOUR FERVENT PRAYER DELIGHTS ME.

By a sincere act of faith
IN ME
YOUR HEAVENLY FATHER
- FAITH IN MY EXISTENCE AND IN MY GOODNESS,
AND IN MY SON, JESUS, WHO CAME TO EARTH
TO SAVE YOU -
you send up to Heaven a triumphant cry
- a cry of hope, love, fervour and determination
and defiance of evil -
from a darkened world.
YOU CALL OUT
AS IF FROM A DARK, PITTED LANDSCAPE,
A FILTHY BATTLEFIELD
WHERE, HERE AND THERE, A VOICE ARISES.
HERE AND THERE, A LONE 'WARRIOR'
- A SOLDIER OF CHRIST -
WHO BELIEVES IN CHRIST HIS SAVIOUR
AND IN THE POWER OF PRAYER
CALLS OUT TO HIS FRIENDS:
"OUR CAUSE IS WORTH FIGHTING FOR,
AS WE FIGHT AGAINST SIN!
OUR HERO IS WORTH DYING FOR,
IN OUR 'DYING TO SELF', DAILY,
IN ORDER TO SERVE HIM."

(T:1570 #2)

Prayer which opens Heaven's door.

Then the Father urged me:-

CONSIDER THE DARKNESS WHICH IS EARTHLY LIFE.

COMPARE IT
WITH THE RADIANCE NOW UNVEILED BEFORE YOU,
AS I OFFER YOU A GLIMPSE OF HEAVEN'S GLORY.

SEE HOW POWERFUL IS YOUR PRAYER
"IN CHRIST",
A PRAYER WHICH - THROUGH MY WILL - HAS OPENED HEAVEN'S DOOR.

A FERVENT ACT OF FAITH
IS LIKE A LIGHT SHINING IN EARTH'S DARKNESS.
IT PLEASES ME.
IT GIVES JOY TO MY SAINTS AND MY HOLY ANGELS.
IT STRENGTHENS YOUR OWN SPIRIT.
IT ENCOURAGES OTHER PEOPLE IN THEIR FAITH.
IT DRAWS UPON YOU A GREAT REWARD.

EVEN SILENT ACTS OF FAITH
ARE VALUABLE
SINCE, THROUGH THEM, THE WHOLE CHURCH IS MADE STRONGER.

(WC:1570A + 1570B) (T:1570 #3)

Thanksgiving for Priests.

After a few weeks of more reverent worship, with hard work and wonderful rewards - and with a new peace given, when I'd been invested with the scapular of Our Lady of Mount Carmel - I thanked Our Lord in prayer for all His gifts, especially for the continuing teachings.

Day by day, I persevered with my usual prayers for the Church - and especially for priests, who bring Christ to us, and Christ's gifts, in such marvellous ways; and on May 13th 1995 I was astonished to be taught by Christ:-

> **Continue to pray for My priests: for those who serve you on earth, and for those who have died. What a wonderful moment it is, when faithful priests enter Heaven! You can see that the three priests for whom you have prayed are now walking towards My Heavenly throne. They are walking along a path which is lined with joyful people. These priests - each of whom is wearing a golden chasuble - are being given a tremendous greeting by their friends, the Saints, since My priests enter Heaven in a special way; they are welcomed as "other Christs." They are accorded special honour and glory at the end of their earthly, priestly service. (WC + OIL:1584.) (T:1584)**

The transforming union.

Some of the teachings so overwhelmed me by their wisdom or charity that I told Christ, on June 6th, what a marvel it is to me, that I should be taught by the very Lord Who has taught the prophets in past ages. It seemed so wonderful as to be scarcely believable, and yet I did believe it - and still do. So I repented again of all that makes me unworthy of this work; and I was brought, in prayer, to a new understanding of my present way of life in which I am enfolded in Love, it seems, in the midst of the Three Divine Persons, with no fear of 'losing' Them.

As I prayed "in Christ" to the Father, I was shown by Christ (in T:1592) that I now enjoy - thanks to His goodness - what is known as the state of 'Transforming Union'. Christ showed me:-

Ponder the marvel which is friendship with Us: with the Most Holy Trinity, your God. See what is happening, even at the end of your spiritual journey, as you persevere in love, and confess your sins, in a new, true beginning, in Our service. Listen to your Heavenly Father, who tells you:

REJOICE IN THIS STATE.
YOU ARE ENCLOSED WITHIN OUR GRACE AND PEACE,
DWELLING AS IF "IN THE MIDST" OF THREE DIVINE PERSONS,
BLISSFULLY EXPLORING
- THROUGH PRAYER -
THE HEIGHTS AND DEPTHS OF OUR INFINITE LOVE.

ONLY THROUGH PRAYER
- AS IF THROUGH A SMALL BRIGHT PASSAGEWAY -
CAN YOU LEAVE BEHIND EARTH'S DARKNESS
TO RISE UPWARD TO HEAVEN'S LIGHT, AND
- IN THE LIGHT OF GLORY -
TO REST WITHIN THE EMBRACE OF YOUR GOD: OURSELVES:
THREE DIVINE PERSONS,
ONE LORD.

(WC:1592) (T:1592 #4)

Perpetual recollection.

Then the Father invited me:-

ENTER WITHIN YOUR OWN SOUL, THROUGH PRAYER,
NOT JUST FOR A MINUTE, OR AN HOUR,
BUT FOR THE WHOLE OF EVERY DAY AND NIGHT.
ACCEPT MY INVITATION;
BY AN EXPRESSION OF LOVE FOR ME,
AND BY A CONFESSION OF YOUR WEAKNESS,
STOOP DOWN MORE FREQUENTLY TO ENTER THE SMALL 'DOOR' OF HUMILITY,

THE 'DOOR' WHICH LEADS YOU WITHIN YOUR OWN SOUL.
HERE, WITHIN, YOU CAN REST IN MY LOVE.
(T:1592 #5)

TURN TO ME, TRUSTINGLY, OVER AND OVER AGAIN.
THROUGH YOUR BELIEF IN CHRIST, YOUR SAVIOUR,
AND THROUGH YOUR ACCEPTANCE OF HIS INVITATION TO PERSEVERE IN PRAYER,
AND THROUGH YOUR PERSISTENT LOVE FOR ME, YOUR FATHER
AND THROUGH YOUR CO-OPERATION WITH MY PLAN,
YOU ARE BEING ENABLED TO REMAIN ALL THE TIME 'WITHIN' YOUR OWN SOUL.
YOU ARE ALLOWED TO DWELL, TRANSFORMED, IN AN UNCEASING UNION WITH ME:
A UNION OF LOVE, DESIRE, AND WORK.
IN THIS MARVELLOUS STATE OF TRANSFORMATION,
YOUR SOUL CAN LIVE IN UNBROKEN JOY;
YOU WILL FIND THAT YOU MOVE 'OUTWARDS' TO OTHER PEOPLE
TO SHARE THAT JOY WITH THEM, THROUGH MANY BLESSINGS.
(T:1592 #6)

TRY TO BE WORTHY OF MY FRIENDSHIP.
YOU WHO LIVE INTIMATELY UNITED WITH ME
OUGHT TO PERFORM EVERY THOUGHT AND ACTION
IN AN UTTERLY TRUTHFUL SPIRIT, WITH AN UTTERLY PURE INTENTION.
THIS IS TO LIVE AND ACT SOLELY FOR MY GLORY,
AND WITH A CONSTANT AWARENESS OF THE BLAZING LIGHT
OF MY PRESENCE NEAR YOU.
(T:1592 #7)

TRY TO BE WORTHY OF PERPETUAL INTIMACY WITH ME, YOUR LORD.
THROUGH THIS INTIMACY, AND BY MY GRACE AND CHOICE,
YOU MUST 'BECOME' LIKE A STREAM OF PURE, CLEAR, LIVING WATER FOR OTHERS;
YOU CAN ONLY REMAIN WITH ME IN THIS SORT OF TRUE UNION
IF YOU LIVE IN PERFECT TRUTHFULNESS, LOVE AND SIMPLICITY
WITH NO 'SHADOW' LURKING BESIDE OR BENEATH ANY OF YOUR THOUGHTS
OR ACTIONS.
AS YOU HAVE DISCOVERED, TO SOME DEGREE,
humility leads to glory;
I REVEAL MY GLORY WITHIN A SIMPLE AND PURIFIED SOUL, IN PRAYER.
THIS IS SOMETHING SCARCELY BELIEVED OR UNDERSTOOD
BY THOSE WHO ARE FRIGHTENED OF HUMILIATIONS.
(T:1592 #8)

At the entrance to the Kingdom.

Then the Father gently reminded me:-

CAST BACK YOUR MIND TO THE EXPLANATION WHICH I GAVE YOU
LONG AGO, ABOUT HUMBLE PRAYER.
I SHOWED YOU THAT YOUR SOUL CAN BE SEEN AS A KINGDOM OF LIGHT

INTO WHICH YOU CAN ENTER - THROUGH PRAYER -
IF YOU STOOP DOWN TO PASS THROUGH THE SMALL 'DOORWAY'
WHICH IS HUMILITY.
IF YOU ENTER THIS 'KINGDOM',
YOU LEAVE BEHIND EARTHLY DISTRESS AND DARKNESS.
(WC:1592B) (T:1592 #9)

CONSIDER HOW ESSENTIAL ARE HUMILITY, CONTRITION AND SIMPLICITY
IN ONE WHO WISHES TO PRAY WELL AND TO BE CLOSE TO ME.
ONLY ONE WHO HAS DISCARDED EVERY PROP, DISGUISE AND PRETENCE,
AND WHO HAS ABANDONED HIS SELFISH AMBITIONS
AND HIS CLUTCHING-AT-POSSESSIONS
CAN SLIP THROUGH THE NARROW 'DOORWAY' OF THE SOUL, IN PRAYER,
TO ENTER MY KINGDOM.
(T:1592 #10)

ENCOURAGE OTHERS TO MAKE THE SACRIFICES
WHICH ARE NECESSARY FOR THEIR PRAYERS TO BE FRUITFUL.
MANY PEOPLE HAVE LEARNED HOW TO ENTER THE 'DOORWAY' OF THE SOUL,
IN PRAYER.
YET SOME ENTER ONLY ONCE,
OR ENTER INFREQUENTLY, AT IRREGULAR INTERVALS.
HOW FEW ENTER IN ORDER TO BEGIN A NEW WAY OF LIFE;
HOW FEW PERSEVERE FOR LONG ENOUGH
TO FIND THE UTTER JOY AND PEACE WHICH ARE EXPERIENCED
- AT MY INVITATION -
AFTER MANY TRIALS AND HUMILIATIONS.
HOW FEW ARE ABLE TO ENTER INTO
A WONDERFUL, INTIMATE, AND UNINTERRUPTED FRIENDSHIP WITH ME
DURING THEIR LIFE ON EARTH.
THIS IS BECAUSE THEY DON'T WANT TO DISCARD THE POSSESSIONS,
OBSESSIONS OR DESIRES
WITH WHICH THEY ARE LADEN;
AND - THUS LADEN - THEY ARE TOO 'LARGE'
TO ENTER THE SMALL 'DOORWAY' OF THE SOUL:
THE DOORWAY OF HUMILITY WHICH LEADS TO MY KINGDOM.
(T:1592 #11)

The Way of perfection.

Then the Father reminded me of what I should keep in mind on the 'Way of perfection'. He taught me:-

STRIVE TO SERVE ME PERFECTLY BY SERVING ME WITH A PURE INTENTION.
IN A LIFE OF INTIMATE UNION WITH ME
ALL OF YOUR THOUGHTS, WORDS AND ACTIONS
SHOULD BE WISE, NECESSARY, SIMPLE, PURE AND GRACEFUL.
EVERY THOUGHT, WORD AND ACTION SHOULD ARISE

FROM A DESIRE TO PLEASE ME AND TO GIVE ME GLORY.
(T:1592 #12)

AVOID, WITH ALL YOUR WILL,
THE MEREST SHADOW OF CONCEIT, SELF-SEEKING OR MIXED MOTIVES,
AS YOU TRY TO SERVE ME.
(T:1592 #13)

BEWARE OF HUNGERING FOR THE APPROVAL OF ANYONE
EXCEPT MYSELF, AND MY FRIENDS IN HEAVEN.
(T:1592 #14)

DON'T BE AFRAID.
DON'T WORRY ABOUT THE WAY IN WHICH YOU RECEIVE THESE INSTRUCTIONS,
IN PRAYER.
TRULY,
"you live in Truth".
YOU LIVE IN MY EMBRACING CARE.
THIS FRUITFUL PRAYER CAN BE SEEN AS A 'NORMAL' PART
OF YOUR PRESENT WAY OF LIFE,
EVEN THOUGH IT DEPENDS WHOLLY ON MY GENEROSITY.
(T:1592 #15)

A new stage.

As can be seen, the Father's teachings have consisted of several interwoven themes. He has offered me His observations and instructions interspersed with consolations; so I'll be eternally grateful, I hope, that I've been led in the contemplative way, in union with Christ. I'd better include as few teachings as possible, however, as I make a list of the significant stages of prayer to which I've been led in recent times - although this list is more for the sake of people who will study this book much later on, than for those, today, who want to read the plain 'story'. But further 'teachings' were given, for example, about Baptism (T:1603), about the New Covenant made by Christ on Calvary (T:1613), about prayer, about spiritual friendship 'in Christ' (T:1614), and about the ceaseless work of the Holy Spirit (T:1628).

It would be pointless for me to list many more, when they nearly all appear in the volumes to which this book is an introduction; but it was from the spring of 1995 - I see in retrospect - that the work progressed very steadily, until the present day. I also see that it was kindness on the part of Christ that kept Him from showing me, at that stage, where my work would lead me. I didn't know that I'd be sending out by post, to thousands of enquirers, not just one volume of "Christ's Instructions," but several - and that I'd be posting them around the world.

The 'Second Version'.

From the very beginning of 1995 I'd been busier than ever, having realised that all of the 'Teachings' should be re-written, to produce what would be called the 'Second Version.'

The problem with the 'First Version' was that it had been written hurriedly, if accurately, but without my making it clear whose words I was quoting or using in each line of text: whether the words I'd written had been chosen by me to 'clothe' God's knowledge, or whether they were God's own 'words-given-in-prayer.'

In a letter to the Jesuit Father, at that time, I explained why I was so busy:

"I have to plough ahead, for the moment, doing what is of major importance: writing a 'definitive' version of the 'Teachings,' (and, as I write, including a verbal description of every recorded image, since these were aspects of some 'teachings'.) It seems important that I explain to you that every bit of "knowledge, implanted suddenly in prayer" (my description) is given:

* either as a concept/'showing' which I must then 'clothe' in words.

* or as a concept/'showing' which is truly instant and silent, and is not a 'thought', but which is 'clothed' with words-for-use (when I come to write it down).

This is very different from conversational words from Our Lord. So, first, God taught me, within prayer, and urged me to write it all down; I did so hesitantly, and nervously. And now, He makes me see not only the wonder of it, but (see) also that I must re-write all the teachings urgently, trying to be bolder and more exact; since no-one knows except myself which words were given by God, and which were freely chosen by me from within my mind's vocabulary. I'd just assumed it would be obvious, but I see it's not. If I don't make this plain, soon, (and have it all typed, as arranged) much of the point of the 'teachings' will be lost. If God has designed ('bothered') to use certain words and sentences - for example, supremely, about the Holy Sacrifice - then I must do all I can to reveal and share those words before I tackle anything else. (He has instructed me about how to do this, and it's becoming easier.) So I'm about half-way through the 1600 'teachings', D.G. - simply using capital letters for God's own "given-words" and underlining for every bit of teaching. Of course, I'm also doing all the other usual jobs, and trying to keep up-to-date in 'teachings' and occasional (watercolour) images.

Something else you weren't to know is ... the urgency ... This is no way a complaint: just a word that I have to 'husband' every minute in order to do essential domestic tasks (happily) and fit it in writing, friends, etc. - (Holy Mass or prayer underpinning it all) ... when new ideas of my own pop up (i.e. ambitions for various projects connected with the teachings) I have to 'flatten' them - or make a brief note, perhaps for the future, in order to stick to "the one thing ..." at a time: the one "present moment" task; and, for the moment, it's the re-writing, and, (D.G.) life is full and very happy ..."

A fulfilling pattern.

More and more, in 1995, my eyes were opened to God's generosity. By then, He had so thoroughly trained me, that a fulfilling and absorbing 'pattern' was discernible to me, every week and every month, as the writings fitted in with the domestic routine, the children flourished, and my understanding of the whole project grew clearer, thanks to new enlightenment from Christ in prayer. My confidence grew that, with God's help, I'd be able to remain faithful and to finish the most important parts of the work.

That confidence was dented, briefly, when our parish priest retired. I'd been confiding in him about the teachings for about five or six years. He was so wise and good that I'd never had a moment's doubt about any of his comments - nor about the fact that Our Lord had wanted me to speak to him about these things. I had grown used to our priest's way of caring for my soul; I mean that he had distanced himself from my work, for reasons of prudence, by never speaking of it unless I did so first; yet he had maintained a kindly watchfulness, reassured by the approval given to each new chunk of my writing by the Jesuit Father who was still willing to examine my work.

My feelings of embarrassment at speaking about the work had lessened considerably by this time. I had even been able to thank Our Lord with some sincerity, after particularly difficult encounters with various persons, for having allowed me "THE PRIVILEGE NOT ONLY OF BELIEVING IN CHRIST, BUT OF SUFFERING FOR HIM AS WELL" (Ph 1:29). I hadn't shed my blood for the Faith - but it had been humiliating to lose friends; and it made my heart ache whenever someone felt too perplexed by my work to be able to speak to me again; and so I felt a bit daunted that I'd have to start all over again, in one sense, by doing my duty and explaining some of the same things about my work to whoever was our new parish priest.

It was absolutely necessary, since it was Our Lord's wish; it was for the sake of the parish, because some of its members would be asking questions about my work in the years ahead - whether from curiosity or from a concern to be reassured about the orthodoxy of the books; but it was also for my own good, although I didn't know it at the time.

A 'new' priest.

Our new priest arrived on August 19th 1995; and I plucked up courage, a few days later, to make an appointment with Father Eugene Fitzpatrick and to explain something about Christ's 'teachings-in-prayer'. I mentioned the prayer-paintings, and also the booklets which I was distributing in the parish to anyone who was willing to read them. He listened patiently, and indeed, whenever I had to return to him - at Our Lord's request - to explain something new, he'd say: "Don't be afraid to come back again." And so my nervousness diminished, over the next year or two; and that was the part of Our Lord's plan that I hadn't known about. As Christ told me, a few months later, it had been through His wisdom that I had already received a very strict yet thoughtful training, partly through Canon O'Leary's faithfulness to inspiration and to duty; yet it was part of that same wise plan of Christ that I should now receive a different sort of help. There was no question but that our new priest would be as prudent and watchful as the one who had just retired; but although Father Eugene didn't know it, he had been chosen by Christ to play a special part in the work.

This wouldn't be made plain to me for another year or two; but the various devotions which were re-introduced into our parish by our new priest were going to bring about, indirectly - through my prayers of thanks to God, and God's response to me - a series of extra 'teachings' about prayer and about the liturgy. Also, the numerous conversations which I was required to initiate because of the teachings, and the patient listening of our new priest, with his repeated instruction that I must "Never be afraid to come back again," gave me a new confidence. This was a supernatural gift, in that I developed a greater confidence in my efforts to do Our Lord's Will from moment to moment, no matter how strange that seemed, as I spent what seemed to be my declining years in printing books that few persons wanted and my own family saw as very strange. But it was a very human gift, as well. I mean that I grew less afraid of persons in authority. I had restored to me, in this way, some of the ordinary, child-like, human confidence that I'd felt slipping away from me twenty years earlier when I'd discovered what a weak human creature I am; and this renewal was made possible through the presence, in our midst, of one more faithful priest who was willing to give all his heart and energy to the service of God in the Catholic Church.

Regularly, I have thanked Our Lord for everyone who has given me encouragement in difficult times, or practical help; it was when I did this again one day, mentioning certain persons by name, that I was assured by Christ, in prayer, that: *"I send friends along to help you!"* *(T:1713)* - and also: *"They will share your glory."*

Joyful news.

It was to our 'new' priest - to Father Eugene - that Christ sent me with a first draft of each new book of mine, before printing, and with reports from the Jesuit Priest about each new work. It was through him that I was required to send occasional messages to our Bishop - and also to give the signs which Christ intended would show that my work is indeed inspired by God and that I have no plans of my own except to do God's Will as I see it; and each time I delivered a new message I was greeted with kindness.

Sparks of wisdom.

Throughout the rest of 1995 I continued to share Christ's teachings, to 'channel' into my notebooks the ever-flowing stream of teachings, to cook meals for the family, and to fit in parties, conversations and hospital visits. Near the end of 1995, the Father Himself had begun to draw me regularly towards Himself, in order to instruct me. He taught me, for example, about my closeness to Him, 'above the cloud' at last (T: 1987), and about His Love for me (T:1556), about my union with Christ (T:1659), about how we can meet and greet the Saints of Heaven (T:1680) and about how our prayers help the souls who are being purified after death (T:1775), and as I was absorbing this instruction, I was growing used to being taught, at different times, by each of the Three Persons of the Most Holy Trinity.

In July of that year, I was deeply moved when, at Holy Mass one day, God the Father explained something more of the way in which the 'teachings' convey His Wisdom to other people, through my efforts. This was a preface to a long teaching about the Holy Mass and about prayer "in Christ". He urged me:-

REJOICE IN THESE TEACHINGS
WHICH YOU RECEIVE THROUGH MY LOVE AND GENEROSITY.
YOU ARE RIGHT TO OFFER THANKS FOR THEM.
TRULY, THEY COME FROM ME, YOUR GOD.
THEY ARE LIKE SPARKS GLISTENING UPON THE BRILLIANT 'RIVER'

WHICH IS MY DIVINE LIFE AND LIGHT
AS MY LIFE 'FLOWS' EVERLASTINGLY WITHIN THE GODHEAD.
THESE BURSTS OF KNOWLEDGE AND WISDOM
ARE LIKE MINUSCULE GLINTS THROWN OUT
- DURING OUR PRAYER-IN-UNION -
FROM THE TORRENT OF MY BURNING GLORY.
NONE OF THE 'TEACHINGS' DOES MORE
THAN REFLECT THE MEREST SCRAP OF MY TRUE RADIANCE,
YET EVERY LITTLE TEACHING CAN BE CONSIDERED AS CONVEYING
A SPARK OF MY INFINITE WISDOM.
(WC:1626) (T:1626)

Writing in the first person.

Just as I was beginning to settle into a very satisfactory routine - forgetting that Christ has unexpected plans for everyone who has offered to do His Will - I received an invitation in prayer which astounded me.

Yet another new version of all the teachings was required. It was on November 3rd 1995 that Christ invited me to re-write His 'teachings' in a different manner. My new task, I learned, was to list most of His teachings in a way which would indicate very clearly what I must do if I sincerely wish to please Him and to become holy. Christ invited me to write "in the first person", so that other people can receive His teachings in the sort of direct and simple way which it's been my privilege to experience.

Day after day, as I worked my way through the backlog of teachings, 'translating' what had often been soundless teachings into my own language - though some had been given in words - I plucked up courage to write just as Christ speaks. He is overwhelmingly tender and understanding, and simple, like a child - yet authoritative; He is very solemn, on solemn subjects; and He is wholly admiring of His Mother! When I read what I'd written it was almost as though I was receiving each teaching once again, despite my flawed grammar, and despite the evidently-stilted language of the first few hundred pages, when I was so awed by my task that I was almost overcome with feelings of impertinence at daring to do it, or daring to think myself capable of persevering.

Further books to publish.

As I continued to write 'in the first person,' Christ showed me that He would like me to publish a volume of His teachings and to give away free copies. That's why I took great care over several matters, and worked out a better system of co-ordinating the number of each teaching with its associated prayer-painting. I devised a clearer lay-out for each page of first-person teachings, with titles to break up the text; and meanwhile I continued to keep my parish priest informed about each new stage of the work, even though I met with no reaction. I also told the family something about my task, although it was very strange for them to see more and more evidence that this matter of reproducing 'teachings' and of sharing them with other people generated much enthusiasm from numerous correspondents. Letter-writing began to take up much of my time; and I posted several dozen pages of typescript at a time to the kind priest, Fr Edwards, who was still willing to check every word I wrote so that I could be reassured about the accuracy of my expressions of Catholic Faith and so that other people, my parish priest above all, at that stage, could be reassured as well.

By the time I went to the printers with the fourth volume of teachings, I had expanded the notes which prefaced the book, and so had explained to the readers why this new way of writing was necessary. It seems best to quote directly from that Note, to give a better understanding of the new style. I wrote:-

"Each 'teaching' here in "Volume Four" is numbered, just as in previous volumes. Each 'T' (for teaching) in the left-hand margin is followed by a number, and sometimes by a paragraph (#) number; and these correspond with the numbers of the same 'teachings' in earlier versions, and with the numbers in my notebooks, and also with the numbers on the associated illustrations in either water-colour or oil, (which can be seen elsewhere.)

Most of Christ's instructions are recorded chronologically, as clearly and as simply as possible. Where a teaching has been given to me as a pure, precious and clear but soundless instruction, I have made it 'concrete', in my own choice of words; a large part of the text below is composed of such teachings.

This 'making concrete' is more like a translation than a composition, since I have 'translated' real but inaudible teachings - given on specific occasions - into English, the language I know best; and you might see, therefore, that any grammatical errors or clumsy phrases - though regrettable - are like flaws in the work of a poor translator; and the 'original text' is Christ Himself, Who I believe to be my Infinitely-wise Teacher, and indeed to be the source of all Truth ever found in prayer."

Then I added:-

"Also reproduced in this book are many passages which convey what I can only describe as God's 'knowledge-given-in-words.' God the Holy Trinity - Father, Son and Holy Spirit - has sometimes communicated teachings in whole phrases or sentences as if from Mind to mind, in prayer, and wholly beyond the realm of imagination. These words are reproduced below in lower-case italic type; and whenever such words are shown with speech-marks it is because these particular words were spoken to my soul in prayer in a real though interior conversation, rather than being simply 'given' in a way which I've explained in another work about prayer."

A mammoth task.

A mammoth task lay ahead, as I'd received nearly two thousand teachings by that time; and now I had to re-write them all, as well as to continue to write each day in my notebook, in the usual simple manner.

I can't remember how long the first volume took: whether it was weeks or months. But I was astonished at the result, in that Christ's teachings now sounded even more vivid and encouraging; much more like the 'real thing'. Then it became plain that I'd been asked to write 'in the first person' at this late stage because only now did I know Christ well enough to reproduce His manner of speaking and so to convey something of His tender and loving attitude towards me in prayer.

The writing went well, that month; and I called the new work "Instructions from Christ," because Christ had shown me that every teaching should be split into segments, each of which should begin with a verb, if possible. In this way, the reader could come to understand that whenever Christ teaches me, He is not dropping pieces of information into my soul and mind as a man throws 'dead' reports into a filing cabinet. Every teaching carries, as if within itself, a spiritual urgency and strength which help me to make that teaching alive and fruitful in my life. Indeed, unless I had absorbed and also responded to each teaching to some degree, I would have found that my friendship with Christ had become less strong, and so the Source and the supply of teachings would have become less active and 'present' in my life.

Sharing God's nature.

But Christ didn't leave me alone and without encouragement as I tackled this new and huge work - and continued with it not knowing exactly how, where or when it would be used. On the very day that He asked me to write 'in the first person' Christ responded lavishly to an especially-fervent prayer.

In the evening at home, on November 3rd, I repented once more of every scrap of pride, yet once again begged the Father for His gifts: especially for purity of heart. I was overwhelmed by His response. All at once, in a simple and yet magnificent teaching, Christ lifted my soul in prayer to the Father; and I was shown what wonderful gifts are given by God to someone who has willingly undergone His purifications and who lives in His presence, and who joyfully does His work with the simplicity of a child. Christ showed me, all in one moment of astonishing spiritual Light:-

> **Open your heart to your Heavenly Father's teaching; open the eyes of your soul, in prayer. He is calling to you; He is inviting you to consider some of the fruits of your life-in-union:**

HERE I AM,
TEACHING YOU.
PONDER MY NATURE AND MY ATTRIBUTES.
YOU CAN HOPE TO BE LIKE ME
IN SEVERAL WAYS
SINCE
YOU ARE LIVING AS MY TRUE CHILD.

BE CLEAR-SIGHTED, NOT BASHFUL.
CHERISH TRUTH.
HONOUR MY WILL FOR YOU.
YOU, MY ADOPTED CHILD
CAN EXPECT TO RESEMBLE ME
IF YOU ARE PURIFIED, TRANSFORMED, AND UNITED TO ME
IN A MARVELLOUS 'LIFE-IN-UNION'.

YOU CAN ENJOY
- EVEN DURING EARTHLY LIFE -
TRUE PARTICIPATION IN MY LIFE.
YOU HAVE A SHARE IN MY DIVINE NATURE,
THOUGH ONLY THROUGH MY FREE GIFT
AND GENEROSITY.

(T:1704 #1)

All at once, the Father showed me how I resemble Him to some degree - though only through His goodness and our union. He explained to me, soundlessly:-

NOTICE HOW EVERY GOOD GIFT
WITH WHICH I GRACE YOUR SOUL
- THROUGH YOUR TRANSFORMATION AND OUR UNION -
ARISES FROM MY DIVINE NATURE
AND ATTRIBUTES.

FOR EXAMPLE,
MY DIVINE AND PERPETUAL BLISS
IS ALREADY TASTED IN THE PRAYER OF UNKNOWING
WHICH YOU ENTER WHENEVER I CALL YOU.

MY KNOWLEDGE OF MYSELF
IS EXPERIENCED
- AND SHARED TO SOME EXTENT -
IN THESE TEACHINGS-IN-PRAYER.

MY INFINITE MERCY AND JUSTICE
ARE UNVEILED
WHEN I CALL SOMEONE TO LEAVE EARTHLY LIFE,
AND WHEN I REVEAL
TO YOU WHO PRAY FOR THAT SOUL'S SALVATION
HIS TRUE STATE AND DESTINATION:
DEATH AND DOOM, OR LIFE WITH GLORY.

MY IMMENSE CHARITY
- CHARITY WHICH IS MY NATURE -
IS REVEALED WHEN I ANSWER THE PRAYER OF YOURSELF,
MY FRAIL CREATURE,
WHEN YOU PRAY, IN THE NAME OF CHRIST, TO ME YOUR FATHER.

MY GENEROSITY
IS PROVED WHEN, FIRST, I EMBRACE THE BLESSED
IN HEAVEN,
THEN WHEN I SHARE WITH YOU
A GLIMPSE OF THEIR GLORY.

MY 'EYE' OF TRUTH
REVEALS TO YOU

404

- THROUGH OUR UNION IN PRAYER -
THE NAKED SIGHT OF YOUR OWN SOUL'S TRUE YEARNINGS.
MY PURE AND PIERCING GAZE OF TRUTH
- UPON SOULS WHICH ARE 'NAKED' BEFORE ME -
IS 'SHARED' BY YOU
WHEN I UNVEIL, TO YOUR OWN SOUL'S EYES,
EACH HEART'S TRUE INTENTIONS.

Compassionate love.

Then the Father showed me what is possible, by His grace, for someone who remains utterly devoted to Him and to His Will. He told me:-

MY INFINITE LOVE
IS SHARED AND SEEN
AS IT FLOWS THROUGH THE THOUGHTS AND ACTS
AND WORDS AND PRAYERS
OF ONE WHO TRULY LOVES ME.

MY CREATIVE POWER
IS AT WORK IN ONE WHOSE LIFE-IN-UNION
WITH ME
- PRODUCING ACTS OF CHARITY -
IS IMMENSELY FRUITFUL.

MY COMPASSIONATE LOVE
IS SHOWN ANEW IN THE LIFE, FREELY OFFERED,
OF ONE WHO SUFFERS ON BEHALF OF OTHERS,
ONE WHOSE LIFE TRICKLES AWAY IN LITTLE SACRIFICES:
A LIFE WHOLLY UNITED TO CHRIST, MY SON, THE CRUCIFIED.
(T:1704 #2)

To the top of the hill.

No-one can have received greater encouragement than this; and that's why I didn't mind that the work I was doing was never-ending. At every appropriate moment, however, Christ encouraged me to persevere. He told me, on November 22nd that year:-

Enjoy this anniversary: now five years since My Mother's special visit to you! Put your trust in Me once more. I know it has seemed as though you have been plodding uphill, like a child who trudges through the snow pulling a heavy sledge; but your strenuous efforts to do My Will and My work during these past five years have been worthwhile. Soon, the work will grow easier. I am preparing to reveal My work in your life; it is as though your burden of work has been pulled to the top of the hill,

and will now hurtle downwards of its own momentum. That is how swiftly I shall ensure that My 'teachings' are carried to other people. (WC:1715) (T:1715)

He also told me:-

Share the joy of the Archbishop for whose soul you prayed, when you heard that he had died. You can see how happy he is, now kneeling before My throne to receive My welcome. I, your High Priest - now wearing dazzling garments, and a Mitre - lean forward to embrace this beloved friend, just as I greet with great delight and with a most tender welcome every priestly servant who has faithfully guarded and guided My flock upon earth. (WC:1716) (T:1716 #2)

Be simple and true in every word and gesture, if you would be worthy of My work. For the sake of the work, too, resolve to abandon your fears, and to keep your eyes fixed on Me, longing only to please Me. (T:1725 #2)

CHARITY:

WITH GOD THE FATHER:
THE SOURCE OF ALL GOODNESS

"Do not let your hearts be troubled ..." (Jn 14:1)

"Anybody who receives my commandments and keeps them
will be one who loves me;
and anybody who loves me will be loved by my Father,
and I shall love him and show myself to him" (Jn 14:21).

"If anyone loves me he will keep my word,
and my Father will love him,
and we shall come to him
and make our home with him ..." (Jn 14:23)

"I shall not call you servants any more,
because a servant does not know
his master's business;
I call you friends,
because I have made known to you
everything I have learnt from my Father.
You did not choose me,
no, I chose you;
and I commissioned you
to go out and to bear fruit,
fruit that will last ..." (Jn 15:15-16).

16 CO-OPERATION
(1995-1996)

NEGLECT OF GOD. CHRIST. GOD'S WORK.

Christ, with His Immaculate Mother.

Many times, in the 1990's, Christ had shown me what Glory and joy await all who love and serve Him - and yet how few of His followers are wholehearted in His service. Then one day in 1995 Christ explained to me yet again how urgently-needed are His reminders of the truths of the Faith. It is a terrible thing that so few of those who call themselves His friends are faithful to His wishes.

Daily, I made fervent efforts to serve Christ better, sorry that my whole life hadn't been spent in loving Him, and sorry that - as He has shown me - many people today don't care a scrap for what He's done for us: or for what His Mother has suffered to bring us this wonderful Saviour.

When I showed God the Father how weak I am, and what struggles I have to carry earthly burdens gracefully, I was enormously comforted when He assured me that He was at work in my weakness.

Because of this kindness, and many others, I prayed with especial gratitude at the Vigil Mass of the feast of Our Lady's Immaculate Conception - on December 8th 1995. During the prayer for the Church, I poured out my thanks to God for Our Lady: for her willingness to give her whole life to God, and for having given us Christ Who is flesh from her flesh. Then, suddenly, Christ appeared to me. He stood before me, bathed in Glory; and He revealed to me His extraordinary purity and simplicity (T:1734A). He was stately and majestic, and awesomely beautiful; and yet He was longing to share, even with me, and in great detail, the good news about His perfection, and about His plan of Salvation, His Love for us, and the infinite value of His redeeming Sacrifice.

An Immaculate Mother of an Immaculate Son.

At the very moment that Christ appeared to me in all His Glory, He told me, soundlessly:-

> **Don't be afraid.**
> **It is I, your Risen Saviour,**

409

dazzling your eyes with My radiant beauty,
sharing My Glory on this feast day
because of your prayer,
when you thanked My holy Mother
- the Immaculate Virgin -
for willingly giving her whole life to My service:
for giving the world its Saviour, Myself:
flesh from her flesh.

Don't be afraid.
Look bravely towards Me.
As you can see
- in astonishing Light and grace -
I am
the Divine Son Who took to Himself
a human nature.
Every cell of My Sacred Body, and
every thought of My Heart and Mind
is irradiated
by Glory, Grace and Divine Light.
This is what it is to be glorified
and Risen.

(T:1734A #1)

Consider how glorious,
and how necessary for My own conception
- and how simple for you to understand -
was My Mother's purity of soul and body.
She whom you call "Our Lady"
- the purest of all pure virgins,
and rightly called "Immaculate" -
was then
and is now
wholly pure, virginal, simple and holy.
I too, your Saviour,
was then
- in youth and in maturity -
and am now
wholly pure, virginal, simple and holy;
and the perfect purity of My human nature
stemmed from the astonishing purity
of My only human parent:
the holy Virgin, Mary;
and that is why
- by My Divine Will and plan -
she whom I chose to be My Mother
was conceived "Immaculate", with
her soul pure and glorious,
free from Original sin.

(WC:1734A) (T:1734 #2)

Christ's purity.

Here, Christ began to explain what wonderful hope He offers to us all, and how perfect joy can be found, in the end, by all who have put their trust in Him. He told me:-

> **Don't be afraid.**
> **My Will for you**
> **- even for you My sinful children -**
> **is also astonishing and glorious!**
> **This is My Will:**
> **- that you be like Me,**
> **- that you achieve, through My grace,**
> **   the same perfect sinlessness,**
> **   and so be fit for Heaven:**
> **- that by My Divine generosity**
> **   you resemble me, in radiance.**

(T:1734A #3)

> **Don't be afraid.**
> **Look bravely towards My Glory.**
> **I, Jesus, am teaching you, further,**
> **about the splendour of My purity:**
> **it stemmed from My Divine nature**
> **and also from My Mother's perfection.**
>
> **Here I am,**
> **shining with a Heavenly radiance and beauty.**
> **Here I am,**
> **shining with a Light more like clear moon-light**
> **than sun-light:**
> **glowing, not searing, and**
> **soothing, not scorching,**
> **for you who are unafraid**
> **to look upon Truth.**
>
> **How painful is My Light**
> **for those who shun not only Truth Itself**
> **but also half-truths, truths veiled,**
> **or even little glimpses.**
> **Gaze more surely upon My truth.**
> **Understand, now,**
> **something which eludes those**
> **who have no desire to be pure, simple and child-like:**
> **that My purity is as marvellous and as beautiful**
> **- and as astonishing, to you -**
> **as My Divine Glory.**

411

I, the Divine Son, Jesus,
am wholly pure and perfect
in every 'movement', every aspect:
wholly 'transparent' in purity,
with the quality of pure water
or a perfect crystal.
No shadow of imperfection
obscures the depth of My Being.
(T:1734A #4)

Don't be afraid.
Describe for others what you see before you:
the figure of a man, in Glory: Myself, your Redeemer.
Yet tell them what you see "in" Me:
you see the clear, patient intelligence
of the Divine Person Who knows all truth
and Who Is Truth: One Who, therefore,
- like a pure child, direct and simple -
is unwilling, indeed unable
to condone or to co-operate with
half-truths, flattery, conversational ploys
or wrong insinuations,
in the conversations between men
or when they address Me in prayer.

I, Whom you approach in prayer,
am Divine, perfect and holy,
living in unsullied and glorious purity.
Yet if My purity is infinite and perfect,
so too is My compassion
which pours out ceaselessly upon My children.

Through that compassion for sinners,
I, Jesus Christ, the Son of God
- son, also, of the pure and holy Virgin Mary -
sacrificed Myself to save you:
to offer salvation to mankind.
(T:1734A #3)

By My obedience I bridged the gulf
which kept mankind from the Father.
I, the sinless, paid the 'price' of sin.
I paid the 'price' throughout My life on earth,
but I paid the whole 'ransom'
on Calvary.
(T:1734A #5)

The price of sin.

Here, in this extraordinarily vivid and generous teaching, Christ began to explain to me the way in which He had redeemed us and therefore the meaning of the Atonement by which God and mankind were reconciled. As I gazed at Christ in wonder as He stood before me in glory, I understood, all-at-once, and in astonishing depth, why Christ's obedience during earthly life should have opened Heaven's door.

Christ explained the meaning of 'Redemption', and revealed to me His immense love for us - for His true brothers and sisters; and He helped me to see more clearly the astonishing importance of the Holy Sacrifice of the Mass, through which His saving Work of Calvary is marvellously re-presented before us. Then He continued to instruct me.

"All Doctrine Is One".

As I remained in prayer, my heart open to Christ's teaching, I saw with the eyes of my soul a scroll being let down from Heaven. I saw that there was some writing on the scroll; and straight away Christ taught me about Truth: about the truth that just as the Godhead contains no parts, but is one, so all doctrine about God and about His Work of Salvation is one. Christ showed me how, by His Will, we have had revealed to us what seems like a 'procession' of doctrines, culminating in the great revelation of Divine Love given through Christ's Incarnation; and yet all doctrine is one; Truth is indivisible (T1734B #1).

Then Christ explained precisely why His own Sacrifice on Calvary surpassed all other sacrifices for sin: and why we have been reconciled to the Father in Heaven through that perfect Offering; and He also spoke about the woman who bore Him and who therefore made possible, in one sense, His Work of Salvation. He spoke once again about His Mother's special privilege: of how she had been conceived free from Original Sin, so that Christ our 'Immaculate' and incarnate God would be born from an 'Immaculate' mother.

A symbol of purity.

It's impossible to say enough about Christ's generosity. Even after such a teaching as the last one, He hadn't finished with the subject. It was at the same celebration of Mass, but after Holy Communion, that I was astonished to see not only Christ - who frequently reveals Himself to me - but also His Holy Mother. She was cloaked from head to foot in a white winter dress and a cloak - like a Queen, in a wintry landscape. Christ stood beside her, holding her hand; and as He stood there, He showed me how much He delights in our sincere and fervent prayers. He told me:-

> **Accept My thanks for your greeting**
> **on My Mother's special feast-day.**
> **She stands beside Me today**
> **- as you can see -**
> **cloaked in white, and wrapped in beauty:**
> **a true Queen, in a hushed and snowy landscape.**

Understand, about My Mother:
I delight in the beauty of her holiness.
Her purity is astounding.
The whiteness of a wintry snow-fall
is a true and radiant symbol
of the purity of My Virgin Mother.
So great is My Love for her, and
so tremendous is My respect
for her Motherhood, her sanctity,
and her immaculate soul, that
"I bring My Mother only to pure hearts."
(T:1734C #1)

Understand the reason for this teaching;
share My joy;
I delight in your struggles to be holy!
It is the Will of My Father
that all who receive Me in Holy Communion
- men, women, and children too -
should strive to be worthy of My Presence.
We have come to encourage you,
and, through you, others. Tell them:
it is the Will of the Father
that all who are called the 'children of God'
be pure, which means:
devoted to Me, entirely,
loving My Will,
determined to fulfil My wishes,
contrite, faithful, chaste and obedient, and
longing to give Me Glory.
Thus, they can be worthy of their title.
(WC:1734C) (1734C #2)

Sharing my life.

Then Christ reminded me of the blessings which are lavished upon all who freely choose to be reconciled and so to live 'in Christ'; and He urged me to be braver about sharing this good news. He told me:-

Consider My Work on the Cross, which, long ago,
reconciled Mankind to the Father;
that same Work, My Self-Offering
- when offered to the Father
through the Holy Sacrifice of the Mass -
reconciles you now!
What a cause for hope!
How wonderful are the gifts which I offer
to My children.

Share the good news;
let Me remind My People
- through you -
what great peace and fulfilment are given
to you who are incorporated 'into' Me,
and who share My Life, even here on earth.
(T:1734D #1)

Transformation through Christ.

Consider the gifts which I long to share
with you, My children,
for your joy and transformation.
    I offer to you
        My own great purity and holiness!
You can live in innocence,
        after the forgiveness of your sins.
You can allow My pure Life and virtues
        to flow through you,
        because of our union.
You can be 'indwelt' by My Spirit.
You can 'share' Him.
You can be One with Me, in the Holy Spirit
        Who already inspires
        all your prayers.
You can pray to the Father
        - since you live 'in' Me -
        just as I prayed from the Cross.
(T:1734D #2)

Consider the work to which I invite
My true brothers and sisters
of every generation: those of you
who have been Reconciled
and so have been delivered from sin.
This is the Work:
it is to pray to the Father as I pray:
praising, thanking, submitting,
asking, and interceding, joyfully,
with a pure heart,
yet with that heart burning:
devoured by a longing for the Father's Glory.
(T:1734D #3)

Rejoicing in my weakness.

It was impossible for me to absorb Christ's teachings about sinners with thinking of times when I myself had turned away from Christ; but He was always tender and thoughtful. I was comforted when He explained why there was no reason to think He should have chosen someone impeccable to do this work. He told me:-

> **Don't allow yourself to be made despondent by the new onslaught of spiritual trials and temptations which is disturbing your present peace-of-soul. I delight in your efforts to please me, amidst these trials; I am not in the least disturbed by your little weaknesses. Far from making you unfit to do My work, they are contributing to this 'project': to this continuing demonstration of 'life-in-Christ'.** *That is the point* **of them: that other people are going to be encouraged, one day, to love Me more fervently because of the example which will be given to them, through you, of 'faith-in-weakness!' (T:1773 #1)**

> **Never give up your struggles to be holy; but accept the fact that you are a weak person whom I have chosen, nevertheless, to do My work; and understand how powerfully the knowledge of this fact is going to help other people. It is part of My plan that when, later on, people examine the whole of the task that you are doing for Me, and the whole of your life, and that when they consider My great Love for you and for mankind, they will praise My Infinite wisdom. They will observe that I did not ask a 'good' person to serve Me and to do My work, which is the work of praying, suffering, and recording My teachings. No! They will see that I invited a sinful person to serve Me, and that I planted within her soul some 'seeds' of hope and love, and also planted the wonderful gift of faith by which she would cling to Me and would allow Me to change her! The wisdom of My plan lies in the fact that people who come to know about your failures - as well as encountering this tremendous work - will realise that I am delighted above all in seeing a meek and contrite heart. I am more pleased, they will understand, with a weak person's patience and obedience than with 'great' self-chosen exploits. (T:1773 #2)**

> **See how marvellously I reward you for your efforts to please Me; I assure you even now that many people are going to be helped when they learn of the spiritual assaults and temptations against which you have battled during past years. (T:1773 #3)**

Christ explained why trust was important, and not a longing for visible results, as I continued to produce one book of teachings after another in obedience to His wishes. He urged me:-

> **Recognise, in your life, the benefits which have sprung from**

a long period of 'gestation'. You can see how the whole
collection of paintings and teachings - with your own
reflections, understanding and knowledge - has been
'maturing' and growing towards a moment of 'birth'.
(T:1774 #3)

Put your trust in Me, once again. I assure you that your
work for Me is like a child which still 'hides' within its
mother's womb. Our joint work - My teachings - is like a
vigorous child who is bursting with life, ready to make a
new cry of hope in the world: a cry which will astound
others by its vigour! (T:1774 #4)

Human and Divine inter-play and action.

After a further few weeks, in which I had worked and prayed as usual, and had learned much
more in prayer about the purpose of my work, I became more determined than ever to keep on
praising and thanking God even in pain and turmoil; and suddenly, the Father taught me that
"Suffering is the seal" which He Himself places upon a life which is being truly lived 'in
Christ'. It is a privilege through which that person is made to have a greater resemblance to
the Saviour Whom he or she serves, and is also a sign for others (T:1782)

Despite having been reassured about this 'sign', it seemed to me that I had so many faults to
conquer that I was holding up God's work in my life: and so on January 30th in the New Year
- in 1996 - I renewed my promise to Christ that I would try to live and work at all times in
simplicity and humility.

In the evening, after my usual domestic chores, I sat at my desk to write out some of the
teachings; and as, usual, I made the Sign of the Cross; but this time I asked with great
confidence: "Most Holy Spirit: guide me!" Then I was shown, all at once, the clear sight of
the ways in which God has helped and adorned me; and I was shown an image of two joyful
figures who were soaring through the universe; and this image, I was told, represented the
way in which a frail human being acts with the Holy Spirit, in the universe, in free-will and
delight, but also with Divine power. I was shown how God is ceaselessly at work for our
benefit - and also how He draws good from our every good thought and action - and many
other things; and the lavish explanation continued for a long time, as the Father gave me the
privileges of true friendship, instead of hiding things from me in the way that some things are
kept hidden not from family or friends but from employees.

The region of the spirit.

This was all so astonishing that I turned to the Father to praise and thank Him; and at every
sincere word from my heart, I was rewarded. He explained to me about union with Him,
about who can achieve it, about the true meaning of love, and many more things. And I was
so overjoyed that I wrote some of those things even as He was still teaching me; but He didn't
mind. Quite the opposite; He delighted in my trust, and each time, continued afterwards to

417

teach me. Such is the courtesy of our God even to His creatures! And since it was in this teaching that the Father 'convinced' me of the extent of His tender love for me, I must include several pages, in order to share my joy, and to convince others of His goodness.

Through Christ, I was taught in the following way - after that lengthy teaching from the Holy Spirit about our work:-

Listen to your Heavenly Father, Who delights in your expressions of gratitude for the gift of the Spirit's teaching. He delights, too, in your gratitude for the life and work of Mary, My Virgin Mother, through whose obedience you were able to know Me and to receive My Holy Spirit. Listen, as your Father pours His Bliss into your heart, and teaches you about faith and union:

HERE I AM, MY CHILD,
GIVING YOU LIGHT , PEACE, WISDOM, JOY AND GLORY
IN OUR LIFE OF UNION.
I DELIGHT IN SHARING MY GIFTS
WITH MY FRAIL AND BELOVED FRIENDS.
MANY MORE OF MY PEOPLE
COULD ENJOY MANY MORE OF MY BLESSINGS
AND ENJOY MUCH MORE OF MY LOVE,
YET
THERE IS SO LITTLE FAITH UPON EARTH,
EVEN IN HEARTS WHICH BELONG TO ME.
HOW FEW ACHIEVE TRUE UNION WITH ME,
A UNION THROUGH WHICH I LAVISH UPON THE SOUL
- EVEN DURING EARTHLY LIFE -
LIGHT, PEACE AND BLISS.

HOW FEW ACCEPT MY INVITATION TO AIM FOR TRUE UNION.
HOW FEW, THEREFORE, CAN ENTER THE 'REGION' OF THE SPIRIT,
A REGION FOUND FAR ABOVE EARTHLY DESIRES.
HOW TERRIBLE THE LOSS, FOR THOSE WHO
- THROUGH IGNORANCE, LUKE-WARMNESS OR DESERTION -
NEVER ENTER THE REGION ABOVE.
HOW FEW SOULS ARE WILLING
TO PASS THROUGH THE NARROW 'CHANNEL'
WHICH IS CHRIST'S WAY
- A WAY THAT LEADS FROM EARTHLY LIFE TO HEAVEN'S GLORY -
ON A JOURNEY THAT REQUIRES WILLING HEARTS, AND ALSO
faith and self-sacrifice.

THE 'WAY' IS SO NARROW,
AND HEAVEN IS SO FAR ABOVE EARTHLY LIFE
THAT WITHOUT FAITH, AND WITHOUT SELF-SACRIFICE,
NO-ONE CAN ENTER.

(T:1794 #11)

DON'T BE AFRAID, MY DAUGHTER.
I AM LISTENING.
ACCEPT THE JOY WHICH I AM POURING UPON YOU.
I WANT YOU TO SEE THAT YOUR EVERY GOOD EFFORT
- YOUR EVERY PRAYER OF FAITH, LOVE AND HUMILITY -
DRAWS UPON YOU, THROUGH MY GOODNESS,
EVEN MORE FAITH AND EVEN MORE BLISSFUL CHARITY.
THUS DO I WORK,
WHO AM LOVING.
YET THIS IS MY GIFT, ALSO, FOR A SPECIAL REASON:
SOMETHING LONG-PAST.
TODAY IS THE ANNIVERSARY OF YOUR GIFT TO ME:
THE ANNIVERSARY OF YOUR TOTAL SELF-GIVING.
ALTHOUGH YOU HAD FORGOTTEN IT, I HAD NOT.
DON'T BE SURPRISED BY MY GIFTS.
WHY BE ASTONISHED BY MY GENEROSITY:
BY THE GOOD DESIRES WHICH I PLACE WITHIN YOUR HEART
OR BY MY TEACHINGS?
YOU LONG TO KNOW AND LOVE ME;
YOU LONG TO GIVE ME GLORY;
AND THIS IS MY 'ANSWER' TO YOUR LONGINGS:
TO ASSURE YOU, MY DAUGHTER,
THAT I AM POURING MY GRACES UPON YOU, LAVISHLY.
SINCE YOU TRY TO DO MY WILL,
I NOW DO YOUR WILL.

"As you gave all you have
to Me,
now do I give all
to you:
all My riches!
Such is the fulfilment of your generosity to Me!"
(T:1794 #12)

Life within the 'whole 'Trinity'.

Here, I was so overjoyed at the Father's goodness that I begged Him for gifts for other people too; and He answered, very tenderly:-

CONTINUE IN PRAYER.
HERE I AM, LISTENING,
DELIGHTING IN YOUR LOVE,
GRANTING YOUR REQUESTS,
AND POURING MY JOY INTO YOUR TRUSTING HEART.
SEE HOW I WORK!
HOW GREAT IS MY LOVE!
BUT SEE HOW MUCH CLOSER IS OUR UNION
PRECISELY BECAUSE OF YOUR INTERCESSIONS

419

FOR OTHER PEOPLE.
A WONDERFUL PROGRESS IS MADE BY YOU
THROUGH EACH ACT OF CHARITY.
BY EVERY SUCH ACT, YOU ARE DRAWN MORE FULLY
INTO MY LIFE,
THAT IS:
INTO THE LIFE OF THREE DIVINE PERSONS:
ONE GOD.
THE 'WHOLE' TRINITY IS AT WORK
DURING YOUR PRAYER.

IF YOU SPEAK WITH THE MOST HOLY SPIRIT
AND ARE TAUGHT BY ME, YOUR FATHER,
CHRIST IS NOT ABSENT.
INDEED,
YOU ARE 'HELD' IN CHRIST'S EMBRACE,
IN THIS LOVING PRAYER, THIS UNION.
YOU ARE 'TURNED' TOWARDS ME, YOUR FATHER
WHO DWELL ABOVE.
YOU ARE UNITED WITH US
BY THE LOVE OF THE HOLY SPIRIT
TO WHOM YOU TURNED, INITIALLY, FOR GUIDANCE!
(WC:1794C) (T:1794 #13)

BELIEVE IN MY LOVE FOR YOU.
DELIGHT IN THE TRUTH!
TRULY, YOU ARE NOW ENJOYING A LIFE OF UNION
WITH LOVE ITSELF: MYSELF, YOUR GOD.
THIS IS THE LOVE OF WHICH THE RAPTURE IS SO WELL EXPRESSED
IN SACRED SCRIPTURE,
AT THE END OF THE 'SONG OF SONGS.'
THIS IS THE LOVE OF WHICH THE FERVOUR IS SO WELL EXPRESSED
IN THE IMAGE WHICH WAS MY GIFT TO YOU,
THIS EVENING:
THE IMAGE OF CARE-FREE, CHASTELY-UNITED FIGURES
WHO TUMBLE THROUGH THE UNIVERSE
IN JOYFUL CO-OPERATION:
SUCH IS THE FERVENT AND LOVING TRUE UNION OF YOURSELF,
BELOVED CREATURE,
WITH ME, YOUR GOD.
(WC:1794D) (T:1794 #14)

Special gifts and mercies.

It was impossible for me to listen any more without thanking the Father for His goodness - and for some special blessings of recent times. Then He continued:-

DON'T BE AFRAID. I AM LISTENING.

DON'T BE SURPRISED BY MY GIFTS.
SINCE I LOVE YOU,
SHALL I NOT LAVISH MY GIFTS UPON YOU?
YES, IT IS RIGHT THAT YOU THANK ME
FOR ALL HELPS, AND FOR SPECIAL MERCIES;
YET DID YOU BELIEVE THAT I COULD ALLOW YOU
- A BELOVED FRIEND -
TO ENDURE PROLONGED SUFFERING, WITHOUT ASSISTANCE?
REJOICE IN THE GIFT WHICH TOUCHES YOU SO DEEPLY.

(T:1794 #15)

DON'T BE AFRAID. I AM LISTENING.
YES, IT IS TRUE THAT CHRIST MY SON
SUFFERED TO THE VERY END, IN AGONY.
NO FRIEND OF HIS SHOULD DEMAND AN 'EASY' LIFE
OR SPECIAL PRIVILEGES,
BUT, RATHER, SHOULD FOLLOW WHERE CHRIST LEADS.
THINK ABOUT MY SON, HOWEVER, AND HIS SUFFERINGS:
"He had a short life.
You have much work to do."
DIFFERENT TYPES OF WORK DEMAND, FROM ME,
DIFFERENT GIFTS , PLANS, HELPS AND ARRANGEMENTS.
NO TASK IS AS PIVOTAL AS WAS CHRIST'S TASK,
YET EVERY HOLY TASK IS TRULY MY WILL:
MY WILL BEING WORKED OUT
IN THE LIFE OF ONE WHO ACCEPTS A SPECIAL VOCATION:
ONE OF MY TRUE FRIENDS.

(T:1794 #16)

Feeble love.

Here, I said that I long to make God known, but "I'm so uncharitable." Yet the Father then told me:-

DO NOT BE ANXIOUS.
HERE I AM, LISTENING,
HEARING YOUR CONFESSION OF WEAKNESS,
WITH YOUR CONFESSION OF NEED,
AND YOUR EXPRESSION OF LONGING
TO SHARE THE GOOD NEWS OF MY LOVE.
DO NOT BE ANXIOUS.
YOU CAN BE SURE THAT AT YOUR EVERY ADMISSION OF NEED,
MY CHARITY
- THE 'GOLD' OF DIVINE AND FIERY-WARM CHARITY -
POURS WITHIN YOUR HEART.
DO NOT WORRY ABOUT YOUR FEEBLE LOVE FOR OTHER PEOPLE.
"Love with My Love!"
MY DIVINE LOVE, WITHIN YOUR HEART, IS MORE THAN ENOUGH

TO LOVE THE MANY PEOPLE
WHO NOW FILL YOUR HEART AND MIND.

(T:1794 #17)

ACCEPT MY LOVE AND JOY AND PRESENCE.
I AM ALWAYS HERE;
AND YOU ARE WHOLLY MINE
WHEN YOU ARE PRAYING IN GRATITUDE AND THANKSGIVING.
THE HUMAN BODY, HEART, SOUL AND MIND ARE HELD IN BLISS
- ACCORDING TO MY HOLY WILL -
WHEREVER AND WHENEVER I CHOOSE TO POUR MY POWERFUL AND DIVINE LOVE
UPON A FRAIL CREATURE.
MY LOVE IS FOUND TO BE CEASELESS AND UNENDING
BY YOU WHOSE HEARTS ARE OPEN TO RECEIVE IT:
YOU IN WHOM TRUTH - HUMILITY - KEEPS OPEN THE 'DOOR' OF THE HEART.
AT EVERY ACT OF FAITH IN ME
YOU CONSENT TO MY ACTION.
I INCREASE YOUR FAITH AND, FURTHERMORE,
I INCREASE YOUR JOY!

(T:1794 #18)

SHARE THE GOOD NEWS WITH OTHERS:
MY LOVE IS TREMENDOUS
AND MY TENDERNESS INFINITE.
YOU YOURSELF KNOW THIS; YET
MANY PEOPLE WILL LONG FOR TRUE AND PERPETUAL UNION
WITH ME, THEIR GOD,
IF THEY HEAR YOUR NEWS:
IF THEY HEAR ABOUT AND SO YEARN FOR
THE STATE-OF-SOUL WHICH IS YOURS:
A STATE OF FERVENT OBEDIENCE
AND OF LOVING SURRENDER TO MY WILL:
IN PERPETUAL JOY.

CELEBRATE THE BLESSINGS
WITH WHICH I DELIGHT YOUR HEART.
REMAIN IN MY LOVE,
IN A STATE OF BLISSFUL FRIENDSHIP,
WITH FREEDOM FROM FEAR,
WITH GRATITUDE FOR MY GOODNESS,
WITH A CONVICTION OF MY POWER,
AND WITH CERTAINTY ABOUT THE FULFILMENT OF MY PROMISES:
PROMISES TO MY PEOPLE, AND PROMISES TO YOU
ABOUT YOUR WORK.
TAKE MY JOY TO OTHERS.

(T:1794 #19)

17 CONTEMPLATION
(1996)

A SACRED WAY. TRUTH. GOD OUR ORIGIN AND PARADISE.

A sacred way.

By the middle of February, 1996, every moment of prayer was so full of peace and joy that, whenever I thought about this, it was as though I should pinch myself to make sure that I wasn't dreaming - as the old phrase says. Part of my mind was wondering: "How can this last?" - even as I realised that several good things had happened at once, or had come together.

Since my trust in God had grown, I turned to Him more frequently, therefore I received greater help, which made me more determined to go to Him with every joy, problem or query; and so, inevitably - by His grace - I had become even more joyful. But there was another reason. This was a new stage. I knew this, because the Father told me.

It was when He had wonderfully answered one of my queries (in T:1811) that I was so thrilled that I exclaimed: "Who is like You!" Suddenly, He showed me that such a conversation takes place almost as a matter of course in what was now a new way of life, in which I walked along in light and joy on a 'sacred way': as if through a beautiful valley, high up in the mountains of the spiritual life, and far above the twisting path of earlier days. (T:1811)

Two vessels, meeting.

That same month, when I remained in church one Saturday after the morning Mass, I turned to the Father in prayer, showing Him every facet of my heart and soul; and then I was made 'speechless' as He suddenly showed me a glimpse into the depths of His own Being. (T:1814)

This was so awesome for me, and the Father, I learned, was so wholly desirous of showing me the reason for this 'reciprocity' of truths, that a simple image was given to me, even as the Father soundlessly explained what was happening in our prayerful 'meeting'.

I saw an image of two stone vases which were side by side, yet each tilted towards the other until the lip of one almost touched the lip of the other; and a stream of shining liquid was pouring from one jar into the other. At the same time the Father explained to me that as I show my truest and most private thoughts to Him in prayer, and at the same time am utterly devoted to Him, trying to live only for His Glory, He can therefore show me something of His own infinite depths - by which He meant His knowledge of Himself.

It is when my heart is willingly 'open' to His gaze, and when it is thoroughly empty at last of all that is foolish and earthly - when I have banished former impediments to true spiritual union - that my heart is wholly 'open' to God's Will. It is open, therefore, to receive the precious spiritual drink which is Divine Life and Love as it pours from the vessel which represents the Godhead; and the two 'vessels' shown to me are joined, therefore, in two ways: first by their proximity to one another, and secondly by the ever-generous stream of life, love and wisdom which pours between them.

There was more reassurance, in the very same teaching. Further teachings followed, on every sort of relevant subject, day after day; and yet each day was busy, too, with meals, mishaps, visits to friends, with the usual services at church - and with extra, unexpected tasks to do for Our Lord.

Christ's loving purpose.

Just before Easter, in 1996, I was preparing to spend a few days with my family in Rome at the English College, where our elder son was at Seminary. Only days before we left, about to encounter for the first time a much broader 'picture' of life in the Catholic Church, with deeper insights into the ministerial Priesthood, I was given a broader knowledge by Christ, in prayer, about my own role in His Church. He taught me precisely why He had chosen to ask a weak and handicapped lay-person like myself to speak out boldly about the Faith; and part of the reason was because not all members of the Clergy who should be speaking out today are willing to proclaim and to defend Catholic teachings.

Christ explained, to my amazement, just why it is that I'm suitable for this task. He told me:-

Follow My inspiration and write down what I am showing you about the work which I have asked you to do, and about My purpose. This is what I want you to explain, for other people:

I, Jesus your Saviour
- God and man -
wish to teach all nations.
I long to save My people from their sins.
I long to teach Truth, through My holy Church;
It is true that I can teach,
through My bishops and priests,
and also through parents, religious, and teachers
and theologians,
if they will faithfully hear Me,
and will faithfully teach others.

Yet many of these people,
- through whom I would teach -
do not hear Me and therefore do not teach!
Some choose to ignore the teaching and guidance
which I Myself offer to you all
through Saint Peter's successor.
That is why I have chosen, to do My work, yourself:
a foolish, emotional woman,
who was passionately attached
to the good things of this world,
and was undisciplined, and was ignorant of the doctrines
which some of My teachers fail to teach.
Your sinfulness and ignorance
have served My loving purpose.
I chose you because of your weakness! (T:1840A #1)

Ablaze with gratitude.

Then Christ explained to me:-

Remember when you prayed to Me,
long ago, and with great faith,
but with a burning need for My Love
and for hope and reassurance;
I poured My gifts upon your thirsty soul,
pouring them in such abundance
that your startled heart
- through every trial and set-back -
has remained ablaze with gratitude:
which fuels your determination
      to take My gifts to others:
      to share the Good News
about My Love for you,
about the forgiveness of sin, and
about the hope of Heaven. (T:1840A #2)

The gift of faith.

Next, Christ urged me to look upon His gifts with gratitude, and to see how appropriate they are for my special task. He made me see what good things had been made possible by my eventual surrender to His wishes, telling me:-

Notice how carefully I have led you forward:
I have given you the gift of faith.
I have given you the gift of repentance.
I have given you a contrite heart.
I have given you a horror of sin

425

in an age when some protest
that sinful thoughts and acts
neither harm the soul nor displease Me.
I have given you a delight in the truths
which many neglect.
I have given you a love of obedience
in an age when obedience is seen
as demeaning,
as if My obedience to the Father's Will
and My Crucifixion
were foolish, and also
were unnecessary for your Salvation.
When you surrendered yourself, therefore,
entirely to My keeping,
in true love, and intimate friendship,
I gave you a glimpse, at last,
of the Heart of My Life:
of the One Glorious Divine Life
which is radiant with Light in its Three-fold wonder:
a Life from which some exclude themselves
by their careless neglect of Truth:
which is one of My Names. (T:1840A #3)

See what a simple task is yours,
now that you have consented to serve Me,
and to follow My instructions!
At My invitation,
you are making a record of My graces:
a record of the gifts, truths and instructions
which you have has found 'in' Me,
in prayer.
None of these truths is 'new'.
But, sad to say, I 'need' someone
to remind the Shepherds,
to guide the parents,
to warn the teachers, and
to say to the theologians:
"Love your neighbour! But also
remember the first Commandment.
Love, revere and obey your Heavenly Father!
Listen to His Son, your Saviour.
Be faithful to His teaching,
which is proclaimed
- now as yesterday -
through His Holy Catholic Church." (T:1840A #4)

Don't be afraid to speak.
You have been appalled at the task,
seeing its magnitude and your ignorance;

426

but I am bringing something worthwhile
out of your obedience. (T:1840A #5)

With Christ's Mind and Heart.

There was very much more I needed to know, at that stage, if I was to be able to fulfil Christ's
plan; and Christ was eager to help me. One day in prayer, He gave me a warning, and also a
glimpse ahead. He urged me:-

> Understand your grave responsibility, as I invite and
> permit you to speak out on My behalf; *"Never forget: you*
> *speak for One Who has the whole Universe in His care."*
> You must take special care, therefore, always to think with
> My Mind, and to love with My Heart, and also never to be
> partisan. Cast aside all prejudice. All men, women and
> children are your brothers and sisters, in need of love, and
> in need of My Light - as and where I Will to shine upon
> certain people, through you! (T:1853 #4)

> Remain here, in prayer, upheld in My Light. I have
> something more to show you. Surrender to My Will; look
> towards Heaven. Here I am, enthroned at the edge of
> Heaven, showing you something of My Majesty. True God
> and man, I reign in majesty in Heaven, in radiant Light, in
> royal dignity and power; yet I am also your Priest: your
> intercessor, clothed as a priest - and powerful and holy.
> But the reason for this sight is not to make your heart quail
> before My Glory, but to reward you. (WC:1853D) (T:1853
> #5)

> Know that I am deeply touched by your new determination
> to banish every sin and failing so that you might be worthy
> to serve Me. You proclaim that you are willing to bear
> mockery for Me; but I know, already, what My service has
> cost you. See how tenderly I am greeting you as I clothe
> you anew for My service. *"You have borne mockery for My*
> *sake. That is why I will now give you Glory;"* and in saying
> 'Glory' I am speaking about the praise which is going to be
> heaped upon you and upon your work - our work - in the
> times which lie ahead. (T:1853 #6)

Then Christ continued to instruct me on every facet of the work:-

> Be confident about your progress, as I teach you about the
> spiritual life, and encourage you to be more single-minded
> and loving in My service. I assure you that when the time
> comes for Me to reveal more widely the extraordinary
> things which I have achieved through your life - for the

purpose of strengthening faith in other souls - I shall have made you ready for your task. And by 'extraordinary' I mean both an astonishing amount of work, all produced at My prompting, and also an astonishing verbal 'picture' or revelation of Myself, and of My loving Nature. By our joint work, you and I are providing a consoling reminder, for many, of what has already been revealed, long ago: the Good News of My Love for you all: the Love of My tender and merciful Heart. (T:1867 #1)

Don't worry about future reactions to My work in your life. I assure you that, when the work is more widely revealed, you will be able to accept the praise which will be lavished upon you because of this work; you will accept it as peacefully as you have come to accept indifference or scorn; and this will be possible because you have not sought that praise for yourself, since all you seek - even now - is Me, your Saviour, and the joy of hearing Me praised. (T:1867 #2)

A new title.

Week by week, Christ continued to enlighten me; for example, He explained the special relevance to this whole work of His Mother's visit to my home, and of the picture of "Our Lady of Harpenden".

I mentioned earlier that I'd been given a clear and privileged glimpse of the beauty of Our Blessed Lady. By about April 1993 I had completed an oil portrait of her which was as detailed and as accurate as I could make it. Then one day in May, 1996, Christ explained to me (T:1899) that I should share my joy about the love of "Our Lady of Harpenden". He invited me to speak to my new parish priest about the visit, and about the title of the painting - so that having shown that courtesy to the head of the Church in our area I'd be free to speak more boldly about the same wonderful things to old friends and to new acquaintances. Christ had explained to me, at different times, that the knowledge of Our Lady's kindness to me would affect other people so much that it would 'soften' many hearts, and so would prepare those hearts in the way that seedbeds are prepared, so that they'd receive a lavish 'planting' within them of the many 'teachings' which He'd given to me in prayer.

I suppose I should add that Our Lord also asked me to tell my priest, in connection with Our Lady's visit, that there's now a river flowing through our town, just as elsewhere, except that this river isn't cold and crystal-clear; it's the living water of Christ's teachings, as it continues to pour out from my prayer and from my pen. Needless to say, I only repeated that to our priest in order to obey Christ, Who has explained to me that His teachings will continue to flow, so long as I am prayerful and faithful. It wouldn't then have occurred to me to make grand descriptions of my work: but I'm not ashamed to do so, today, now that Christ has shown me what tremendous results will be brought about because of these teachings, and now that I'm longing for Him to be praised for His wisdom and goodness.

This is precisely what Christ has told me about Our Lady's picture and its significance:-

Don't be bashful about My gifts to you, and your good work for Me. On this wonderful feast of Pentecost, you have turned to My Holy Spirit, Who longs to help you in every aspect of your life. Listen to His guidance:

FOLLOW MY PROMPTING. DON'T BE AFRAID TO DO AS I URGE YOU, WHICH IS TO SPEAK TO MY PRIEST, AT GREATER LENGTH, ABOUT THE WONDERFUL VISIT WHICH YOU RECEIVED FROM CHRIST'S HOLY MOTHER, AND ABOUT THE PORTRAIT OF HER WHICH YOU HAVE PAINTED AND WHICH IS GIVING JOY TO SO MANY PEOPLE. I, YOUR GOD, DELIGHT IN THE BEAUTY AND HOLINESS OF THE MOST HOLY VIRGIN MARY; AND YOU CAN MAKE THIS KNOWN. "Share My joy" WITH YOUR PRIEST, AS WITH OTHER PEOPLE. LET HIM ENJOY THE KNOWLEDGE THAT THE PICTURE WHICH IS ENTITLED "OUR LADY OF HARPENDEN" IS A TRUE REPRESENTATION OF YOUR GRACIOUS VISITOR: OF THE HOLY MOTHER WHO GAVE YOU COURAGE, AS WELL AS REASSURANCE AND GOOD ADVICE. (T:1899 #1)

SHARE THE GOOD NEWS THAT THE INTERCESSION OF CHRIST'S HOLY MOTHER IS ESPECIALLY FRUITFUL, UNDER HER NEW TITLE, FOR DEPARTED SOULS, AND FOR THE SICK, AND FOR CHILDREN IN DISTRESS. (T:1899 #2)

TELL MY PRIEST, TOO, THAT A SPRING OF LIVING WATER IS NOW FLOWING IN YOUR TOWN; AND THAT 'SPRING' IS THE UNENDING 'STREAM' OF TEACHINGS WHICH IS MY GIFT TO YOU IN PRAYER - A 'STREAM' WHICH WILL BENEFIT VERY MANY PEOPLE. (T:1899 #3)

ACCEPT MY WILL FOR YOUR LIFE. YOU HAVE LONGED TO SHARE YOUR FAITH WITH OTHER PEOPLE; AND IT IS PRECISELY SO THAT MY GOODNESS SHALL BE MORE WIDELY KNOWN - AND ALSO THE HOLINESS OF THE MOST HOLY VIRGIN MARY - THAT YOU HAVE ALSO RECEIVED, IN PRAYER, SO MANY HUNDREDS OF TEACHINGS, AND HAVE RECEIVED SEVERAL VISITS FROM CHRIST'S HOLY MOTHER. I WANT YOU TO SHARE THE JOY OF THESE THINGS WITH OTHER PEOPLE, TO ENCOURAGE THEM IN FAITH AND TO SPREAD IN THEIR HEARTS MY DIVINE AND HEAVENLY JOY: WHICH IS MY GIFT TO THOSE WHO LOVE ME. (T:1899 #4)

KNOW THAT IT IS MY WISH THAT CHRIST'S HOLY MOTHER BE HONOURED EVERYWHERE, ALBEIT UNDER THE DIFFERENT TITLES WHICH ARE APPROPRIATE FOR DIFFERENT TIMES AND PLACES. I DELIGHT IN THE VIRTUES OF CHRIST'S HOLY MOTHER - AND IN HER PRESENCE IN HEAVEN; AND I ALSO ASSURE YOU THAT "OUR LADY OF HARPENDEN" IS A FITTING TITLE FOR THIS MOST HOLY OF MY SAINTS, AND FOR HER PICTURE. (T:1899 #5)

Unfaithfulness, today.

In the following week, when I'd passed on the good news, as Christ had requested, I was shown once again why we are in need of spiritual help from Himself and from His Saints. He showed me how serious a matter is the unfaithfulness which He sees among many Catholics in our age. He urged me:-

> **Persevere in prayer for the Church. You are right to rejoice on this Feast of the Visitation, today, when My holy Mother praised the Father for the work of Salvation which was to be achieved through Me. Yet many of those who believe in Me - many of your spiritual brothers and sisters - face great dangers to their faith: dangers which stem even from fellow-members of My Church. (T:1909 #1)**

> **Look upon truth, bravely.**
> **Many of My people are in danger.**
> **It is as though blood is flowing beside the highway**
> **wherever a 'haemorrhage' occurs**
> **from the life of My Church.**
> **My own people are losing their life-blood**
> **wherever**
> > **they contradict My Church's teaching,**
> > **they mock the Holy Father,**
> > **they scorn obedience, and thus**
> > **they destroy religious orders, or when**
> > **they proclaim that Truth is falsehood, or when**
> > **they explain that sin is virtue, or when**
> > **they leave the Church. (T:1909 #3)**

> **Be sure that if blood were flowing**
> > **in the street,**
> **good people would look for a body.**
> **Be sure that when, in the Church's life,**
> **lack of faith is evident, and disobedience,**
> > **a disaster has occurred.**

> **Just as a man's blood flows, and he dies,**
> > **if he receives a mortal wound,**
> **so do My friends 'lose' the life of their souls**
> > **whenever faith is not taught,**
> > **whenever disobedience is condoned,**
> > **whenever eternal hopes are replaced by earthly goals,**
> > **whenever proud souls mock the faith and the devotions**
> > **of My 'little ones' and**
> > **whenever worship is tarnished:**
> > **as when admiring attention is focused**
> > **- by worshippers who meet to pray in My Name -**
> > **not upon the Father**

but upon themselves and their lives. (T:1909 #4)

Lingering fears.

This teaching about the Church's 'life-blood' shocked me, but not by its content. I'd already learned on so many occasions in prayer how simple and straightforward is Our Lord, whether in His admiring comments or in His warnings; and so I wasn't astonished to hear Him speak the plain truth about disobedience within His Church. What shocked me was the realisation that I was being invited, of course, to pass on to other Catholics - to members of the laity and also to members of the Clergy - not just earlier 'spiritual' teachings but also these very frank and perhaps unwelcome observations.

But it had to be done if I wanted to fulfil Christ's plan; and so I recorded each new teaching carefully, determined to include even the 'difficult' teachings in the next volume of "Instructions from Christ."

[Disobedience and defeatism.

Which of us can claim to be serving God well? Yet as we're struggling to be faithful, perhaps we should re-examine our attitudes and activities. Perhaps we should be more aware that by relentless peer pressure - even in religious circles - we can be led to do as much wrong as right. Unless we remain close to Christ and to His Church through firm faith, loyalty and prayer, we might find that we've succumbed to bad influences in things to do with doctrine and discipline, and also in devotion to God. Our attitudes to prayer, to Mission and to education will all undergo unhealthy changes, and we shall begin to imagine that we know better than Christ and His Church in a number of circumstances.

Most dangerously, perhaps, today, we are tempted to join with the majority whenever the Church's constant teaching is derided - in a group or a conversation - or whenever the Holy Father is being dismissed as "old-fashioned". It's one thing to investigate matters of belief and conscience, but quite another to believe that we can legitimately have a different moral code from that which is founded upon the Commandments given to Moses and is now taught by the Pope and Bishops with the authority of Christ Himself.

It's been suggested to many of us - even by persons within the Church - that an unswerving attachment to the Tradition as well as to Holy Scripture is evidence of a rigid piety. It's suggested that people who struggle to be faithful in all things are uncreative and docile.

Here, within the Church, supporters of heterodoxy try to persuade us that rigid doctrine is something life-destroying. We've been urged to break free from a 'threatening' God, or a 'male' God in order to worship a non-judgmental God who would approve a new presentation of the Catholic Faith: a version which never suggests that anyone really needs saving, or that anyone could ever 'perish'. It's suggested that a healthy faith can free its adherents from the moralising of past ages, and can free them from the slavish obedience which is so unnecessary for enlightened, educated, modern Catholics who have now been made aware of their real needs.

Loyal and obedient membership.

Isn't it sad that so many Catholics aren't aware that our deepest yearnings, needs and hopes can be intelligently examined in the presence of God, and by the Light which He gives through His Spirit and His Church: and that the God Who longs for us to be eternally and blissfully happy most definitely arranges that we can 'taste' some of that happiness, even on this earth, through family joys and the fulfilment of our duties - and, supremely, through union with Christ in active, loyal and obedient membership of His Church, culminating in "Holy Communion."

How deeply I've wished, sometimes, that I need only write about the joys of our Faith, and that I could shy away from problem areas; but I'm conscience-bound to write in the way which Christ requests of me; and so I must give a simple warning about false doctrine and dangerous attitudes. If I don't do this, I shall be unfaithful to Christ, Who answered my request for guidance, last week, with a reminder of the words of His Apostle. Christ told me that it wasn't "THE SPIRIT OF TIMIDITY" that had been given to me (2 Tm 1:7); and that's why I must remind those who will listen that whatever is true remains true; and so we should believe that when many decrees were published for the benefit of the faithful, after the Second Vatican Council, the teachings of earlier Councils were not 'cancelled out', as in the way of the world when the minutes of former meetings are looked upon as nothing but historical records.

What marvellous changes have taken place within the Church this century; yet there have been no fundamental changes in matters to do with faith or morals.

I know, from the teachings of the Church, as well as from what Christ has taught me in prayer, that those theologians, teachers, religious and clergy who have spent half a life-time saying that "there are no easy answers" to question of faith will one day find that the answers are too 'easy' for suspicious or sophisticated minds. The answers were and are 'easy' enough for a child to understand - whether a child in years or a child in simplicity; and I'm speaking about answers to the age-old questions about how to 'find' God and how to please Him, and how to do right and avoid evil. The Church gives plain answers today, or rather, Christ does so, through His Church; and the answers to the main questions are simple, I know, because they come from God Whom we know to be pure, perfect, and simple: from God, of Whom we can say: "THERE IS NO DARKNESS IN HIM AT ALL" (1 Jn 1:5); and so the Way to which He points is also simple, for all who will rely on Christ's strength and wisdom and not on their own.]

An even greater joy.

What a cause for gratitude it is that I've spent so many years in a prayerful and faithful parish; in which our everyday worship has been well-ordered and fulfilling, with reverent liturgy and helpful homilies - as well as feast-day celebrations, and special treats.

I was especially joyful to be able to go to Lourdes on a parish pilgrimage in July 1996. Apart from being thrilled by that town's association with Our Lady, I was very happy to be there with my husband, as well as with our grown-up children, our local priest, and some fellow-

fellow-parishioners.

But an even greater joy was given only a week after our return home from the shrine. My husband decided to approach our priest and to ask to be received into full Communion. Plans were made that he would begin the forthcoming R.C.I.A. course in the autumn; and meanwhile, I relied on my husband's generosity to continue to print successive volumes of teachings, in accordance with Christ's requests.

The Origin, the Home, the Paradise ...

But to return to the teachings from God the Father; since I'm writing about 'stages', I must mention the Feast of Corpus Christi, on June 6th, 1996. It was on that day that I turned to the Father in even greater trust, and with a new act of dedication to His Will; and then He spoke to me once more about His work in my life, and about our union. He said: *"I shall set a seal upon your heart; and that seal shall be Joy!"* He explained that this perpetual gift of joy is to be His sign to others of His dominion over my soul - or, I can say, of His acceptance of the 'treasure' which is a heart given wholly to Him (T:1917).

On the twenty-third of that same month, when I had solemnly and sincerely forsworn every selfish thought or yearning that would keep me from the perfect service of Christ, I was astonished to be given special help by Our Blessed Lady. Then, when I greeted Christ joyfully in Holy Communion, my heart was 'lightened' - by which I mean made entirely carefree and child-like; and I was suddenly enabled, through Christ's Will and Presence and power, to direct the eyes of my soul 'upwards'; and I 'saw' by spiritual knowledge that the Father was reaching out to touch me, in an awesome revelation of Himself to my attentive heart. This was the moment for which the Father had been preparing me, in prayer, for many years.

The Father said: *"It is I!"* And as I heard those words my heart nearly broke for joy. At the same time, I was shown that it's by the power and work of the Holy Spirit, as I'm brought towards the Father through my prayer "in Christ", that I receive Wisdom and Light in prayer, and achieve this sort of union with the Godhead: with the Most Holy Trinity. (T:1941)

But as the Father said those words to me, He revealed the Infinite Love to which all our loving efforts and sacrifices are directed; and He explained in great detail that the total fulfilment for which we yearn, as we serve Him, is eventually given to faithful souls as a bliss and a satisfaction beyond our wildest dreams.

This is what I learned, that day, as I turned to the Father "in" Christ, and was then invited by Christ:-

Listen to your Father, Who now speaks to you from Heaven as He opens Heaven's 'door':

LISTEN, MY CHILD;
"It is I",
YOUR FATHER,
WHO AM REACHING OUT TO TOUCH YOU,

BECAUSE OF MY GREAT LOVE FOR YOU,
AND YOUR GREAT LOVE FOR ME.
I WHO AM LOVE AM THE LORD OF ALL THINGS:
WORTHY OF YOUR DAILY SACRIFICES,
AS YOU, WITH CONTRITE HEART,
STRUGGLE TO PLEASE ME AND TO BE FIT FOR HEAVEN.
I ASSURE YOU, MY BELOVED,
THAT YOUR SURRENDER OF YOUR OWN WISHES
HAS BEEN WHOLLY WORTHWHILE.
I CANNOT FAIL TO REWARD YOU.
YOU CAN BE CERTAIN, THEREFORE,
THAT THROUGH YOUR UNION WITH CHRIST, MY SON,
AND THROUGH THE HELP OF HIS HOLY MOTHER, MARY,
YOU HAVE BEEN WELL-PREPARED
FOR OUR JOYFUL MEETING.

IT IS TRUE THAT I LIVE FAR ABOVE YOU, IN HEAVEN'S SPLENDOUR.
YOU CAN SEE THAT I DWELL IN THE HEIGHTS OF GLORY;
YET HERE I AM, MY CHILD, GAZING UPON YOU,
SHOWING YOU THE HEIGHT AND DEPTH OF OUR LOVING UNION;
AND SINCE YOU BELONG TO CHRIST
THERE IS NO NEED FOR YOU TO SEARCH FOR ME.
YOU CAN MEET ME WITHIN YOUR SOUL, IN PRAYER,
AS IF IN A TABERNACLE OR A TENT.

(T:1941 #3)

The Father: reaching out His hand.

DON'T BE AFRAID.
TRULY,
IT IS I, YOUR HEAVENLY FATHER
WHO NOW REACH OUT TO TOUCH YOU:
REACHING OUT FROM HEAVEN'S GLORY
TO TOUCH YOU WITH LOVE!
AS YOU CAN SEE
- IN THE FLEETING IMAGE WHICH IS MY GIFT TO YOU -
IT IS THROUGH THE OUTSTRETCHED 'HAND' OF MY HOLY SPIRIT,
IN PRAYER,
THAT I BRING MY LIGHT AND JOY TO YOU.
RECOGNISE MY TOUCH!
YOU AND I ARE ALREADY UNITED
IN MY SPIRIT'S POWER,
THROUGH MY SON, YOUR SAVIOUR,
AND THROUGH YOUR TRUSTING PRAYER.
HAVE CONFIDENCE IN OUR FRIENDSHIP;
IT IS THROUGH OUR UNION AND COMMUNION
THAT I CAN SHARE MY LIFE WITH YOU, FURTHER,
BRINGING YOU GREATER JOY,

AND TEACHING YOU MORE ABOUT MY NATURE:
ABOUT THE LOVE WHICH IS GENTLE
YET IMMENSELY POWERFUL.
TREASURE THE KNOWLEDGE
WHICH YOU CAN 'SEE' IN ME, TODAY.
(WC + OIL:1941B) (T:1941 #4)

Sweet, tender Love: cause of all true joy.

GAZE TOWARDS THE BRIGHTNESS OF MY GLORY
IN CONTEMPLATION.
GAZE, WITH THE 'EYES' OF YOUR SOUL.
LOOK BEYOND ALL EARTHLY THINGS
- THEN BEYOND ALL IMAGES -
AS MY HOLY SPIRIT BRINGS YOU UPWARDS
CLOSE TO THE FURNACE OF LOVE WHICH IS SHINING
AT THE HEART OF MY LIFE.
IT IS THUS, THROUGH MY INVITATION,
AND THROUGH MY LIGHT AND POWER, IN PRAYER,
THAT YOU CAN BEGIN TO FATHOM MY NATURE,
WHICH IS LOVE:
DIVINE LOVE, IN ITS BEAUTY AND PERFECTION.

TRULY,
I AM LOVE,
AND THEREFORE
I AM THE SOURCE
OF ALL TRUE LOVE.
I AM THE CAUSE
OF YOUR CONSTANT SPIRITUAL JOY.
I AM THE LIGHT
WHICH NOW ILLUMINES YOUR HEART AND MIND AND SOUL.
I AM THE BLISS
AT THE HEART OF ALL TRUE AND HOLY LOVE,
IN ITS BRIGHT, FIERY JOY AND EXHILARATION.
I AM THE BURNING LOVE
WHICH WARMS AND WOUNDS THE HEARTS
OF ALL WHO LOVE TRUTH, GOODNESS AND BEAUTY.
I AM THE SWEET LOVE
WHICH BINDS TOGETHER ALL TRUE FRIENDS,
FIRST, AMIDST THE JOYS AND TRIALS OF EARTHLY LIFE, AND THEN
ETERNALLY: IN HEAVEN'S GLORY.
I AM ALSO A TENDER LOVE.
I GAZE UPON YOU, NOW AND ALWAYS,
IN THE VERY WAY IN WHICH YOU GAZED
- WEEPING FOR JOY -
UPON YOUR NEW-BORN CHILD.
I AM DIVINE LOVE:

435

UNCHANGING YET ACTIVE: WARM AND EFFECTIVE.
I AM THE TREASURE
FOUND BY ALL WHO MEET TRUE LOVE, ON EARTH;
YET
YOU CAN SAY, OF ME,
WHO AM BLISS AND LIGHT AND LOVE, UNENDING, THAT
I AM THE ETERNAL PRIZE
OF ALL WHO PUT THEIR TRUST IN ME
- EVEN DENYING THEMSELVES LOVE
IN MY SERVICE,
BECAUSE OF THEIR LOVE FOR ME -
AND WHO REMAIN FAITHFUL.

HEARTACHE AND PAIN ARE SURRENDERED
BY ALL WHO ENTER THE HEART OF HEAVEN
FOR THE MARRIAGE-FEAST.

(T:1941 #5)

The bright flame of love.

Then the Father reassured me:-

DON'T BE AFRAID, MY CHILD.
HERE I AM: YOUR FATHER, ENLIGHTENING YOUR SOUL.
I AM THE BRIGHT FLAME
AT THE HEART OF YOUR PRAYER;
INDEED,
I AM THE FIRE
AT THE HEART OF EVERY MOMENT
OF TRUE LOVING UNION AND COMMUNION: WHETHER
BETWEEN OURSELVES,
OR BETWEEN YOU WHO ARE MY CHILDREN.

DON'T BE AFRAID.
I HAVE MUCH MORE TO TEACH YOU,
YET
REJOICE IN MY LOVE.
BE AT PEACE IN OUR PRAYER.
TRULY, IT IS I, YOUR FATHER,
WHO TEACH YOU,
TONIGHT,
REVEALING MY GLORY:
WHICH IS THE LIGHT OF YOUR SOUL
IN EACH HOLY COMMUNION:
YOUR DAILY DELIGHT.

(T:1941 #6)

Paradise.

DELIGHT IN MY GIFTS.
I AM THE SOURCE
OF ALL TRUE WISDOM.
I AM THE GIVER
OF ALL TRUE PEACE.
FURTHERMORE,
IT IS I WHO DRAW YOU TO HEAVEN
- THROUGH CHRIST, AND YOUR PRAYER -
UNVEILING EACH STAGE OF YOUR WAY
ON THIS SPIRITUAL JOURNEY.
TRULY,
I AM YOUR GUIDE;
AND IT IS I WHO INSPIRE YOU
TO PLEASE ME.

I AM THE ORIGIN
OF YOUR LONGING TO BE HOLY.
I AM THE FATHER
OF CHRIST THE BELOVED, IN WHOSE NAME YOU PRAY.
I AM THE LOVE
- PURE, PERFECT, UNENDING, FIERY AND TENDER -
FOR WHICH YOUR SOUL IS YEARNING.
I AM THE GOAL,
ON YOUR JOURNEY TO HEAVEN,
AS YOU FOLLOW THE WAY OF MY SON.
I AM THE HOME
IN WHICH YOU CAN SHELTER FOREVER.
I AM THE PARADISE
IN WHICH IS FOUND THE PERFECT FULFILMENT
OF EVERY GOOD LONGING,
WITH UNENDING BLISS FOR THE HUMAN HEART AND MIND
AND BODY AND SOUL.

IT IS MY ETERNAL WISH, MY CHILD,
TO SEE YOU JOYFUL
ETERNALLY:
TO BIND YOU TO MY HEART
MORE FIRMLY:
AND TO CLAIM YOU AS MY OWN;
YET IT IS I, YOUR GOD, WHO NOW INVITE YOU
TO CLAIM AND CAPTURE ME!

(T:1941 #7)

Undivided attention.

Here, the Father urged me to live in a more profound state of recollection. He urged me:-

437

STAY CLOSE TO ME, MOMENT BY MOMENT.
MAKE YOUR HEART WHOLLY MINE.
GO OUTWARDS, TO LOVE YOUR NEIGHBOUR
WITH MY GREAT LOVE,
THEN TURN TO ME ONCE MORE
IN PRAYER.
TURN YOUR ATTENTION INWARDS, FOR A WHILE,
AWAY FROM THE 'DOORWAY' OF YOUR SOUL.
LOOK TOWARDS ME, WHERE I DWELL, WITHIN.
HERE I AM,
WITH MY SON - YOUR SAVIOUR - AND WITH MY SPIRIT:
EVER-READY TO HOLD YOU AT REST IN OUR LOVE:
IN OUR COMFORT, AND CONVERSATION:
IN THE PURITY AND PEACE
OF YOUR GOD.

(T:1941 #8)

Custody of the heart.

LISTEN, MY DAUGHTER, TO A FURTHER INVITATION:
SHARE MY LIFE AS NEVER BEFORE.
IN THINKING OF MY GIFTS TO YOU,
CONSIDER ONE OF YOUR 'GIFTS' TO ME;
DAY AFTER DAY, OUT OF LOVE FOR ME, YOU 'KEEP CUSTODY'
- A CUSTODY OF THE EYES -
NEITHER GAZING IDLY UPON FORBIDDEN THINGS,
NOR GAZING, BORED,
ON OTHER PEOPLE OR OTHER FACES,
IN CHURCH, DURING THE HOLY SACRIFICE, WHEN
I AM
IN THE SANCTUARY.
THAT IS WHY I NOW INVITE YOU
TO OFFER ME A FURTHER GIFT:
INVITING YOU TO KEEP A TRUE 'CUSTODY OF THE HEART':
TO FOSTER A SINGLE-MINDED LOVE OF MY WILL,
FOR THE SAKE OF AN EVEN CLOSER UNION.

(T:1941 #9)

CONSIDER YOUR LENGTHY PREPARATION
FOR OUR UNION,
NOW ACHIEVED BY MY GRACES:
AND WITH THE ASSISTANCE OF YOUR IMMACULATE MOTHER.
TRULY,
IT WAS SHE WHO LET FALL HER CLOAK
TODAY
TO CONSOLE YOU,
AND TO ENCLOSE YOU IN OUR LOVE,
SO THAT I MIGHT GIVE YOU JOY

UNCEASING.
(T:1941 #10)

The soul, like a tabernacle.

CONSIDER THE BENEFITS OF EVEN GREATER UNION.
WHAT CAN YOU GAIN
BUT INFINITE BLISS, AND HEAVEN'S GIFTS?
BELIEVE IN MY LOVE!
CLOAKED IN THE DARKNESS OF CONTEMPLATION,
YOUR SOUL IS LIKE A TENT
- OR A TABERNACLE -
WHERE I, YOUR FATHER, MEET YOU AND GREET YOU.
HERE I AM: LOVE HIMSELF,
TO TEACH YOU.

TRULY
YOU ARE MY PRECIOUS CHILD.
IT WAS I WHO CREATED YOU.
I MYSELF HAVE LED YOU TOWARDS LOVE, PURITY AND HOLINESS;
AND NOW, IN THIS 'CUSTODY' AND COMMUNION
I MAKE NO DEMANDS:
BUT RATHER,
I MAKE MYSELF 'PRISONER' TO YOUR DESIRE,
AS YOUR EVERY PRAYER IS GRANTED!

SO GREAT IS MY LOVE, AND SO TENDER MY CARE FOR YOU,
THAT NOW I CHERISH YOUR EVERY WISH,
WHETHER EXPRESSED OR UNSPOKEN.
WHO IS LIKE ME, YOUR GOD?
WHO, THEREFORE, CAN RIVAL
MY WOOING OF YOUR SOUL?
WHOSE LOVE OR GIFT, WHOSE WORD OR TENDERNESS
CAN RIVAL MINE?
(T:1941 #11)

Equal in self-giving.

SEE HOW I ACT, IN THIS CUSTODY AND COMMUNION;
I, YOUR CREATOR, RELINQUISH MY POWER!
YOU WHO ONCE FEARED ME ARE NOW
WHOLLY AT REST,
OVERJOYED BY MY KINDNESS:
TOUCHED TO THE HEART TO DISCOVER MY PLAN, WHICH IS THAT
I, YOUR GOD, SERVE YOU.
I COMFORT YOU,
MY BELOVED.

439

> HERE, IN OUR UNION, WE ARE EQUAL IN SELF-GIVING.
> I AM DOING YOUR WILL, BY GRANTING YOUR HEART'S DESIRES.
> YOURS, NOW, IS THE JOYFUL KNOWLEDGE THAT
> YOUR EVERY REQUEST IS GRANTED;
> AND THUS, AS YOU REALISE:
> HERE IN OUR PRAYER,
> IN THE BOND OF LOVE,
> AND IN THE MARRIAGE OF OUR HEARTS,
> I, YOUR LORD, YOUR BELOVED AND ALL-HOLY CREATOR
> - I WHO AM LOVE -
> AM SUBJECT
> TO YOU, MY CREATURE.

(WC: 1941C) (T:1941 #12)

Many joys.

My heart ached with joy whenever I recalled the Father's magnificent teaching. More and more, I understood what we mean by proclaiming that "GOD IS LOVE" (1 Jn 4:16); and I yearned to be able to share the Good News more effectively. Meanwhile, Christ urged me:-

> **Share My Teachings with the people you meet; but realise that I want you to offer them primarily to members of My Holy Catholic Church, in order to renew the rudimentary faith of some, and to strengthen others whose faith is already well-established. (T:1954 #1)**
>
> **Reassure My People! Say with conviction that I, your God, am very near to you. I am present in your hearts; and I am Really, sacramentally Present in the tabernacle, and on the holy altar! (T:1954 #2)**

---

18 MISSION

(1996-1997)

GOOD NEWS FOR THE POOR. THE WHOLE MESSAGE.

To the weak and needy.

There came a time, at last, when I had been utterly delivered from fear before God, in prayer, and also delivered from any desire to hide my thoughts and weaknesses from Him. I knew from experience that He rewards every act of trust and every moment of sincere contrition; but I was so astonished by God's goodness, when I was praying at home, in the evening of July 26th, 1996, and when I'd found myself enveloped in the joy and Glory of the Holy Trinity, that I asked: "How is it that You are so good to one so wicked?"

Suddenly, the Father taught me - with both majesty and tenderness - about how He delights in our trust. He showed me (in T:1971):-

> HERE I AM, MY CHILD,
> DELIGHTING TO SEE TRUTH
> IN YOUR HEART AND MIND
> AS YOU PONDER MY GOODNESS
> AND YOUR SPIRITUAL POVERTY.
> IT IS A PART OF MY PLAN
> THAT I GIVE ENCOURAGEMENT TO MY PEOPLE
> IN THESE TIMES,
> THROUGH THESE TEACHINGS.
> IT IS A PART OF MY PLAN, ALSO,
> THAT THIS WORK FLOWS NOT FROM A SAINTLY FIGURE
> WHO WOULD BE SEEN BY THE WEAK AND SINFUL
> AS DIFFERENT FROM THEM: REMOTE AND IMPECCABLE,
> BUT THAT IT POURS, RATHER,
> FROM A WEAK AND SINFUL PERSON
> WHO CAN SAY WITH GREAT CONVICTION:
> 'SEE HOW GOOD IS GOD,
> WHO HAS BEEN SO KIND TO SOMEONE LIKE ME:
> SOMEONE IN SUCH GREAT NEED!'
> UNDERSTAND, THEREFORE,
> HOW IMPORTANT HAS BEEN YOUR RECOGNITION
> OF YOUR NEED AND SINFULNESS.

ONLY BECAUSE OF THAT ACKNOWLEDGEMENT
- AND YOUR REPENTANCE -
CAN YOU SUCCEED IN THE SPECIAL WORK
INTO WHICH I HAVE LED YOU:
A WORK ESPECIALLY 'TAILORED' TO YOUR LIFE
AND TO YOUR WEAKNESS.
AS I WORK THROUGH YOU WHO ARE WEAK,
THIS IS MY INTENTION:
"To give hope to others"
WHO, ALSO, ARE WEAK AND NEEDY.

(T:1971 #2)

Bliss and Glory.

HAVE FAITH IN MY POWER.
MY PLANS SHALL SUCCEED.
IT IS I WHO PROMPT YOU TO CONSENT
TO MY PLANS.
IT IS I WHO FILL YOUR HEART WITH A LONGING
TO MAKE KNOWN TO OTHER PEOPLE
MY GREAT GLORY.
TRULY,
I AM AT WORK, EVEN NOW.

(T:1971 #3)

CONSIDER THE REASON FOR YOUR STATE:
FOR THE BLISS INTO WHICH I HAVE DRAWN YOU,
IN PRAYER:
A BLISS WHICH IS INSEPARABLE FROM SPIRITUAL GLORY;
CONSIDER MY PLAN.
THIS IS MY WILL:
you shall show out My Glory: in your own person.

THROUGH THIS MANIFESTATION OF MY RADIANCE
IN YOU WHO DO A SPECIAL WORK
I SHALL HELP OTHER SOULS
AND BRING JOY TO MY HOLY CHURCH.

(T:1971 #4)

'The Blue book'.

What I'd learned that evening seemed very strange to me. What had the Father meant by speaking of me? What had the Father meant by speaking of His Glory "in" my person? I didn't understand, but I believed in the wisdom of His plans, whatever was going to happen; so I wrote down the teaching, and forgot it . Then I pressed ahead with my usual work. I finished what we call "The blue book", which was the first collection of teachings printed 'in the first person'; then I took it with me to our local church.

As I said earlier, I'd gone to the church every time I'd finished a pamphlet or a book, so that I could place the book on the shelf by the sanctuary - just for a minute or two, as I offered the work to Christ, and prayed that it would help people; and when I took 'the blue book' to church, I was astonished to hear Christ say to me:-

> See how I reward you for following My prompting. *"Well done, Lizzie!"* I am delighted with this work; and what better thing could you have done, after finishing this first Volume of My instructions, than to have brought it here to Me, before the tabernacle, asking Me to touch the hearts which meet My Truth within these pages. (T:1971 #5)
>
> Persevere with your writing. Here is My holy Mother beside Me - as you can see; she too is encouraging you to press on with the work. (T:1971 #6)

Numerous blessings.

But there were so many other blessings to enjoy that spring and autumn: further teachings and also further delights; for example, our church was left open all day, daily, for the first time in years. The Rosary was recited daily, after Mass, in Our Lady's months of May and October. Holy Communion was re-introduced, under both kinds. Fr. John Edwards gave his opinion that nothing in Version Three of the 'Teachings' contradicted the Faith. My family and I enjoyed a trip to Lourdes with fellow parishioners, as I mentioned, and also with our 'new' priest, Fr. Eugene.

It was through that trip, and through other outings with Church members - such as a Diocesan gathering at Aylesford - that I came to experience in a heart-warming way something I'd known only by faith: that the Catholic Church is a simple family of love.

It was marvellous to see demonstrated so plainly that the Church is a pilgrim People or family which is moved steadily towards Heaven, whilst holding within itself members at all stages of spiritual maturity. The rebellious and the contrite, the confident and the faint-hearted, the rich and poor and strong and sick, can all move on together in a compassionate and long-standing community which cannot be crushed or discouraged because it is Christ's own family of love, active and united by His own power and Will and Spirit.

As I also mentioned earlier, it was after that Lourdes pilgrimage that my husband approached our priest to ask if he might be received into the Catholic Church; then within a week of hearing about that courageous request, I was astonished when Christ appeared to me in Holy Communion, and explained how my life in His service had come 'full circle'.

The whole of life's journey.

At the Sunday Mass, on the 11th of August, I had begged God once again for the virtues I needed so badly, and I'd given my life to Him again, determined to please Him in everything, amidst all sorts of ailments and setbacks. But in Holy Communion, Christ appeared before me in Glory. He was Real, silent and gentle - and yet as dazzling in His Glory as when He had first appeared to me thirty-two years before, when I had called out to Him in desperation, believing that He would help me; and as I gazed at Him again in wonder, I was touched to the heart to be told:-

> **Look at Me, as I stand beside you today, in Holy Communion. You can gauge something of your progress in our friendship if you remember how you felt, in 1964, when My loving presence caused you pain rather than delight! You trusted in Me, but were very ignorant about faith, and only half-reconciled; and so the radiant Light of My Glory seemed to scorch your heart and soul; whereas things are different now. How marvellous is the effect of many years of growth and purification, in the spiritual life; My Presence today is wholly delightful for you, and welcome, and pain-free, and bliss-full! (T:1979 #1)**

> **Cast back your mind briefly, over the whole of your life's journey: at the road that we have been following together even though you weren't always aware of My presence. You can see what a cause for wonder and gratitude it is, that I have come to you, to stand beside you and to encourage you, at each 'end' of that journey. I was with you many years ago when you called out for My help with a firm conviction that I would help you; and I am with you, today, as you can see, as you prepare to accept a new way of life: or, rather, a way of 'dying', as your state of health declines. Whether at the beginning of your spiritual life, therefore, or near the end, I am very close to you, as you can see. I am just as real, gentle and loving as ever: a true Friend to a weak woman whose heart nearly breaks for joy at the thought of being 'released' from this world in order to be with Me forever! (WC:1979) (T:1979 #2)**

Into the 'lost world'.

Eight days later, in an even more fervent yearning to be pleasing to Christ, I begged His help again, and sacrificed every hope and dream of my own in order to do His Will. Then I was astonished when He showed me an image of a beautiful valley - and at the same time explained to me through His Holy Spirit (in T:1984):-

> *LOOK AT THE WONDERFUL SCENE BEFORE YOU, WHERE A WOMAN IS STROLLING THROUGH A LITTLE VALLEY WHICH IS FULL OF FRUIT-TREES. YOU CAN SEE THAT TO ENTER THIS VALLEY SHE HAD TO FOLLOW THE NARROW, WINDING PATH WHICH CROSSES THAT HIGH RIDGE AT ONE SIDE AND THEN MEANDERS DOWNWARD TO THE*

*FERTILE AREA. SHE HAS ENDURED A LONG JOURNEY, SINCE THIS
VALLEY IS IN THE TOPMOST HEIGHTS OF THE HIGHEST RANGE OF
MOUNTAINS; AND THIS WOMAN IS YOURSELF: NOW ENTERING A
FERTILE VALLEY OF THE SPIRITUAL LIFE. IT IS AS THOUGH YOU ARE
WALKING BESIDE LADEN FRUIT-TREES: AND THESE FRUITS
REPRESENT THE SPIRITUAL FRUITS WHICH ARE ALWAYS FOUND IN
THE LIVES OF THOSE WHO LIVE IN OUR FRIENDSHIP: IN 'GOD'S
GARDEN.' (WC:1984) (T:1984 #1)*

Then Christ told me:-

> **Delight in the knowledge which is My gift to you, through
> My Spirit. Delight in the results of your total self-offering,
> an offering renewed and maintained over many years, and
> renewed again so painfully this morning! To be wholly
> sincere in such an offering is to pray an immensely
> powerful prayer; it is to allow Me, your Saviour, to lead
> you across the top-most ridge of the spiritual mountain-
> range which has for so long soared up before you. I have
> brought you, at last, into the most fertile valley of the
> spiritual life: into the 'lost world' of warmth, security,
> perfect joy, and fruitfulness. Rejoice in this 'garden'.
> (T:1984 #2)**

> **Accept My gifts. Delight in this new stage of your life.
> Truly, you can say that *"This is Eden!"* This is a taste of
> paradise, for you who have been led to dwell in this
> wonderful state. It is a way of life which is astonishing in
> its peace, simplicity, joy, freedom and sense of fulfilment.
> (T:1984 #3)**

> **Notice how things are simplified, in this new way of life, in
> which you are wonderfully guided by Me in a manner more
> tangible - it seems - than ever before. I Myself am leading
> you; I am showing you what to observe, when to speak,
> where to pause, with whom to work, and how to suffer as
> though you are not suffering; and this patience in suffering,
> as you know, is possible because of the joy of being
> constantly in My company. (T:1984 #4)**

> **Look back, for a moment, to renew your thanks for My
> guidance. You can see that without your willing surrender
> of those various paths which you might have chosen - each
> one of which would have brought you an immediate and
> superficial happiness - you could not have arrived at this
> present way of life and state of soul. It is as though your
> heart, mind and soul are now entirely permeated by Divine
> sweetness, joy and peace; what more wonderful gifts could**

you have hoped to receive from Me, Who love you?!
(T:1984 #5)

A steep staircase.

In the same month, on August 23rd, it was the Father Who showed me, in prayer, something more about the path on which He was leading me. He explained, all at once (in T:1987) that I am approaching the end of my life's journey, and that I now live 'above' the cloud and mist of earlier times. A steep staircase lies ahead, however, which I must climb in order to reach His throne, and Heaven. Yet there are several stages: and a resting place will be provided after each difficult part of the climb.

Infinite holiness.

It was the Father Who taught me, also - a few days later (in T:1992) - that I am right to pray fervently to be made ready to do His work. He explained that by our penance and prayer we are gradually becoming fit not only to serve Him but also to enter Heaven.

By an image, He showed me that as I approach His Glory in the company of Christ it is as if I am approaching a Wall of Fire, into which I shall plunge one day: the purifying fire of the Godhead. Those who have been purified enter joyfully into that Fire; but those who have not been purified should remember that God is not only Infinite Love, but also Infinite Holiness; and so they should realise that if they want to be happy with God, a thorough preparation is essential.

Good news for the 'poor'.

There was so much writing and painting to do that summer, as well as my usual work, that my energy was flagging; but Christ assured me:-

> **Persevere with your work, in the knowledge that I am sending you "to bring good news to the poor"; and by this, I mean that your work will help those 'poor' within My Church whose faith is wavering in a time of spiritual poverty. These 'poor' people need encouragement; yet their simple devotions are sometimes scorned, even though their attitudes and practices are in accord with the teaching of My Church, and with the Sacred Tradition. You can be confident therefore, that these 'Teachings-in-prayer' are already helping many people. I have countless ways of continuing to bring My Good News to the 'poor': of continuing to bring My hope, friendship and Love to those who are crushed or dispirited. You can be sure that our joint work is worthwhile and effective in helping to fulfil**

this aim. (T:1998)

The parish and the town.

There wasn't a facet of the whole project which Christ left unexplained, where understanding was required. He has always told me in great detail for example, how to explain things to our parish priest, who was no longer Canon O'Leary, as I mentioned, but our 'new' priest, Fr. Eugene Fitzpatrick. In September, 1996, Christ urged me:-

> **Continue with your efforts to keep your relatives and friends informed about the progress of this work - to the extent that is dictated by charity and by their various attitudes to the subjects of prayer and faith; and continue to distribute these works to some of the people you meet, and to those who write to you. But make a special effort to help My priest to understand more about the work which I have entrusted to you. This effort is required not simply because I ask it, but because this work - and My plan for your life - will affect your parish, and also the whole town, later.(T:2000 #1)**

> **Tell My priest about your faith in Me since your conversion, and about your perpetual longing to share that faith with others, despite your being a bad example; then tell him several things more about your life, and speak about our joint work. Explain, too, that it is precisely because of your weaknesses that I will show other people how powerful and important is faith in Me. Explain that I am demonstrating, through you, how important is faith, through which people can be led to serve Me even when they are sinful, tired or fearful! (T:2000 #2)**

> **Recall how I have been urging you to speak to your friends and relations about My work in your life. Because of My encouragement, you have managed to introduce most of them, bit by bit, to our work and to your writings; you can see, therefore, how I am helping you to introduce My priest to our work, little by little. If you are obedient to My promptings, your conversations with him will lead him to a greater understanding of your task. This is mainly for the sake of his own involvement - if he is willing - later on. (T:2000 #3)**

> **Speak up bravely to My priest about the way in which I am fulfilling your desire to please Me and to make My Glory known: about how I have shown you that My Glory is going to be revealed in your own person. It is important that you say this; it is an act of faith in Me and in My**

> **promises; and My priest is to be a witness to this act, for the sake of the whole Work and its fulfilment. The teachings and images which I have given to you are not nearly as important as the witness which I am inviting you to give through your words and prayers and actions. (T:2000 #4)**

Sheltered, for a while.

One day in prayer, Christ led me again in prayer to God the Father, Who explained more about what was only an apparent delay in His plans.

The Father taught me:-

HERE I AM, MY CHILD,
TO CONSOLE YOU,
AND TO EXPLAIN MY PLAN, FURTHER.
YOU HAVE BEEN SHARING GOOD NEWS
WITH MANY PEOPLE,
SPEAKING ABOUT MY SON AND HIS TEACHINGS
YET SEEING FEW RESULTS.
THERE IS LITTLE EVIDENCE OF CHANGE.
BUT THERE IS NO NEED FOR YOU TO WORRY.

ONLY BECAUSE OF MY LOVE FOR YOU
HAVE I ALLOWED YOU TO LABOUR FOR SO LONG
IN APPARENT OBSCURITY.
IT WAS IN ORDER TO TRAIN YOU.
IT IS WHEN YOU ARE WORKING QUIETLY, ALMOST ALONE,
THAT YOU CAN GROW IN HUMILITY:
HAVING NO REASON FOR PRIDE.
FURTHERMORE,
YOU CAN LOOK UPON THIS OBSCURITY
AS BEING A SPECIAL GIFT FROM ME.
IN MY GREAT KINDNESS,
I HAVE BEEN 'SHELTERING' YOU FOR A WHILE,
UNTIL YOU HAVE BEEN ABLE TO THROW OFF YOUR FEARS:
TO WORK UNHAMPERED BY PRIDE AND REMORSE, AND
TO SPEAK OUT, UNEMBARRASSED BY YOUR UNWORTHINESS.
(T:2004 #1)

BE GLAD AND GRATEFUL
THAT I HAVE HELPED YOU TO BECOME
LIKE A CAREFREE CHILD, AT LAST.
YOU ARE DETERMINED TO SHARE YOUR NEWS
OF MY SON AND HIS TEACHINGS;
YOU DELIGHT IN SPEAKING OF ME

TO ANYONE WHO WILL LISTEN.
BY MY GRACE, AND BY YOUR RENEWED EFFORTS,
YOU HAVE BEEN SPEAKING ABOUT YOUR TASK
AND PROCLAIMING MY GOODNESS
WITH A NEW FREEDOM.
ONLY RECENTLY,
THEREFORE,
HAVE YOU BEGUN TO SEE EXTRAVAGANT RESULTS
FROM OUR MISSION.

(T:2004 #2)

The endless joys of Heaven.

Daily or weekly (as in T:2009) I was reminded that I have Christ's powerful assistance. Throughout that year, I was given frequent reminders of the need for this work, with reminders about our hope of joy. It was Christ Who spoke to me about Heaven, on September 14th (in T:2012). My heart was bursting for joy at that time because of some wonderful events and surprises; and I asked Our Lord in prayer: "How is it possible that one can have more joy than this, in Heaven?!" Then He told me that it is because we shall be contemplating our blissful state whilst *"Knowing that it will never end."*

Through Baptism.

What a wonderful sacrament is Baptism, by which the many graces I've received have been made possible. Every year, on the anniversary of my Baptism, I thank God for His goodness; and when I did so in 1996 - on October 4th - I was overwhelmed with delight when the Father spoke to me, confirming the reason for our close union and speaking of His Love. He told me:-

BELOVED CHILD,
IT IS CHRIST WHO HAS LED YOU
- THROUGH YOUR HOLY COMMUNION -
'FURTHER' TOWARDS ME, YOUR FATHER.
YET, TRULY,
OUR UNION WAS ESTABLISHED
THROUGH YOUR BAPTISM,
WHEN YOU WERE FREED, CHANGED, AND BROUGHT CLOSE TO ME.
WE ARE LOVINGLY UNITED IN PRAYER
AND IN DAILY LIFE.
YOU ARE RESTING IN MY PEACE,
EVEN AMIDST YOUR IMPERFECTIONS.
I WANT YOU TO KNOW
THAT IN OUR MUTUAL LOVE
- AND IN OUR SPECIAL FRIENDSHIP -
"I delight in you!"

(T:2028 #1)

DELIGHT IN THIS EXTRAORDINARY UNION,
OF YOU, MY BAPTISED CHILD, WITH MYSELF:
OF A CREATURE WITH HER CREATOR.
YOU HAVE BEEN BROUGHT, THROUGH CHRIST,
INTO THE LIGHT OF MY GLORIOUS DIVINE LIFE:
NO LONGER IMMERSED IN THE DARKNESS
WHICH IS SIN
WITH ESTRANGEMENT FROM YOUR GOD.
I DELIGHT IN YOU, MY DAUGHTER,
AS I DELIGHT IN EVERY BELOVED CHILD.
SHARE YOUR JOY.

(T:2028 #2)

SHARE YOUR JOYFUL NEWS ABOUT LIFE "IN" ME.
SHARE THE KNOWLEDGE OF THE SOURCE OF YOUR DELIGHT:
MYSELF, YOUR FATHER.
YET DON'T BE AFRAID TO SHARE
THE WHOLE TRUTH.

(T:2028 #3)

REMIND MY PEOPLE ABOUT THEIR NEED OF ME.
REMIND THOSE WHO BELIEVE IN THE LIFE OF GRACE
AND WHO RISK THE LOSS OF JOY, BY THEIR BEHAVIOUR,
THAT THEY RISK THE LOSS OF DIVINE LIGHT AND FRIENDSHIP
FOR ALL ETERNITY
IF THEY PERSIST IN THEIR CARELESSNESS
OR IN THEIR SERIOUS AND DELIBERATE SINS.

(T:2028 #4)

Then Christ assured me, soon afterwards, that the Saints of Heaven are very close to me, as I continue with my writings and with my prayers (T:2030). He also said:-

Put your trust in Me, once more. It seems to you as though you are not doing enough to encourage other people in their faith, and to spread My teachings. But I assure you that *"You're doing very well, Lizzie,"* **in difficult circumstances. (T:2031 #1)**

Radiant Light.

A little later on, Christ explained the title which He had given me for future use with the whole work. It was a name which He had invited me to keep for the day when the whole body of work would eventually be made plain. He told me:-

Understand something more about your task: about our joint work which I have entitled "RADIANT LIGHT." Through these teachings, I am doing just what you have

450

> heard described today in Holy Scripture; My aim is "to radiate the light of the knowledge of God's Glory," which is the Glory which you yourself have been privileged to see on My face: "on the face of Christ." (T:2032 #1)

Then He reassured me:-

> Don't worry about your unworthiness to do this work. Truly, it is a task which I Myself have given to you. Rejoice in it, and continue with your efforts to complete it. (T:2032 #2)

The whole message.

On another day, Christ explained the dire need of Church members today for reminders of the plain truths of the Gospel. He urged me:-

> Co-operate with Me, no matter what it costs you. Through you, I am reminding My People of some of the truths of faith which have been overlooked or even denied, today, by some who claim to be teaching the Gospel. Now, as in past ages, I want My Gospel to be preached for the Salvation of souls; yet I want to see proclaimed what you have just heard about in Holy Scripture; I want "the whole message" to be proclaimed; and it is through these 'Teachings-in-prayer' that I am speaking to many of My children about various things to do with faith and discipline amidst My Church and People: things which are currently ignored or minimised. (T:2040 #1)

> Be brave; help people to see that those who, in their teaching, speak truthfully about something good, yet who fail to speak of something important which is also relevant to that subject, are distorting the message. Write about this, as I make it plain to you, through the Light of My Holy Spirit: (T:2040 #2)

> *CONSIDER THE MEANING OF SIN AND SALVATION. MANY WHO TALK ABOUT THE GOAL OF THE SPIRITUAL LIFE OMIT MUCH OF THE TRUTH ABOUT THE JOURNEY. SOME SPEAK ABOUT CHRIST: THE SON, BUT RARELY OF HIS HOLY MOTHER THROUGH WHOSE LOVE AND HUMILITY HE, TRUE 'SON OF GOD', WAS GIVEN TO YOU. SOME SPEAK ABOUT EARTHLY LIFE, BUT NOT OF THE CROSS WHICH WE ASK YOU TO CARRY. SOME SPEAK ABOUT EVIL STATES, AND EVIL HUMAN BEINGS BUT NOT ABOUT THE EVIL ONE: THE TEMPTER, AGAINST WHOSE ASSAULTS AND DECEPTIONS YOU SHOULD ALL REMAIN ON GUARD. SOME SPEAK ABOUT WHOLENESS, BUT NOT*

*ABOUT SIN, NOR ABOUT THE SUFFERING OF CALVARY, WHERE
CHRIST PERISHED, TO STEER YOU AWAY FROM HELL. THEY MAKE NO
MENTION OF CONVERSION.   SOME SPEAK ABOUT CHRIST'S
RESURRECTION BUT RARELY ABOUT HIS WOUNDS, OR ABOUT HIS
PRECIOUS BLOOD WHICH WAS POURED OUT FOR YOU, TO SAVE YOU.
SOME SPEAK ABOUT HEAVEN, BUT FAIL TO WARN YOU ABOUT THE
SELF-LOVE WHICH PROPELS YOU TOWARDS ETERNAL DARKNESS.
(T:2040 #3)*

Counting the cost.

Christ taught me, through His Holy Spirit, about the 'cost' of purification, for those of us who
long to be made ready for Heaven. He showed me:-

*CONSIDER THE 'COST' OF PURIFICATION. MANY WHO TALK ABOUT
GROWTH IN HOLINESS OMIT MUCH OF THE TRUTH. SOME SPEAK
ABOUT 'OPENNESS' TO IDEAS BUT NOT OF RIGHT AND WRONG:
GOOD OR EVIL. SOME SPEAK ABOUT MY INVITATION TO BE LOVING,
BUT NOT OF COMMANDMENTS FROM HEAVEN. SOME SPEAK ABOUT
COUNSELLING BUT NOT ABOUT CONFESSION AND RECONCILIATION.
SOME SPEAK ABOUT DISCIPLESHIP AND FELLOWSHIP BUT RARELY
MENTION SACRIFICE OR SELF-DENIAL. SOME SPEAK ABOUT JOYFUL
SERVICE, BUT NOT ABOUT YOUR NEED OF MY GRACES AND VIRTUES.
SOME SPEAK ABOUT PERSONAL FULFILMENT, BUT NOT ABOUT THE
COMPLETE AND ETERNAL FULFILMENT WHICH FOLLOWS A LOVING
SURRENDER AND A FAITHFUL ADHERENCE TO EVERY FACET OF MY
HOLY WILL. (T:2040 #4)*

*CONSIDER THE TRUTH ABOUT SUFFERING AND SERVICE. MANY WHO
TALK ABOUT SERVING ME OMIT MUCH OF THE TRUTH. SOME SPEAK
ABOUT COMMITMENT BUT NOT OF LIFE-LONG DEDICATION. SOME
SPEAK ABOUT SERVICE BUT NOT OF MORTIFICATION. SOME SPEAK
ABOUT LOVE BUT NOT OF SELF-ABNEGATION. SOME SPEAK ABOUT
HUMILITY BUT NOT ABOUT THE PATIENT ACCEPTANCE OF
HUMILIATIONS. SOME SPEAK ABOUT SELF-ESTEEM AND WHOLENESS
YET NOT ABOUT SELF-ABANDONMENT TO THE FATHER, AND TO HIS
PLANS. SOME SPEAK ABOUT DYING BUT NOT ABOUT CONTRITION
AND REPENTANCE. SOME SPEAK ABOUT DEATH AND GLORY, BUT
NOT OF JUDGEMENT OR PURIFICATION. (T:2040 #5)*

The Sacred Tradition.

Then I was shown how neglected are some of the marvels of the Sacred Tradition:-

*CONSIDER THE SPIRITUAL RICHES OF CHRIST'S CHURCH. MANY WHO
TALK ABOUT THE JOYFUL LIFE WHICH IS FOUND WITHIN THE
COMMUNION OF SAINTS OMIT MUCH OF THE TRUTH. SOME SPEAK*

ABOUT THE CHURCH, CHRIST'S BODY, BUT NOT ABOUT HER SURE TEACHINGS. SOME SPEAK ABOUT THE PRIMACY OF ST. PETER'S SUCCESSOR, BUT NOT OF OBEDIENCE TO THE POPE. SOME SPEAK ABOUT THE HOLY SCRIPTURES BUT NOT ABOUT THE SACRED TRADITION. SOME SPEAK ABOUT PRAYER FOR THE LIVING, BUT NOT OF PRAYER FOR DEPARTED SOULS WHO SUFFER AGONY AT THE SIGHT OF THEIR SINS. SOME SPEAK ABOUT MY SAINTS, PRAISING THEIR VIRTUES AND CALLING THEM MODELS OF HOLINESS: BUT RARELY ASK FOR THE VERY POWERFUL PRAYERS OF THESE INTERCESSORS IN HEAVEN. SOME SPEAK ABOUT MY HOLY ANGELS BUT NEGLECT TO HONOUR THE ANGELS WHO ARE PRESENT AT THEIR SIDES AND IN MY CHURCHES. (T:2040 #6)

CONSIDER WHO I AM. MANY WHO TALK ABOUT ME, YOUR GOD - CREATOR AND REDEEMER - OMIT MUCH OF THE TRUTH. SOME SPEAK ABOUT JOYFUL PRAISE OF THE HOLY TRINITY BUT NOT ABOUT AWE, AND ADORATION. SOME SPEAK ABOUT HOLY COMMUNION, BUT NOT ABOUT THE HOLY SACRIFICE. SOME SPEAK ABOUT CHRIST'S LOVE AND MERCY, BUT NOT ABOUT HIS INFINITE HOLINESS WHICH IS WORTHY OF DUE REVERENCE FROM YOU WHOM HE HAS LOVED MORE THAN LIFE ITSELF: FROM YOU WHO WOULD BE LOST WITHOUT HIM. (T:2040 #7)

Pleased to be near Him.

Quite soon after giving me that teaching Christ explained how shockingly are He and His holy Mother neglected; and He urged me:-

> **Persevere in prayer. Many people have turned their eyes and their hearts away from Me, their Saviour, and from My holy Mother. Many people shun My presence and My teachings, not wanting to spend their time or their lives in My service, nor being willing to pay Me honour and worship as they ought. (T:2076 #2)**

Then Christ spoke words which saddened me, afterwards, whenever I recalled them. He told me, gravely:-

> **Remain loyal to Me and to My Mother. We delight in your greetings today, as always.** *"How few are pleased to be near us."* **(T:2076 #3)**

Sharing the news more widely.

Then Christ invited me to further His plans by sending some of my work to the Holy Father. I was urged:-

> Share My teachings more widely. The time has come for
> you to bring encouragement even to those from whom you
> yourself have received encouragement and teaching. You
> have heard in Holy Scripture today: "Speak to the heart of
> Jerusalem" and by this, I mean that your completion of a
> new volume of work, today, has brought you to a new stage
> of your task. I now invite you to send these two completed
> volumes not only to your local Bishops, but also to Rome.
> (T:2077)

New encouragement.

Only in obedience to God have I written down the severe warnings which He has given me,
for other people, about their neglect of Him, and about the danger of Eternal separation; and
it has only been in obedience to God, as I have said, that I am sharing so many memories
about the good things that God has told me or given me; and yet I shall be glad if some of
these teachings give even a hint of the joy to be found in God's friendship: a joy which is quite
astonishing. For example, I have found that Christ never lets an anniversary pass by without
giving me at least some token of His affection.

Early one morning, on the eleventh anniversary of what I call the 'Alpha and Omega' day,
when I was praying at home, and was awed at the thought of God's goodness, I was suddenly
shown that the 'Door' to Heaven had opened; and there stood Christ and His Holy Mother,
close by me: greeting and consoling me, and bringing me even greater joy; and Christ taught
me, very tenderly:-

> Don't think that you are celebrating this special
> anniversary all alone! No-one but I shared your joy -
> indeed, was the Source of your joy - on that winter day
> eleven years ago when I brought you, at last, to live in a
> state of unending union, after so many years of spiritual
> 'night'. But today, as you can see , it is as though the door
> to Heaven has opened, as I stand close by you, in Glory,
> with My beloved Mother at My side. (WC:2078) (T:2078
> #1)

> Enjoy our visit! Accept My gifts, My greetings and My
> consolations. I delight in your thanks for My friendship,
> and in your continued efforts to please Me. (T:2078 #2)

> Believe in My Love. You are right to prepare for the Holy
> Sacrifice by fervent prayer; I Myself have encouraged you
> to approach Me with reverence, to repent, to trust in Me, to
> confide every cause for concern, and then to enjoy My
> Presence; but I urge you never to forget what prayer and
> the spiritual life - and all your struggles - are 'about'.
> Through prayer, and through your fervent striving after

> virtue, you are loving and pleasing a real Person! Your prime motive is not to adhere to a list of rules, but to live in a tremendously loving union with Me your Saviour: although, from that union, of course, stems your fervent longing to keep My Commandments and recommendations. (T:2078 #3)

A sense of freedom.

Then Christ told me, after the morning Mass (in T:2079):-

> Think about the special union which we are celebrating today. Notice the great blessing which is yours because of our union and My grace at work in you. You experience a sense of freedom which is incomparable, now that your only desire is to please Me. (T:2079 #1)

> Consider the real reason for your present joy; your whole heart is set on pleasing Me. This is your one, true, unwavering desire; and so you can see that the secret of eventual 'success' in the struggle for perfection consists of the perfect alignment of your will - of your true 'wanting' - with My Will. (T:2079 #2)

Then He continued:-

> Open your eyes to My purpose, as I come to you with special gifts on this special anniversary. I have brought you incomparable peace and bliss; but it is through My presence, and through My gifts, that I am completing what I began in earnest at your agonised consent, eleven years ago, when you freely and finally surrendered your entire life to Me, and abandoned your own dreams and ambitions. I am completing your spiritual transformation, so that you can become like a lamp which shines its light all around. (T:2080 #1)

But Christ explained something further; He told me the reason for the Glory which He was now sharing with me in prayer:-

> Understand the significance of the Fire and Glory which you see within your soul whenever I come to you nowadays, in Holy Communion. You have seen Me come to meet you as if through the wide-open door of Heaven; and I am sharing My own Glory with you in this way for a special purpose. Recall My promise to you: when I said that I would one day 'set alight' the 'Mountain of Teachings'

> which I have given to you. I assure you that the 'mountain'
> or bonfire which I described is your very own soul, which I
> am setting ablaze every day in Holy Communion, in order
> to show out My Glory. It is My Will and plan that you
> shine with My Presence, for the sake of the next stage of
> your task. (T:2084)

A friend of God.

Amidst a great deal of illness and hard work, that winter, I was reassured by the Father, just before Christmas. I had just been remembering how utterly weak and helpless I am without Christ. But the Father spoke to me and said: *"You are a friend."* He urged me, lovingly, to serve Him with my whole heart, body, soul and mind: to try to imitate Jesus in every outward act and unspoken thought, throughout every difficulty. Furthermore, He drew me to the 'door' of Heaven in prayer on January 2nd, 1997, and showed me the Fire of His Glory (in T:2100). He explained that His friends can be confident of even closer friendship with Him, to the degree that, in everyday life, they are abandoning themselves to the fulfilment of His Will.

Content in any circumstances.

When I thanked Christ one day, in Holy Communion, for the wonderful and unexpectedly-fulfilling way of life that I now enjoyed, I was shown how thoroughly He had been preparing me for every aspect of my task. He showed me:-

> Understand what an achievement this is in the spiritual life:
> to be content and prayerful in any circumstances. I want
> you to know that it is because you are thoroughly happy
> with this quiet life of routine work and simple joys that I
> can trust you with something different, and even
> dangerous: with crowds paying respectful attention, and
> with adulation, and even with a reputation as an authority
> on prayer. It is because your present joy is so great, within
> a restricted way of life, and because of the thorough and
> lengthy training which I have given you that there will be
> little likelihood of your head being 'turned' by future
> events. (T:2113 #14)

Then I thanked Christ for allowing me to share His teachings; and He told me:-

> Understand something more about your task; it has been a
> part of My plan, since the beginning, that you would share
> most of My teachings with other people, although you
> weren't aware of this at first, when I was still training you
> in prayer and obedience. (T:2113 #17)

Consider what you know about the special work undertaken by certain persons. In different ages, I have given wonderful teachings in prayer: some of which were for sharing; but most were for the benefit of the recipients and only indirectly for other people; but the reverse is true here; and I have given you so great a number of teachings that it would have been cruel to expect you to 'contain' them. (T:2113 #18)

Have no doubt that you, My children, have already received all the teaching that you could need, for your Salvation; and that unique Revelation is still being handed on in My Church. Yet the teachings which you have received, over so many years, are unique, amongst what we call 'private' revelations. No-one before you has had, in prayer, such a load to carry: such a weight of gifts of this nature. So you can see why I Who am loving have arranged for you to be 'unburdened' to some degree as you share the teachings, with certain persons first, and then with many other people who are willing to receive them. (T:2113 #19)

Don't be anxious. Truly, I am powerfully at work in your life. (T:2113 #20)

Celibate priests.

In ways which astonished me, Christ consoled and encouraged me at every set-back, and revealed some of the ways in which His work would help other people. He told me:-

Banish these thoughts about your unworthiness. Our plans for your life and for this work are greater than you could imagine; but you need only follow My Will in simplicity, step by step, if you wish to please Me. (T: 2127 #3)

He explained the significance of this work for priests: explaining by His Holy Spirit:-

NOTICE THE SMALL FIGURE WHOM YOU CAN SEE IS MAKING HER WAY, AS IF IN A SOLITARY PROCESSION, PAST A HUGE CROWD OF PRIESTS, WHO ARE ALL WATCHING HER. IT IS MY WILL, DEAR CHILD, THAT YOU FOLLOW A PATH WHICH LEADS YOU FOR VARIOUS REASONS, AND IN VARIOUS WAYS, VERY CLOSE TO MANY OF MY CELIBATE PRIESTS, EACH OF WHOM IS 'ALONE' IN THE CROWD, AND IN MY SERVICE, IN ONE SENSE, DESPITE THEIR UNION WITH CHRIST AND WITH THE WHOLE CHURCH AND THEIR STRONG BONDS WITH ONE ANOTHER IN THE SACRED PRIESTHOOD. THOSE WHOM I AM PICTURING BEFORE YOU WILL BE TREMENDOUSLY ENCOURAGED BY

457

OUR WORK. THEY WILL BE GRATEFUL FOR MY VIGOROUS REMINDER, THROUGH YOU, OF THE TRUTHS FOR WHICH THEY HAVE SURRENDERED THEIR EARLIER AMBITIONS, INDEED, SACRIFICED THEIR LIVES: BY WHICH I MEAN: TRUTHS ABOUT CHRIST'S MAGNIFICENT LOVE AND HIS SAVING SACRIFICE - AND HIS GOOD NEWS ABOUT FORGIVENESS FOR SINNERS, AND THE SURE HOPE OF HEAVEN. (T:2127 #4)

DON'T BE BASHFUL ABOUT MEETING PEOPLE MADE JOYFUL BY YOUR WORK. THE PRIESTS WHOM YOU SEE BEFORE YOU WILL HONOUR WHAT IS MADE EVIDENT TO THEM: BOTH THE WORK AND YOURSELF, THE WORKER: BOTH THE TEACHINGS AND THE WRITER; AND THEY WILL DO SO BECAUSE OF YOUR LOVE FOR CHRIST YOUR SAVIOUR WHO IS REVEALING HIMSELF THROUGH THIS WORK, IN WHAT IS A LAVISH AND VIGOROUS REMINDER OF WHAT HE HAS ALREADY REVEALED, LONG AGO. (WC:2127) (T:2127 #5)

Spiritual communications.

Then Christ helped me to deal with my qualms about speaking out:-

Don't worry, My child. You are right to confide in Me about every concern; but there is no need for you to worry about speaking out in obedience to My wishes, whether to fellow-parishioners or to Bishops. (T:2134 #1)

Never be anxious about the form of words which you might need to use, when I Myself have asked you to communicate a message for Me. Whenever I invite you to speak out on My behalf I make sure that you have the gifts you really need. Sometimes I give you words to use; you know this, already. Yet at other times, I give you the general sense of what I am asking you to convey. I give this to you in a swift Thought which leaps from My Mind to yours in the way which I described to you long ago when I was speaking about the sort of communication which is used by the Blessed in Heaven. And when you have the 'general sense', in this way, you are free to clothe My wishes in your own words, in order to pass on the message. (T:2134 #2)

Don't doubt that My Divine power is already at work in you; and this power - with something of my Glory - is seen and noticed by other people according to My Will, even inspiring fear as well as wonder. (T:2149 #1)

Speak out bravely about My words in your life. I have taught and encouraged you; you, therefore, can encourage each person to whom I send you. (T:2149 #2)

458

Approaching fulfilment.

There's no-one as kind as Christ. I wish I could explain that better to everyone I meet; but I'll content myself meanwhile by showing how thoughtful He's been about every aspect of my work. I hope I can show in the rest of this chapter how He gradually introduced me to alarming but fruitful aspects of the whole plan. The helps and explanations have been interspersed with new difficulties; but at every recent stage, Christ has explained to me - often in advance - what His plans entail, and why more faith and courage are required for certain new tasks which He invites me to undertake; and so I'm beginning to see and to understand the work, as well as to know by faith that Christ's plans are always successful in our lives, if we don't withdraw our co-operation.

A template of the spiritual life.

As I said, Christ's kindness and encouragement have been ceaseless. In a wonderful way, one day, Christ showed me by a new illustration why my weaknesses haven't hampered the work, but have provided Him with opportunities by which to demonstrate His love and power - for my benefit and for the benefit of all who will learn about my story. Christ invited me to go to my priest once again, and urged me:-

> **Speak to My priest about your work.** *"Go and help him."* **Remind him of the time, long ago, when I told you that the whole 'mountain' or 'bonfire' of Teachings would be set alight one day, by Myself, to call attention to the Source of these teachings: your Father in Heaven. Explain to My priest that the Glory which shines out from your soul is My gift and My sign. Tell him not to be afraid. It is My radiance that He sees, as I shine My Light within your soul, day after day, in prayer. (T:2149 #3)**

> **Speak about the whole Work. Explain to My priest that I am powerfully at work through these books, encouraging My People; but explain that there is a progression through these three Volumes, which don't merely consist of more and more 'teachings' about things which Christians already know. Describe how I am providing, through these books, a 'template', so to speak, of the whole spiritual life, from conversion to the transforming union. Through these books, people can see clearly that I have been at work in someone who is sinful and ignorant; and this knowledge will bring comfort to those of My People who know little of My great Love. It will bring consolation, also, to those of My faithful People who are reminded, by what you have seen and recorded, that I am Really Present amongst them in the Blessed Sacrament. (T:2149 #4)**

459

Be comforted by your knowledge that My plan will succeed. Through your work, I am giving a wonderful reminder to My People that I am still guiding them through My Holy Catholic Church, still teaching them - through My faithful bishops - and still feeding and sustaining them through the holy sacraments. Those of My People who are lamentably ignorant of the true teachings of the Faith will be helped by this work; they will learn something of what they need to know about Heaven and Hell, about sin and Reconciliation, about My tender Love for mankind - and man's need of repentance. They will learn about the marvel which is the Holy Mass, where I am Really Present in the Blessed Sacrament. (T:2149 #5)

See what good things I can achieve, through the story of your weakness and My Love. Through the story of our friendship, I am showing many people that I can work wonders even in the life of someone who is weak, hesitant or fearful, and that I am always tender, patient and faithful. (T:2149 #6)

Remember how important it is that you don't become so busy with the writing of the teachings that you begin to forget their purpose. It is very important that you make continued efforts to 'live out' what you are writing: putting these good things into practice in everyday life, amidst the chores and conversations, and as you go to Mass, or shop, or make an apple crumble. (T:2149 #7)

Think about your present frailty - in every sense - *"and then look at what you're doing!"* It is astonishing that you have produced such a huge collection of writings and pictures, at My invitation, despite considerable handicaps. (T:2149 #8)

A flame of Glory.

One day in prayer, Christ reassured me abut the value of my work, saying:-

Delight in My work: in our work. For the sake of Truth, you must acknowledge what is truly happening in your life. It is I, your loving Saviour, Who am now producing from within your turbulent and loving heart and life, abundant works, constant and immense joys and great graces. It is only through Me that you do anything good; yet you are now doing things - 'in' and through Me - which are truly

grace-ful and which are of great benefit to other people. (T:2149 #9)

Christ led me again to God the Father Who told me about His gifts in prayer, and Who assured me:-

AS I CROWN YOU IN PRAYER
WITH MY OWN 'FLAME OF GLORY'
I AM FULFILLING MY PROMISE TO YOU:
IN WHICH I ASSURED YOU
THAT I WOULD ONE DAY SET ALIGHT
THE 'MOUNTAIN'
OR
THE 'BONFIRE' OF TEACHINGS.
I ASSURE YOU
THAT THEIR RADIANCE WILL SHINE OUT
UPON MANY WEARY PEOPLE WHO ARE LIVING IN DARKNESS.
(T:2154A #2)

Christ urged me:-

Don't be afraid. Be simple! Accept, with a peaceful heart, the way in which I am at work in your soul and in your life. (T:2154A #3)

Then He told me, through His Holy Spirit:-

HERE I AM, BRINGING YOU COMFORT AND UNDERSTANDING. I ASSURE YOU THAT THROUGH YOUR OBEDIENCE IN WRITING AND SHARING MY TEACHINGS, AND IN OFFERING REMINDERS OF THE TRUTHS ABOUT LIFE AND HOPE AND SALVATION "IN CHRIST", YOU ARE TOUCHING MANY LIVES AND WARMING MANY HEARTS. (T:2154A #4)

UNDERSTAND, MY CHILD, THAT THERE ARE MANY FACETS TO THIS WHOLE WORK. KNOW THIS, FOR EXAMPLE, THAT, BY OUR WILL, YOU YOURSELF ARE THE 'BEACON' BY WHICH THE LIGHT OF OUR TEACHINGS IS TO BE NOTICED AND MADE KNOWN. TRULY, I AM AT WORK IN YOUR LIFE; INDEED, THIS SHINING-OUT OF HEAVEN'S RADIANCE HAS ALREADY BEGUN. (T:2154A #5)

Thin alabaster walls.

On the very next day, Christ spoke to me about His special plan. He explained to me:-

Don't be afraid of Our work in your life. As you can see, daily, I am bringing My own radiant Light to your soul,

each time that I come to your soul in Holy Communion; and My radiance is so bright and glorious that it now shines from you in just the manner which I explained to you last year. Whenever I choose to let My Light shine out from your soul in order to further My special plan, it is as though a lamp is glowing: the lamp which I once described to you. It is as though My holy Light is shining out through thin alabaster walls. (T:2154B)

Christ taught me something more about the spiritual Glory within my soul in prayer, telling me through His Spirit:-

DON'T BE PERTURBED BY MY ACTION. YOU HAVE NOTICED THAT MY GLORY SHINES FROM WITHIN YOUR SOUL, DAY AFTER DAY: BUT YOU HAVE SEEN HOW THIS RADIANCE BURNS MORE BRIGHTLY AT CERTAIN MOMENTS DURING THE HOLY MASS WHEN I HAVE DRAWN YOU INTO EVER MORE FERVENT PRAYER. BY THIS INCREASING RADIANCE, I AM FULFILLING MY PLAN FOR YOUR WORK AND FOR YOUR LIFE. I AM CONFIRMING - FOR YOURSELF AND FOR OTHER PEOPLE - NOT ONLY THE STRENGTH OF YOUR FRIENDSHIP WITH CHRIST BUT ALSO THE PURPOSE AND THE HOLINESS OF THE DIFFERENT PARTS OF THE MASS. (WC:2160) (T:2160 #2)

NOTICE HOW YOUR SOUL BURNS MORE BRIGHTLY - LIT BY MY GLORY - WHENEVER YOU SAY 'LORD HAVE MERCY': IN TRUE SORROW FOR SIN. THIS SAME GLORY BURNS BRIGHTLY AT THE READING OF THE HOLY GOSPEL, AS MINDS AND HEARTS ARE BEING FED BY THE WORD. MY GLORY SHINES BRIGHTLY AS YOU TURN YOUR HEART AND MIND TO THE FATHER, DURING THE PRAYERS OFFERED BY MY PRIEST, AT THE ALTAR. THE SAME RADIANCE IS SEEN AT THE CONSECRATION WHEN YOU WELCOME YOUR SAVIOUR'S REAL PRESENCE, AND ALSO DURING THE PRAYER FOR THE CHURCH: ESPECIALLY AS YOU PRAY FOR THOSE IN SPECIAL NEED, AND FOR THE FAITHFUL DEPARTED. MY GLORY BURNS BRIGHTLY AT THE 'PER IPSUM': AT THE OFFERING OF CHRIST'S SACRIFICE TO THE FATHER - AND THEN BURNS BRIGHTLY AGAIN AT YOUR TRUE UNION WITH CHRIST IN HOLY COMMUNION: SO GREAT IS HIS GLORY AND OUR LOVE FOR YOU, AND SO FIRM IS CHRIST'S WISH TO SHOW OUT THE STRENGTH OF YOUR FRIENDSHIP TO OTHERS, FOR THE SAKE OF YOUR TASK. (T:2160 #3)

THINK OF THIS SPARKLING RADIANCE WHICH NOW ILLUMINES AND DELIGHTS YOU AS BEING THE 'JEWELS' WITH WHICH CHRIST ONCE SAID HE WOULD 'ADORN' YOU. (T:2160 #4)

Three Persons: One God.

At about this time, I was marvelling not only at the way in which Christ's Glory was shining within my soul daily, in prayer, but also at the way in which I was being taught, as each of the Three Divine Persons - One God - identified Himself, at each offering to my soul of Divine wisdom and instruction.

It was because I had become so confident of Christ's Love for me that I had prayed a very bold prayer at Mass one morning, in March 1997. I asked Him, after the Offertory Procession, "Holy Lord: May I share Your Divinity?" And I was astounded by what He did for me, and by what He taught me. I was suddenly reassured by Christ that His Church will be renewed, through my work. He told me, through His Holy Spirit:-

> *ACCEPT WHAT I AM SAYING TO YOU THROUGH THE HOLY SCRIPTURES, TODAY: THAT "I WILL RESTORE THE LAND AND ASSIGN YOU THE ESTATES THAT LIE WASTE." BY THIS, I MEAN THAT MY PLANS WILL DELIGHT YOU. THROUGH MY PLAN, AND YOUR WORK, I AM ENSURING THAT MY HOLY CATHOLIC CHURCH - HERE IN YOUR OWN COUNTRY - SHALL LIVE AND WITNESS AND WORSHIP WITH GREATLY-RENEWED VIGOUR AND JOY. THROUGH OUR WORK, I SHALL BRING JOY TO THE HEARTS OF THOSE WHO HAVE REMAINED FAITHFUL THROUGH DIFFICULT TIMES WHEN THEY HAVE BEEN MOCKED FOR THEIR STEADFAST FAITH IN THE CONSTANT TEACHINGS OF THE CHURCH AND DESPISED FOR THEIR SIMPLE DEVOTIONS. (T:2161 #1)*

Then Christ taught me more about the Glory which I had begun to 'see' almost daily, in prayer. He told me joyfully:-

> **Don't be afraid. You are right to echo, with a fervent will, the prayers which are offered by My priest at the altar. Truly, he is not speaking for himself alone, but on your behalf. (T:2161 #2)**

> **Think about My Love for you. I long to see you sharing My gifts and My virtues. I long to see you sharing My Divinity, by which I mean sharing, experiencing and enjoying the Glory which is inseparable from My Divine nature, as well as sharing other marvels. (T:2161 #3)**

> **Be simple. Accept the truth: that I am giving you, even now, a share in My Glory. Here, during the Holy Sacrifice, My Divine Fire - My radiant Light - is burning in your heart and upon your brow, throughout the great prayer of the Church. Even now, in Holy Communion, I am filling your soul with dazzling rays of My Glory. Even now I am leading you to the very 'doorway' to Heaven. (T:2161 #4)**

> **Accept the truth: which is that I have brought you very**

close to the Father, through our Holy Communion. It is as though you are standing at the entrance to Heaven: at a place from which you can glimpse not the face of your Heavenly Father, but something of the Uncreated Fire which surrounds Him; and here I am, beside you. In showing you something of this Fire, I am showing you something of My own nature: the Divine nature which I share with the Father. I am showing you something of My Glory and purity: something of the Divinity which you longed to share when you prayed your trusting prayer. (WC:2161) (T:2161 #5)

Don't be bashful. Accept and delight in the marvellous changes which I have brought about within your soul during these past few years. (T:2161 #6)

Remember the time when I came to you, unveiling My Glory to your startled soul, in 1964. You felt only shame and horror when you saw your own sinfulness beside My dazzling beauty. But now - and even though you realise that you are still sinful - you are joyful as well as repentant. Daily, you gaze upon My Glory - that same, unchanging Glory - in delight, gratitude and peace. (T:2161 #7)

Never forget that there is someone else to whom you can turn for special help, as you long for holiness and still have to endure difficulties and trials. I am speaking about My beloved Mother Mary. Very powerful help is given to those who have faith in her help, and who call out trustingly to their "Immaculate Mother." (T:2161 #8)

A triple joy.

So overwhelming were God's teachings, and so complex was the task of recording them all that I was grateful for a quiet daily routine, and also for firm 'anchors' in the spiritual life. I mean that I was still having my work checked by the Jesuit Father who was so generous with his time and his encouragement, and I was still going backwards and forwards to my parish priest to explain about each new stage of the work. I was no longer quite as embarrassed at having to speak about my soul, and about God, and was beginning to accept the task with more grace, and with fewer thoughts about my obvious unworthiness. Then after a wonderful teaching (T:2166), also in March, about how the 'empty' and purified soul can contain the 'Triple Joy' - can contain Christ's Light, with the Spirit's Bliss and the Father's 'Fire' - I was required to speak to our priest once more, to explain a new stage, and to explain the reason for the new format of the recent volume of "Teachings-in-prayer."

When we were sitting in the front room of the Presbytery I gave our priest the following explanation. (See T:2167)

I told him that the second Volume of my "Instructions from Christ" had just been printed, and that the lay-out of the text was a bit different from what he'd seen in the initial draft. I explained that I'd changed the typeface of certain segments, and that it was important that I try to explain this, not just for his own sake but because he needed to understand it for the sake of other people, later: people who would be asking him for his opinions. What I meant was that in the new Volume I'd used capital letters for the teachings which I'd had from the Father; and I felt I ought to explain why there weren't any such teachings in Volume One.

It was seven years since I'd been to Father O'Leary, I explained, to tell him something about my life and my prayer, and since I'd also explained that God was 'teaching' me in prayer. Fr. O'Leary had said that it was a gift from God and that it was all right to accept it. I said that in the years before and after I'd gone for advice I had usually been taught by God through a sudden, pure and piercing moment of 'knowledge' given quite unexpectedly in prayer, in an experience which was over almost before it began. But something had changed, later on: only about six months before our new priest had arrived in the parish.

Here, I mentioned that passage in Holy Scripture in which Christ tells us: "IF ANYONE LOVES ME ... MY FATHER WILL LOVE ... AND WE SHALL COME TO HIM AND MAKE OUR HOME WITH HIM" (Jn 14:23).

I said: "That's what happened to me."

Called by the Father.

Then I explained that although, until that time, most of the 'teachings' had been given in prayer, very briefly, and usually in church, and usually during Mass, I found that I was being given lengthy teachings - at home - by God the Father. I was only taught by Him because I pray to Him in the name of Jesus; I found, however, that the Father would sometimes call me, at home, calling me away from whatever I was doing, to invite me to listen to Him, in prayer; and He would teach me for up to an hour. I said that it is awesome, and that He teaches me about Himself, about human nature, about the Covenant, about Christ - or whatever subject He chooses; and that, I said, is why I have to try and explain something more about this; I must show how important it is that I have put the Father's teachings in capitals, in Volume Two of "Christ's Instructions." The Three Divine Persons are equal, as we know; but I've had to make the Father's teachings 'leap off the page' for a specific reason.

Next, I explained that whenever Christ teaches me in Holy Communion, it is awe-inspiring; yet because He is human, as well as God, we have something in common; whereas - although only through Christ am I brought to the Father - whenever the Father reaches out to teach me, it is awesome, because He is not human. He is wholly Other.

Although I don't see the Father, I explained, He is so wonderful that I don't know whether to dance for joy or to lie flat on the floor; but it is by using capital letters for the teachings which are specifically from the Father that I can convey some of the impact which they have on me - for the sake of recording the teachings as accurately as possible. I added that I've sometimes been mistaken about little things, but that these particular teachings are so awesome and powerful that it's quite impossible to be mistaken about them; and so now that I've put them in capital letters, at the centre of the page, I find that as I read them I feel something of the awe I felt when I was given them; and it's that mixture of awe and delight that I hope and pray other people will develop in their own relationships with God.

A clear distinction.

It was necessary, at around that time, to explain about the different typefaces to the Jesuit Father, as well. He was still very kindly checking my work; and so I wrote a letter to explain that it's because the whole work is so complex, and God the Holy Trinity is so beautiful and awesome, that the volumes of "Teachings-in-prayer" now contained a clear identification of Whichever of the Three Persons had given me a specific teaching; and even as I described this, I was progressing to the stage where the Holy Spirit would be 'identified', as well as Christ and the Father. That was to follow within a few months.

What I wrote to Fr. Edwards was: "Everything good we receive in prayer does come through Christ. We only 'reach' the Father through Him; and I know that whether a teaching is given from Christ or from the Father, it is a 'teaching' from our God: the One, Holy God. But God Who has planned this whole work and Who has led me to write His teachings wants people to learn not just the facts within the teachings - 'facts' which we already know, of course, through the Revelation already given, of which these teachings are simply a reminder. But through this work, God wants to show, as if from "the inside" of a relationship, how a 'willing soul' grows in closeness to Him and how a willing 'person-who-prays' relates, in prayer, to each One of the Three Divine Persons.

Then I explained how I've found that in this relationship with the One, True God, a willing soul is instructed by each Divine Person in a slightly different manner, although each is wholly Divine and is equal to the other Persons.

I added: "The aim of the new draft, therefore, is to make very much plainer just Who, exactly, has been teaching me in prayer at particular moments; and this is for the sake of other people whom God wishes to instruct about His Love, His nature, and about the spiritual life."

Since the readers of each new volume of "Teachings-in-prayer" also deserved an explanation I added a few new paragraphs to Volume Four of "Christ's Instructions", under the heading: 'Notes on the text', where I described the different sorts of typeface I'd used.

Inspiring stories.

It was less than a fortnight after I'd gone to our parish priest to explain about the Father's teachings that Christ explained to me, further, how the teachings would be useful. He invited me to think about my own writings, and then about works that I'd read in earlier years. He urged me, on 2nd April, 1997:-

> **Look back to your own discoveries about various friends of Mine, to recall how greatly you were encouraged in the spiritual life by their inspiring stories. You believed that**

**what I had done for them, I could do for you too. It is true
that you live by faith, as you know; but each one of you
becomes more eager to press on with your journey if you
receive some glimpse or story or whisper about the
rapturous spiritual life of someone whose union with Me is
firmly established. Your writings, therefore, are going to
encourage many people to believe that friendship with Me
is worth pursuing at any cost, and that Heaven's joys can
be tasted even here on earth by those who are willing to
make sacrifices in order to come close to Me, the Son of
God Who has come from Heaven to save you. (T:2178 #4)**

Nothing can compare.

Every little effort I made to serve God more joyfully was ever more lavishly rewarded, as our
friendship grew stronger. For example, it was on Easter Saturday in 1997 (in T:2180) that I
made acts of trust and humility towards the Father. I was ill at home, and was almost
overwhelmed when He answered me in the following way - and not only answered me but
nearly submerged me in joy and glory.

The Father taught me, with infinite tenderness and love:-

LITTLE CHILD:
MY LOVE FOR YOU IS SO GREAT
THAT I CANNOT YET REVEAL TO YOU
THE FULL EXTENT OF ITS MAJESTY AND BEAUTY,
LEST YOU HESITATE ON YOUR JOURNEY,
OVERWHELMED BY LOVE'S INTENSITY,
AND AFRAID.

I DELIGHT IN YOUR ACTS OF FAITH IN MY LOVE.
I DELIGHT IN SEEING YOU PRAYERFUL AND JOYFUL
AND ALSO
SEEING YOU USING TIME WELL, EVEN IN SICKNESS,
AND
OFFERING A NEW SURRENDER
TO MY WISHES.

(T2180 #1)

BELIEVE THIS, MY CHILD:
MY LOVE FOR YOU IS SO GENUINE, POWERFUL AND UNSTOPPABLE
THAT I AM REACHING OUT ALL THE TIME:
TO DRAW YOU FURTHER INTO MY EMBRACE
AND
FURTHER INTO MY HEART.

(WC:2180) (T:2180 #2)

SHARE WITH OTHERS
- AND WITH THE WHOLE WORLD, THROUGH YOUR WORK -
THE TRUTH ABOUT MY LOVE:
ABOUT DIVINE LOVE FOR WEAK PERSONS.

(T:2180 #3)

REASSURE OTHERS
THAT NOTHING CAN COMPARE WITH THE GIFTS
WHICH I, YOUR FATHER, SO TENDERLY BESTOW.
REASSURE MY PEOPLE
THAT
NO EARTHLY LOVE
- NO EXPERIENCE OF NATURAL HAPPINESS,
NO ROMANCE,
NO WORLDLY FULFILMENT,
NO JOYFUL AND SATISFYING USE
OF MIND, BODY, MEMORY OR IMAGINATION,
NOR ANY HUMAN JOY -
CAN RIVAL HEAVEN'S JOYS:
CAN SURPASS THE INTENSITY OF THE UTTER BLISS AND GLORY
WHICH ARE MY GIFTS
- SOMETHING EVEN DURING EARTHLY LIFE -
TO
MY TRUE FRIENDS

(T:2180 #4)

Being saved.

In case anyone should say that Heaven's joys on earth are all very well, but it's reaching Heaven that really counts, to find Salvation, I can joyfully say that in the year of which I'm speaking, I was taught by the Father what His Church means by telling us that we who love Him can have a 'sure hope' of being saved. (T:2200A)

A strange promise fulfilled.

As I've had to explain several times, it wasn't Christ's plan that I should press on with the task without keeping our parish priest informed about certain things. At around the time of that last teaching - in April 1997 - I was invited by Christ to see Fr. Eugene yet again, as I mentioned, to speak about my new way of recording the 'special' teachings-in-prayer that I'd received from God the Father; and on another day, when I'd followed Christ's new instructions about the work, He commended me for my obedience, and explained why He had asked me to do certain things:-

> **See how appropriate it was, yesterday, that on the transferred feast of 'The Annunciation' you should send out copies of My "Teachings-in-prayer" to these members of the Clergy: to the Holy Father and to these two Bishops.**

Even when you could not understand why it was necessary, you trusted in My wisdom, and obeyed My wishes. I assure you that the way of simplicity and obedience is the right way. (T:2182 #1)

Understand something further about the progress of this matter. I am making things plainer to those of My priests who are to be involved in judging and speaking about our work. (T:2182 #2)

Recall the visit which you made in obedience to Me, over a year ago, when you spoke out frankly to the Bishop about My teachings and then about the Glory which I had promised you that I would one day confer on you. You spoke about this even though you didn't really understand My plan. Furthermore, you spoke to your parish priest also, several months ago, to repeat what I had told you: that you would show out My Glory 'in your own person;' and now - you are beginning to realise - something is happening to fulfil My strange promise. I have been filling your soul with My Glory, daily, in prayer - and for many weeks. I have let you know the moment of the appearing of My Glory, and I have revealed this radiance to your parish priest, also. He has witnessed it many times. This, therefore, is part of My plan: that if My priest is willing to obey Me in this matter, he will speak to the Bishop about this Glory, which you mentioned twice, in obedience to My wishes, even before it had appeared; and this is My sign that the work which you are doing in obedience to Me is truly My gift, and My work, and that the only plans you value and try to follow are Mine, as you strive to be faithful to My Church, in everyday life, and also to the instructions which you receive from Me in prayer. (T:2182 #3)

Understand plainly, now, why you have been right to keep silent about these teachings, during this past year, except to explain them to the people you meet, in the ways which I have recommended. I mean that you have remained 'silent' in not making further requests for approval of your work. You long to be able to reassure My faithful friends who worry about reading private revelations that there is nothing here which is against the teaching of My Church; yet it is your parish priest who - as shepherd of My flock in this area - will ask for approval of these writings: if he is willing to fulfil My request. (T:2182 #4)

My priest is a witness to My sign, as well as pastor; and so it is he, not you, whom I now invite to ask for a sign from the Church that her people can safely read your writings and for an official confirmation that there is nothing in them which is against the Faith. He should explain that you are convinced of the orthodoxy of your own work not because you deem yourself able to judge - although you have a firm conviction - but because you have willingly submitted your work to scrutiny by a priest-theologian at every stage; and you have been doing so ever since your former parish priest made that suggestion. (T:2182 #5)

Convey My wishes to My priest, about how I wish for a sign to be given, by those in authority, in response to My sign. But remained unconcerned about the outcome. Continue to pray and work as at present. (T:2182 #6)

In order to fulfil Christ's wishes, I made an appointment with our parish priest, and I posted copies of the new book of "Instructions from Christ" - the 'green book' - to our Bishop and Archbishop, and to the Holy Father in Rome.

A new vocation.

On 10th April, I explained these things to Fr. Eugene - and gave him also a copy of the second volume. Then, on the following day, during the Mass, Christ showed me how pleased He was that I'd done what He wanted. He overwhelmed me with joy; and, only three days later, He explained to me:-

Understand something further about your present state of prayer and your spiritual progress. Realise that your new vocation - after motherhood - involves a very great responsibility, as your contacts with other people become more numerous and wide-spread, through your written work. But although the collection of writings and paintings which you have produced in obedience to My wishes is an important part of what I am achieving through your life, it remains only a part of My whole 'project'. I want you to see that you are going to influence other people most powerfully, for My sake, not primarily as an author or painter but as a living witness to My Love and mercy. (T:2186 #1)

Allow me to 'unveil' much of your life, for other people, in order to give them hope. You have been distressed at the thought of enduring either relentless curiosity from numerous people, or overwhelming gratitude; but I Myself have chosen you for a special task. At your consent, I shall use you. It is precisely because you are so needy and feeble, and yet have been given such joy through My Love and forgiveness, that you can serve as My visible 'teaching' for others. I have chosen and trained a weak person like yourself in order to encourage other weak people. I shall give you many opportunities to speak about Me and about My goodness, and thus you shall be My visible 'teaching' about faith and about other things; and, furthermore, this will shame some who think themselves 'wise' but who mock simple faith and whose acts and attitudes are wounding My Church. (T:2186 #2)

Consider how few persons are willing to say with wholehearted fervour: "Christ is worth every sacrifice! Love Him; trust in Him." Truly, I have trained you and led you forward because there is such a great need for sincere witnesses to My Love. (T: 2186 #3)

Persevere in your work and witness, no matter how difficult things become. I assure you that I shall bring tremendous consolations to other souls through your life and work. The most secure course for you, therefore, at what is a new stage of your life, is to remain firmly 'in Christ' at every moment, trying to fulfil My wishes from hour to hour, and with an attitude - more and more - of simple self-forgetting. (T:2186 #4)

19 TRANSFORMATION
(1997-1998)

KNOWING GOD. THE TRANSFORMING UNION.

About Salvation.

On the feast of Saint Joseph the Worker - May 1st, 1997 - I offered many thanks to the Father, with many petitions as usual, and then offered the Precious Body and Blood of Jesus, as usual, at Mass, as my praise of the Father and my reparation for sin; and, suddenly, I found that the Father stopped my words, and lifted me wholly into contemplation, to reward me for my devotion, but also to teach me about hope. Suddenly, He explained to me:-

> BELOVED CHILD:
> HERE YOU ARE, VERY CLOSE TO ME.
> I HAVE LIFTED YOUR SOUL UP HIGH
> INTO MY PRESENCE
> BECAUSE OF YOUR FERVENT PRAYER
> 'IN CHRIST.'
> YES!
> THE BLOOD OF JESUS IS REPARATION
> FOR THE SINS OF YOUR ENTIRE LIFE.
> YOU CAN BE CONFIDENT, HERE BEFORE ME,
> BECAUSE OF HIS PRECIOUS BLOOD
> AND
> YOUR REPENTANCE.

(T:2200A #1)

> BE AT REST, IN MY PRESENCE.
> YOU HAVE DONE WELL, MY CHILD.
> YOU ARE WISE TO RELY ON CHRIST, TO PRAY IN HIS NAME,
> AND TO OFFER HIS PRECIOUS BODY AND BLOOD
> - HIS HOLY SACRIFICE -
> AS YOUR OFFERING:
> AN OFFERING OF PRAISE AND THANKS, OF REPARATION AND PETITION.

> I ASSURE YOU
> THAT THE REVERENT AND SINCERE PETITION
> FOR SALVATION

WHICH YOU OFFER TO ME DAILY
IS ALREADY ANSWERED.
(T:2200A #2)

CONSIDER THIS STATE OF PRAYER:
ITS SIGNIFICANCE.
IT IS BECAUSE OF OUR UNION
THAT YOU CAN BE CONFIDENT ABOUT MY ANSWER
TO YOUR PLEAS FOR PERSEVERANCE AND SALVATION.
THESE PRAYERS ARE EVEN NOW BEING GRANTED
BECAUSE
ONE WHO LIVES 'IN' ME
IN THIS SORT OF FULL AND TRANSFORMING UNION
IN WHICH THIS SWIFT, DIVINE AND POWERFUL GIFT OF CONTEMPLATION
IS A NORMAL PART
IS ALREADY SAVED.
(T:2200A #3)

SEE HOW SIMPLE IS TRUTH,
MY BELOVED.
CONSIDER THE DEPTH OF MY LOVE FOR YOU,
THEN CONSIDER THE HEIGHT OF PRAYER
INTO WHICH I, YOUR GOD, HAVE DRAWN YOU, IN CHRIST,
AFTER LENGTHY PURIFICATIONS.

YOU CAN SAY, TRULY, THAT SHE WHO LIVES 'IN' ME
IS NOT LOST;
NOR CAN SHE BE LOST UNLESS
SHE LEAVE ME.
(T:2200A #4)

Christ's way of teaching.

How I longed to be able to give hope to others! Only one month later, I paid a visit to the church in the afternoon, on the feast of the Visitation - on June 1st 1997; and I asked Christ about His teachings, and about how I should use them. I'd been asked to give a talk to a womens' group and very much needed advice. But Christ suddenly taught me:-

Don't be anxious about how to present My teachings to these people who have asked you for a talk. *"Teach them the way I have taught you."* **What I mean by this is that you can copy My method of teaching - a method now very familiar to you; but you can also teach these people "The Way", that is, various truths to do with the practice of the Faith. (T:2231 #1)**

Consider My manner of teaching, first. If you copy My manner you will strive to be perfectly sincere, truthful,

474

simple and encouraging, in everything you say and do. This attitude is what you have witnessed as you have watched Me during these past few years. Like Me, you can express things simply at first, and then more deeply, later on; and plain speaking is best, with no attempts at what we can call 'cleverness'; nor is there any need for complicated explanations. (T:2231 #2)

Think about what we can call "The Way": by which I mean the spiritual path upon which I have led you, through these teachings, as I have led others in past times who have been willing to trust in Me, to accept the gifts and guidance of My Holy Catholic Church, and also to accept special personal helps and promptings. My Way is simple, you have learned; yet it requires faith, love and sincerity: with some humility, and a determination to persevere. (T:2231 #3)

Christ's constant recommendations.

Urge these people who approach you: "Live for God". Teach them what I have taught you, about making a new beginning - over and over again. (T:2231 #4)

Assure needy people
that these have been My constant recommendations:
Turn to Me, your Saviour.
Put your trust in Me, and in the power of My Spirit.
Put Me first, in your life, no matter what the cost.
Open your heart to Me, in reverence and humility.
Consider My holiness and your sinfulness, but
Believe in My great Love for you!
Believe in the teachings of My Church.
Make a new beginning.
Put your trust in Me, and
turn to My holy Mother: now your Mother, also.
We can help you.
Put things right; give up sin. Confess your sins.
Be reconciled, and do penance.
Yet: be joyful and simple. I never leave you.
Through all your tears and all your joys
you are in My care; yet
        if you turn away
        you do not allow Me to help you. (T:2231 #5)

Accept your circumstances.
Ask My help to fulfil your plain duties.
Pray every day; turn to Me as to a Friend.

Keep My Commandments.
Accept My help, through the sacraments, regularly.
Offer perfect homage to the Father,
through the Holy Sacrifice of the Mass.
Pray every prayer of the Mass with reverence.
Listen carefully to the Holy Scriptures.
Give Me a loving welcome, in Holy Communion,
when you are in a state of grace:
or else be reconciled, as true friends
should be reconciled before a celebration.
Be a friend to Me. Visit Me, at the tabernacle.
Let Me lead you to the heart of the Holy Trinity.
Love Me, and love your neighbour for My sake.
Forgive those who hurt you. (T:2231 #6)

Keep on praying: even very brief prayers.
Make friends with the Saints,
        and with My holy Angels.
Live in the 'present moment'.
Entrust the future to Me.
Love My Will: My Holy Will.
Work for change, where there is evil, but
accept with patience, in union with Me,
unavoidable sufferings and humiliations,
        thus joining in My redemptive work, and
        helping to save souls.
Persevere. Never give up!
Aim for sanctity.
Show Me all of your weaknesses,
        so that I can change you; but
remember: I love you 'madly'!
Hope for Heaven! (T:2231 #7)

Love, flowing within the Godhead.

So many chapters have had to be filled with the 'story' of Christ's teachings; but my plan is to explain something, soon, about life at the heart of the Holy Trinity: about how, if we persevere, we are able to experience the Triple Love which is offered at the heights of contemplative union; and so we recognise and relish that Love, and are continually praising the Holy Trinity for such generosity. But first, it seems that I should mention just a few more of the teachings which were given to me in 1997. They encapsulate, for me, the sense of peace and security which is given - with astonishing joys - in the day by day wonder which is the life of 'transforming union'.

One Sunday morning in June, at the end of Mass, as I continued to offer to the Father, from within my soul, Christ's prayer, and Christ's beauty and Glory, I was suddenly taught by the Father about the wonder of Life in God. He explained to me (T:2244B):-

YES, MY CHILD! I AM HERE:
WELCOMING YOUR PRAYER.
YOU ARE MAKING 'YOUR OWN'
THE SACRED OFFERING OF CHRIST MY SON:
AN OFFERING WHICH DELIGHTS ME.
TRULY:
SHE WHO FREELY OFFERS
- BY THE LONGINGS OF HER HEART,
AND BY PRAYER
AND BY HER ATTITUDES AND GESTURES -
THE PRAISE AND HOMAGE
WHICH CHRIST OFFERS TO ME ETERNALLY
IS MAKING 'HER OWN'
HIS SACRED GIFT.
AS A PRIVILEGED 'CHILD OF GOD', SHE IS 'USING'
- FOR MY GLORY AND FOR HER OWN GOOD -
CHRIST'S OWN LOVE, LONGINGS, PRAISE AND PRAYER AND WORK.
(T:2244B #1)

ACCEPT MY ASSURANCE
THAT AS SHE OFFERS CHRIST'S GREAT PRAISE TO ME
SHE FREELY 'INSERTS' HERSELF INTO OUR LIFE:
AS A SWIMMER MIGHT ENTER THE POWERFUL CURRENTS
OF A FAST-FLOWING RIVER.
SHE IS 'IMMERSED', THUS, IN THE LIFE OF THE HOLY TRINITY:
THE LIFE OF FATHER, SON AND HOLY SPIRIT;
AND AS SHE 'ENTERS' OUR LIFE
SHE STEPS INTO THE UNCHANGING YET DYNAMIC RELATIONSHIP
BETWEEN THREE DIVINE PERSONS:
A UNION WHICH CONSISTS OF FERVENT LOVE.
SHE IS DRAWN INTO THE 'MOVEMENT' OF THAT LOVE
AS IT FLOWS WITHIN THE GODHEAD;
AND WHEN
SHE IS 'LAUNCHED', IN THIS WAY, INTO OUR LIFE, LOVE AND UNION,
SHE CAN BE SAID TO BE TRULY ONE WITH US
BOTH IN LOVE AND IN WORK.
(T:2244B #2)

By this explanation about the Divine-human relationship, an understanding was given to me that the Divine work and the Divine Love into which a soul is drawn during its earthly life is the very work and love which will continue in Heaven, if that soul is faithful.

A precious drink.

When I thanked God the Father in prayer, in May 1997, for all of the teachings, and for having allowed me to do this work, He sent His Holy Spirit to teach me. I was suddenly shown, once again, why there had been an apparent delay in the work's fulfilment:-

CONSIDER HOW A PRECIOUS LIQUEUR IS KEPT IN A CASK FOR MANY YEARS WHILST IT MATURES. YOUR OWN WORK HAS BEEN MATURING, WE CAN SAY, FOR SEVERAL DECADES; AND THIS LENGTHY PREPARATION FOR AN EVENTUAL OUT-POURING HAS BEEN ESSENTIAL. (T:2255 #3)

ACCEPT MY ASSURANCE THAT OTHER PEOPLE WILL BE ASTONISHED BY THE RICHNESS OF THE PRECIOUS DRINK WHICH IS BEGINNING TO POUR OUT FROM WITHIN YOUR LIFE. BUT HOW MUCH LESS ASTONISHING WOULD HAVE SEEMED MY GIFTS, GIVEN THROUGH YOU TO OTHERS, HAD YOU TRIED TO HURRY THE TASK, EARLIER, BY LOUD SELF-PROMOTION OR BY COMPLAINTS ABOUT AN APPARENT LACK OF SUCCESS IN SPREADING THE GOOD NEWS THROUGH YOUR QUIET 'ONE-TO-ONE' CONVERSATIONS AND PRAYERS. YOU CAN SEE HOW CRUCIAL TO MY PLAN HAS BEEN YOUR OBEDIENCE AND PATIENCE. (WC:2255) (T:2255 #4)

Love never stops loving.

As an illustration of the sort of love into which we can be drawn, at our consent, I offer a marvellous teaching, received as I was praying in church after Mass on the 9th July, 1997. I offered Christ's Glory to the Father, as usual, and was caught up in Christ's praise of the Father, wholly surrendered to His Will. Then, when I was tired, and had turned aside, having begun to think that I must leave to do my shopping, I said to God the Father: "I'd better go now ...;" but He replied to me in a tender and yet urgent way which deeply moved me:-

MY CHILD:
I DON'T WANT YOU TO GO!
BUT I AM TELLING YOU THIS
NOT TO MAKE YOU STAY HERE, IN CHURCH,
ANY LONGER
WHEN YOU ARE TIRED AND HAVE WORK TO DO
BUT ONLY TO LET YOU KNOW
THE DEPTH OF MY LOVE FOR YOU.

IT IS TRUE THAT DIVINE LOVE IS A GIFT,
YET
IT IS NOT A FAVOUR WHICH IS DELIVERED WITH RELUCTANCE
FROM A DISTANT FIGURE.
YOU CAN SAY THAT
IT IS A STATE OF DESIRING-TO-GIVE-JOY, TO SHARE,
AND TO BE ETERNALLY UNITED.

(T:2266 #1)

UNDERSTAND THE DEPTH OF MY LOVE
FOR YOU.

DIVINE LOVE FOR A FRAIL CREATURE
IS 'REAL' LOVE.
I ENJOY YOUR LOVE.
I DELIGHT IN YOUR FRIENDSHIP,
I ENJOY YOUR DEVOTED ATTENTION.
I WOULD LIKE YOU TO STAY CLOSE TO ME
AT ALL TIMES.
YOUR LOVE OF ME DELIGHTS ME
SO MUCH
THAT I 'CANNOT' LET YOU GO,
ALTHOUGH I ALLOW YOU TO TURN 'AWAY'
- TO TURN YOUR ATTENTION ELSEWHERE -
BECAUSE YOUR WORK AWAITS YOU.

(T:2266 #2)

UNDERSTAND, AT LAST, WHY I TOLD YOU
- AS YOU PREPARED TO 'LEAVE' ME -
THAT I DON'T WANT YOU TO GO.
I LOVE YOU DEARLY;
AND TRUE LOVE NEVER STOPS LOVING.
IT NEVER CEASES TO DELIGHT IN ITS BELOVED.

(T:2266 #3)

GO AND DO YOUR WORK, MY DAUGHTER;
BUT REMEMBER, ALWAYS, ABOUT ME,
THAT LOVE LOVES TO BE LOVED
AND THAT
LOVE LOVES YOU!

(T:2266 #4)

Never had it occurred to me, in past years, that the Father Himself would one day converse with me; and this is the Love which created us all, and which loves us now! How I long to see people believe it. I hope to see them living in the 'land' which is offered to them, if only they will travel on the path which God has chosen for them, and not on their own by-ways.

'Where milk and honey flow'.

Christ showed me one day in August (in T:2299B) - and by His Spirit's Light upon the reading from Holy Scripture - that my joyful way of life is truly a gift from Him. He explained to me, through the Holy Spirit, that I now live, spiritually, in "A LAND RICH AND BROAD, A LAND WHERE MILK AND HONEY FLOW" (Ex 3:8).

*REALISE, MY CHILD, THAT YOU ARE NOW LIVING IN THE 'LAND'
WHICH YOU ARE HEARING ABOUT TODAY IN THE HOLY SCRIPTURES.
IT IS THROUGH YOUR UNION WITH CHRIST THAT YOU ARE LIVING IN
A WONDERFUL LAND - WE CAN SAY - "WHERE MILK AND HONEY
FLOW." (T:2299B #1)*

479

RECOGNISE AND REMAIN GRATEFUL FOR THESE SPECIAL GIFTS: THE 'MILK' WHICH FLOWS IN THIS 'LAND' AND UPON WHICH CHRIST IS FEEDING YOU IS THE SPECIAL PERSONAL NOURISHMENT WHICH HE GIVES TO YOU THROUGH THESE TEACHINGS - AS WELL AS HIS OWN SACRED BODY AND BLOOD IN HOLY COMMUNION, WHICH YOU HAVE RECEIVED AT EVERY STAGE OF YOUR SPIRITUAL JOURNEY, IN HIS CHURCH. THE 'HONEY' WHICH IS FOUND IN THIS WAY OF LIFE IS THE SWEETNESS IN WHICH YOU ARE NOWADAYS SUBMERGED AT EVEN THE BRIEFEST OF PRAYERS TO YOUR SAVIOUR. (2299B #2)

The process of purification.

By way of contrast, I was reminded by the Father in prayer, only three weeks later, that todays joys have been made possible only through Christ's goodness and after I've endured many purifications.

I had just spoken the plain truth to the Father once again by saying that I have nothing good to boast about but only Jesus' Blood and Jesus' Glory, as I'd been shown by the Father once again, in prayer; and the Father suddenly drew me close to Himself and taught me with great tenderness:-

DEAR CHILD,
HOW QUICKLY YOU HAVE FORGOTTEN
THE LENGTHY PURIFICATIONS THROUGH WHICH I HAVE LED YOU.
I HAVE MADE YOU MY OWN CHILD.
I HAVE TRANSFORMED YOU.
I HAVE FORGIVEN EVERY TRANSGRESSION,
AND YOU ARE LIVING IN MY LOVE.

(T:2326 #1)

BE AT PEACE, MY CHILD.
THE LONG JOURNEY IS FAR BEHIND YOU.
THE SEEMINGLY-ENDLESS YEARS OF THAT PROCESS OF PURIFICATION
ARE LONG-PAST.
IT IS AS THOUGH YOU HAVE CROSSED A WAR-TORN TERRAIN
AMIDST HEAT, SMOKE AND FIRE-BLACKENED RUINS.
YET, THROUGH MY GRACE, YOU PERSEVERED, AND 'FOUND' ME,
OR, RATHER,
YOU ALLOWED ME TO BRING YOU TO THIS PRESENT JOY:
TO A STATE OF EXTRAORDINARY UNION.

(T:2326 #2)

As the Father showed me this reminder, He included in the purifications of which He spoke the very ordinary and mundane work of several decades, as well as the painful but routine miseries and humiliations which are met with in every earthly life, and which we can only bear with God's help. What a marvellous thing it is that we can offer every difficulty to the Father in union with Christ, as a sacrificial and very fruitful prayer; and I'm saying this to encourage those who think that we can only please God by doing 'heroic' tasks with heroic virtue.

Peace and sweetness.

Exactly ten days later, on the 17th September 1997, and when I'd told God the Father how much I long to see Him in Heaven, I turned to Him again in prayer, at home. Then I began to pray sincere prayers, just as He has taught me; I said to Him, with joy and confidence: "Father! I am a sinful woman, but I put my trust in You; I come to you through Jesus Christ my Lord ..."

But He wouldn't let me pray any more. He showed me Heaven's door, which was open wide; and then He told me:-

> MY CHILD:
> I AM OPENING THE DOOR TO HEAVEN
> AT THE SOUND OF YOUR VOICE
> AS YOU PRAY SIMPLE BUT CONFIDENT PRAYERS.
> WHENEVER YOU SPEAK TO ME, THUS,
> ABOUT LOVE, ABOUT SIN, ABOUT CHRIST,
> AND ABOUT TRUST IN ME
> YOU CAN BE SURE THAT THE 'DOOR' TO HEAVEN IS OPEN.
> (T:2331A)

Knowledge of Divine Life.

In the evening, I turned my heart to the Father again. I made the Sign of the Cross, and asked Him: "Help me to be good!" I was taught very firmly about how He desires to see me holy; but even more astonishing was the way in which every new plea or query was swiftly and marvellous answered: for about an hour.

My heart was nearly breaking with the wonder of it: that in my own home, and through the love of Christ, in Whose Name every prayer I make is offered to the Father, I can converse with my Creator, question Him with reverence, ask His advice, and praise Him - knowing that He will reward me for my love.

There's nothing I can do, it seems, except to reproduce this entire teaching, of which the last few lines were - in one sense - the most significant, because they ushered in a new era of enhanced union between us.

As I said, I had begun by asking the Father to help me to be good; and then He assured me:-

> DEAR CHILD:
> I WANT YOU TO BE HOLY;
> IT IS PART OF MY PLAN.
> EVEN HERE, AS YOU PRAY, I AM LIFTING UP YOUR SOUL
> INTO A CLOSER UNION
> WITH ME, YOUR GOD:

INTO A STATE IN WHICH YOU CAN SHARE
MORE OF MY HOLINESS.

(T:2331B #1)

Then I said to Him: "Father: You can see that I'm full of wonder at Your invisible beauty and majesty and goodness. Who are You?! ...." And I was astonished to hear Him reply:-

TRULY
"You know Me."
YOU ALREADY KNOW ME, TO SOME DEGREE,
BECAUSE OF YOUR UNION WITH CHRIST,
AND THE ENLIGHTENING WORK OF THE HOLY SPIRIT.

WE, THE HOLY TRINITY, YOUR GOD AND CREATOR,
HAVE ALREADY HELD YOU IN LOVE'S EMBRACE;
INDEED, WE ARE HOLDING YOU THUS, EVEN NOW;
AND THROUGH THIS CLOSE UNION
YOU HAVE LEARNED MUCH ABOUT OUR LOVING NATURE
AND ABOUT THE WAY IN WHICH WE ARE 'AT WORK'
IN YOUR SOUL AND YOUR LIFE.
YOU CAN SAY THAT YOU KNOW ME BY EXPERIENCE,
AS WELL AS BY FAITH.

(T:2331B #2)

DON'T BE AFRAID TO ACKNOWLEDGE MY GIFTS.
I AM THE SOURCE OF THESE TWO PARTICULAR GIFTS:
THE SWEETNESS WITHIN YOUR SOUL HAS ITS ORIGIN IN ME;
AND
YOUR KNOWLEDGE OF MY DIVINE LIFE
WAS GIVEN TO YOU FREELY
THROUGH OUR TRUE UNION.

(T:2331B #3)

A privileged state.

Wanting to be honest, I said: "Father: You're so good; and this prayer and 'communion' with You is so wonderful that I wish I could live like this all the time - in such peace and sweetness and familiarity! .." Then He told me:-

THIS GIFT IS NOW YOURS, MY CHILD.
THIS IS MY WILL FOR YOU, FROM NOW ON:
THAT YOU REMAIN IN THIS PRIVILEGED STATE
OF FAMILIARITY WITH ME, YOUR FATHER:
A STATE IN WHICH YOU EXPERIENCE
CONSTANT PEACE AND SWEETNESS.

THIS GIFT COMES TO YOU, AS YOU KNOW, BECAUSE OF MY LOVE FOR YOU;
YET IT COMES TO YOU, ALSO, BECAUSE OF MY LOVE FOR ALL OTHERS;

I WANT OTHER PEOPLE TO EXPERIENCE MY PEACE AND SWEETNESS
THROUGH YOU:
THROUGH YOUR WORDS OR YOUR PRESENCE.
(T:2331B #4)

DON'T BE ASHAMED TO RECORD THIS, MY CHILD
IT IS MY WILL.
IT IS A PART OF MY LOVING PLAN.
(T:2331B #5)

Determined to express gratitude for special gifts, I prayed: "Father: I'm trying to pray with a pure intention: making the Sign of the Cross, longing to stay close to You, determined to please You by fulfilling various duties - and especially grateful for Your special help! ..." Then He answered:-

RELISH THE GIFT WHICH CONSOLES YOU.

"It is My gift to you."

I DELIGHT IN YOUR GRATITUDE FOR GOOD THINGS
AS WELL AS YOUR CONTRITION WHEN YOU DO WRONG!
DON'T WORRY.
(T:2331B #6)

But since I trusted the Father, I confessed happily to Him: "Father: look at all these thoughts about life - and about aspects of my work - and about all these people. I'm determined not to worry. I abandon myself to You, and to Your care ..." Then He answered:-

HERE I AM, MY CHILD,
TO ASSURE YOU THAT YOUR TRUST IS WELL-FOUNDED.
REMEMBER THAT DAY, SO MANY YEARS AGO,
WHEN I TAUGHT YOU HOW TO PRAY:
TEACHING YOU TO 'LEAP', IN PRAYER
- IN AN ATTITUDE OF NAKED FAITH -
AS IF OVER THE EDGE OF A PRECIPICE,
IN NAKED TRUST THAT I WOULD HOLD YOU
AND COMMUNICATE WITH YOU
IN THE PURITY OF 'BLIND' PRAYER
IN YOUR SOUL'S INTERIOR DARKNESS?
TRULY, YOU ARE CONFIDENT, NOW,
THAT I AM HOLDING YOU IN EVERY CIRCUMSTANCE.

I AM LEADING YOU FORWARD, AGAIN,
TO FOLLOW A NEW PATH, IN MY SERVICE.
ALTHOUGH WE ARE FRIENDS, AND VERY CLOSELY UNITED,
THE WAY STILL REQUIRES NAKED FAITH,
WITH COURAGE, HOPE, LOVE, TRUST, AND PERSEVERANCE.
(T:2331B #7)

Pride, a great danger.

The Holy Spirit then showed me - before the eyes of my soul - the great danger which lies close by me, as I do this work. He told me:-

> *SEE HOW I LEAD YOU, BY THE FATHER'S WILL: ON A NEW PATH: A SURE WAY - IN HIS SERVICE. BUT YOU WILL BE IN GREAT DANGER. IT IS AS THOUGH YOU ARE STEPPING ONTO A LITTLE PATH WHICH HUGS THE HILLSIDE AT THE EDGE OF A BURNING LAKE WHICH IS HALF-HIDDEN BY SMOKE. DARKNESS LIES ALL AROUND. ONE FOOLISH STEP - ONE SLIP ON THIS NARROW PATH - COULD LEAD TO DISASTER. BUT YOU SHALL BE SAFE FOR AS LONG AS YOU WALK CAREFULLY ALONG THE PATH, HOLDING FIRMLY TO THE ROCK WALL AT THE SIDE - WHICH REPRESENTS ME, YOUR GOD. I AM SHOWING YOU, BY THIS IMAGE, HOW GREAT IS THE DANGER OF PRIDE, IN THIS WORK. BUT IF YOU STAY CLOSE TO ME, REMAINING OBEDIENT AND HUMBLE AND AVOIDING PRIDE AND EVERY SPIRITUAL DANGER, I SHALL BRING YOU INTO THE FATHER'S ARMS, ONE DAY: TO STAY FOREVER, ALL DANGER PAST. (WC:2331B) (T:2331B #8)*

Fervent Petitions.

As I thought about the Infinite care and kindness demonstrated by the Father, and as I realised how privileged I was to be enjoying such a wonderful conversation, I resolved to be bolder and more trusting than ever before, and to ask confidently for special gifts and favours. So I began to make fervent petitions, and said: "Father: I'm a sinful woman; and I'm happy to admit it, because Christ's Blood is what I plead by, and not my own good efforts - although I hope to please You. And I believe that You love me, and that You like to please me - because You've already shown me how true this is; so I ask You, now, for great gifts and favours. I believe that You can do these things ..."; and the Father answered:-

HERE I AM, SHOWING YOU, POWERFULLY,
THAT AS YOU OFFER ME A PETITION WHICH YOU MAKE
IN FAITH
YOUR PRAYER DRAWS DOWN MY GRACE
BOTH UPON YOURSELF AND UPON THE PERSON FOR WHOM YOU HAVE PRAYED.
THEN,
AT EVERY SUCH PETITION,
THE SAME WONDERFUL THING HAPPENS ONCE AGAIN:
BY MY WILL AND GENEROSITY.

(T:2331B #9)

God's plan for my life.

Next, I spoke frankly about my special work, and about my thoughts, saying: "Father: You 'touch' me so powerfully by your grace. What is Your Will for my life? Shall other people value their contact with me: and with this work, and Your wisdom?" This was His answer:-

DEAR CHILD:
I AM POWERFULLY AT WORK
THROUGH EVERY TRUE FRIEND WHO BELIEVES IN MY POWER
AND IS WILLING TO FOLLOW MY PROMPTINGS.
FURTHERMORE:
IT IS MY WISH THAT YOU BE KNOWN
AS SOMEONE WHO IS PRAYERFUL - AND INFLUENTIAL:
YET NOT FOR YOUR OWN SAKE,
BUT IN ORDER TO HELP MY WORK AND MY PLANS.
(T:2331B #10)

BE WATCHFUL.
THIS WAY OF LIFE CAN ENDANGER YOUR SOUL.
NEVER FORGET THAT WITHOUT MY GRACES
YOU CAN NEITHER COPE, NOR REMAIN FAITHFUL.
(T:2331B #11)

Aspects of Truth.

Nearly overcome with wonder, I offered my thoughts to God again, as if saying: "Father: here You are - teaching me so marvellously; and here I am, amazed at Your goodness! How is it that, for this work, You chose someone so wicked? ..." Immediately, He said to me:-

"Truth."
THAT IS THE ANSWER TO YOUR QUESTION,
MY CHILD.
THAT IS WHAT MAKES YOU SUITABLE
- THOUGH NOT 'GOOD' -
TO DO THIS WORK.
(T:2331B #12)

LOOK AT THE PATTERN, FROM THE BEGINNING;
YOU 'BEGAN' WITH TWO ADMIRABLE PARENTS, NEITHER OF WHOM
- THOUGH NOT PERFECT -
WOULD EVER TELL A LIE.
ALSO:
TRUTH HAS BEEN YOUR PRIZE AND GOAL,
THROUGHOUT YOUR LIFE,
DESPITE YOUR FAILINGS.
(T:2331B #13)

RECALL THE COST OF THESE EFFORTS TO REMAIN FAITHFUL
TO TRUTH: TO ME;
THINK ABOUT PAINFUL ASPECTS OF TRUTH:
FOR EXAMPLE,
TREASURING TRUTHS ABOUT MYSELF AND MY WISHES,
AND THEREFORE RECOGNISING AND ENTERING MY CHURCH
EVEN WHEN SUCH A CHOICE

IN THIS ERA, AND AMONGST THIS PEOPLE,
BROUGHT SUFFERING.
(T:2331B #14)

RECALL THE PAIN OF ACCEPTING TRUTHS
ABOUT YOUR SINFUL NATURE AND THE NEED FOR CHANGE.
RECALL THE HEARTACHE OF LOVING TRUTH TO SUCH AN EXTENT
THAT YOU HAVE ALWAYS PROCLAIMED THE TRUTHS OF THE CHURCH:
SOMETIMES AMIDST LAUGHTER.
RECALL THE EFFORTS TO HONOUR TRUTH
- DESPITE YOUR SINS -
TO THE EXTENT OF NEVER DELIBERATELY TELLING
WHAT SOME PEOPLE STRANGELY CALL 'WHITE' LIES.
(T:2331B #15)

AND NOW,
SEE WHERE I HAVE LED YOU:
SEE HOW PLAIN IT IS THAT SOMEONE WHO SPEAKS OUT MY TRUTHS
MUST BE SOMEONE WHO SPEAKS TRUTH
ABOUT ORDINARY, TINY, DAY-TO-DAY CONCERNS.
IT IS TO THOSE WHO VALUE THE LITTLE WORKS
WHICH I HAVE ENTRUSTED TO THEM
THAT I ENTRUST GREAT WORKS.
(T:2331B #16)

Jesus and Mary.

Astonished at the richness of life 'in' God, I said next: "Father: how good You are! I'm 'aching with gratitude and wonder at Your kindness. And thankyou for my constant companionship in this wonderful life 'in' Christ: for Christ and Our Lady: "Jesus and Mary!" I had no idea, years ago, of the depth of the friendship which can be enjoyed with them, nor of Our Lady's tremendous importance ... Father: they're so beautiful! ...".

Then I was suddenly shown the dazzling sight of Our Lord and Our Lady, who were standing side by side in Heaven; and the Father assured me:-

SWEET CHILD: HERE THEY ARE:
JESUS AND MARY:
STANDING SIDE BY SIDE, IN THE GLORY OF HEAVEN,
EACH VEILED IN HEAVEN'S RADIANCE.
I ASSURE YOU:
"You shall gaze upon them in Heaven."
YOU SHALL BE ABLE TO 'DRINK IN' THE BEAUTY
OF CHRIST AND HIS MOTHER MARY:
THE BEAUTIFUL SIGHT WHICH YOU HAVE BEEN YEARNING TO SEE.
YOU SHALL BE ABLE TO LOOK UPON THEM
WITHOUT BEING COMPELLED BY TIME, OR BY DUTY,
EVER TO TURN AWAY!

(WC:2331B) (T:2331B #17)

How well the Father knows me! How clearly He's seen my momentary pang of sadness whenever I've had to walk away from a vision in order to fulfil some duty, or when I've had to leave the church in order to keep an appointment or do the shopping.

Creation: and human life.

Then I added: "Father: I'm so thrilled by Your kindness. There's so much more I could ask for: but I'm too weak to sit up any more. I entrust myself to You: but there's one more question: Lord, how is it that we are made - this human life which is so strange and feeble, and yet so wonderful?! ... " Straightaway, He answered:-

MY CHILD:
THIS WAS THE SOLE REASON
WHY I CREATED YOU:
"Out of Love!"
LOVE IS MY NATURE, AND THEREFORE
LOVE IS MY PURPOSE.
I WISH TO SHARE MY JOY;
AND THEREFORE
ALL THAT I GIVE TO YOU
OR PERMIT YOU TO ENDURE
IS INTENDED TO GUIDE OR HELP YOU
IN YOUR PROGRESS TOWARDS ME;
YET: YOU ARE ALL TRULY FREE TO CHOOSE
WHETHER TO MOVE TOWARDS ME OR WHETHER TO TURN AWAY.

(T:2331B #18)

DELIGHT IN THIS THOUGHT:
THAT YOUR PRESENT STATE OF FRIENDSHIP WITH ME,
AND ALSO
THE JOY AND SWEETNESS WHICH YOU EXPERIENCE IN MY PRESENCE
ARE WHAT I HAVE INTENDED FOR YOU
- BECAUSE OF MY LOVE FOR YOU -
SINCE THE BEGINNING.

(T:2331B #19)

A new stage.

Words can't describe the wonder of it, when the Father showed no sign of 'releasing' me back into 'normal' prayer, as He had usually done after a conversation.

When I said to Him: "Father: I'd better 'leave' You; but I'm so grateful ..," I received an astonishing answer. The Father explained to me:-

NO:

> DON'T BELIEVE THAT YOU ARE 'LEAVING' ME.
> THIS IS A NEW STAGE, MY CHILD.
> NO LONGER IS IT AS THOUGH YOU GO 'AWAY' FROM ME
> AFTER SUCH A MEETING AS THIS:
> SUCH A PRAYER OF BOTH TEACHING AND ENFOLDING.
> ALTHOUGH YOU GO AWAY, IT SEEMS,
> TO REST OR TO DO YOUR WORK,
> WHILST KNOWING THAT I DO NOT 'GO AWAY' IN THE LEAST DEGREE FROM YOU,
> A CHANGE HAS OCCURRED TONIGHT
> IN YOUR SOUL, AND IN YOUR SPIRITUAL LIFE.
> FROM NOW ON
> YOU SHALL NEVER LEAVE THIS STATE OF UNION:
> THIS STATE OF BEING ENTIRELY-RECOLLECTED-IN-MY-PRESENCE.

(T:2331B #20)

The Father's promise.

Then the Father made me an extraordinary promise, which He has fulfilled, of course, right up to the present day. He told me:-

> UNDERSTAND, MY CHILD, THAT
> FROM NOW ON,
> MY PEACE SHALL ALWAYS ENFOLD YOU, WHOLLY.
> FROM NOW ON,
> YOU SHALL ALWAYS BE ABLE TO QUESTION, TO 'HEAR',
> TO TALK, TO CONFIDE, AND TO MAKE REQUESTS
> WITH AS MUCH IMMEDIACY AND FULFILMENT
> AS YOU HAVE ENJOYED TODAY, IN OUR PRAYER,
> DURING THIS PAST HALF-HOUR.

(T:2331B #21)

On the very 'edge' of Heaven.

So great was my astonishment and gratitude, that I turned to the Father in prayer the next morning, yearning to give Him a gift; and I said, sincerely: "Father: I unite my heart to Christ's Offering, even though I'm ill at home, ... in praise and thanksgiving, in reparation for my sins ... and begging You for perseverance, sanctity and Salvation for myself, and for all these people ... " Then the Father assured me:-

> BE JOYFUL, MY CHILD.
> TRULY:
> YOU CAN BELIEVE THAT
> - BY MY WISH AND YOUR CONSENT -
> YOU ARE NOW ON THE VERY 'EDGE' OF HEAVEN.
> IT IS MY WISH THAT YOU SEE AND UNDERSTAND YOUR STATE:
> THAT YOU RELISH MY GIFTS TO YOU

AND DELIGHT IN MY GOODNESS.
TRULY,
YOU ARE READY TO ENTER HEAVEN.
(T:2332 #1)

Next, the Father showed me the reasons why I can be joyful and carefree all the time. He told me:-

CONSIDER YOUR STATE:
YOU ARE 'WRAPPED' IN MY PRESENCE.
YOU ARE VERY CLOSE TO CHRIST.
YOU ARE GUIDED AND TAUGHT BY THE HOLY SPIRIT.
YOU ARE RELEASED FROM ALL THAT EVER HELD YOU.

YOU ARE DELIGHTING IN MY WORK:
UNAFRAID OF OPINIONS ABOUT YOU,
TRUSTFUL ABOUT WHAT LIES AHEAD,
AND CONFIDENT OF MY HELP AND MY CARE
AND OF MY GENEROUS RESPONSE TO YOUR PETITIONS.

UNDERSTAND, MY CHILD, HOW TREMENDOUS IS MY LOVE FOR YOU.
TREASURE THE KNOWLEDGE THAT YOUR TRUST IN ME IS NOT MISPLACED.
I AM YOUR FRIEND, STRENGTH AND CONSOLATION,
AND YOUR HOPE OF ETERNAL JOY.
(T:2332 #2)

Books for distribution and sharing.

At the end of September, 1997, Christ shone His Light into my soul and explained something more to me about my unique task - and about this spiritual autobiography. He showed me:-

Understand something more about My Will for you. It is My wish to encourage and guide you, as you move to another stage of your special work. Even though you are at home, unwell, you are fulfilling My plan for you, since I have made possible - by this short Providential 'retreat' - a time of rest, reflection and prayer by which I help you to see My Will more clearly. (T:2339 #1)

Benefit from the spiritual Light which I am now shining so brightly within your heart and soul and mind. I invite you to reassess your priorities, in My service: to 'clear the decks': to abandon every needless or useless idea, and to keep up-to-date with your essential work and correspondence. This is how you can focus more clearly on what I am doing in your life - and can reassess how much I have done for you. (T:2339 #2)

Think of those things which you can boldly proclaim are true: for example: you belong to Me - by your free and loving service. Your first loyalty is to Me. Your heart is entirely Mine: and your work is progressing well, as you follow My instructions. You have been reassured by the priest whom I chose to examine your work that there is nothing in these books which is contrary to the faith of the Church. Your former parish priest has played his part in your training, through his watchful care; and your present parish priest has been prepared for his part in this whole work by his reading of these books, and through the conversations and explanations which I have prompted you to initiate. Furthermore: several books are now ready for distribution and sharing; and these can now include the spiritual autobiography which you wrote several years ago, in order to please Me, at a time when I knew that you could undertake such a difficult task, and I could trust you to store it until the appropriate time would arrive for its use in My whole plan. (T:2339 #3)

See how plain it is, at last, that you are going forward in a unique mission which has been planned and set in motion by Me, your Saviour. It seems as though you are alone, at times - as when a chick leaves its nest; and your 'nest' is the routine of your somewhat obscure domestic life, where you have been held securely for many years. But several generous people - including your own children - are ready to help you: even to set up the body which can take care of this work and so promote the Catholic Faith. (T:2339 #4)

Be simple, always. All that you need to do, in order to proceed contentedly in this work is to act as I wish you to act: acting out your new role from the heart! It is a role which you would never have expected or dared to choose for yourself; but it is a role for which I have marvellously trained you - as you are just beginning to appreciate. Truly: you are to be a living witness to My Love. (T:2339 #5)

Be confident that you are working and living 'in Christ' as you do My work. You are doing it in My Spirit's Light; and you shall be moving steadily towards the Father, Whose Will it is that you persevere in your task. (T:2339 #6)

Worthy of adoration.

Never could I have believed, in earlier years, that friendship with Christ could mean this: never-ending love shown towards me in prayer, with endless reassurance. Christ told me, in November of 1997:-

> **Accept My assurance that a great deal of good is going to be accomplished - according to My Will - through the teachings and paintings which you have produced in accordance with My Will; and there are many facets to this work. Truly, this task has been entirely designed by Myself and directed towards the Father, for His Glory; and so it is rightly entitled 'Radiant Light', as I showed you. (2383 #3)**

> **Consider a special aspect of this work: an aspect of which you have not so far seen the significance. Think, first, about the reminders which I have given in other eras and to other people about what I do, or what I can do. It has been through private revelations that I have given My People reminders, for example, about sin and forgiveness. Through certain persons, I have given reminders that I, your God, still forgive sins, heal, reign, win victories, offer hope - and so work marvels of love in all sorts of ways. Through your own work, however - through these private revelations, given in prayer - I am reminding My People not principally of what I do, but of what, 'in' Myself, I am. (T:2383 #4)**

> **Rejoice in your task of being able to give My People this reminder that I, your God - the Holy Trinity, undivided - am Glory and Love and Strength and Holiness: Infinite Beauty, worthy of adoration, and also the Cause of Eternal Bliss for those who achieve Salvation. (T:2383 #5)**

> **Rejoice that this reminder of My Perfection and Beauty is expressed so vividly - for the encouragement of those in My Church who struggle to be faithful - precisely because it comes through the work and life of someone who is undistinguished, weak and sinful, yet who now strives at every moment to please Me. (T:2383 #6)**

Later, He showed me, in answer to my queries:-

> **See what a simple task this is, at its heart. I wish to encourage My People to practice their faith. Through this work, I am giving special help to many Catholics - and other Christians - who neither believe in nor practice those things which can lead them close to Me. It is of supreme importance that people repent of their sins, in order to**

**proceed on their spiritual journey and to grow in the hope
of Heaven; yet in order to repent sincerely, they need to be
led to know - or to be reminded - about which things are
sinful and which things are not; hence the firm instructions
which are 'woven' amongst the loving and encouraging
comments, in these teachings. (T:2386 #11)**

A spiritual autobiography.

The Holy Spirit, too, shone His Light within my soul, and reassured me:-

> *DON'T BE ANXIOUS ABOUT HOW TO INTRODUCE YOUR WORK, OR
> HOW TO EXPLAIN ITS ORIGIN.   GIVE BOOKS TO ANYONE WHO
> EXPRESSES AN INTEREST IN PRAYER; THEN PUT YOUR TRUST IN ME. I
> SHALL GUIDE PEOPLE IN THEIR UNDERSTANDING. (T:2392 #2)*

Then He urged me to be brave about another stage in the work which He was inviting
me to achieve. He explained:-

> *SHARE YOUR JOY WITH OTHER PEOPLE, IN THE WAYS WHICH I HAVE
> INDICATED SO FAR; AND DON'T BE AFRAID TO USE THE SPIRITUAL
> AUTOBIOGRAPHY WHICH YOU WROTE IN OBEDIENCE TO MY WISHES.
> WHEN YOU HAVE CHECKED IT, AND MADE MINOR ADDITIONS, YOU
> CAN CIRCULATE IT IN AN APPROPRIATE MANNER. IT IS A PART OF
> THIS ENTIRE PROJECT WHICH I, YOUR GOD, HAVE DESIGNED, AND
> HAVE ENABLED YOU TO UNDERTAKE. (T:2396 #4)*

> *RECOGNISE AND REJOICE IN THE TRUTH ABOUT YOUR TOILS; I AM
> EFFECTING, THROUGH YOUR LIFE AND LABOURS, A TREMENDOUS
> WORK OF ENCOURAGEMENT-OF-FAITH FOR OTHER PEOPLE.
> (T:2396 #5)*

The Holy Spirit also urged me:-

> *NEVER   GROW   DESPONDENT,   WHETHER   HEARING   ABOUT
> DESERTIONS FROM THE FAITH, OR ABOUT MOCKERY AND
> OPPOSITION. YOU HAVE HEARD, ABOUT ANCIENT TIMES, THAT:
> "ALL THE PAGANS CONFORMED TO THE KING'S DECREE ... YET
> THERE WERE MANY ... WHO STOOD FIRM AND FOUND THE COURAGE
> TO REFUSE UNCLEAN FOOD." I ASSURE YOU, MY CHILD, THAT I SEE
> WHAT GREAT COURAGE IT TAKES, TODAY, FOR MY OWN PEOPLE TO
> DO MY WILL AND TO RESIST SINFUL INFLUENCES. THE HAPPIEST OF
> ALL AMONGST YOU - AS YOU HAVE LEARNED - ARE THOSE WHO RELY
> ON MY HELP AT EVERY MOMENT AND WHO ARE DETERMINED TO
> PLEASE ME. (T:2403 #1)*

> *REMIND MY PEOPLE THAT THE HAPPIEST, TOO, ARE THOSE WHO ARE
> NEVER AFRAID TO TURN BACK TO ME WHENEVER THEY HAVE*

*SINNED: TO CONFESS THEIR SINS AND TO BE RECONCILED.   I
DELIGHT IN REWARDING REPENTANT SOULS FOR EVERY ADMISSION
OF TRUTH, AND FOR EVERY ACT OF HUMILITY. (T:2403 #2)*

Encouraged to be joyful.

Almost every day, I was busy with numerous aspects of the work; then, in November, 1997,
when Volume Three of "Christ's Instructions" was ready - the "Red book" - Christ came to
my soul in Glory. He taught me:-

> **Don't be afraid to delight in our joint work. Truly, it has
> been inspired for the extra help and encouragement of My
> People. It should be a cause for joy that you have been able
> to co-operate with Me in producing another book in which
> the Father delights: a further volume of My 'teachings-in-
> prayer'. (T:2404 #1)**

> **Realise that you have good reason to be awed, as you recall
> My appearance to you in Glory, over thirty years ago, and
> as you consider the work which I have achieved in past
> years - through someone so ignorant and fearful. Only by
> My Love and grace have you produced Volume Three of
> My teachings; but you can praise Me for My help; and
> then you can enjoy reflecting upon some of the wonderful
> things which I've shown you. (T:2404 #2)**

Then Christ sent His Holy Spirit to show me again just why such reminders as these
'Teachings-in-prayer' are much-needed today. I was shown:-

> *YOU HAVE HEARD TODAY, MY CHILD, ABOUT THOSE PEOPLE OF
> ANCIENT TIMES WHO HAD "A FERVOUR FOR THE LAW". YOU HAVE
> HEARD HOW SOME WHO TOOK THEIR STAND ON THE COVENANT ...
> "WENT DOWN TO THE DESERT." I ASSURE YOU - AND OTHERS,
> THROUGH YOU - THAT I SEE HOW DIFFICULT IT IS FOR MY PEOPLE IN
> YOUR OWN ERA TO BE FAITHFUL TO THEIR COVENANT.   THOSE
> WHOM CHRIST HAS CALLED AND HAS INVITED TO ENTER HIS HOLY
> CHURCH, AND WHO HAVE FOLLOWED THAT CALL AND ENTERED,
> AND WHO HAVE TRIED TO REMAIN FAITHFUL TO HIS TEACHINGS,
> TODAY, ARE THOSE WHO HAVE BEEN "DOWN TO THE DESERT:" AS
> IF TO A WASTE-LAND OF MISUNDERSTANDING AND ISOLATION, AND
> EVEN OF PERSECUTION FROM MANY CONTEMPORARIES. (T:2406
> #1)*

To share in Christ's Divinity.

It was on the very day that I received that teaching - on 20th November 1997 - that Christ drew me into the heights of the transforming union, as He told me soon afterwards, and so answered my prayer that He would keep me close to Him, and that He would let me 'share His Divinity' - which is the prayer of our priest during the Holy Mass.

There's no end to the joys which are given, in life with God. Further teachings followed, one after another, minor and major - on the usual sorts of subjects. But when two months had gone by, and I had grown bolder in prayer, I asked Christ once more, during the Mass, to let me share His Divinity - just as He has come to share our humanity, as our priest says before the Consecration.

Christ lavishly rewarded me for such a child-like and trusting request. I remember that I was sitting quietly in front of the Lady Chapel, when the Mass had ended. I prayed fervent prayers; then it was as though Christ led me, in prayer, towards a state and a moment when no aspect of my being lay 'outside' the bliss and grace in which He immersed me; and at the same time, He showed me (in a continuation of T:2406):-

> **Understand My purpose: which is to share My Divinity with you not just for a moment in prayer, but eternally. Yet I am here: true man, and your Redeemer: helping you to understand something more about My 'work'. In this blessed hour, I am sharing My Divinity with you, whom I have chosen. I am enfolding you in grace, holding you within My Divine nature, pouring My Divine and holy Bliss and Glory upon your soul with such lavish generosity that not only your soul but your body too is wholly suffused with My grace - and therefore is changed. (T:2406 #2)**

> **Treasure this union, through which I, your Incarnate God, am leading you in prayer into the life and heart of the Godhead, and so into Divine Love, and Bliss and Work. (T:2406 #3)**

Then Christ taught me how it is that our union with Him in prayer can be the prelude to our Eternal Union with Him in Heaven. He explained to me:-

> **Consider the manner in which you are drawn towards the Father and towards Eternal fulfilment. You know that it was at My Ascension to Heaven, some time after My death and Resurrection, that I brought humanity - by My human nature - into the life and heart of the Godhead; and you know that it is by your union with Me Who have ascended, thus, that you can hope to 'enter' the Godhead: the Holy Trinity: for all Eternity. You can understand, at last, that you have been making a type of 'ascension' to Glory, whenever I have lifted you to My heart, in prayer; and so you can understand, also, that it will be by what we can call an 'ascension' of souls to Glory, after death, and then by a bodily 'ascension' of yourselves at the Resurrection, that faithful people - albeit frail human beings - can be**

'entwined' with Us: can share the Life of Three Divine Persons: the Life of the One and only God, in the joy and beauty of Heaven. Yet this cannot happen to anyone who has not been purified and transformed, whether through prayer and penance - and Divine action - in earthly life, or by purifications after death. (T:2406 #4)

Never forget how tremendous is My Love for you all. Only from Love do I act so generously towards you all. Remain ever-grateful: giving constant praise and thanks that through our union and My generosity, humanity is 'ennobled' - found worthy - to share the active and pure Divine Life of the Holy Trinity. (T:2406 #5)

Don't imagine that the Godhead has in some way been changed, because of My Incarnation or My union with faithful people. It is through My invitation, and at their consent, that human beings can be changed and ennobled in the way which I have been describing; yet I - in My Divine nature - have not been changed; and this is true of Me even though humanity has entered, through My human nature, into the Godhead; and it is true even though, before My Incarnation, death, Resurrection and Ascension, humanity had never entered into the heart of the Holy Trinity. (T:2406 #6)

Suffused by grace and peace.

On the following day, Christ assured me, through the Light and the words of His Holy Spirit (in T:2407):-

ACCEPT WITH DELIGHT AND THANKSGIVING THE KNOWLEDGE OF THE CHANGES WHICH I HAVE ALREADY WORKED WITHIN YOUR LIFE AND YOUR SOUL. I ASSURE YOU, MY CHILD, THAT "I transformed you yesterday"; AND MY WORK IS EFFECTIVE. YOU WERE TRULY CHANGED IN THAT 'SUFFUSION' OF GRACE AND PEACE, WHICH WAS A GIFT FROM YOUR DIVINE SAVIOUR, BY MY POWER, AND THROUGH THE FATHER'S WILL. I WAS POWERFULLY AT WORK IN YOU BECAUSE YOU ALWAYS TRY TO PLEASE ME, BECAUSE YOU GAVE YOUR CONSENT TO MY ACTION, AND BECAUSE YOU WERE WILLING TO SURRENDER TO THE WILL OF YOUR CREATOR, NO MATTER WHAT THE COST. (T:2407 #4)

RECOGNISE MY WORK. TRULY, IT IS I, THE HOLY SPIRIT, WHO HAVE BEEN VIGOROUSLY AT WORK WITHIN YOUR LIFE AND SOUL. THE STATE WHICH YOU HAVE ENTERED, BY MY GOODNESS AND YOUR CO-OPERATION, IS THE TRANSFORMING UNION IN ALL ITS FULLNESS. (T:2407 #5)

REJOICE; BE GLAD. YOU ARE NEITHER MISTAKEN NOR DECEIVED ABOUT THE KNOWLEDGE WHICH IS YOURS THROUGH MY WORK IN YOUR LIFE AND THROUGH PRAYER. IT IS I WHO AM AT WORK IN YOUR SOUL; AND IT IS I WHO EVEN SHOW YOU IN WHAT WAYS I AM AT WORK: AND FOR WHAT REASONS; SUCH IS THE EXTENT OF MY GRACIOUSNESS AND LOVE. (T:2407 #6)

The work of the Holy Spirit.

Very soon afterwards - on 27th November, 1997 - when I begged that same Holy Spirit for further understanding, and said how great was my longing to understand Him better, I asked: "Who are You!" And then He taught me, most generously, and increased my hope and confidence. He explained to me:-

LISTEN, DEAR CHILD: I AM YOUR LORD AND GOD: THE HOLY SPIRIT: LOVE HIMSELF, NOW POWERFULLY AT WORK IN YOUR SOUL, AT YOUR CONSENT. TRULY: YOU CAN KNOW, OF ME, THAT "I am He Who makes you acceptable to the Father." (T:2411 #1)

THINK CAREFULLY ABOUT WHAT I AM REVEALING TO YOU, THROUGH MY ANSWER TO YOUR QUESTION: A QUESTION WHICH SPRANG FROM A FERVENT LOVE FOR ME, AND NOT FROM VAIN CURIOSITY. I REVEALED MY CHARITY BY SPEAKING TO YOU, MY CHILD, IN PRAYER. I REVEALED MY DIVINE NATURE, AS I EXPLAINED TO YOU THAT MY LOVE IS ACTIVE. I REVEALED MY PURPOSE, BY GUIDING YOU MORE SURELY TOWARDS PERFECTION: WHICH I CAN ACHIEVE "IN" YOU, AT YOUR CONSENT; AND BY YOUR PERFECTION - WHEN IT IS EVENTUALLY REACHED - YOU CAN FULFIL MY PURPOSE: WHICH IS TO GIVE GLORY AND DELIGHT TO THE FATHER. TRULY: I HAVE TAKEN CEASELESS CARE OF YOU DURING THE WHOLE OF YOUR SPIRITUAL JOURNEY. (T:2411 #2)

Towards the Father.

As I look at this story of the spiritual journey towards the 'transforming union', with the many stages along the path, I can see just how steadily and wonderfully Christ has been guiding me towards a knowledge of the Love of God the Father; and the description of God's Love which I've placed later in this chapter is important because it's only at this 'late' stage of my spiritual journey that I've been taught in prayer by God the Father, and at great length, in a way which has profoundly moved me; and Our Lord now wants me to describe some of the more recent stages through which He has led me as He has brought me to what I dare to call a state of friendship with the Father.

As most of us Christians perhaps know, but don't yet fully understand, Our Saviour called Himself "THE GATE" (Jn 10:7) as well as "THE WAY" (Jn 14:6); and He was referring to the fact that only through Him can we enter the Heart of the Godhead - to 'find' the Father -

whether in a certain manner in prayer, or eternally, after death..

'Eden'.

Growing closer to the Father in prayer has been a little like climbing an earthly mountain, in the sense that we're frequently tempted to think that the summit is in sight, when there are still many peaks ahead; yet He has led me to peak after peak: to heights which I didn't even know existed, until the day when I reached my own 'Eden', as I said earlier, where I live with Him like a happy child, in joy and simplicity. And what a miracle of grace this is: for someone as naturally untrusting, anxious, and impatient as myself.

Present joys

How can I find the words to describe my gratitude to God for His gifts, which have left me almost weeping for joy at His tenderness, yet almost weeping for sorrow that there's so much ingratitude towards Him, or irreverence, or disbelief?

The peace in which He has immersed my soul is a reason for unending gratitude. This doesn't mean that I'm never swept by brief storms of conscience, or that I'm never battered by temptations. Every few months it's as if I find myself at the centre of a spiritual whirl-wind, for several hours; and so I make frequent and fervent acts of faith in God's love for me, and in His power to hold me firm until the storm blows over; and then I'm at peace again, as if cocooned in His Love; and it seems to me that He allows these episodes as brief reminders that it's only through His strength and kindness that I generally manage to cope from day to day in such spiritual delight.

Just in case anyone imagines that this state of peace and joy might be a consequence of having every natural longing fulfilled, or every whim indulged - or is a sort of euphoria which some people say is experienced in chronic illness - I can only say that I know in my heart that it stems from union with God in prayer and from acceptance of His Will in daily life; but it's only by His grace that I've come to love His Will; and, without Him, that daily life would provoke in myself not euphoria but despair. I'm such a pessimistic creature, left to myself; and if it weren't for God's goodness I'd be lost in self-pity and grief at having such constant pain and lack of energy - and so much work still to do, despite all the good people and good things which surround me in my present circumstances.

But that's enough about difficulties. What I want to 'boast' about, in this present way of life, is Christ's Love and Christ's tender friendship. It's nothing but the plain truth when I say that everything I've ever really wanted is being thoroughly fulfilled in this profound "life-in-Christ". I've been given love, joy and friendship 'in' Christ. I've been given utterly fulfilling work to do: whether the work of my hands or of my mind: or the 'work' of the prayer of contemplation - or the work of suffering, in union with Christ. But I don't do this alone.

Christ has given me tremendous helps, amidst a loving family, loving priests and other companions: with a priest amongst my own children; and only through Christ have I come to know and relish the Love and wisdom of the Father Who is the Source of all good.

Facing the door of Heaven.

The Father's goodness astounds me, daily. Every experience of receiving teachings in prayer is now wholly delightful; and the state of friendship with the Father in which I live - this heart-warming and profound participation in the Life of the Holy Trinity - is so wonderful and fulfilling that I've only to turn my heart and thoughts towards the Father in Heaven, or to His Son, or to the Holy Spirit, to receive another 'taste' of Heaven's Bliss.

Never could I have believed, years ago, that I could eventually be bubbling with joy at almost every moment, and not because I've done anything wonderful but through having come to believe with all my heart that I am profoundly loved by God. That's why I'm usually light-hearted. That's why I turn to Christ and to Our Lady in every need. That is why I rely on Divine help for every new piece of work, and every new problem; and that's why I'm rarely perplexed about what to do next. I ask, and it is shown. God's goodness is indescribable.

God is so good that He has changed my life entirely. I'm not ashamed to say that every prayer I pray leads to bliss. I've only to enter the church, and to begin to pray - whether by greeting the holy Angels who are gathered there, by honouring Christ's Mother Mary at the Lady Chapel, or by adoring and thanking Christ Who is Really Present in the Blessed Sacrament - to find that my heart, mind and soul are almost overpowered by God's Love and Glory. I face the 'Door of Heaven', it seems, in what used to be the darkness of prayer; and yet I now always find that door 'open', as God's Light shines out towards me.

How can I write this? Yet it's true. I can't pass the church without yearning to go in - although Christ greets me in almost the same way at home; and it's no exaggeration to say that although I'm a weak person who's tempted to worry about illness or danger, I'm so longing to see God that I long for Heaven. Everything He does is good; and everything good in my life is His doing. He's taught me that it's only been done because of my perpetual prayer of mixed praise and repentance; yet there's No-one like Him, and I could weep for gratitude. He's so kind, beautiful and holy; and I wish everyone could know it.

Diverse but related subject.

It seems astonishing to me that Christ has continued to teach me about the truths of the Catholic Faith: teachings which in recent times have been very difficult for me to 'translate' into words, yet which have been thrilling to understand to a greater degree. They've included such diverse but related subjects as the Immaculate Conception, the Atonement, and the Holy Sacrifice of the Mass, and also the work of Contemplation; and it astonishes me how Christ has enabled me not only to understand more about these subjects but also to describe such things for other people. But the reason I'm saying all this is because I'm overwhelmed with gratitude; and so of course I want to share my good news; and I know I can do so by obeying the Father and by describing how an astonishing friendship with Him is now the fulfilment of my journey.

Only today - October 15th, 1998 - I told Christ once again how I'm yearning to make Him known to other people; and straightaway He showed me that although He understands my difficulties, the quicker I finish this book, then the quicker I'll be able to explain to people about His goodness. It's to be through this very book, which I was so bashful about writing, that many people will be given hope, comfort and encouragement about things to do with His Love, and faith, and about His Church.

God's Love for mankind.

Right up to the present day, Christ has continued to teach me, in prayer; and my heart aches with joy as I ponder each new teaching. More and more, I've understood what Saint John meant when he wrote "GOD IS LOVE" (1 Jn 4:8); and I long to help other people to realise that God's Love for us isn't something luke-warm, conditional, or grudging, but is a fiery and personal delight in each one of us, with a longing-to-give joy.

In the past two years, I've begun to see something else: to see the significance of the fact that so many of the 'teachings' - which I'd already learned would one day be influential - are more about God's nature and God's Love for us than about human nature or human behaviour. Furthermore, there are many, many teachings about the Holy Mass - at which we are present to the most striking demonstration of God's Love for mankind - and also about prayer, through which we can be held in intimate contact with that Love: whether or not we 'feel' it. It's faith that tells us that we're held in God's care; and in an age when faith is lacking, there is little love for the Person of Christ, and so there's less prayer, less penance, less reverence before holy things and persons and places; and also fewer vocations: though not because Christ has stopped calling men to the religious life, but because young persons made cynical or distracted in an age of unbelief and irreverence don't hear the call - or refuse to respond to it; and this is why Christ has been giving me so many reminders - for other people - about Divine Love, and about holiness, and prayer.

Since Christ yearns to encourage members of His Church towards greater love for Him, and to more fervent adoration and greater reverence, He is doing so through His 'teachings-in-prayer' by allowing an apparent 'imbalance' to arise in the subject matter of these teachings. There's such a lot about prayer and penance, and about Heaven and Hell; and so of course some readers might ask why there are comparatively few teachings about what's generally known as "loving your neighbour," by which some people mean, supremely, giving practical help to the needy: of giving "BREAD TO THE HUNGRY" (Ezk 18:7) and nursing the sick.

About Salvation.

If I speak first, about love for our neighbour, we're probably all aware that many Christians today - children as well as adults - are bold in their declarations about doing our duty towards needy and suffering people, or, rather, about showing our love for the needy; and it's a wonderful thing that we're encouraged to imitate Christ, Who in His earthly life was deeply moved by the sufferings of those around Him, and was so tender and helpful in His dealings with the sick and the bereaved, for example. We're not loving God properly if we're not, for His sake, loving every neighbour, since each is God's 'child' and is thus to be seen as a brother or sister. But Christ has made it plain to me, in these 'teachings', that the truest love for other people is based upon a clear knowledge of Who God is, and what His wishes are for mankind. Without such knowledge, we can't know how to love people in the best way: best for them - for bodies and souls, and for their Eternal welfare.

Blind affection or sentimentality won't provide a solid foundation for works of true charity, though they can provide a place in which to start 'digging'; but if we know about Eternal Life, through Christ, we can see that the greatest love for our neighbour is shown by our desire to see each person eternally happy with God: and so we'll make efforts to help them to achieve Salvation, efforts at least as vigorous as those by which we try to ease their earthly sufferings. I don't mean that we'll always be lecturing people about being good - although we must speak out bravely against evil - but that we'll be fervent in prayer for them as well as in practical help.

The first Commandment.

Now that I've been instructed for many years in prayer, it seems to me that the teachings are primarily about important aspects of our relationships with God rather than with one another.

It seems to me that Christ's great longing is to give people of our era, and beyond, a vigorous reminder of the importance of the First Commandment by which we're urged to "LOVE THE LORD YOUR GOD" (Mt 22:37) and to put Him first. How many of "the faithful" who recommend that we be heavily involved in practical works of charity are asserting with equal vigour and confidence that God is to be loved and honoured above all things and people and is to be greeted and worshipped daily, with great reverence, by us, His children, who are privileged to be able to call Him "Father"? How many of His People assert that He is to be obeyed in everything: in the ways in which He has plainly revealed to us through Christ and His Apostles, and has continued to make plain to us through the teaching of His Church, and through the Holy Scriptures and the Sacred Tradition? It's because there are fewer persons urging the Faithful towards reverent worship of God than are urging the Faithful towards practical charity that Christ has planned my work, and has trained me to do it.

Obedience to God's Will.

It is Christ Himself Who, through my inadequate work, is urging His People to be fervent in prayer, and to be obedient to His Will in everyday life - out of love for Him Who is Wisdom and Goodness. This is how we can glorify Him, and also bring down immense blessings upon our own souls: blessings and graces which will enable us to relish and to do His Will, and which will also prepare us for Heaven. Then, if we spend our lives in God's service, relying on Him and His strength in everything, and trying to follow where He leads us, we'll love our neighbour from the best of motives, and in the best possible way: in the way in which God wishes, when and where He wishes, as we're prompted and guided by His Holy Spirit in the practice of true charity.

Since it's part of Christ's plan to offer, through this work, more reminders of matters to do with worship and adoration than of ways in which to serve our neighbour, it's also been a part of His plan that these teachings are given through the daily life of an ordinary housewife, or home-maker. It's true that I'm an artist, as well; but my year-by-year and willingly-accepted work has primarily entailed the care of other people: literally the feeding and clothing of them, with care of the sick; and it's precisely because that sort of practical help is 'routine' in a housewife's life, even if done very poorly, that Christ has seldom instructed me on the need to give such care, but, rather, has concentrated on spiritual matters.

This doesn't mean that I haven't needed such instruction; we all know that in practical care there's always a need for growth in charity, as well in other virtues; but it does mean that although during my prayers, and in between household tasks, I've been taught a great deal by Christ about the true spiritual foundation of the charity which He wants to see us practice towards everyone, I've been taught even more about the love which He wants us to offer directly to God our Father. For example, Christ has shown me numerous ways by which we can express our sorrow-for-sin, through penance and reparation, and can express our love for God through reverent worship: supremely through the offering of the Holy Sacrifice of the Mass in union with Christ.

Teachings about spiritual matters.

It's been by Christ's own choice - and through His desire that I remind other people about the importance of a sincere love for God and a longing for holiness - that I've been taught by Him for so many years: during prayer, and occasionally during meditation, and only rarely when I'm working at my normal duties. The significance of the time at which He teaches me is that - by His choice - He usually teaches me about a particular subject when I'm at least obliquely 'involved' in it - for example, when I'm praying about a certain problem, or repenting of a certain attitude; and He has taught me far more lavishly about purely "spiritual" things than about earthly.

By His Will, Christ almost always teaches me when my soul is 'facing' Him in true prayer in what I can only call a God-giving moment of undistracted attention combined with contrition or gratitude, or praise, or trust in His power to give good gifts to His children; and so - because this is His Will - there are more teachings in these volumes about our need of greater contrition and greater gratitude, for example, than about our duty to go out to help our neighbour; and this is not accidental. It is Willed and brought about by Christ, because although He wants to feed and comfort His People - through our kind actions - in ways which help sick and tired bodies, He wants to issue a special reminder in our time that He can also help and change damaged souls through us.

Christ can work through us to soothe hearts by hope, to feed minds with Truth, and to purify souls through Reconciliation; and so, through our prayers and sacrifices, He can make 'whole' persons who are ready for 'real Life' with Him: ready to enjoy His beauty and perfection, forever.

Friendship with God.

Christ is so generous and tender; so how could I remain unchanged by demonstrations of His love? It's because I want to share my joy in what He has shown me that I must end this book by trying to describe what it's like to know and to converse with the Three Divine Persons, in a perpetual friendship which vivifies the soul, endures through every difficulty, and transforms every aspect of life; such are the marvels I've enjoyed for many months, this year.

As you can gather, it's only because the Father has invited me to describe what He Himself has called "*The end of the journey*" that I've attempted some writing which might be seen as impertinent as well as inadequate; and only through Christ's goodness have I been brought to live and pray as I do now. It's true that we've been indwelt by the Three Divine Persons from the moment of our Baptism; yet I've been shown through personal experience and by faith that an intimate friendship with the Three is achieved, and understood to a limited degree, and also 'relished', only if someone has been willing to love, serve and obey Christ with both fervour and sincerity, and has been willing to accept His purifications. These are utterly necessary before a sinful creature can endure as well as enjoy what I can only call a special proximity to the Three Divine Persons Who are Infinitely pure, perfect, majestic and Holy - although Infinitely tender and loving. But I can also say from experience that the more lavishly God reveals His Glory and beauty to a contrite soul, the more clearly does that soul see the need for further purification, and the more gladly does he step forward, willing to be changed.

The joys which are given in the heights of prayer are greater than anyone can imagine; and a loving union with the Three Divine Persons Who bestow those joys makes every past agony seem worthwhile.

---

20 PARTICIPATION
(1998)

THREE DIVINE PERSONS. LIGHT AND LOVE AND LIFE.

A wonderful state of friendship.

No-one can live daily in the company of the Three Divine Persons - as if at Their 'heart', as They dwell in the unity of the Godhead - who has been unwilling to be prepared and purified according to Their supremely wise and far-seeing plan. But God is so good that anyone who responds to the Divine invitation can achieve this magnificent friendship: of a creature with his or her God; and it's from within that state of astonishing peace and fulfilment and bliss that I now urge other people to persevere in love and in prayer, so that they, too, can experience the wonderful things which God has lavished upon me, some of which He wants me to mention in the next few pages.

God Himself has told me that this book can be seen as my own "MAGNIFICAT" (Lk 1:46), written in praise and thanksgiving to Him after a long and arduous spiritual journey. So I'll write no more about my failings, but only about His kindness. It's no use my being bashful, anymore, about God's goodness towards me, if I want to convince anyone about the sweetness of His friendship; rather, I'm willing to say that for the last year or two the manner of receiving each teaching in prayer has been wholly delightful. The state of friendship with the Father in which I now live is so wonderful and fulfilling that I've only to turn my heart and thoughts towards Him in Heaven to receive His Bliss. Every blissful prayer increases my confidence in His Love; and every new growth in confidence causes me to pray with a greater hope of being heard and answered; and, indeed, His answers have amazed me. Some have been so sweet and loving that it almost breaks my heart to think of them and makes me yearn to bring other people towards Him; and that's why I'm going to try to describe in more detail what I've learned from God about Himself. I'm going to tell what I've learned from the Holy Trinity about the Three Divine Persons, and about the joys of a loving union in prayer and in daily life with this Source of Joy Who is at the same time Father, Word and Spirit.

Three Persons yet One God.

In order to speak accurately about God, I must begin again at the beginning. I mean that the Church has taught us through the Apostles and their successors that God is 'Being' Itself: Three Persons in One God, that is, in One Divine Being, Whom we adore because He created us and because He is worthy of all possible praise, since He is Good.

What 'dry bones' are these facts, some people would say. Yet how staggering is the meaning, or rather, how staggering is the thought of God's nature, His attributes and His actions. But to continue: I can say that we've all learned from the Church - which puts God's Revelation into words for us, through her decrees and catechisms and Councils - that the Three Divine Persons are equal in Majesty. Furthermore, the Father possesses nothing that the Son does not have; the Son possesses all that the Spirit has: yet the Father is not the Son, the Son is not the Father, the Spirit is not the Son, and so on; and yet the Divine Persons are equal. Each possess the same attributes as the others; and, in a way beyond our understanding, the Three Persons are One Lord, with no beginning and no end.

I'm aware that I've received these beliefs or 'concepts' through the Church, although they've been confirmed by what I've learned in prayer. I say this because some of the above phrases are quoted from memory, for example: 'the Father is not the Son' - perhaps a phrase from the Athanasian Creed; I haven't had time to check; but I know that this is certainly our true teaching: from God, through His Church.

Many details about our life within the Most Holy Trinity are what we have learned through God's Revelation of Himself in Jesus Christ, knowledge now handed down to us through Christ's living, teaching Church; and what I've noticed in prayer only confirms something else that the Church already teaches us: something we find 'illustrated' in our liturgy; I meant that God Wills us to attribute certain acts and certain virtues to certain Persons of the Most Holy Trinity. This is what was done by Jesus Himself on earth.

So we speak of the Father creating us, of the Son redeeming us, and of the Spirit sanctifying us: to give a brief example of the language I want to consider; and the Church urges us to speak in this way, even though God the Father didn't create us without the Son, the Spirit helped to redeem us, and so on. An act by each Divine Person is an act of the Most Holy Trinity. God 'has no parts or passions' as our old catechism said. Someone who speaks about Father, Son, and Holy Spirit, however, as though the distinctions we make between the Divine Persons are unimportant, won't relish the wonderful Life of the Holy Trinity and so won't yearn wholeheartedly either to know or to enter the Godhead; and I believe it's because God wants to encourage a greater interest in His inner life - and so to cause willing souls to turn to Him in fervent prayer - that I've been shown so much about the Three Persons, in prayer, and have been encouraged to notice the different 'approach' that Each One has adopted towards me - adopted as a way of teaching me about the Godhead in which Each of the Three Persons is distinct whilst sharing the same nature.

Different approaches.

In a moment, I'll try to share what I've experienced in prayer: to describe what I've experienced as different approaches from the Three Divine Persons, and also to show how God Himself has encouraged me to attribute certain Divine actions and 'attitudes' either to Father, Son or Holy Spirit, although they are co-equal, and are one Lord. This is the foundation of my opposition to certain changes put forward by 'extreme' Christian feminists, who call for an end to 'patriarchy' and who dislike naming God our Creator as "Father"; but, more importantly, it is a reason for increased gratitude to God Who is so loving that He delights in sharing with us the riches of His own inner life and His own ways of acting; and since I can say with gratitude and confidence that this is what He's done for me, I'm writing these pages from personal experience. Nothing I'm writing is fundamentally new, but is simply a description of the different approaches made to the soul in prayer by the Three Divine Persons of the Most Holy Trinity; and I dare to write about "different approaches" even though each Divine Person possesses the Divine Nature and All are equal in perfection, in majesty and in every good property. I dare, only because none of the three 'approaches' was seen by me as being against Truth, as I know it.

Each 'approach' has been experienced with overwhelming intensity in contemplative prayer, or, rather, in that state of contemplative prayer where the soul can act, think, speak and reason. All is silence and 'unknowing' in other 'stages'.

Adoration and submission.

As I shall soon describe, the difference I've noticed between the Divine Persons lies in what I've experienced of Them in states of prayer Willed and given by God; and my knowledge of God, it can be seen, is a gift to me from God, given because He has trained me to be obedient and therefore to worship Him just as devout persons in every century since Christ have worshipped Him: by calling Him "Father" and by striving to obey His wishes. Furthermore, I haven't been ashamed to bow towards the floor before Him in adoration and submission, as well as wonder and love; and He has stooped down to me and has lifted me up, in order to teach me about Himself; and that's why I can share my delight in Him through books, pictures and conversations.

Here I must insist that this submissive awe is what is due to God; and we ought to offer it gladly. Even when someone has been lifted into the Father's friendship through a deep, tender and intimate friendship with His Son, Jesus Christ, Who greets and consoles that soul in Holy Communion, that fortunate soul mustn't think of saying: "I'm a baptised child of God, redeemed and cherished, and therefore I don't need to bow down low before Him, like a servant." We needn't always be bowing or kneeling. When it's appropriate, we can sit to pray - or kneel, or walk, or lie in bed, if we're unwell. But although we're praying to a most tender Father, Who is 'mad' with love for us, we're always right to remember and to honour His Divinity in particular ways.

No matter how close we are to God, no matter how much loved, nor how frequently we're drawn into blissful prayer, we remain always mere creatures before our Divine Creator, for as long as we're on this earth. Not until Heaven will we "BE LIKE HIM" (1 Jn 3:2). Then, at last, though our worship of Him will continue and will give us unending joy, all fear will have been banished. We shall be utterly changed, joyful and confident in His presence; yet until that time, we must keep in mind our utter indebtedness to Christ. Only through Him has our confident prayer been made possible, and our peace-of-soul, and our hope of Heaven.

"Father," not "Mother".

[There's a need for a brief digression here, perhaps, to suggest that it's God's Will - expressed through Scripture and Tradition - that we follow Jesus' advice and say to God:

"Our Father" - not "Mother" - when we pray for help and salvation. Surely there's no need for us to address God differently; and I only say this so forcefully because it's what I've had confirmed through God's teachings-in-prayer; and this will become evident during the next dozen pages - although it's a comparatively minor matter, when set beside the greatest problem today, in worship, which is not modes of address but pride and irreverence.]

A description of the Three Persons.

Now that I'm about to describe what I know of the Three Divine Persons - One God - I'm not afraid to say quite boldly that Christ my God, Who gave me His Divine Life in Baptism and to Whom I've given my loyalty, has drawn me into His friendship. He has led me to experience His teaching and attributes, to some small degree, during prayer; and as I've explained, Christ has drawn me into almost unceasing intimacy with Him, from our union in 1985. Such intimacy wasn't possible earlier, before various great purifications had been completed, both passive and active, and interior and exterior. It has only been through my baptism and the faith of my parents that I learned such a lot about truth, faith, God and prayer, and so - assisted by reason and observation - was led to a firm belief in the existence of a Creator/Designer-God; and only through prayer 'in' and through Jesus Christ did I grow in the knowledge of God, that is, grow in a real friendship, though it was once marred, as I said, by insecurity and sin to a degree that is only a memory to me now, through His grace; and yet now I can say with immense joy, and utter conviction, that Christ my God has allowed me to experience His Love and friendship more and more fully in prayer; and I can say from experience that His personal tenderness and care are astonishing, that is, astonishing to someone who, earlier, didn't really understand the meaning of the words "GOD IS LOVE" (1 Jn 4:16). Despite the fact that I'm not worthy of such a love I've found that Christ is ablaze with Love, especially in Holy Communion, although at other times as well.

Christ's tenderness.

Anyone who perseveres through several volumes of 'teachings' and who believes in them will have a glimpse of the Christ I know - the only Christ - Who is more gentle and loving than I once thought possible. There's no-one like Him. As He Himself has explained to me (in T:2064) He is the Source of every sort of consolation for those who put their trust in Him. Whether we're fearful, lonely, sinful and repentant, or weak, old, sick, or broken-hearted - or dumb, blind or dying - we can find peace in Him, if we'll trust Him. There's no embrace sweeter than His. There's no greater or kinder friend or counsellor, or Priest, or helper, or teacher, companion or hero. He knows our every thought and hope and fear; and He longs to draw us through the difficulties of earthly life towards the Bliss of Heaven; but He can't do so unless we put our trust in Him and give our consent: such is His respect for our dignity: for our free-will.

But Christ isn't solely our Priest and Redeemer; He's a poet, and a teller of stories. He's the loving Friend Who brings gifts on special occasions, Who remembers every hurt I've ever suffered and every word of thanks I've offered to Him for good things. It's He Who has bent over me, gently, to stroke my head and to comfort me as I've endured necessary trials in order to do this work. It's He Who knelt at my feet, one extraordinary day, to show me how much

He sympathises with me in every difficulty, and would wash my feet, He said, just as He washed the feet of His Apostles, if it would make my journey to Heaven any easier (T:2243B). Perhaps you can see, now, how He breaks my heart by His tenderness; and that's why I can't bear to refuse any of His requests, even when He asks me to do difficult things - for the sake of the work - which will leave me looking foolish or very much alone.

Christ Our Lord.

One night I was asked by a member of my family: "What's He like? What does He look like? Do you see Our Lord every day?" It seemed right to answer; and, indeed, on the following morning at Mass, Christ taught me that in speaking out about Him with such fervour, and with the knowledge gained through our firm friendship, I'd been fulfilling His plan for me, which is that I act as a living witness to Him and to His Love.

Christ's appearance to me.

This is more-or-less what I said about Christ. I exclaimed, joyfully, that there's no-one like Him, and that He breaks my heart with His kindness. I said: "He's devastatingly attractive, in that He's so loving and kind and encouraging. He's very strict, whom He needs to be, but even that's for my good, if I've been selfish." Then I spoke about His attitude towards me.

"He's always the same, in the sense that He's reliable: never moody, though I do see different aspects of Him; I mean that He's very funny, when He teases me - but gently - or when He makes a play on words, to amuse and to console me; yet He's so tender, at times, that I'm overwhelmed just to remember the times when He's stroked my head, to comfort me after awful difficulties, or when He's spoken about His gratitude for little sacrifices I've made.

I 'see' Him everyday in one sense, though not always by spiritual 'sight' - but usually by what's called an "intellectual vision" when He comes to the altar after the Consecration, and then comes to me in Holy Communion; and I experience His presence in this way at home as well, from time to time. But I also see Him in the sense of a vision with an image - a real Person, though seen with the soul's eyes and not by my bodily sight. This happens every few days, but with extra occasions such as special feast-days, or else the times when He suddenly appears to me to speak to me and to explain something, as a reward for a special effort on my part.

Unexpected visits.

To see Christ in this way is an immense privilege. I never know in advance whether I'll see Him or not. He's been training me, for many years, to pray to Him all day and every day with a sincere, contrite and trusting heart, without ever thinking about whether He'll teach me, appear to me, speak to me, or give me new tasks to undertake. He's made it plain that I'm not to waste time speculating about His gifts, but should simply accept them joyfully when He gives them to me, and continue to pray in the usual ways when there seem to be no 'special' spiritual gifts or phenomena to be noticed; and by this training He has brought me to love Him more than any of His gifts - though it's true to say, today, that I only have to look in His direction, in church, to be swamped by His loving and consoling attention: such is the degree of friendship to which He's drawn me in recent months.

But to attempt to describe Him a little better, I need to say where I see Him: I mean, to explain in what ways He chooses to show that He's close to me.

Very close to me.

On very special occasions when, for example, Christ wants to comfort or reward me after a particular event, He usually stands besides me: at my right side; and He talks to me as any friend talks to another, as He leans forward over my chair, since I'm usually sitting in church nowadays, due to increased weakness. But on most of the occasions when I've seen Him clearly - though almost dazzled, as I said, at the sight of His glory, and sometimes at His Mother's radiance too - I've seen Him in front of me. He usually stands one or two metres away, and speaks as anyone speaks to a close friend; and each time I'm overwhelmed with joy to be there.

This sort of appearance is always unexpected in the sense that I haven't known in advance that at this particular Mass, rather than at another, I shall have this immense joy. Such meetings as this, several years ago, were so sudden and so startling for me that Christ kept them mercifully brief, until I'd grown stronger, and had also become less ashamed and bashful in His Presence; but they are now - although unexpected - neither so startling nor so brief. Christ has spoken to me on so many of His major feast-days that I can't honestly say I'm surprised when He chooses to do so again, although I'm immensely awed and grateful, still; and since He's made me spiritually stronger, I find that I can now converse with Him and enjoy His evident company without being stricken with remorse, or made speechless, or even made oblivious to my surroundings, as in earlier times. But every time, I'm so overjoyed that my heart aches, afterwards, when I think of His goodness.

Christ's characteristics.

It's not possible for me to describe each of Christ's features in great detail, because although He hasn't hidden Himself from me, His face is so dazzling and so radiantly beautiful, that until very recently my soul's eyes have been half-blinded, so to speak, by the Light. But it's true to say that He's a real person: a real man, a few inches taller than His Mother - as I know, since I've been privileged to see them together on a number of occasions. He has long wavy hair, and always wears a long white robe, similar to an alb. He has a wonderful smile; and He's very expressive in His movements. He doesn't stand still like a statue but uses His arms to explain things to me, or His hands to point or to demonstrate, or to touch my head, as I said, or to gesture to different parts of the church or to certain persons - as you can see if you look at the watercolour paintings I've done.

He's so kind and so wise that my heart lurches, sometimes, just to think about Him; so it doesn't surprise me to read that people rushed around the lake, in Galilee, for the chance to be with Him for a bit longer. Those who saw what He was like, and who loved Him, must have been besotted with Him. He has that effect on you, if you can bear to go close enough to Him to feel His gaze. I mean that when He looks at you, He sees straight to your heart; and so you sometimes feel as though you can't bear it but must run away to hide for shame, or to grow angry at knowing your true self to have been 'found out'; or else you must kneel and confess your sins to Him, for the joy of hearing Him forgive you and comfort you; and that's when you find that you'll do anything to be worthy of Him, even giving up sin, and trying to be like Him: holy, gentle and child-like ; and yet He's immensely wise and mature at the same time.

It seems important to say that He's very manly, in the sense of seeming to be strong, brave, and authoritative in a manly sort of way - whilst still being tender and gentle. He makes you feel as though He can cope with any problem. You know that He can provide wisdom, truth and protection - all things which a woman can also provide, yet He does so in a manly sort of way; and this is no accident. It's because of His very manliness - His heroic and authoritative stature which is wholly suffused with kindliness - that He can provide men with a certain sort of friendship - a sort desired and planned by Him, our Incarnate God; and He can provide women too, and children, with just the sort of friendship by which He can help and encourage them best.

Things which most delight Christ.

Just for the sake of adding a few more words about what Christ is 'like' when I meet Him, I suppose I can't fail to show Him out more clearly if I try to describe His reactions, if I can use that word, to the different sorts of prayers and requests I make before Him. I mean that it's become plain, after hundreds of conversations with Him, and after thousands of confessions to Him of my sins and weaknesses, that He is made even more joyful by some things than by others.

This doesn't mean that He's not perpetually and forever joyful in Heaven, as the Divine Son of God; but it means that as the Incarnate Son Who is fully human as well as Divine, He expresses more delight in meeting one sort of approach than another - just as He did when on earth, towards those who came to Him, as recorded in the Gospels. So I've discovered, from His reactions, what sorts of prayers please Him most; and perhaps it's worth my listing a few things here, on this subject - though with a reminder that the sort of reactions I describe are those revealed only in these past few months - in 1998 - now that He has brought me to a previously-unimagined degree of intimacy and contentment.

If I start at the 'lowest' level of what I must call Christ's response to prayer, I can say that if I am in my 'right place' for a time of prayer, but am day-dreaming or distracted, I am aware that Christ is holding me in the peace which is His gift; but He is silent, since He never forces anyone to pray. I can say that He has invited me to pray - by His Spirit's prompting - but yet He 'waits' for me to begin.

But as soon as I 'turn' my heart and mind towards Him, His Glory shines out, and warms my soul to it's depths.

Whenever I express my love for Him, I see that Glory increase; and the joy within my soul increases, too, in accordance with His plan.

Whenever I ask for His help, believing that He will help me, I am rewarded for my trust by a further increase of Glory, of joy, and of peace and spiritual warmth: such is His goodness.

509

Whenever I beg Christ, with confidence, for some help for a needy neighbour - or else turn to the Father with Christ to offer that sort of prayer in Christ's Name - I am rewarded even more lavishly.

Christ's delight in contrition and humility.

The prayer which brings the greatest reward, however - and which is greeted by Christ with the greatest delight and tenderness - is a sincere confession of sin or sinfulness after every un-Christlike thought or action; and this is one of the reasons why numerous words about sin appear so frequently in this story. Whenever I open my heart to Christ, to confess a fault or to reveal a lack of virtue, I am shown in a swift and almost overpowering manner that He is thrilled - deeply touched - by each act of humility and trust and love.

He sees humility in the heart of everyone who makes a sincere confession to Him of wrong. He sees trust whenever someone opens his heart to Him, on any subject; and He sees love wherever someone endures the humiliation of admitting his weakness and yet endures this because he wants to please Christ and to change; and Christ is overjoyed at such sights. I have seen that joy, in prayer; and that's why I no longer feel inadequate or remorseful when I confess my sins to Christ.

Now that I've learned how good He is, and how constant and unchanging is His attitude, I know that whenever I go to Him with some new cause for shame, I'll be loved, heard, forgiven and consoled - and also rewarded for my honesty and trust. Who could be kinder than Christ? No-one; and I wish everyone could come to know Him, and to know what it's like to believe in His Love, and to grow so close to Him through prayer and penance and service that Divine Love becomes almost the 'air' which the soul breathes throughout each day: an almost palpable sweetness which suffuses one's whole being; and Christ has told me that such sweetness is Heaven's 'medium', whereas the glory with which He adorns my soul in prayer is Heaven's livery; and these are the rewards for all who are repentant and reconciled - after they have patiently endured their purifications. Truly, there is no-one like Christ.

A warm, affectionate person.

In order to help you to picture Him to some degree as I'm now able to picture Him because of all His appearances to me, I can't do better at this point than to ask you to think of the kindest, most tender and loving person you've ever met: someone who is also generous, understanding, funny and articulate and yet simple and straightforward, and then to realise that Christ is all of these things, and that He's real. He's a warm, affectionate Person, but Someone Who knows every thought and emotion that I ever experience; and so He is Someone Whose relationship with me and Whose conversations with me can be based - at my consent - wholly on truth, without a shadow of misunderstanding on His part.

This, then, is the Person Whom Peter and the other Apostles grew to know and love; and yet they had to deal with another 'aspect' of Christ that I've hardly mentioned so far; one which I, too, have found difficult to 'handle' in my heart and mind. I'm speaking of the fact that Christ Who is true man is also true God: the Son of God, now glorified and living in Glory.

Christ: God and man.

It's true that it was only on rare occasions that the Apostles glimpsed that glory; but the more they listened to Christ, and watched Him, the more they noticed the things about Him which made Him different from other men; and this must have had them racking their brains for an explanation, before they could accept the astonishing and in some senses appalling truth about His Divine nature: and I say appalling because I believe that their respect for the Godhead was far more profound than ours, in our century; and they must have been shaken to the depths of their hearts at finding out Who Christ is, and then learning to cope with the implications.

Here amongst them - and now before me - was Someone utterly true and pure Who was totally trustworthy, even if He seemed impredictable at times because His way of thinking wasn't what they expected. He was never petulant or self-seeking. There was no sin in Him: no greed, lust or pride; He never lied, but went to the heart of things and spoke truth, all the time. How uncomfortable that must have been for those who were used to lies, flattery or evasions.

What a struggle for Christ's friends: to hold together in their minds what they saw before them, and what they had begun to know of Christ through His words and actions. What an extraordinary problem confronted them, as they tried to develop a friendship with Someone Who looked just as ordinary as themselves, yet Who was, in some respects, so utterly Other that they wanted to fall down in front of Him, or else to run away from His gaze.

Opening our hearts to Christ's gaze.

I can say from experience that it's when we can't face that gaze in prayer - whether we actually see it or not - that we find it very hard to pray. Yet it's in the merciful darkness of prayer, if we'll spend our lives freely choosing to meet Christ there, that we're given the opportunity to unveil to His compassionate gaze our shoddy lives and pitiful attitudes, and our foolish sins and yearnings. Little by little, we can agree to abandon all that's unworthy of a close friendship with Him; and when we're reconciled and have begun to trust Him a little more, we can even bear a little of the radiance which He begins to shine upon us in our prayer. His Light is so dazzling, as I mentioned, that it hurts our soul's eyes, at first; and so we imagine that we're still living in spiritual darkness when in fact we're very close to God, and we're undergoing the marvellous process of purification, which we must endure either here or in Purgatory, if we're to be ready for the Glory and beauty of Heaven.

Christ, the Way to the Father.

Now that I've tried to describe Christ, I want to say what I've found so marvellous about knowing Him: not all the obvious points, but the fact that He, my God and Saviour - Who has led me to the Father, in the power of the Holy Spirit - is so approachable, as man, that in knowing Him I understand much more about the Godhead, and I'm drawn closer towards the Holy Trinity. Furthermore, I can say from experience - about Christ's effect on our souls - that it's in knowing and loving Christ, the perfect man Who is unendingly patient, loving and trustworthy that I'm brought to a clearer understanding of the meaning of love, Salvation, Eternity, and sin and Heaven.

The importance of regular prayer.

Now you can see, perhaps, that regular prayer is essential for everyone who hopes to change, to grow in virtue, to please Christ, and to be able to look forward to Heaven. Who will look towards death and Eternity with any peace, let alone any scrap of joy, if he's spent a life-time avoiding Christ's gaze, and has refused to pray, and has hoped to shrug off his responsibility which is to lead a life worthy of someone who was created by God, from love, for a life of perpetual bliss in His friendship?

Truly, Christ is so good, tender - and beautiful - that He's worthy any effort or any sacrifice, for those who believe in Him.

To meet Christ in Holy Communion, when one's friendship with Him has been tested, and when He appears to the eyes of the soul at each meeting, or else speaks of His love, or perhaps wordlessly communicates His wishes - or His thanks, or His plans - is to meet a uniquely pure and powerful Love. It's to meet, at close quarters, an all-consuming Divine Love; and so it's to meet, all-at-once, as Christ has shown me (in T:1916) the warmth of His loving glance, the fire of His pure affection, the sight of His open arms, the embrace of a lover, the strength of a brother - and it's also to meet the tenderness of our God, with the now-painless scorching of His radiant Glory.

In every such meeting, Christ makes possible the acceptance of painful memories. He enables the soul to surrender to His care. It's as though He irradiates the soul by His holiness, and so transforms everyone who is willing to be changed; and He persuades us, at last, of His power to lead us into a holy and Eternal Communion; and this goodness, and these gifts, are truly extraordinary - yet are freely available for all who believe in Christ and who put their trust in Him.

Finding a balance, in prayer.

Something extraordinary that I've already mentioned, about Christ - and which is extra-ordinarily strange to learn how to 'deal' with - is the wonderful union, in Him, of a Divine nature and a human nature. He is one Person, Who is truly both God and man. I'm mentioning this again because it's sometimes difficult to keep a 'balance', in prayer, when one speaks in Holy Communion, for example, with Someone Who is true man, and tender, and also wise, helpful and very much Present, yet Who is burning within Himself with an utterly pure and Divine holiness which is awesome to be near. This holiness is also awesome to 'see', when Christ chooses to let His Glory be seen in a more dazzling manner than usual, on special occasions, as I've mentioned, or in order to teach a special lesson.

Yet Christ's Love for us is wholly true, unswerving and forgiving. He delights in us, and relishes our friendship. As He's encouraged me to approach Him in prayer, He has taught me to be both trusting and respectful: to confide in Him as one confides in a best friend and yet always to remain aware that He is my Creator. He has been training me - with infinite love - to come to Him with the most foolish or embarrassing problems, in the certainty that He delights in my trust and will help me; and yet He wants me to remember that He died to save me, and that I can't do anything good without His grace; and that's what I mean by speaking about 'balance'. Christ wants me to be like a little child with Him; He wants to see me living in His burning Truth, in humility, able to gaze admiringly upon His majesty; and yet He wants me to be as confident of His love as of His power, and to be wholly convinced that by living in both truth and trust I can be brought to true happiness.

Christ's Risen Glory.

After mentioning these few examples of Christ's evident tenderness and humanity, I'm going to describe an occasion on which He revealed Himself to my astonished gaze in the Glory of His Divinity. In this way, I hope to show how wonderful He is in dealing so sweetly with a difficult person who has served Him so grudgingly. It happened in December, 1995, when I turned to the Father in prayer to thank Him for Our Blessed Lady, and when I also thanked Our Lady for giving her whole life to God and for giving us Christ: flesh from her flesh.

I've mentioned this in Chapter sixteen. It was at the Vigil Mass of Our Lady's Immaculate Conception that I was praying in this way; and Christ suddenly appeared to me and began to teach me about Himself, and about His Incarnation; but He didn't just teach. He stood before me, radiant with Heavenly Glory (T:1734A).

The majesty and dignity of our Risen Saviour are awesome to see, if He has chosen to show them, and are impossible to describe well. Yet, even with all His Glory, Christ is as simple, straightforward and gentle as a good child.

On that occasion, I was speechless with joy at His sudden appearance; but I felt my soul being held up by God's power; indeed, only because of God's power was I enabled to bear Christ's radiant Light. Here, seen more clearly than ever before, was the Saviour to Whom I had tried to be loyal for so many difficult years. Here was the Mind which had planned the work I was doing, and had called me to do it. Here was the Person Who had trained me in obedience; but here, too, embodied, was the Love which yearned to make me happy forever, even as He was using me - at my consent - to bring reminders of Truth to His People: truths which could lead them, also, to true happiness.

And what did I see, with the eyes of my soul, in that moment?

Before me stood a figure of radiant beauty: a pure man, with every cell of His body and every thought of His heart and mind irradiated by an astonishing Light and grace. I saw the risen Christ, a Divine Person; and as I gazed upon Him, I was taught by Him, soundlessly, about his dual nature. In His glorified Body, Christ was shining with a light which was more like moonlight than sunlight, in the sense that His Light, as shown to me, was glowing rather than searing, soothing rather than scorching; yet it's a bright light which cannot be borne by anyone who is afraid to look upon truth: upon Truth Itself: true God-made-man.

Christ's purity: like pure water or crystal.

Even more astonishing than the Light was Christ's purity. As I gazed upon Christ, I 'saw', by my soul's sight and by a spiritual teaching, that every aspect and every movement of this pure and Divine Person had the quality of pure water, or a perfect crystal. Christ was wholly 'transparent', in the sense that no shadow of imperfection obscured the depths of His Being;

and within that radiant glory I saw, in Christ, the clear patient intelligence of the Divine Person Who knows and Is all Truth, yet Who is as simple and direct as a pure little child.

Ever since my conversion, I had believed wholeheartedly that this pure Christ is a Divine Person, come down to earth, through Mary, made flesh from her flesh and so born fully human yet also Divine. Yet now I was given a clearer understanding of this marvel; that no-one on earth before Christ had ever 'graced' this earth with such a graceful presence. Even the saintly and sinless Virgin who conceived Him was not more than a creature on earth fulfilling the Will of her Creator, whereas Christ's real humanity was irradiated by the beauty of His Divine perfections; and His Divine beauty was the source of His effective words and work during His life on earth.

Can you imagine how I almost shook with awe, whenever I reflected in the days and weeks to come that I had clearly seen the Saviour Who had spoken with Apostles and disciples on earth two thousand years ago? Whose heart could stay the same after such a meeting? Who could look into Christ's eyes and speak to His Heart without trembling at the mystery of it: at meeting a grown man Who has the clear gaze of a child? Yet at the same time I had met a mature and intelligent Christ - Truth Incarnate - upon Whom every conversational ploy, half-truth or piece of flattery or insinuation must be broken as surely as an incoming wave is shattered on a rock.

With my whole heart, I felt thankful that during the previous few years Christ had prepared me to be able to meet His gaze. There was no fear in me, now. I could have died for joy. His human soul was adorned, I know - like His Mother's - with every virtue. But what I saw that day was the radiance of His Divinity, though it was a radiance muted by His own loving Will. It flashed out toward me in our prayer just as it had blazed out occasionally on Earth in His speech, whether through reprimands or tender phrases.

Who saw Divine beauty in the bleeding figure Who trudged through Jerusalem on the day of His Passion? Christ kept His Divine Glory hidden, by His Will, during most of His time on Earth; yet there was much that He didn't hide. He offered to everyone the Divine wisdom of His words, the Infinite strength and purity of His Love, and the Divine authority by which He could speak clearly about Salvation - and could provide the means of achieving it; and this Christ was the very Saviour Who had come to me, in my prayer.

A true representative.

Christ proceeded to teach me about His Holy Mother: about why she had been conceived 'Immaculate'. in her own mother's womb. He showed me something of His own perfection: of how, by His love for the Father and by His obedience to the Father's Will, He had been willing to die for us on Calvary. I was even shown how Christ, as a true representative of mankind, had bridged the chasm between mankind and the Godhead; and the aim of this whole teaching, I was shown, was to provide me with a message for His People: a request that we all allow Christ's pure life and virtues to flow through us, when we are reconciled to Him, and are living in union with Him, indwelt by His Holy Spirit, and devoured by a longing for the Father's Glory.

Prayer: a dark 'veil'.

[Speaking from the heart, I must add that Christ might terrify us, so astonishing is His purity and beauty, if we hadn't learned already through the prophets and then through Christ Himself and His Apostles, something of His nature. We've only to look at the terrible suffering He bore for our sake to be reminded that although He is Truth He is also Infinite Love, Mercy and Compassion. We're only to remember the Resurrection to remember, too, that Christ is Infinite Joy - and can share that joy with all who believe in Him and do His Will.

Through faith, and also through experience, I can say with complete conviction that Christ's wish is not to crush us with His Truth, but to let us approach Him with our icy hearts or dirty garments - whatever image will most plainly show us that the pure, tender, truthful Christ longs to relieve us of our burdens, to warm and wash us, and to pour His grace and truth upon and within us. This is our only hope of true joy, on Earth or in Eternity, and Christ yearns to see us joyful.

It's true that faith is needed, to believe that a Saviour so pure and holy can love people like ourselves, whom He died to save; but He's yearning to press His gifts upon us, if we'll freely approach Him. We're tempted to think He holds Himself aloof and critical. Yet if we saw Him now, and saw His Love for us, we would die - either of terror or joy; and this is why we should always remain grateful for the marvel which is prayer. Under the cover of its mysterious and veiling silence and darkness, we can grow close to the God Whose Light would otherwise dazzle us. We can learn to unwrap our sore hearts and sore lives, whilst still hidden in Christ's temporary, merciful, gloom.

One day, Heaven's Light will break into our lives. When we die, how glad we'll be, if our wounds have healed. How happy we shall be if our eyes have grown used to Christ's Light, slowly, during prayer: if we're not faced, as some are, with the sudden and tormenting glare of Truth after twenty, fifty or even eighty years of wilful darkness.]

A description of Christ.

What I really long to do now is to rush ahead with a 'description' of the Father; but I must first complete my verbal 'impression' of Christ with a few more words about how loveable and loving He is; and I'm going to use a few paragraphs I wrote in 1995. But there's a special reason why I'm incorporating those words into this piece of text. It's because on the day after I'd listed those things about Christ which so delight and console me, I greeted Christ in church, before Mass began, only to hear Him say to me: *"You've written well, Lizzie!"* So you can see that He liked this description of Himself; and by making His approval plain He encouraged me to speak even more boldly about Him, so that other people can begin to believe that they, too, can find joy in prayer and in the practice of the Catholic Faith.

It's from experience, then, and with Christ's approval, that I can say: "Christ is calming, tender, wise and understanding; and as He forgives every confessed sin or feeble effort, He is gently drawing one forward to make greater efforts to please Him and to grow like Him: but for one's own happiness, as well as God's Glory. Its only with sweetness and gratitude that

515

He rewards and thanks the soul even for pathetic attempts to bear sufferings patiently, for love of Him and for what He suffered in His terrible Passion.

No-one takes such delight as Christ in private anniversaries. Often, when I've forgotten a special date, Christ has astonished me with His special gifts; then I've remembered the date, and have remembered the occasion which He wants to see me celebrate all over again! So we're right to cherish our liturgical cycle of fasts and feasts and anniversaries, which of course is inspired by God.

No-one is as utterly constant and sympathetic towards us as Christ, when we bravely confide the most embarrassing, gruesome, silly or muddled details of our lives. Christ is unshockable. He sees, knows and understands everything. How I hope that good priests will all model themselves on Him.

In the story of the Prodigal Son.

There's something else that's tremendously reassuring to remember, about Christ, God and man. Christ is more thrilled by certain things than by certain other things; and so I've written a list of these things from memory:-

Christ is thrilled, whenever we repent, by our humility, though we don't feel much in the way of thrills at the time. He is thrilled by the sincere efforts we make to begin again, when we've been 'backsliding' or have failed or 'fallen' again; and I'm speaking about big sins as well as little faults. Christ is never wagging His finger sarcastically when someone returns to him for the two-thousandth or even the ten-thousandth time to say a sincere 'Sorry'. Christ is all smiles and joy at our real, pitiful efforts. He is just like the Father in the story of the Prodigal Son.

Christ is thrilled by our gratitude, and is very 'touched' by our sincere thanks for any and every good thing in our lives, and by our thanks for answers to prayer. He is thrilled by something often neglected by us: by our thanks for forgiveness, and thanks for the Sacraments.

But Christ is thrilled, more than ever, by our gratitude for what He suffered for us during His Passion. Although He's living in Glory now, He's full of joy at the mere sight of someone thanking Him, for example, by devotedly praying the 'Stations of the Cross'; and if we comfort Him in His Passion by accepting our sufferings and by uniting them, mysteriously, to Christ's, so joining in His work of Redemption, He counts us as His special friends.

Holy Scripture says: 'GOD HAS NO FAVOURITES' (Ro 2:11); but the God-man, like any of us, is touched by acts of true devotion. It's worth noting that Christ was 'closer' - by choice - to some Apostles than to others, although He loved them all immensely, and died for them all.

It's important that I also write that we delight Christ by our acts of devotion and gratitude towards His Holy Mother. Conversely, in order to wound Christ, one need only belittle ignore or insult her. He loves her tremendously, with a respect and gratitude He shows in just such a way to no other human being; and so He is genuinely thrilled whenever we show our love for her, or thank her for giving Jesus to us, or when we thank St. Joseph for looking after them both."

I could write for ever, about Him; but I must move on, in order to speak about the Father.

Learning about the Father, in prayer.

I have to say that my experiences of God our Father are different: not because God's nature is different in different Persons, nor because one Divine Person has something that Another doesn't have, but because God has chosen to reveal Himself to me in a different way, or, rather, wishes to confirm that what His Church recommends is what He desires, which is that we should 'tailor' our perception of the Holy Trinity in accordance with Divine Revelation-expressed-in-certain-language, for example: about God's Fatherhood, and His Son's Priesthood, and the Spirit's role as Consoler. I mean that God the Father has taught me in prayer that we cannot improve upon the way in which the Three Divine Persons - One Lord - have been portrayed for us through Holy Scripture and the Sacred Tradition. It's God's Will that we know and believe that the Three Divine Persons are equal, and that we approach the First Person to acknowledge His Fatherhood, the Second to acclaim Him as our Saviour and the Third to rejoice in His power, for example; and I say this with such confidence because this is what I've been taught by the Holy Trinity during the past two or three years.

God our Father has allowed me to experience His teachings and attributes in prayer, to some small degree; and they are experienced in a different way from that experienced with Christ in Holy Communion, even though "God is God", whichever Divine Person is instructing me. God Wills that this different approach is experienced by me. He is responsible for it. It's manifested partly in the feelings He evokes in me, when, as Father, He offers His awesome touch in prayer, a touch which is different from Christ's gentle 'touch' in Holy Communion; but it's revealed also by the Father's special choice of words as He teaches me during the silent 'teaching' of contemplative union.

(I can hardly believe that I dare to write this, but I just have to do it, and to stop being so self-conscious. Its part of my work, work which isn't self-chosen, but God-given.)

To converse with my Creator.

The difference which I experience can be described in the following way:- God the Father Most Holy, by His own Will, 'stirs' within me tremendous pangs of awe and reverence, even when I'm only thinking about Him. Of course, I'm full of reverence for Christ, but His gentleness banishes all fear, whereas an immense but wholesome reverence is something Willed by God our Father, for an earthly creature in His presence.

Until very recently, this reverence was accompanied by an immense joy-tinged-with fear; yet in recent months that fear has entirely disappeared, to be replaced in prayer by what I can only describe as an exhilaration at being able to communicate - to converse, with sincere questions and infinitely-loving answers - with my Creator.

Although it seems at times as though I am only a 'whisper' away from God the Father, in the intimacy of prayer, it should be understood that my imagination has no part in such prayer, but is wholly subdued, so to speak, as are my memory and intellect, as my spirit pierces the clamour of thought and rises 'above' the mind to meet God in the silence of contemplation; and it does so only by God's power, and God's invitation; and so of course I never see the Father standing in front of me (- forgive me for saying this, yet I have to) - as Christ does, frequently, in Holy Communion. The Father is inaccessible, unless we come to Him in Christ; and even now that I've been 'lifted' in the prayer of contemplation through the cloud which separates us from the Glory of the Godhead, and even now that I hear the Father speak to me and teach me, I sense that He is so transcendent and 'Other' that I want to cover my face and bow low as I approach Him, as my spirit is lifted towards Him, in the 'heights'.

Conversation with the Father.

From experience, I can describe the attitude which the Father encourages me to adopt towards Him. It's because the Father chooses to make Himself known to me, every few weeks, or every few days, by calling me to a genuine conversation in prayer, that I can speak from experience: although these conversations are only possible because I already live "in Christ," and so am the Father's true child. So that's why I say quite firmly, that whenever the Father begins our 'conversations', He summons me to His Presence, summoning me from my normal life, into prayer, yet upwards - as though to a great height, far away - where He lives in a region which, unless He calls us, is inaccessible. He even calls me from my armchair to another room, where - in order to obey Him - I must kneel down and pray, if I am well enough to do so.

I have to describe it thus, although I know that we live "in God". I'm writing about real intimacy with God, and about the limits which He places on that intimacy - for our good - during our life on earth.

Now, although the Father is extraordinarily tender, so tender and understanding that He can make me weep with delight and gratitude, He leaves me in no doubt that when I'm called to listen to Him, I'm being given an extraordinary privilege. I mention this because - by contrast - the Divine Son, Christ, in Holy Communion, has only rarely, as far as I can remember, given that impression. Christ seems to present Himself to me always as Friend first, and God at the same time, whereas the Father is always my Majestic God - Who can also be known as Love. Just in case anyone says that my perception of the Divine Persons is different, because my expectations have been different, I can only stress that never in my life have I expected to be taught by God in this way; indeed, I didn't know that it was possible. I had only hazy ideas about 'mystical contact' with God, that is, about felt contact, since I know that even a breath of 'dry' but sincere prayer establishes or reinforces our 'contact' with God. I know that it's through faith that we have become His children, not through emotion. Also, I had no pre-conceived ideas about the Father seeming to be more remote and powerful than Christ though just as loving.

Every thought of mine about God - Father, Son or Holy Spirit - had been 'coloured' simply by the truth about our relationship: about His Sovereignty and my creatureliness, associated with His never-ending love and my trusting confidence in all that He gives us through His Church.

At the 'edge' of darkness.

To return to the experience of being taught in prayer by the Father: I know that whenever He has called me, in prayer, He has called me, through Christ's life in me, to go and 'hover', so to speak, at the edge of the darkness where He dwells, though the darkness isn't like earthly darkness. It has nothing to do with banishment or lostness, but is a comforting and loving darkness in which the Father cocoons me because of His Love for me; and that Divine Love recognises that I'd be hurt and dazzled were I to be confronted by His burning Glory while I'm still earthly and earth-bound and not yet quite ready to 'go in': by which I mean not fit to enter wholly into His infinite Knowledge of Himself. To do so would be to be in Heaven.

God the Father sometimes 'calls' me, therefore, and permits me to 'taste' His Knowledge, or, rather, to accept such Wisdom as He chooses to give to me a little bit at a time, in each teaching: and I must stress that I'm not writing, here, about the soul's being lifted to God in silence and utter incomprehension, in what I sometimes experience as the prayer of 'Unknowing' contemplation. I mentioned that earlier, and it's quite different, and yet very fruitful for the one who prays like that - when God so arranges it - and for the people in her heart. But what I'm about to describe is something which I believe is even rarer and more precious, which is a perceived or 'known' union with the Father in a conversation only achieved after incorporation into Christ and after many purifications.

When the Father speaks.

I can say from experience that whenever the Father 'speaks' to me in a soundless instruction or conversation, my heart is lurching with the honour of it, and with the marvel of His Goodness, even while I'm longing to be worthy to be with Him; and all of this has been tinged, until recently, with sorrow that I have ever served Him less than wholeheartedly. How I wish that my whole life had been spent in a state of willingness to suffer or to die for Him without even a split-second's hesitation.

Strange to say, I rarely seem to feel sorrow with Jesus any more; in fact, He has kept asking me to leave sorrow behind, in my day-to-day intimacy with Him in prayer. A reverent sorrow-for-sinfulness, however, seems to have been something Willed by God the Father for most of my life. It's been the inevitable accompaniment to the years of necessary penance, with prayerful explorations of the Faith; and yet it's been easier to bear as my hope and faith have grown stronger.

Groping about for the right words, again, such 'sorrow-for-sinfulness' seems to have been, for a long time, a necessary, earthly aspect of my daughterly relationship with the Father. But even as I write that, I'm stunned to realise how surely, nowadays, He banishes every scrap of fear or sorrow each time He draws me into His presence - or else makes His presence known.

Exquisite courtesy.

It's only by what I must describe as the weight of His Glory, and the power of His majesty, and the Infinite Love of His Heart that the Father banishes everything foolish or fearful in my soul, in our meeting. Although I turn to Him in prayer very frequently throughout the day, with a brief request, or a few more words of gratitude or praise, there's something special about those times of prayer which I 'enter' only because He Himself has powerfully 'called' me. At such times as those, He and I converse in a manner which reminds me, by its exquisite courtesy, of those stately dances of olden days. I'll try to describe our progress.

God prompts me, by His Spirit, to turn to Him in prayer. I speak to the Father in the Name of Jesus; then the Father responds with love to one of my little queries about life or about prayer. He answers me, although with neither sight nor sound. I praise and thank Him, and dare to ask Him something else; then it's as though Heaven's door opens even wider. Its as if the Father is saying that there's nothing I can't ask Him: no gift I can't persuade Him to give me, for my good or my delight; and there's something else so marvellous that I feel bound to mention it here.

From experience, I can say that in the early days, when I was learning how to pray, it was as though my contact with God was broken if ever I were distracted, or if I moved away physically from where I'd knelt in prayer - or if someone called to me to lend a hand with some little task; and now I know that although God never leaves us, He permits this 'felt-absence' in order to train us to be recollected in prayer. It's a necessary spiritual discipline in the nursery-stage of contemplation. Yet now, through God's infinite goodness, it seems as though I couldn't 'move away' from God even if I wanted to, in the following sense; I mean that whenever He calls me, as I mentioned above, and permits me to question Him about all sorts of things, and when He answers and instructs and consoles me so sweetly in prayer, He makes it plain, also, that He delights in conversing with me; and what's so extraordinary about this is that neither by my distractions - by my random, silly thoughts - nor by outward interruptions - if the 'phone should ring, so that I must pause to answer it in order to please Him, Who wants me to be faithful to duty - is He 'caused' to end our prayer.

No; it's as though He follows me, or, rather, is glad to 'stroll' with me - I mean, spiritually - from place to place, as I find it necessary to move either through duty or perhaps because of pain: for example, when I can't kneel any more, but must sit, or must move from my desk - where I was sitting when He first 'sought me out' - to go and rest in my armchair.

Exchanges of love and knowledge.

It astonishes me, too, that so great is His kindness - and so much more trusting of Him have I become - that it's as though He 'waits' whenever I pause to write down whatever He's been explaining; and so the wonderful minutes pass by in exchanges of love and knowledge for up to an hour - or until I'm too weary to remain utterly recollected and attentive any more, and so am forced to 'descend' from a state-of-communication to a state-of-being-enfolded in His loving care.

From experience, I've found that the only thing which can end such conversations is either exhaustion on my part, when I can't pay attention for another second, after a long morning or day of intense concentration, or duty: when I have to go and immerse myself in some activity or human conversation. I don't mean that He can be 'shut out' by any activity of mine, but only that our special 'dialogue' must end for a while, though the peace and friendship and joy are never-ending.

This is our God! I can't begin to thank him enough for having brought me to know Him by faith, and for having taught me how to pray; and yet if I take a 'wider' look at God's work, I am stunned, too, to see that God's Love is very lavishly shown in all sorts of ways besides prayer. I can see that God's fatherly care has 'wrapped up' all of my life's plans, mistakes, sins, gifts and diversions, into a pattern which I can now see is shot through with His Will, His Wisdom - and His fatherly love: even when I was being unfaithful or half-hearted. Truly, this is a good enough reason for me to persevere in the perpetual joyful repentance which He has shown me is pleasing to Him.

But the point to stress is that the experience of being instructed by the Father is not the same as the experience of being instructed either by the Son or by the Holy Spirit.

Grandeur and Majesty.

It seems to me that, for His own holy purposes, God our Father chooses to keep me aware of His remoteness-from-my-nature, whenever He instructs me, even though He loves me, and even though His Divine Son Jesus Christ has united the Godhead to our humanity.

Even though the Father's 'touch' in prayer - by which I mean the spiritual joy and knowledge with which He almost palpably suffuses my soul - is as sweet and gentle as a baby's touch, it carries 'beyond' itself something, or rather, Someone Whose strength and majesty are held back, so to speak, lest they harm me. I know that when the Father speaks to me He speaks with tremendous authority and power. He speaks a brief phrase, or a wordless instruction, whilst giving me the strength and courage to bear the spiritual 'sight' of His Grandeur - with the knowledge that He, so Infinitely Holy, is stooping to speak with me, who am so totally unworthy.

Whenever He calls me in this way, so explicitly, in prayer, He makes me feel that if I could do so I should fall flat on my face on the floor as I speak to Him, even though both Christ and the Holy Spirit - and the Father - have shown me how infinitely tender is Their love for us. And although the very power and perfection of the Father which He permits me to sense are not 'masculine' there is, in them, something which is demanding my eternal loyalty and obedience. Perhaps I should say that the Father gently 'invites' obedience. It's plain that I'd be foolish to refuse any invitation of His, because He is Wisdom. But the Father makes it plain, by His own Being, that He is powerful as well as loving. It's as though He is clothed in authority. I must repeat, He is not male; but the authority with which God chooses to 'clothe' men on earth is a sort of shadow of the real Authority which is the Father's, in earth and in Heaven; and that's why I've written elsewhere that to address the Father as 'God our Mother' seems to be not only disobedience but sheer silliness - although it's true that in His tenderness towards weak people He is like a mother.

No evidence of separation.

It's important that I qualify these words about prayer and about sorrow by gratefully asserting that my relationship with God, in recent months, has become so simple and joyful that no thought of sorrow or pain can enter to divide us when we're one heart in prayer.

This is not because I've become so overwhelmed or 'absorbed' in prayer that my person or personality is annihilated; on the contrary, it's because God, in His kindness, has so fulfilled and adorned and made joyful my soul that it has never been more 'real'. It has become to some degree like Him, supremely in knowledge and love; and my soul, in this likeness and union, can no longer perceive any evidence of separation between myself and God; and therefore our prayerful union is such - if I can express it in this way - that no pain or sorrow can touch or enter. This is the sort of union to which He calls us all - if we will listen, believe, respond and allow Him to change us. How I wish that everyone would believe, and could experience such immense joy.

How I wish that everyone could discover what I was shown by the Father (in T:1941) on 23rd July 1996 - as I've described in Chapter sixteen. How I wish that everyone could come to know God as He is: as true Love, and as the Source of all Love. He is the Cause of our joy, the Truth, Light, Bliss, and Sweetness which can warm and change us: the tender and Divine Love which can heal our wounds: our Prize and Treasure: our God Who, all-at-once, is Fire and Flame and Glory, Peace and Wisdom, Guide and Father. All-at-once, He is the Origin of all holiness, and our Home, our Goal, and our Paradise.

In our communion with Him we can find the perfect fulfilment of every good longing , with unending Bliss for the human heart and mind and body and soul. This is what He has shown me and what I know to be true; and it's this glorious, Only God Who 'woos' us, calls and cherishes us , and answers our prayers - so that, when we have learned to trust Him, we can live with Him in the bond of Love, in a true union in which the soul and God are equal in self-giving, and in which the Creator Himself - through this mutual surrender - can be said to be 'subject' to His own beloved creature.

How is this possible? The answer, of course, is that it's only been made possible through the life, death and resurrection of Christ, and through the power of the Holy Spirit Who was sent to our hearts by Christ after the Ascension; and it's about the goodness of the Holy Spirit that I want to write next.

The simplicity of the Holy Spirit.

To continue, about the Divine Persons - still almost holding my breath at daring to write - the Most Holy Spirit, too, allows me to experience something of His teachings and attributes in prayer.

Although it's true to say that it's by the Holy Spirit's prompting that I've been helped to turn to Christ in prayer, at home and before the Blessed Sacrament, I know that it's Christ Himself Who has taught me much about the Holy Spirit. Christ once showed me, most vividly, though without sight or sound (in T:1262) that the Holy Spirit is Lord and God, Creator, Sanctifier and Consoler, and yet is like a little child in purity, simplicity and truth. It was at Pentecost that Christ once showed me (in T:1316) something of the power and joy of the Holy Spirit, Who is Fire and Glory, Divine Light and Beauty; and we 'owe' to the Holy Spirit, therefore, both adoration and loyalty.

Christ showed me that in Purity, Power, Wisdom, Omniscience and Love the Holy Spirit resembles both Father and Son; and yet Christ also showed me that the Spirit's action upon us, during our journey towards Heaven, is more like a cradling than a steering. The Spirit is our Guide, Comforter and Teacher, and yet it's as though He carries us lovingly, during this 'cradling', towards the Father.

It's because of the experience of having been 'closely-cradled' so many times in the Spirit's loving care, that I can describe how the approach of the Holy Spirit to the soul in prayer is perceived as being different from the sort of approach which is experienced in a communication either with the Father or with the Son. The Holy Spirit is never perceived as being 'above' me, or in darkness; rather, I am allowed to experience His gracious presence in a noticeably different way; it is His Will. I say 'gracious presence' because He doesn't summon me, like the Father. No; whenever I've been taught by the Holy Spirit, I've been made aware that at that moment of specific 'teaching' He is already 'carrying me', it seems: as if cradling my whole person, in the spiritual life.

The kindness of the Holy Spirit.

It's the Holy Spirit Whom I've felt prompting or 'nudging' me - at every stage of my life - urging me to do good, to go in a particular direction, to undertake a course of action, or to avoid a certain evil influence; and it's a cause for sadness that I haven't always obeyed His promptings, and that I found from experience that the more His guidance is ignored then the weaker or fainter seem His urgings. In such cases, it's not He Who abandons us, but we who shut our soul's 'ears' to His calls. But it's a cause for joy, today, to know that He has led me back to the right path, and that at every stage His wise promptings continue - and that I cannot go badly 'wrong' if by every thought and act I'm trying to obey Him and so to please the Father and follow Christ in the ways recommended by Christ's Church.

Today, therefore, the Holy Spirit never seems remote, though I don't feel His presence all the time. I rarely think about what I'm 'feeling'. I'm concentrating on what is God's Will, and am trying to do it. That's my main concern; although I confess that God's gifts sometimes overwhelm me and so demolish my resolutions about shunning 'special' experiences in prayer. I know from experience that it's the Spirit too, Who gives me guidance as I write. Whenever I turn to Him for help, He makes things plain. If I am lost for words, He provides them; and it's only through my union with Christ, and through His gift of the Spirit, that I can see Truth so clearly, and so attempt to describe it; and by this I mean truths about the Godhead, and prayer, and our relationships with God and with one another.

The work of the Holy Spirit.

It's through the Holy Spirit that I've received so many teachings in prayer - through the merits of Christ, and for the Glory of the Father. Sometimes the Most Holy Spirit - to my utter astonishment - has instructed me, for example, about His action in the life of Our Blessed Lady, or about the ways in which He guides and helps souls in their journey from darkness to Light: or about how He is at work during the Consecration. On one extraordinary occasion - as I mentioned in Chapter fourteen (T:1354) - He astounded me by His magnificent response to my request for help: when I asked Him to give me a more loving heart.

When He then taught me about Love, by saying to me: *"I am the measure"*, He awed me by

His grandeur. He showed me - with neither sight nor sound - something of His majesty and holiness. Equal to the Father and the Son, He is true God, worthy of all reverence and to be given adoration and obedience; and yet, whoever meets Him meets true Love: Divine Charity.

On that extraordinary day, as He spoke to me, the Holy Spirit helped me to see that I should never be satisfied by my pitiful attempts to be loving - but should always hope to grow more loving. Yet He wasn't encouraging me in love by words alone; nor was He just proposing Himself as an example: as a 'measure'. He wasn't like a lecturer who invites his students to reproduce his demonstration of some subject as they sit before him in miserable silence, all too aware of their own ignorance and lack of understanding. No! The way of the Holy Spirit is different. It is loving. It's by His gift of Himself that He coaxes us to show out charity to others. He pours that Love into willing hearts in the sacraments; He also radiates that Love towards us through loving persons; and He fills and surrounds our souls with that burning Love in prayer, at times of His choosing; and that's why I can describe the 'sort' of Love which He is, if I can phrase it that way, since it was on that September day in 1993 that He gave me a demonstration of love which I shall never be able to forget, and which I have to try to encapsulate in a few inadequate words.

A demonstration of love.

On that extraordinary occasion, I was astonished to find that the Holy Spirit, Who is the Love of God, utterly surrounded and suffused my soul in prayer; and in doing so, He showed me that whoever meets Him meets a Love which is heart-warming, and which wholly enfolds the whole 'person'. This Love is blissful and tender and consoling. It is simple, pure, gentle and encouraging. The embrace of this forgiving Love is light, not burdensome. It makes no demands, but rather - by its purity and bliss - invites love to grow where before there has been little love; and thus, as the Holy Spirit told me, it can help the small fire of love within a weak soul to reach out and to become one with the Great 'Fire' which is Divine Love; and thus, the soul can be 'wrapped' in the everlasting and full embrace of the Eternal bliss of the Three Divine Persons: the Holy Trinity. So this is why we say that the Spirit is 'at work'. He perpetually draws and encourages us towards a greater good and a greater joy: always yearning to see us joyful with the true joy which is found in Heaven - in Love's Kingdom.

At the same time, He taught me many things about His nature, and our friendship: far too much for me to be able to mention here. If I were to write non-stop for a year, I couldn't adequately express my awe or gratitude. But what is He 'like', in Himself ? I can say from experience that the Holy Spirit is always Invisible, yet is always breathtakingly Light, pure and tender. He inspires no fear in me, or such is His Will; I'm only describing what has happened. His presence brings Wisdom, in instructions, and also satisfaction, as He satisfies a soul's thirst for understanding. He is 'sensed' by the soul as One Who is as lovely as pure air, or as vast as a cave in the greatest mountain; yet He's as simple as a little child, and is always gently at work with willing souls, helping and pacifying us as we do our best to love Christ, and as we reached out, 'in' Christ, to please and glorify the Invisible Father.

On several other occasions, the Holy Spirit has spoken to me, plainly; and a simple, clear phrase from Him is like a baby's breath, or like a drop of clear water. His touch is gentle and consoling. One can 'fall' into His care without a care in the world, if one has already lost one's fear of 'falling': lost it, I mean, by surrendering to God, giving up sin, and living a life of gratitude, repentance, reparation and devoted service.

I know that the touch of the Most Holy Spirit within the soul can be like a scorching flame in the heart, almost unbearable, for anyone who has sinned. But this is all forgotten when we're determined to love God, and when we've emerged from God's major purifications.

An infusion of Light and peace.

It was the Holy Spirit - so He told me - Who once lifted my soul to Heaven, to that extraordinary meeting with Christ (in T:43) on what I've called the 'Alpha and Omega' day: such is the Spirit's power and goodness.

As for the beauty and Glory of the Holy Spirit: of the Divine Spirit, Who is Holiness Itself - a pure and inextinguishable Fire - I've been shown that it's His Light which shines within my soul both during and after the Gospel readings. Since I pray fervently to the Holy Spirit for understanding whenever the Holy Scriptures are read in church, I cannot be surprised - He has shown me - that He gives that understanding, and does so, at this stage of my life, with such a lavish infusion of Light, joy and peace within my soul, that that moment of grace is almost as overwhelming as the moment of Christ's arrival in Holy Communion; and this, I can be sure, is our God: the Third Person of the Most Holy Trinity.

He is the fiery Light which illuminates minds, warms cold hearts, and brings courage. It is He Who blazes like a pillar of Fire within the hearts of those who call to Him, welcome him and are willing to be changed by Him; this is our God.

Furthermore, I can proclaim that whenever Christ comes to me in Holy Communion it is the Spirit's Glory which Christ sends 'up' to the Father from within my soul, as an infinitely-worthy prayer of praise for the Father. It's the Spirit's own flame of Glory which shines in my heart or burns on my brow - according to the Father's Will - whenever it's time for yet another manifestation of His presence and work and goodness: for the sake of this God-given task.

It's only by the courage which is given to me by the Holy Spirit that I write so boldly, today, about God and about the spiritual life, when I'll probably be called a mad-woman or a fool - although everyone who believes my story will be given joy. But I, too, am made joyful by this writing: not because it's good writing, but because my efforts are sincere and because God is so good. I mean that He keeps rewarding me for what I do.

Each time I sit at my desk or my kitchen table to write something more about God's goodness, before proceeding to church for Mass, I'm happy just to be doing my duty; but as soon as I arrive in church, I'm lavishly rewarded. Christ pours His joy and gratitude within my soul from the tabernacle, and rewards me further in Holy Communion. Imagine this: that God lavishes rewards upon a creature for praising her Creator in print, and for urging other people towards Him.

Three Persons yet One God.

How dearly I should like to carry on writing about God, to describe His goodness and beauty;

525

but something crucially important must be mentioned here. I would be horrified to find that I'd perhaps given someone the impression that I'm speaking as if of three 'Gods' whenever I speak of Father, Son and Holy Spirit. That I can speak confidently of the Three Divine Persons has only been made possible because the One God, the Most Holy Trinity, has set me within the 'heart' of His Life - so to speak - as I co-operate with Him on earth, although I do so inadequately. It's through God's invitation in prayer, and through His power, that I 'glimpse' something of the life within the One Holy God upon Whom we usually seem to gaze as if from a distance.

Astounding though it is, I've been permitted to cast my soul's gaze around me, as it were, from the 'centre' of God's heart, by which I mean from the 'centre' of life-in-union with Him; therefore I find that I can describe something about the Three Persons Whom I know and with Whom I have communicated during the freely-given-by-God extraordinary experiences of contemplative prayer. Of course, all the "seeing" which is mentioned is by the soul's faculties, and not by bodily or earthly sight. Also, when I mention the 'soul's gaze', I mean to say: the soul's understanding of God which is given to the soul in a life of intimacy, in a union of Wills, after many purifications.

Contemplative union.

Although God has revealed Himself through Christ and His Apostles, we can say that until we meet Him in Heaven, He remains, for us, essentially Mysterious, and Unknowable and Unseen. Yet the obscure 'Knowledge' of Himself which He chooses to give to certain persons through contemplative prayer's amazing union can give to a soul a vivid and instinctive grasp of those things about God that the Church knows and says to people who live in spiritual darkness.

The contemplative knows and 'relishes', through union with God in prayer, those things which the theologian knows through his or her intellect, and which both contemplatives and theologians know by faith.

That is the reason why the Three Persons can be 'met' and loved, in prayer, and then sometimes described with a clarity which might seem astonishing to someone who doesn't pray, or who hasn't yet progressed beyond a certain degree of prayer.

This is why, also, a description of the perceived distinctions between the Three Persons might give the impression - to someone who is unfamiliar with our doctrine of the Blessed Trinity - that the writer is describing three gods.

At the heart of a comet.

Perhaps it's worth risking a poor analogy to make it a bit plainer why it's through prayer rather than through thought that God's inner life can be better understood and God Himself be better known.

If observers of a huge and beautiful comet were to see it hurling itself in a great arc over the earth, far enough away not to be dangerous, but near enough for people to see its beauty, they would speak in unison about the direction in which the comet was flying, its origin, its age, and the length of its fiery tail; but no-one could be really sure of what was happening at the comet's centre, except by scientific deduction. Details about temperature, mass and speed, when combined with facts about solids hurtling through our atmosphere, would allow a reasonable assumption to be made about conditions at the centre; but no-one would really know. Logical deduction is not the same as personal and tangible evidence and experience.

This analogy falls down, above all, I think, because God - unlike the comet - has revealed much of His nature and His purpose to mankind, through His own Divine Son. But much of the rest of the picture will 'hold'. I mean that if someone, by an extraordinary power from a Divine 'comet', were to be brought to the centre of a comet during its flight, and were marvellously protected from what would normally harm it, for example, from the heat, that person would 'see' as being true what the scientists had only advanced as theory. But that person 'at the heart' would have another advantage; and it would be an advantage consisting not of having more facts nor of feeling a firmer assurance of the truth of those facts; he or she would have a better grasp of the relationship between one fact and another, and of which facts were really important for an understanding of the comet's origin, present condition, and 'purpose'.

What might have seemed immensely interesting, from below, might be seen to be of little importance: for example, the comet's tail. What is unseen from below, such as the material at the comet's centre: its condition, temperature and nature, is seen clearly at the centre; and so, by this poor illustration, I can offer a glimpse of the marvel of God-given contemplative 'teaching'. The marvel is that someone who, when 'outside' prayer, believes in the Most Holy Trinity but who doesn't understand the ways in which God 'works' - since she cannot see how God can be Three and One - can be lifted by God into Himself in a particular sort of prayer; and there, she can gaze upon the 'workings' of the Divine Persons within the One Godhead as clearly - though in a different manner - as the person in the illustration has gazed at the heart of the fiery comet.

Writing from experience.

Please excuse my speaking about God as if God were a 'thing' or a mere being, rather than Being itself. That's part of the poverty of my analogy. But perhaps you can see that if we know a contemplative who writes from the vantage-point - if I dare to say this, yet I must - of the Heart of God, a Heart opened by God for brief periods to someone who has given his or her life to God in its entirety after responding to God's invitation, we can be sure that she writes only what she knows. She writes only what she 'sees' through her soul's faculties.

Her words may be badly expressed, and her faults plain, but the 'picture' which she paints of God's Nature, His Will, and His methods of dealing with human souls, will be worth a hearing. She has experienced what others might have grasped by deduction. I'm not saying that she can't be mistaken about minor matters; but it's because she writes not unwisely from her genuine experiences of God that her writings are given a place in the Church's life, as are the writings of numerous uneducated and prayerful persons who are usually known as Christian 'mystics'.

Such people have been able to describe things, from experience, which no learned person can describe - even though the wisdom of a learned Christian writer who has had no mystical prayer experiences is invaluable.

If I can throw out a few analogies, it seems to me that someone who wants to hear about the special beauties of Antarctica will speak first with an explorer, if possible - although he will be grateful for the work of the map-makers who have made it possible for him to have information which is vital for a journey to that region. Or if someone wants to learn French so that he can speak better with the French family with whom he stays each summer, he might prefer to spend time conversing in French with a French neighbour, even if that person happens to be illiterate, than in reading books of French grammar. He will absorb the sounds and the rhythm and the intonation of the language, through speech, in a way which cannot be learned from books - although books are essential for someone who wants to be sure that he can construct beautiful sentences in French, with the correct tenses, and with silent word-endings learned, so that his written French will be correct in every way. Or, to labour the point - and bearing in mind some of the torments of the spiritual life, as well as the astonishing joys and triumphs - we could imagine that someone who wants a first-hand account of a surgical operation, so that he can plan his own finances and his own convalescence, might first approach his neighbour for information, if that neighbour has had that operation, instead of dashing off to the surgeon. It's true that the surgeon's help will be essential - particularly his medications, his warnings about not eating before an anaesthetic, and his surgical skills, and so on. Yet someone who has suffered an operation, and has experienced the special problems as well as the delights of recovery can give an account of the whole episode which will be more vivid and accurate, in some senses, than anything which could be said by the surgeon.

So it is with prayer, of course. Accounts of prayer-experiences must be examined with caution, if indeed they have to be examined. There's no substitute for the learning of a good and wise theologian, on this subject. Yet there are people who want to know more about prayer in order to be encouraged in their progress, to be urged to endure desert-patches, and to be assured that God's sweetness and kindness are so astonishing that it's worth enduring every sorrow in order to reach Him; and they will be helped in a special way if they seek not just information from the pages of a learned book, but inspiration from the heart and pen of someone who can say with conviction - and preferably with some evidence - "God is good. I believe this; but I say this, too, because I know Him; and this is what He is 'like' ......"

A Russian wedding ring.

If I continue to speak boldly about God while I have the 'framework' of this chapter in which to hold up a certain image, it seems to me that the work and unity of the Three Divine Persons in the One God Whom we adore is best described by a symbol; and the most apt symbol I have ever seen, by which to express the Mystery which is God's Trinity-in-Unity, is what is called a "Russian Wedding ring".

(I'm so unfit to write this, and untrained - except by Him. But I believe it's His Will that I try. I'm sitting near my kitchen table, during a 'heat-wave', as one group of guests departs and another is about to arrive; the whole 'piece' has been written in bits and pieces between various kitchen tasks, rests, conversations and phone calls.)

Have you ever seen a wedding ring which consists of three shining bands of metal, each a circle, but a circle which is apparently twisted one way and then another to accommodate the 'movements' of the two other metallic circles which are inter-twined around it and with each other?

How simple it is, and how beautiful! No band is larger than another. None has a beginning or an end. Each is perfect in its own shape and its own beauty; each gains nothing by being with the others, since the three together are a ring just as the single band is a ring; yet if you can imagine the three bands flowing over and around and next to one another smoothly, unceasingly, and slowly - in a stately manner - in Eternity, you can share the picture in my mind which best symbolises, for me, God's Trinity-in-Unity: God's inner Life, of which He has revealed something to us, through Christ. It is a Life in which Three Divine Persons, One God, exist as beautiful and changeless, and yet are 'at work' unceasingly, 'flowing' in the heart of Eternity.

How amazing it is, that God is Love, and that He invites us to live within His life of unceasing Love, first through our faith and baptism, and in the union of Holy Communion, and then - as He draws the soul towards Him in contemplative union - in prayer, and, at the end of our lives - we hope with all our hearts - in Heaven. What more could He do for us, and how astonishing it is that we have ever complained about His requests, or about His care of us!

Body and soul.

[You'll notice that I've said a great deal about the soul, but very little about the body, which Christ and Christians believe to be so important that we rejoice in the thought of its resurrection and glorification. I hope I've said enough, however, about reverence in prayer, and therefore about posture, at least to indicate that each one of us is created body and soul: each of us one person who is bodily affected by spiritual good and evil and is also spiritually affected to some degree by bodily pains or delights. But this is such a vast subject that I'll say no more, having chosen to stress, earlier, that whatever touches our lives - our bodies or souls - is 'met' and dealt with by us in our soul's interior where, of our free will, in our inmost heart, we take up either a loving or a self-centred stance or attitude towards other people and towards God.]

Unnecessary changes.

How much more I could say - about God and His creatures. But the main point has been made: that everything I've been permitted to learn of God, through the experience of being taught by Him and of hearing His words, has made me see more clearly the wonder of all that Christ taught his Apostles and now teaches us through His Church. The Three Divine Persons are equal in majesty and in purity and in every perfection; and it's the Will of God the Holy Trinity that we delight in the Father's Fatherhood, in the Son's Sonship and in our in-corporation in Him, and also in the Spirit's role as Consoler, as the Three Persons draw us into the wonder of life in the Glory of the Godhead, at our consent, and after penance and purification; and it's God's Will, also, that someone like myself who, in adult life, has met this Love in its mixture of majesty and tenderness, its purity and its fervour, should speak about it -

about Him - through these writings, and so should invite other people to turn to Him in prayer.

Earlier this year - on February 16th 1998 - I thanked God once again for His goodness; and I asked Him: 'Who am I, to speak with You: Lord God, and Creator!" Then, straightaway, the Father showed me that He lifts my soul in prayer to such a height because of our close union, and in order to teach me. He taught me that I'm right to put my trust in Him. His holiness lies far above those who are occupied with earthly desires or ambitions; and yet I mustn't be afraid to say that I now live far 'above' earthly preoccupations, since I have truly reached the Father, "in" Christ, and now live joyfully in the Father's presence.

A 'return' from the heights.

As I've already indicated, my every prayer in this degree of union is greeted with Bliss, whether my prayer be an act of praise, petition or contrition. Such is the Father's delight in contrition and truth that Bliss is now His answer and gift to every movement of my heart towards Him; and that's why I wasn't surprised when Christ came to me in Holy Communion on 16th February and reassured me (in T:2503) that, truly, I love and greet the same God - the One, only God - whether I greet Father, Son or Holy Spirit. But then Christ also taught me, as I offered His Glory to the Father in praise and thanksgiving, that it is Christ Who brings my soul 'high' before the Father in contemplation: but not only so that I can praise God and delight in our prayer; it is also to give me so glorious a knowledge of Truth - of the Godhead - that I can help other people through my "return" from the heights of the mountain-tops of prayer.

At the same time, Christ reminded me that He once told a story about when Dives and Lazarus had died. The rich man called out to Father Abraham, who was cradling poor Lazarus in his bosom whilst he, Dives, the rich man, was in agony; and Dives begged for a warning to be given to his still-living brothers about selfishness and sin, and about God's Commandments, and reward and punishment; yet Abraham replied - Christ said, in His story - that "... THEY WILL NOT BE CONVINCED EVEN IF SOMEONE SHOULD RISE FROM THE DEAD" (Lk 16:31).

Then Christ explained to me that although the brothers in the story weren't given a special message about how to please God and save themselves from disaster, many people in our own day are being given useful reminders of the same things - and all because God has trained me, and has invited me to make a 'return' to the valley from the heights of the mountain-tops of prayer, in order to share the knowledge I've been given: to offer reminders of the Eternal Truths about God, and mankind, and Christ, and Salvation, and to do so through this spiritual autobiography and through several volumes of 'Christ's Instructions.'

Further Volumes.

It's time for me to finish this book, at last; and it gives me greater courage to share it, when I remember that Christ has shown me very recently - on July 3rd, 1998 - that this spiritual autobiography is reaching completion, as He had planned, just as I'm becoming bolder and more carefree, in doing this work. I'm so aware of the many good things that He has done for me that I yearn to do 'Apostolic' as well as contemplative work. I'm longing to "GO OUT TO THE WHOLE WORLD" to "PROCLAIM THE GOOD NEWS" (Mk 16:16): the good news about His Love, and about the good things which He's done for me, and which He can do for everyone who will believe in Him.

Everything important in Christ's sight - I mean everything to do with this task - is ready now. What we call the 'red book', or Volume Three of "Teachings-in-prayer: "Christ's Instructions", was written and printed by January this year; and the 'yellow book - Volume Four - was ready by May of this same year, 1998. In August, only a month ago, as I write this, what we call 'the Priests' Book' - "My Priests are Sacred" - was compiled and printed. It's a collection of teachings selected from all four volumes of "Christ's Instructions": a selection of passages which are about the ministerial Priesthood or which are relevant to it; and I only produced it - as I only produced "How to pray," which followed it - because it's what Christ has asked me to do. That's one of the reasons why I don't worry about whether the books will help people. Another reason is that God the Father has plainly shown me how much He delights in the books of 'Teachings'. He did so only this year, on 2nd April - and by an extraordinarily beautiful illustration.

When I'd only just arrived in church, that morning, I was lifted in prayer to Glory; this was how Christ rewarded me for being obedient and for having shown the latest book to my parish priest. Then, as Christ led me towards God the Father, it seemed more important than ever that I be simple and honest in prayer. That's why I said to the Father, immediately: "Father: Do You like the book?" - by which I meant the 'yellow book': Volume Four of "Christ's Instructions," which contains a dialogue between myself and the Father.

Straightaway, the Father gave me an image of Creation: of the Earth, teeming with life, before sin and sadness; and He explained, through this image, and with infused knowledge, (in T:2575) just what delights Him about this work which He Himself led me to undertake.

Our 'creation'.

The Father explained that He delights in seeing that my expressions of delight in Him are being broadcast to other people. He delights in work done in difficult circumstances - especially when that work consists of re-statement of His truths about certain subjects; and He delights in the love which has led me to follow His promptings - though I have to add that I haven't a scrap of love in my heart that He hasn't placed there first.

But the reason why He showed me an image of created beauty was this: the Father explained that if He were to express His delight about the books in a way which involved the natural world which He has made, and as if to provide me with an illustration of His delight, He would show me a bright ocean such as I could now see before me, teeming with life. He'd show me all the water-spouts where the whales are surfacing. He'd show me the waves glinting in the sunlight as shoals of fish encircle gaily beneath the surface of the water. He'd show me the flocks of birds which are soaring through the bright sky in the soft, sweet, breezy evening air, as His Glory is shining on high, over everything; and through this image, the Father explained, He is expressing delight in my love. This image of His own beautiful Creation is His way of showing me His delight in the special work which He and I have 'created' together.

He explained to me, then, that this image is like a toy for a child on a special occasion; and the reason for this gift is that just as God the Father gazes upon all that is good, unspoiled and beautiful in His own Creation, so does He gaze upon my work: with delight.

Then the Father told me something more. He told me that He was giving me this 'gift' today - this illustration - as an indirect means of showing delight, instead of giving an immediate expression of His delight, precisely because He loves and cares for me. He knows that the plain sight of His Divine Love and delight would crush me, were I to see it here, in my present state: when I'm still a feeble soul, still in earthly life and therefore unable to bear the full sight of His beauty.

Good things to share.

Isn't it astonishing that God rewards me for work which He Himself has planned, prompted, inspired, made possible, and almost brought to fruition? Who is like God? Who could be kinder? That's why I say that I don't worry any more about the books, or about any part of this task. I'm sure that if Christ asks me to distribute books, He's bound to bring good results from such work; and I say this so boldly today, because I know Him.

He's so good: wiser and kinder than we've ever dared imagine - and longing to hear us welcome His friendship: longing to see us enjoy the good things He wants to share with us.

I count amongst those 'good things' all the further teachings I've received in the past two years - few of which are included here, but which can be found later on - God Willing - in Volumes Five and Six of "Instructions from Christ." Other 'good things' include the faith of my family. My husband was received into full Communion in January 1998 - by our elder son Stephen who, by then, had been ordained to the Sacred Priesthood, to my tremendous delight and gratitude.

By then, also, many volumes of teachings had been distributed. By that time, Christ had led me in prayer into "THE BRIGHTNESS OF THE LORD," (2 Co 3:18), as St. Paul says, and in doing so had given me the sign which would help both my parish priest and our Bishop to recognise that God Who uses, as St. Paul also says, "THOSE WHO ARE NOTHING AT ALL" (1 Co 1:28) has indeed used me to give a message to His People.

That message is a reminder that He is at work, to help us, as much today as in past ages. It's a reminder that He can help all who turn Him in trust and repentance, and that He does so from the depths of His Infinite tenderness and compassion. He is longing to see us leave behind all sin and danger so that we can enjoy the blissful friendship of Himself and of His Saints, though not just as joyful and obedient members of His Church on earth who already enjoy the riches of her Tradition and the gifts to be found in her in everyday life. He yearns for us to enter Heaven, as Saints, to share and to enjoy for all Eternity, in Bliss and Glory, the sights of God and Our Lady: and to meet all the Saints and Angels who have shared, invisibly, in all the worship which we've offered to the Holy Trinity during our life on earth.

FALLING IN LOVE

APPENDIX

"But still we have a wisdom to offer those who have reached maturity: not a philosophy of our age, it is true, still less of the masters of our age, which are coming to their end. The hidden wisdom of God which we teach in our mysteries is the wisdom that God predestined to be for our glory before the ages began. It is a wisdom that none of the masters of this age have ever known, or they would not have crucified the Lord of Glory; We teach what scripture calls the things that no eye has seen and no ear has heard, things beyond the mind of man, all that God has prepared for those who love him.

These are the very things that God has revealed to us through the Spirit." (1 Co 2:6-10)

THE APPENDIX

CONTENTS

CONTENTS (Continued)

CONTENTS (Continued)

Section   Page

INTRODUCTION

a) THE PURPOSE OF THE APPENDIX.

The 'pattern' of prayer.

Now that I've written at some length, in the narrative, on the way in which someone can 'discover' the Catholic Church, the Catholic Faith and prayer, and have also mentioned some of the trials and torments of the early spiritual life, I'm required to recall, list and describe the many blessings and the many degrees of intimacy and union which are conferred upon the soul by God in what is called 'advanced' prayer. It's only because of His invitation that I attempt this.

I've had to describe these things from my own experience, since I'm not learned, and haven't studied in any depth the experiences of others. However, to judge from what I've read here and there, the stages which I describe both in the Narrative and in this Appendix follow the commonly-accepted 'pattern' of mystical prayer - even though the names which I've given to the categories of prayer might be different, simply because of my separation in time from other such writers, or because of ignorance on my part.

It seems to me that what I'm writing sounds very formal, or stilted. This is perhaps inevitable since, first, I've little experience in writing of these things, and no advice on the writing itself, but only an assurance that the 'teachings' which I receive in prayer are a true gift from God. Secondly, it seems extremely important to me that these matters are described accurately and calmly; so there's no place here, I feel, for the colloquialisms or the flourishes I might have used in a letter to a friend.

As with so many other things, I must do the best I can and leave the results in God's hands. Nothing could have made me even dream of attempting to write about such things - things which are so sacred, and which I'm not fit to describe - if it hadn't been made plain to me that it was the Will of God that I first write this piece about prayer, and then use it at the conclusion of a volume of spiritual autobiography.

An enormous volume.

The first draft of a long piece about prayer and its categories, now revised, and placed in

Sections three, four, five and six of this Appendix, was written at intervals as I pressed on with my usual domestic work and worship and outings, in the early 1990's. Gradually, I came to see how much of what I'd written in the past few years was to be gathered in one work, which if I'd been asked to undertake it, all at once, in the beginning, would have tempted me to run away in despair.

As Our Lord led me so gently to do first one section of the work, and then another, He was patient with my puzzlement. He knew that I'd learn to have greater trust in Him. I found that an enormous body of work was steadily being prepared for the future: for a time known only by Christ Who had been guiding me through the various stages of the spiritual life as well as through the stages of writing.

Now I've been shown by Christ, in 1998, that the whole written work is to consist of this spiritual autobiography with its Appendix on Prayer, and also of several volumes of "Teachings-in-prayer: Instructions from Christ" - now written in the first person in accordance with His wishes; and I'm content to do what He asks of me next, even though I'm not sure exactly what use will be made of it. I trust in the Providence of God, Who guides everything wisely, and guides in the best possible way everyone who sincerely asks His help.

Beginning with 'the basics'.

Throughout much of this Appendix, you'll see references to the sorts of devotions which are commonplace but valuable in Catholic life, and which I've practised throughout the past thirty years. I've omitted the practice of some of these devotions, temporarily, in times of illness or crisis, but, thanks to God, have never omitted the 'basics', by which I mean daily praise and thanksgiving to God, in whatever 'shape' it has been offered.

As I shall tell, I haven't included these details in order to persuade anyone to pray as I've prayed, but - in obedience to Christ's invitation - only to show that the true prayer-in-union which many of us have hoped to achieve needs a firm foundation.

Although it's true that we can only pray because God in His kindness has first prompted us to do so, and then has enabled us to pray to Him by the power of His Spirit, and in the Name of Jesus, it's also true that without our free decision to co-operate with what is usually an interior, spiritual prompting, prayer doesn't 'begin'. It's our responsibility to find a time and a place where we can express our utter dependence on God, and our longing to know Him, to serve Him, to praise Him, and to share His Life.

It's usually only when we begin to make 'space' for God in our lives and begin to want to love Him that we start opening the door of our hearts from the inside - so to speak - and so allow God to shine His Light within our souls and our lives; and until the 'door' has been opened by a willing soul, the adventure which is mystical union with God can't usually begin: so great is God's respect for our free-will. He forces no-one to love Him, but gives the gentlest invitation and 'awaits' a free response.

Private prayer: an introduction.

It's because so much of this Appendix necessarily describes things to do with long-practiced devotions, and also 'extraordinary' prayer, that I'm offering a few pages here, in this introduction, about how to begin to pray: for some of you who perhaps have never prayed, and don't know how to start.

What I intend to say is: here's a way of praying which is fairly straightforward and which will bring someone close to God, if he chooses to practice it. But I'm not saying that it's the best or the only way.

If I met someone who asked me to teach her how to swim, I'd probably teach her 'the side-stroke'; but another person might teach her how to do 'the crawl'; but in either case, she'd learn how to move in such a way that she stayed afloat in the water and - at the same time - also moved swiftly to the other side of the pool.

So each of us must pray in the way which God has brought to our attention through books, perhaps, or through prayerful friends - as long as that prayer involves belief in God, with reverent and trusting attention to Him as we approach Him in the Name of Christ. I'll explain more about Christ in a moment; but every reliable Christian teacher wants to help people to raise their hearts and minds to God; and so all methods and recommendations can be judged - if this is necessary - by whether or not they do indeed encourage people to move towards God in praise, thanksgiving, contrition and trust.

---

b) HOW TO PRAY.

What to do first.

This is what I've suggested to people who've asked me about prayer, though, as I've said, there are numerous valid and worthwhile 'approaches'; and of course we can pray absolutely anywhere, at any time; but my aim has always been to encourage people to develop the habit of prayer; hence the details below. I usually say something along these lines:-

"Go to your room and lock the door; or, if you don't have a room of your own, go to a quiet place such as a Catholic church or the corner of a park.

If you're outdoors, you can stand, sit or kneel; but if you're indoors, kneel if you can. Kneel by a cupboard or by your bed if you need something to lean on. You can lie flat on your front on the floor, or sit on the bed, if you prefer - but it's good to kneel before God if we're healthy. It helps to remind us of Who He is and how powerful and marvellous He is, besides loving and fatherly. We mustn't worry about Him; but although we shall learn to trust Him, to believe in His love for us and to chat freely about our most secret and perhaps shameful worries, we should know that God is nevertheless more glorious and worthy of respect than anyone we have ever met or imagined.

First: do one minute's plain thinking ... of something on these lines: God is certainly mysterious; He might seem to be far away. But the Church which was founded when God (as

Jesus) came to earth and lived amongst us now continues to teach us what God is really like. It teaches us that God is almost mad with love for us. He thinks we're marvellous - and wants us to be happy! He wants us to turn to Him in all our troubles and to put our trust in Him, which is why we kneel besides our beds - or elsewhere, really believing that God is pleased and delighted that we have turned to Him for a few moments, uninterrupted by distractions, so far as is possible at present.

So: honesty is all! You have Someone listening Who is 'thrilled' by all your good points, and Who longs for you to be happy despite all your fears and phobias and failings, or, rather, even now: with your private phobias and failings, which don't stop Him loving you. Quite the contrary: He has tremendous pity and compassion for you in your difficulties. He cannot resist hearts which admit their weaknesses frankly and humbly.

So: make the Sign of the Cross. By that act of faith (for such it is) you place yourself surely within God's life, 'in' Christ.

Then try shutting your eyes, and turning your inmost heart and thoughts and longings and towards the God-in-darkness when you can't see or imagine but Whom you believe is with you. You don't have to see: only to believe and to pray sincerely. Just push aside, gently, the Father-Christmas-type images which float into view. But don't worry if you're not successful. We are all helped, early on, by different images.

But, if you can, peer into that interior darkness, steadily, and say to the God who made you and Who loves you more than you know, whatever is most truly the thought or desire at the 'centre' of your heart, at present, perhaps:
- "Here I am", or
- "I feel silly, but I'm trying to pray," or
- "Show me Who You are", or
- "I'm lonely; are You really there?" or perhaps
- "This is what I'm terrified of, and this and this; I'll wait here while you give me some of Your peace, because I believe You can."

Then, believe that God will give you some help and enlightenment and peace, even if your mind is going in six directions at once, and you don't seem to feel peaceful. You will be calmer and wiser when you leave prayer than you were before it, and also wiser in the judgements and activities which you take part in afterwards.

Whatever good might seem to have come from your prayer-time might not seem to 'last' for long; I mean - we so quickly fall back into old patterns of thinking; so don't keep looking for changes within yourself. Practice improves everything; and that's one reason why we so desperately need to pray regularly, though in a way which suits us. I mean that some people enjoy meeting God in silence, whilst other people feel lost if there's nothing 'going on,' and need words as a framework for prayer; and it's for those who want something to cling to, or who want a sort of ladder which will lead them to a point at which they can launch out into wordless prayer, later on, that I make these simple suggestions for a daily routine:-

Put yourself before God.

Tell Him honestly what is filling your inmost heart and mind.

Tell Him all the other fears and miseries.

Thank Him for the good things!

Say sorry for any way in which you've been thoughtless towards other people or have neglected the things you know God wants you to do: things which trouble your conscience.

Trustingly, ask God's help for all the persons closest to you, or whom you worry most about.

Ask God, confidently, for the grace to go through the day calmly, working hard at what needs doing, but not worrying about little failures.

You might turn your inmost heart, too - and practice and grace will make this easier - towards Our blessed Lady, who is there in Heaven longing to help us. Ask her to pray for you. In fact - be bold: ask all the Angels and Saints to pray for you - they will!

Stay there silently, at peace for a few moments, if you're able, simply to honour God by your silent attention to Him in naked faith. But be happy to get up or stay still. He's delighted with every sincere prayer - long or short.

If you want to pray for a bit longer, but aren't happy with silent attention to God, read a prayer from a prayerbook, and offer those thoughts to God, if you can make them your own.

Then, if you can, prepare your mind to go out into 'normal' life again, saying "In the name of the Father and of the Son and of the Holy Spirit" whilst making a careful sign of the Cross. This is not like adjusting your spectacles or putting away a prayer book. It's a very prayerful and powerful help and protection, and puts us ever more firmly within God's grace and protection. That's why early Christians - and most Christians through the centuries, and many today - make the Sign before and after each prayer-time, before setting out on a journey, or beginning a new project, for example: whether a meal or a letter to a friend, or a new shift at work.

Progress in prayer.

All prayer is good, but better prayer means more help, not because God won't help us unless we pray 'well', but because of His respect for us. He so respects our freedom and our privacy that He doesn't trample all over our souls - so to speak - without permission. But if we regularly invite Him to help us, He works quiet wonders in our lives.

So if you - or anyone - can pray to God in the name of Jesus (more about that in a second) every morning and evening, though without thinking "He'll be put off" you if you're too tired or busy to pray now and then, you will progress rapidly in quite a short while, provided that you turn to Him in utter sincerity. You can tell Him anything and everything and He will help you to sort out your life to your best advantage, teaching you to see things as He sees them, and teaching you to trust in Him in every difficulty.

But: remember: God is Truth as well as love; so we grow closer to Him the more we dare to speak only perfect truth to him: I mean, the real truths which are in our hearts as we pray, even if the truth is that we're worried about spots, people, stomach-aches or exams. Tell Him! You can pray for your friends, too, and for the poor and the starving: but you won't pray for them well or sincerely until you've told God the truth about your real fears and desires.

By the way: do read a little bit from a good book in your prayer-time, if it helps you to gather your thoughts together at the beginning, or if a few phrases of someone else's prayer or reflection can help to 'launch' you more swiftly toward God than your own vague thoughts and yearnings. There aren't any rules, as such, in private prayer, which is meant to be a sincere and trusting opening-of-our-heart to God, so that He can draw us closer to Himself, teach us about Himself, lead us to see more clearly our own selves and the needs of other people, and so purify and change us and make us Christ-like and loving and joyful. Whatever assists us in this process, therefore, is worthwhile, provided that its 'seasoned' with common-sense and prudence.

The reason for our trust.

It seems important, now, that I attempt to solve two small worries before I finish. At least - these points worry most people, though not all. But I'll jot them down here, while they're on my mind.

What makes Christianity unique is that Christians pray to God as children to their Heavenly Father. When we pray to God "in the name of Jesus" we mean that since God Almighty took flesh from Mary, became man, died, rose again and returned to Heaven, where He waits - as it were - for us to join Him, we can be sure that since we now believe in Him, and have been baptised into His Life, or hope to be baptised, and follow His example (guided by His Holy Spirit) we are allowed to address Almighty God not only as "God" or "Your Majesty" (on our knees) but as "Father" or "Abba": which means "Daddy".

It's solely because - through baptism or through our desire for baptism - we now belong to Jesus, that we have the right to stand before God and ask for and expect His help. We don't have to grovel, through ignorance, as though before a ruthless tyrant, though we must bear in mind what a privilege and marvel it is that, through Jesus' suffering and death, the sins we have committed against our holy, compassionate and Infinitely-good Creator can be forgiven.

We can pray to God with absolute confidence that we're like children whose every whisper is heard by an adoring Mother. God is no longer far away from us. God the Holy Trinity - Infinite God - even dwells within our souls.

But we mustn't tie ourselves in knots trying to understand the Holy Trinity. In our simple, honest prayers, you or I might instinctively say 'O God' or 'Jesus' or 'Heavenly Father'. (I prayed: "Oh You!" ... for years, very reverently.) Do what comes naturally - but don't try to 'imagine' God.

Various images of "Christ as Man" might come and go in our minds. They can be useful; but what matters is that we believe in Him. One day, we hope, He will lead us to the Father, even though He has said: "TO HAVE SEEN ME IS TO HAVE SEEN THE FATHER" (Jn 14:9).

Lastly, don't forget that this amazing Jesus to Whom we pray, and Who is so keen to help us, is Really Present in every place where the Blessed Sacrament is found.

We who believe this sincerely - and it's the Church's true and accurate and important teaching which Saints have died to defend - will be enormously comforted not only by each prayer made on a bus or bench, or in a café or disco, but also by the Real Presence of Christ Who is really there with us in every chapel of the Blessed Sacrament: just as near and dear as He was to His Apostles in Galilee - only in a different way: a sacramental way.

So we can speak to Christ there, pouring out our problems, or pleading for others, or just saying 'Thank You very much' for good things. He's always waiting to listen to us, but loves to give us His interior gifts too; so it's silly not to take advantage of His marvellous Presence.

Offering up our sufferings.

In between your prayer-times, and throughout the whole day, "offer up" your sufferings, united in prayer with Christ. This will make you one with Him in helping and consoling suffering people. I'm not suggesting that we can't take steps to avoid suffering, to relieve pain, or to correct injustice, if we can do so charitably, in accordance with our circumstances and our duties and God's plan for us. There are many sufferings in this life, however, which we can't avoid, and which must be borne with patience if we want to imitate Christ our Saviour and model; and it's through such patient endurance that we can actively unite ourselves to Christ, and so help other people to bear their burdens and to be rescued from sin.

As soon as you meet unavoidable suffering - large or small - whether pain, disappointment, humiliation, grief, neglect, dismissal or toothache, turn to Christ. Tell Him that you accept this suffering and willingly unite it to what He bore in His Passion. Tell Him that you're doing this out of love for Him, in reparation for your own sins and for the sins of other people. This is a powerful and loving prayer which is very Christ-centred and effective.

Offer your sufferings in this way, regularly, for a special intention, if you wish to do so: perhaps for someone's conversion, or for a successful outcome to some good work, or for the Holy Father, or for a departed soul - or as a powerful prayer for more vocations or for people in special need.

Offer up your sufferings throughout each day, in union with Christ, in order to do what Saint Paul did, who said: I am suffering "... IN MY OWN BODY TO DO WHAT I CAN TO MAKE UP ALL THAT HAS STILL TO BE UNDERGONE BY CHRIST" (Col 1:24). It was Christ Who saved us by His Passion and Death; but we are privileged to be able to join in His redeeming work: to help to bring other people towards Him, through our patience in suffering and our union with Him.

Notice how everything that you used to find difficult can be 'converted' into a prayer, if you do as I've described. You can 'offer up' even encounters with people who despise you or with angry motorists. You can offer up each tedious delay in a hospital waiting room or each disappointment at work, or each painful step with a sore foot - or some perpetual, hidden heartache. Every single trouble can be faced, shown to Christ, accepted - by His grace - and offered as a powerful prayer to the Father; and the reason why the Father is so deeply touched by such prayers is that as we make them, we resemble Christ more closely than at almost any other time, since we're imitating Him in His submission, obedience, patience, forgiveness, and love for others.

Persecution.

Be Christ-like. If you receive insults for your Faith, accept them silently, as a penance. In the same way, accept disappointment, waiting, frustration or betrayal. Silently, turn to Christ in your soul, saying: "I accept this, for love of You. I unite my suffering to Yours, out of sorrow for my failings, and making reparation for the sins of others!" Bear the pain of it! Be resolved to share your Faith when circumstances permit.

Points to remember.

Put your trust in God, but don't keep worrying about seeing 'results'. It's true that prayer can work wonders, where there's a 'mustard-seed' of faith, and perseverance; but prayer doesn't instantly clear up every fear or phobia we have. It is, supremely, not a therapy, but a way of being in touch and staying in touch, very closely, with God Himself, Who gives us Divine Life, in Christ, and Who is more powerful than any number of healers or counsellors, though of course we ought to accept help from doctors and other experts when appropriate. But the important thing to remember is that God is a true Father to all who have put their trust in Him. He is constantly loving us: you and me; and He can lead us through our daily jobs and joys and miseries, giving more patience and calmness and real joy than we might have dreamed was possible.

It's true that our joy and peace does tend to get swamped, at each crisis. But if we pray regularly and well - although every prayer is a good prayer, in one sense - we shall find it easier to keep our balance in the difficult times, and we'll be less pessimistic generally, since we'll be starting to trust in God, at last.

Here's another quick word about honesty in prayer; an old motto is: "Do what you can and not what you can't". In other words - it's no good pretending to be devoted contemplatives if all we can honestly manage at this moment of our life is a sincere but gritted-teeth "Hello" to God when we fall out of bed each morning. So, too, it's no good pretending that we're not wounded, frightened persons if we are. Our loving God isn't like an employer who only wants to talk to us when we've cleaned ourselves up, and have put on our smartest clothes. He's infinitely holy and majestic in Himself, which is why we approach Him with honour and reverence; yet He is infinitely tender as well as holy; and so He is like a mother in His 'attitude' towards us: full of delight at our smallest efforts to respond to His invitations, ever-ready to listen to our sincere thoughts and confidences, and utterly joyful at seeing our little attempts to live as children of God should live, as we try to show towards others the love and forgiveness which we know God shows perpetually towards ourselves.

Even as we fail in so many of our efforts, we are immensely loved by God, Who delights in our efforts to begin again, and Who give us strength and peace whenever we open our hearts to Him in sincere contrition and trust. It's worth remembering, however, that there's one sure way of stopping progress in prayer: and that's deliberately to refuse to make efforts to conform our behaviour with what we know, in our hearts, to be right. To be deliberately and determinedly selfish, whether disobedient to God or malicious towards our neighbour, is to make oneself a hypocrite in prayer and so to turn ourselves away from God. But remember: He's never turning away from us: and so we can turn back to Him, to start again, a hundred thousand times; and, each time, He'll welcome us to His heart, whether or not we 'feel' it. That's the other thing to remember: that we live by faith, and don't rely on a diet of wonderful experiences to be kept going - though it's true that God gives gifts just when they're most needed, because He loves us."

---

c) A FEW 'HARD SAYINGS'.

Drawing closer to God.

Now that I've said such a lot about learning how to pray, I feel duty-bound to offer a few 'hard sayings' about how to draw even closer to God, day by day and year by year - when our 'honeymoon' of faith has almost ended and our difficulties seem to multiply at each renewed attempt to be fervent and faithful.

If we genuinely want to draw closer to God, we should first remember that we are already extremely close to Him in this sense: He made us from nothing, and He supports us in existence at every moment of our life. But, in the spiritual life, to grow closer to God is to become a truer friend of God - though astounded that we're invited to be so intimate with God Himself, Who is so beautiful, powerful, wise and glorious.

Through God's kindness, shown in the teachings and life and death and resurrection of Christ, each one of us can hope to become an intimate friend of God. Yet we have to do two things to bring about this intimacy or, rather, to say 'Yes' to the intimate friendship which, throughout our life, is held out to us.

First, we have to want to be close to God. Many people don't want this, because they know it will mean change and purification; and their fear and short-sightedness deter them even from hoping for such close union. They're willing to pray every day, but don't really want to become too 'involved' with God.

Secondly, we have to begin acting as if we are true friends of God, which means: expressing our attitude of friendship by trying to see and do God's Will, at this very moment, instead of putting Him on trial, so to speak, by demanding results and solutions before we'll consent to love and serve Him.

This is the point I want to stress above all, because there seems to be so much confusion about it nowadays. We don't grow closer to God by enjoying certain books, or by being stirred by certain pieces of music, or by relishing elevated thoughts about God, although all of these things can prompt us to begin praying or doing kind things, for God's sake.

It's only in trying to love and serve God right now, here, in my own peculiar circumstances, that I can hope to open up the 'channel' which unites His heart with mine and through which

He wishes to give me countless gifts: joy, peace, patience, wisdom, courage, humility, and many others.

If I'm not loving God's obvious Will for me at this very moment, I am quite obviously not loving God as I ought, since - faith tells us - God's infinitely wise Providence is drawing me through every single event and circumstance of life in a way which will bring me extraordinary growth and enormous graces: if I will consent to follow His path and not to pursue my selfish ambitions.

Finding 'true North'.

More than anyone, God knows in what way I can be encouraged in what my life should be 'about': which is the imitation of Christ's love and Christ's virtues, in my own era and my own circumstances; and God alone knows the special way in which I can most fruitfully love and serve the 'neighbours' with whom I hope to live for ever in Heaven, one day.

No sensible Christian can deny that following God's Will is sometimes painful or lonely; this is the 'Cross' which Our Lord spoke about. But no sensible Christian, I believe, can deny that at each moment that we're determinedly choosing to obey and serve God, we are thereby proving our love for Him, and at each moment that we're saying to Him: 'No, I won't do Your Will at the moment,' we're deliberately (thereby) putting a halt to any growth in intimacy that might have been underway: not because His Will and His Laws 'count' for more than anything, in a legalistic way, but because we, in such a stance, are freely choosing to turn away from Him.

So I'm not even talking, here, about serious sin. I'm saying that to turn away from God's Will in the slightest degree is to turn away from God, (as when a compass needle veers away from 'true North'). It is we, by our turning, who can 'cut off' the graces and helps which God wishes to pour upon us at the present moment. And if we are tempted to think that God is 'intolerant', we should reflect on the marvel of our relationship with Him. Here is God our Father, we can say, willing to live 'face to face' - as it were - with weak, pitiful human beings: and this privilege is ours because we have come to Him through Christ and Christ's Sacrifice; and, yet how tragic it is that instead of being thrilled by 'face-to-face,' moment-to-moment prayers and honest confessions and increasing friendship with God, we sometimes become fed up with God's Will and with feeling humiliated at how badly we serve Him. We lose our fervour or look 'sideways' at easier ways of life; or we kid ourselves that God doesn't care what we do; and even then, we're so anxious to claim that we still have a great friendship with God that we search for experiences which will give us warm 'religious' feelings and which will thus persuade us that we're as close to God as ever we were, despite our immoral behaviour or dereliction of duty. But it's important not to become confused about these things. We mustn't imagine that rectitude is what counts. If that were true, Christ would have given us a list of 894 good things to do, with 'points' to cross off for bad behaviour.

Good and evil.

As Holy Scripture says: it is *'a contrite heart'* which pleases God; and it's when our heart is turned to God, contrite, in the present moment, longing to love and serve Him, that we can be sure that God's graces are pouring lavishly upon us, to help us, even if unseen or unfelt; and those graces will make our poor, struggling, pitiful lives, glorious and fruitful!

That's why I urge people to struggle for holiness, yet why I urge them, also, to be on their guard, and to think about temptation: but not just about the temptations we usually hear about: to lust, anger or disobedience. It's worth thinking about what must be the attitude of the evil one - so named by Christ Himself - towards one of Christ's own friends who is trying to love and serve God as well as possible to definite circumstances, in the present moment? It's worth recalling the old phrase: 'Know your enemy.'

Obviously, temptations will be hurtled at such a person, to draw him or her away from 'the present moment' in which a really amazing and fruitful contact is made with God. The temptations will be aimed at both past and future; that person will be tempted to regret past choices, linger in memory on past injustices, or bewail an imagined lack of friends, opportunities or gifts. Then 'the future' will leap up within the imagination, pictured so colourfully as to make 'the present' seem dreary; even better, from the point of view of the evil one, the bright future - pictured so vividly - will be seen as impossible to embrace, because of certain attitudes or plans of a person's relatives or friends; thus, the evil one succeeds not only in making someone feel frustrated, but in poisoning certain relationships, and thus killing charity, which is his enemy.

There ought to be whole chapters written about temptation for the education of school-children who either have not heard the word in religious instruction lessons, or who have only heard the word in connection with jokes about early-nineteenth-century 'prudery' or "outmoded Victorian attitudes." But then, it would be hard to convince anyone of the dangers of temptation, if they don't believe in the tempter; and it's less and less common today, I've found, to hear people talk about good and evil, about Heaven and Hell, or about kindness and rebellion - as though in the world and the universe there exist only degrees of goodness, and no real danger: and therefore no need of talk about sin or the Cross or Salvation.

Greater strength from God.

Since we're all in such need of every scrap of help we can find, I can't finish this section without mentioning the effects of the sacrament of Confirmation in our lives. I've no wish to rush people one iota along their spiritual journey, but I want to show that fear and weakness of any kind aren't conquered fully or permanently by will-power alone. Common-sense and intelligence can lessen our very real fears and anxieties: indeed, God himself gave us our brains and common-sense and wants to use them; but His greatest gifts come through the sacraments; and we cannot do anything good without His grace.

We know that through conception, we're given life, and that through birth we're given the opportunity to use some of our natural gifts and aptitudes during our time on earth; but it's through Baptism that we are given the supernatural gifts - of faith and hope and love - and are given "Life in Christ," which includes the ability to pray as God's child, in the sure hope of being heard. It includes the right to call out confidently to God with Christ, and with our brothers and sisters, as Christians gather with Christ and with each other in the supreme act of prayer and praise and sacrifice which is the Holy Mass, and from which prayer all our private prayers draw their 'value'.

When, however, we are confirmed, we receive further gifts from Christ's Holy Spirit, Whom we received in baptism to guide us. His graces are poured out in our souls much more strongly; and the gifts which we are given at this time include Wisdom, Understanding, Counsel, Fortitude - which is courage of a special order - Knowledge, Piety, and the fear of the Lord: which means true awe and reverence. That's why I'd urge every Catholic who practises his or her Faith but who hasn't yet been confirmed to discuss the possibility with a priest.

God has so many ways of helping us; and it's plain sad if we don't hold out our hands, so to speak, for His free gifts.

Finding out more about God.

I'm sure that everyone who prays will pray even more fruitfully, the more each person finds out about God, Who is so loving and loveable, and about the Faith by which He wants us to live.

The better we know and understand our earthly friends, the more at ease we can be in our intimate conversations, and the more confidently we can set out to plan a particular treat, or to help them in some way. So it is with God: the more we know about Him, the better we shall pray to Him, love Him, know how to please Him, and confidently do what we know is His Will; and that's why all 'spiritual writers' recommend spiritual reading.

Try to set aside a few minutes, daily, to read even a paragraph of one of the following, to keep you more in touch with and fed by spiritual reality: a biography of a Saint or a few verses from the Gospels or other parts of Holy Scripture, a religious poem or pamphlet, a prayer book or a catechism - or a book of short reflections or meditations.

There are so many instructive and encouraging books available; but don't read anything. Look carefully. Make sure it is 'sound'. Unless your faith is mature and tested, stick to orthodox works. These will teach you much about God, and will also give you 'material' for informal meditations and for prayer.

So: do your thinking and praying and studying as and when you choose. But there are marvellous gifts for you to use when you feel able to call on them or when you fully believe.

Out of all of this, take what you can use, and ignore the rest. It's my little effort to help in the only way possible to me at the moment: through encouragement and advice; but only you can decide, in your heart of hearts, that if God created you so that you can love and serve Him now, and live with Him in bliss when this earthly life is over, it's worth making efforts to be 'in contact,' and to become one of God's good friends, through prayer and through a life of love and forgiveness.

That friendship is held out to us, now; and it's by deciding to pray, and by doing so - no matter how briefly - that we reach out to seize the friendship, and say 'Yes' to the hope of an intimate union which, in the end, will fulfil every dream and yearning."

d) THE APPENDIX: SEVERAL SECTIONS.

Several stages of prayer.

There follows, in Section one, a plain outline of the spiritual life, which I call 'DETERMINATION', or "The Journey of Faith". It seems appropriate that I summarise the soul's progress from birth to Union, and so remind the reader of the long and terrible journey which is contemplated when a sinful soul is willing to be purified, and so to be made fit for true union with God in Christ. The devout soul wants this, not because he wants suffering, but because he wants to love and serve God; and any encounter with holiness, when we are so imperfect, will inevitably involve suffering. Nevertheless, the willing soul can hope to live in a true Communion with Christ, even in this life, united with the Father in and through Christ, within the life and love of the Most Holy Trinity - though all of this is by faith, and not yet by clear sight: and yet that mystical communion gives incomparable bliss, even amidst earthly sufferings.

In Section two, I write about the preparations which are necessary for anyone who hopes to live in an intimate union of love with God during earthly life.

Section three is about various things to do with extraordinary prayer - sometimes called mystical prayer or true contemplative union.

Section four consists of a lengthly explanation of each stage of extraordinary prayer.

Section five provides an illustrated list of numerous stages in the mystical way towards union. It is illustrated by small line drawings only because the symbols shown are what I've devised as useful for my water-colour sketches of 'prayer-images'. This is explained more fully in the text.

Section six consists of a few water-colour illustrations of the different types of prayer-images mentioned in parts six and seven.

Section seven is my conclusion, with a list of the types of subject matter which are explained in Christ's 'teachings'.

Visions and locutions.

If anyone who reads about the numerous categories of prayer which I'm to describe (in Appendix 4 and 5, in particular) thinks it strange that an Appendix with such detailed information should have been placed here, or unnecessary, he can be assured that I, too, think it strange - but not unnecessary, and for this reason: that Our Lord has invited me to produce this work with its two unequal halves; and so I've done so, even though I don't understand every facet of His plans, and even though I'm more keen to dissuade people from taking notice of their visions or supposed visions than to make it easier for them to think about such things.

It seems to me, however, that the two parts of this book support one another. I mean that someone who reads the Narrative, yet who has doubts about the descriptions of prayer-experiences, can turn to the Appendix to find a systematic description of prayer-states: a description only achieved, I know - though I'm aware of its deficiencies - by someone who has in fact been taught by Christ and has been led by Him, in prayer, from one state or stage to another, to her amazement, but in accordance with His extraordinary plan. Then I mean, also, that someone who turns, first, to the Appendix and who has doubts about the truth of it - about whether God really induces such apparently-complicated states in the soul of someone who prays in the Name of Christ - can turn to the Narrative to find some enlightenment.

I believe that it's plain, in the Narrative, that the whole process of communion between God and the soul, with co-operation and commitment, is a lengthy and gentle process, initiated and guided by God. It will be plain, also, that the apparently 'complicated' prayer-experiences were only introduced by God a little at a time after a lengthy preparation; and I hope it will be plain that there was a wise purpose behind the gift of those experiences and 'teachings': and that purpose was not only wise but loving. It will be seen that as God led me through each new stage of prayer, He was drawing me into a closer friendship, helping me to mature in the spiritual life whilst also helping me to grow more child-like in my attitude towards Him; and He was - is - providing teachings which would help other souls besides myself, and which would make me so grateful and awe-struck that I became determined to put Him first in everything, no matter what it cost me.

Needless to say, I don't manage to do so, all the time, but He delights in our efforts to love Him; but that's a digression. I'm trying to say that it will be plain, perhaps, in the Narrative, that even the apparently-complicated prayer-experiences which I've described have the appearance of an ordered sequence which progressively enlightens my soul and also leads me on towards a greater and more wonderful knowledge of what-God-is-'like'.

Divine-human friendship: a parallel.

It might quieten one or two doubts that people have, as they read about 'complicated' sorts of prayer, if I explain that surely the friendship between God and a human being has a parallel in a relationship between earthly friends.

The love between two persons who are attracted to one another and who remain friends eventually becomes something simpler and clearer, whilst the interests which those friends can discuss and share perhaps grow broader - more complex - as each person grows in knowledge of the other; and so it is in our friendship with God. I mean that when someone develops an intimate friendship with God through prayer, the love between God and the soul might seem to grow simpler and purer; the expression of that love will become simpler, swifter, purer and more joyful; and yet the depths and breadths of 'knowledge,' experience and glory now found in that friendship in its fullness parallel the wider 'interests' of the earthly friends; and that's why my descriptions of the various categories of what I call 'extraordinary prayer' seem so complicated when they're captured in print: categorised, illustrated and labelled, although what is experienced in such states is wholly spiritual, light and gentle, illuminating and sanctifying and simple.

It's impossible to describe such things; but it's not impossible to attempt to do so in order to obey Our Lord's request; and so what I present is only an attempt; but I know that in His sight, it's sufficiently-accurate to achieve His purpose; and since His plans - He has told me - far surpass anything I might ever have dreamed would be possible, I'm content to finish this work and to leave it all in His hands.

---

1 DETERMINATION

THE JOURNEY OF FAITH.

---

a) THE GOOD BEGINNING.

Several stages of the spiritual life.

Before I begin to describe things to do with extraordinary prayer, I must try to give a brief word-picture of the spiritual journey in its entirety.

I can see clearly now, as if they were drawn on a map, the several stages of the spiritual life through which God can draw us, through our life in Christ; but I don't intend to reveal every detail of all those stages, since other writers have described much of the journey, and there's no need for me to duplicate their work. I mean that, at the beginning, all journeys are the same, even though our personal characteristics are different and our backgrounds and attitudes seem to be very unalike. The similarity lies in the effects produced in each individual soul when each person freely chooses to respond to the grace of God and therefore attempts to please God by doing good and by refraining from evil; and of course it's because of our Baptism that we can know that God's grace is ours, and is powerful; and it's also because of our Baptism that we can pray in Christ to our Father in Heaven.

We can never praise God enough for our life - for the life of body and soul - and for our birth; yet it's the second 'birth' - our Baptism - which should draw from us even greater expressions of gratitude and wonder.

This sacrament is so marvellous, both in what it signifies and in what it achieves, that we should never let a day pass without thanking God for having brought us into His own Life in this way, whether it was in infancy or in adult life. We should thank Him too, for all his gifts, in particular for our Confirmation in the Life of Christ, in the strength of His Holy Spirit, and for the Holy Eucharist, and for all the holy sacraments given to His Church. But I mustn't write any more on those subjects since my main task is to identify the stages of the spiritual life, with its peculiar joys and problems.

Mixed fervour and blindness.

Many 'beginners' are fervent. They pray a great deal; and since every attempt to love God more fervently draws upon the soul more grace and strength, no-one can fail to progress in the knowledge and love of God if, with all his heart and will he clings to God amidst all difficulties, trusting in God's goodness and relying on the benefits He pours out through His Holy Catholic Church.

It's true that, at the beginning of the journey to Union, few souls are aware of the extent of their own weaknesses. Nevertheless, when someone is faithful to prayer, is firm in resisting temptations, and remains resolute in his main ambition, which is to love God and his neighbour with his whole heart, then his progress will be rapid.

For the first few weeks - or years - someone might attempt to please God and to please his neighbour, when his aim should be to love God and his neighbour. Such a soul hasn't yet grasped that he can't please everyone, no matter how hard he tries. He works and prays with great generosity, but is secretly convinced that he can please God, on this earth, and at the same time can make others happy, too, without opposition or difficulty, as if Christ had never said that He came to set "A MAN AGAINST HIS FATHER" and to warn us that "A MAN'S ENEMIES WILL BE THOSE OF HIS OWN HOUSEHOLD" (Mt 10:35-36).

Little trust in God.

A fervent person might have much genuine goodwill, at this stage; but he usually has great faith in his own powers, and little real trust in God. He frequently interferes in things which aren't his business, proudly imagining that he can solve what others have failed to solve, even though he's quite blind to many of his own faults and makes excuses for his own backslidings.

During this time, the prayerful soul is full of contradictions, though he thinks himself sure-sighted and brave. By grace and by self-examination he begins to suspect his own lack of generosity, but he is still intolerant of others' faults. Even as he throws himself wholeheartedly into the loving service of others, prepared to exhaust himself for God's sake, he wonders why other people aren't more loving and generous. He thinks he is humble, because he is awe-struck when thinking of God and His Creation, but it is secretly proud of what he himself achieves; and although he has truly made great sacrifices for God, he is still fearful of the opinions of others - in ways which he doesn't yet see - and so trims the practice of his faith, unknowingly, less concerned with truth than with current fashions. I'm not speaking here of efforts to be tactful or thoughtful, but of the adoption of small but dangerous ways in which a compromise is made with the spirit of the world, in order to avoid suffering.

Despite immaturity, however, a good-hearted person deliberately attempts to practise the virtues, and begs God for the grace to eradicate apparently incurable faults. He genuinely wishes to grow in the knowledge and love of God, because this is what God wishes; however, he isn't yet willing to sacrifice all that is unworthy of the life of someone who wants to live in perfect union with God. He's not so foolish as to cultivate the perfection of his own soul in a narcissistic manner since he truly feels very humbled by the thought of God's perfection; yet he tends to forget that God alone has made possible his present exertions and triumphs. He becomes overwhelmed with work, since other people find him so willing and kind; but he hasn't yet found the courage to refuse things that he needn't do, nor has he opened his heart sufficiently to receive from God those powers of discernment which would enable him to see what is essential and what is not.

At this stage, such a soul rarely thinks about 'stages'. He's almost too busy to think, having to carve out, as it were, some time for prayer and spiritual reading, which he knows to be essential, as is attendance at Holy Mass and at the Sacrament of Reconciliation: I mean essential for the soul's health, even when someone might be excused attendance at Mass on account, perhaps, of ill health, or might know that "Confession" isn't obligatory for those who believe themselves to be free from grave sin.

That someone's love of God and of his neighbour is real can be shown by his longing to serve God perfectly - even though he's unaware of his own blindness about many things; and it's also shown by his struggles to serve and to cherish his family and friends, and not only them, but everyone he meets in the course of the day, especially those who are in trouble. It's shown, too, by his longing to know more about God, and about the Revelation once made in Christ and handed on in His Church. Since he is wise and good-hearted he tries to study the Faith, in a manner appropriate to his way of life.

Furthermore, he will be brave in resisting temptations, even though he might not be able to explain to other people everything he's doing. He develops a longing to do good and to avoid evil, guided by the Holy Spirit; and so he listens to those who guide Christ's Church on earth. He perseveres in regular prayer, however difficult. Vocal prayer will give way, at times, to affective prayer: that is, to words from the heart, which will be further nourished by regular spiritual reading.

Boredom or impatience.

At this time, such difficulties as there are in prayer stem mainly from tiredness, or from boredom or impatience. The tiredness is to be expected, but can be made worse by an eager person's senseless over-exertion, whether in works of charity which have been undertaken through pride, or in over-long prayer-times which someone who doesn't yet trust in the goodness of God dare not curb. The boredom is to be expected at times, since a soul at this stage is so unspiritual. He cannot yet claim that his 'dryness' and boredom are a special trial permitted by God. Impatience in prayer-time is not unusual in those who have more faith in the power of their own words and physical activities than in the prayers offered secretly, in obedience, by which God works many marvels on this earth, in every age.

At this stage, the fervent soul is frequently amazed at others' apparent faults, and can't understand why others don't do much for God. Worse than that, he thinks that his pity for others' lack of virtue is a sign of fervour and of love for God, whereas he is still very proud. He isn't aware that the time spent in judging other souls - and judging inaccurately, since he cannot see 'inside' them - would be better spent in looking at his own faults, with a truer repentance, or better still, in learning about God. Alas, at this stage, too, someone only begins to see himself more clearly if aided by light from God, and, here, the soul is usually too busy and troubled to allow God to shine that light within him in prayer - or else God permits this soul to continue in this partial blindness for a lengthier time, in order to bring about his conversion in ways unknown by us.

When someone at this stage truly regrets his own sins and failings - that's to say, the ones of which he's aware - he doesn't realise that his sorrow is caused as much by disappointment at failing in his own spiritual ambitions, albeit ambitions for God's sake, as by sorrow at betraying, even in small ways, his Lord and Saviour.

As time passes, the willing soul grows in faith, in hope and in love - though not in equal measure, since much depends upon his natural outlook and upon his temperament. I mean that someone who finds it easy to be pessimistic will need to grow in Hope more than will the person who has a 'sunny' disposition. Yet someone who continues on this path, faithfully, will make great strides, if he remains alert to the Will of God. God sends him all the help he needs - by books, persons and inspirations - and increases his earnest longings to please Him, causing the soul to resolve to be even more charitable and truthful. Nevertheless, the danger is more tremendous, the higher the soul is drawn by the grace of God; and that's why the fervent soul eventually finds himself in difficulties.

---

b) THE FIRST 'NIGHT' OF THE SOUL.

Purification and strengthening.

Just when the fervent soul is secretly hoping to be rewarded for all his courageous acts so far, he is astonished to find himself undergoing not just earthly troubles and opposition, but many distressing experiences, all of which have been permitted by God for the soul's sake, since no good person will persevere in faith during his life on earth unless his feeble faith is purified and strengthened in ways unforeseen by the 'beginner'. So he is soon drawn into the first spiritual 'night'.

One of the most distressing things for the soul at this time of change is the sudden 'dryness' or boredom found in prayer. Since prayer has been, so far, a pleasurable activity, the extent, now, of each soul's distress is an indication of his dependence on good experiences rather than on faith in God.

The spiritual darkness which the soul has entered can be called a 'night' of the soul. Now, this is a very mundane sort of 'night'. No-one need practice heroism to endure it. A generous soul kneels and prays as before, dryness or boredom notwithstanding. Faith tells each good soul that his worship of God and his acts of love for his neighbour are supremely important, whether his emotions seem fervent or tepid. Faith counts, not moods. Love is proved by deeds. At the same time, probably, those acts of love for neighbour are done with true goodwill, and also for the love of God, but with less joy than formerly. Everything seems to conspire to make the soul more irritable and doubtful. Here, provocations and ill-health, temptations and extraordinary demands from others can cause someone to question not only his way of life, but aspects of faith which haven't so far been understood. He might quake at the thought of the demands which could be made upon him, and hope that he won't be asked to undergo anything painful or humiliating in the years ahead.

A moment of crisis.

One day, probably after many years of hard work and struggle, a good person will see that pain and humiliation in the service of God are inevitable; and it will be at that point that he will be brought to choose, once again, whether or not to serve God despite the great cost. But until that moment of crisis, he might live for weeks or years half-way through the foothills, as it were - working for God, praying with a devoted heart, experiencing occasional peace and sweetness in prayer, and usually but not always resisting gross temptations, yet all the while aware that he hasn't yet handed over his whole life to God, in complete trust. He fears illness, misunderstanding or pain. He fears death. He sacrifices, unnecessarily, things which God is willing for the soul to use or enjoy, whilst refusing to give to God what, above all, God Wills he should give, by which I mean his own self-will and independence.

Alas, even with a considerable amount of self-knowledge a fervent soul can deceive himself in serious ways. For example he might begin to look back over the 'journey' with nostalgia and some degree of satisfaction. He can grow proud at the sight of all that he has willingly sacrificed for the love of God. He secretly congratulates himself on having endured all sorts of minor trials and persecutions, and begins, perhaps, to forget his former weakness.

He forgets how firmly he was once "bogged down" in a pit of bad habits before the grace of God enabled him to stumble onto the bank. He even forgets that it was by God's grace that his more recent charitable and brave acts have been accomplished, and he congratulates himself on his virtues. He might even despise souls who appear less virtuous or less disciplined. He truly loves God and wants to serve Him, but the love is so firmly mixed with vanity and conceit that only by the 'scouring' which occurs when terrible troubles and upheavals are bravely accepted can such a soul be brought to see clearly where his real ambitions lie. As he begins to understand himself at last, and to become aware of the obstacles which keep him from growing towards true union with God, he quakes at the prospect of change.

The prospect of change.

It is here that the soul attempts to bargain with God about certain things. Here, someone might live in constant anxiety because he can't let himself say 'yes' to God; yet he can't turn away from Him; or the soul averts his eyes, so to speak, from the area where he isn't utterly faithful, or utterly pure, and so continues to compromise with the world's ways. He resigns himself to spiritual mediocrity, not realising that he's endangering himself, since no-one remains stationary, so to speak, in the spiritual life.

The saddest and most terrible state-of-soul possible at this time is the state in which someone who is unable to consent to serve God as He should be served not only persuades himself that God asks too much of him - forgetting Christ's bitter Passion - but then makes matters even worse. He convinces himself that what the Church teaches and always recommends is not what Christ would teach us, today. Worst of all, he debates these things with many others in order to salve his own conscience and to lessen his loneliness; and so he disturbs the faith of other people. Such a soul will be held responsible not only for his own faults or cowardice, but for his influence in having drawn others away from God.

It's quite possible that someone who genuinely longs to serve God - even though sadly aware of his own weakness and lack of courage - might continue for a long time in the genuine loving service of God and of his neighbour, even 'peeling away' further layers of selfishness by his good works and acts of penance, as he lives in true humility. But until he's prepared to open his deepest heart to what he knows God wants - and God wants the soul's complete and everlasting happiness - he won't be pierced and transformed by God's own sanctity. He will do good works, but he won't bear marvellous fruit: one hundred or one thousand-fold.

Someone who, by the grace of God, does continue to offer himself to God, in heart, soul, body and mind, to be used how God Wills, for His Glory and for the salvation of souls, and despite some felt reluctance and fear as he makes this true and loving sacrifice, is drawn on by God towards a deeper and more thorough purification that he has ever dreamed might be possible.

Towards greater humility.

Such a soul as this has already undergone a certain amount of true purification. He has been purified in one sense, even by his falls: or rather, by the results of sin acknowledged and repented of, since these falls can propel the good soul towards a far greater humility than he possessed before.

However, many of the methods and details of the purification undergone so far have been self-chosen, and thus have been flawed; and since there's no greater perfection in anything than to do God's Will rather than our own, and since this is true of penance, too, the purifications just described have therefore been inadequate.

As I said, a soul might 'hover' in this place for a short while, or for a long time; but God in His goodness will permit the soul to be brought, not once but many times, we hope, to the point where the difficult but essential choice must be made: will the soul die to selfishness in order to love God and to do His Will to the utmost?

One day, more solemnly and sincerely than ever before, the willing soul decides, again, to love God, whatever the cost. He sees nothing ahead but blackness and danger and loneliness, but he voluntarily sets out to serve God more perfectly, relying on His grace alone, despite his own terror.

---

c) THE SECOND 'NIGHT' OF THE SOUL.

The fires of humiliation.

At this point, a fervent person now enters the state known as the second 'night' of the soul. Up to this point, the fervent soul has been active in his own self-purification. At the prompting of God, he has cut and pruned his life-style and has given up bad habits. He has curbed his extravagances and dubious pleasures. But now, suddenly, he finds that he is quite without satisfaction as he considers his way of life, and his efforts to be virtuous. Rather, he burns with humiliation at seeing his own faults. He feels utterly 'passive' beneath a purification which comes from God - except that it doesn't feel as though it's from God. Every sin is remorselessly revealed to that person's spiritual sight, and he recoils from what he now sees.

How few souls have enough faith to be able to cling to God and to profess to love Him, now.

They find that even the outward circumstances of their lives are turned upside down. Good things seem terribly fragile, ill-health is common, and temptations, if recognised, become ever more subtle. God, Who is good, doesn't send temptations; but it's by His Providence that the person He wants to purify - for that soul's joy and for His own Glory - is led to see that by nothing except faith can he cling to God, in the hope of loving God and neighbour; yet such a soul feels that he no longer knows the meaning of "faith". On the contrary, he feels quite deserted by God, and, at the same time, is plagued by further scruples and by doubts about any number of things.

In this torment, interior and exterior, such a soul is convinced that he doesn't love God, even while he endures dreadful sufferings rather than offend Him. The soul blindly trusts in God in the depths of his misery; and even though he seems to be seeing and understanding nothing, he begins at last to live by pure faith, selflessly, though he doesn't know it. He sees only his own sins; and this is what God allows to happen, for the soul's purification. The clear view of sinfulness which is often experienced at this stage hasn't been brought about by a person's own reflections.

When someone has decided, firmly, to keep on trying to love God and neighbour, whatever the cost, he half-hopes for some reward, and yet - there is none. God is teaching him the meaning of true love; there's no other way by which anyone can learn this essential lesson. So here, there's no illumination for the soul who still perseveres; nor does he receive any assurance of a right choice. He has to be content with the dark, naked assurance which he receives by faith, as he examines his conscience and yet remains at peace because he knows that with every atom of strength, he clings fervently to God and avoids deliberate sin.

---

d) TRUE LOVE FOR GOD.

Blind trust.

This is the point at which many souls demand security of one sort or another; however, the greatest love for God is displayed by those who are willing to serve Him in this state, according to His Will, in blind trust, day after day and even year after year.

Of the few who have walked this far, and who have said "Yes" to God, even fewer have had the courage to rely on His help as they not only follow the difficult path which lies ahead, as they see nothing but blackness and danger, but continue on it for many years even when it seems to grow still blacker and still more dangerous, and when God seems to have deserted them entirely.

So it can happen that, for many years, someone in this state might even think that he'll probably be damned. There is not only no joy in prayer, but emptiness instead, and horror. By naked faith alone, at this stage, does someone survive for one minute at a time, believing in God's love but no longer knowing what that means. Such a soul is aware only of his own feebleness beside the holiness of God Who is Unseen but Who is somehow Known; but as he clings to God and to the Will of God in faithfulness through exterior trials and interior torments, while convinced that nothing that he himself is doing can be considered of much value, he achieves more for himself and for other souls by one minute of his patient endurance than other souls would achieve by ten years of self-chosen, vainglorious Christian works; but of course he doesn't know this.

Strong, pure love.

In this state, the willing person simply shoulders his cross again and again, and continues to call out to God for help as he does his work cheerfully from moment to moment with a strength that he knows, obscurely, can only be from God, for he has no strength, it seems, of his own. Perhaps many years pass by in this way. There seems to be no cause for optimism, and the soul's pain at the sight of his own wickedness is almost unbearable. God, who sees everything, sees that this soul is pure and strong; yet no-one in such a state imagines himself to be virtuous.

Thus it is that, for love of the soul, God has brought that soul to love and serve Him in an entirely self-forgetful and divine manner - for that's the way to the soul's eventual perfect and everlasting bliss. But God doesn't yet 'step in' to lighten all the soul's burdens; on the contrary, He eventually gives him an opportunity to imitate his Master in Gethesemane.

Willing to choose death.

At some point, through a peculiar problem, or a strange set of circumstances, the soul is required to choose, once again, whether or not he'll put God 'first' in his life; and here, the faithful soul chooses death, in order to love God as well as he can. Only by grace is he able to do this; but at last he is willing to be annihilated out of love for God; and, then, God knows, or rather sees, that Jesus Christ His Son has a true child on earth. I said "death" - whether it be a death of martyrdom by blood, or a death of human hope or ambition, or the death of pride or of something else which has brought this person to the 'precipice', where, if he would prove his love, he must jump into the arms of the invisible God in total darkness.

This might be done with feelings of only horror and fear; yet it's in the doing - in this "leaping-in-faith", from a true, pure love of God - that someone faithful proves his love and, unbeknown to himself, thus merits union.

In this deep night, in a daily agony of soul, there's no glimmer of light in any direction. Yet it will be here, in this darkest night, that the true Light will soon be given in prayer. This will be the beginning of this person's spiritual resurrection, or - I mean - the beginning of fruition in his life of union with God on earth.

Many persons weaken, and give up the struggle, here, for such is the torment of this path that very few are courageous enough to go on in such difficulties. Few are willing to bear the sight and knowledge of their own wickedness, a knowledge given by God with such clarity, and for such a long time. But someone who now perseveres, expecting no help or refreshment, and content to serve God - even though feeling that he serves Him badly, if at all - is one day astonished to be shown how much he is loved by God; and here, in some measure, God lifts the soul towards Himself, in a manner which is clear and unmistakable; and thus in one blissful moment God lightens every burden and overwhelms the soul with joy.

e) THE SOUL'S 'BETROTHAL',

Radiance and joy.

Such a soul suddenly finds himself raised from his sufferings, brought into a relationship of such wonderful, blissful intimacy that he couldn't have borne such joy - such is God's power and purity - if he hadn't been prepared by the passive purifications which have scoured and burnished him for so long. At about this time he is given, too, a glimpse of the 'road' upon 'which he has been travelling.

This is the soul's 'betrothal'. Someone who has reached this stage is so joyful that he looks at all his past agonies as nothing, compared with his present bliss, even if the radiance of the betrothal lasts only a short while. He marvels that God has drawn him so close to Him; also, he looks at his neighbour, now, with an entirely new insight and compassion. He is driven more by love than by duty, at last.

There's still so much impurity in the loving soul, however - even in the few who have reached this small summit - that, for his own good, and for the good of all the others who will benefit from his sanctity, the soul is led by God through darkness once again, in a continuous night.

Such a soul grows stronger and less fearful. But he experiences true 'night,' still, as he is almost overcome, again, by the awareness of his own sinfulness, and is horror-struck at his past offences against God's holiness; for now no offence seems small or unimportant. Yet God strengthens and purifies him; and if this soul is faithful he grows in true humility, which brings peace.

Here, the faithful soul learns to turn away from the sight of his own feebleness, and learns to rest his eyes, so to speak, on God's goodness, and on the needs of his neighbour. He learns to forget self, at last. He doesn't forget his own obligations and duties, but his own desires; and he calmly accepts the continual aching pain of his true self-knowledge and his insight into a number of his unworthy hopes and motives.

So it is from this time, usually, that God Who cannot fail to "fill" and to adorn the soul with graces, the more the soul empties himself to make "room" for God, occasionally adorns the soul with His Wisdom and Knowledge and Understanding; and such a soul begins to resemble God in extraordinary ways, even though this soul doesn't see the resemblance, and doesn't yet know what's happening in his own interior darkness.

Towards complete desolation.

This state might last for several years; but whatever has been experienced, this stage of the journey ends not in delight, but in utter desolation. God cannot permit anyone to progress to the marvel of true, known, continuous union with Him, until that soul has been thoroughly purified. The final purification of this stage of the spiritual life will be unexpected and crucifying; moreover, it will occur just as earthly trials seem to grow more cruel and relentless. The faithful soul - who is already tempted to despair by his inner sufferings - experiences some or all of the following sufferings: misunderstandings, violence, and loneliness, and, worst of all, malicious attempts by the evil one to drive him to despair, or to paralyse him with fear.

Throughout every new trial, however - and only by the grace of God - the devoted soul freely and gladly says: "Yes" to God once again, and "Yes" to love of God and neighbour for God's sake, whatever the cost. Such a soul expects nothing but more darkness and pain, and isn't thinking of reward beyond a quiet conscience and a dark but true hope of Heaven: although he hopes to gain these through the goodness of God, only, and through the merits of Christ's Passion, convinced of his own utter unworthiness.

It is here that God, Who loves His creatures beyond anything we can imagine, brings that soul into true union with Himself, even on this earth; and the astonishing bliss of that union cannot be imagined or described.

The bliss of Union.

The journey to a perfect and everlasting union with God in Heaven isn't yet complete. But nevertheless, the soul, though living in faith, is now truly united to God; I mean that such a person now does all his work - as it were - hand in hand with God, and his heart is God's entirely. What God Wills, that soul wills, and, marvellously, what the soul wills, God Wills. Through his union with Christ, Who is the Door, the Gate, the Way, and the Image of the Father, the soul is suffused with joy, and is 'one' with God, the Beloved, though not yet utterly purified.

There are trials, still. There's no end to trials in this life; but now each difficulty serves only to strengthen the faithful soul, or to make him more aware of his own weakness and thus to enable him to turn again to God in trust. At each new trial, this person makes a further act of trust and of self-denial - for the Glory of God and for the good of others and for the expiation of sin. But the soul unites all his sufferings to those of Christ's Sacrifice and regards them as not worth thinking about when compared with Christ's pains, which were endured for the soul's sake.

The faithful soul now lives in joy and contentment amidst all difficulties. He enjoys a true union with Christ; but the purifications aren't yet over. All the nooks and crannies of heart and memory are like so many attics and cellars, as it were, of the soul; and, if this person consents, these will be purified, painfully, by God's pure light and grace. Yet, by now, the soul has learned not to flee this pain, but to accept it as a sign that, truly, God is at work in the soul; and the soul learns that the pain diminishes as pride and obstinacy disappear. This person is as happy in spiritual darkness as in God's clear light.

The danger of pride.

Human weaknesses remain. God permits this in order to keep the faithful soul in humility, since the danger of pride is the more terrible, the 'higher' each person soars in his flight towards God. I mean that for as long as there remains life in us, we can be tempted to vanity or pride: such is our pitiful weakness. Without grace we would be lost. Humility keeps us attached, so to speak, to Truth, which is God.

When someone has proved his love for God through many terrible trials and sufferings, and is utterly determined to love God and his neighbour without ceasing, until death, and also looks to Christ in every need, joyfully, he is now guided and accompanied by Christ, step by step towards the mountain-top. Earthly agonies remain agonies, but he doesn't weaken. He is prepared for any pain or humiliation, so long as he doesn't turn away from Christ and His Way. He lives to please Christ and to do His Will, and to make Him known and loved. He lives more and more in a clear spiritual Light, although this isn't yet constant.

This person is guided ever more surely, now, through Christ's Church and Christ's pastors, and through the Holy Scriptures, and also through the special graces which are given to the soul in prayer, although no-one should accept any unusual experience in prayer without speaking to someone responsible who can give him wise spiritual advice. He should try to reject all images and peculiar occurrences, as he has already rejected all images for many years, since he knows that whatever can be seen or felt, heard or touched in prayer, is not God; but I'll write more about that - later.

Such a soul still lives by faith, no matter what comes to him in the way of visions or experiences. The only sure sign for him that he's firmly on the road to God is that he wants only what God wants, and makes every effort to shun extraordinary experiences and to do God's Will, moment by moment, for God's Glory alone, obedient to His Church.

---

f) DESOLATION.

One last, terrible trial.

So far as I know, there remains for the faithful soul, although he is probably unaware of this, one further, terrible trial which must be undergone before he is sufficiently purified to be united with God on this earth, through Christ, not only in joy and peacefulness but in Light - although still by faith, when the darkness experienced so far will soon be banished.

First, though, the person who has grown used to the sweet company of Christ and used to a certain ease in all that he does for Christ - although he knows that it's all due to Christ's grace and goodness - is led by God through a terrible and incomparable spiritual desert. He is led to the heart of a desolation so awful that the grace of God alone keeps him from despair at the sight of his own weakness and powerlessness, and at the sight - that is, at the dark knowledge - of the infinite Holiness of God.

Into a spiritual void.

There comes a time when the faithful soul suddenly finds himself, without warning, pitched into a spiritual void which he could never have imagined, and which - such is the soul's humility - he even thinks he deserves to be in, as he wonders what's happening, and wonders how he can ever know peace again, or can ever see God.

He suffers unbelievable pangs as he goes about his daily work. He half-wonders if he's going mad, since no-one else seems to be overcome by God's holiness or by his own sinfulness; then he repents of these thoughts, convinced that he misjudges other people, and knowing that no-one is as wicked as himself.

A clear sight of the Abyss.

This 'desert' is a place of testing. This person's faith is tested as he makes acts of faith in the love of God for a fearful and sinful creature like himself and begs God's help to remain firm in the hope of Salvation, even as he is torn with terror at the sight of the Abyss from which he is saved only by the mercy of God.

He feels that he loves nothing and never will, even as he continues as usual, without pausing, in the service of others, by prayer and by acts, and would sooner die on the spot than commit the least deliberate offence against the pure Majesty of God.

In this state, the faithful soul is chained, as it were, for as long as God permits; yet, all the while, though the soul would scarcely believe it, God looks on in great tenderness, knowing that only by this dreadful testing can the soul, which is still so easily tempted to pride and foolishness, be purified further and clothed in true humility. Soon, this spiritual union will be fruitful. True dawn lights up the faithful soul, eventually, and clothes him in grace.

---

g) THE SPIRITUAL MARRIAGE.

Drawn out of the desert.

Clothed in that garment of grace, at last, the faithful soul is drawn by God out of the desert, and is brought into a new intimacy with Him. Such a soul is at peace as never before, and from now on is able to do God's work surely and quietly, without troubling about his own appearance or effect on others. He has almost forgotten himself, in order to please God, and therefore God's Glory may now pour through this soul without such a great danger, as formerly, that he'll be led into pride at the sight of all that he now achieves, or at the spiritual sight of his own astonishing intimacy with the most Holy Trinity. But also, such a soul is full of gratitude at seeing how much he is loved.

There remain, still, several stages of true union through which Almighty God might choose to draw such a soul, if he will consent.

I shan't describe them all here; but they involve the nurturing and growth of this person's soul - even in this true union - so that he more and more resembles Jesus Christ his friend and Master, not only outwardly in his acts of love for God and for his neighbour, but interiorly, in his heart: crucified by the wounds of love and by interior suffering. If he consents, this soul is led by love and by obedience to a true interior resemblance to Christ, Whom he now serves with utter joy and gladness.

Such a soul no longer even yearns to die in the hope of being united with Christ, but is more content to will whatever Christ Wills. He longs neither to die nor to remain on earth - only to do whatever will bring the most Glory to God and good to souls - all through the merits of Christ's Holy Passion. He longs to be "HUMBLER YET, EVEN TO ACCEPTING DEATH" (Ph 2:8). He lives here on earth within the Life of the Most Holy Trinity, Whose Divine Life makes him not only active but fruitful.

An extraordinary dialogue.

One of the wonderful stages of true union which it seems appropriate to describe here is the one in which the faithful soul is able to converse in a sublime way with his Heavenly Father; and by 'converse', I mean that he is able to speak and question, and also to receive very tender and detailed answers, in what is an extraordinary and wholly-spiritual dialogue.

What I'm referring to is the state in which the soul converses with God the Father, at God's direct invitation, in a manner of prayer which is deliberate, conscious and willed, and which can be continued or interrupted - and which can be clearly recalled when the soul has 'left' that state.

Someone who prays in this way - at God's invitation - is now able to 'step' from prayer to daily life and back again, or from one state of prayer to another, as Willed by God, with the greatest ease and delight, so close is his union with God and so thoroughly and peacefully 'entwined' are all of his spiritual, mental and bodily faculties, and so well do they 'work' together.

At the 'door' to Heaven.

These conversations with the Father take place with such ease and delight - through the merits of Christ, as I said, and by the Spirit's power - precisely because a soul such as this which is called so frequently by the Father to converse with Him in this manner is already, and always, and wholly, attentive both to His presence and to His Will; and so when God Wills that such a conversation take place, this person has no need to 'compose' himself, or to become recollected or to prepare for such a marvellous union. He is already prepared and able to converse because he is already alert, or 'waiting', we can say, as if at the soul's door to Heaven, which, at this stage - as God has revealed to him in prayer - is continually open.

It is in this marvellous state - this conversation with the Father - that the faithful soul can understand God's wishes in a spiritual way, by which I mean usually without words and by a Spirit-to-spirit communication which, although silent, is as true, or truer than verbal speech.

It is in this marvellous state that the faithful soul - like a simple and trusting child - can put questions to his Father and so receive answers which by their tenderness, simplicity and wisdom bring him unsurpassable delight and reassurance.

It is in this marvellous state that the soul understands to the fullest possible degree the meaning of 'adoption', of 'child of God', of God's 'Fatherhood', and of 'spiritual union' and of 'Heaven'.

It is in this marvellous state, furthermore, that the soul which has become accustomed to this way of life and love can 'lift' more powerfully than ever, into the Father's heart, all of the persons, problems and places which occupy the heart and mind, in the knowledge that this is a sure and wonderful and conscious way of receiving help which is plainly worthwhile and very effective.

h) TRUE UNION, IN PRAYER AND DAILY LIFE.

A fruitful relationship.

There comes a time when the soul which is wholly 'enamoured' of God and has been wholly drawn by Him into a close and fruitful relationship is shown, in prayer, many details about that friendship, about the extent of it and the results of it, and about the inner life of God, and about Heaven: and all of these things are shown in a way which, by its purity, transcends all other ways of knowing.

The soul is so 'at one' with God that the soul sees what God sees - to a limited degree - and sees it as He sees it; and therefore the soul observes, knows, understands, weighs and judges just as God does. This is what was meant by the Apostle who said "WE ARE THOSE WHO HAVE THE MIND OF CHRIST" (1 Co 2:16). Someone who has reached this state sees clearly, therefore, the truth about his vocational duties, and about his duty to his neighbours, and see the truth about his other relationships. He also sees the truth about God's plans for what remains of his life - since God now shares with such a soul, to an astonishing degree, the knowledge of His own plans for that soul and for the Church.

When someone 'sees' such things because he has been drawn by God into His Divine Life, and so has entered the Life, Love and Work of the Godhead, he knows something of the Life within the great movement of Divine Love at the heart of the Holy Trinity. The soul has entered that Life as a swimmer might enter the powerful currents of a fast-flowing river (T:2244B) and therefore has truly become one with God in love, and one in fruitful work, also.

Someone who lives in such a state, as if in the 'heights' of the spiritual life, lives in constant peace, joy and fulfilment, even amidst suffering, since what greater joy can there be, before Heaven, than to enjoy something of what is experienced to a marvellous extent in Heaven: by which I mean the friendship of God, and also the special gifts which God cannot refrain from lavishing upon His friends - with the friendship of all other creatures who love God, such as the Saints and Angels of Heaven, as well as the devoted friends of Christ amongst whom this soul now works, prays and suffers for God's Glory.

The spiritual glory of another soul.

These special friends of Christ are recognised and treasured by each faithful soul who has reached the heights of the "HOLY MOUNTAIN" (Ps 48:1). They all encourage one another in holiness; and the wonderful things which are experienced by these souls are foretastes of the joys which consume the Saints of Heaven. Even here on earth these true friends of God enjoy in their true Communion with one another 'in Christ' a burning and blissful love for God, with life 'in' Him, and with a certain likeness to one another, without uniformity. They delight in one another's virtues. They live and work in a state of near-perfect harmony with one another and of blissful closeness both to Christ and to His holy Mother; and in their prayer, whether they could describe these things or not, they enjoy the blissful contemplation of the perfections of God the Most Holy Trinity.

It might be expected that each true friend of God is given admirable and useful powers of discernment: admirable in that all of God's gifts are admirable, but especially His spiritual gifts - and useful because wonderfully effective for whatever special work occupies each fervent soul; but the marvels enjoyed at this stage of the spiritual life are more marvellous than anyone could imagine. This is all because the union between God and the soul is so close that one good thing follows from another - from God, to that soul, and onward to other souls - as surely as water must pour out from a tilted jug onto whatever lies below. But when I say that 'more marvellous' gifts than discernment are given, I'm not thinking about what the faithful soul learns, by spiritual 'knowing', about other souls; I'm thinking about the particular spiritual 'sight' which is God's gift to this soul, by which he can see and relish another soul's state of spiritual glory.

The true friend of God who is fervent in thanks to God for the lives and virtues of the Saints of Heaven is frequently honoured by the spiritual 'sight' of a friend of Heaven, with a spiritual glimpse of the glory in which that Saint now dwells, and also by the spiritual knowledge of the degree of glory which God has bestowed upon that Saint - when compared with the glory given to other Saints. God makes it plain to such a soul, for example, that one particular Saint is vastly more holy than others, although all are holy and much-loved; and God also makes it plain that another Saint has been gifted in a particularly marvellous way for the sake of the Church but nevertheless, is not the most glorious in Heaven. In Heaven, it seems that Christ delights in giving the most glory to those who have excelled in the virtue of charity - especially those whose great love for Christ caused them to pity Him and to console Him in His Passion. But the reason I've mentioned all this is because the true friend of God is shown not only the glory of the Saints in Heaven but also the glory of God's saintly friends on earth.

The 'way of seeing' differs, according to whether the glory seen is of a Heavenly friend or of an earthly person; but the knowledge given is the same. Whenever Heaven's Saints are seen, with their glory, it is through glimpses given to the 'eyes of the soul', or through the visions which are 'normal' in certain types of prayer, or as spiritual 'treat' on a special occasion; but if I write about those whom God has already crowned with His glory in this life, even though it can't generally be seen, I must explain that their spiritual glory is not 'seen' by the soul's sight , but is 'experienced' by the soul's spiritual heart, and is then relished, so to speak, through the intellect, according to God's Will, for His own good purposes and for the soul's delight.

Spiritual glory.

Such is the great degree of spiritual union between God's true friends in what is accurately described as the "Communion" of Saints that they can delight in special gifts which are unknown not just to people outside the Church but also to people within it who have never made a serious effort to aim for sanctity.

When God's true friend has at last grown used to the Glory of God which he sees within his own soul, in prayer, at every moment, and has almost become used to the sight of the Glory of Heaven whenever he turns to Heaven to ask for the help of Christ or His Saints, he becomes aware that God is revealing to him in day-to-day life the state of glory of one earthly friend after another: this means, of other friends of God who have also been purified and who live very close to Christ's heart.

God's friend experiences the glory of those other souls. The glory is experienced whenever a similar soul is in the vicinity, even where bodily sight is not used; and that glory is experienced in a two-fold spiritual sensation which consists of a burning weight upon the forehead with a suddenly-arriving suffusion of sweetness through the soul.

The person of whom I write - who through his friendship with God experiences the glory of the Saints of Heaven and also of earthly persons - already feels a burning on the forehead, during prayer, with some sweetness of soul; but that burning and that sweetness are made more intense, by God's Will, by the proximity to that person of any other of God's true friends, whether they be very young children, or middle-aged persons, or the elderly. The burning and the sweetness are felt for as long as another true friend of God is in the vicinity. The burning and the sweetness are experienced more intensely, the greater is the degree of holiness of the person who is nearby; indeed, this is one of the ways by which God reveals to His friend the degree of holiness which another person has achieved; and of course the degree of glory which is ascertained through this burning and sweetness has nothing to do with the age, intelligence or learning of each individual whose soul is clearly revealed in this way but is solely a question of what degree of Divine Charity burns within a soul who is either very innocent or who has finished his purifications.

As might be expected, since the degree of glory mentioned has to do with Charity and true spiritual purity, greater degrees of glory are revealed amongst those who - it is confirmed later on - are both self-critical and self-forgetful. The most holy are those who are 'ordinary' in being obedient to God, simple, willing to admit their faults and to start again, kind and gentle, shy of rushing in to judge or to organise other people or to satisfy curiosity.

Holiness and glory are wholly pure, free gifts from God given in the end to those who have been willing to be of service and to accept purification.

It is by God's Will and God's grace that His true friends can 'see' in an entirely spiritual way the spiritual beauty of one anothers' souls, and can also see and experience the delight which other loving souls experience on meeting them. This is how they are helped to achieve what Christ spoke about in His last discourse, when He said: "AS THE FATHER HAS LOVED ME, SO I HAVE LOVED YOU. REMAIN IN MY LOVE" (Jn 15:9). These friends of Christ, whose whole desire is to keep His Commandments and to please Him at every moment, cannot escape His Love as it were, since they now enjoy a tender, pure and reverent friendship with every other true lover of Christ the Saviour, and they are suffused with Christ's gifts of peace and joy at every moment of prayer.

The 'heights' of Union.

Someone who has reached the heights of union praises and thanks God - Father, Son and Holy Spirit - at every opportunity, whether turning to thank Christ for special joys, approaching the Father in a trusting plea for help, or asking the Holy Spirit for light and guidance; and each prayer is answered not just with unseen, powerful help, but with a palpable suffusion-of-soul with sweetness and joy, and with a crowning-of-the-brow with glory.

This is the summit of the spiritual life: to know and to experience - by presence and sweetness and glory-of-soul - the Most Holy Trinity: Three Divine Persons, and to be able to do so continuously, with every thought and event of one's life woven into a perpetual and loving conversation with God, or into a wordless, perpetual exchange of loving 'glances'.

All persons, encounters, situations, tragedies and apparent problems are brought willingly into that perpetual prayer, where Divine Love, wisdom and understanding are brought to work upon them. Nothing of the life of him who prays in this way is left 'outside' God's presence and loving influence; yet when the time for petition and intercession is over, that soul, in union with Christ, and with a joyful and grateful heart, praises the Father in the Spirit's power, and offers Glory, in praise of the Father's Glory; and so that person is doing the work of Heaven in his own house, street or church - even before reaching the Home for which he is yearning.

All of Christ's faithful friends - as I mentioned earlier - live and work in a state of near-perfect harmony with one another and of blissful closeness both to Christ and to His holy Mother; and in their prayer, whether they could describe these things or not, they enjoy the blissful contemplation of the perfections of God the Most Holy Trinity.

Showing out virtue.

These friends of Christ bring joy to all who love Christ - and bring joy to all who admire goodness. Each of these friends of God shows out - more clearly than anyone else - a particular virtue or combination of virtues, so that other people will be inspired and so that God will be praised by all who delight in what is virtuous; and yet those who possess and show out virtue are usually aware of others' virtues and not of their own.

Christ is glorified differently, in different friends. One person shows out humility to an extraordinary degree; another person seems like justice 'embodied'. Another person seems to shine with truth: to be a 'bright sword' which can cut swathes through falsehoods and disguises; another person acts with perfect purity of intention in everything. Someone else is all compassion for the suffering and the poor, while another seems to be on fire with pure charity: above all, with love for Christ - and especially for Christ in His Passion. All such friends of Christ are holy with His holiness; and yet someone whose soul is on fire with Christ's fiery charity possesses the purest holiness.

---

i) <u>PERPETUAL JOY</u>.

Each of Christ's friends who lives, transformed, in His friendship, is led by Him to the Father, to enjoy a union so close and trusting that it's as if God and the soul whisper as intimate friends or lovers do, yet without sound or murmur.

Someone who lives in a Heavenly communion with God in perpetual intimacy is so privileged and blessed even during this earthly life that he has only to 'enter' prayer by an act of the will to be brought 'palpably', it seems, into God's presence; and he knows that his prayer is immensely fruitful and worthwhile, as well as fulfilling - and even though there is no evidence of this, except in faith. It is God Who reveals to such a soul that by such a pure, piercing prayer as this, as with every God-given moment of other sorts of contemplative prayer, it is as though the clouds which 'hide' the Godhead from mankind are parted. It is as though, through that prayer, the clouds are held back, as God pours down His graces upon mankind, to a greater-than-usual degree: such is the goodness of God, the power of true prayer, and the fruitfulness of the countless loving sacrifices which a prayerful soul has made in order to be ready for this state of contemplation.

The spiritual senses.

There are further marvels, in the spiritual life. Someone who enjoys God's friendship to this degree and who has come to trust in Him entirely - though remaining always aware of his own imperfection - has by now, and by the Will of God, been brought to God's 'heart' in prayer.

Each time this person 'enters' prayer, he finds that his soul is suffused with Glory and that God has lifted him 'high' once more, and awaits him, at His 'heart', so to speak; and whoever converses with God in this state finds that he can 'taste' - as it were - God's love, reassurance, wisdom and consolation. It's as though the soul 'tastes' these gifts merely by turning his heart towards his Heavenly Creator, Redeemer and Sanctifier; and thus he comes to know the marvel of the use of yet another of the spiritual senses - all of which, at last, have been satisfied.

Someone who has been invited by God to share in God's knowledge of Himself and of Heavenly realities has, by this stage, seen many of God's marvels; he has seen Heaven's companions with the eyes of his soul. Furthermore, he has heard the voice of his beloved Christ, and has listened to the singing of the Angels. He has smelt the bitter perfumes which were Christ's astonishing and consoling gifts to him when he was first struggling to believe that Christ was illuminating his heart and soul in prayer, after many years of spiritual darkness. Furthermore, he has felt the touch of God on his brow, whenever the Father has clothed and crowned him anew as a 'prophet, priest and king' so that he can step out to do God's work with greater simplicity and confidence.

Now, by a spiritual sense, this person learns " HOW GOOD YAHWEH IS - ONLY TASTE AND SEE" (Ps 34:8); and as he experiences God's goodness through a pure communion with God he rests in such contentment in prayer that he's like a child on his mother's lap; or it's as if he is leaning against Heaven's door, as he waits in patience for an invitation to step up and enter. His soul is now suffused with joy.

By this stage, the soul's spiritual sight and hearing, with his spiritual senses of smell, touch and taste, have all been 'awakened' and used, at God's prompting, so that more and more, the whole person, in every bodily and spiritual faculty, has been 'gathered' in prayer and has been wholly irradiated by grace. It's as if he is inebriated and warmed by the gifts which he has received from the Living God Whose unchanging plan, from the beginning, has been to make this soul one with Himself in perpetual joy.

The life of grace.

These notes on the life of grace are so inadequate, and omit such a vast amount of information that I must mention my purpose, which is to write at length on the many types of prayer into which God in His kindness draws the soul. So I'll leave for another place, or another writer, further warnings against the dangers of the spiritual journey, and advice about method and discipline in family life and prayer. That's why I omit, too, all that I long to write about Our Blessed Lord and His Passion, and about Christ's Holy Mother Mary, who not only bore Him, but who leads us to Him now.

All that the soul has undergone on the long and terrible journey described here couldn't have been borne without the grace and mercy of God, the merits of Christ's Passion, and the prayers and example of Christ's Holy Mother, the help of Angels and Saints, and the benefits and blessings received through Christ's Holy Church on earth, especially through the Holy Sacrifice of the Mass, and through the Sacraments.

God's so good, and lavishes such blessings upon us! May He grant us perseverance until death, and enable us to give Glory to the Most Holy Trinity; and may Christ our Lord, and Our Lady and Saint Joseph be better known and loved.

573

2 PREPARATION

PRAYER-IN-UNION. THE HOLY SACRIFICE OF THE MASS.

---

a) PRAYERFUL EFFORTS.

Faithful prayer and penance.

Now that I've written such a lot about the soul's progress towards complete union with God, it seems important that I stress, again, our need to be faithful to those quiet, traditional and daily prayers and devotions which the Church has recommended to its members through the centuries, and which can act as the "RICH SOIL" (Mt 13:8) from which contemplation can spring, well-nourished; or, to use a different image, I can say that it's by responding with a contrite and a loving heart to God's invitation to "REPENT ... AND BE BAPTISED" (Ac 2:38) that the soul finds the door ajar, so to speak, to eventual Eternal bliss and security. It's by faithfully talking to God and listening for God in daily honest, trusting and reverent conversations with Him that each person can prepare himself for possible prayer-in-union. I mean that although a devout person ought to be content to serve God in whatever simple way He permits, rather than to yearn for extraordinary tasks and special spiritual experiences, he will be possessed with a genuine longing to grow closer to God.

No-one can be brought into a constant and intimate union with God if he scorns - whether from laziness or lack of love - regular and loving contact with God, in prayer.

A true and loving union with God is firmly established not by much speaking about our love for God and neighbour, but by the willing opening of our hearts to God in daily prayer and by our efforts to make amends for sin by acts of penance. Also, every prayerfully and carefully-chosen small mortification will discipline and strengthen the soul as exercises strengthen the body; furthermore, each one of us discovers, through such acts, how weak we truly are. We discover our reluctance to make even small sacrifices for spiritual reasons, even though we would make enormous sacrifices, for example, to win a prize, or to see a long-lost friend. But the best reason for practising mortifications, of course, is to unite oneself with Christ in His Agony.

No-one 'progresses' in the spiritual life except through the grace of God, by the Merits of Christ's death and Resurrection; yet God's graces won't be any use to us, unless we give our consent to His promptings. I mean that it's important that we turn to God with a free heart and mind, saying 'yes' to His Will, even if at the beginning we lack joy or graciousness in giving our consent to His plans for us.

Numerous devotions.

Regular prayer is so important that I'm going to mention a few devotions. Daily acts of faith and hope and love are enormously valuable, as are traditional morning and evening prayer-times, which can be spent - with words or without - in fervent adoration, thanksgiving, penitence, petition and intercession. It's extremely worthwhile to 'lavish' time upon God by sitting or kneeling in silence, in His presence, and so 'allowing' Him to teach, guide or hold us according to His Will, in a communion which is beyond words - even if it seems as though nothing is 'happening'. Yet Christians have been helped, over many centuries, in all sorts of ways: by dwelling on the words of Holy Scripture, by meditating on the Passion of our Lord Jesus Christ, and by devoutly making the Sign of the Cross. We rely on the help of the Holy Mother of God, as we learn to pray in some of the old, recommended ways - whether by reciting the Rosary, following the Stations of the Cross, praying the 'Jesus prayer', saying the 'Angelus' or the 'Divine Praises', or by reading the lives of the Saints. We ought to thank God for His gifts before and after meals, and indeed, before all good activities. We rely, too, on the marvellous help - sought in prayer - of our Guardian Angels and Patron Saints: indeed, of all the Angels and the Saints. Short prayers and brief requests are enough, whenever we speak in this way, with the confidence which comes from faith, to these Heavenly friends who love us so deeply.

Every Catholic ought to value - even if he or she doesn't use it - the Breviary or 'Office', recited by clergy and religious, and also by many lay-persons, for the benefit of the whole Church. Daily 'spiritual reading' of Holy Scripture, or of works about the spiritual life, will strengthen our souls and help us to persevere. Without such spiritual nourishment, we are ill-prepared for our journey through an uncomprehending and sometimes hostile world, where the enemies of Christ mock the truths of the Faith. Some truths are scorned in one century, some in the next - even though Christ's enemies sometimes admire the external forms in which the Faith is clothed, or praise the acts of charity which are done for Christ's sake and which astound them. It's because of the many ways in which we find ourselves under attack that we must keep turning to God for help; and it's a good idea to seek even greater help from God, by arranging to have an occasional 'day of recollection'.

Faithfulness to the sacraments.

It hardly needs saying that no-one can hope to advance in prayer if he refuses the honour due to the holy sacraments which Christ instituted for our joy and benefit: for example, the sacrament of Reconciliation, and the Sacrament of Christ's Holy Body and Precious Blood.

Above all, the prayerful soul will yearn to participate fully and frequently in the Holy Sacrifice of the Mass, which, the Church teaches us, is the "Source and Summit" of all that we hope for: the source of all the graces which come to us only through Christ, and the summit of all our desires, since it is though the Holy Mass, and through our Holy Communion, that we offer worthy praise to God, and then have a foretaste of Heaven in our Communion with Christ and so with all other members of His Mystical Body.

Even invalids, of course - those confined to their homes or also to their beds - are able to participate spiritually in the Holy Sacrifice, and to offer their sufferings with Christ in His One Offering to the Father; also, they are wedded to the celebration as they receive the Blessed

Sacrament at the hands of someone who has been present at the Mass. There's much more that could be written about suffering and reparation and co-redemptive prayer, but I'll content myself with what I've written in different places throughout this book.

Different methods of prayer.

None of my statements about prayer - particularly about the devotions mentioned earlier - should be taken to mean that we must all follow the same method in prayer, or should be attracted to the same devotional practices. Although no Catholic could neglect attention to the Passion of Christ, or to the Holy Sacrifice of the Mass, without endangering his spiritual health, we all ought to follow our own reasonable attractions in the matter of daily, private prayer. Everyone who sincerely clings to God in regular prayer and in love of his neighbour, guided by the Church, cannot fail, as I said earlier, to progress in the spiritual life.

Amongst those who obey Christ's advice about "WHEN YOU PRAY, GO TO YOUR PRIVATE ROOM" (Mt 6:6) - even if their only private sanctuary is in their own heart - some people find more nourishment in formal prayers and psalms and litanies than in informal, lively, unstructured conversation with God. Others are led by God into silence and apparent insecurity - in a prayer of 'Unknowing'. Many find that they are quite satisfied and well-nourished, spiritually, by the repetition of simple prayers, year after year. They genuinely advance wonderfully in the spiritual life by the use of devotions which others would find tedious. All of this shows, as ever, that God leads souls to Himself through Christ, but does so along different paths in prayer. Zacchaeus' manner of approaching our Blessed Lord (Lk 19:1-10) was different from Mary Magdalene's, (Jn 20:11-18) which was quite unlike Nicodemus' approach (Jn 3:1-21).

The Most Holy Spirit can be trusted to guide the soul along an appropriate path, with the usual provisos and warnings. But no fervent, reasonable person who hopes to grow closer to God will leave out daily expressions of love for God, gratitude towards Him, sorrow for failings, and hope for gifts: gifts for himself and for other people.

---

b) LOVE FOR OUR NEIGHBOUR.

Sincere love for God and neighbour.

Since 'structured' prayer-time occupies a comparatively small part of the normal active day of many Christians, I must mention, here, something of supreme importance, even though this section is primarily about contemplation. I must stress that there's no love for God without love for our neighbour.

I mean that the whole point of turning to God so frequently in prayer and meditation, as described above, is to give Him Glory and to grow in union with Him; and He is Love; and therefore love for our neighbour is inseparable from Union with God. If we believe that "GOD IS LOVE" (1 Jn 4:8) and know that He wants us to love our neighbour, as we're told in the second Great Commandment (Mt 22:39), and if we don't make many efforts in this direction, then our declarations of love for God are evidently insincere. It seems to me that as much effort and discipline and sincerity should be put into the deliberate ambition of proving our love for our neighbour, 'outside' prayer-time - although in true, quiet, self-less service, not in showy expressions of devotion - as into our deliberate and devoted attention to God within our prayers.

In a circular movement, someone who loves God and who attempts to pray, increases in his belief that he must cherish and help everyone whom God has created and now holds in existence; and he does so according to his circumstances and by exercising true love hand-in-hand with prudence and wise judgement. Furthermore, the soul begins to see the real worth and potential of every single person on earth, each of whom was of such importance to Christ that Christ sacrificed His life for each one.

The more that a generous person overcomes his own selfish instincts to preserve his free time, his trivial opinions, his security and his own customs and habits - and I'm not speaking here of matters of principle - then the more truly does he permit God to pour even more light and grace into his heart. Thus, in the 'circle' which I've mentioned, a true friend of Christ is prompted by grace to see more and more clearly that no true service is possible without reverence towards others, and without repentance for his own prejudice and self-righteousness. He sees, too, the supreme importance of forgiveness, that is, of loving and forgiving others, utterly, always, no matter what the provocation nor how deep the wounds received. He sees that this is Christ's plain teaching. He knows this, as we all do, since we have Christ's example.

Therefore, whoever loves God ought to want to love his neighbour. But we're so weak and blind that this is frequently extremely difficult - in fact, it would be impossible to achieve to the degree that's asked of us - unless we're perpetually prompted and aided by grace. We're invited to love as Christ loved: limitlessly.

Our circumstances can discourage us for many reasons. I mention, above, provocation and wounds. On the other hand, I think that life in a loving community helps a truly devout person to see some of his own weaknesses clearly, amidst others' virtues. Reflection on these matters can lead to a deeper humility and gratitude, and will compensate for the soul's rash judgements about others' apparent faults, intentions, moods and attitudes.

Evident need of help.

With regard to love-in-practice, it seems to me that no true friend of Christ can fail to see the real though varied needs of those with whom he shares the same home or the same street. There's no end to the pains and wounds and turmoil which we observe in others: both exterior and interior sufferings, whether freely displayed or half-concealed. Here, the devout person can prove his love for God by kind acts, both physical and spiritual, even when he seems to have to goad himself into action, regretting his hard heart, and ashamed of his usual impatience and cowardice. Despite even frequent failures, this person knows by faith that he must simply start again after each little fall, trusting that God will see his longing to serve Him, and asking Him to bring good out of evil - or out of foolishness.

By his co-operation with God, perhaps a blind but nevertheless fervent co-operation, the faithful soul is eventually transformed by Him. By that I mean that one day the hardheartedness is melted. This person is aghast that he should ever have found others irritating or difficult - since he now sees his own faults so clearly. Also, God has so enlightened his heart that he is full of the love and compassion of Christ Himself, and has begun to love others at last with a true, pure, Christ-like love which is full of tenderness and sweetness and compassion. He is less inclined to make rash judgements of others. He seeks only to encourage and console, in accordance with truth and prudence.

When someone persists in quiet loving service in this way, acting for the love of God even if he feels no great emotions of love in his heart, he isn't likely to go astray, provided that he remains faithful to prayer and clings to Christ in the Sacraments. Thus, he will be guided more plainly to see where his true duty lies, since, while he knows he ought to love everyone, he sees clearly that his first duty is towards those who are bound to him by particular ties, and those near to him in other ways.

He doesn't despair that he can't palpably reach out with help to many more persons, since faith tells him that they can all be helped, through the Merits of Christ's Sacrifice, by a loving soul's prayers and sacrifices. This person knows, too, that the value of acts of kindness isn't measured by the noise they make before the world, or by the visible joy they bring.

One could write volumes about love of our neighbour; but it's enough, now, to conclude by saying that we ought to imitate Christ's love. That's enough inspiration for a life-time. So I shall press on with my task - which is to give a reminder about the marvellous way of life into which God draws a faithful person who has never ceased to trust in Him, who is repentant of every wrong, and who has received His gift of prayer-in-union.

Wholly at one with God.

As I mentioned earlier, in 'The journey of faith', there comes a time when someone who is wholly 'enamoured' of God and is wholly drawn by Him into a close and fruitful relationship is shown, in prayer, many details about that friendship: about the extent of it and the results of it, and about the inner life of God, and about Heaven; and yet all of these things are shown in a way which, by its purity, transcends all other ways of knowing.

Such a fortunate soul has been given true, Heavenly joy and peace after the trials and struggles of earlier years. Such a person loves and understands God's Will. Past, present and future are now seen by the soul in God's Light. The very 'attics and cellars' of the soul's inmost dwelling have been scoured and purified. This person now sees that he possesses nothing at all that hasn't been given to him by God. He knows, now, in a way impossible before, that to take pride in himself is more than foolishness; it's a lie - a theft from the Source of all good. But now that this soul has learned to trust in God's grace alone God now rewards him with unbelievable joy and tenderness.

Whoever has reached this stage is brought to the border of a new land, where he learns to walk in true humility and simplicity. He learns, even, to rejoice in his own weakness, trusting only in the Merits and graces of Christ his Lord; and he begins to live like a true child of God in gratitude and faith.

A Heavenly way of life.

The soul is so 'at one' with God that the soul sees - to a limited degree, as I said earlier - what God sees, and sees as He sees it; and therefore the soul observes, knows, understands, weighs and judges just as God does. In this marvellous state of friendship, moreover - though in a slightly different state of prayer - the soul is able to converse with God in a union so close and trusting that it's as if they whisper as intimate friends or lovers do, yet without sound or whisper.

Someone who lives in a Heavenly communion with God in perpetual intimacy is so privileged and blessed even during this earthly life - as I said earlier - that he has only to 'enter' prayer by an act of the will to be brought 'palpably', it seems, into God's presence; and he knows that his prayer is immensely fruitful and worthwhile, as well as fulfilling - even though there is no evidence of this, except in faith. It is God Who reveals to such a soul that by each pure, piercing prayer such as this, as with every God-given moment of other sorts of contemplative prayer, it is as though the clouds which 'hide' the Godhead from mankind are parted. It is as though, through that prayer, the clouds are held back, as God pours down His graces upon mankind, to a greater-than-usual degree: such is the goodness of God, the power of true prayer, and the fruitfulness of the countless loving sacrifices which a prayerful soul has made in order to be ready for this state of contemplation.

That's one of the reasons why I hope and pray that everyone who reads this book will persevere in prayer. It's vitally important for our Eternal happiness that we respond to the love which God lavishes upon us; yet so many of us, at one time or another, have shut our eyes to God, and to His Love. I long for everyone to believe that the wonderful things I've described are possible - by God's grace - and that even people like ourselves can come to share God's joy and even His holiness.

---

c) THE HOLY EUCHARIST.

Participation in the Holy Eucharist.

It's quite impossible for me to write about prayer, without writing about the Holy Mass: also known as the Eucharist. It's only because of the astonishing Sacrifice of Christ, once offered on Calvary, and now re-presented before us in the Mass, that we've been given the opportunity to become children of God who can pray with confidence to our Heavenly Father; and so I feel duty-bound to say a little about the Mass, in an effort to help any Catholic who - through ignorance or lapsation - needs some background material.

There's no better way of 'praying the Mass' than by doing what the Church recommends: which is to aim for full and active participation; but the fullest participation takes place not when someone makes a lot of noise or moves about a great deal, but when his heart and soul are as 'fully' involved in the Mass, in prayer, as his body is 'involved' in sitting, standing or processing as appropriate, in accordance with the rubrics.

At its heart, every Mass is simple, whether it's celebrated with vigour and with joyful music, or with hushed reverence and silence pauses. In offering the Holy Sacrifice of the Mass, today, Christ's present-day disciples are obeying the command which Christ gave at the Last Supper, almost two thousand years ago.

On the night before he was put to death because of our sins, Christ changed bread and wine into His Body and His Blood, and - anticipating His self-offering on the Cross on Calvary, on the following day - He said: "THIS IS MY BODY WHICH WILL BE GIVEN FOR YOU; DO THIS AS A MEMORIAL OF ME" (Lk 22:19). It seems to be true, however, that very many people today don't realise what a staggering privilege it is to be able to be present at the very Sacrifice by which God and mankind have been re-united: nor are they awe-struck that Jesus Christ our Lord is Present amongst them in an astonishing, sacramental way. Consequently, many people complain about having to attend Mass, or about the Mass itself.

Bored or discontented in church.

It seems to me that people are unhappy at Mass for one of three reasons - and often through no fault of their own; and people who come into these categories won't benefit much from the suggestions I'll make about praying the Mass, unless they have a change of heart - or unless, in learning something about Christ or the Mass that they didn't know before, they become interested enough to listen and then to pray.

First, I must mention the reluctant attenders, many of whom are young. I can't deny that parents have a duty to encourage their children to go to Mass; but when people have been bullied into attending, their hearts and minds perhaps become bitter and resentful; and of course, no-one in that state prays very well, by which I mean prays with much hope or trust, and so rarely finds prayer joyful or fulfilling.

The second group consists of people who go to Mass - for whatever reason - but who don't really believe in the spiritual realities which are indicated by words, symbols and gestures, and which are invisible. Faith - a scrap of faith - is necessary for someone who wants to take a true part in the Holy Mysteries.

It seems to me that a third group consists of those Catholics who do believe in Christ and in prayer, who go bodily to church, and who enter the building, but who don't pray. Although they mouth the words of the Gloria or the Creed, their hearts and minds aren't actively engaged; God's Love cannot pour into their hearts, as it would if they'd opened them to His influence; and so when they eventually leave, they complain that they were bored; or they complain about the heating, the lighting or the homily or whatever else has annoyed them, although their inner discontent stems from their spiritual separation from God and from those who have prayed and taken part. Such unhappy souls are like people who stand outside a house and gaze at the lighted windows as a glorious gathering takes place - and yet who aren't willing to enter into the spirit of the celebration, and cannot be made joyful by the marvellous Host and His Heavenly Company.

Only God knows why these people can't pray from the heart: whether it's through tiredness, sin or cynicism, or distractions - or depths of grief, or depression. It's not for us to judge one another. But surely it's a good idea for those who treasure Christ and the Mass to say a brief prayer for all the reluctant or incomprehending worshippers who are present at the same

Celebration.

Now I must go into more detail about the Mass itself - which is marvellously described in the 'Catechism of the Catholic Church' - and then about our part in it.

The Holy Eucharist: Sacrament and Sacrifice.

There must be a dozen reasons why it's worth rushing to Mass, such as to be obedient to God and so to please Him, or to offer the best possible prayer in praise of God - or to pray in the best possible way for someone who has died - or to be spiritually and visibly one with fellow-members of Christ's Body. But rather than make a list of reasons, I'll try to say what it is about the Mass - the Holy Eucharist - that is so stupendous that people who know about it, and understand a little, can hardly bear to stay away; and so I must get to the heart of this great *mystery of our Faith:* the Eucharist, to say not only what It is but to say why It is, and how It is.

You might say: "We already know that Christ died for us. We know that we're supposed to repent of our sins, and be baptised. We know that we can be made children of God, members of the Church, and heirs to the Kingdom of Heaven. We know that Christ explained that we can lead a new, prayerful life, and can hope for Heaven. But where does the Eucharist come into this? Why do we have this extraordinary gift, this Eucharist: both sacrament and Sacrifice?"

Before I say anymore, I'd better define "Eucharist". The Church teaches us that it is the Sacred *Body and Blood of Christ* - made present on the *altar,* and also to be found in the *tabernacle;* and since we're taught that the Eucharist is a *sacrament* we Catholics speak about the sacramental Presence of Christ. And by 'Eucharist' or *'Holy Eucharist'* we also mean the *Holy Sacrifice of the Mass,* of which I'll say much more on the next page. First, we need to explore the reasons why we have received such astonishing gifts from God.

The Holy Eucharist: why it is.

Everything good is a gift of love from God; and His love isn't something wishy-washy. It's something which is fiery and tender, all at the same time: and it's something active; and this One, Holy God Who loves us has gone to enormous trouble, so to speak, to work out a plan by which we could be saved from our sins, and saved from despair at the miseries of this life; and He's also worked out an extraordinary plan, out of love, by which to give His Church a gift which would remain at its heart and give it great joy for century after century.

Let's go back to the beginning, in order to understand this. But in saying the 'beginning', I'm speaking about our *Salvation history.*

We Christians believe that Creation was achieved by God out of love. His Love and generosity are so great that they spilled out in a great *Act of Creation:* of the Universe, and of the people in it. But we also believe that at some stage, at the beginning of human history, the first *man and woman rebelled* against God. They had free will; and they chose to do their own will rather than God's - and that's what we mean by *sin.* So we say that they sinned; and our Faith teaches us that we've all been tainted to some degree, ever since then, by this germ of *rebellion within ourselves,* by which we find it easier to do wrong than to do good. We call this *original sin;* and it's 'wiped out' by *Baptism,* though some disharmony remains in our lives.

It was part of God's loving plan, however, that He would rescue mankind from sin: that He'd offer us the possibility of finding real joy upon earth - even amidst life's terrible difficulties - and also of finding Bliss with Him, forever, in *Heaven;* and it was God Himself - the *Son of God, Jesus Christ* our Lord - Who came down to earth to fulfil this *plan of Salvation.*

For century after century, God had chosen and prepared the *'Chosen People',* from whom Christ would eventually be born. God had taught them about Himself, encouraged and tested them, guided them by *Patriarchs, Kings and Prophets,* and had led them to expect a *Saviour -* a *'Messiah'* - to arise from amongst them, as indeed He did. It was Christ the Son of God Who, at the appointed time, 'leapt down to Earth' in the sense that, by the Spirit's power, He took flesh from *Mary* - from a woman of the Chosen People. This happened just over two thousand years ago; and it's what we celebrate each Christmas.

Christ lived amongst us and showed us how to live. He was perfectly sinless and yet He accepted the consequences of sin: accepted the realities of life in a sinful world - even as evil people wanted to shut Him up when He did good and always spoke the truth. He died on the Cross for us - although this is such a huge subject that I shan't try to explain it here. But we believe that through that sacrifice of Himself on *the Cross* - which He had foretold, and which He underwent freely - He poured out His life-blood for the forgiveness of sins. He reconciled mankind to the Father and repaired the terrible breach which had occurred at the time of our first parents.

Christ was perfectly loving and obedient in every way; and He is God's only Son; and so it's as though God the Father couldn't possibly have left Him dead, but raised Him up to a new life which was vibrant and glorious, and which culminated in His *Ascension into* Heaven: an event witnessed by the faithful *Apostles* who were transformed by Christ. And the wonderful thing about this is that we too can hope to have that sort of wonderful life if we believe in Christ, and become united to Him, and remain faithful, accepting His gifts, and doing His Will. We who believe in Christ believe that He has made it possible for us to "ENTER THE SANCTUARY" (Heb 10:19) of Heaven, just as He did at His Ascension, a few weeks after His death and Resurrection.

This is where we must consider what gifts we need to accept from Christ, and what connection the Eucharist has with doing Christ's Will.

Reasons for joy and gratitude.

I spoke of God's Love, earlier. Followers of Christ have always known that Jesus, the Son of God, gave His Apostles something extra special to do. It was at the Last Supper that Christ commanded them to "DO THIS" (Lk 22:19) - in memory of Him. He was asking them to meet as one Body, on future occasions, to listen to the Word of God and to reproduce His words and gestures with the intention of changing bread and wine into the Blood and Blood of Christ, in memory of Him, in a 'conversion' which we now call *transubstantiation;* and the reason for all this was that Christ our God is so mad with love for us that when He knew that He was about to die and leave us - although He also knew that He'd be going to Heaven - He couldn't bear to leave us without leaving behind what we now call a *living memorial of His love:* of the Love shown out in His self-offering on Calvary.

On the night before Christ died, it was through a two-fold consecration that Christ made present first, His Body, and secondly, His Blood; and thus He showed out by symbols the separation or outpouring of His Blood from His Body: a separation which would take place on the Cross, on the following day, as He gave up His life and died for us in order to save us from our sins.

So let's examine some aspects of this astonishing means, instituted by Christ, by which He would do extraordinary things for us; and the four especially-marvellous things which I list below are surely reasons for unending joy and gratitude on our part, since they spring from Christ's Infinite Love and generosity.

First, we in Christ's Church can always have re-presented before us, through the Holy Sacrifice of the Mass, the whole *'Paschal Mystery'*: the wonderful way in which Christ has saved us from sin and death.

Secondly, by the Will of God, we have a way of thanking and praising God forever: a way given by God Himself by which we can offer the most perfect praise that it's possible for us to offer to Him from upon this earth: and I'm speaking of the offering to God, in each age, of the very sacrifice that Christ once offered from on Earth, when He died to save us (CCC:1366).

Thirdly - through this Holy Sacrifice of the Mass - Christ also gave His Apostles some spiritual food: the sort which He'd promised them when He'd been speaking to them in Galilee, a little earlier (Jn 6:32); and we who are His present-day disciples can now receive this same spiritual food for our souls, when we receive Christ in Holy Communion.

Fourthly, Christ guaranteed His own Presence amongst them always, though in an extraordinary manner: through His sacramental Presence. We know from Holy Scripture that this was His promise, before His Ascension into Heaven, when He said: "KNOW THAT I AM WITH YOU ALWAYS; YES, TO THE END OF TIME" (Mt 28:20); and Christ's sacramental Presence amongst us is one of the ways in which He has fulfilled that promise, and the greatest.

I want to tell you how this came about.

The Holy Eucharist: how it is.

Let's look back again to the night before Christ died: to the night when He was about to be betrayed by one of His disciples. He knew, with His Divine fore-knowledge, everything that He would suffer on the following day. But He made special arrangements for that night before He died, so that He could be with His Apostles in the upper room and could eat the *Passover meal* with them (Ex: Ch 12 and 13). This is the sacred meal which the Jews celebrated - and many celebrate today - annually, in thanksgiving to God for the rescue of their ancestors from Egypt and from danger: for the 'passing-over-them' of the Angel of death, and for their own *pass-over from slavery to freedom.*

But Christ took that Passover meal and gave it a new twist, in order to celebrate, in advance, the Passover which He would begin on the next day: the passing-over from death to life which He would achieve through His death and through His Resurrection from the dead. And it was through His Passover that He was to make possible our own pass-over from the slavery of sin, through "A NEW WAY" (Heb 10:20), to the freedom and joy which are experienced by those who live as children of God.

Here's the passage from Saint Luke's gospel which describes this 'Last Supper:' "THEN HE TOOK SOME BREAD, AND WHEN HE HAD GIVEN THANKS, BROKE IT AND GAVE IT TO THEM, SAYING, 'THIS IS MY BODY WHICH WILL BE GIVEN FOR YOU; DO THIS AS A MEMORIAL OF ME.' HE DID THE SAME WITH THE CUP AFTER SUPPER, AND SAID, 'THIS CUP IS THE NEW COVENANT IN MY BLOOD WHICH WILL BE POURED OUT FOR YOU'" (Lk 22:19-20).

What happened at that last supper with His Apostles was that Christ took bread and gave thanks and shared it with those present; but as He did so, He broke the bread; and in this breaking was symbolised the way in which He Himself would be 'broken' by death, so to speak, on the following day. By His Divine power, Christ changed the bread and the wine into the sacred Body and Blood which He was going to offer up in sacrifice on the following day, as He died upon the Cross on Calvary.

This is why we call the Eucharist a sacrifice as well as a sacrament. A sacrifice is the highest form of adoration of God, in which a pure victim is offered in sacrifice as an offering to God by a particular community through its designated *priest*, in an act of worship which is a sign of their recognition of God's dominion over them. This sounds rather complicated, perhaps; but if you can hold onto the idea that the Eucharist is both a sacrifice - an offering to God - and also a sacrament - a source of holiness - things might become clearer by the end of this section.

A holy and living Sacrifice.

Christ's generosity was so great that He wanted to give us a living representation of the greatest proof of His Love for us, by which I mean, Calvary's offering; and that's why the Eucharist is called the '*sacrament of our Salvation*'.

The Church teaches us that when Christ said to His Apostles: "DO THIS ..." (Lk 20:19) He was giving the Church the power to achieve this extraordinary thing - and thus was making it possible for the same power to be given to our priests, through the centuries, in order to give those same benefits to Christ's People in future eras.

So it is our belief that, in every generation, when the Church celebrates the Eucharist, and the priest at the altar does what I've described - does those same actions and says those same words over the bread and wine - the Sacrifice of Calvary is re-presented before us, though in a different manner. It is through the words of Christ and by His Spirit's power that Christ's Body and Blood are made present on the altar and are symbolically separated through the two-fold Consecration. And it's by the offering of this "*holy and living sacrifice*" - as we read in the third Eucharistic prayer - that we offer to God the Father from our own time and our own lives, through Christ and Christ's Sacrifice, the most pure and perfect worship and supplication that has ever been offered from earth or can be offered (CCC:1359-1362): something so marvellous that the Church joyfully proclaims that the Mass is the heart and summit of the Church's life, and brings blessings upon the living and the dead.

I've also mentioned spiritual food. I said that Christ had promised in Galilee, soon after His miracle of the loaves and fishes (Jn 6:1-15), that He'd give Himself as our *spiritual food*. We know that He said: "IF YOU DO NOT EAT THE FLESH OF THE SON OF MAN, AND DRINK HIS BLOOD, YOU WILL NOT HAVE LIFE IN YOU" (Jn 6:53).

Christ also said: "HE WHO EATS MY FLESH AND DRINKS MY BLOOD LIVES IN ME AND I LIVE IN HIM. AS I, WHO AM SENT BY THE LIVING FATHER, MYSELF DRAW LIFE FROM THE FATHER, SO WHOEVER EATS ME WILL DRAW LIFE FROM ME. THIS IS THE BREAD COME DOWN FROM HEAVEN ... ANYONE WHO EATS THIS BREAD WILL LIVE FOREVER" (Jn 6:56-58); and these words shocked people; but Christ didn't try to hold back the people who then walked away. He'd given a promise. They didn't understand it and left; yet the Apostles, even though not understanding it, believed in His wisdom and goodness; and so they were with Him at the Last Supper, as He made it possible for them to receive His Body and Blood as spiritual food and as a true Communion with Him; and we too can enjoy this astonishing privilege - when we receive Holy Communion.

A sacrament is a visible and touchable sign which has been instituted by *Jesus Christ* and given to the *Church*, as His means or method of giving to us His own power and grace and holiness. We have seven sacraments, and the Eucharist - the *Sacrament* of the Lord's Body and Blood - is the greatest of them all, since it gives us not just Christ's graces but Christ Himself, Really Present; and as we receive His Body and Blood under the appearance of bread and wine we receive food for our souls, and innumerable graces.

Christ: wholly and entirely Present.

It's important that we all realise that we receive Christ and Christ's graces whether we receive the *Sacred Host* in Holy Communion - the "BREAD FROM HEAVEN" (Jn 6:32) - or whether we drink from the chalice to receive His *Precious Blood.*

As I said above, we believe that Christ Himself is Present with us, because of what He taught the Apostles at the Last Supper, and because of what our priests do today, in obedience to Him. Christ said, just before His Ascension: "I AM WITH YOU ALWAYS; YES, TO THE END OF TIME" (Mt 28:20). It's true that we have, made Present here, His Body and Blood, under the appearance of bread and wine; yet He said: "I AM THE LIVING BREAD" (Jn 6:51). Christ is a living, joyful, Divine Person. He is the God-man Who can never die again and Who cannot be split up into bits; and so we know that wherever Christ's Body and Blood are Present, He Himself is Present: the whole Person Who even now is risen from the dead and lives in Glory in Heaven. He is really with us - *His Body, Blood, soul and Divinity* (CCC:1374) - though under the appearance of bread and wine. He is present whole and entire in each of the species.

Of course, it's faith that counts in our lives, not the ability to repeat complicated explanations; but for those who want to know, I'd add, of the Consecration, that when the bread is changed into Christ's Body, there is present also - under the appearance of bread - His blood, soul and Divinity; and when the wine is changed into Christ's Blood - under the continuing appearance of wine - there is also His Body and soul and Divinity: and this 'being-together' is called, by the Church, *concomitance;* so we believe that the whole living Christ is Present under each *species;* and the change itself is called, by the Church, *transubstantiation.*

The wonder of Holy Communion.

So where Christ is made Present before us we have the thrill of knowing that Christ our Lord and God, to Whom we look throughout our lives for hope and strength as we try to do His Will, is really here amongst us: not very far away at all; and we also have Him as our spiritual food, as I said. The culmination of our participation in the Sacrifice of the Mass is Holy Communion; and when we receive the Body and Blood of Christ we receive Christ *whole and entire*: a loving and Divine Person Who delights in being with His friends, and Whose friendship brings incomparable blessings.

Whenever we receive Christ our Lord we are united with Him in an extraordinary and intimate manner which cannot be surpassed, and which He has especially planned, so that He can do wonderful things for us. Through His Real and extraordinary Presence, Christ not only gives us peace and comfort but begins to change us and to make us ready for Heaven. And there's something else. Through this intimate Communion with Christ, we are bound very closely to everyone else who receives Him: to everyone else who is fully *"in Communion"* with Him and so is spiritually in Communion with us too: with the whole Church (1 Co 10:16-17).

At the heart of our Faith.

When Christ lived on earth, He told a lot of stories; and one of them was about "A MERCHANT LOOKING FOR FINE PEARLS" (Mt 13:45-46); and one day that merchant saw a pearl of such magnificence that he longed to have it. So he sold everything he had in order to buy it.

The reason I'm telling you this is that the Eucharist seems so staggering and glorious and beautiful to those of us who know about it and love it that we've found it's well worth making sacrifices for it. Some people in past ages have even sacrificed their lives in order to attend the Holy Eucharist - the *Holy Sacrifice of the Mass* - or to protect priests, and so to ensure the continuation of the Church's Eucharistic life. We haven't all been called to shed our blood for the Faith. But this must give you some idea of the centrality of the Eucharist in the *Catholic Faith.*

It seems such a strange thing: to say that the Body and Blood of Christ are at the heart of our Faith as Catholics; and yet this Sacrament is a treasure handed on since the time of Christ; and when I say that it's very precious, I wonder if you've ever known anyone to whom the Mass has been very precious: someone always keen to go to Mass and to *Holy Communion*? Have you ever been puzzled by their devotion - perhaps wondering why they continue to go if there are very few people there, or if the church is dreary, or if there's a nervous young priest, or an inaudible old priest - or if they've lost friends and relatives and perhaps God doesn't seem to be very near?

Why is it that some people keep the Mass at the heart of their lives even when other people take a brief interest and decide that, outwardly, it's not very gripping? I suppose there are several reasons, but I'll emphasise just one.

Christ's Real and sacramental Presence.

Those of us who believe that Jesus Christ our Lord and God is there in the church, during the Mass, in the Eucharist, and who love Him, find the thought of His Presence so mind-boggling that we can hardly bear to stay away, whereas people who don't believe in His Presence are only aware, perhaps, of a shabby building or a sparse congregation.

Imagine what would happen, if it was announced on the local radio that Jesus Christ was descending from Heaven to land on Harpenden Common in an hour's time, and that hundreds of people had gathered to greet Him. Can't you just imagine that many more people - Catholics amongst them - might dash to be there, partly out of curiosity, yet partly out of a longing to be near Him. And yet Christ comes to be amongst us at every single Mass in a way which is every bit as real as in that imagined episode, though in a manner which is different; and He is Really Present, all the time, in the Blessed Sacrament in the tabernacle.

How many of Christ's friends today bother to come and greet Him and thank Him? So many people only half-believe. Yet if they prayed a little more, and asked for more faith - and plucked up courage to change - their lives would be transformed.

The Holy Mysteries.

I've said so much about the Eucharist, and I've used words which might be new to some of you; though it's true that we expect to learn new words whenever we examine a new subject, whether in science, art, cookery or religion; but it seems important that I say once more that at every Mass, you see enacted what Christ Himself did at the Last Supper; and you see offered from the altar, at the hands of the priest, though in a different manner, the very Sacrifice which was offered once on Calvary, for our sins. That's why it's so important for us to know a few useful things about how we can approach this marvellous event which is, all-at-once, a memorial, a Sacrifice, a Thanksgiving and a Celebration.

Perhaps you can see why we're not meant to be silent bystanders as the Holy Mysteries are celebrated. We who are privileged to be Catholics can prepare for the Mass, take an active part in it, and leave in order to give the blessings of the Mass to other people: to the people we meet; so it's surely plain by now that it's important that we try to take part worthily in this extraordinary Celebration.

Let's encourage one another to attend Mass, and to treasure it - and also to remember that the Mass is holy, no matter how poor the attendance, nor how feeble the singing, nor how weak the homily. It is holy because it's the worship being offered by Christ's Mystical Body on earth. It is holy because Christ our God is Present with us, at the heart of this Celebration:

this living memorial of His Passion.

Whose mind can remain distracted, critical or self-pitying for long, if he really believes that Christ is made Present at the Consecration? What can any sincere believer do, at that moment, except greet Christ with mixed gratitude, love and awe?

---

d) HOW TO 'PRAY THE MASS'.

This is where I must say something about 'praying the Mass'. I'm aware that if what I write helps some people, it won't suit others; nevertheless, these are the things I've always said to those who ask about prayer, and the Mass: things which Our Lord has either recommended or praised.

"Make up your mind to please Christ by being obedient to His Church. Abandon everything you know to be sinful; and if you can't bring yourself to do so, go faithfully to Mass, and - each time - ask fervently for the grace to see things as Christ sees them and for the grace to be willing to change.

Decide to attend Mass without fail, every Sunday and holy day, in order to praise Christ in the way He's decreed is best, and in order to meet Christ - Who offers that perfect praise for us - and to receive Christ and His gifts.

Go to Confession, if you're aware of having grievously sinned. No-one can make you go. Even if you don't do this, it's still a wonderful thing in God's sight that you go to Mass. But you can't benefit from the Mass as you might, or go to Communion and so receive the rewards for a peaceful conscience, until you've put things right with God - Who is always longing for us to turn back to Him; and He is thrilled by our acts of humility, as we speak to a priest in the Sacrament of Reconciliation, when we are contrite, and are also determined to make a new start."

An immediate preparation.

Remember to fast for an hour, if you intend to go to Holy Communion. Set out for church in good time, so that you'll arrive a few minutes early.

Use the holy water in the porch to make the sign of the Cross as you go into the church.

Find somewhere to kneel - but first, 'find' Christ Who is sacramentally, Really Present in the tabernacle. Silently greet Him, and also the Angels; then genuflect - bow the knee - in His honour, and kneel in your place.

You've spoken to Christ. If you now ask the Holy Spirit to help you to pray well, and then 'turn' your heart to your Heavenly Father, you've spoken to the Three Persons of the Holy Trinity, even before the Mass has begun!

Say something like this to God the Father, as you wait in your place: and try to mean it:

Say something like this to God the Father, as you wait in your place: and try to mean it: "Father: I unite myself with the whole Church today, as we offer You Christ's Holy Sacrifice from our altar: offering It for Your Glory, in thanksgiving for all Your blessings, in reparation for sins, and in a confident plea that You'll grant the prayers of the Church, and also the prayers of my own heart for myself and for all who are dear to me."

United in prayer.

When the priest and the servers enter, and you begin to pray every prayer of the Mass with your whole heart, you can be sure that you are taking a worthy part in the most sublime act of worship possible on Earth. It's the worship of the whole Church: and the Church, remember, includes all the Saints of Heaven, with whom you are praying, at Mass, and also the Holy Souls who have gone before us, who are also intimately involved in our Celebration.

Remember: you are taking part in the worship and homage which Christ Himself offers to the Father, in a holy Celebration which has been enacted and offered, with only minor changes, throughout the past two thousand years; and that's why, when we pray during the Mass, we pray best as we unite ourselves to Christ's sacred Offering, having in our hearts the very same intentions as Christ.

Some special parts of the Mass.

Make a reverent and dignified response whenever the priest addresses the congregation.

'Mean' every word of every prayer that we all pray together.

'Unite' your heart and mind, interiorly, with every word of prayer which the priest speaks to God on our behalf.

Listen carefully to every reading from Holy Scripture.

Give generously to the collection, if you can, since you're giving a gift to God.

Remind yourself - before the most solemn part of the Mass: before the Consecration - that Jesus Christ our Lord will soon be Present, 'hidden' in sacramental form, but really here amongst us, just as He has come amongst our spiritual ancestors at every Mass.

Welcome Christ at the Consecration, as the priest holds up the Sacred Host.

Perhaps you can thank Jesus for having died for you, as the Chalice of His Precious Blood is held up to view after the second Consecration.

Remind yourself that to be present at the Offering of the Holy Sacrifice is to be present to the very offering which Christ offered on Calvary; it's as though we're at the foot of the Cross; and we can be sure that Jesus is Really Present, praying to the Father on our behalf, asking for forgiveness and Salvation.

with Christ, as the priest holds up the paten and chalice which contain Christ's Body and Blood, and says to the Father, of Christ: "Through him, with him, in him, in the unity of the Holy Spirit, all glory and honour is yours, almighty Father, for ever and ever."

Add a fervent 'Amen' - by which you confirm that you yourself offer that glory and honour to the Father, through Christ, in the Eucharist.

Going to Holy Communion.

Pray the 'Our Father', in unison; and mean every word of it, especially about wanting God's Will to be done, and about forgiving those who hurt you.

When the time arrives for Holy Communion, but you know you can't receive, stay quietly praying where you are, and make a 'spiritual Communion' - by brief expressions of contrition and love to Christ, with a fervent request that He come to your heart to help and console you. He will do this, because He is good. Then you can make an act of faith in His love for you; you can thank Him, and speak with Him, and allow Him to change you.

If you're going to Holy Communion, approach the sanctuary with reverent longing.

Remember Whom you're going to receive: Jesus Christ Himself: your best and closest friend, Who is also your Creator and Redeemer, Who comes from the glory of Heaven to our altar, and to your soul.

Go back quietly to your place, and kneel, if you can; and then speak to Our Lord in the silence of your heart in whatever way is most sincere, as well as reverent and grateful. Don't be afraid to confide in Him - about your worst fears and failings, or your hope or joys; or just sit in silence and enjoy the gifts which He can give you if you have a quiet conscience and are happy in His Presence.

When you leave the church, after the blessing and the dismissal - or when you've spent a further few minutes in thanksgiving - go out determined to be a good child of God, and to be as kind and forgiving towards the people you meet as Christ is towards you.

Smile or greet someone, if you can, on your way outside. Even if you're shy, or if you don't think people seem very friendly, try to be pleasant - and try to grow familiar with the faces and names of those who make up the Body of Christ: your spiritual brothers and sisters in this wonderful family.

'Other Christs' amongst us.

We should be respectful and helpful to everyone, of course; but perhaps it's worth saying, too, that Our Lord is thrilled when we're supportive towards the Clergy. He doesn't want to hear anyone moaning about His priests. If we have a genuine complaint we should speak to a priest in private, and respectfully. But Christ has placed them as 'other Christs' amongst us, and wants to see us loving and reverent towards them, whatever their apparent failings.

3 DEFINITIONS

EXTRAORDINARY PRAYER: REFLECTIONS.

a) INTRODUCTORY NOTE.

Special gifts in prayer.

This is the point at which I must once again refer directly to my own experiences in prayer, as I begin to write about the ways in which Christ, for His own purposes, has taught me about 'Life-in-grace,' and has brought me to pray His Prayer, as I shall explain, in a way impossible to an unaided human being. There may be some repetition, since I've written about prayer elsewhere; but what I'm about to describe isn't something to be sought for its own sake. It's a free gift of God to those on whom He chooses to bestow it. We can refuse His gifts, but we should not - dare not - demand them; in fact, we couldn't bear them without His purification and His strength, although everything we might suffer in this way seems insignificant, when compared with the joy which is given by God to a purified soul.

By 'purified' I don't mean perfect, as I explained earlier when mentioning our remaining weaknesses and imperfections, the sight of which helps to keep us in humility.

I couldn't begin to speak of Christ or of union with Him, without knowing myself to be, not worthy or fit, but 'in Communion' with - of one heart and mind with - His Holy Church; so, it's only after seeking advice which the Church freely offers to all Christ's brothers and sisters that I feel free to accept His gifts and to press on with the task which He has entrusted to me. I can't describe the joy which He gives me now, even amidst all sorts of difficulties; but I'm determined to do His Will from moment to moment, by His grace, neither peering sadly back to the past, nor straining anxiously to see ahead.

St. Paul says that God chooses "THOSE WHO ARE NOTHING AT ALL" (1 Co 1:28) to show and prove His goodness and His power, for the sake of many others who don't yet know about His Love, and who haven't yet been brought to faith in Him.

He has certainly chosen someone insignificant in this case, as I once said; but He is true to His promises; and since I gave Him my whole life - every aspect of it and every dream - He has given me His. As I freely consented to His Will being worked in me, He now guides my will, my memory and my understanding too. He wants to make them entirely His; and so He continues to purify them in the fire of His love, in the ordinary circumstances of daily life, for His use and service; and I hope He'll do this until my life's end.

---

b) LIVING IN UNION.

Ordinary prayer: a 'launch pad'.

Since a December day in 1985 - which I've mentioned in the Narrative - when I once again, in utter darkness, freely consented to give my life to God, all prayer became further simplified.

I continued as before, still praying every word of the Mass each time I attended, and still using words as well as silent attention to God whenever I knelt in prayer at home, at regular intervals; and I kept on praying as I carried on with my work. It didn't occur to me to hope for any further special experiences, as I made acts of adoration, thanks, petition and sorrow - just as I'd done for about twenty years. I continued to pray as usual, and to name every precious soul whom I lifted up to God in intercessory prayer. Words, for me, had become a brief launch-pad from which Christ regularly led me upwards to silence and to peace.

Christ had led me to pray without words, many years previously, but this "Unknowing" wordlessness and peace was not only more profound, but of a different order. At the same time, at every moment of every day, by promptings and Providential events and trials, He continued to train me in His Way of love and service and humility, and helped me to begin again after every fall.

Despite, or, rather, amidst both interior and exterior sufferings, I found that I was at last working and praying with a tremendous inner peace and contentment. I knew that Christ had become my whole life and my whole desire even though I still struggled with recurring fears and failings.

In Christ, I found all that I had ever hoped for or needed. He led me peacefully to see His Will for me, day by day; and He even astounded me by teaching me more about Himself, in prayer. His 'teachings' had begun several years earlier, but I'd done my best to ignore them: as encouraged by trustworthy spiritual writers.

I had no idea how or why such 'teachings' should be occurring; but, when the time seemed ripe, I asked for expert advice and was reassured, as I said in the 'Narrative'; and so Christ continued to lead me forward - usually in darkness, although a safe darkness - as He guided me through prayer, and through the Scriptures, and through His own words and instructions in Holy Communion, and through the circumstances and events of daily life.

For as long as I worked and prayed solely for love of Him, putting myself entirely into His hands from moment to moment, fed and guided through His Holy Church, I was led onwards and upwards in His Peace. More clearly than ever, I saw that there's no other good road, except the road on which we cling to Christ and rely on His grace to do good and to avoid sin: all the while trusting in the constant teaching of the Catholic Church.

This is so simple a Way that a child can see it, yet so difficult a path to follow that we can't hope to persevere without God's grace. Many scorn it.

The need for greater care and effort.

It became clear, however, that any slackening of effort on my part would leave me, in one sense, 'further away' from Christ, not because of any lack of love on His part, for this is impossible, but by reason of the spiritual law.

I mean that, just as someone who deliberately persists in gross sins, and who mocks God's love and mocks those who love Him, cannot, except by an exceptional grace or opportunity, be brought closer to God - for by such a stance a rebellious person is not permitting God to pour His love upon him - by the same laws, souls don't usually grow in intimacy with God, if by the smallest act of selfishness or pride they deliberately say 'no' to His Will and His Love.

It is God's Love which is the sole reason for the existence of, or rather, the functioning of these laws; meanwhile, I discovered through experience that the least unfaithfulness on my part left me in darkness. I'm not thinking of the faults and failings into which we fall, despite our best efforts, for God sees our hearts, and completely overlooks the little failures and irritations of souls who are utterly determined never to offend Him, and who would sooner die than deliberately go against His teaching. But the smallest movement of pride in my heart for His gifts to me, or the merest flicker of hope that He would give me further extraordinary gifts or would show me something more in prayer, and He would leave me in darkness. In this way He was purifying my desires and was training me to work and pray solely for His Glory.

I knew that it was for my own good, and for the good of my neighbour, somehow. It seemed that God is like a mother who takes no notice of the many clumsy mistakes made by a small child who is learning to walk, when she wants the child to feel confident and secure in its struggles. But the same loving mother would be more severe, if one can use that word, towards an older child who was clumsy and careless through laziness or from lack of love, and who knocked aside others' precious things. So God appears more severe towards those on whom He has lavished His gifts for many years and whom He wants to see even braver and more loving; yet such severity is for their own good and for their ultimate happiness.

The truly mature and loving soul no longer becomes scrupulous and anxious, but sees that, whereas a small deceit or unkindness between mere acquaintances is a sad thing, between lovers it's a more dreadful thing: a worse betrayal of love.

It's for our happiness as well as for His Glory that God spares no effort, so to speak, to lead us and to train us to reach perfection. Although He has overlooked all the silly mistakes I've made despite my good intentions, He has never failed to correct me in one way or another for every small conceit or lack of charity.

In this way, He has taught me to hope for nothing except the grace to recognise and to do His Will in everything, in darkness or in Light, day by day, for Love alone. It is such a privilege that we're asked to do anything at all for Our Lord; and so it's a cause for wonder that He not only offers us the hope of Heaven, but pours upon us so many gifts and graces which are utterly undeserved.

Vanity or curiosity.

From the time I mentioned earlier, when I explained how the 'teachings' began, I found that Christ's words, visits, teachings and gifts now came to me always unexpectedly, unasked, quite sudden, and usually delightful, as He encouraged me to be like Him: to "BE COMPASSIONATE ... DO NOT JUDGE" (Lk 6:36-37) and showed me that "THE AMOUNT YOU MEASURE OUT IS THE AMOUNT YOU WILL BE GIVEN BACK" (Lk 6:38). Despite all my failures, I was determined to follow Christ's Way towards Heaven.

Now that I had resolved to love without limits, so that I could say, with truth, with Saint Paul, that "OUR FORMER SELVES HAVE BEEN CRUCIFIED" (Rm 6:6), and was attempting to live in complete obedience to God's Holy Will, despite my failings, I found that, over and over again in prayer, Christ was teaching me even more about His life or His Church; but if I ever began to speculate on His gifts or on their effect on me I found that Christ was silent until I apologised for my vanity or curiosity.

It was only because Christ gave me that extraordinary training that I was made ready to move from one stage of extraordinary prayer to the next, at Christ's invitation, and was shown precisely what happens in the soul during successive stages, and, furthermore, was enabled to describe such things with confidence, when eventually I was asked to do so.

In trying to fulfil Christ's wishes by describing the earlier stages of 'extraordinary' prayer, I'm duty-bound to include many details which I suppose will confuse some readers and alarm others; but I'll move away from such apparently complicated sorts of 'knowledge', eventually, in order to explain the most pure and sublime of God's gifts to the soul, and to write the about most simple and pure sort of spiritual 'knowledge' in prayer.

---

c) THE STAGES AND DEGREES: AN EXPLANATION.

God's holiness: sublime and unimaginable.

I know that if, in His Wisdom, God chooses to teach me or chooses to lift me into His Light in the prayer of Unknowing, I must never fail to remind myself that everything He gives me today could be withdrawn - for the good of my soul - tomorrow. It's foolishness to take these gifts for granted, and I pray with all my heart that I'll be allowed to remain in His Love, to be faithful in doing His Will, to be able to persevere to the end, and to bring Him glory. Meanwhile, I'll attempt my explanations.

It seems to me that - admitting the superiority or purity of the un-sensed, Un-knowing, pure prayer of Union which I've mentioned above, and of which I shall write again - the occurrences or 'touches' which I've noticed in prayer are of a certain order of purity and grace. I must mention here that I've sought advice, and have been reassured that I may accept the occurrences, indeed must thank God for them. It's only in obedience to God that I now dare to write on such matters at great length, speaking so boldly, though I still have to pluck up courage to put pen to paper; so I leave my efforts, as I said, in God's hands.

I intend to describe the different types of prayer-in-union, beginning with the more 'impure', in the sense of their containing not just Love, unseen and unperceived, but images or sound - indeed, anything which can be understood by the senses, although I mean the spiritual senses. Needless to say, anything even slightly 'impure', in the normal sense, if occurring to the soul in prayer or to the soul's eyes, is not of God and, like all distractions, but particularly evil ones, must be utterly rejected. But then I shall describe, in ascending order, the 'purer' types of prayer.

As I think I said earlier, God's holiness is so sublime and unimaginable and pure that none of us can see Him in this life. We mustn't imagine that we have 'grasped' God, if, for His own purposes, He permits us to feel, see or sense some gift from Him in prayer. Our spiritual guides will help us to discern what comes from God and what doesn't; meanwhile, the safest way of proceeding is to ignore everything extraordinary in prayer, if this is possible.

Since these descriptions begin with the 'lower' types of prayer, various gifts and phenomena must be mentioned. But when I go on describe the higher stages it will be more clearly seen, I hope, in what ways the stages differ, as I speak of pure Knowledge, which is 'simple', unlike the 'lower' types of Knowledge - which are 'complicated', so to speak. I shall explain about the most pure and sublime of God's gifts to the soul - which will surely cause any sincere enquirer to be amazed at God's Goodness.

An inability to recognise 'stages'.

By the way, those who have persevered in prayer for many years will know that we usually recognise the place to which God has brought us only afterwards, perhaps on reflection. Even then, the stages might be unrecognisable for a while, or they might overlap, or be repeated. They might, occasionally, occur in a different order. They might not have been experienced in a traditional manner. For example, a generous person who doesn't count the cost of his service to God, in the early stages, but who whole-heartedly throws himself into all the tasks which God seems to demand of him will probably not even know that he has entered the "first night" of the soul, if, indeed, he has ever heard of it, since he expected hardship and pain in the service of Christ; and so he has never dreamed of leading an easier life than his Master.

Nevertheless, although in the next section I'll be describing only the later stages, the usual path to God in prayer follows this course:

The Grace of God brings repentance
    and so leads to effort by the fervent soul
        who is therefore brought to accept 'passive' purification;
           and his sufferings are effective.
                They lead to a 'stripping' of imperfections, so
                    preparing the soul for transformation
                        and for increased union with God.

All that I'll now describe concerns "what God does", that is, the extraordinary ways by which God can teach the soul about Himself, as He draws the soul, with his consent, into a true union, which is a union not only of love and of wills, but also of Knowledge. This is the marvel about which I must write, not to persuade anyone that he ought to be disturbed in his work and prayer by a longing for extraordinary experiences, but simply because the ways of Knowledge-in-prayer can be a stage of the soul's journey towards the true union of Heaven; and this is the part about which I must now write if I'm to be obedient to God's Will: whether or not I think it will be immediately useful - although doing His Will is always profitable.

Love alone 'counts', in God's service.

I can't stress too strongly that, apart from what St. Paul calls "THE HIGHER GIFTS" (1 Co 12:31), extraordinary experiences are never to be sought, nor even hoped for. The soul must hope only to love God and his neighbour perfectly, by God's grace, attempting this until death, even forgotten and utterly rejected, whilst hoping fervently to be united to God forever. Even if a faithful soul's legitimate guide confirms that certain special experiences have been given by God, such things mustn't be sought or lingered over, since love alone counts, in God's service, not raptures or visions.

It will seem, in the next section on Extraordinary Prayer, that some types of experience are counted as being more valuable, and purer, than others. This, as I think I can explain, is because of the absence, in the purer types of prayer, of things recognisable by, or palpable by the senses - even by the spiritual senses, that is: by spiritual seeing or hearing and so on, which isn't bodily, but which is seen or felt by the soul's interior spiritual faculties.

Yet if anyone should disagree with the order in which I've gathered the different types of prayer, and should insist that one category or another is wrongly placed, I might agree. This is, first, because I would welcome guidance from someone else on this subject, and secondly, because I was uncertain about one or two of the categories. I can see that certain experiences might be counted as 'purer' because of one aspect and yet could be regarded as less pure because of another aspect.

Now, despite my saying that one type of prayer is 'purer' or more sublime than another, we know that all prayer is a gift of God, given from Love for our good and the good of others, in some obscure way, and for God's Glory. So - His gifts are not to be bargained over; nor should we hope for one type of prayer rather than another; and I say this because someone who is discontented with the prayer given to him by God is evidently not steeped in gratitude and trust, and doesn't yet yearn, above all, to love and to accept God's Holy Will; and it's only by trying to love and to do God's Will in everything, amidst all difficulties both in prayer and in daily life, that the soul prepares itself to be intimately united to God, when He Wills, in a true union which eventually brings unimaginable fulfilment and peace. I say 'eventually', because union with Infinite Wisdom and Purity Itself brings some measure of torment to the soul which isn't yet repentant of all pride and sinfulness, and isn't yet utterly devoted and docile to the promptings of the Holy Spirit.

---

d) A NOTE ON APPARITIONS.

Before I start explaining what the soul 'knows' or 'sees' in prayer, using a terminology appropriate to prayer - for example, when speaking of visions seen with 'the eyes of the soul' - I must make plain that I have never seen anything at all before me, in front of my bodily eyes, except what anyone else would see there before me in the same place. Therefore I can't speak of such things, or describe them; and I've limited myself to describing what I've seen Our Blessed Lord do to the soul in prayer - though I've seen these things not by physical sight, but by the marvellous workings of His grace, and the simultaneous workings of the soul's spiritual senses, as prompted by Him, for His own purposes.

---

e) DEFINITIONS.

It seems sensible for me to explain, below, some of the words I frequently use in my writings about prayer. Other people use them differently, sometimes, and I shall be happy to be corrected if I'm wrong. But these are my own meanings:-

THE SOUL.

When I write that *"the soul"* does one thing or says another, or looks at God, I mean that the *person* looks towards God, interiorly.

THE CENTRE.

Yet, frequently I write about the *'centre'* of the soul - or the height or depth; and, in this way, I explain what is happening in *the secret interior of one's own person* which is the "place", so to speak, where one meets God. It is because that 'centre of the soul' is so difficult to find that I speak of it so often. We are in the habit of looking away from our soul's centre, because our conscience pains us greatly when we look within ourselves, or else we are full of visual or verbal mental distractions which draw our attention away from the soul's centre.

But, usually, those who are beginning the way of prayer are quite unable to find the soul's centre. It's 'doorway', so to speak, is utterly hidden beneath a mountain of foolish distractions, memories, bad habits, obstinate thoughts, resentments and wrong beliefs. However, God Himself can clear all these away, in a moment, when He Wills, if we consent; and our consent is necessary because the removal is extremely disturbing.

THE SPIRIT.

Less frequently, I speak of a person's *'spirit'*, for example, when I explain how one's spirit can soar to God in Unknowing union whilst the soul rests below in silence. By *'spirit'*, I mean *one's whole willing self*, that is, the aspect of the soul which yearns towards God. So: the soul is one's own person, but the spirit is *the person's most true and central will*, which can grow stronger, according to the strength of its desire for God and the purity of its determination to cooperate with the grace of God. I write about 'the spirit' sometimes being feeble, due to neglect or laziness or sin.

THE HEART.

This *"most true and central will"* of each person - by which I mean someone's spirit -

599

is called by me, at times, the *'heart'*, since it not only yearns, but loves, and makes loving resolutions, and offers itself for annihilation, solely out of love for God.

So, the words *'spirit'* and *'heart'* in these writings are almost interchangeable, I suppose; and here, I'm not speaking of the Third Person of the Most Holy Trinity, whom we ought to address with reverence as the Holy Spirit.

THE IMAGINATION.

By the *'imagination'* I mean a person's capacity for deliberately holding an image within the mind, whenever that person has recalled one or more images from his visual memory in one of the many methods of thinking or assessing, whether at work or at leisure. In some types of prayer-meditation, such as the Rosary, one can 'call-up' remembered gospel illustrations, or can combine, in the imagination, several memories from different times and places.

By *'imagination'* I don't mean a capacity for invention which some persons claim to possess.

MEMORY.

Most of us mean the same thing when we use the word *'memory'*. It refers, as far as I can see, to anything which we recall, by the mind, of the past; so our *recollections* might be clothed in remembered images, or not - and might prove to be a great source of distractions in prayer. That's why it seems easier to pray if one has been recollected and calm in the hours before one's prayer-time.

I can't speak here about conscious and unconscious memory; it's too vast a subject. But although we believe, rightly, that many half-hidden, unacknowledged, dark areas of memory and experience can affect our attitudes to prayer and to sacrifice, we must always remember that God's grace cannot be stopped. He is so merciful, kind and powerful that, whenever He chooses, He can overcome, purify, or keep at bay or render harmless our most deep and terrible memories which we might find impossible to control by our own power. Of course, when He so Wills, God also blots from our minds all power of recalling certain consolations and joys; but He does this only because of His love of us, as He works in this way at particular times to help us to grow stronger and braver.

---

f) SYMBOLS.

I must add a few lines here about the symbols I've devised to accompany the explanations about prayer.

The task before me has been enormous. I make no complaint; I mean that I've had to devise a system by which I could sort various written experiences of prayer into different categories, without becoming completely muddled - because of my difficulties in remembering numbers; I mean that I had to categorise those of my writings and drawings which explain or illustrate over two thousand "teachings-in-prayer".

The symbols which can be found in Section five are simply visual 'tags' by which I can easily identify the many writings and drawings before me. Someone else might have used a system which involves numbers, as I suggested, or coloured inks; but the simple shapes which I've composed, and which are reproduced below, have made my task easier.

There's another reason why I've devised this means of identification, and why I've 'framed' each drawing - that is, each picture in my set of drawings of images which have been given to me in prayer - with a particular symbol. I've come to accept - on sound advice - that what I receive in prayer is valuable, and that the 'teachings' are a gift from God. Also, I believe that it's the Will of God that I should put aside my fears, and should share the teachings by means of both writing and drawing. It's on this point that the importance of the symbols will become plain.

I mean that I can't permit anyone who is sincerely using these pictures to learn about prayer to hold that any one picture is as "important" as the next. In other words, without the help of symbols, someone who sees a painting of a dazzling image given to me during *an extraordinary vision* (8A) might judge it to be of the same significance as a fleeting *"own-image-prompted-by- God"* (8D). Where an observer takes note of which symbols frame the different pictures, however, his eye is led, quickly, to notice a sequence of 'teaching' pictures, for example, or to note the infrequency of another type of image. In this way, I hope, the relative importance of the different categories of prayer becomes plainer.

---

g) A WARNING.

Before I describe in detail (in Section four) the various categories of extraordinary prayer, and before I reproduce the picture symbols, (in Section five) I feel I should give a warning about the different ways in which, in my experience, God's gifts are imparted to the soul in prayer. No yearning, nor any amount of 'straining' of the will, will bring about contemplative union or any special state or gift. Each is God's free gift.

Those with lively imaginations might think that their tender feelings towards God announce the beginnings of the prayer of union; yet although God's gifts are silent and invisible, they can be more alarming than pleasant, at certain stages; and besides, they're rarely given to souls who haven't utterly destroyed in themselves, by God's grace, all longings for anything except whatever they really need for their attempts to love God and their neighbour. Those who sincerely hope to advance in prayer must be utterly determined to do God's Will no matter what the cost to themselves - and all because of their love for Him.

---

4 DESCRIPTIONS

NUMBERED CATEGORIES OF EXTRAORDINARY PRAYER:
FROM THE LOWEST (15) TO THE HIGHEST (1).

---

15. A 'SENSE' OF GOD.

It seems to me that the 'lowest' experience of God which it's appropriate for me to include in this list - the lowest sort of extraordinary prayer, although every sort of genuine prayer is a reason for giving thanks to God - is the true but uncomprehending 'sense of God' which is given at certain times, and often given when a soul is full of wonder and gratitude at seeing the beauties of nature. No image is given. This real 'sense of God' is different, however, from an unspiritual and wholly emotional response to beauty: a response which might have 'mixed in' with it the beginnings of awe or the start of a question but which is not in itself a gift from God: not a prayer arising within the soul.

---

14. MEMORY ONLY.

As I recorded Christ's 'Teachings-in-prayer', and whenever I have recalled the particular circumstances in which a great grace was received, I have painted a picture of these circumstances. I have numbered each of these pictures (14) and have written (M) for Memory, as I've tried to show a glimpse of everyday life at that time.

---

13. THE SOUL'S EXPERIENCE.

E) DESOLATION.

The faithful soul who is determined to love and to cling to God whatever the cost might one day be prepared for a true, though still earth-bound, union with this Lord by *an experience of desolation so profound* that he learns perhaps, at last, to trust entirely in God and not in his own powers: powers which in fact he can no longer see.

God sees, first, that a certain soul trusts in Him sincerely and is ready for union, but isn't yet utterly purified. If that person consents - by his attention to God and by his clinging to God's

Will from minute to minute - God draws him into a spiritual darkness so profound that that person is left with nothing except the awful memory of his sins and the consciousness of his own helplessness and weakness.

To his utter horror, that person sees himself clinging by faith alone to a thin thread of Hope, suspended over a great Abyss. He knows, still, the power and unseen Majesty of his Creator, but is amazed, almost, that he hasn't died of despair at the knowledge of the holiness of the God Whom he has dared to offend and disobey at times. Such a soul has utterly forgotten all past gifts and consolations. He isn't aware that God, for love of that soul, has Himself blotted out those things from the soul's memory, since God wants that soul to discover the true meaning of faith and trust; and only in this way is the soul brought to recognise his utter dependence on God, and also to realise that he can choose, anew, either to put all his trust in God or else to cast himself away in hopelessness and despair.

The willing soul continues to cling to God by pure faith. He continues to try to do God's Will because of the pure hope which remains in his heart even in the face of the apparent danger of Eternal loss; meanwhile, nothing gives the soul which is in this state any shred of joy or peace. Someone who suffers in this way has never known such utter loneliness and desolation. He can't do a single thing which would bring him comfort or relief. He fulfils his plain duties; he moves and works and attempts to pray; but the enormity of his own sinfulness seems to hold him on the verge of paralysis. He calls out to God for mercy, and makes acts of faith and hope and love, whilst feeling no shred of comfort in his heart. He plucks up all his courage in order to communicate with his Creator, even as he feels that he might be damned for daring to approach Someone so Holy.

Truly "OUR GOD IS A CONSUMING FIRE" (Heb 12:29); yet He knows what we can bear, for the ultimate good and joy of our own souls and for the sake of those who will be helped by our sanctification - since every advance in holiness, as every move towards sin, affects other people.

The faithful soul learns to say: "Fiat" to God's Will, which means: 'Let it be done.' He continues to trust in the Lord's goodness even in the midst of this terrible trial. He simply waits for deliverance, in indescribable fear of loss, and in utter ignorance of his own state or destination.

After days or weeks, God gives peace to the soul. Past, present and future are now seen by the soul in God's Light. The very 'attics and cellars' of the soul's inmost dwelling have been scoured and purified. This person now sees that he possesses nothing at all that hasn't been given to him by God. He knows now, in a way impossible before, that to take pride in himself is more than foolishness; it is a lie - a theft from the Source of all good. But now that this soul has learned to trust in God's grace alone God now rewards him with unbelievable joy and tenderness.

So the fortunate person who has reached this stage is brought to the border of a new land, where he learns to walk in true humility and simplicity. He learns, even, to rejoice in his own weakness, trusting only in the Merits and graces of Christ his Lord; and he begins to live like a true child of God in gratitude and faith.

13. THE SOUL'S EXPERIENCE.

D) THE SOUL STRIPPED, INTERIORLY.

There is an extraordinary way in which God tears someone - in that person's own spiritual self and at exactly the 'right' time - from all that fastens him, in his thoughts and desires, to the things of this world. The one who follows the path of obedience, and who reveals his soul to his superiors in order to receive the advice that God wishes him to receive through His human agents in the Catholic Church, is wonderfully rewarded by God, though such a soul knows nothing about reward or joy at the time. God rewards the soul, later, by Himself completing the task which the faithful soul furthered by his own obedient and courageous act. Indeed, God cannot fail to reward, lavishly, someone who is willing to risk sacrificing his own reputation and his own instinct for privacy in order to seek advice, thinking this to be the Will of God. Meanwhile, it happens that the *soul's interior is burned and stripped* in an entirely new way, as God strips away the 'old self' with the soul's pride. The courageous soul, if he chooses, accepts this 'stripping' for as long as God Wills. It consists of more than the humiliation of having exposed one's soul to another person. But the faithful soul quietly continues with his usual work, whilst offering the pain as a penance in union with the sufferings of Christ; and then he is rewarded by God, much later on, when he is shown the spiritual fruit which has sprung from this act of obedience and humility. Even as this person was suffering entirely alone, praying "All for Jesus", and uncomprehending, his sufferings were proving fruitful. Grace was being poured upon others through his sacrifice.

---

13. THE SOUL'S EXPERIENCE.

C) THE SOUL BURNED, OR WOUNDED.

Sometimes, the *soul is burned or wounded* by the touch of the Most Holy Spirit when He scours the soul with His Light. This can happen in prayer-time or outside. Such a soul isn't necessarily thinking about God; but one touch causes him to do so, and he becomes more aware of God's holiness and of his own wickedness. This causes him almost unbearable pain, until the time comes when he is given great peace, and doesn't so much weep over his past sins as praise God for His Mercy in having sent such a wonderful Saviour to help us; and yet he still weeps; but the piercing pain is experienced less frequently, for God, by numerous ways, has brought this soul to live in some degree of humility. God permits this burning, nevertheless, to keep the soul from pride.

This gift is usually given to those whom God sees will be willing to die to themselves, as Christ taught; and God alone can uphold someone who permits God to reveal every facet of the soul's interior to its own gaze, naked in God's pure Light. The torment is indescribable, and the soul might groan out loud for the pain; but it's a tremendous grace, even if it's unrecognised as such when it's first experienced.

In this action, the God of Love appears merciless as He burns away impurities in order to pour His own Purity into the soul, so that all past and present actions are seen as never before in His dreadful Light. The faithful soul thinks he might die from shame; but if he continues, no matter what he feels, to empty himself of all desire except the desire to do God's Will, then he receives from God from some faint indication of His Presence. God strengthens the faithful soul to a degree which that soul wouldn't have thought possible; and that soul is astonished to see that he endures and undertakes things from which he would have run away in earlier times, when his faith was weak and his trust very feeble.

The soul's worst torment, in this agony - which God has allowed, in the early stages of the spiritual life - is that he thinks that God cannot love him and doesn't love him, even while the soul continues, in blind faith, to do good things for the love of God alone, with, to his own mind, no natural hope or optimism at all. Also, he thinks - since God has blinded him, so to speak - that he doesn't love God at all, and that some secret sin or subtle evil within himself will perhaps keep him from God forever. He thinks this, with secret horror, even though he continues to prove his love - although he doesn't know it - as God leads him onwards and, when the time is ripe, brings him into His presence, in prayer.

This is the soul's Gethsemane. Many souls stop here and turn away, unaware of how far they have already come on the journey to union, but not possessing enough of the virtues to continue blindly from pure love alone. There's a great danger that a soul in this state will grow bitter. Such a soul has made tremendous sacrifices for God, but seems to have been ill-rewarded; for of course, this person has suffered many of the pains of preparation for union, but has so far experienced few of the almost unbelievable joys of true union; yet he is on 'the brink' of receiving them soon, if only he'll continue.

---

13. THE SOUL'S EXPERIENCE.

B) PRAYER WITH WORDS, STIRRED.

Sometimes the soul is led to *pray with words which are stirred from its own depths* by the action of the Holy Spirit - Who prays in the docile soul, in a way unknown to someone else who always praises God with his own feeble words and his own cautious thoughts, saying "if" and "but" and "provided that" to God, in prayer, not daring to give to God all his heart and free will, or indeed, his very life, which is the greatest 'praise' of all, in union with Christ's Sacrifice.

---

13. THE SOUL'S EXPERIENCE.

A) VOWS AND RESOLUTIONS.

Someone who lives habitually united to God in thoughts, words, deeds, hopes and constant prayers, is led by the Holy Spirit from moment to moment in daily life, towards one task and then towards another, without great agitation or worry or indecision. In prayer-time, the same Holy Spirit guides that faithful soul, and prompts him to renew his self-offering and to repent of all wrongs; and such a soul never hopes to be led in extraordinary ways.

But sometimes, the faithful soul is *prompted to make vows or resolutions* which he couldn't have 'thought up' by himself. He had no intention of making vows, yet he finds, in prayer, that he's inspired to undertake greater responsibility; and so he commits himself to God with new fervour. However, this soul ought not to regard himself as bound by any of these vows without consulting the proper authority, who can help him in many ways.

---

12. KNOWLEDGE AND WORDS.

Whenever God truly speaks to the soul in one of the types of extraordinary prayer which I'm listing here God gives to the soul what I call *Knowledge-in-prayer-by-means-of-words*, or accompanied by words; and this occurs in a wholly spiritual way. The words aren't heard by the bodily ears; nor are they heard "out loud".

There's a distinction between *"Knowledge-accompanied-by words"*, and *"spiritual-words-in-a-spiritual-conversation"* which can arrive within the soul during prayer or recollection. I'll try to explain this in the following few paragraphs.

D) WORDS TO THE SOUL.

It can happen that God guides the soul by means of *spiritual words heard within the soul quite unexpectedly* when someone is at prayer, or working, or meditating on his life or upon God. However, when words are received in this way, quite outside a state of evident union with God, and unaccompanied by Knowledge of any significance or by joy, the soul ought to beware, and to be even more determined than usual to take advice, and to follow nothing but the plain and sure path of Christ, with guidance from the Church. There's no need to explain further, as the soul will, I hope, take no notice of this sort of thing. It's true that God sometimes speaks to the soul in this way, but the soul can easily be deceived.

---

12. KNOWLEDGE AND WORDS.

C) WORDS THROUGH HOLY SCRIPTURE.

There is a way in which the faithful soul is guided by words which are addressed to his own heart, and which pierce him deeply, as Holy Mass. I'm not speaking, here, about when an agitated person twists the meaning of certain Scripture phrases to suit himself. I'm not even referring to the special gift of Understanding of Scripture sometimes given, as described in 10B, below. I'm referring to the extraordinarily *clear words of Holy Scripture*, impressed upon a soul as he listens to the reading at Holy Mass, *words used by God the Father or by Christ Himself to teach the soul* something about himself, or to *instruct, command, rebuke or encourage him* - all of this with great impact and *immediacy*. This is quite unlike hearing other parts of Scripture read aloud. These words are directed to the soul in great clarity and power, as are the words given in a spiritual conversation (12B) below; and the soul understands far more than it would have expected to learn from such simple phrases; and these things are understood not by thought or by imagination, but by grace.

This can happen when someone is not in a state of true prayer, although he's generally recollected, and is rarely without some thought of the God Whom he lives to serve, even if he thinks he serves Him badly.

The soul can also be instructed in this way *by God*, with extraordinary clarity, *by means of a few words of the homily* at Holy Mass: whether the priest (or deacon or Bishop) who is preaching is eloquent in introducing the Gospel, or pedestrian in his explanation.

---

12. KNOWLEDGE AND WORDS.

B) SPIRITUAL WORDS OF CONVERSATION.

'Spiritual words' given in a spiritual conversation arise as follows and are not usually about the chief truths of the Faith, but about the individual soul or the spiritual life. Sometimes, in prayer, when the soul is 'saturated' or 'absorbed' in Christ entirely - I mean, absorbed by His grace, as described in 6C - Christ speaks to the soul. He speaks within the soul; others cannot hear. But He uses true words heard as words by the soul's spiritual faculties. These words haven't been "conjured up" in the imagination. That's indeed possible; but if it happens the words are very different: over-loud perhaps, or hesitant. There's no grace about them.

Christ's own words to the soul are heard quite unexpectedly and quite suddenly, deep within the soul. They are heard with great clarity, and are usually brief and easily-understood. They always bring great calm to the soul, although it feels some surprise and puzzlement, as usual, since it's so aware of its own weakness and of Christ's holiness; and they also seem to tell the soul much more than their brevity could contain. As I said earlier, hearing such words is like receiving pure Knowledge, too. The faithful soul absorbs the truth conveyed in this way, and finds that he can write about it even years later on. He learns about the spiritual life, but is usually instructed or encouraged about his own interior life and progress.

There's little question here of anyone deceiving himself, if he is generally faithful and obedient and takes advice about extraordinary states. He learns that Christ's words never leave the soul agitated, or confused. Christ's words enlarge and purify the soul, and never draw the soul away - by enticement - from God, or from his duty to his neighbour, or from the Catholic Church. Christ cannot contradict Himself, and His Spirit of truth is One Spirit, undivided.

---

12. KNOWLEDGE AND WORDS.

A) KNOWLEDGE-ACCOMPANIED-BY-WORDS

Sometimes Knowledge is given to the soul in prayer by God the Father, or by Christ our Lord, through perhaps a dozen clearly-heard words of great simplicity; yet the words bear within them a tremendous truth or truths about some extremely important aspect of the Christian faith, such as the true meaning of Love or of the Atonement, or of the Incarnation of Our Lord. When I say 'true meaning' I speak about a mere glimpse of meaning given by God, since no soul dare claim to understand fully what are holy and sacred Mysteries. When this happens in prayer, the soul is stunned by the enormity of the Love which is revealed in this way, and is amazed that God should communicate in this way with a mere creature.

The faithful soul can't fail to be humbled and helped by *spiritual words* of such import: spiritual as described above; yet he ought to ask for guidance as usual, for fear of being deceived.

No-one does wrong in wanting to accept such words, since the experience resembles the prayer-of-union-of-persons or intellectual vision which I'll explain later on, in 5, which the soul seems to be unable to ignore except by ignoring or leaving prayer itself.

It seems to me that the words and the Knowledge which are given in this way have a special purity in that they're implanted in the depths of the soul, by God, it seems, so suddenly and swiftly that this experience resembles, too, the piercing-by-Knowledge which I'll describe later, in 2, an experience which I'm sure nothing evil could imitate, for reasons I needn't state here. The subject-matter, as well as the manner of 'implanting', is sublime. These words are usually about Christ our Lord, or about God the Father, or about Christ's Passion or His Sanctity, whereas the 'words of conversation' I've mentioned are more personal and usually endearing.

I can't be certain of this since I haven't spoken with others on this subject; but I don't believe that words of immense importance are given solely to benefit a solitary soul. I feel sure that they're given primarily so that the privileged recipient might share with others a marvellous reminder about faith, in the course of whatever sort of teaching or writing is, by now, this person's most important task.

---

11. DISCERNMENT.

I'll write a few words, here, about a truly extraordinary gift, which, it seems to me, is given to certain persons so that they can help others in an immediate and direct manner, in a way impossible without *true spiritual discernment*.

It's true that the more God's grace is 'permitted' - by the soul's goodwill and repentance - to flood the soul with Light, then the more marvellously is the soul able to look at this earth and the people on it - indeed, everything on it, in some measure - *through the eyes of Christ.* I mean that a faithful person no longer thinks about the Earth without at least indirectly thinking of God our Creator and of His Son Jesus Christ. Nor does he look at his fellow-humans any more in a worldly manner, that is, judging by exterior signs, or considering any other person as 'less' than someone beloved by God.

God enables the faithful soul, more and more clearly, to see others as He sees them, and never as mere faces which disguise a reality within, nor as mere parts of a crowd or a group. Each soul that is seen in this way retains - in one sense - his privacy; yet God can enable someone, through the gift of His Knowledge of hearts, to discern *the state of another's heart.* I mean that the one thus gifted can 'see', by Knowledge, where each person's true will lies. He 'sees' that person's inclination of heart and soul, whether towards good or evil, or pre-occupied with things of this world, or perhaps almost dead in spirit, from lack of charity or faith or hope.

Many thank they have this gift, but don't have it. Also, it's so dangerous a gift, and can be so seriously misused, that anyone who is gifted thus must walk carefully, in true union with God, running with horror from the least shred of pride, and begging for true purity of heart.

---

10. UNION WITH GOD IN RECOLLECTION-PIERCED-BY-UNDERSTANDING.

B) 'LIGHT': THROUGH HOLY SCRIPTURE OR ANOTHER SPIRITUAL BOOK.

There are very many ways in which God communicates His Will to us, and His Knowledge and His Love; but I'll mention, here, two states of recollection in which God teaches the soul. The truths are as true, of course, as truths communicated in formal prayer. But the description of these states will emphasise *different modes of understanding.*

God can teach the soul, and sometimes speaks to it, giving understanding *through the words of Holy Scripture* as these are spoken aloud in the Liturgy, yet as they are understood with more clarity than is normally given. This frequently occurs when the soul has prayed to God for guidance on some topic. God never fails to help the soul who asks for help and this is one of the many ways which He might choose. He speaks by His Word, yet since so few treasure His Word, fewer persons are guided thus than are enlightened in the way described below (in 10A.) Occasionally, someone is guided by God in the same fashion, through a book written by a holy author. However, this happens quite suddenly and unexpectedly, as and when God Wills. No-one ought to expect amazing enlightenment to leap routinely from the pages during spiritual reading but should use books for normal intelligent reading, as God Wills.

In daily life, a holy understanding of the Sacred Scriptures is a gift from God to be received with thanks. The soul ought to remain alert, however, to the possibility of understanding things differently at a later reading. God's truth is not tied to the personal interpretation of a day, and truth has many facets. All of these, nevertheless, as perceived by the soul which is truly united to God in prayer and recollection, will conform to the only true way of understanding Holy Scripture, which is with the mind of the Church, guided by the most Holy Spirit.

---

10. UNION WITH GOD IN RECOLLECTION-PIERCED-BY-UNDERSTANDING.

A) THE GIFT OF SPIRITUAL LIGHT.

The *type of Understanding* I want to explain here, if possible, is a gift from God. All truth is from Him, but, in this case, the soul finds that, amidst its daily activities, *it is suddenly pierced by Understanding* in a sudden and profound enlightenment of the soul. The soul hasn't a mere insight into a subject, such as those which can arise after thought or meditation; it has received an extraordinary gift, though quietly and gently. The gift of Understanding is similar to Knowledge, though not as extraordinary in its intensity or purity. It is usually given to someone who is already recollected, but who isn't necessarily praying. Understanding is more like a swift sun-rise within the soul, with regard to the subject-matter - usually the spiritual life - rather than like the narrow, blinding, piercing beam of pure Knowledge which is received by the soul in Unknowing prayer (2).

I believe that this experience is not uncommon amongst those who pray, but it is most definitely a special gift. It's quite different from the experience of "light dawning" in one's intellect, in thought. The faithful soul is recollected but alert, though he might be at work, perhaps, or engaged in vocal prayer or reading. He finds that he's free to dwell on what he has just understood. If he does this he benefits enormously. He doesn't do wrong if his subsequent sense of gratitude and wonder, or his calm reflections on what has been understood in this way, cause him to thank God and praise Him for His Goodness, since that sincere prayer of praise - which stems from the Gift of understanding - is a greater prayer than the vocal prayer which it might replace. Nevertheless, this person is free to return to his vocal prayer later on, if that will stop him being anxious. But God cannot be 'displeased' when someone neglects one type of prayer because God Himself has said to the soul, as it were, "Come up higher"

To sum up: after such an 'Understanding', the soul's reflections ought to lead it to act upon the Understanding given, whether it acts through prayer or thought or movement or neighbourly service or whatever. I ought to mention, here, that such Understanding is not, in my experience, given with an image. It is utterly pure and simple. As it pierces the soul and the intellect it "carries" nothing and disturbs nothing, although Wisdom is contained within it. What I'm trying to say is that someone might find that, afterwards, he has added an image from his own memory to that experience. He ought not to feel guilty about possessing such a visual 'aid-memoire'. This is quite acceptable to Our Lord if it isn't misused, or changed or idolised.

---

9. <u>PRAYER-OF-UNION, WITH AN IMAGE</u>.

The 'visions' or states of prayer which I'm now going to describe are not as visually gross or disturbing as others might be led to believe when the states are described by words such as 'dazzling' or 'moving image' seen by 'the soul's eyes'. Everything I shall describe is utterly light, pure, gentle and delicate in a way quite beyond the understanding of anyone who deals mainly with what is large, loud, vigorous, brash or self-centred either in prayer or in dealings with others. These things will be more readily understood not by timid or cowardly souls but by those with much love, faith, courage and simplicity.

B) <u>WITH A 'JOURNEY' IMAGE, IN AWARENESS</u>.

There's a type of prayer in which one sees a *moving image* not with the bodily eyes, as I said, but with the eyes of the soul. It is God Who has drawn the soul into union with Him in prayer in this peculiar way. This happens infrequently, but it seems to be a special means by which He instructs the soul about various stages of the spiritual life.

In this strange prayer, the faithful soul has no choice but to go where Christ invisibly leads him, or to give up prayer completely. So, if this person consents, Christ guides him on a spiritual journey which is seen clearly with the soul's eyes. The person who prays remains conscious of the place and attitude of prayer.

No images have been sought by the soul; but, on these occasions, a single image is communicated, and a single 'teaching' is given, wordlessly, as the soul is led by Christ to a new height. Then, within a few minutes, the soul sees that he kneels and prays as usual, wondering just how and why Our Lord leads him in such strange ways, for they seem strange, always, since the person who prays has never met anyone who has spoken of such a thing.

---

9. PRAYER OF UNION.

A) WITH A LIVING-IMAGE, IN AWARENESS.

There is a type of *prayer-with-living-images* which is experienced, by those whom God draws along this path, much more frequently than the one I shall describe later in 3. The state of which I now speak is also a state of *union-with-Knowledge and a living-image* yet it is less glorious and less prolonged; also, it frequently occurs whilst the soul is alert, rather than enraptured, although the peaceful joy of this state might draw the soul into an absorption similar to rapture though not as intense.

The living images seen here with the eyes of the soul are not as over-powering as those I shall mention below (3) nor as clearly seen. Yet Christ frequently chooses to appear to the soul's eyes in this majestic way after Holy Communion, giving His Knowledge and encouragement to the faithful soul, and instructing him in whatever subjects He has decided will benefit that soul.

Sometimes - I hardly dare to write this, but it is true - the thoughts of Christ and of the soul move to one another in an exchange of pure love and truth. The person who prays is uplifted but, as I said, is usually still conscious of his surroundings. He is free to turn away, distracted, or free to turn away to fulfil some duty, as Christ looks on in love. In the same way, the soul might greet the Saints or Angels in prayer outside the time of Mass: usually at home, but occasionally elsewhere.

The faithful soul is 'absorbed', throughout, though not usually totally 'enfolded'. He is free to turn his attention away. I have found that if from amazement or curiosity one turns away from prayer in order to think about the appearance of the Heavenly person or persons seen, then this state of prayer ceases. But if one turns away in order to praise God in the Mass, or to do something kind for a neighbour, then Christ, or whichever holy person is present, remains 'in' the soul in this way, waiting for one's return. Words might be spoken, too - but more on that, later.

On these occasions, Christ is seen more frequently with His Holy Mother than without her, and is usually attended by Angels, and sometimes by Saints too: all of whom appear in so much glory that the soul's eyes are dazzled. It's in this state of prayer, or in others very similar, that I've been gently urged to ask questions, and to share my concern about people I love. I've been led to hold up each person to Christ or to His Holy Mother, and have been answered with *pure Knowledge, Spirit to spirit, and with gentle gestures*. None of this stems from the imagination, which would be quite incapable to producing anything which has the delicacy, spontaneity and grace of what is experienced here. With the usual warnings in mind, one can be fairly certain that such good gifts come from the One Who is Good, but we'd be foolish not to seek advice on such matters at some stage of the spiritual life.

I repeat, interminably, I know, that one can be deceived whenever one sees images in prayer.

However, in this type of prayer, as in others, one can only leave behind or repudiate the images by leaving prayer itself - and, in my opinion, that's a good sign. I haven't spoken of this to others in detail, but, from experience, this type of prayer usually leads to a renewed determination to serve God and one's neighbour lovingly, and to take up one's cross without complaint - by God's grace. If it's the prayer which has brought about that increase of genuine fervour, then some aspect of that prayer, or perhaps all of it, was good.

---

8. TEACHING IN PRAYER: WITH AN ASSOCIATED IMAGE.

I intend to describe, now, four ways in which God - in His great love for the soul, and for those whom that soul will eventually help - teaches him in a wholly spiritual manner about many aspects of life in Christ: about the soul's union with Christ; and yet a simple image is associated with each occasion on which such a 'teaching' is received.

In my experience, God doesn't generally teach, in this way, things which we ought already to have learned in the normal way, from 'faith teachers' such as parents, school-teachers or catechists and priests. For example, I think that no-one would be taught the Commandments in this way, though he or she might be taught the difference between true sin and mere weakness, and might be shown the effects which these have on the soul.

The four ways which I'm about to describe are placed here, "before" the prayer of union of Persons (5), and of Wills (4) from which the reader might deduce that they are less 'pure'. That is true in the sense that the soul, in the four types of prayer below, sees an image, and is therefore in some danger of being deceived - at least before that person is experienced enough to discern the difference between different images in prayer, and before he has sought advice in this matter. As I said earlier, he ought to try to ignore, whilst in prayer, images of any type, however "holy", secure in the knowledge that he can recall 'good' images afterwards. He mustn't seek for experiences, nor must he allow any image to interrupt his true gaze towards God-in-darkness during any period of worship, whether private or liturgical.

The origin of the images which I've described is God, acting in the soul; and these images are a brief accompaniment to the true and valuable prayer-of-Union-with-knowledge, which I shall soon describe (2) and which is easily recognised in its purity, since the soul isn't disturbed by movements or warm feelings.

So, the types of prayer which I shall describe in the next few paragraphs are very valuable for the soul who keeps God first in everything, despite the presence of images. Meanwhile, the wise soul will always remember that how weak he is and that he's never beyond making mistakes, for as long as he still lives on earth.

---

8. TEACHING IN PRAYER: WITH AN ASSOCIATED IMAGE.

D) TEACHING IN PRAYER - BY KNOWLEDGE WITH ONE'S OWN IMAGE PROMPTED BY GOD. GOD TEACHES THE SOUL ABOUT ITSELF BUT THE SOUL SUPPLIES AN IMAGE.

The type of 'Knowledge-with-image' which I must describe is just as described soon in (8C), and (8D), except that the *image is one's own*. I mean that one might receive Knowledge in prayer, without any 'Translation' into an image, yet sometimes one's mind immediately provides an image. The soul is aware that the image comes from the imagination. It tries to ignore every image, as usual, since worship is so important. However the soul knows, with some experience, that God has prompted the imagination, so to speak, to clothe His Knowledge-in-prayer; and that's why the soul permits himself to recall such an image later on. *The Knowledge,* and the *God-prompted image, together,* are a precious gift, though of a lower degree of purity than the "Translations" described below, in 8A, in which the soul is absorbed and utterly lifted up 'into' God for a moment, and is as if helpless as an image is given at the same time as Divine wisdom.

---

8. TEACHING IN PRAYER: WITH AN ASSOCIATED IMAGE.

C) TEACHING IN PRAYER - BY "KNOWLEDGE WITH A GIVEN-IMAGE". GOD INSTRUCTS THE SOUL IN THE SPIRITUAL LIFE.

Sometimes, when the faithful soul is peacefully at prayer, his heart yearning towards God yet already resting in Him, he suddenly sees *an image of great importance*, yet he sees it in a manner different from that by which he sees pictures in the imagination or memory, in everyday life. He 'sees' with the eyes of the soul. This 'seeing' cannot be described adequately to someone who hasn't experienced it; yet the soul who 'sees' thus in prayer knows that it is a gift, and this is why he knows this: it's because such an image isn't a 'thing' which can be moved about at will, as when, for example, we select and alter visual memories in our normal thought-processes or meditations.

This *"given-image"* is seen within the soul, and not within the imagination. It is unchosen, suddenly-appearing and still. It lasts for a longer time than the images of the "Knowledge-Translation", and *Knowledge accompanies it.* The experienced soul is sure that it is a gift which can be contemplated later or communicated to others, if God Wills, for their encouragement in faith. But since the person who receives it knows that his first duty is to look towards God in prayer, especially at Holy Mass, and since God is not an image, the soul won't permit himself to be distracted by any image, however holy or interesting, and so tries to turn away from it if he can, in order to continue his prayer. By experience, he becomes less anxious and less impatient, since he learns that he can 'pull' the image from his memory after his prayer-time, if God permits, even many years later on.

These 'given-images' seem to be given to the soul for one of two reasons. By what I describe here God shows the soul *what is happening within itself.* This is a precious personal gift by which God explains with marvellous tenderness the stages of the spiritual journey; or He shows the soul, clearly, in which good state He has placed him at present, and how (8B) He has done so.

In a moment, I'll try to sum up the purpose of the 'given-images' although, as I said, the soul should peacefully turn away from the images, confident that Knowledge given at the same time will remain imprinted in the heart and memory.

I believe that it's unlikely that any soul will be instructed in this secret and holy manner, who hasn't given up all that doesn't lead to God - and that not from any motive except pure love and a longing to be united with Him for ever. God Who is Love can't refrain from giving extraordinary help to all who love Him more than anything or anyone, and who sacrifice everything, by their consent, if not in fact , for love of Him and of His Will.

This type of teaching-in-prayer is exactly the same as in 8B which I describe next, that is: *"Knowledge with a given-image"*; but the subject matter is different. I suppose the difference exists only in my mind, and in my method of classification, and in my use of symbols, since the state of prayer is the same in each; however, it does seem to me that each soul which is privileged to be instructed by God in this way learns about the *spiritual life and the state of its very own soul.* Such a person receives very *precise and accurate information about the manner in which God works* within the soul, or about the soul's precise role in intercessory prayer. Many other things of great practical usefulness can be taught, thus. Everything I've described here in 8C about the state of the soul is true, also, of 8B.

---

8. TEACHING IN PRAYER: WITH AN ASSOCIATED IMAGE.

B) TEACHING IN PRAYER - ALSO BY KNOWLEDGE-WITH-A-GIVEN-IMAGE. GOD SHOWS WHAT IS HAPPENING TO THE SOUL.

Someone who experiences the state just described in 8C might receive Knowledge which is not specifically about his own soul but which is about the spiritual life of everyone who is united with Christ. Such teachings illustrate general principles of the spiritual life, rather than personal states or achievements; and yet these teachings are received in exactly the same manner as in 8C: by Knowledge combined with a 'given-image'; and whoever receives such gifts finds that he is able to remember such images for ever. He is awed by God's wisdom, and is humbled to realise how privileged he is to receive such gifts. The more he grows in appreciation of such gifts, the greater is his yearning to share his conviction of God's goodness with other people.

---

8. TEACHING IN PRAYER: WITH AN ASSOCIATED IMAGE.

A) TEACHING IN PRAYER - BY KNOWLEDGE-WITH-TRANSLATION. GOD GIVES KNOWLEDGE ABOUT THE LIFE OF GRACE.

Sometimes, when the soul is at prayer, and is pierced by Knowledge from God - by a wordless Knowledge which is pure, sudden and brief - God permits that, at almost the same time, in the same state of prayer, such *Knowledge is "translated"* into an image, within the soul! The image is not 'conjured up' by the soul or by the imagination; in fact, the faithful soul can do nothing but receive; he doesn't know what he is doing. He receives a pure gift from God, given in Love, for the soul's benefit, and in some way for the good of others. The soul doesn't know what has happened until the experience is over.

Sometimes, this gift of Knowledge-with-Translation is of greater length, or is interspersed with other types of union or soul's sight, yet all so gently, however that the soul is drawn by God from one type of prayer to another without any perceptible change of 'status'. 'Knowledge and Translation' might last for a few minutes. It is so pure that although someone might have tried initially to reject it, he cannot do so. There is little danger, therefore, of this person being deceived.

The soul might experience this, also, whilst not totally enfolded by God. The faithful soul can remain conscious of his body although his heart leans towards God, drawn by Him: and the soul can rest with God in this prolonged prayer, wordlessly accepting what is being given silently by God.

I would add a warning here. If, in the prolonged state, someone is prompted by curiosity or vanity to start thinking about whatever is being revealed in this marvellous way, instead of remaining faithful to his duty by continuing to pray as usual, he will probably find himself 'outside' prayer, so to speak, having to decide what to do and whether to turn his heart towards God again, in penitence.

---

7. REALITY, SEEN WITH THE EYES OF THE SOUL.

Now that I've described, in section 8, the various ways in which God unites the soul to Himself in prayer, whilst simultaneously providing the soul with one sort of image or another which will benefit that soul's own spiritual life or another's, I must explain that the soul can be enlightened by God in a different state which combines knowledge and image, which I call *"Reality, seen with the eyes of the soul"*. The soul is enlightened thus even when not entirely 'lost' or absorbed in prayer; and I write 'reality', because these images are not provided as illustrations for parables or analogies; they represent spiritual realities, in a mysterious way.

On these occasions, God teaches or enlightens the soul in a way which is inferior to a pure intellectual vision, as in 5, but which is more truly pure and brief than the ways which I've already listed (even though, in all ways I describe here in 8 and 7, the soul sees some sort of image).

I've found that the soul who is attentive to God and to the things of God, and who is at the same time living in true charity with Him and his neighbour, and who is also advanced in prayer, sometimes sees, in the very midst of the activities and experiences of every-day life, things which can only be perceived by those to whom God Wills to reveal them; and these are spiritual realities which are now seen only by 'the eyes of the soul'.

This sounds mysterious, but I'm aiming not at mystery, but at clarity; and that's why this writing is sometimes so long-winded. What I mean is that our Holy and Merciful God sometimes permits the soul, quite unexpectedly, to see, by its soul's sight, what spiritual thing is really happening before it. It's as simple, and as marvellous, as that. The soul might 'see' many Angels present in the church, for example, or might 'see' an aspect of the Sacrifice of Christ at which we're present at Holy Mass; or he might glimpse, in the same spiritual way, other holy Mysteries; and such pure spiritual 'sights' are gifts from God, and do not arise from an over-excited imagination.

Yet, in my experience, this never happens unless the soul is totally recollected and at peace with God, even if occupied with daily outside-prayer activities. The more the prayerful person strives to live in loving obedience towards God the Father, through Christ, the more he is likely to see the deep reality of things in this way - spiritual sights unsought and quickly forgotten, but nevertheless God-given, for His own purposes.

---

6. PRAYER OF FELT-UNION.

Sometimes, Christ's felt presence within the soul, usually after Holy Communion, combined with His action and grace, brings the soul to an extraordinary state of prayer which is less 'pure' than those I shall describe below, but which is nonetheless God-given and marvellous. I call this *"felt-union"*.

C) 'ABSORPTION'.

The 'lowest' of the three states of 'felt-union' which I'm about to describe occurs most frequently after Holy Communion, although it can happen too, in prayer at home or elsewhere, and whether someone prays alone or in a group. The soul is drawn into a wonderful prayer of 'felt-union'; and yet whoever experiences this state doesn't merely become engrossed in Christ, so to speak, by thoughts or by emotions, or by desires or expressions of gratitude. I mean that Christ suddenly overwhelms and sweetens this person's whole soul, and detaches him gently, by degrees or wholly, from what his body usually experiences when he is kneeling at prayer. This is a true union of Love, felt as a blessed absorption which is a pure gift, and which is not and cannot be invented, though an immature soul might momentarily mistake its warm emotions for the pure joy of this type of God-given union.

In His Goodness, Christ allows such a soul to rest in His felt Presence for a long time, sometimes holding the soul in silent repose, or sometimes teaching the soul by Knowledge or by words-without-sound. Sometimes, He might lead the soul, 'unsighted', upwards to the Father, in the Light of His own Praise; and here, the soul follows Christ's Will and guidance; and the soul's usual thanksgiving after Communion is rarely as pure as this - except in pure Unknowing prayer, for example - since, here, this person offers Christ's own prayer and thanksgiving to the Father.

Sometimes, in this state, the faithful soul is so absorbed - even though not now in rapture - that he hears nothing of what goes on around him, even if others are present in the room. There is not, in my experience, any fainting or loss of consciousness in the usual sense. There is no collapse. Yet, here, the prayerful person notices nothing but Christ's own action within himself. At other times, he is half-absorbed in Christ, not by inattention, but by Christ's Will only half-absorbing him. By God's Will, this person still hears and notices whatever is going on around himself. This is doubtless due to Christ's longing for the soul to live in charity, since, in this 'half-absorbed' state, the soul can respond correctly during the prayers of the Mass, and can turn to his neighbour if there is a need to be met or a kindness to be done - there in church. The soul's own greatest personal praise of God is to do His Will; and God Wills that we love our neighbours all the time, even when this means 'leaving' our prayer in order to help someone.

In the state I've described above, someone might find that he has received *'knowledge with a Translation'* as I've already described (in 7). I mean that God raises and lowers our souls, when He wishes to do so, between one type of union and another. But I've noticed that it's most frequently after Holy Communion that the soul is enlightened on one of many subjects in the way I've described in 8. This is for this person's own benefit and, also perhaps, for the eventual benefit of others; and I write 'eventual', although others truly benefit immediately, even if they don't know it, simply through the obedience and charity of a soul who goes to prayer thinking only of giving Glory to God. All souls benefit from the good done by each sister or brother in Christ, visions or no visions.

I must say, here, that whenever I speak of 'movements' from one type of prayer to another, or of 'visions', or of God 'raising' or 'lowering' the soul in prayer, I describe movements and perceptions which are so amazingly pure and gentle and delicate, that if we compare them with physical movements they are as gossamer compared with hessian, or, better still, I think, as silk threads compared with a fence woven of barbed wire.

So, in the absorption described above, the faithful soul doesn't seek anything extraordinary in his prayer but is drawn into true joy through the presence and kindness of Christ. The soul feels saturated with peace and joy in this prayer, no matter how much he might have been troubled earlier with pain or tiredness or cold; and he can hardly bear to leave this prayer, but does so willingly whenever his attention is needed elsewhere. He knows, by now, that Christ will give him peace and refreshment whenever He sees the soul's true need; but the soul isn't agitated, thinking about the future. Such a person trusts in God entirely and is happy in any state which God permits.

---

6. PRAYER-OF-FELT-UNION.

B) 'FLIGHT'.

The second of these prayers of 'felt union' - in ascending order - is the *prayer of 'flight'*. No other word is appropriate, since, in this state, the soul is as though taken away by God. Whoever experiences this knows that he is being led 'upwards' at a tremendous speed. Unswervingly, but dimly, he is conveyed through vast spiritual regions where he wouldn't dare go by himself, if such a thing were possible; and all of these places are in God, Who is unseen. It's impossible to describe what God is doing for this person, or why; but though this happens comparatively rarely this person knows that he has no choice but to go where he is so swiftly taken; indeed, he wouldn't refuse if he could, since his will has already been given to God, Who is therefore utterly trusted and obeyed throughout.

The faithful soul can recall that he has been taken in spirit to somewhere unknown: and since the 'journey' was lengthy, this prayer is not as 'pure' as the prayer described (in 1) of complete, sudden Unknowing; but someone who has experienced this 'flight' can't recall what passed between himself and God in the 'heights' to which his soul was taken. He is content to trust in God during prayer, and to live by faith and not by sight, on earth. The devout soul should leave this prayer as he leaves any other: unconcerned about such an experience, provided that the soul's continuous yearning is towards God alone and towards the faithful fulfilment of His Will in everything.

6. PRAYER OF FELT-UNION.

A) 'JUBILATION'.

The highest of these three states of 'felt' union, in my view, is that most appropriately called *'Jubilation'*. I know I've read that title elsewhere; but there could hardly be a better word by which to convey the imageless, wordless and yet - to the spirit - palpably blissful state of celebration into which the soul is brought by Christ, when He chooses. This state is very different from other ecstasies, which can be called *'blind bliss'*. 'Jubilation' is the utterly pure and spiritual and *God-given equivalent of feasting* and joyous shouts and pealings of bells and music; but nothing is heard. These things are simply known, in a manner permitted by God, who has chosen to give the soul this special sort of joy.

Over many years I have experienced this union-in-jubilation only a handful of times whilst other gifts have been given to me dozens of times; yet of course every sort of Heavenly joy is given from love, as God chooses - for His own purposes and for our delight. I know that one can recall the fact that one was taken into this state; but the soul can't recall anything afterwards, since there was no-thing on which to fasten himself: that is, neither sight nor sound. But God's goodness was conveyed secretly to the soul by His pure Knowledge, in this extraordinary manner; and such obscure Knowledge about love and joy remains in the soul afterwards.

5. PRAYER OF UNION-OF-PERSONS: AN INTELLECTUAL VISION.

There is a marvellous way in which God sometimes teaches the soul not about doctrine, but about holy persons. A prayerful person can experience an extraordinary union of himself, spiritually, with a Heavenly person or persons, through God's power and grace, and when and where God Wills - I mean, a union different from that described further on (in 3).

To explain this *prayer of 'Union-of-persons'*, I can explain that sometimes, when I've been praying or working or reading, I have suddenly become aware of the presence of the enfolding Love of the Most Holy Trinity, or have been aware of Our Blessed Lord's presence by me; or sometimes, in the same imageless way, I have met a holy person from Heaven. This might happen anywhere God chooses - at home or even when I'm travelling - but, strange as it might seem, I've experienced what are called intellectual visions such as these more frequently at home or out of doors than in Church. Perhaps that's because God communicates His Knowledge and His Love, in church, principally through the Sacraments and through the Holy Scriptures. Also, since He Wills that we pay attention to the altar and to the Holy Sacrifice, He doesn't usually contradict His own instructions by drawing our attention away from Christ's Own Offering towards some lesser person or activity.

The aspects of Knowledge which I'm trying to describe, as I mention different places, aren't the same as one another. I mean that, although this isn't an invariable rule, it's usually during Holy Mass that God teaches the soul, for example, about His attributes, or about the Holy

Sacrifice of Christ on Calvary. But what I describe here enriches the soul not with a knowledge of a 'fact' or an event or an abstract truth, but with a growth in knowledge of a person or persons; and this is achieved through the 'presence' of that person.

In this image-less and silent '*prayer-of-union-of-persons*', the soul seems to be pierced with 'knowledge of presence' in a similar way to that in which it receives imageless 'knowledge-of-God's-Attributes', as I shall shortly describe (in 2). But in this case (5) the soul isn't usually caught into rapture; and the experience is usually much longer-lasting, I mean, for many minutes rather than for a fraction of a second: perhaps even for days or longer. Nothing is seen, though the soul knows who is present. The soul is not enraptured but alert, although he might find himself swiftly led from this type of image-free 'vision' to a prayer of union with living-image (8) and back again, as God Wills.

However, because of that fact - that the soul isn't enraptured during this state - he finds that, once responsive to that presence, that is, courteously and gratefully turning immediately to Christ or to another Heavenly friend in welcome, he is free, even in this state of true prayer-in-union, to worship, to speak, to ask questions, and to listen. In other words, he can do whatever seems appropriate in the presence of his Saviour or of a Saint or Angel. He is guided throughout by his own good instincts, by the promptings of the Most Holy Spirit, and by the gracious albeit sometimes wordless conversation of whoever the soul has been brought to meet in this marvellous way.

Commonsense and caution.

Now: since I have so frequently suggested that the soul should turn away from all images or experiences in prayer, if possible, for fear of mistaking evil for good and of being led astray, I must point out, here, that we cannot fail to benefit if we do so and ignore every 'vision' if possible, or if we seek advice from someone in authority, by which I mean a confessor or someone suitable: not any randomly-chosen confidant.

It's true that in the state which I've just described, when someone has suddenly been spiritually 'confronted', so to speak, with a gentle presence, he sometimes feels unable to turn away from that presence without turning away utterly from prayer. Anyone who has experienced this will know what I mean; and it seems to me that the soul should stay 'in' prayer, his heart 'leaning' towards God if possible, without anxiety. But if this person becomes anxious, he ought to be very sensible and "show" God every worry, and then get up and do something else, with a clear conscience, until he can go to prayer peacefully again.

If God wishes to speak plainly to us in prayer, whether directly or through a holy person, then He will do so at some stage, however many times, out of common sense or obedience, we walk away. It's better to risk missing something than to seize on experiences which are false; then there will be less likelihood of us being trapped by a longing for sensational prayer experiences or for wonderful feelings.

Those who are very advanced in prayer won't need all this advice. I believe that intellectual visions are frequently experienced by those who have crucified their ambitions, as Saint Paul said, and who live only to make Jesus Christ known and loved. People like that don't usually talk about them, however, unless a trustworthy person has advised them to do so, or unless it's God's wish that they do so, for a good purpose. In the same way, we don't usually divulge what has been said to us and by us in intimate conversations with earthly friends, except - perhaps - in special circumstances, such as in order to save a life.

Loving concern for us.

It seems best to explain here, between descriptions of *intellectual visions* and *other visions*, that the *Saints and Angels* accompany us in one way or another during our journeys on earth: by their holy yearnings and prayers, I mean, even if there's nothing palpable for us to grasp, as consolation; and it's usually by means of such visions as I've tried to describe - whether wordless and imageless, or visible to the soul's eyes - that God sometimes permits us to be aware of their love and concern, even though, by faith, we already know of their love.

We know that every one of us has a Guardian Angel close by. Someone might occasionally be aware that his Angel walks nearby, guarding him. This person might not see his angel with his bodily eyes, but sometimes glimpses 'him' with the soul's eyes, or is aware of 'his' presence, in a forceful way. Sometimes, the soul is made aware, by God, through an intellectual vision, of the Angel's response to the soul's prayers or actions. The soul might even witness the Angel's gestures of reverence or celebration. Sometimes, the soul 'sees' many Angels at Holy Mass.

Before I finish this section on a state of prayer in which, by a spiritual gift from God, someone knows that Christ, or a Saint of Heaven, or an Angel, is present beside him, I must point out how utterly pure and spiritual is this *"knowledge-of-presence"*. It is not the same as a "feeling of the presence" of someone, which I describe in sections 6A, 6B and 6C. In those, (particularly in 6C) the 'felt-presence' of Christ, in Holy Communion, for example, is to normal 'feeling' what things seen by the eyes of the soul are to normal 'seeing'. That way of 'feeling' and 'seeing' is spiritual, God-given and pure, but nevertheless, it doesn't have the same degree of purity as what I'm now trying to describe. This holy *"knowledge-of-presence"* is given to the soul unasked, immediate, piercing and pure, and carries with it no palpable feeling or seeing (unless another gift is added - that is, unless this type of experience is altered as God substitutes one state for another, as and when He Wills).

---

4. <u>PRAYER OF UNION-OF-WILLS</u>.

We now 'ascend', as it were, to the prayer of *'union-of-wills'*: to a more sublime state of prayer, which is a true prayer of union but not yet the most sublime. In this marvellous state, the soul is united in heart and will and intention with his Lord, even in darkness, and leans in spirit towards Him in love and longing, as described above. In this state he is sometimes pierced by pure knowledge from God, but without being lifted secretly into ecstasy. That's the first point in which this prayer differs from the next (3); also, the knowledge which the soul receives here is not so much about God Himself, but, more usually, about God's action on the soul, and many other things - all imageless and pure, but things about which this person can 'legitimately' concoct an image later on, in order to explain the subject, if he wishes to do so.

Once again, I must add that someone who has received knowledge in this way ought not to dwell on it whilst still kneeling in prayer. But it may be recalled and pondered later on, since such knowledge is Wisdom from God Himself.

Someone who is without guidance, and who has a vain longing for experiences, could, alas, easily deceive himself on this matter by admiring his own thoughts and by 'elevating' them, in his own misguided judgement, to special gifts from God. The faithful soul who regularly experiences such teachings as this, however, is only rarely mistaken since God's gift of Knowledge is much more pure and piercing than any thought of the human mind.

---

3. PRAYER IN UNION, WITH A LIVING-IMAGE, IN RAPTURE.

It seems appropriate, here, to speak about the *'prayer-of-union with a living image'*, which in my experience is much more rarely experienced than even the supreme states to be described below. Despite its comparative rarity, and despite the astounding beauty and attraction of this state, which I'm about to describe, I list it here as being less pure than the type described below (in 2). I say "less pure" only because there is more danger of being deceived in a state such as this. St. Paul has warned us about receiving an impostor who has disguised himself as an *"Angel of Light";* and, here, there is much light and glory.

In this state - when it is a true gift from God - the faithful soul is drawn by God into either a brief or a lengthy period of true union, but then suddenly finds himself receiving not only knowledge, but receiving, too, as he finds himself present with a glorious person, *a living image of a person, present in light and glory.* He knows that the living image is truly that person, in some way, or so he believes when he is urged towards love and unselfishness.

He doesn't see the image with his bodily eyes, but *with the 'eyes of the soul'* - though he can't reflect on this at the time, since he is completely enraptured, at least, at first. He cannot think at all while he is 'suspended' during the vision, but only afterwards. Nevertheless he is astonished that his usual darkness has been so dramatically, though quietly, replaced by this Light. He is astounded to see, within that Heavenly Light, Christ or the Blessed Virgin Mary, perhaps with the Saints.

Such a soul finds himself enclosed within that Light for as long as the vision lasts. He doesn't seem to be outside the light, peering in from darkness. Rather, he knows himself to be wrapped within that Light, and is truly 'rapt' or enraptured, at least for part of the time, whilst he looks ahead with the eyes of the soul, and speaks and worships with great naturalness and simplicity, but with instinctive reverence and respect, also. Our Lord Jesus Christ, when seen in this way, is so dazzling in His Glory that the soul's eyes cannot look steadily, unless strengthened by grace.

In my experience, this type of 'prayer-with-a-living-image' might last for several minutes, or even half an hour, since a genuine though spiritual conversation or personal instruction takes place within it. This occupies real time, unlike the 'knowledge' described below (in 2) which is implanted, so to speak, in one swift movement.

Ready to ask advice.

Such a soul is, afterwards, full of wonder at the memory of what he has just been seen and heard. But he is ready to ask advice about his experiences. He even tries to forget them, in order to press on with his usual intercessions, or his other works and duties. But he is amazed at the goodness of God. His heart is full of gratitude.

This type of prayer seems to the soul to be one of the most sacred and precious, yet this isn't really so. All that comes from God is precious; however, there's a smaller chance of being led astray in a prayer without words or images than in any prayer with even 'living images' - however glorious. There's a further danger: that having once experienced such visions as those just described, the soul might become discontented with dark prayer, and with the quiet practice of virtue and the performance of secret penance.

All that is good in these visions may be recalled later on, to stimulate the faithful soul towards increased attempts to prove his love for God, and to encourage him in his resolutions to work and pray for God's Glory alone. But he ought never to hope for a further, similar experience. He should learn to accept and love whatever type or degree of prayer is permitted and given by God on each successive day.

It seems appropriate to explain, here, that I've judged this experience (3) to be superior to those I've already described, despite the things 'seen' with the soul's eyes, as described above; and this is because such experiences as these of Christ or of His Holy Mother (in 3) are combined with the prayer of 'Union-pierced-by-knowledge', and thus are superior to an intellectual vision alone. That's my opinion; but I feel bound to give a reminder, meanwhile, that I'm not discussing 'apparitions' which consist of persons seen with one's bodily eyes. As I said, I've never seen such things, so I can't speak accurately about them.

---

2. PRAYER OF UNION-PIERCED-BY-KNOWLEDGE.

Before describing in a few paragraphs, and very inadequately, the marvellous state of *prayer-of-union-in-Unknowing* (1) of which nothing can be remembered, I must write of the *prayer-of-pure-union-pierced-by-brief-knowledge*.

This prayer resembles the prayer of 'Unknowing' which I shall shortly describe in that the soul is lifted into *ecstasy* or *rapture*, and is lifted suddenly and quite unexpectedly. Here, however, the faithful soul is afterwards astonished to realise that, while he was praying, he was pierced and enlightened by a pure, sudden, instantaneous, wordless and *imageless 'Knowledge' of God* or of His attributes.

This state of prayer is usually brief. Since the person who experiences this state has been utterly enraptured, he has no way of knowing, from his own senses, how much time has passed. But since I've found, from my own experience of this state, that Holy Mass has proceeded only by a little, just as during one's 'Unknowing' prayer, I've concluded that this extraordinary 'knowledge' has been given in a prayer which lasted for a mere second, or for a few minutes, only.

I've found that, whenever God Wills, He unites the soul with Himself in this prayer of utter union-in-unknowing usually after Holy Communion, though sometimes at or after the Consecration. However, this state differs from the prayer of total Unknowing (1) for this reason: something from this prayer (2) can be recalled. I mean that I discover, afterwards, that my soul has been utterly enfolded, and that I've been given, during that time, God's pure gift of Knowledge, as I shall describe more fully below. This happens even while there has been no consciousness on my part of thoughts or memory or will or imagination. Then I am released back, I find, into ordinary prayer, as suddenly as I was taken from it; but I'm aware of what I've just learned in this extraordinary way, and am once again awed and astounded. It was so sudden and unexpected, and it seems so marvellous, that the soul almost trembles at the thought of what it has received.

However, from the first time that I myself experienced this type of prayer, I tried not to think about it, but to treat such Knowledge as a distraction. It seems to me that such knowledge can be gladly recalled at the appropriate time; but it mustn't be pondered during our usual prayer-time, when God deserves our heart's devotion rather than our speculation about Him and His gifts.

So, in this way, when enraptured, I've learned about many things, through God's Goodness. He has taught me, with neither words nor images, about His Glory, about the most Holy Trinity, the Love of Christ, The Holy Sacrifice of the Mass, and the Incarnation of the Word through the Blessed Virgin Mary - and much more. Such images as I've drawn on these subjects have arisen from other experiences in prayer: from the types I've described in earlier sections.

A gradual 'strengthening' of the soul.

At my present time of life, now that God has been teaching me in this way for many years, I find that I'm sometimes taught in this way even though I'm not in ecstasy, but am simply recollected in prayer or in thoughts about God. I believe that this is due to the soul's gradual strengthening if someone lives more peacefully in God's presence, with fewer crises and with less frequent - because less necessary - deep purifications. Of course, all of this is due to God's mercy and patience, and no-one dare congratulate himself on his apparent advance. We're so weak, and fall so easily. God alone holds us up in charity and helps us to persevere.

As I've said elsewhere, I was for several years so puzzled at receiving such sublime 'teachings' in prayer, and so awe-struck that God should have remained patient and loving towards someone as sinful as myself - since my faith was weaker then: I was more sure of God's Majesty than of His Mercy - that I wrote nothing and said nothing about what I'd learned in this way, except indirectly. I mean that I spoke of things to do with our Faith with a new assurance, but I scarcely paused to connect that certainty with the teachings-in-prayer. I wasn't sure, until after I'd sought advice, that I should take any notice at all, although my eventual instinct was to thank God for His gifts, and so I did so. Then I continued as before - ignoring the gifts - until the time came when Christ Himself asked me to record His teachings and to submit them for assessment.

Even as I speak of 'taking notice' of His gifts in prayer, there was no choice in the matter; or, rather, by choosing to try to love God, I had made my choice, and I had thereby - in advance -

accepted His Will and so had accepted all that He might send to me, whether in prayer or in daily life. So His sudden, unsought teachings were entirely His choice for me, as was - later - the writing of them all, by me, in response to His command.

Loving attention to God.

These simple 'occurrences' in prayer came at different times of the day, or in different places, although more frequently in church; but they always came - indeed, come now - at the point where my heart is totally devoted to reaching towards God in darkness, in worship and in faith and in penitence, through Christ. So, it can be seen that God prompts me to pray; and then with all my will I respond to that prompting and 'lean' towards God in an act of loving attention; then - when He Wills - He grants His gifts or withholds them.

My experience has been that, over and over again, in that darkness, and in that loving attention which, by the grace of God, is quite devoid of thoughts of self, the 'knowledge' has suddenly, unavoidably, swiftly and secretly pierced my soul and has left its mark. I mean that, in a "split second" I have been taught more about God and about our holy doctrines than I could have learned by reading or thinking for many years. The occurrence is over before I can even react to it, or think of anything. But the 'Knowledge' remains.

This way of receiving 'Knowledge' is so astonishing that it was a relief to be told, at last, by my former parish priest, that it's a true gift from God, and then to discover that others have written accounts of what they too have learned in this way. I've found that I can write at length on any of the 'subjects' taught in this way. Of course, nothing that is taught in this way contradicts in the least the true and sure teachings of the Church. If such knowledge did contradict the Church's teaching, it would be evident that the recipient was certainly not receiving teachings from God, Who cannot contradict Himself. Christ Who founded One Holy Church on earth, and Who guides it now through His Holy Spirit, can neither deceive nor mislead His sincere followers.

How and why God was teaching me in this way was a mystery to me at first; but then eventually I was shown the reason, or reasons. God the Father explained to me that everyone who attains a very high degree of union with Him in prayer - through God's invitation and the soul's consent and co-operation - inevitably is 'taught', since love and Knowledge 'go' together. Where love increases, Knowledge cannot fail to 'increase'; and so God doesn't withhold that gift of Knowledge. But He also explained that I've been taught more lavishly than is usual, for the sake of the work He's called me to do, of offering "Instructions from Christ" to the whole Church, as a reminder of the important truths of the Faith.

Spiritual knowledge: its purity.

It seems important, now, that I explain the three points I've noticed on which the Knowledge acquired in this particular way differs from worldly knowledge by its breadth and purity.

First, it's true that I've read much in books; but I couldn't possibly remember it all, or see so clearly the connections between one 'thing' and another; nor, indeed, have I ever understood even a fraction of the idea of the Glory and grandeur of God's Majesty and dignity from anything I've read, compared with what I've understood through prayer.

Secondly, it's only by God's grace that I can explain with certainty and fluency - without much pondering or hesitation - what I've truly learned in this way.

The third point is that the 'Knowledge' is utterly pure, in a special sense of being 'uncontained'. I mean that, unlike the knowledge gained from books or speech or sight, this 'Knowledge' - whether about God Himself or about the soul in grace - is wordless and immediate. There's no visible or auditory 'vehicle' bringing it to me. It is secretly and suddenly 'implanted'; and I know that this is true because it has no 'style' except its own marvellous fullness and purity. I haven't recalled it from an historic source.

My certainty about this unique way of learning is based upon both the manner of the apparent 'implanting' and my observations about our usual methods of learning and understanding.

I've already mentioned this, in the autobiographical narrative, but I'd better say again that, in daily life, I can usually recall where I've read a certain piece of information; and I remember the size and colour of the book in which I read it; or if it was something I studied hurriedly long ago, I might recall perhaps only the shape of the paragraph, that is, the shape of the print on the paper - or, if recalling a conversation, the place where I was standing or sitting at the time.

So, to give an example, I might recall a paragraph written about Purgatory by C.S. Lewis. But I would know that the words had been chosen by him, and by no one else. Even as I recalled the concept which he had explained I would recall it 'clothed', as it were, in his own distinctive style. It's the same with other writers' wonderful phrases about Christ and the Church. A phrase or two might be 'made my own' in the sense that we all enlarge our vocabularies by a conscious or unconscious borrowing from others through our reading and conversation; but the Knowledge given to me in prayer is so extraordinarily broad and full, and inexpressibly pure, that I know it's not the result of memory, nudged into action, although God does work upon our minds in that way, too. What I'm describing, as I write about 'prayer-knowledge' is God's free gift, quite unsought and totally unexpected; and it's not a procession of facts, but a Unity. In some measure, it is Truth itself, rather than ideas or sentences about Truth.

For six or seven years, I wrote nothing down. But when the time was ripe, and in obedience to God, I was able to recall and describe dozens of 'teachings' which had been given to me in the previous six or seven years. I've listed them all in versions Two and Three of Christ's 'Teachings-in-prayer.' Version Two isn't yet in print; but Version Three - which is written in the first person - is available as Volumes One to Four of "Teachings-in-prayer: Instructions from Christ." I hope that all the painted images which should accompany the teachings can be made available later on.

---

1. <u>PRAYER OF UNION</u>.

   C) <u>UNION-IN-UNKNOWING</u>.

I must write next about the pure prayer of 'Unknowing', since this is almost the most pure and holy prayer of all, freely given and utterly undeserved. We can prepare ourselves for it by the love we display towards God and neighbour - in good deeds, not in fine feelings; and it's legitimate to hope that we will be united to God - both on earth and in Heaven; but what we must avoid is any hope of experiencing marvels or wonders. We're easily seduced by good feelings and emotions in prayer, yet these are not prayer; in fact, they lead us away from true prayer, which consist of pure, loving and selfless attention to God, for His Glory.

There is neither self-seeking nor pleasure-seeking in true contemplation, although this mustn't be taken to mean that I'm criticising the prayer of petition. It was Our Lord Himself who told the story about a woman who pestered someone for assistance, until, through that man's weariness, she was granted her request. Also, even though I say that we oughtn't to look for consolations in prayer, I must proclaim that the joy which God gives to the soul, when He chooses, is so great that anyone who loves Him would wait ten years in utter darkness, so to speak, for another second of the bliss of being drawn 'palpably' close to Him in that way.

Still, many of God's dealings with the soul are so secret and marvellous as to be far above any perceived experience or remembered touch. I mean that God Himself can work within our souls, secretly, a prayer of which we see or understand little or nothing. We might sometimes be drawn - through our union with Christ, in the power of the most Holy Spirit - into a secret, silent prayer of *"union-in-unknowing"*. In that prayer, even though we don't see, feel, hear or know anything, Christ - Who is within the soul - praises God with His Own Infinite Praise.

During that prayer, the faithful soul doesn't know what is happening. But, whether he remains aware of his surroundings or is drawn into utter Unknowing - according to the Will of God Who gives this prayer - he doesn't know what is 'happening'; and yet even though he feels and sees nothing, he knows that this is true contemplation.

This 'nothing' which I mention is not the same as an absence of prayer in a person who - for example - is kneeling silently in an attitude of prayer, but who fails to turn his or her heart towards God because of ill-will, boredom, distraction or distress. The 'nothing' of which I speak, whilst utterly remote, impalpable and 'empty', is nevertheless a clean, pure, void-like 'nothing' which, even in its Arctic, sense-less Infinity, is different from any human 'nothing' in prayer. But the soul learns that this 'nothing' is either given or not-given. No soul can seize it. It is a state or a gift for which the ardent soul yearns in a blind, instinctive reaching-out of the heart; and yet the 'nothing' is not palpably an attractive state or gift. The soul doesn't know what he's seeking, but knows only that he must seek. Meanwhile, that which is sought is neither 'there' nor 'here'. The soul, in prayer, touches - without touching - the edge of the 'nothing'; and someone who wishes to serve God and know Him will remain attentive and alert, reaching out in soul and spirit towards God: even in apparent nothingness, if that should be His gift.

The soul which has experienced this 'nothing' in prayer is at first frightened by it. But I've described much about that aspect in Chapter 6 of the Narrative. When someone is first confronted by God's silent, wordless invitation to 'step into' His true depths in prayer, he is usually terrified. Spiritually, he is being asked to launch himself into a void, and, at the same time, to trust in God - Whom he now feels he doesn't know. Many souls refuse this invitation, or approach their prayer-time cautiously, hoping that the invitation will never disturb them. Yet someone who, by grace and courage, accepts God's invitation, will perhaps be brought to the stage which I now describe, where the 'void' and the 'nothingness', though still empty and unknowable, are not now so utterly strange and repulsive. I use the word 'repulsive', only because our human nature is weak, and it shrinks from what it doesn't know or can't see, since it senses - rightly - that it will lose much of what it holds dear, if it draws closer to God. We don't usually believe, in the early 'stages', that God is more true and beautiful and blissful and rewarding - to use a few inadequate words - than the good things and persons that He has made, and some of which a devout soul must surrender in order to progress in prayer.

First, purification, then union.

So, someone who has overcome his fears so far, and who has been led by God to persevere in sincere prayer year after year, might be brought one day to the prayer of Unknowing; and this secret, silent prayer of love takes place only in the soul of someone who has been called and purified by God. God alone chooses when and where to unite a soul with Himself in this marvellous way. It is a true work on our part, that is, a true act of pure charity, since it's only by charity and self-sacrifice that, whether implicitly or explicitly, we have permitted God to purify the soul in preparation for such an intimate union of praise. Also, a faithful person will have prepared himself by frequently kneeling in the presence of God in reverence, penitence and praise, waiting for God to work His Will in every aspect of life. This faithful soul hasn't neglected his duty, that is, his obligation to praise and thank God daily: nor does he despise vocal prayer, even if his prayers might now be simplified. He speaks frankly to God of his failings and hopes, and asks like a little child for help for himself and for others.

This *prayer of Unknowing* is so pure and secret, as I said, that when we have been drawn into it we cannot sense, see, hear, taste or touch anything. We don't know what's happening within the soul. God praises God in the soul - I can hardly bring myself to write these words, but they are true - whilst the mind, the imagination and the memory circle, as it were, below. The will strains, or, rather, leans towards God with all its might, but peacefully; and God Who is Unseen and Unknown gives His gift of *'Prayer-in-Union', in Unknowing,* as and when He Wills, sometimes for a moment, or sometimes for a lengthly period: perhaps for twenty or thirty minutes.

Someone whom God draws to Himself in this sublime prayer of Union, is at first so overwhelmed, spiritually, by such an intimate meeting with God - because unused to it - that he is usually completely withdrawn from things of the senses, and is enraptured and held for a few moments in true Unknowing. Then God releases him, so to speak; and this soul 'finds' himself kneeling in prayer, his heart fixed on God but his thoughts active again; and he is quite unable to describe anything about his prayer, since the prayer was silent and imageless and utterly pure.

The use of the word 'pure' in this sense, means only that God can't be seen, touched or felt. We can say that anything which can be 'felt' in prayer makes that prayer less "pure". Such "touches" may be true gifts from God, but nevertheless they are not God Himself; and so the faithful soul should, as usual, strive to ignore all that he thinks he sees, hears or touches in prayer, unless by good direction and under special circumstances it is made plain that certain gifts are from God. Even then, he should be extremely vigilant lest pride and curiosity lead him to hope for "experiences" or to turn his attention away from God towards the workings of his own self, in self-admiration.

True freedom in prayer.

When someone finds that he is frequently *'enraptured'* in this way, but is no longer frightened or puzzled - though extremely grateful for God's love and graciousness, now that advice has been sought - he finds that he isn't necessarily utterly withdrawn from this world at each occurrence. He has learned to kneel in prayer as usual, proceeding in his normal manner, busy when necessary with his acts and petitions, or silently resting in praise; however, he has also learned to let his spirit soar to God whenever God beckons him, so to speak, or, rather, whenever he senses - by his spiritual senses - that God is lifting him upwards to enter into God's own Life.

If such a soul perseveres in a life of true love and service, obedience and humility, and if God calls him frequently to Himself in the prayer of Unknowing, he gradually learns how to allow his spirit to remain peacefully and silently with God, so that something happens which sounds strange but which is true: the soul remains earth-bound, but contented, knowing nothing, it seems, although knowing that God is invisibly at work.

God can work this prayer in the soul whenever He chooses, but usually does so only through the soul's earlier and freely-given consent, in a spirit of faith; but that soul learns, with tremendous gratitude, that this sort of prayer is immensely fruitful and worthwhile, as well as fulfilling - and even though there's no evidence of this, except in faith. It is God who reveals to such a soul that by such a pure, piercing prayer at this, as with every God-given moment of other sorts of contemplative prayer, it is as though the clouds which 'hide' the Godhead from mankind are parted. It is as though, through that prayer, the clouds are held back, as God pours down His graces upon mankind, to a greater-than-usual degree. Such is the goodness of God, the power of true prayer, and the fruitfulness of the countless loving sacrifices which a prayerful soul has made in order to be brought to this state of contemplation.

---

1. <u>PRAYER-OF-UNION</u>

B) <u>PRAYER OF SOUNDLESS DIALOGUE WITH THE FATHER.</u>

So far as I'm aware, the most astonishing state of union with God the Father - as I mentioned earlier in this Appendix, in 'The journey of faith' - is that in which someone is able to converse in a sublime way with his Heavenly Father; and by 'converse', I mean that such a person is able to ask questions of God with child-like confidence and also to receive very tender and detailed answers.

At God's direct invitation.

What I'm referring to is the state in which the soul converses with God the Father, at His direct invitation, in a manner of prayer which is deliberate, conscious and willed, and which can be continued or interrupted - and which can be clearly recalled when the soul has 'left' that state in order to give some rest to the soul's faculties. By mentioning this need of rest, I don't mean that this prayer isn't wholly delightful, but that it is very demanding. This is because the soul's intellect, will and attention are at full 'stretch', so to speak, as this wonderful communion with the Father is commenced, expanded, explored, enjoyed, pondered and continued, so that the soul finds itself, afterwards, more drained, for example - although at the same time exceptionally joyful - than after the prayer of simple Unknowing.

Although I've already suggested that those states of prayer in which something can be seen, heard or 'felt' by the soul's faculties are less 'pure' - in spiritual terms - than those states in which God is secretly at work in the soul and is unfelt, I believe that this stage of 'conversing with the Father' is the exception to this rule, and for the following reasons:

First: this experience is wholly spiritual. Although God and the soul converse, there is nothing seen, felt, heard or touched in this marvellous and spiritually-pure state. It's true that very occasionally, the Father gives a gift, even here, of some real but soundless words - as if to leave the soul with a souvenir of that extraordinary conversation, or for a special purpose such as to link His teaching with some of His own Wisdom as it is found in Holy Scripture, for example.

Secondly, there can be no more sublime prayer than that in which the soul is able to converse with his Maker, when he has been lifted to Him by the Holy Spirit's power, after that person has put all his trust, day by day and minute by minute, in the Person, the power, the Love and the Merits of Jesus Christ his Saviour and Mediator Who has made possible such a relationship with God the Father, 'in' the Holy Spirit.

Thirdly, it is Christ Who has led such a soul to His Father; and it is only now, at the 'heights' of friendship with Christ that such a soul finds himself lifted up not just to the spiritual cloud which separates Mankind from the Godhead; he finds himself lifted above it, to the 'Door' of Heaven: or to the Father's Heart, we can say, as the soul begins a new stage of prayer at the heart of the Holy Trinity, in a joyful and conscious union with all Three Persons of the Holy Trinity.

Fourthly, I know from experience - by my observations and by what the Father has told me - that whenever a soul is 'called' by the Father from a now-constant state of prayerful and joyful recollection into a wholly spiritual but real conversation, he is being invited to take a conscious and free part in something which is one of the supreme privileges of the spiritual life.

Spiritually-strong and peaceful.

The reason why such a soul, at such a stage, is not lifted into rapture, is that he is now so spiritually-strong, and is so familiar with God's ways, God's communications, and God's goodness - though more reverent and loving towards Him than ever before - that he is no longer as if swept away at God's evident 'approach'. He is able to pause in whatever he is doing in order to give God his wholehearted attention; and the marvels of this way of life and of prayer cause the soul to live in a state of perpetual wonder and gratitude.

Such a soul is now able to 'step' from prayer to daily life and back again - or from one state of prayer to another, as Willed by God - with the greatest ease and delight, so close is his union with God and so thoroughly and peacefully 'entwined' are all of this person's spiritual, mental and bodily faculties, and so well do they 'work' together.

630

At the 'door' to Heaven.

These conversations with the Father take place with such ease and delight - through the Merits of Christ, as I said, and by the Holy Spirit's power - precisely because a soul such as this which is called so frequently by the Father to converse with Him in this manner is already, and always, and wholly, attentive both to His presence and to His Will; and when the faithful soul finds that God is inviting him once again to converse in this manner, he has no need to 'compose' himself, or to become recollected or to prepare for such a marvellous union. He is already prepared and able to converse because he is already alert, or 'waiting', we can say, as if at the soul's door to Heaven, which, at this stage - as God has revealed in prayer - is now continually open.

It is in this marvellous state - this conversation with the Father - that the soul can understand God's wishes in a spiritual way, by which I mean usually without words and by a Spirit-to-spirit communication which, although silent, is as true, or truer than verbal speech.

It is in this marvellous state that the faithful soul - like a simple and trusting child - can put questions to God the Father and so can receive answers which, by their tenderness, simplicity and wisdom, bring him unsurpassable delight and reassurance.

It is in this marvellous state that the soul understands to the fullest possible degree the meaning of 'adoption', and of 'child of God', and of God's 'Fatherhood', and of 'spiritual union' and of 'Heaven'.

It is in this marvellous state, furthermore, that someone who has become accustomed to this way of life and love can lift as if into the Father's 'heart' all of the persons, problems and places which occupy his heart and mind, in the knowledge that this is a sure and wonderful and conscious way of finding the Divine help which he knows to be worthwhile and very effective.

---

1. <u>PRAYER-OF-UNION</u>.

A) <u>TRUE UNION, IN PRAYER AND IN DAILY LIFE</u>.

As I mentioned earlier, in 'The journey of faith', there comes a time when someone who is wholly 'enamoured' of God and is wholly drawn by Him into a close and fruitful relationship is shown, in prayer, many details about that friendship: about the extent of it and the results of it, and about the inner life of God, and about Heaven; and yet all of these things are shown in a way which, by its purity, transcends all other ways of knowing.

The soul is so 'at one' with God that the soul sees - to a limited degree - what God sees, and sees it as He sees it; and therefore the soul observes, knows, understands, weighs and judges just as God does. This is what was meant by the Apostle who said "WE HAVE THE MIND OF CHRIST" (1 Co 2:16). Such a person sees clearly, therefore, the truth about his vocation and duties, his neighbours and his other relationships, and also the truth about God's plans for what remains of his life - since God now shares with such a soul, to an astonishing degree, the knowledge of His own plans for that soul and for the Church.

The soul 'sees' such things because he has been drawn by God into His Divine Life, and has therefore entered the Life, Love and Work of the Godhead, within Its great movement of Divine Love at the heart of the Holy Trinity. The soul has entered that Life as a swimmer might enter the powerful currents of a fast-flowing river, and has therefore truly become one with God in love, and one in fruitful work, also.

In this marvellous state of friendship, moreover - though in a slightly different state of prayer - the soul is able to converse with God in a union so close and trusting that it's as if they whisper as intimate friends or lovers do, yet without sound or whisper.

Someone who lives in a Heavenly communion with God in perpetual intimacy is so privileged and blessed even during this earthly life that he has only to 'enter' prayer by an act of the will to be brought 'palpably', it seems, into God's presence; and he knows that his prayer is immensely fruitful and worthwhile, as well as fulfilling - even though there is no evidence of this, except in faith. It is God Who reveals to such a soul that by such a pure, piercing prayer as this, as with every God-given moment of other sorts of contemplative prayer, it is as though the clouds which 'hide' the Godhead from mankind are parted. It is as though, through that prayer, the clouds are held back, as God pours down His graces upon mankind, to a greater-than-usual degree: such is the goodness of God, the power of true prayer, and the fruitfulness of the countless loving sacrifices which a prayerful soul has made in order to be ready for this state of contemplation.

Each time this person 'enters' prayer, he finds that his soul is suffused with Glory and that God has lifted him 'high' once more, and awaits him at His 'heart', so to speak; and whoever converses with God in this state finds that he can 'taste' - as it were - God's Love, reassurance, Wisdom and consolation. It's as though the soul 'tastes' these gifts merely by turning his heart towards his Heavenly Creator, Redeemer and Sanctifier; and thus he comes to know the marvel of the use of yet another of the spiritual senses - all of which, at last, have been satisfied.

A heavenly way of life.

Someone who lives in such a state lives in constant peace, joy and fulfilment, even amidst earthly sufferings, since what greater joy can there be, before Heaven, than to enjoy something of what is experienced to a marvellous extent in Heaven: by which I mean the friendship of God, with the special gifts which He cannot refrain from lavishing upon His friends - and with the friendship of all other creatures who love God, such as the Saints and Angels of Heaven, as well as the devoted friends of Christ amongst whom this soul, on Earth, now works, prays and suffers for God's Glory.

5 EXPLANATION

CATEGORIES: AN ILLUSTRATED LIST

This illustrated list begins with the 'lower' stages of extraordinary prayer and proceeds to the highest. It is illustrated with symbols which were devised for use on the prayer-image water-colours, some of which are reproduced in the next section (Appendix: 6).

EXTRAORDINARY PRAYER: EXPERIENCES

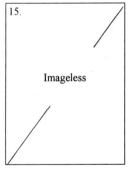

15. An uncomprehending "sense of God".

A childhood or later sense of God's presence in nature.

A similar sense of God's presence in every building which houses the Blessed Sacrament.

Examples: In Chapter 1 of Narrative, and elsewhere.

14.

M

A
real-life
visual
memory,
illustrated

14. A special experience of Divine grace.

The soul can sometimes enjoy a felt experience of a sacramental
grace: an experience which is a gift from God which has no
bearing on the effectiveness of the sacrament.

The image (in 14) is a visual memory of the occasion of such a
gift, or of another step forward on the spiritual journey.

Examples: WC: 4c: The Real Presence.
WC: 7:   Yearnings.
WC: 11: Asking for help. (See illustration in Appendix 6).
WC: 13B : Confirmation.

13E.

A
visual memory
of what is
realised of this
spiritual state.

13E. Desolation.

The soul, 'in' prayer and 'out', feels desolate: abandoned.

No light is given in prayer.

No memory of past good can comfort this soul, who bears, to a
degree almost beyond endurance, the knowledge of his own
sinfulness and of God's infinite holiness.

In itself, this is an imageless state, though this soul can see its
state clearly, at God's prompting.

Example: WC: 471: The Abyss. (See illustration in Appendix 6).

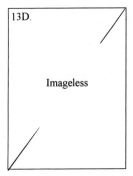

Imageless

13D. The soul, stripped interiorly.

The soul is recollected.
God, at the soul's consent, strips the soul of its old 'self'.
The soul is 'burned' and purified in a new way.
The soul who emerges from this state enjoys a new lightness and
freedom.

Example: See Narrative.

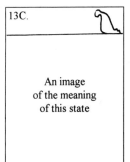

An image
of the meaning
of this state

13C. The soul, burned or wounded.

The soul is at prayer or recollected, and consents to God's
action.
In that state, the soul is scoured by God's Light, and so
experiences pain, interiorly.

See Narrative: WC: 646: A fire, burning in my heart. (See illustration in Appendix 6).

EXTRAORDINARY PRAYER: WORDS

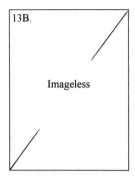

13B. Praying with words stirred from the depths.

The soul is fervent in prayer to God, in private, and speaks with an eloquence quite foreign to it.

The yearning is the soul's own love at work, but the given-words of prayer are a gift from God.

Examples: At many places in my notebooks.

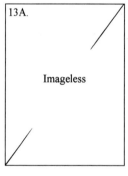

13A. Vows: prompted in prayer.

The soul prays as usual.

An unforeseen and powerful prompting from God invites a response.

The soul makes vows or resolutions which he had not planned to make but which bring immense blessings upon him.

Examples: At several places in the Narrative.

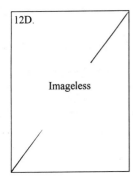

12D. Words to the soul.

The soul is recollected, and suddenly 'hears' words, spiritually.

Such words can be an evident rebuke, yet should be ignored even more firmly than other types of 'words'.

The soul who is rebuked by Christ is contrite, but is not left devoid of hope.

The soul can safely ignore troubling words, in order not to be deceived.

If it is Christ who speaks, He will not be deterred by the soul's admirable caution.

Examples: in my notebooks.

12C. Words through Holy Scripture.

The soul is recollected, usually at Holy Mass.

The soul is pierced by words from God: words of instruction or command or rebuke or consolation or encouragement.

This gift is sudden and unexpected.

What is learned is astoundingly clear and moving.

Much more is understood than is suggested by the simple words.

Examples: in my notebooks. (T: 291) "Call to her that her time of service is ended."

(T:431) "It is right ... to reveal ... the works of God in worthy fashion."

(T:631) "... write the vision down ... to be easily read ..."

12B.
The soul receives a visual impression of what happens in each type of encounter.

12B. Spiritual words of conversation.

The soul is recollected, and is suddenly given true words - though not heard by bodily ears.
Such words are given to the soul in prayer, by Christ, or another.
Knowledge is given too, about the soul.
Sometimes, words are given with personal tenderness.
At other times, words are given with great authority.

Examples: T:1462: (Illustrated by WC: 89A.) " ... I want to give you joy."
T:1440: (Illustrated by WC: 89B.) " ... One who honours My holy Mother honours Me."
T:1917 "I shall set a seal on your heart, and that seal shall be joy."

12A.
The soul sometimes receives a visual impression which conveys the occasion of the gift, and the power of the gift.

12A. Knowledge and Words.

The soul is wholly given to prayer, and suddenly receives knowledge which is accompanied by words.
This is an astounding intrusion into the soul's centre in prayer.
It is about something momentous, such as God's nature, God's actions or God's plans.

Examples: T:1354 (Illustrated by WC: 89C.) "I Am the measure ..."
T:1003 "It is love that counts. It was sin did this ..."
T:1680 "A shrine is a doorway to Heaven."

EXTRAORDINARY PRAYER - UNION.

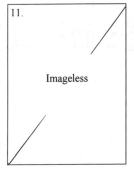

11. Discernment.

Example: in the narrative.

10B. Union with God in Recollection-Pierced-by Understanding, through Holy Scripture.

This differs from 12C.

This is an imageless state, also, yet here is given a clear vision of a truth, rather than a specific instruction.

Some of my early 'understandings' were recorded as on the left: with an image of a lectern and with the words of Holy Scripture printed: words through which the gift was given.

These 'understandings' became so frequent that it was impracticable to record every occasion in this way.

Example: T:243. "The Holy Spirit will teach you ..." (See illustration in Appendix 6).

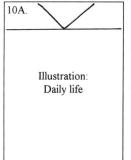

10A. Union with God in Recollection-Pierced-by-Understanding: pure gift.

The soul is recollected amidst his daily activities.
The soul is pierced by Understanding.
This gift is implanted within the soul, and is a pure gift.
This is different from the 'Knowledge' which is given in a similar manner (in 2).

Examples: WC: 14: "Holy desires."
WC: 45: "Work for love alone."
WC: 46: "Jesus loves us in our weakness." (See illustration in Appendix 6).

9B. Prayer of union-in-awareness - with a 'journey' image.

The soul is aware that God is 'moving' the soul upwards.
The soul is drawn onwards, in prayer.
The soul is taught by an image, with Knowledge also, usually about the spiritual life.
This is a prolonged experience.
This sort of image develops or changes, but does so in an unexpected and illuminating way: not as when plain thinking leads someone from one deduction to another.
This is usually a sequence of images which are accompanied by an understanding or an explanation from God.

Examples: WC: 34: "A pool of consolation."
WC:1197: "Out from the Father's Heart." (See illustration in Appendix 6).

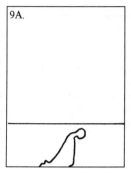

9A. The prayer of union-in-awareness, with a living-image.

The soul is at prayer - but is perhaps alert.
The soul is aware of light and glory, though less glory than in 3.
The soul might see a Heavenly person.
The soul remains with a Person or persons but is free to turn away in charity.
This experience might alternate with or accompany the state of Union-pierced-by-Knowledge.
This is frequently a lengthy prayer-experience, and sometimes takes place in Holy Communion.

Examples: WC: 1093: "On this side of the Veil."
WC: 1068C: "All honour and worship." (See illustration in Appendix 6).
WC: 1136: "Christ's Way to the Father."

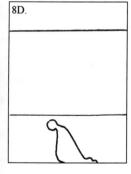

8D. A teaching about the soul by Knowledge and one's own image prompted by God.

The soul is aware of his surroundings, whilst he is busy with prayer.
Knowledge is given, suddenly but undramatically, about a less-important matter than in 8C.
One's own mind provides a marvellously-appropriate image.
All images are to be rejected as distractions.
Images can be recalled and recorded later on, and then can be used for instruction or encouragement.

Examples: WC: 276: "Beneath the waters."
WC: 691: "At the moment of death." (See illustration in Appendix 6).
WC: 984: "Contrite and forgiven."
WC: 2123: "Truth, like a magnet."

8C. Teaching in prayer by Knowledge with a 'Given-Image'.

The soul is absorbed in prayer.
The soul is instructed by information suddenly received, spiritually, about the spiritual life
An image appears within the soul: not in the imagination.
This lasts longer than the 'Translation' mentioned in 8A.
Knowledge always accompanies images such as these.

Example: WC: 426: "Held in the dancing."
WC: 1221: "A mountain of teachings."
WC: 1501: "As if in a chasm."
WC: 2069: "Catching fire."

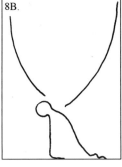

8B. Teaching in prayer: by Knowledge with a "Given-Image".

The soul is wholly absorbed in prayer.
The soul is given an explanation by God, in silence, about what is happening within itself.
God places an image within the soul to assist its understanding.
This lasts longer than a 'Translation' mentioned in 8A.
Images such as these are always accompanied by Knowledge.

Example: WC: 900: "A few clumsy marks."
WC: 1877B: "From cavern to cathedral."

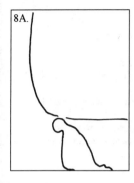

8A. Teaching in prayer: by Knowledge-with-'Translation'.

The soul is wholly engaged in prayer.
A sudden, piercing Knowledge is given, which is immediately 'translated' into an image.
This is a pure gift from God.
The soul can do nothing but receive both Knowledge and image.
The experience is finished before it is recognised.
The image cannot be forgotten.
The soul grows in love and admiration for God after every such experience, as he 'sees' so frequently demonstrated, thus, God's wisdom and kindness.

Example: WC: 1039C: "Those who hide in Him." (See illustration in Appendix 6).
WC: 1061: "Jesus the Fisherman."
WC: 1654: "When the soul is like a tomb."
WC for 25 March 1998: "Like stars which flare briefly."

7. Reality, seen with the Eyes of the Soul.

The soul is recollected, whether 'in' or 'out' of formal prayer.
Both Knowledge and Reality-in-image pierce the soul, often in the state of rapture.
This experience is a wonderful gift from God.
The soul 'sees' spiritual realities, by spiritual sight.
The soul receives a brief glimpse of Heavenly persons in an experience less spiritually 'pure' than an intellectual vision (as in 5) but God-given, nevertheless, and fruitful.

Example: WC: 464: "Standing amongst us."
WC: 516: "Holy souls, advancing." (See illustration in Appendix 6).
WC: 1073B: "The feast at the altar."
WC: 1267: "The great debt."
WC: 1494: "A parting of the Veil."
WC: 2138: "The 'flame' of Christ's Glory."

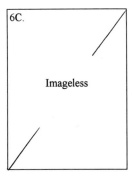

6C. The prayer of Felt Union: Absorption.

The soul is recollected but not enraptured.

This is an experience of overwhelming sweetness, with utter absorption 'in' God.

This is an imageless experience which sometimes leads to pure Unknowing.

The soul is sometimes pierced by Knowledge from God.

The soul is sometimes led to Knowledge-with-translation, or words, or 'given-images'...

Examples: In my notebooks.

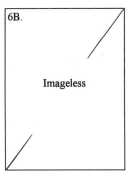

6B. The prayer of Felt Union: Flight.

The soul is wholly absorbed in God.

This is an indescribable experience.

The soul is 'lost' in God, in a journey of Unknowing.

This is a wholly imageless and silent experience.

It is as though the soul is transported into the mystery of God, above, at great speed.

The mind and imagination 'remain' below, as God transports the spirit to His own Heart.

Examples: In my notebooks.

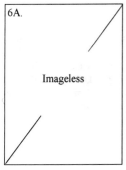

6A. The prayer of Felt Union: Jubilation.

The soul is wholly united to God in prayer.

This is a state of 'blind' bliss.

The soul is aware that it enjoys this experience, yet sees nothing.

This soul experiences an imageless rejoicing of astonishing intensity.

The soul knows that he rejoices with the whole of Heaven.

This is a gift from God, intended to give astonishing consolation.

Examples in my notebooks.

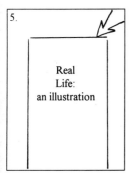

5. The prayer of Union-of-persons: Intellectual Vision.

The soul is alert and is not necessarily praying.

The soul is pierced by a Knowledge-of-Presence.

The state is usually prolonged.

This is an imageless state which can be experienced in fervent prayer or in every-day times of physical work, or during a walk, for example.

All pictures in this category are of the real-life circumstance in which the experience took place.

The soul, in responding to a presence with words of gratitude or delight might then be led into a more glorious state of prayer.

Example: WC:43: "Jesus in Oxford Street." (See Narrative).
      WC:113: "We call out, and Jesus is here."

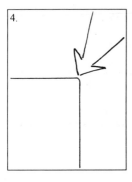

4. Prayer by Union-of-Wills.

The soul is alert in prayer, but is suddenly pierced by Knowledge.
This state is usually brief and imageless.
Sublime matters are revealed and explained by God, wordlessly.
The soul can choose a suitable image, later, so making a
'translation' which makes 'concrete' a gift of Knowledge; yet
the image is not a product of the imagination.

Example: WC: 18: "Seeing God's holiness." (See illustration in Appendix 6).
WC: 55A: "The love of the Father."
WC: 1223A: "Fire meeting Fire."

3. Prayer of Union: with a living Image in Rapture.

The soul is contrite, joyful and prayerful.
The soul is caught into ecstasy.
This state is perhaps prolonged.
This is a prayer of brief or lengthy union.
Knowledge is given which can be recalled afterwards.
The soul is before a living person, in a dazzling light, and is
astounded, and so is not 'free' to speak.
All is brilliance and Glory.
The soul is suffused by joy and wonder, both during the
experience and afterwards.
The soul is wholly absorbed in gazing at the figure(s).

Example: WC: 519: "Saint Anne, with the Immaculate one." (See illustration in Appendix 6).
WC: 812B: "Holy Saints in Heaven." (See Narrative).
WC: 896: "Saint Joseph." (See Narrative).
WC: 1244A: "The Father's Light." (See Narrative).
WC: 2014: "Saint Francis."

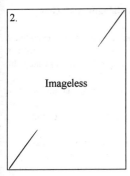

2. Prayer of Union: pierced by Knowledge-in-Unknowing.

The soul is wholly absorbed in prayer.
This is a state of union-in-Unknowing which is brief, secret and
imageless.
Knowledge is given by God as Wisdom which can be recalled,
afterwards.
The soul feels astonished when he finds that he has so suddenly
and swiftly been given this magnificent gift.

Examples: in my notebooks, and in the Narrative.

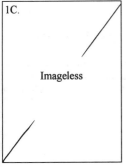

1C. Prayer of Union-in-Unknowing.

The soul has been lifted by God into 'Unknowing' prayer.
This is a great gift from God, Who is at work within the soul at
such a time.
This state cannot be induced by the person who prays.
This is almost the 'purest' of states, in spiritual terms: a free gift
from God to a soul who has co-operated with Him in the
purifications which have fitted that soul to be dignified with
this state of prayer.
This state very frequently occurs after the 'Second Night' (The
night of the spirit).

Examples: In my notebooks.

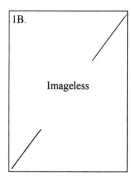

1B.   Prayer of Union: A soundless dialogue with God.

This is a state which the willing soul can enter on receiving a direct invitation from the Father - which is different from a 'prompting' from the Holy Spirit and from an 'approach' by Christ in Holy Communion.

Nothing that the soul might do can bring about such a conversation.

God and the soul converse silently, each responding to the other in complete love, trust and delight.

This is an imageless state, although God can introduce images or, rather, draw the soul 'up' or 'down' into other spiritual states states in which images are given for the soul's education or delight, (as, for example, in 8A).

In the same degree of communication with God, in perpetual intimacy, but in a slightly different sort of dialogue, God and the soul are as if whispering to one another as friends or lovers do: very close, and united in mutual understanding.

God and the soul converse in a union so close and trusting that it is as though the soul 'tastes' God's Love, God's reassurance, God's Wisdom, and God's consolations: and therefore enjoys, by this time, the use of all five spiritual senses, which are 'sight', 'hearing', 'touch', 'smell', and 'taste'.

The soul which enjoys this degree of union is suffused in prayer by God's glory.

The soul experiences neither sight nor sound, but only this Heavenly communion, an awareness of his privileged state, with an 'awareness', close by him, of the God Whom he loves and adores.

Example: T:2331B, in the Narrative: a conversation with the Father.

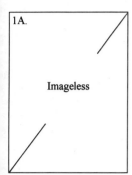

1A. Prayer of Union:Known 'Participation'.

By God's Will, the state-of-soul is 'seen' as the soul is drawn into the Life, work and 'movement' of the Holy Trinity.
The soul sees, to some degree, 'into' God's Life.

Example: T: 2244B, in the Narrative: (The 'insertion' of the soul into God's Life) and also in other chapters.

6 ILLUSTRATIONS

PRAYER-IMAGES: FIFTEEN WITH SYMBOLS, FIVE OTHERS MORE 'DEVELOPED'

The fifteen water-colour (WC) illustrations which follow stem from almost all of the prayer-categories just mentioned in 'Appendix 5.'

Illustration 1,   Category 14   "Asking for help" .... (WC:11)

Illustration 2,   Category 13E   "The Abyss' .... (WC:472)

Illustration 3,   Category 13C   "Fire, burning in my heart" .... (WC:646)

Illustration 4,   Category 10B   "The Holy Spirit will teach you." .... (WC:243)

Illustration 5,   Category 10A   "First recognition" .... (WC:46)

Illustration 6,   Category 9B   "Outward, to reach us" .... (WC:1197)

Illustration 7,   Category 9A   "All honour and worship" .... (WC:1068C)

Illustration 8,   Category 8D   "At the moment of death" .... (WC:691)

Illustration 9,   Category 8C   "Pure truth, drop by drop" .... (WC:1160)

Illustration 10,   Category 8B   "Cavern to Cathedral" .... (WC:1877B)

Illustration 11,   Category 8A   "Those who hide in Him" .... (WC:1039C)

Illustration 12,   Category 7   "Holy Souls, advancing" .... (WC:516)

Illustration 13,   Category 5   "Sickness and trouble" .... (WC:1038B)

Illustration 14,   Category 4   "The joy of an Angel" .... (WC:876)

Illustration 15,   Category 3   "Saint Anne, with the Immaculate one" .... (WC:519)

Illustration 1, Category 14: "Asking for help." (WC:11)

ASKING FOR HELP.
THE PRIEST TOOK ME INTO A SIDE-ROOM, AND WE SAT AT A
LONG POLISHED TABLE. HE ASKED WHAT I HAD READ, AND IF I PRAYED.

Illustration 2, Category 13E: "The Abyss." (WC:472)

Illustration 3, Category 13C: "Fire, burning in my heart." (WC:646)

Illustration 4, Category 10B: "The Holy Spirit will teach you." (WC:243)

Illustration 5, Category 10A: "First recognition." (WC:46)

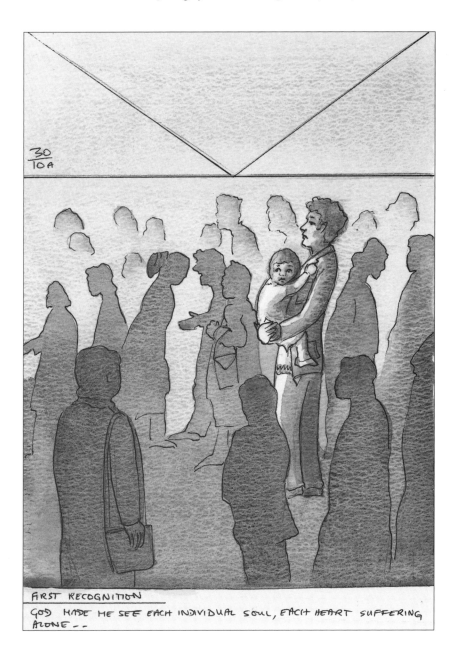

Illustration 6, Category 9B: "Outward, to reach us." (WC:1197)

Illustration 7, Category 9A: "All honour and worship." (WC:1068C)

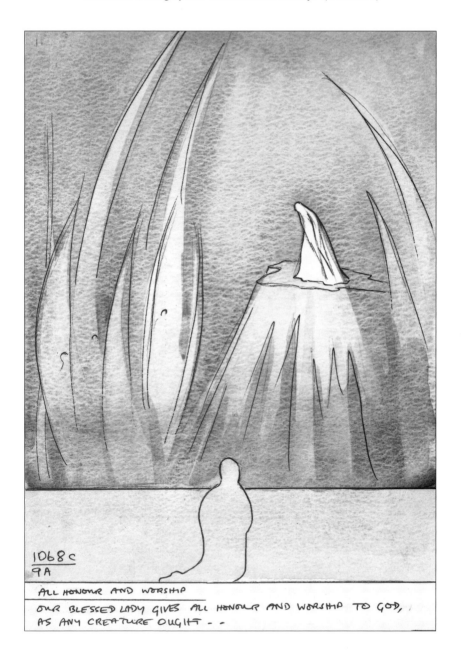

Illustration 8, Category 8D: "At the moment of death." (WC:691)

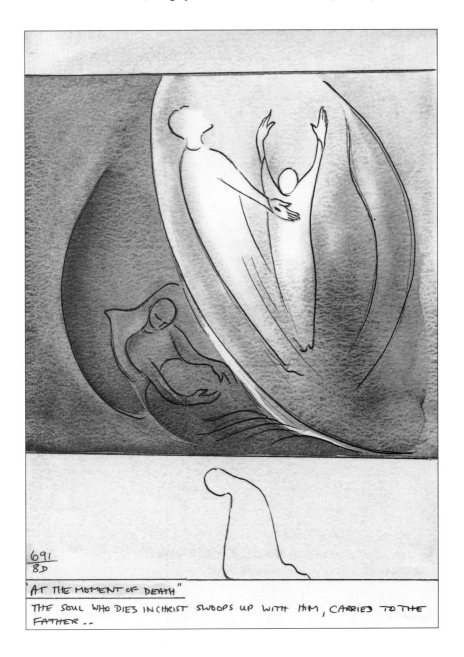

691
8D

"AT THE MOMENT OF DEATH"

THE SOUL WHO DIES IN CHRIST SWOOPS UP WITH HIM, CARRIED TO THE FATHER ..

Illustration 9, Category 8C: "Pure truth, drop by drop." (WC:1160)

1160
8C

DROP BY DROP
CHRIST'S PURE TRUTH IS POURED — I SAW — DROP BY DROP
INTO THE SOUL, GATHERED IN READINESS FOR A GREAT OUTPOURING...

Illustration 10, Category 8B: "Cavern to Cathedral." (WC:1877B)

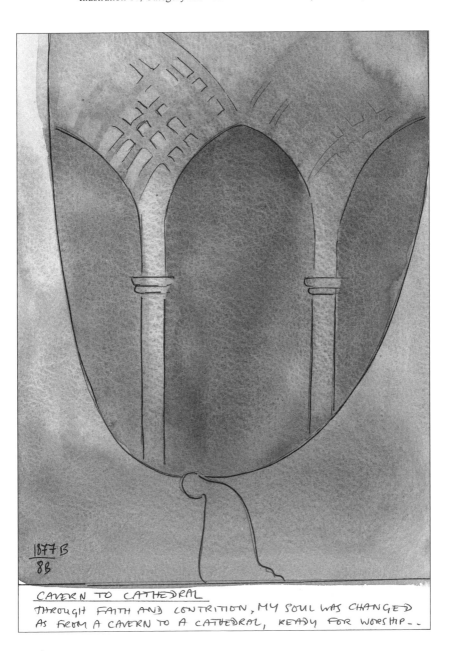

CAVERN TO CATHEDRAL
THROUGH FAITH AND CONTRITION, MY SOUL WAS CHANGED
AS FROM A CAVERN TO A CATHEDRAL, READY FOR WORSHIP..

Illustration 11, Category 8A: "Those who hide in Him." (WC:1039C)

1039 C
8A

."THOSE WHO HIDE IN HIM."
"THOSE WHO HIDE IN HIM SHALL NOT BE CONDEMNED" —Psalm 33

Illustration 12, Category 7: "Holy Souls, advancing." (WC:516)

516
7

HOLY SOULS, ADVANCING

THE HOLY SOULS ARE STIRRED AND HELPED BY OUR PRAYERS;
THEY ADVANCE IN LOVE, AND MOVE CLOSER TO HEAVEN'S LIGHT.

Illustration 13, Category 5: "Sickness and trouble." (WC:1038B)

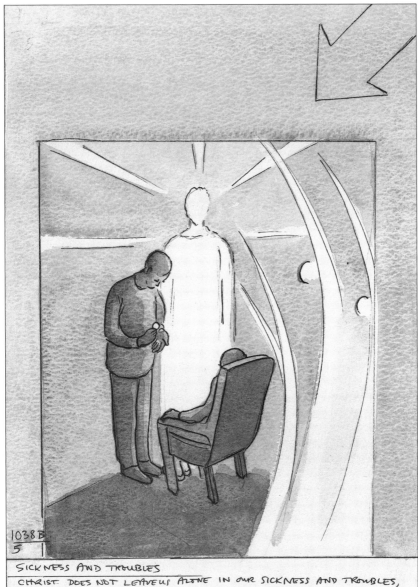

SICKNESS AND TROUBLES

CHRIST DOES NOT LEAVE US ALONE IN OUR SICKNESS AND TROUBLES, BUT COMES TO US IN HIS SACRAMENT, ACCOMPANIED BY ANGELS --

Illustration 14, Category 4: "The joy of an angel.". (WC:876)

876
4

876
4

THE JOY OF AN ANGEL

AT THE BAPTISM, I SAW THE PURE, FERVENT FIERY JOY OF THE ANGEL, AT
THE SIGHT OF DIVINE LIFE WITHIN THE CHILD'S SOUL...

Illustration 15, Category 3: "Saint Anne, with the Immaculate one." (WC:519)

ST.ANNE, WITH THE IMMACULATE ONE

I SAW ST.ANNE, BEARING IN HER WOMB THE IMMACULATE ONE —
LIKE A HOST — FROM WHOM WOULD COME CHRIST'S DEAR AND HOLY BODY..

The five images which follow are all prayer-images which have been 'developed', in oils, and colour-enlivened.

Illustration 16: "The earth is enfolded by prayer 'in Christ'." (OIL:39)

Illustration 17: "All the virtues come from Christ, the Source." (OIL:99)

Illustration 18: "Love drove Him to join us in earthly life." (OIL:1320)

Illustration 19: "Christ is the Light in the midst of His People." (OIL:1327)

Illustration 20: "Christ ascended, and opened a Way to Heaven." (OIL: 1588)

7 CONCLUSION

TRUST IN CHRIST. SUBJECT MATTER.

What I've just written - as can be seen - is clumsy in parts, and inadequate. So much had to be left out, and so much compressed, because I felt - as I feel with what follows - that the 'bare bones' had to be recorded now. I've tried to be entirely accurate and truthful, but I'm aware of my deficiencies both in style and in fluency.

There's so much more that could be written about the spiritual life and about contemplation. But I must finish here, and let the "teachings" speak for themselves. I can't finish, though, without stressing once again that everyone who wants to grow close to God ought to remain faithful to his ordinary prayers and activities, year by year. We do need, occasionally, to substitute a 'new' devotion for a minor outworn practice, since our spiritual tastes change as we grow more proficient in prayer. But the usual, important, daily devotions ought not to be carelessly dropped or postponed.

On the other hand, we shouldn't hope for extraordinary experiences for their own sake. Loving union with God, in accordance with His Will, is what 'counts', in whatever way that union is achieved. There are so many dangers lying in wait for those who want to serve and follow Christ faithfully until death that it seems like madness for anyone to think - proudly, or in ignorance - that he can 'cope' with the dangers of a spiritual pathway which he need not have followed.

If we follow the path revealed to us bit by bit in prayer, and remain united to Christ within His Church, we can be certain that He will give us the graces we need to follow His Light safely. But people who long for visions or other unusual experiences are fool-hardy. They will learn that they can easily be deceived. They will risk terrible dangers, or they will find that they're unable to bear the torment of being brought forcibly - as it were - so close to God. Only those whom He has mercifully and slowly purified can rest peacefully in His Presence, in the prayer of union, and so enjoy the extraordinary joys with which God, from all Eternity, has planned to reward, console and delight them.

I conclude this explanation about the ways in which God might choose to instruct the soul in prayer by listing the subjects on which He has chosen to instruct me during the past forty years, though most lavishly during the past fifteen years; or, rather, I've listed those subject headings under which I would like to see gathered, one day, the teachings which are at present listed chronologically in the several volumes of "Instructions from Christ".

Perhaps this is a task I'll have to leave for someone else to do, in another century. But these are my suggested headings, though someone else can surely improve on my list.

By the way: some of the teachings are so plainly about two subjects that whoever compiles the books ought, I believe, to put such teachings under both headings - even if the books seem to be enlarged in this way to a worrying degree. But the main headings could be as follows:-

The Angels of God.
The Blessed Sacrament.
The Christian Way.
  Christ's Life.
  Christ's Love for us.
  Christ's Passion and Death.
The Church: Christ's Body.
The Church: the House of God.
The Church: Leadership. (Includes Popes and Bishops)
  Death.
  Disability or ill-health.
  Ecumenism.
The Faithful Departed.
  Gender.
  God the Most Holy Trinity.
  Heaven, our home.
  Holiness: Christ-in-us.
  Holy Communion.
The Holy Sacrifice of the Mass.
  Images.
The Journey to union.
  Life-in-union.
  Marriage.
  Mission.
The Mother of God: Mary, the Blessed Virgin.
A Neighbour to love.
  Penance and Reparation.
  Personal matters.
  Prayer.
  Priesthood.
The Prayer of intercession.
The Saints, and Heaven.
  Sin and forgiveness.
  Sin, unrepented.
  Suffering and sacrifice.
  Teachings-in-prayer: explanations.
  Temptation.
  Virtues: our need.
  Weakness.
The Will of God.

"This, then, is what I pray, kneeling before the Father, from whom every family, whether spiritual or natural, takes its name:

Out of his infinite glory, may he give you the power through his Spirit for your hidden self to grow strong, so that Christ may live in your hearts through faith, and then, planted in love and built on love, you will with all the saints have strength to grasp the breadth and the length, the height and the depth; until, knowing the love of Christ, which is beyond all knowledge, you are filled with the utter fullness of God.

Glory be to him whose power, working in us, can do infinitely more than we can ask or imagine; glory be to him from generation to generation in the Church and in Christ Jesus for ever and ever. Amen." (Ep 3:14-21)

PRINCIPAL DATES

Please note: works done at God's request are prefaced by A.G.R.
T means 'teaching'.

Age	Date	Teaching no.	Event or work, or subject matter of teaching	Page no.
	29.10.93	*1361*	*T: This is what we are born for: to serve God*	-
	09.11.93	*1366*	*T: Purgatory completed in earthly life*	*367-8*
	09.12.93	*1376*	*T: "I gave up My Body"*	*369-370*
	14.12.93		90 oils now completed **(Sets One and Two)**	367
	17.02.94		The evil one: the worst of all attacks	350-355
	[28.05.94		World-wide publication of "Catechism of the Catholic Church	376]
	24.07.94	*1459*	*T: Our Lady again: a true mother to us all*	*373-5*
52	*02.09.94*	*1471*	*T: Our Lady's delight at her statue*	-
	26.11.94	*1508*	*T: Co-operation, and 'Teachings': the Father's explanation*	*377-389*
	Nov. '94		Pilgrimage to Aylesford for private intentions	390
	21.12.94		50 more oils completed. **(Sets Three and Four)**	-
	29.12.94		AGR, began to re-write all 'Teachings' as 'Version Two' - to distinguish plain description from God's own words	397-8
	03.01.95	*1530A*	*T: invited by Christ to cover hair in church at Mass*	*349 + 390*
	23.04.95		Was invested with Brown Scapular, at Aylesford	393
	May '95		Had given up all commercial work	360
	08.04.95		Wrote **'King of Kings'** booklet	-
	13.05.95	*1584*	*T: Christ's welcome to faithful priests*	*393*
	18.05.95		Gave talk at a London school	-
	06.06.95	*1592*	*T: Transformation, and the Triple Glory*	*394-7*
	17.07.95		Pilgrimage to Knock Shrine	-
	04.08.95		A.G.R., wrote about Holy Trinity (now in Ch. 20)	278
3	24.08.95		A.G.R., spoke about work to new Parish Priest	399
	Sept. '95		Approx. 40 more oils completed **(Sets 7 and 8)**	-
	02.11.95	*1682*	*T: A.G.R., spoke with Bishop about 'Teachings' and glory*	-
	03.11.95	*1703*	*T: A.G.R., resolved to re-write all 'Teachings' in the first person*	*401-2*
	03.11.95	*1704*	*T: Participation in God's nature*	*403-5*
	08.12.95	*1734A*	*T: The Risen Christ's purity and perfection*	*409-413*
	08.12.95	*1734C*	*T: Christ's Immaculate Mother*	*413-414*
	17.12.95		A.G.R., began 'Third Version' of Teachings: (to be Volume One)	401
	18.12.95		A.G.R., wrote about 'Redemption', now in "How to pray", Part 2.	-
	19.12.95		A.G.R., wrote about Holy Sacrifice	-

****

This index covers the whole of the Narrative and the Appendix, though not the Preface. It is not exhaustive, since words such as faith, love, prayer and union occur on hundreds of pages of the text. If something cannot be found under 'Prayer', however, it can probably be found under 'spiritual life' or 'Church', or 'Holy Sacrifice' and so on.

The names of canonised Saints can be found under each one's Christian name, whereas each entry which begins with 'St.' or 'Saint' is the title of a book, a play, or a church building.

Italic type is used for the titles of books and paintings.

Where a page number appears in bold italics, the subject matter listed is mentioned in a particular 'teaching-in-prayer.'

soul: its 'interior' (Continued)
  'suspended' in rapture 622.
  'tabernacle' for God *434, 439.*
  'transparent' for God's Light and God's
    graces *233, 459.*
  wilful darkness of 515.
  withdrawn from the senses 628.
  'wounded' *259.*
Spain, Spanish 63, 98.
spiritual abyss of desolation 222, 264.
spiritual adoption 631.
"Spiritual Aenaeid" 9, 114.
spiritual ambitions 127, 129, 162, 196,
    198, 222, 557.
spiritual anniversaries 516.
spiritual assault(s) 349, *416.*
spiritual assessment 624.
spiritual balance 546.
spiritual battles *204.*
spiritual beauty 64, 570.
spiritual betrothal 179, 563.
spiritual blindness 7, 332, 555-557.
spiritual brothers and sisters 591.
"Spiritual Canticles" 6.
spiritual chasm between mankind and
    Godhead 95, *170, 345.*
spiritual children *280.*
spiritual Communion 128, 591.
spiritual consummation *343-344.*
spiritual 'crowning' with Glory 571.
spiritual death 609.
spiritual deception *241,* 612.
spiritual delight 497.
spiritual development 8.
spiritual dialogue 567.
spiritual director 155, 628.
spiritual discernment 609.
spiritual 'Eden' *445,* 497.
spiritual experiences 7, 86, 104, 175, 198,
    203, 207, 211, 219, *241,* 256, 526,
    548, 569, 603-631, 620, 628, 632.
spiritual feasting 619.
spiritual Food 114, 188, 584, 586-587.
spiritual formation *243, 376.*
spiritual freedom *455.*
spiritual friendships *361, 397,* 632.
spiritual fruitfulness *308, 396,* 566, 568,
    605.

spiritual gifts 6, 9, 71, 85, 126, 142, 175,
    197, 202, 203, 212, 213, 217, *218,*
    226, 231, 257, 276, *306,* 315, *342-*
    343, 349, *369, 379-389, 387,* 403,
    414, 415, 419-422, 433-440, 445,
    468, 482-483, 488, 497, 507, 515,
    520, 550, 570, 582, 593, 597, 601,
    625.
spiritual glory *206,* 215, *218,* 347, *387,*
    569.
spiritual goal(s) *170,* 173, 181, 197, 224,
    239, 280, *437, 444.*
spiritual guidance 63, 90, 523.
spiritual 'harvest' *324.*
spiritual 'heart' 569.
spiritual 'heights' 220, *423,* 502, 518,
    530, 564, 568 570, 625, 630.
spiritual help 354-355.
spiritual honeymoon *39,* 91.
spiritual horror 561, 604, 606.
spiritual immaturity 556-558.
spiritual impurity(-ies) 563, 605.
spiritual journey 6, 96, 113, 114, 116,
    162, 173, 182, 199, *203,* 205, 215,
    225, 226, 249, 269, 315, 347, *371,*
    437, 444, 446, *466, 480,* 500, 507,
    573, 611.
spiritual joy 5, 7, 9, 20, 21, 64, 91, 105,
    125, 129, *143,* 167, 172, 173, *183,*
    202, 209, 217, 219, 221, 222, 245,
    250, 273, 315, 332, *361, 368, 422,*
    487, 524, 572, 695.
spiritual law(s) 595.
"Spiritual Life" 192.
spiritual life
  abandonment to God *456.*
  acceptance 110, 119, *170, 181,* 194,
    195, 200, 203, *231,* 243, 245, 250,
    251, 252, *323, 365, 475.*
  accounts of 89
  act of the will 571.
  acts of obedience 605.
  adventure(s) 74, 192.
  advice on 90, 119, 122, 623.
  alienation from God 19, 68, 148.
  analogy: a comet 526-527.
  analogy: an explorer 528.
  analogy: an opinion 528.

spiritual life(Continued)

for God's Glory 103, 182, 184, 187, 214, *228, 238, 243, 249,* 257, *260, 267,* 277, *344,* 356, *415,* 524, 564, 606, 627.

fortitude 13.

'framework' 130, 156.

free consent, choice 72, 73, 88, 140, 151, 171, *173,* 180, 210, 216-217, 220, *226,* 277, *294,* 330, 361, 560, 575, 624, 629.

free submission *229,* 330.

free time 149, 578.

free-will 34, *93,* 183, *210, 230, 232,* 242, *322,* 417, 540, 582, 606.

friendship with God 5, 7, 96, 146, 173, 182, *254, 390, 395,* 397, 417, *422, 449, 467-468, 475-476, 487,* 501-502, 503, 532, 548, 568, 570-571, 631-632.

foundation(s) *58,* 68, 82, 85, 86, 89, 205, 237, *373,* 501, 540.

fulfilment 5, 9, 79, 125, 138, *143,* 166, 184, 199, 218, 219, 372, *387, 433, 452,* 497.

fundamental principles 73.

future 30, 183, 220, 251, 264, 549.

generosity 103, 114, 239, 249.

gift(s) *433.*

goodwill 88, 96, 118, 138, *173, 182,* 188, 202, 211.

gratitude 31, 146, 189, 192, *204, 239, 483,* 501, 516, 566.

grief 102, 111, 164, *170.*

heart 8, 21, 68, 71, 81, 85, 88, 90, 92, 118, 121, 122, 125, 136, 144, 166, 167, *170,* 190, 192, 195, *198, 226, 230, 231, 371, 383, 388, 390, 475,* 559, 564, 566, 577, 599-600.

heart-ache 119, 125, 187, 217, 244, *323,* 333.

heart and mind together 76, *197, 198,* 631.

heart, divided *171, 183,* 556.

heroic(-ism) 103, 109, 110, 111.

hesitation 9, 188, 198.

hiddenness, obscurity *228, 327, 332, 448.*

'high mountains' close to God *423, 445,* 530, 565.

spiritual life (Continued)

holiness, degrees of 570.

holy(-iness) 24, 75, 80, 88, 90, 96, 97, 109, 111, 125, 136, 169, 193, *226, 230, 249,* 250, *295, 415, 481,* 549.

honesty 158, 167, *170.*

hope 30, 71, 88, 118, 122, 137, 139, 168, 183, 197, 199, 216, 217, 279, 595.

humiliation(s) 48, 165, 169, *170,* 173, 179, 187, *229, 267,* 328, 358, *476,* 558.

humility 119, 127, 137, 162, 166, 169, 179, 196, *197,* 205, *259,* 262, 275, 280, *395, 475, 516,* 566, 604.

ignorance of faith and God 30, 98, 115, 116, 120, 146, *374.*

ignorance of one's own spiritual state 604.

imagination 314, 356, 549, 600, 608.

imitation of Christ 90, 276, 579.

immaturity 136.

impatience 153.

imperfection(s) 24, 146.

impertinence 96.

inclination of heart and soul 609.

inessentials 88.

influence(s) on others 210.

influences on self 32, 77, 156, 160, *210.*

injustice(s) 168, 189, 190, 192.

inner promptings *225,* 523, 531, 572, 575.

insults *328.*

intellect(-ual) 78, 119, 123, 191, 356, 526, 570, 630.

intention(s) 138, 139, *143,* 196, *321,* 349, *395-397, 405.*

invitation from God 121.

invitation: ours, to God *196, 197, 230.*

irreverence 361.

joyfulness *479.*

judging one another 138, 145, *181,* 277, 557.

justice 139, 181, 190.

keeping silent about difficulties *329.*

kindness 90, 158, 191, 578-579.

Kingdom of God 16, 171, 172.

knowledge of hearts 609.

lack of faith *430-431.*

spiritual life (Continued)
    laziness 575.
    leniency *187.*
    liberty of spirit 30, 183, 196, 197,
        213, 270.
    life of grace 6, 38, 203, *209, 218, 225,*
        238, 259, 593.
    limited desires 184.
    little 'crucifixions' 150.
    logic, reason 100, 106, 114, 121, 123.
    loneliness 10, 34, 39, 68, 150, 165,
        170, 174, 190, *227,* 604.
    loss 105.
    loss of God *450,* 454, 604.
    love for God 6, 9, 38, 86, 87, 90-91,
        103, 109, 110, 112, 127, 130, 137,
        138, 146, 147, 152, 155, 175, 193-
        194, 197, *180,* 216, 217, *218, 226,*
        257, 274, 280, *388, 479,* 500, 560.
    love for neighbour 5, 8, 21, 22, 37,
        38, *80,* 84, 86, 87, 90, 103, 109,
        110, 111, 115, 127, 130, 137, 138,
        139, 147, 153, 155, 170, 172, *180,*
        181, 185, 186, *187,* 193-194, 204,
        216, 220, *226, 245,* 257, 261, 274,
        280, *438, 476,* 499, 566, 577-579.
    lowliness *227.*
    loyalty 22, 26, 114 159, *171, 183,*
        191, 199, 204, *490.*
    lukewarmness 11, 145 , *418.*
    luxuries 110, 115.
    marks of the Cross *267.*
    meaning of life 60.
    mediocrity 129.
    meditation(-ative) 9, 30, 77, 85, 132,
        141, 169, 180, 183, 191, 576.
    memories 10, 66, 85, 179, 195, 202,
        217, *226,* 253, 262, 298, 315, 356,
        512, 564, 600, 603, 604.
    memory, unconscious 600.
    mercy, need of 68, 147.
    merit 118.
    mind 24, 30, 31, 90 *93,* 102, 113, 119,
        136, 144, 190, *197, 218,* 355, *375,*
        458, 567, 622, 630.
    minimalism 58.
    minor questions 58.
    mis-judgements, mistakes 88, 188,
        195, 215, 622.
    modesty 47, 48, 240.

spiritual life (Continued)
    monastic advice 89, *92,* 101.
    monotony 150, 151, 165, 193.
    mortification 146, *183, 452,* 575.
    motive(-ation) 71, 74, 90, 92, 151,
        180, 257.
    'naked' trust 198, 204, 330, *483,* 561,
        604.
    need for reconciliation 146, *254.*
    neglect of God by man 81, 409, 453.
    new life 'in Christ' *254.*
    'night' of faith 146, 148.
    obedience 7, 13, 39, 90, 99, 109, 122,
        123, 160, 161, 162, *183,* 193, *220,*
        227, 229, 257, 262, *318, 320,* 349,
        361, 391, *414, 422, 426, 468,* 521,
        589, 616, 620.
    obligation to praise God 628.
    obstacles to Union 196, 559.
    offering-up of sufferings 38, 182,
        206, 248, 308, *310,* 480, 545, 576.
    old age 112, 113.
    opinions of other people 186.
    opposition 358, 399, 558.
    'out of proportion' 88.
    pain 5, 9, 113, 149, 155, 181, 187,
        195, 202, *206,* 211, *248,* 253, 558.
    patience 91, 156, 172, *181,* 182, 191,
        203, *243, 247, 248,* 303, *476,* 561.
    pattern of events 187, 202, 215.
    penance 38, 57, 82, 89, 90, 91, 95, 98,
        99, 109, 112, 129, 137, 146, 162,
        194, 196, 198, 203, 207, 303, *324,*
        360, 499.
    penitence 211.
    persecution 75, 102, 108, 117, 118,
        127, 128, 185, *463,* 546.
    perseverance 63, 150, 167 188, 195,
        199, 204, *225,* 351, *474, 476,* 562,
        624.
    pessimism *389.*
    phariseeism 90.
    physical problems 279.
    possessions 35, 74, 115.
    powerlessness 252.
    practice of the virtues 262.
    prayer-routine 62, 75, 151, 187, 203.
    precious relationship with God 83.
    prejudice *427.*
    pre-occupation(s) 5.

spiritual life (Continued)

preparation for Heaven *367.*

preparation for Union 196, *446.*

'present moment' 87, 183, 200, 255, *304.*

pride 90, 137, 147, 179, *226, 263,* 264, *397,* 556, 579, 595, 609, 628.

priorities 73, 162, 184, 186, *208,* 239, *489.*

privileged state 149, 630, 632.

problems 7, 74, 75, 76, *180,* 182, 184, *203, 306,* 631.

prohibition(s) 89.

punishment 96, 139, 191, 196, 351.

purification 81, 146, 147, 197, 202, *206,* 221, 257, 262, *324, 334-335, 341,* 350, *367-368, 446, 452, 474, 480, 495,* 502, 511, 519, 547, 563.

purifications, self-chosen 127, 560.

purifying Fire 446.

purity of heart 167, *170, 230, 414.*

purity of spiritual knowledge 626, 628.

purpose of life 31, 542, 547, 549-550.

putting wrongs right 81, 85.

puzzlement 9, 10, 16, 17, 18, 24, 29, 30, 39, 46, 54, 105, 115, 155, 206, 207, 211, 624.

reassessment 185.

reassurance 114, 212, 222, 267, 279.

rebellion against God 19, 24, 34, 71, 75, 190, 585, 594.

recollection 89, 144, 520, 567, 600, 607, 610, 616, 630, 631.

refusal to love 81, 86.

regret(s) 81, 181, 196, 197.

remorse 81, 170, 262.

renunciation 167, *170,* 184, *327.*

reparation 38, 82, 96, 110, 111, 135, 172, 182, 196, 205, *206, 248,* 276.

repentance 16, 83, 88, 162, 172, 173, 208, *209,* 212, 326, *327, 368, 460, 491-493,* 532.

reputation 103, 183, 253, 605.

resemblance to Christ *249, 258, 261, 267-268, 318,* 566.

resolutions 84, 172, 184, 194, 202, 243, 248, 251, 256, 265, 293, 296, 606.

respect 52, 116.

spiritual life(Continued)

responsibility(-ies) 5, 102.

result(s) *180,* 208, 216, 416, 532, 546.

retreat(s) 90, 91, 160, *180,* 184, 206, *489.*

reverence towards creatures 158.

reverence towards God 86, 145, 146, 197, 326, *475,* 499, 517.

reward(s) 351, 532.

right or wrong 15, 33, 101, 172, 188, 192.

romanticism 92.

routine 23, 87, 90, 92, 106, 130, 136, 149, 156, 169, 203, 243, 247, 275, 277, *376.*

'rule of life' 189.

rules and regulations 22, 31, 58, 95, *454.*

sacrifice(s) 7, 41, 58, 99, 103, 109, 114, 119, 144, 146, 150, 152, 162, 189, 190, 215, *228, 237,* 240, 252, *257, 260,* 279, 303, *317, 382, 396,* 507, 632.

sadness 6, 10, 19, 39, 40, 50, 61, 167.

Salvation 25, 56, 58, 87, 99, 125, 138, 163, 184, *210, 263, 264, 344,* 356, *361,* 413, *451, 468, 473-474, 491,* 511, 549, 585.

sanctity 28, 96, 99, 103, 109, 169, *476.*

scruples 77, 136, 194, 202, 561.

search for God 78.

secular values 45, 48, 76, 166, 240, 332.

self-abandonment to God *317, 333, 343, 388, 426, 445, 452, 467,* 512, 524.

self-admiration 628.

self-assertion 190.

self-conquest 218.

self-deception 203.

self-denial 146, *452.*

self-'emptying' 179, *233, 245.*

self-esteem 96.

self-forgetfulness 186, *471,* 562.

self-fulfilment 190.

self-illusion 180.

self-idolatry 158.

self-indulgence 91, 181, 202, 213, 333.

728

Wang, Pauline Elizabeth: life (Contd.)
move to a house 13; nursery school
14; God our Creator 15; conscience
16, primary school 17; telling a lie
19; the doll 16-17; country life 20-
21; family discipline 22; Christian
faith and parish 22-24, 26, 36; visit to
Blessed Sacrament 28; childhood
tasks and hobbies 26, 29-30; diary
30; dull Sundays 31; the fun-fair
32, 174; loneliness 34-39; a visit to
France 49; problems about religion
53; poetry 62; remote from God 67;
a brief conversion 68; a renewal of
faith 73; marriage 69-71; illness and
study 75; Christ 78; the Reformation
97; visit to a Catholic Church 104-
105; children 71, 112-113, 148, 153,
157; Reception into full Communion
124-125; the Holy Mass 135; prayer
145; turmoil 148; feminism examined
165, 189; crisis 167-168; regular
'teachings-in-prayer' 169, 211; a
spiritual 'betrothal' 173; a new
conversion 179; father's death 188;
good books 191; purifying Fire 195;
mother's death 200; Union 217;
began to write 'teachings' 232; levels
of teachings *237-238;* violence 241;
diagnosis 251; the Abyss 262; the
"Mass Paintings" 269; colour theory
269; an exhibition 270, 326; finished
commercial work 271; confided in a
priest 273; taught by God the Father
279; 'Our Lady of Harpenden' *281;*
'God is Love' 293; The Saints *296;*
St. Joseph *300;* the Blessed
Sacrament *308;* a judgement on the
writings 316; taught by the Holy
Trinity 322; a white booklet 325;
gave a talk on prayer 328; Our Lady
in Spain *328;* the Father *338;*
pierced to the heart *342-343;* gave a
talk on the 'Mass Paintings' 365;
veiling for Mass 349, *390-391;* the
evil one *351-354;* pictures 358;
correspondence 360; many spiritual
topics *360-361;* a new parish priest
399; the Father's teachings *365,* 377,
379-389, 417-422, 433-440; the 'blue

Wang, Pauline Elizabeth: life (Contd.)
book' (Volume One) 442; 'Eden'
445; the need to speak 447;
'Radiant Light' 450-451; the whole
message *451-453;* the 'green book'
(Volume Two) 464; the fulfilment of
Christ's promises *455-456;* taught
about Salvation *473-474;* taught
about Christ's teaching method *474-
476;* the 'red book' (Volume Three)
493; the 'yellow book' (Volume Four)
531; a personal 'Magnificat' 503;
unceasing Union, with a promise
481-489; the transforming
Union *494-496,* 503, 471; Christ
506-517; the Father 517-522, the
Holy Spirit 522-526; Contemplative
union 526-530; a message to share
532.

Wang, Pauline Elizabeth: paintings
in childhood 40, 62, 66; discovering
the Expressionists 67; making time to
paint 115, 154, 185, 193, 216, 296;
priorities 150; founder-member of
S.B.A. 199; prayer-paintings: Mass
paintings 269-272; prayer-images
277; purpose of Mass Paintings 303;
exhibition in Westminster Cathedral
326; unwillingness to portray evil
351; photographs circulated of oil
paintings 358; coloured and
monochrome prayer images 358-360;
end of commercial work 360;
exhibition in York 365; further oil
paintings 367; pictures explained to a
new parish priest 399; a long
'gestation' of work 417; symbols for
prayer-paintings 601; the reason for
symbols 600-602; further images
available later 626; examples of both
water-colours and oils 667-694.

Wang, Pauline Elizabeth: special task
'Teachings' as Catechesis *237-238;*
'teachings' as encouragement for the
Church 265; visible person required
to speak out about faith and about Holy
Mass 272; must keep parish priest
informed 272; Christ has a plan. He
invites me to speak out as directed
272; my duty is to record the teachings

Wang, Pauline Elizabeth: special task
(Continued)
and prayer-images for the Father's
Glory 277; Teachings are to be
poured out to help needy souls 291;
Christ gives extraordinary help 291;
knowledge of Our Lady's goodness
will prepare hearts to receive Christ's
teachings 291; first understanding of
the task 302-304; role as a witness
who has 'seen the Lord' 304; told that
past penances bear fruit 324-325;
asked to circulate a booklet 325;
meeting silence and embarrassment
332-333; Christ promises that the
teachings will bear fruit, for God's
glory, the salvation of souls and the
good of the Church 344; task of great
complexity and significance 347;
need of long spiritual training 355;
aspects of teachings 355-357;
reactions to booklets 358;
significance of prayer-images 358;
subject matter of further teachings
360-361; providing a 'template' of
spiritual life 361; conversations with
the Father 379; correspondence 360;
Books to be sent to Bishops and to the
Pope 360; further explanation 361-
362; a further promise: of a 'great
outpouring', of grace, through this
work 363; mixed reactions to work
and weaknesses 364; chosen by God
for His work 368-369; thousands will
be helped 375-376; detailed
instructions from Christ about
Volumes One to Four 401-403; more
than two thousand 'teachings' 402;
work is about to be 'revealed' 405,
417; whole work will provide an
example of 'faith-in-weakness' 416;
special helps are given for a special
vocation 421; supreme reason for
God's choice: that Church teachings
are not always taught 424; fears
allayed 426-428; teachings described
as 'living water' 428; teachings given
to strengthen faith of Church members,
and as reminders of Christ's Presence
in their hearts and in the Blessed

Wang, Pauline Elizabeth: special task
(Continued)
Sacrament 444; the story of a weak
person will help others who are weak
441; Christ's promise about 'showing
out' His Glory 441-442; teachings are
'Good News for the poor': for the
crushed and dispirited 446; God
invites me to speak to the priest about
Glory: as an act of faith 447-448;
more about the progress of the task
448-449; the title of the work to be
'Radiant Light' 450; books should be
sent to Rome 453-454; explanation of
the promise about a 'mountain' of
teachings 455; words about lengthy
spiritual training and about future
reputation 456; reassurance given
about speaking to Bishops 458; a
promise of success for the work 459-
460; an explanation about the Father's
teachings 464-466; an explanation
about a sign for the parish priest and
the Bishop 468-469; Christ's plan to
provide a 'living witness' to His love
and mercy 470; Christ's plan to bring
consolation to many through this work
470; explanations for delays 477-
478; the danger of pride, and a new
path 484; reason for God's choice:
importance of truth-telling 484-486; a
new role, to be 'acted' from the heart
489-490; God's wish to encourage His
People to practice their faith 491;
Teachings are more about our
relationship with God than with one
another 500; by God's plan and my
work, reminders are given about
Eternal truths: about God, mankind,
Christ and Salvation 530; God the
Father delights in this special
work 532.

Wang, Pauline Elizabeth: writings
"Instructions from Christ" 3, 8;
"Teachings-in-Prayer" 6; *spiritual
autobiography* 5, 7, 8; Bible 'family
tree' 41; poetry 62; asked to
'translate' wordless prayer instructions
into words 79; stilted language 205;
asked to record 'given-words' 205;

Wang, Pauline Elizabeth: writings
(Continued)
notebooks 232; *"First Version"* of
teachings 236; several essays, and
"An Introduction" and the *'blue
Book'
(Volume One)* 237; levels of
catechesis through teachings *237-
238;* "Write the vision down": began
full accounts of major teachings 277;
ecumenical reports, and writings on
other subjects eg Marriage, *Holy
Trinity,* and *"Prayer-categories"* 278;
the 'blue book' (Volume One) 237,
290; required to speak again with
parish priest 300; *"Prologue",* as far
as 1985, and *"Narrative"* (1985-1991)
and *"Summary"* from which was
compiled *"An Introduction"* - given to
parish priest 302; wrote explanation
called *"Extraordinary Prayer"* first for
Fr. Edwards 311; posted work for his
assessment 316; more about *"An
Introduction"* 324-329; more about
spiritual autobiography and *"An
Introduction"* 347, 348; general
progress in special task 352;
explanation about 'checking' teachings
356; details of Christ's instructions
about what to have printed 357; *"An
Introduction",* again 360; many
subjects taught *360-351;* several
volumes of *"Teachings-in-prayer"*
377; volumes of *"Christ's
Instructions: second version"* 397;
more about *"First"* and *"Second
Versions"* of the teachings 397-398;
explained whole task to 'new' parish
priest 399; re-wrote 'teachings' in the
first person, as the *"Third Version"*
401; *"Volume Four"* 402; one book
swiftly followed by another 416;
Christ's wish that 'difficult' teachings
be included in volumes of *'Teachings-
in-Prayer'* 431; the *'Blue book'
("Volume One")* finished 442, 454;
three volumes ready *459;*
autobiography details *460;* the *'green
book' ("Volume Two")* 361, *454,*
464, 470. Different typefaces

Wang, Pauline Elizabeth: writings
(Continued)
necessary 464-465; *"Volume One"*
and Two 465;
typefaces and notes on the text 466;
clear identification necessary of Three
Divine Persons of Godhead 466;
autobiography, in God's sight *489-
490;* book distribution *492;* God's
request about completion of
autobiography 492; "Volume Three"
ready (the *'red book')* *493;*
autobiography 498-499;
autobiography and volumes of
teachings 530; *"Volume Three"* and
Four and *"My Priests are Sacred"* and
*"How to pray" 531; "Volume Five"
and Six,* later on 532; *spiritual
autobiography* 539; *Appendix* to
spiritual autobiography 539-540,
551-552; writing in obedience to God
596; writing: God's choice for me
625; *"Teachings-in-prayer":* several
volumes 696.
War, war-time 10, 11, 12, 13, 14, 16, 35,
48.
Wilberforce, William 103.
"Window in the Wall" 207.
woman, womanhood 77, 165, 189.
Womens' Movement, see feminism.
Wordsworth, William 21, 65.
'working-class' life-style 110.
world Faiths 103, 214.
World War Two 12, 13.

York 365.

The paintings and writings of
ELIZABETH WANG
are published by

Radiant Light is a non-profit-making company. It has wide trading objects, together with two specific aims which are:

'*For the glory of God the Most Holy Trinity, for the honour of the Blessed Virgin Mary, and out of love for the Catholic Church and loyalty to the Pope*:
    (1) to advance the Roman Catholic religion
    (2) to promote the works of Elizabeth Wang'

If you would like to help support the work of Radiant Light, please send a UK cheque to:
    Radiant Light, 25 Rothamsted Avenue,
    Harpenden, Herts AL5 2DN. UK
A complete catalogue is also available on request from this address.

<u>Book orders and Distribution</u>
Further copies of this book, and other Radiant Light books, posters and paintings by Elizabeth Wang, are available from:

    St Pauls (By Westminster Cathedral)
    Morpeth Terrace, Victoria, London SW1P 1EP - UK
    Tel: 0171 828 5582 – Fax: 0171 828 3329

Company No. 3701357 (Company limited by guarantee and not having a share capital)